ASIAN THOUGHT:
TRADITIONS OF
INDIA, CHINA, JAPAN & TIBET

Volume I

HINDUISM
INDIAN BUDDHISM
TIBETAN BUDDHISM

by
Robert B. Zeuschner, *Ph.D.*
Professor of Philosophy
Pasadena City College

Published by Echo Point Books & Media
Brattleboro, Vermont
www.EchoPointBooks.com

Asian Thought (volume 1)
ISBN: 978-1-63561-702-3 (paperback)

Cover design by Alicia Brown
Cover image: An old Hindu man praying, by SoumenNath, courtesy of iStock

BUDDHIST SITES IN INDIA

INDUS VALLEY SITES IN INDIA

CHINA

TIBET

MODERN
PAKISTAN

Indus
River

●Harappa

● Mohenjo-Daro

Ganges River

MYANMAR
(Burma)

INDIA

●Bombay

Bay of
Bengal

SRI LANKA
(Ceylon)

CHINA AND JAPAN

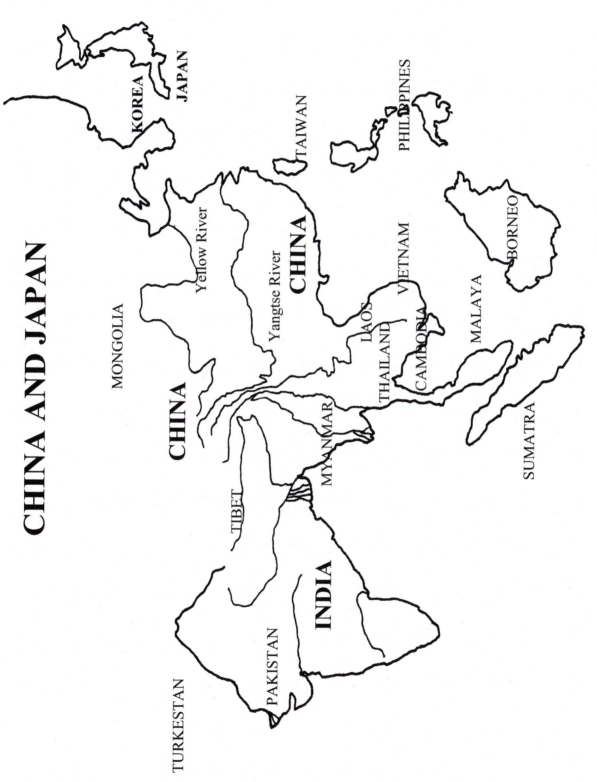

KOREA

JAPAN

TAIWAN

PHILIPPINES

MONGOLIA

Yellow River

Yangtse River

CHINA

CHINA

BORNEO

LAOS

VIETNAM

THAILAND

CAMBODIA

MALAYA

MYANMAR

SUMATRA

TIBET

INDIA

TURKESTAN

PAKISTAN

TABLE OF CONTENTS

ASIAN THOUGHT: Volume I
TRADITIONS OF INDIA AND TIBET

by
Robert B. Zeuschner

INTRODUCTION TO VOLUME I

These books are intended to serve as an introduction to some of the most important and enduring religious, spiritual and intellectual traditions of India, China, Tibet, and Japan. Because this material is introductory, these discussions cannot be exhaustive or comprehensive. Consequently, the chapters do not go into extensive detail into any specific subject although the author has tried to provide enough detail so that key concepts are not distorted.

This book is not concerned with trying to persuade the reader to change his or her religious orientation. The author has no interest in encouraging you to be more spiritual, to take religion more seriously, to make you more religious, or less religious, and has no interest in converting you from one religion to some other religion. What the author does want is for you, the student, to find the topic of Asian[1] thought to be interesting, stimulating and challenging. These systems provide new perspectives to enrich and broaden one's world-view, new possibilities of thought which seem obvious to other civilizations, but often unrecognized or under-appreciated by the wide variety of Western traditions. There is much to appreciate in non-Western traditions. Studying religion requires us to be objective, to commit ourselves to rigorous academic standards, with the goal to be an appreciation of the complexities found in the non-Western traditions.

The focus in **Volume 1** will be on South Asia, stressing India and Tibet. The importance of the traditions of this area is evident when one considers that the South Asian subcontinent (including India, Pakistan, and Bangladesh) contains twenty-percent of the world's population. We will begin with India and the ideas found in the earliest sacred texts called *Vedas* and the numerous forms of Hinduism which acknowledge the sacred authority of the *Vedas* and trace their origins to the *Vedas*. We shall also discuss the ideas of the **Bhagavad Gita** and several devotional developments in Hinduism. In addition, there are many Indian traditions that reject the *Vedas* and reject Hinduism, such as all the

---

[1] Some books refer to this area as "Oriental," however "Oriental" has been used to describe areas as widespread as northern Africa, the Middle East, eastern Europe, and Persia, as well as India, China, Korea and Japan. That is quite diverse. As noted above, the focus of these two books will be India, China, Japan, and Tibet.

various Buddhist traditions and the Jains. The major intellectual traditions of Tibet are a creative confluence of the ancient Bon religion combined with many varieties of esoteric Buddhism.

In **Volume 2** we will focus on East Asia, specifically China and Japan. We will begin with China, where we find Confucianism, Taoism, Legalism and other early thought systems, plus later developments in Chinese Buddhism and Neo-Confucianism. In Japan we will focus on the several varieties of Buddhism, including the Pure Land and Zen, and the ancient religion of Shinto. Each and every one of these various traditions is quite complex, and so the author cannot avoid using generalizations. Whenever we make historical, cultural, and philosophical generalizations, there are always exceptions.

Although most books freely and uncritically use the English term "religion" to describe many of these systems, this book does so only hesitantly, firstly because in defining religion we tend to make the Eurocentric assumption that there must be some universal essence to all the things we call religions, and despite numerous attempts to find and define that essence, no such essence has ever been found. In addition, in assuming that all religions share important commonalities, we feel safe and comfortable using Western assumptions to predetermine the forms that questions will take before those questions are even posed, such as questions about a "god" or a "savior."

The problem is that we discuss systems of thought that are much broader than the limited meaning for the term "religion" as it is used uncritically in Western Christian cultures. The author has found that many of his Western students tend to assume that anything called a religion will be sectarian and centered around beliefs in some divinity. Isn't a religion simply a belief system with a list of things one must accept on faith, the major difference being that other religions use a different name for the divine being they worship? The answer is "no." Many of the systems of thought traditionally described as Asian religions stress actions over belief or faith, and encourage critical responses. As used in the field of world religions, the term "religion" is incredibly more broad than concepts like "belief" and "faith" would suggest.[2]

WHAT ARE RELIGIONS?

In recent decades, it has become recognized that even asking the question "What is religion?" is based on assumptions that are not as straightforward as we used to think. In fact, these assumptions are quite controversial. The religious categories we use to answer the question "What is religion?" are historically specific and culturally relative, not universal.[3] Some scholars have argued that the word "religion" is too Western in its associated meanings to be

---

[2] "Belief appears as a universal category because of the universalist claims of the tradition in which it has become most central, Christianity." Donald S. Lopez, Jr., "Belief," in Mark Taylor, ed., *Critical Terms for Religious Studies* (Chicago: University of Chicago Press, 1998), p. 33. In assuming that all religions are alike, that they are universal in some important way, then we can safely assume that because "belief" is important in Western religion, then "belief" must also be an important element in non-Western religions, and we will put special energy in looking for something which would play the same, or a similar role in non-Western religion. We look for "belief." In doing so, we distort the non-Western tradition with our presuppositions.

[3] The introduction to Brent Nongbri's *Before Religion: A History of a Modern Concept* (Yale University, 2013) states "For much of the past two centuries, religion has been understood as a universal phenomenon, a part of the 'natural' human experience that is essentially the same across cultures and throughout history. Individual religions may vary through time and geographically, but there is an element, religion, that is to be found in all cultures during all time periods. Taking apart this assumption, Brent Nongbri shows that the idea of religion as a sphere of life distinct from politics, economics, or science is a recent development in European history—a development that has been projected outward in space and backward in time with the result that religion now appears to be a natural and necessary part of our world. . . . in antiquity, there was no conceptual arena that could be designated as 'religious' as opposed to 'secular'."

INTRODUCTION

useful.[4] Leading scholars have pointed out that both "religion" and "religious experience" are not universal categories of human experience, but instead are a relatively late and distinctively Western invention, which certainly will cause problems for any author trying to create a textbook introducing world religions.[5]

These issues of the general nature of religion as discussed by scholars in the field of religious studies go well beyond the purposes of this textbook.[6] There are dozens of definitions for "religion" yet there is no single agreed-upon definition for this central term.[7] This textbook will gently sidestep these scholarly controversies, and instead use the term "religion" as a general albeit vague term, flexible enough to have some relevance to both Western civilizations and non-Western civilizations.

In the West[8], there is a tendency to assume that world religions share some common essence with Western religions, perhaps involving unquestioning reverence for an institutionalized ancestral dogma.[9] In the West there is a tendency to believe that the categories based on a divinity who requires submission, adoration, belief, and faith, are universal categories. However, recent scholars have argued that this cluster of ideas is related specifically to Western culture, and does not apply universally to many non-Western religious traditions. For many in the area of religious studies, religions are concerned with how we respond to fellow humans and to the world in which we live. It may be impossible to separate out religion from philosophy, history, politics, economics, art, literature, sociology, psychology and anthropology, although we in the West have attempted to do so. Can religion be separated from cultural institutions? As pointed out previously, early human civilizations seem not to have made any distinction between religion, culture, economics and political structures.[10]

Are religions just a list of beliefs one must accept on faith? Certainly, some of the systems we call religions fit this description. However, there is much more to religion than accepting beliefs generated from ancestral dogmas, or even accepting supernatural beings. In Western religions, religious questions often involve theories of human nature (do we possess a soul and how can we tell? is soul different from mind or consciousness?), morality (is something good because God commands it, or does God command it because it is good?), mortality (is there life after death? reincarnation, heaven, hell, or something else?), society (how can we apply the Golden Rule to our neighbors and to other cultures?), history (who are the real authors of our scriptures? is the universe really six-thousand years old?), and

---

[4] Daniel Dubuisson, *The Western Construction of Religion: Myths, Knowledge, and Ideology* (Johns Hopkins University Press, 2007).

[5] The issues are complex, but several excellent discussions are available. See "Experience" by Robert H. Sharf, and "Religion, Religions, Religious" by Jonathan Z. Smith, both in Mark C. Taylor, ed., *Critical Terms for Religious Studies* (Chicago: University of Chicago Press, 1998). Should we understand religion through the lens of modernism, post-modernism, structuralism, post-structuralism, or some other methodology? Professor Taylor's introduction to the volume summarizes the most important issues in this debate.

[6] For example, see Tomoko Masuzawa, *The Invention of World Religions: Or, How European Universalism Was Preserved in the Language of Pluralism* (University of Chicago Press, 2005), or Brent Nongbri, *Before Religion: A History of a Modern Concept* (Yale University, 2013).

[7] For a good discussion of many different attempts to define "religion," consult Steven Brutus, *Religion, Culture, History: A Philosophical Study of Religion* (CreateSpace Independent Publishing Platform, 2012).

[8] The term "West" is quite problematic, for there is no single unitary religion or philosophy typical of all the countries included by the term "West." It is not even clear precisely which groups or nations are included in the umbrella term "West." We cannot restrict "West" to just North America, or just North America and Europe. It would have to include South America and many other regions. In this book, the term "West" is intended to refer to a vague yet still useful generalization whose purpose is to contrast typical Greek, Roman, Christian, Northern European Anglo-Saxon-descended cultures, and North American assumptions with the religions and systems of thought of India, China, Japan, and Tibet. The term "West" is also used in the study of societies. For example one might study "WEIRD" societies, that is, "Western, educated, industrialized and democratic."

[9] This is how Christian missionaries explained the meaning of the Western term "religion" to the Japanese and Chinese.

[10] For more on this, see Brent Nongbri's *Before Religion: A History of a Modern Concept.*

anthropology (did humans evolve over the millennia or are humans some kind of special creation?). In fact, religions serve many purposes and fulfill many functions.[11]

All civilizations attempt to explain what humans could not explain. Questions about the causes and meaning of an eclipse, an earthquake, a flood or tsunami, an illness, about the possibility of some life after death, or the general meaning of existence, are in need of explanation. Out of these kinds of questions come systems of symbols which encapsulate a world-view which will guide the choices and lives of those who participate in the system.

THE MANY FUNCTIONS OF RELIGION

Systems of thought we label "religious" provide symbols which followers use to filter ideas and make sense of experiences. Sometimes priests interpret dreams and make predictions for the future which can fill us with fear or give us comfort.[12] Religious world-views tell us whether there are such things as supernatural sacred realities, and how to relate to sacred realities if such things exist. Religions open up some new possibilities of thought, and close down other possibilities.

Religions transmit these world-views to succeeding generations because religions are not separable from culture. Religions do not merely influence our spiritual beliefs, but they can and do influence our politics and our science and our expectations in general.

Those things we call religions can help humans to find meaning in and provide structures to make sense out of the stages of life, birth, childhood, marriage, old age, and death. Religions can help us deal with a fear of death, and sometimes offer the possibility of a continuation of life. Within the culture's system of symbols are guides to what we can eat, who we can marry, and which holidays are to be celebrated, and in some traditions, they tell us what sorts of sexual activities are acceptable and which are unacceptable. Indeed, it is not uncommon for religions to claim the authority to provide absolute moral standards.

Events in nature like eclipses, earthquakes, and floods can be explained by religious stories and myths. Perhaps if we offer sacrifices, or purify ourselves of things offensive to supernatural powers, or pay money to religious institutions, these dangers can be controlled, minimized, or avoided.

Many religions provide systems of symbols that inspire art, architecture, literature, music, garden-design, martial arts, and even food rituals such as feasting and the tea-ceremony. Religions can provide a structure for a life guided by particular moral rules and can provide a place for artistic creativity as a religious activity.

Sometimes, religions are closely intertwined with politics. Religious leaders gain political power and their religion becomes the handmaiden of politics, legitimizing some policies and rulers and excluding others. There is the phenomenon of "ingroup" versus the "outgroup" which has been studied extensively. Yet politics is primarily about central authority, privilege, and power—the power to influence, the power to suggest, the power to control, the power to transfer wealth—not spiritual issues. In recent analyses in the field of religious practice, scholars have argued that the study of the religious sphere is inseparable from the overall production and circulation of power within society.

In the name of protecting society, politically-based religions have claimed the right to oppress, to censor what citizens can read, what they can write, how they dress, and put limits on what songs can be sung and limits on what

---

[11] The student might find it instructive to read the first chapters of several different textbooks on world religions, and notice the great variety of definitions for the term "religion." There is no single agreed-upon standard definition for this important term. There is even disagreement about the meaning of the Latin root for the term.

[12] We are all aware of Western religious leaders who regularly predict the end of the world, and have been doing so regularly for two-thousand years and more.

artists can create, simultaneously seeking to suppress unwelcome political ideas, thereby operating as a tool for the religious government to regulate the behavior of its citizens. A quick examination of the historical record reveals that institutional religion is never isolated, never just religion–religion is tied to politics, resource distribution, ideology, wealth and social control.[13]

One of the most important aspects of religions is their social function, providing us a community of like-minded individuals who cooperate and share. This community supplies husbands, wives, friends and people who care about us and share with us. Certainly this is one of the central functions of a great many religions.

For those who worry about the meaning of existence, religions can lessen anxiety by assuring us that the apparent chaos and meaninglessness of life is only apparent, and that there is some ultimate meaning which we do not yet understand, and that ultimate meaning underlies all the inequity, the evil, and the suffering. In short, religion is a uniquely powerful and pervasive social force in human life.

All of us are aware that there is a dark side to religions. There are intolerant and even violent strains of what are often called religious fundamentalism. These have been associated with racism, genocide, and slavery. We can note that many of the systems we call religions claim to teach ultimate truth and demand absolute loyalty from followers. Their power derives from their claim to represent and convey a cosmic or divine order (powerful forces which transcend this world), and which expect to govern every aspect of our lives, personal, social, and political. Often, religious leaders expect to direct our thoughts, our language, and our behavior. Countries organized around religion each claim a unique destiny for their society, which can lead to a religiously motivated mission to draw boundaries of identity (discrimination) and uphold a social order with political leaders now being religious leaders who claim to possess ultimate authority because they communicate with the sacred ultimate.

Nations interact with one another throughout world history guided by their understanding of specific values directed by divine forces. Populations are mobilized to go to war by religious leaders who tell followers what their deity wants. Politicians have fanned religious fear, hatred and violence against subgroups within their own culture. Humans are very sensitive to who belongs to the "ingroup" (the group of God-followers) and who belongs to the "outgroup" (the group of Satan-followers) and frequently religions have manipulated this tendency to demonize those who do not agree with the ingroup. In the past and in the present, religions have condoned and inspired torture, violence, genocide, beheadings, discrimination and even slavery for members of the outgroup. History is filled with examples of religious followers torturing and killing those who seem not to share their own religious world-view.[14] Some religions have resisted scholarly findings that seemed to be contrary to their beliefs. Repeatedly, some religions have tried to suppress scientific knowledge and research, to control the publication of books and limit artistic expression, to control sexual expression, and to control women.

Yet at the same time we know that religious thought (theology) has inspired some of the greatest philosophical concepts within world civilizations without a hint of discrimination and prejudice. We do not want to lose sight of the complexity of this wide variety of behavior which can be called "religious." One way to ensure that we do not get confused is to simply minimize the use of the potentially misleading term "religion."

ASIAN THOUGHT

Western people tend to draw a distinction between religions and philosophies, but these lines are due to

---

[13] As noted previously, scholars have pointed out that in past civilizations, religion and politics weren't distinguished.

[14] Scholars have noted that historically it is within the monotheistic religions that coercion and worse ("conversion by the sword") are employed to convert others; polytheistic and non-theistic religions do not seem to be so concerned.

conditions unique to Western thought, and are artificial and inappropriate when used on non-Western traditions discussed in these volumes. Rather than try to impose the Western distinction between religion and philosophy on Asian thought systems to which the distinction is foreign, in these books more often we will use an Asian category. In Chinese and Japanese there is a two-character compound **ssu-hsiang**, or **shi-so** 思 想 which we render in English as "thought." It can include what we call spirituality, or philosophy, and what we call religion as well.[15] Thus, the title of this book is *Asian Thought*.

Over many centuries, Western people traveled to Asia and noticed that many Asian practices and rituals resembled what Christians do in the West, and that these practices and rituals seemed to fulfill functions similar to Western religion. They found a wide variety of very different creation myths and sacred stories. Sometimes there were explanations of the universe or the origin of good and evil. There were sacred texts and goals that guided individual behavior and choices. In the West, these sorts of activities tended to fall under the category of religion. Consequently, Western people called these Asian systems "religion," assuming that in essence, these were similar to Western religions. However, despite similarities, westerners did not realize that these non-Western systems simply did not have similar presuppositions, did not share the same concerns or ask the same questions that those Judeo-Christian religious traditions asked.

For example, many of the non-Western systems did not wonder if a single god existed, and explicitly rejected the idea that a single god created all of reality. They did not conceive of a divinity who required submission and adoration. They did not interpret the world as a battleground between an omnipotent good god and an evil being or devil. They did not believe that humans needed a divine savior. For some of these thought systems, the question of the existence of a god was simply not interesting. Some wondered "where did god come from?" and searched for the impersonal ultimate source of all divinity and considered worship of a god to be spiritually immature.

Athens versus Jerusalem

Non-Western systems tend not to have the same tensions between faith and reason which are part of the history of Western religion. The history of Western thought could be described as an ongoing tug-of-war between ideas originating in Athens and ideas originating in Jerusalem. In this book we will explore thought traditions whose world-view does not originate in either the Jerusalem of Judaism, Christianity, and Islam, but also neither do these traditions have their origins in the Athens of Socrates, Plato, and Aristotle. In religions originating in Jerusalem, obedience and faith tends to be valued over reason, over empirical observation, over science. In Athens, it is reason, critical thinking, empirical observation, and science which tend to be valued over faith.

In India, China, Japan, and Tibet, there never was anything like the sharp tension between these two approaches of Jerusalem and Athens, the tension between reason and faith, between science and religion, which dominates the history of Western thinking. Thus the demarcation in the West between religion and philosophy applies perfectly well to the history of Western Christian civilization, but dividing non-Western thought into these two rigid categories is simply an inappropriate structure to impose upon these non-Western traditions of thought. It gives us a distorted understanding of the ideas and their assumptions.

The tension between science and religion in the West is found only recently in Asian systems and it arose in

---

[15] In Japanese the term *shukyo* renders "religion," however the Japanese two-character compound *shukyo* (*zongjiao* in Chinese) is not ancient; it was created by Jesuit Christian missionaries in Japan. Because the Japanese did not have words for anything quite like Christian beliefs, the missionaries made up the two-character compound in an attempt to capture the Western concept of religion as an institution with authority derived from a historical lineage (such as that of the Catholic pope). Interestingly, the literal meaning of *shukyo* is something like "essential principle-lineage teachings," "tenets-teachings," "sectarian-tenets" or "lineage-teaching," a respected teaching handed down in a line of teachers. According to Professor Dan Lusthaus, the compound implies reverence for an institutionalized ancestral dogma. The Chinese borrowed the two-character compound from the Japanese.

modern times as a result of conscious political manipulation, not devotional conflicts. We cannot assume that Asian thought systems are opposed to critical philosophical analysis, or opposed to science and contemporary scientific discoveries.[16]

Westerners who have never taken a course in world religions tend to assume that anything that is called a religion will be like Christianity. It will have a god or gods as its central core, and would believe that this divinity lays down moral and social rules, believe that humans have an eternal soul, and that there is life after death when one will be judged. Similar concepts are true for a few Asian thought systems, but not all.[17]

Some Asian thought systems do have similarities with Western Christianity, but also have significant differences. Asian and Western systems are both filled with creative insights and have inspired countless followers to guide their lives by some features of each system. In Asia what we might call religion, philosophy, and even proto-science have interfused and interacted in many fecund ways. This is what we will explore in this book, and try not to get distracted by the issue of how to use specifically Western labels to describe non-Western systems.

We must be careful also not manipulate one religion to appear better than another. One easy way to do that is when we compare the **ideals** of one religion with the actual **practices** of another. Some people say "My religion says that we should not kill, but followers of your religion do kill." To be accurate, we should compare the ideals of one religion with the ideals of another. Then we may discover that both teach "do not kill." We can also compare the actual practices of one religion with the practices of another. Then we may discover that both have had followers who killed in the name of their religion.

RELIGION: THE GRAND TRADITION AND THE LITTLE TRADITION

In recent times some Western scholars have pointed out that there is a way to think about religions that is not related to content or beliefs, but a more sociological understanding related to the attitudes and training and social position of those who hold the religious beliefs.[18] Some sociologists have pointed out that religious understanding in a culture may vary depending upon wealth and education. There is a continuum of beliefs and practices between the literate and powerful minority at one extreme, and the illiterate yet hard-working majority at the other extreme. This distinction is *not* between ancient tribal traditional followers and modern industrialized religious followers. In contemporary America we find both traditions existing side-by-side.

The religious understanding of those elite members of the well-educated segments of society are those people who are not only literate, but also familiar with a wide variety of world views, acquainted with critical thinking and philosophy, knowledgeable about current science, and this segment of society attempts to understand religion in a way that is consistent with the best science and philosophical and critical traditions. The religious beliefs of this group are perfectly compatible with science, with evolution, with the age of the universe, with the fact that the earth is not the center of the universe, with quantum physics, with anthropology, with the findings of geology, with the wide variety

---

[16] A book which deals with how Chinese Buddhists understood the relationship between Western science and their doctrines is Erik J. Hammerstrom, *The Science of Chinese Buddhism: Early Twentieth-Century Engagements* (New York Columbia University Press, 2015).

[17] For example, see Stephen Prothero, *God is Not One: The Eight Ritual Religions That Run the World – And Why Their Differences Matter* (New York: HarperOne, 2010).

[18] This distinction began with Max Weber in his *The Sociology of Religion* (Boston: Beacon Press, 1963) but has been discussed extensively by Robert Redfield, *Peasant Society and Culture* (Chicago: University of Chicago Press, 1973). Examples of the application of this dichotomy are found in Robert Ellwood, *Cycles of Faith* (New York: AltaMira Press, 2003).

of human sexuality, and evolutionary biology. For many of these thinkers, if god did create the universe and everything in it, then science will be discovering the details of the mechanisms which god used to make our world and our selves. Thus science and religion must be compatible. This compatibility is not generated by rejecting science, but rather by offering skillful interpretations of sacred scripture.

It is often the case that the religious leaders of the major Christian churches and denominations are educated at high-quality secular universities taking classes in science, philosophy, critical thinking, anthropology and history alongside the scientists and philosophers, and the views and understanding of this group has been referred to as the **Grand Tradition** of religion. Thus, the term Grand Tradition refers to the elaborate ideas, teachings, values, and practices of the well-educated elite members of the institutional churches.

The Grand Tradition will be interested in trying to date accurately when their sacred scriptures were composed, and perhaps debate the actual authors of these sacred texts, and in doing so they utilize a complex array of scientific tests, combined with linguistic and historical data. Because of their education, social position, and wealth, often these same people may wield political power as well as religious power. If one considers this as a continuum, at the far left are those scholarly in ancient languages and ancient history, as well as other well-educated members of the religion, and at the other end of the continuum, at the far right, are those who never had the benefit of a quality education and may never have encountered many people whose ideas were different from those of their own insulated community. Of course the majority of people belong in the in-between area. This distinction between Grand Tradition and Little Tradition lies along a continuum, with the majority of the people in the vast in-between grey area.

Until very recently in human history, the majority of people in a civilization were not literate and had very little formal education, no training in scientific methods or the mathematical underpinning basic to science, little understanding of empirical testing and how science works, and had little interest in historical methods, or critical thinking. The religious beliefs and attitudes of this segment of society tends to be interestingly different from the explicit beliefs of the Grand Tradition church leaders.

There are groups of basic religions whose followers preserve their religious beliefs in stories, in oral form. They could not, or have not preserved their ideas in written form. In fact, in general this aspect of religion is not focused on the historical analysis of texts, or focused on beliefs and ideas at all; rather it tends to be about behavior. Popular religion is less concerned with the conceptual justification of what people think and believe, but rather tends to be about what people do.

This popular oral manifestation of religion is at the other extreme of the continuum, and is often referred to as "Folk Religion" or the **Little Tradition**. The term "little" is not meant to be demeaning to popular folk religion. Some scholars prefer to refer to the Little Tradition religion as Popular Religions, Oral Religions,[19] or Basic Religions.[20]

The Little Tradition covers a quite wide range of trends and practices, but tends to be more focused on personal needs, subjective spiritual feeling, visions, dreams, spirit beings, personal experience, anecdotes and pious tales, and has little interest in abstract theology or theory. Religious tales and scriptures are taken at face value and the conclusions of informed historical analyses are rejected. History and mythology are not clearly distinguished. The Little Tradition has greater reliance upon ongoing miracles, stressing apparitions and relationships with a spirit realm filled with divinities or angels who can provide concrete blessings in response to rituals, personal sacrifice or devotional vows. Little Tradition religion can see images of saints and divinities in an oil slick, in a pattern of wood on a door, in a cheese sandwich. This is "popular religion" or "folk religion."

The Little Tradition can be conveyed with song, with dance, with celebrations, and community festivals. The

---

[19] Michael Molloy, *Experiencing the World's Religions: Tradition, Challenge and Change* Second Edition (Mountain View, Ca.: Mayfield Publishing Company, 2002).

[20] For example, see chapter one of Lewis M. Hopfe and Mark R. Woodward *Religions of the World*, 10th edition (New Jersey: Pearson-Prentice Hall, 2007).

INTRODUCTION

Little Tradition is transmitted orally through family and community, transmitted through charismatic figures who are often local church officials, or perhaps "holy men" and "holy women," who might include miracle workers who enter trance-like states. It might include such activities as "speaking in tongues" or ecstatic states where the participants may believe that they can predict the future.

Shamanism

The Little Tradition also includes shamans. **Shamanism** is the name for the world-view of those who believe that there are two realms which make up reality: the physical world that humans inhabit and a parallel realm inhabited by a wide variety of spirits who can intrude into our world to communicate with us, to help us, or to hurt us. Things with spirit could be animals, trees, stones, rivers, mountains, seas, human beings who have died, and heavenly and underworld beings. People who claim to "channel" spirits or communicate with the dead belong to this tradition.

Shamanism holds that these spirit beings can bless or curse humans. Thus spirits provide an explanation for why bad things happen to us. These spirits can enter and possibly take over the body of a human and cause illness. Often, the shamans explain that dreams are a connection between us and the spirit realm. **The shaman is the person who has the ability to interact with these spirits, to enter the spirit realm and communicate with and perhaps manipulate these dangerous forces**. Contemporary people who claim to offer us the opportunity to communicate with departed family members are modern inheritors of the shamanistic tradition.[21]

Shamans must be concerned with practical matters as well. Success in hunting and in planting and harvesting are central, but so too is dealing with evil spirits, curing pain and disease by bringing about spiritual healing and expelling demons. Evil spirits can sometimes be frightened off by fearful gestures or by loud noises, like the sounds of firecrackers. Sometimes the shaman may have to leave his or her body and travel to the realm of spirits. Sometimes the spirit will take up residence in the body of the shaman and the shaman will speak with the voice of the spirit.

Shamans provide talismans[22] which can ward off sinister or evil forces and shamans can interpret dreams for supernatural significance. The shamanistic aspect of religion places its stress on a world filled with unseen realms and invisible spirits who can cause our lives to change for the better or worse. Illness and bad luck must be the result of negative forces and spirits. Using rituals and various devices to induce a trance-like state,[23] the shaman is able to perceive and communicate with these spirits, hopefully to improve the lives of the individual or community. These are the kinds of activities which are the domain of the shaman.

The Questions of the Grand Tradition and the Little Tradition

Although "Grand Tradition" and "Little Tradition" are merely the extremes of a grand continuum with almost all religious people falling somewhere in the middle, we can discuss some qualities associated with each extreme. The questions which dominate the Grand Tradition tend to be the abstract ones. What is the meaning of existence, what is the nature of the sacred, why are we here, what is our purpose, how should human beings relate to supernatural beings, or relate to one another? They might ask why we human beings suffer? What is it that we are ignorant of that causes human beings such misery? Why is there something instead of nothing? The Grand Tradition might attempt to define the nature of the supreme being, or explain how a trinity of gods is monotheism, or attempt to explain how

---

[21] Shamanism is found in movies, in books, in popular entertainment. Any movie with ghosts or demons is drawing on shamanism. One cannot but note that Grand Tradition religious leaders show little interest in this aspect.

[22] A talisman is some physical object which is believed to have magical powers, or perhaps will confer powers or protection on the bearer. Something that will ward off evil influences because of its protective powers is a talisman. A good luck charm is a talisman.

[23] These devices could include ingesting psychoactive substances, chanting, drumming, dancing, isolation, fasting, sleep deprivation and meditation.

a universe created by a perfectly good deity could have so much undeserved evil in it.[24] The Grand Tradition might ask why a divine being would create a universe with so many flaws—what was the plan or purpose? Literacy and reason are important tools of the Grand Tradition.

Generally, followers of the Grand Tradition understand how reason works, and understand what makes some reasons good and other reasons worthless, understand the difference between a good explanation and a poor explanation, know why some arguments are logically very strong, and other emotionally appealing arguments can be weak or invalid. In a weak or invalid argument, the evidence offered does not support the conclusion.

The Little Tradition questions tend to be more literal, more immediate, personal and practical. For the Little Tradition believers, if one's sacred text says that giants mated with human women at the beginning of the world, then this must have happened. If one's sacred text says that a deity took three steps across the universe, creating morning, noon, and night, then this must have happened. If the sacred text says that a god came to earth and incarnated as a chariot driver on a battlefield, then this must have happened. Generally, practical questions dominate the Little Tradition of religion. For example, how can we influence deities to bring rain, or cure grandmother's illness? How can we ensure that our next child will be male, or how can I improve my luck when I gamble? If I sacrifice something of value as an offering, will the spiritual beings respond with blessings, with protection, with what I desire?

There is a tendency for the followers of the folk traditions to regard the Grand Tradition as too liberal and too abstract. If science is incompatible with their interpretation of doctrines and beliefs, then it must be science that is mistaken and empirical evidence and empirical testing are irrelevant. The followers of the Little Tradition are the ones who perform magical conjurations to summon the rain or bring about a miracle that could cure an illness or save the crops from insects. Often this is the realm of the shaman.

All the world religions exhibit both Grand and Little Tradition aspects, including Western Christianity. Hinduism and Buddhism have the intellectual component, but among the majority of people it is a wide range of folk religion which dominates. China and Japan also have these two traditions. The various Grand Traditions of these civilizations can be compared with one another very fruitfully, but the many Little Traditions are more varied and less conceptual, and thus more difficult to explore. As noted before, this distinction between Grand Tradition and Little Tradition is a continuum, not an either/or relationship.

Emic and Etic

"Emic" and "etic" are useful technical terms in the field of religious studies. Scholars of religion use the term **"emic"** to denote the understanding of a religion as explained by a committed believer, or possibly a priest, a minister, a pope or bishop. These people provide an insider's sympathetic view of a religious tradition, an appreciative view, a committed view. However, the view of one insider within a religion might be wildly different from the view of another insider. Insiders within the same church will often disagree vigorously with one another. Sometimes insiders will not acknowledge the legitimacy of other ways of practicing the very same religious tradition. For a clear understanding of a particular religious tradition, we cannot restrict ourselves only to the emic perspective.

The term **"etic"** is used for the knowledgeable outsider's view of a religion, the view of a scholar who wants to be respectful yet objective,[25] dispassionate and honest about the claims and practices of a particular religion, and also someone who wishes to make useful and reasonably accurate cross-cultural comparisons between religious traditions. To understand religions of different cultures, we need both **emic** appreciation and **etic** studies of religions.

---

[24] The Grand Tradition might try to answer the question of undeserved evil (i.e., senseless murder of small children) with free will. The Little Tradition response might be to say that the undeserved evil is punishment by an angry god for the sins of those among us, that god wants us to change our ways. These two approaches are interestingly different.

[25] The author is **not** suggesting that the emic perspective, that of religious believers, must be biased or that all outsiders are objective. The question of what objectivity is and whether it is even possible for anyone, is outside the purview of this book.

INTRODUCTION

We need objectivity, but we also need empathy.

As the purpose of this book is to provide an appreciative scholarly study of Asian thought, the obvious stress will be on the etic, a scholarly study of the dominant literary Grand Traditions in India, China, Japan, and Tibet. However, there will also be discussions of the Basic Religions, the Oral Religions, or the Little Traditions in each culture as well.

Because this book on Asian thought is incorporating both religion and philosophy, and because this is directed primarily at students who are likely to have some background in Western ways of thinking about spirituality, let us begin with some distinctions that Western scholars might make between religion and philosophy.

DISTINGUISHING PHILOSOPHY AND RELIGION IN THE WEST

In using the phrase "Western Thought," the term "thought" is intended to encompass both religion and philosophy. Although neither the Chinese nor Japanese find a problem with the term "Asian Thought," in the West we have distinguished philosophy and religion. Let us pursue this distinction as it appears in contemporary European and American thought.

The origins of Western philosophy are found in Athens, roughly four-hundred years before the common era. The term "philosophy" has its roots in the Greek language, and literally it can be translated as "love of wisdom." For the Greek thinkers, philosophers seek wisdom. Socrates and Plato offer a new understanding of wisdom. Wisdom is not merely repeating fixed truths inherited from previous generations. Wisdom is the ability or skill to make careful choices which lead to a good life, a meaningful, worthwhile, and fulfilled life. Wisdom leads to happiness. For philosophy, this wisdom is acquired by a combination of critical thinking and knowledge gained by sense experience. Education was not mere memorization of culture; it was based on critical discussion.

The etymological roots of the term "religion" are in Latin, and the verb *religio* probably meant "bind" or "tie fast." A common explanation is that *religio* refers to that aspect of society which binds people together in a community-unifying attitude of respect for and cultivating a special relationship with various forces, powers, or divinities. The Roman world had numerous divinities, and was aware of the religious practices of other cultures, and never insisted that the Roman religious beliefs were the only true beliefs. The Latin term *religio* did not refer to an exclusive belief system or symbol system which rejected other religions. In this more ancient sense, religions, like cultures, bind us together into a common attitude of respect for powers that control human destiny. Quite often these forces were associated with forces of nature and not divine beings who had human-like personalities.[26] Some interpret *religio* to mean "binding" people to what is good, and avoiding evil.

However, for most people in the West religion is identified with the problems and viewpoint of Jerusalem, the original source of three major world religions. In general these are referred to as "followers of the book," the Jewish, Christian and Islamic followers. Among these groups, the term "religion" denotes an exclusive group to which one belongs. In addition, throughout much of human history, religious education was memorization of sacred texts, not critical discussion of these texts.

---

[26] An extended discussion of the numerous interpretations of the Latin *religio* can be found in many books. A good discussion is found in Steven Brutus, *Religion, Culture, History: A Philosophical Study of Religion* (CreateSpace Independent Publishing Platform, 2012). One might also consult the introductory chapter of David Hicks, *Ritual & Belief: Readings in the Anthropology of Religion* (New York: McGraw-Hill, 1999).

INTRODUCTION

Theology

  Christianity is primarily a monotheistic devotional religion (many non-Western religions place little or no emphasis on gods or devotion to gods) and the intellectual aspects of Christian religion are explored in **theology**, the aspect of religion closest to philosophy. "Theology" is a Christian term derived from the Greek, and basically it means the study of the nature of the divine as explored by those committed to forms of Western religion including Christianity. Theology is the rational conceptual justification of what members of the religious group think and believe to be true. Theology uses reason to justify and explicate doctrines and dogma.

  Many people assume that non-Western religious traditions are pretty much like Western religions. For example, almost all Western religions are exclusive, which means that in joining one religious group, one must reject all others as wrong, possibly as evil.[27] This is not common in non-Western traditions, which tend to be non-exclusive, and tend not to understand their own tradition as possessing the sole truth. Students are often astonished that in other cultures, one can easily move between two or three religious traditions without any problem.[28] This fact lends support to the position that non-Western systems are really not religions in the way the West uses the term.

Western Philosophy and Theology Share a Number of Basic Problems

  There are several problems common to both religion and philosophy in the West such as concern with the fundamental nature of human beings, the existence of a single omnipotent creator god (if any), the source and structure of ultimate reality, the nature of the good life for human beings, and both have a shared concern with morality and the basis for morality (i.e., ethics), and questions of what we should value and why.

  In terms of content, religion and philosophy also have problems that are unique to each and not shared. For example, the nature of valid inference or a cogent argument (in logic) and the explication of the notion of "cause" are purely philosophical; the function of baptism or the proper age for baptism is purely theological or doctrinal.

  Although philosophy and religion share many common problems, neither are defined just by the content of what they study. It is more in the *approach* to these various problems that philosophy and theology differ so profoundly.

The Approach of Theology and Philosophy

  To distinguish theology and philosophy is to distinguish the world-view of early Athens from the world-view of Jerusalem. These differences provide the historical foundations for the distinction we in the West make between philosophy and religion. What differentiates these two is the approach they take and the assumptions they make.

What Is Assumed to be True?

  A major distinction between philosophy and theology lies in **what they assume to be true**. Christian

---

[27] As with any generalization, there are exceptions. Scholars have noticed many of the students in Buddhist groups are Jewish and Buddhist simultaneously. Some Roman Catholic priests and nuns have been recognized as Zen Buddhist teachers (see the bibliography) at the same time. Often, Quakers and Unitarians feel that they belong to multiple traditions. Native Americans in the southwestern states will often follow both their own traditional religions and either Roman Catholicism or some form of evangelical Protestantism.

[28] It is common to note that in traditional China, everyone is Confucian in their moral, familial and political lives, Buddhist in the realm of matters of life and death, Taoist in matters of alchemy, medicine, and cosmology, and also participants in "Little Tradition" forms of popular religion including ghosts, spirits, and gods in heavenly realms. Nevertheless, in China politics was important for Confucianism, Buddhism, and Taoism, and because of power politics, each group separated itself from its rivals in the competition for political influence.

theology begins by assuming the existence of a supernatural dimension of reality, traditionally interpreted as a single spiritual being who created and continues to sustain all that exists, and the transcendent realm inhabited by that being or beings. In English-speaking Christian cultures that spiritual being is called God (from the pagan pre-Christian German word "gott" or fluid) and this being is described as omnipotent, omniscient, omnibenevolent[29] and the creator of all that exists.

If a being with these characteristics does not exist, if in fact there is no supernatural dimension of reality, then theology is the study of things like the Marvel universe of the X-Men, like studying Middle Earth[30] or the civilizations of Barsoom[31] or the content of fantasy fiction novels such as the Harry Potter series. If there is no supernatural realm, then an expert in theology is like an expert in the history of and architecture of Hogwort's Academy. One can be an expert in unicorns or dragons as well. Such a person is a genuine expert in the area, but what she studies need not exist. Thus, theology assumes that God exists.

It is popular to say that philosophy demands justification for every claim; that nothing is simply assumed to be true. Since the days of Socrates and Plato four hundred years before the Christian era, philosophers have been very wary of accepting anything as true unless there is substantial evidence to justify the claim. Philosophy strives for clarity about what we think is true and why we think it is true, which means to be critical with respect to all assumptions and not accept a claim too easily. A thorough philosopher will require that all conclusions exhibit their truth or probability in the light of reason or sense experience before being accepted. It is very difficult to imagine any absolute assumptions without which philosophy would cease to be.

If you assert that a statement is true, the contemporary philosopher will think it is perfectly appropriate to ask how do you know? How do we know that the sun is 93 million miles from earth? How do we know that the square of the hypotenuse of a right triangle is equal to the sum of the squares of the other two sides? What evidence supports the claim that the universe is nearly fourteen billion years old, or that it is merely 6,000 years old? What evidence is there for the existence of free will, and what do we mean by the term "free will"? How do we know what year Henry VIII was born?

For a philosopher, before any statement can be accepted as true, there must be good reasons which justify and support the claim. For philosophy, the fact that authorities in the past asserted the claim, or that a sacred text makes such a claim, does not constitute good evidence or reasons (how does the authority know? sacred texts do not agree and highly regarded interpreters of sacred texts do not always agree).

Thus, the philosopher does not start out assuming that a god exists or that a god does not exist; rather the philosopher will ask the person or group which makes the assertion if there is any evidence at all which can justify the claim that such a being exists. And for those who hold that no god exists, the philosopher will ask if there are good reasons to conclude that, as defined, such a being is self-contradictory or impossible. Based on argument and evidence, some philosophers reject the existence of a divine creator, and others accept the claim as reasonable or probable. This philosophical approach is also found in some religious scholars (theologians) and it generated numerous attempts to find an argument which could prove that the God of Christianity exists, or at least provide some evidence or justification to make probable the claim that some sort of a god exists.

The Goals of Philosophy and Theology

---

[29] This standard list is glossed as infinitely powerful (omnipotent), knows all that is true (omniscient) and is infinitely and perfectly moral or perfectly good (omnibenevolent).

[30] A reference to J. R. R. Tolkien's classic book trilogy, ***The Lord of the Rings***, which was made into a very successful movie trilogy by Peter Jackson. ***The Hobbit*** trilogy of films is also set in Middle Earth.

[31] A reference to Edgar Rice Burroughs' fantasy realm based on Mars, found in his classic novels ***A Princess of Mars***, ***The Gods of Mars***, and ***The Warlord of Mars***. The realm of Barsoom was the setting for the 2012 Disney film *John Carter*.

INTRODUCTION

The goals of philosophy and theology are interestingly different. The **goal of theology** is to understand the nature of the divine and the proper relationship between that divinity and human beings. The primary activity to accomplish that is the explication and interpretation of religious truth or religious doctrine as contained in sacred scriptures from the past (for Christians this is the Bible), or found in the writings of the leaders of the tradition. In this sense, theology is not independent of religion; rather, theology serves religion. The basic orientation of both theology and religion is usually otherworldly and focuses in the ultimate direction of the eternal as opposed to the merely temporal.

In general, the **goal of philosophy** is wisdom (remember "philosophy" means "love of wisdom"). This wisdom is often interpreted as a clarity which provides the ability, knowledge or skill to live a good life. It is also the wisdom to realize how little we really know for sure, and philosophy makes us less confident in the simple answers accepted by those of the past.

Philosophers know that we cannot simply discard everything we think we know and start fresh. We must have confidence in our current understanding and use it to live in our world, and yet we cannot allow ourselves to be so confident that we are unable to modify our current understanding, or even to reject it when new compelling evidence is presented. Even our most cherished beliefs could be wrong (maybe the earth is *not* the center of the universe after all, maybe large amounts of vitamin C will not lessen the duration or intensity of a cold), and recognizing that is the strength of science. We must be willing to value evidence, and study it even if it leads to contradiction of some of our most deeply held beliefs.

We all realize that one group's or person's common sense can be another person's absurdity.[32] Philosophers understand that human thought is fallible; we may be wrong about what we believe to be true. Not only were ancient societies wrong about many of their beliefs, but when we analyze his arguments, we may conclude that Socrates may have been wrong. Plato and Aristotle may have been wrong. Kant may have been wrong. You and I may be wrong. Ideally, philosophers are willing to change their minds when an alternative view has very strong evidence to support it. Philosophers tend to think that wisdom is acquired by way of some kind of comprehensive intelligent and critical understanding of the nature of human beings, the nature of the world which human beings inhabit, and the relation between the two.

Attitude Towards Legitimate Sources of Knowledge.

Philosophy and theology have quite different attitudes towards sources of knowledge. Both philosophy and theology accept (1) **reason** and (2) **sense experience** as sources of relatively reliable knowledge. Reason tells us that the square root of 2 is ±1.41428 . . . , and sense experience tells us that the sun is shining outside our window.

But philosophy rejects two additional sources which theology accepts as a source of genuine knowledge. Theology accepts (3) **authority** and (4) **scripture** as sources of reliable knowledge. An important source of knowledge for the Christian tradition is pronouncements made by church dignitaries and officials.[33] For many Christians, when church authorities pronounce some practice praiseworthy, and a different practice to be sinful, most followers accept these authorities and accept the statements as true and certain, and use them to guide their choices and their lives. For many followers, scripture and church authorities are accorded a sacred status which exempts them from critical challenge.

---

[32] For much of the world, reincarnation or rebirth is common sense. For others, it seems to be absurd.

[33] It is common to observe that some Little Tradition church leaders imagine that science is simply *whatever scientists believe* thus turning science into a faith system like Christianity. Of course, no scientist accepts something as true simply because Newton or Einstein stated it. When one believes a statement to be true because there is sufficient evidence, we call that knowledge, not belief. The question scientists ask is: What is the evidence? Where does the evidence lead? Are there any possible observations which could show the claim false? What predictions are made by the hypothesis? Science does not produce certainty; rather it seeks for the best explanation consistent with reason and observation.

Philosophers do not do this. Concerning authority, philosophers ask, "How does the authority know?" or "Where did the authority gain her knowledge?" or "When two different authorities disagree on a doctrine, how can we tell which of them is correct?" Thus philosophers do not treat authority alone as a reliable source of knowledge. Similarly, no scientist accepts a claim merely because some famous scientist has asserted it. A Nobel-prize-winning scientist may make a claim, and fellow scientists ask, "What is the evidence that supports the claim?" "What possible tests can confirm or disconfirm the findings?"

The second source of knowledge accepted by theology is the belief that the sacred scriptures of its tradition are without error. Sacred scriptures of Western religions are often called revelation, truths revealed by God. Revelation is treated as more certain than knowledge gained by reason or by sense experience. The philosophical approach rejects the *assumption* of the absolute truth of sacred texts. Philosophy does not blindly reject everything in scriptures, but neither does philosophy treat scriptural statements as sources of certain knowledge when properly interpreted.[34] From the point of view of orthodox Christian theology, properly interpreted revealed scripture cannot err, and thus any statement that contradicts revealed scripture (when properly interpreted) is necessarily false. Of course, the problem as to what a given scriptural statement really means is usually not an easy problem for the theologian. Scripture does not interpret itself. Thus, although scripture may be absolute, interpretations of scripture are diverse.[35]

So, in general theologians accept four reliable sources for knowledge, and philosophy (and science) accept only the first two of those, reason and sense experience. It must be obvious that when two groups disagree on the sources of reliable knowledge, meaningful discussion is very difficult. One group offers support for their claims by quoting scriptures or church authorities, and considers that certain and the issue settled. The other group rejects the claims of authority and scripture without empirical evidence to support the claims.

Attitudes Towards Truth

The attitude toward truth differs between philosophy and theology as well. For the theologian, the ultimate truth has been set forth once and for all and is to be discovered in special sacred writings or teachings of the past. For most Christians, the highest truth was laid out in the writings of the Old Testament (mostly the books treated as sacred in the Jewish religion) and the New Testament (the twenty-seven books originally written in Greek which relate to the message of Jesus, the anointed one).

For the philosopher, there is no one source of complete truth. Philosophy does not look to the past for the ultimate and final truth. Even the greatest thinkers have made questionable assumptions and logical mistakes; we are all fallible and we can and do make mistakes even today (and when these errors are recognized, the mistakes are corrected and not repeated). There are many valuable insights and truths discovered by studying thinkers of the past, but these insights are not ultimate; they can be improved. By studying the philosophers of the past, we find the mistakes committed and expect that we will not repeat those mistakes.

Suppose you are a Platonist, a person who looks to Plato as a great philosopher. Plato's philosophy has problems. Plato was clearly mistaken about many of his claims, and many of his arguments are not very strong or not logically valid. The modern Platonist selectively rejects and reconstructs Plato's positions. The Platonist philosopher does not accept something just because Plato wrote it any more than a scientist would accept something just because a respected fellow scientist like Newton or Einstein wrote it.[36]

---

[34] Do not make the mistake of thinking that philosophers assume that scriptures are false; they do not. Rather, they take a "wait and see" attitude, and test the empirical claims made by these sacred texts, not merely to confirm, but also to see if any observation could disconfirm the claims. This is the critical attitude of science in general, not just philosophy.

[35] For example, take "Thou Shalt Not Kill." This does require interpretation. Can we kill animals and eat them? Can we kill in times of war? Can we kill criminals in the name of the state and justice? Can we kill in self-defense? The early Christians were pacifists and did not fight when thrown to the lions. Note that different Christians disagree on each of these things. Interpretations vary.

[36] Remember that authority is NOT a source of reliable knowledge for science.

INTRODUCTION

The attitude of the creative philosopher will be a feeling of confidence with respect to her or his own views, not as absolute, but subject to revision when errors are revealed. A philosopher tries to start out having learned from the mistakes of the past, tries to establish her claims on as sound a footing as possible, and clearly moving in the right direction. The creative philosopher learns from the past, but also hopes that she or he can learn from and avoid the errors made by those in the past, and as a result can re-conceptualize and produce something more complete than what has ever been set forth before.[37]

ASIAN VIEWS OF SPIRITUALITY AND WISDOM

There is an amazing variety and diversity in what are called "world religions" which are not encompassed by the concerns of Western theology. In Indian thought, philosophy and religion are encompassed by (1) notions of social, ritual, moral and religious duty (called **dharma**), and (2) insight into the ultimate nature of reality (called **darshana**).[38] As we have already noted, in China and Japan, the terms for spirituality are **ssu-hsiang**, or **shi-so** 思 想 and the closest English translation to this is just "thought."

The standard Western way to be religious focuses on faith in, obedience to, and devotion to the one Supreme Being, who is thought of as a supreme king or ruler who hands down laws that must be obeyed upon the threat of severe punishment. Indian models of spirituality include devotion, but are considerably broader than traditional Western models.

Four Ways of Being Religious

In the Indian model, there are at least four ways of being a religious human being living a spiritual life.[39] One can be spiritual by engaging in the pathway of right **action**, that is, certain special sorts of activities which certainly include performing rituals or ceremonies but it might also include one's social and moral duties, perhaps building homes for the homeless, donating money to social or religious groups, or feeding the hungry.

Another way of being spiritual is to engage in quiet, solitary **meditation**, in a deep and profound focusing of awareness until a transformation of ordinary consciousness is brought about. A third way of being religious is the pathway of **reasoned inquiry**. This is to use one's intelligence or reason to question, doubt, explore, challenge and ultimately to achieve liberating wisdom, or achieve profound insight into the nature of the way things truly are (here the student can see where the lines between religion and philosophy are blurring).

---

[37] The author is indebted to Prof. Harold McCarthy for many of the distinctions and points stressed here.

[38] *Darshana* is a term rich with meaning, including "focused religious viewing," which can mean having eye-contact with a sacred statue or an image of the divine, or viewing an image of one's spiritual teacher, or having a face-to-face meeting with one's spiritual guide, and ultimately seeing past the individual into the absolute reality. In modern times a follower can have live *darshana* by watching an icon of a divinity on the internet.

[39] In recent times Western scholars have suggested that there may be many different ways of being a religious human being living a spiritual life. For example, see Dale Cannon, *Six Ways of Being Religious: A Framework for Comparative Studies of Religion* (New York: Wadsworth Publishing, 1996), or Gary E. Kessler, *Eastern Ways of Being Religious* (Mayfield Publishing, 2000).

Finally, another way of being spiritual is the pathway of **devotion**. On this path one will worship the divine, one will love completely, rely upon, and pray to supernatural powers or beings, the majority of which in Asia are neither rulers nor creators.

Although all four of these can be found within the framework of Christianity, Western religion tends to place the greatest stress upon devotion, dogma, doctrine, and ritual out of these four pathways of spirituality. Many of the world's great spiritual traditions focus on the other ways of being religious. It is important to realize that what is typical of Western religion is not typical of all world spiritual pathways.

TERMINOLOGY

In this book, the reader will be led through the many ways of Asian intellectual thought, the many ways of Asian spirituality typical of India, China, Japan and Tibet. Some of these traditions will argue that there exists some sacred reality which interacts with humans, which rewards, which punishes, and which intervenes in human history with miracles. This is **theism**. Some assert that this sacred ultimate is plural or many. We can describe that as **polytheism**. Some will argue that the sacred is one divine being who cares about humans, interacts with humans, rewards, and judges, and we call that **monotheism**. Some assert that there is one divine being but that one divine being takes many different forms or incarnations throughout history; shall we call this one monotheism as well?

We will discuss some Asian spiritual systems which assert that all the world is sacred, everything in the world is sacred, including humans. Western scholars refer to these as **pantheism**. There is one view which seems comfortable with a divinity who gives form and shape to the chaotic universe, but that divine creator does not have any special affection for humans and does not answer prayers or respond to rituals; this is called **deism**. Some will argue that the genuinely real is oneness and when we perceive differences, we are misperceiving the highest ultimate truth. We might refer to these positions as **monism**. Some will argue that sacred reality cannot be numbered at all because all concepts are inadequate, including the concept of "oneness." Sacred reality cannot be described adequately as one or two or many. Some of these can be called **non-dualism**.

Some will argue that there is no convincing evidence that there exist sacred realities which transcend this world or are apart from this world, although if such evidence were produced they could change their minds. They often find the definitions and descriptions of a deity to be self-contradictory and therefore such a deity would be impossible. Because there is no good reason to accept a supernatural being, such people do not accept divinities. This would be **atheism**. Some find focusing on divinities counterproductive, irrelevant or useless for the achievement of a spiritual life. Often these are called **non-theistic**.

A person who is **agnostic** is someone who says although a divinity is possible, there is not sufficient evidence for either accepting or rejecting divinities, and so an agnostic is not sure whether there is any supernatural deity, and thus reserves judgment. It is also true that an agnostic could argue that it is impossible for any limited *finite* human to actually know that an *infinite* being exists.

ASIAN LANGUAGES

The technical ideas and concepts in this book are described in languages like Sanskrit (India), Tibetan, Chinese, and Japanese. In the discussions which follow, we shall find technical terms in many different languages, and we will use words that most students will not have heard of before. Those terms in Asian languages which seem to have fairly close equivalents in English will be rendered by English terms. We will encounter many important technical terms whose meanings cannot be accurately translated into English (i.e., *jnana, Brahman, satori, koan, Nirvana* or *Tao*). Those we will simply describe and define and then proceed to use the foreign term in the text.

None of these Asian civilizations use the Latin alphabet, the "a" and "b" and "z" with which we are so familiar.

So, these Asian technical terms and names need to be rendered using our alphabet, that is, *transliterated* into English so that we can pronounce them. This is also called *romanization*. Even simple things like capitalization is a product of Latin languages; there is no such thing as a capital letter in Sanskrit, Chinese, or Japanese. In their classical forms, these languages did not have commas, periods, or quotation marks.

Even when romanized, pronunciation will be a challenge. It is made even more difficult because there are different forms of transliteration into English, even for the same language. To complicate matters, some languages have sounds that do not exist in English, and scholars use numerous different technical marks (diacritical marks) which indicate subtle sounds that the great majority of students will not be able to hear easily. For example, you may have seen the name of an important Indian deity written as *Shiva*, *Śiva* and also *Siva*. You may have seen the central Buddhist concept written as *shunyata, sunyata* or *śūnyatā*. You may have seen *Ch'ang* and *Chang*, or *k'ung-fu* and *kung-fu*. How are we to pronounce these correctly?

For the ancient Indian language Sanskrit, scholars utilize numerous diacritical marks. However, as an introductory text, we have chosen to omit the diacriticals and try to follow the standard romanization which will allow students to approximate the accepted pronunciation. Thus we will write Shiva for the name of the deity, not Śiva. We will use *ch* instead of *c*, *sh* instead of *ś or ṣ* so that non-specialists can approximate the sounds.[40]

For the Chinese language there are numerous transliteration systems, but there are two which are important currently in the English-speaking world. One is the Wade-Giles system which has been used in English-speaking countries for well over a hundred years, and the other is the Pinyin system, decreed by Chairman Mao in the 1950s and becoming more popular in this country since the 1980s.

This text book will use the Wade-Giles system as the primary system of transliteration of Chinese because it is what the Library of Congress uses, and every English book prior to the 1970s used only the Wade-Giles system. Important texts published this year still use the Wade-Giles system. However, the Pinyin romanizations are becoming increasingly popular and will be included as well for those familiar with that system. When appropriate, the author will also include an approximate guide to proper pronunciation because in many cases, neither the Pinyin nor the Wade-Giles romanizations will be pronounced correctly by the average English-speaking student.[41]

There is more than one way to transliterate Japanese terms, for example we can write kōan, or kooan, or koan (a *koan* is a puzzling question asked by a Zen teacher of the student). Many Japanese terms appear in English dictionaries, in which case we will use the English spellings. For all the others, the standard way to romanize Japanese terms, called the Hepburn system, is the one that will be used in this book.

The case with Tibetan terms is even more complicated. It is impossible for non-Tibetan speakers to pronounce Tibetan words even remotely correctly using the system of transliteration that scholars utilize. The standard transliteration system for Tibetan was devised by Turrell Wylie, but in this book we will use the phonetic system associated with Jeffrey Hopkins.[42] Some Tibetan terms occur fairly frequently in English newspapers and in those cases we will retain the popular spelling.

"Before the Common Era"

Like the great majority of scholarly books in recent decades, this book does not use the calendar abbreviations

---

[40] There are some foreign terms which have become well-known in English spellings, and for these we will follow common practice.

[41] For example, it is not clear to the average reader how to pronounce the Chinese term "Qi" or "Xin" based on the Pinyin romanization, or "jen" or "k'ung-fu" and "kung-fu" in the Wade-Giles system. The term *foxing* in Pinyin is written *fo-hsing* in Wade-Giles. The issue is further complicated by the fact that there are very many dialects of Chinese, and the same term can be pronounced differently depending on where the speaker was born and lives in China.

[42] Dr. Jeffrey Hopkins is a scholar of Tibetan Buddhism and has written extensively on Tibetan religions. He explains his preferences for transliterations in Jeffrey Hopkins, *Meditation on Emptiness* (London: Wisdom Publications, 1983), in the Technical Notes at the beginning of the book, pages 19–22.

INTRODUCTION

"B.C." or "A.D." These two abbreviations for calendar dates seem to imply some special international status and privilege for the Christian religion. Why would a Chinese Marxist date Mao or Confucius by the birth of Jesus? To say that Siddhartha, the Buddha, was born in 563 B.C. (Before Christ) is not relevant to a Buddhist—why would a Buddhist want to date the Buddha by the Christian misunderstanding of the birth year of its founder?[43] In fact, in many Buddhist countries such as Sri Lanka, the current calendar date system is based on their understanding of the date of the death of the Buddha.

Similarly "A.D." means *anno domini*, "in the year of our Lord" — again a uniquely Christian calendar. Without intending to be disrespectful to Christian cultures, or disrespectful to non-Christian traditions, in this book we use the standard neutral abbreviations used in most recent scholarly history books: "Common Era" or **C.E.** and **B.C.E.** or "Before the Common Era."

WHY STUDY ASIAN THOUGHT?

At no time in this text will we argue that any particular religion is best. If you are already firmly convinced that your own personal religious outlook is perfect and cannot be improved, then the study of Asian thought has something valuable to offer to you. Stated simply, when you learn about spiritual systems which have different presuppositions from your own, which offer new possibilities of thought, this gives you the ability to better understand and appreciate your own religion from different perspectives. In articulating the beliefs of others, you can better articulate your own beliefs. As a result you can reflect about your own life and the world; you can try to clarify the basis of your own world-view.

Actually, that works just as well if you consider yourself non-religious. By studying the spiritual patterns of others, you can come to appreciate the variety of ways that human beings are spiritual, and again come to understand where your own views position you in regards to these deep and enduring issues.

The primary purpose of this book is to help you understand ways of being wise or spiritual which arose in Asia (and are not the same as Judeo-Christian systems), but which at the same time have a long history of recognition of worth and importance to fellow human beings. I have learned much from each of these; I hope you will too.

ACKNOWLEDGMENTS

No book that aims to cover so much in so few pages can possibly satisfy all readers and any approach to such a vast task comes with advantages and drawbacks. The advantages have to do with the range of topics, and the drawbacks have to do with details. It should be obvious that the range of perspectives and traditions that this book covers is beyond the expertise of any single scholar, or many scholars. Some of the material in this book comes from personal travel and personal experience, but even more from approximately five decades of reading, studying, organizing, distilling, teaching and discussing Asian thought. It also comes as a result of studying with a great many excellent teachers, including Chang Chung-yuan, Chung-ying Cheng, David Kalupahana from Sri Lanka, K. N. Upadhyaya from India, Eliot Deutsch, and Harold McCarthy, at the University of Hawaii. I have benefitted greatly from ongoing conversations with colleagues at the University of California at Santa Barbara and the University of California, Riverside. I have had valuable discussions with David Chappell, Robert Doud, and others informally and

---

[43] Christian historians are in fair agreement that Jesus was born between 6 and 4 B.C.E. because the most likely date for the death of King Herod (the ruler when Jesus was born according to the New Testament) is 4 B.C.E.

at conferences. Dr. Philip Ricards graciously read early drafts of some chapters and made numerous suggestions and improvements from which I have benefitted. I have also learned from all the students who have taken my classes over the decades. Their questions have prompted me to do further research in many topics, and have allowed me to work on clarification of many obscure issues. I would like to express my appreciation to all of them.

I have tried to provide acknowledgments for each and every book and author whose ideas and words have influenced this text, but fifty years of reading and lecturing means that there is much which I may have remembered but lost track of the original source long ago. In the case of any omissions, please let me know and I will be very happy to make suitable acknowledgment of the sources in future editions.

Although I have learned so much from so many, it should be noted that no work of any size is free from errors. Certainly this volume will have more than its fair share. The author is responsible for all such errors.

TECHNICAL TERMS USED IN THIS CHAPTER

agnostic	The term "agnostic" literally means "not know." An agnostic is someone who thinks a divinity might be possible, but does not claim to **know** that a divine being exists, and is not sure whether any such beings exist.
atheism	Literally "not-theism;" the view that there is insufficient or no evidence to support the claim that there exists a divine being who performs miracles, interacts with humans, rewards, punishes, or judges. An atheist does not claim to possess certain knowledge of the fact that a divinity does not exist. Rather, the atheist concludes that there is not enough evidence to allow one to conclude that such existence is even probable. "Non-theistic" is used in this chapter to mean religious attitudes which acknowledge that gods may exist, but consider the existence of a god irrelevant to spiritual goals.
Bhagavad Gita	The "Song of the Lord," "Song Supreme" or "Song Celestial," a sacred text for many Hindus which tells of Lord Krishna.
darshana	This is to see directly the nature of the sacred, and is pronounced darshan.
emic	The insider's view of a religious tradition, the perspective of a devotee, a believer. These can vary from person to person.
etic	The outsider's view of a religion, the perspective of a scholar, a person trying to maintain an objective standpoint. Scholars of religion hold that both an emic and an etic perspective are required if one is to gain a useful understanding of any particular religious tradition.
monism	The view that all of reality is truly one, not many. All distinctions and differences which we perceive are, in some sense, not real.
omnibenevolent	All-good, perfectly good, infinitely good, perfectly moral.
omnipotent	All-powerful, infinitely powerful, unlimited in power.
omniscient	Knows all that is true, past, present, future.
pantheism	The view that all ("pan-") is sacred, or divine.
philosophy	The love of ("philo") wisdom ("sophia"). Philosophy is the branch of human endeavor which seeks clarity and justification for those things we are curious about, and which we believe to be true or false. The modern philosopher attempts to ask and answer "What do you mean?" and "How do you know?"

INTRODUCTION

"Does your conclusion follow logically from your evidence?"

polytheism | The view that there are two or more sacred beings who care about humans, may answer prayers, interact with history and perform miracles, reward and judge.

shaman | This is the specialist (often either a male or female village priest) who is believed to be able to communicate with and interact with spirit realms.

theism | The view that there exists one or more divine beings who interact with humans, who care about humans, who reward, punish, and judge, who perform miracles and answer prayers, and who preside over a heavenly realm.

theology | The intellectual study of the nature of the divine. In Christianity, the theologian is the believer who attempts to make intellectual sense of and find conceptual justification for the doctrines of his or her church.

theodicy | The problem within Christian theology of trying to account for the existence of evil in a universe created by a deity who is infinitely powerful, perfectly good, and opposed to evil. If God created evil, then the deity cannot be all good. If God did not create evil, then God is not the only creator of all that exists. If God cannot eliminate evil, then God is not all powerful. If God can eliminate evil but chooses not to do so, then God is not all good. If God created everything, then God created Satan.

Vedas | The ancient sacred scriptures of Hinduism, which includes (1) four volumes of sacred hymns, (2) the Brahmanas which discuss ritual, (3) the Books of the Forest Monks, and (4) the Upanishads (all of which are discussed in detail in succeeding chapters).

QUESTIONS FOR FURTHER DISCUSSION

1) It might be an instructive exercise to look up several different definitions of the term "religion" in reference works, and then see if those definitions will describe the beliefs and practices of non-Western religions.

2) Is it possible for a religion to exist only within the mind of a single person, or do religions require a culture and a group of followers? Of course we can say that "Sam makes a religion out of golf," but it is not clear that we use the term "religion" in the same way we might speak of the "Protestant religions." What do you think?

3) How important are shared systems of symbols to religion? Could a religion exist without any special religious symbols?

4) Many students find it nearly impossible to use the term "religion" to describe a group which has no concern with supernatural deities. Yet there are several non-Western groups that certainly appear to have all the trappings of religions, but no concern with gods. Where do you stand on this issue? Is belief in a deity required for something to be called "a religion"?

5) One can adopt an insider's view of a religious tradition (an emic view), or an outsider's view of a particular religious tradition (an etic view). Scholars of religion feel that both emic and etic views are essential to understanding a religion. Is the insider's view always biased, or prejudiced? If so, everyone who belongs to a religion is biased and prejudiced. Can this be true? Is the outsider's view automatically objective and unbiased? Should we trust whatever a scholarly non-believer says about your religion?

INTRODUCTION

6) We discussed the collection of religious attitudes called Shamanism, whose roots go back into ancient prehistory. Do you find any traces of Shamanism in Western religions or in Western culture? You might consider Hollywood films about ghosts and about people who communicate with the dead (i.e., the 1990 movie *Ghost* with Whoopi Goldberg playing a shaman, or the 1999 film *The Sixth Sense* with Bruce Willis).

7) Do you think that belief in an afterlife is essential for something to be a religion? Western religions assert that there is some sort of life after the death for each individual, however this is not true for all non-Western religions. Some accept reincarnation or rebirth. Others assert that the individual is swallowed up in a great ocean of pure consciousness. Still others put their energy into this life because there is no life after death.

BIBLIOGRAPHY

RECENT DISCUSSIONS OF 'WHAT IS RELIGION?'

Brutus, Steven, *Religion, Culture, History: A Philosophical Study of Religion* (CreateSpace Independent Publishing Platform, 2012). ISBN-10: 1479109681.

Dubuisson, Daniel, *The Western Construction of Religion: Myths, Knowledge, and Ideology* (Johns Hopkins University Press, 2007)

Hicks, David, *Ritual & Belief: Readings in the Anthropology of Religion* (New York: McGraw-Hill, 1999)

Masuzawa, Tomoko, *The Invention of World Religions: Or, How European Universalism Was Preserved in the Language of Pluralism* (University of Chicago Press, 2005)

Nongbri, Brent, *Before Religion: A History of a Modern Concept* (Yale University, 2013)

Taylor, Mark, ed., *Critical Terms for Religious Studies* (Chicago: University of Chicago Press, 1998)

GENERAL INTRODUCTIONS TO ASIAN THOUGHT

Bonevac, Daniel, Phillips, Stephen, *Understanding Non-Western Philosophy* (Mountain View, Ca: Mayfield, 1993)

Cannon, Dale, *Six Ways of Being Religious: A Framework for Comparative Studies of Religion* (New York: Wadsworth Publishing, 1996)

Carmody, Denise and T. L. Brink, *Ways to the Center: An Introduction to World Religions*, 5th edition (Belmont, Ca: Wadsworth, 2002)

Coogan, Michael D., ed., *Eastern Religions: Origins, Beliefs, Practices, Holy Texts, Sacred Places* (New York: Oxford University Press, 2005)

Ellwood, Robert, *Cycles of Faith: The Development of the World's Religions* (New York: Alta Mira Press, 2003)

Fenton, John Y., Norvin Hein, Frank E. Reynolds, Alan Miller, Niels Nielsen, Jr., Grace Burford, *Religions of Asia*, 3rd edition (New York: St. Martin's Press, 1993)

Fieser, James, and John Powers, *Scriptures of the East*, 2nd edition (McGraw-Hill, 2002)

Hawkins, Bradley K., *An Introduction to Asian Religions* (New York: Pearson Longman, 2004)

Herman, A. L., *An Introduction to Indian Thought* (Prentiss-Hall, 1976)

Hicks, David, *Ritual & Belief: Readings in the Anthropology of Religion* (McGraw-Hill, 1999)

Hopfe, Lewis M., and Mark R. Woodward *Religions of the World*, 10th edition (New Jersey: Pearson-Prentice Hall, 2007)

Kessler, Gary E., *Eastern Ways of Being Religious* (Mountain View, Ca: Mayfield, 2000)

Koller, John, and Patricia Koller, *A Sourcebook in Asian Philosophy* (Macmillan, 1991)

Koller, John M., *Asian Philosophies*, 5th edition (New Jersey: Pearson-Prentice-Hall, 2007)

Koller, John M., *The Indian Way: Asian Perspectives* (New York: Macmillan, 1982)

INTRODUCTION

Oxtoby, Willard G., *World Religions: Eastern Traditions*, 3rd edition (London: Oxford, 2009)

Potter, Karl H., *Presuppositions of India's Philosophies* (Englewood Cliffs, N.J.: Prentice-Hall, 1963, paperback Westport, CT: Greenwood Press, 1963)

Radhakrishnan, Sarvapali, *Indian Philosophy*, two volumes (London: Allen & Unwin, 1927; reprinted several times)

Schouten, Jan Peter, *Jesus as Guru: The Image of Christ among Hindus and Christians in India*, (Amsterdam/New York: Rodopi Press, 2008)

Van Voorst, Robert, *An Anthology of Asian Scriptures* (Belmont, CA: Wadsworth, 2001)

PART I: INDIA

CHAPTER 1: THE ORIGINS OF INDIAN THOUGHT

1.1 OVERVIEW OF THE CHAPTER

In this chapter we will explain a bit of the ancient history of the subcontinent region which we call India, and which provides some of the background for the modern Indian religious world view. We will explain the origins of terms like "Hindu" and "India," and we will discuss the ancient religious and philosophical language of India, called Sanskrit. We will also explain why the common Western scholarly view on the origins of what is called "Hinduism" is considered controversial by some in India. Finally, we will discuss the ancient civilization known as the Harappan civilization (also the Indus Valley civilization) and what we know of the religious practices of this ancient culture.

The origins of the religious worldviews of this subcontinent area go back at least five thousand years (about 3000 B.C.E.). Our discussion will begin with the very early Harappan civilization, and then the later religion of the Aryan peoples embedded in the first of the Vedic texts, the *Rig Veda* (earlier than 1500 B.C.E.). Although modern Indian spirituality is not identical to these early forms of religion, the discerning student will be able to see elements of contemporary Indian religion whose roots point back to the ancient past.

1.2 GENERAL REMARKS ON THE INDIAN WORLD VIEW

The path of the spiritual or religious life was very highly regarded in ancient India[1] and remains so today. Traditionally, people who are spiritually wise are regarded with great respect and even reverence. There are several pathways possible for the religious life, often involving some form of self-discipline.

One of the many paths of self-perfection and spirituality is the path of worship and devotion—a very common and popular way of being religious. In Sanskrit, the sacred language of classical India, this devotional pathway (*marga*) is called *bhakti-marga*.[2] But in India, this is not the only way of being religious. Those who focus their energies upon the path of ritual, of ceremony, of activity, of action, of doing (*karma-marga*) are also religious. There is also the path of mental discipline, of concentration, of focused meditation (*dhyana-marga*). Finally, there is the path of knowledge,

---

[1] We would be remiss if we did not note that in the times that we are discussing, in the past, there wasn't any country called "India" or "Nepal" or "Pakistan" and the many people who lived on the subcontinent never thought of themselves as unified. There were no borders, and no central authority unifying the broad range of territory that today we call "India." This textbook uses the term "India" or "Indian thought" for convenience but it might be more accurate to describe this as ideas of people who lived in ancient lands which thousands of years later became unified and called "India." Similarly, the indigenous peoples of north American never thought of themselves as "Americans" until very very recently.

[2] *Bhakti* (devotion) tends to be the central approach in Western religion, which sometimes tends to identify all of religious activity with this one aspect. However, Indian religious thought is much broader than this; people are religious in many different ways, and in India each way is effective and acceptable.

the acquisition of liberating wisdom and insight by careful study, thinking and analysis (*jnana-marga*). Each of these four is an acceptable and valid way of following the spiritual pathway. Just about all the Indian traditions can be understood as combinations of these basic four foundational pathways.

A common assumption in much Indian thought is that the true nature of each of us is profoundly spiritual. The ultimate questions in Indian philosophy and religion are related to this presupposition. If we assume that each of us is profoundly spiritual in our deepest self, the next obvious question would be "What is this profoundly spiritual true self, the truest and deepest nature of a human being?" Other questions follow: What is the nature of ultimate reality and how is it related to the true self? How can I discover and realize this inner self? What is the relationship between my deepest, truest self, and the gods, or the sacred ultimate which lies deeper than the gods? Is the ultimate one or many? Is the ultimate neither one nor many? Is the pathway to salvation a personal journey, or can one rely upon a savior? If we need a savior, from what are we being saved?

Various answers to these and similar questions generated many of the religions and thought systems of ancient India. Later in Indian history, more theoretical questions arose about the basis of morality (ethics), the nature and function of society, the sources and limits of knowledge (epistemology), the techniques of logic to assure validity and soundness in thought processes, and the relationship between the way things appear to be, and the way things truly are (metaphysics). We will see all of these issues discussed in Indian spiritual traditions.

We shall begin with some general remarks about traditional Hinduism, and then explore the roots of Hinduism in the indigenous religion of India which goes back to 3000 years before the Christian era began, in the area of the Indus valley and its Harappan civilization.

The region of the subcontinent we call modern India is quite large and is geographically diverse in climate and in environment. Like all the world's early cultures, the inhabitants depended upon farming for survival. The land was generally fertile and supported the people and their crops. The religious traditions of the time reflect the concerns of farmers. For example, a farmer must worry about drought—will there be enough water? If not, it could mean death to the crops, and death to the people who depend upon them. Too much water can lead to similar consequences. Scholars of Indian religion have noted the great importance of water in India's religious observances, which may be due to the natural concern of people who farm. Whatever it was that controlled the weather and rain were thought to be living forces, divinities, gods and goddesses, and they were intimately connected with the fertility of the earth, plants, and human beings.

1.3 WHAT ARE THE COMMON BELIEFS FOR HINDUS?

There is a tendency among Western people to think of religions as a faith system, or a list of beliefs, and assume that other religions have some common lists of beliefs in which people are expected to have unquestioning faith. This model works very well for Christianity. In general, Christians can be identified by having a creed (the Nicene Creed or the Apostle's Creed), by having faith in the Trinity, the divinity of Jesus, and the role of Jesus in Christian Atonement to provide Reconciliation between God and humans.

Hinduism is *not* a faith system like this. In fact, no traditional Asian religion is. There is no common list of things that one must believe in, have faith in, or accept as true in order to be a Hindu or a Buddhist or Jain, or Confucian. There is no special belief about god or gods required in order to be a Hindu. One can be an atheist and be a Hindu. One can be a monotheist and be a Hindu. One can be a polytheist and be a Hindu. One can be a materialist and be a Hindu.

There is no single sacred text, no single deity, or single teacher that all Hindus would consider supreme, or authoritative, the way a Christian would accept the Christian Bible or accept the monotheistic God of the Old or New

CHAPTER 1: THE ORIGINS OF INDIAN THOUGHT

Testament. Hinduism comprises hundreds of local communities and varying sectarian movements, and these groups do not share a common sacred text, or even a common sacred temple or holy place which can serve as the focus of a pilgrimage. Some Hindus considers temples important, and others reject the idea of a sacred temple. They most certainly do not share a common divinity believed to be absolutely supreme. Those features common to Hinduism tend to be foundational ideas in Indian civilization, traditional ideas like hierarchy, difference between classes, and privileges for some and not for others.

1.4 THE TERM *Hindu*

During the period when the British dominated India (the 18th and 19th centuries into the early 20th century), English speakers consciously used the term "Hinduism" to mean the religious cluster of attitudes of the majority of the Indian population, excluding the Muslims, Jains, Christians and Buddhists.[3] Contemporary scholars use "Hinduism" to name the religion whose earliest forms were taught by the specialists in ritual, the Brahman/Brahmin[4] priestly caste of ancient India. In fact, Hinduism can also be called "Brahmanism" for this reason.[5] It is the predominant religious tradition of the subcontinent of India, and is predominant no where else except India. Perhaps 80-85% of the people of India think of themselves as Hindus.

Although Sanskrit is the classical language of Indian Hinduism,[6] neither the term "India" nor the term "Hindu" are from the Sanskrit. "India" is a Greek term. The fourth century B.C.E. Greek-Macedonian armies of Alexander the Great invaded the northern regions (which today is Pakistan) and the area that they first arrived in they referred to as the Sind. That Greek word became "India." Similarly, the term "Hindu" is of Persian origin. The Muslim armies conquered most of the northern areas of India in the twelfth century C.E., and used the term "Hindu" to describe people living in the land of "Hind," which was their name for India. These terms may have been related to the name of the important river, Indus.[7]

1.5 IS HINDUISM A RELIGION?

The Latin Term translated "Religion"

There was no word in Sanskrit, the scholarly and spiritual language of ancient India, which corresponds to the

---

[3] Some have argued that the British created the concept of "Hinduism." This claim is explored in Brian K. Pennington, *Was Hinduism Invented?: Britons, Indians, and the Colonial Construction of Religion* (New York: Oxford University Press, 2007).

[4] The term for priestly specialist in ritual is "Brahman" but the term "Brahman" has several different meanings. It is ambiguous. We will use the common spelling "Brahmin" for the priests in order to minimize confusion.

[5] Later, we will see that the term Brahman has numerous related meanings, including the sacred sound of prayer, the ultimate absolute reality, and even a specific creator deity.

[6] There is an ongoing controversy among scholars as to whether in Indian history there was ever a unified system called "Hinduism," or whether this is a construct superimposed by British colonialists and missionaries who had their own Christian agenda and Christian presuppositions. Were the various religious thought systems of India ever unified, or were they scattered without a common core? A book which discusses the complexities of the issue is Andrew J. Nicholson, *Unifying Hinduism: Philosophy and Identity in Indian Intellectual History* (South Asia across the Disciplines Series, New York: Columbia University Press, 2010).

[7] Scholars point out that in the period prior to Indo-Muslim Delhi Sultanate (approximately 1200–1500), there were well over a dozen terms specifying ideological groups in India and those various groups did not regard themselves as a single coherent entity. None referred to themselves as "Hindu."

English word "religion." Western monotheists think of a religion as an exclusive group that a person belongs to, and if you belong to one religion, then you cannot be a member of another religion. This exclusivity is far removed from the original meaning of the Latin term *religio* in the early Roman empire.

The original meaning of "religion" was **not** something a person belonged to and which excluded other religions. As noted in the previous chapter, the term "religion" comes from the Latin *religare*, "to tie" or "to bind." Religions, like cultures, bind us together into a common attitude of respect. We act with care and we respect powers because we are bound together and share obligations to the powers that control human destiny. Latin was the language of the Romans, and the Romans had lots of different god- and goddess-cults, some from Egypt, some from Persia, some Greek, some Roman, and many of them in competition with one another. Quite often these powers were associated with forces of nature rather than beings with human-like personalities. In Rome, a *religio* was neither a belief system nor a symbol system, but rather was a community-unifying attitude of respect for cults in general. In matters of luck, we might offer rituals to deities which offer good luck. In matters of love, we might offer rituals to the appropriate goddess of love. If we are going to war, we offer rituals to the appropriate gods of war.

Hence, whatever powers we believe govern our destiny will elicit a religious response from us and inspire us to wish 'to tie or bind' ourselves to these powers in relations of ritual obligation, so that we act with respect and care toward them and can be sure these powers will be on our side.[8]

Dharma and *Darshana*

Although no Indian Sanskrit terms correspond to "religion" in modern English, there are two Sanskrit terms which translators often rendered as "religion." The first is *darshana* (pronounced dar-shan) which has a cluster of meanings, such as to see the nature of reality clearly, to see what is, to behold clearly with faith, to see or to be seen by the deity or the holy teacher.

A second Sanskrit term sometimes translated as "religion" is *dharma*. In the context of Hinduism, the term *dharma* can be translated as sacred duty, moral duty, social duty, righteousness, justice, faith, religious obligation, and social obligation. But, *dharma*, stressing action, does not cover all that is sacred. The term "sacred" can include sacred times, places, omens, architecture, music, trees, and plants. It has been noted that there are some topics which Hindu religion considers religious but which would not be considered religious in Western religions. For example, in Hinduism astronomy and astrology, dance, music, phonetics, and even studies on poetic meter, are religious activities.

1.6 CONTROVERSY OVER THE ORIGINS OF INDIAN RELIGION

Although there is a fairly unanimous understanding of the origins of early Indian religious thought among mainstream academic Western scholars, the issue is more controversial in India. Are all Indian religious and thought systems native to India, or did some important Indian religious ideas originate outside of India? Did all the gods of India originate in India as the legends assert, or were some of the gods imported into India by external non-native groups migrating into India?

In accord with religious teachings, traditional Hindu devotees and some Indian scholars assert that the ancient Indian Hindu religion is an eternal tradition whose origins extend before human history to the beginnings of the universe and whose teachings were divinely revealed to sages in ancient India. In traditional Hindu doctrine, it would then follow that the Indian people and all Indian religions must have originated in India. The traditional belief is that

---

[8] John L. Esposito, Darrell J. Fasching, Todd Lewis, *World Religions Today* (London: Oxford University Press, 2002), p. 7.

CHAPTER 1: THE ORIGINS OF INDIAN THOUGHT

the eternal gods of India revealed truths to the indigenous people, who called themselves Aryans.[9] It would be unthinkable (and contrary to Indian religion) that any Indian gods or religious beliefs could have been the result of a historical migration of non-indigenous peoples into India.

Western scholars generally hold that the dominant Indo-European language and the people who spoke it, and religions on the Indian subcontinent did not all originate in India. Instead, an important source for many central features of Indian religions is a group of people who emigrated out of their homeland between 4200 and 3300 B.C.E. and eventually migrated into India around 1500 B.C.E., displacing the indigenous groups of people who were in living in northern India, and gradually replacing the native society with their own religious world view and practices.[10]

A Brief Summary of the Standard Western View

The subcontinent we call India was difficult for humans to get to because to the north, access was impeded by the tallest mountains in the world, the Himalayas, and major desert regions also separated India from the rest of Asia. The primary route for humans to get to India involved traveling along the western coastline, or through mountain passes through present-day Iran, Afghanistan and Pakistan.[11]

Although it was not easy to get to the Indian subcontinent, nevertheless India was inhabited by successive waves of immigrants over the millennia. The earliest evidence of human habitations in India may go back 60,000 years, perhaps more. There is much archaeological evidence that in its early history India was inhabited by numerous clusters of different socio-cultural and linguistic groups who did not interact with one another on a large scale. However, the recent DNA findings have settled the issue: the peoples who are responsible for much of the civilization we call "Hindu" arrived into the Indian subcontinent later in an Aryan migration.

Western scholars find evidence that there were two main groups of immigrants who created the Indian religions that will be discussed in this book. One very early group came initially to the Indus river region of northwest India around 6,000–7,000 years ago, and slowly developed a remarkably sophisticated civilization in the area of the Indus river valley. We call that group the Harappan civilization (centered in northern India, now the area of the border with present-day Pakistan), also called the Indus Valley civilization.

The Indus Valley civilization hit its peak about 4,400 years ago (2400 B.C.E.) and then began to decline. Another wave of immigrants, nomadic Indo-European tribes from the European Anatolia (present-day Turkey) or Ukraine region, arrived around 1700–1500 B.C.E. and displaced the earlier indigenous people, pushing them southward. The new group, calling themselves Aryans, had a spoken language which was an early version of the Indo-European language. The Aryans gradually took control of India, beginning in the north and slowly moved south and east. By about 1000 B.C.E. the Aryans had control of the major institutions of the north and had put themselves on the top of a social, economic, and religious system which ultimately developed into the caste system of India. The Aryans will be discussed in detail in the next chapter, but this view of Aryan migration angered many in India.

Why is that common Western scholarly view so controversial? The reasons are complex. The Western view described above originated in Europe during the 1800s, and became entangled with Christian ideas about the biblical Old Testament story of creation. Many Indian-born scholars feel it is very presumptuous and even biased for non-Indian non-Hindu outsiders to attempt explain the origins of Indian civilization and Indian religion. Why? Because that analysis was originally undertaken within a set of assumptions that are based on the belief that the Christian texts

---

[9] We should note that this story is held by many Hindus, but there are many other religious traditions in India which reject the idea of divinely revealed Vedas, and each holds a different religious view of the origins of their religion.

[10] The influence is not just one way. As one might expect, over the centuries the indigenous religions appear to have exerted a profound influence upon the religion of the immigrating populations.

[11] Of course the country we call Pakistan was simply northern India until recent times.

are eternal truths whose origins go before all human history, were divinely revealed, and were inerrant historical records supporting Christian religion, assumptions that many Indians find to be colonial and imperialistic, and Old Testament and New Testament stories nothing more than popular myths unique to the Judeo-Christian religions.

It is true that the early Western scholars in India were Christian and many were also Christian missionaries. They did bring with them assumptions about the ultimate truths of their Christian religion. However, these people were also curious. In the early 1800s, Christian scholars were interested in trying to find the oldest forms of religion and language, and were certain that the world's most ancient religious texts (the Hindu Vedas[12]) would have the same stories as the Old Testament descriptions of a universe created in seven days, stories of the original parents, Adam and Eve, the story of Noah and a flood which destroyed humankind, and the Tower of Babel. They also assumed that the world's first and oldest spoken language would be Hebrew. Thus Indian religions and history was seen through the nineteenth century presuppositions of European Christianity.

Some Indian scholars consider the Western view of nomadic Indo-European tribes immigrating into India from the European Anatolia (present-day Turkey) or Ukraine region around 2000–1500 B.C.E. as a false view deliberately devised by a European colonial governing power to serve imperial and colonial European interests. These same Indian scholars who consider their own Vedic religious views to be eternal truths, hold that the ancient Aryans are not a 1500 B.C.E. Indo-European migration into India, but rather the Aryans were a noble and enlightened group who were indigenous to India and that Aryan Vedic religion is eternal, existing before the dawn of the human race, long before the stories of the Christian Old Testament. From the Vedic viewpoint, the Aryans must have been native to India, and not an importation from the European Anatolia or Ukraine region around 1500 B.C.E.

Hindu devotees also tend to make the same claims about their sacred texts that the Christians made about their Bible. Many Indian religious followers assert that the stories of the divinities in the ancient Hindu books are divinely revealed and literally true, and are describing an ancient India that goes back to the beginnings of time. If the Western scholarly view disagrees with their religious texts, then the Western scholars must be wrong.

The evidence in support of the Western view includes both archaeology and linguistics, with new evidence coming from ongoing DNA research. In addition to recent scientific discoveries based on extensive DNA analysis of many different populations,[13] there is also archeological evidence (discussed below). In addition, Western views have been strongly influenced by and supported by linguistic discoveries derived from comparative philology. As these philologists wrestled with ancient Sanskrit, to their surprise, European linguists discovered that the Sanskrit language used in the earliest of the Aryan sacred texts seemed to be a cousin language to the dominant European languages including Greek and Latin, English, French, and even Aramaic and Icelandic. In fact, virtually all of the many families of languages called Indo-European languages have shared words which suggest a common mother language.

In addition, Sanskrit[14] exhibited linguistic features that demonstrate that the language originated outside of India (such as very ancient names for snow, for animals like wolves and words for plants and trees not native to India).[15] Because these terms are shared with European cognate languages, this indicated a common origin for Indian

---

[12] The Vedas are the sacred books of the Aryans, the earliest of which date back to perhaps 1500 B.C.E. These will be discussed in the next chapter.

[13] Recent discoveries are summarized in Tony Joseph, "How genetics is settling the Aryan migration debate," in *The Hindu*, June 19, 2017, which can be found online at www.thehindu.com/sci-tech/science/how-genetics-is-settling-the-aryan-migration-debate/article19090301.ece. The various studies are enumerated and explained in this article.

[14] Although Sanskrit is no longer a common spoken language, approximately every three years there are world conferences of Sanskrit scholars who are able to communicate with one another using spoken Sanskrit. The 17th conference is in 2018, and the 18th in 2021.

[15] There are common words in the Indo-European language families for snow, for wolves and bears, and for specific trees that do not exist in India. This would seem to make it unlikely that the mother language originated in India since the family of core vocabulary in the languages have words for things that do not exist in India. Some linguists have argued that agricultural terms are not found in the common core of the various languages, suggesting that these early groups were not farmers. Common terms like "wool," "horses," and

CHAPTER 1: THE ORIGINS OF INDIAN THOUGHT

Sanskrit and for the European families of Indo-European languages which preserved a core vocabulary of shared words (for head, lungs, for star, for snow, for foot, for water, for night, moon, mother, father, and so forth). This also implied that the original language developed where there were wolves, and snow, and plants not native to India.[16]

There are several ways to envision this situation with so many words shared in the family of Indo-European languages. One possible view of this is that the Indo-European family of languages originated in India. In other words, English, Greek, Latin, Icelandic, Swedish, French, Spanish, German and Aramaic and dozens of other Western languages would have originated on the Indian subcontinent. That would mean that early Aryan nomadic groups originated in India, but then migrated north and westward into Europe, bringing their Indian language with them.

There several problems with this first view that India is the land where the mother tongue of Indo-European languages began. It seems very difficult to explain the common words for non-Indic features found in European languages and Indian Sanskrit if the Indo-European[17] mother tongue of the family of languages originated in India. If the common language originated with a westward migrating band of Indo-European speaking nomads who came across northern Europe, then into Iran, and then into India, the common features could be accounted for rather easily.

The common European scholar's view is that the original proto-Indo-European language began outside of India, either (a) among wagon-based equestrian herding nomadic populations in a central region in the Kirghiz steppes of central Asia[18] and then radiated outwardly both south and eastward into Iran and India and also westward into Europe, or (b) among farming groups in Anatolia or farther east into Russia. These groups then gradually moved eastward using wagons and horses, first across Europe and then into Iran and then into India.

However, this discovery of commonalities between Indian languages and European languages created a serious problem for Christian scholars of the early 1800s. Their Christian beliefs led them to conclude that all world languages were descended from Hebrew as the mother language of the two parents of the human race. By the late 1800s comparative linguistics showed that, despite what was written in the Old Testament, not one European language had any relation with Hebrew. There then followed a scholarly effort to discover the mother tongue of all world languages.

Early European discoveries of pre-human fossils (beginning in the early 1800s) and encounters with the civilization of India indicated that the human race was much older than Europeans had believed. A common European belief, based on the genealogy lists in the Bible, was that the entire universe was created around 4000 B.C.E., and the great flood of Noah would have been about 2500 B.C.E. It was clear that Indian sacred books were very old, perhaps older than the civilization described in the Old Testament, and closer to these religious events which should be common to all civilizations. Thus Indian texts could be relied upon to provide additional information which could

---

"livestock" supports the thesis of steppe herders. Other experts believe the Indo-European language arose among farmers seeking new lands to cultivate. See Bruce Bower, "New roots for a big language family: Indo-European tongues are traced back to ancient Turkey," in *Science News*, Vol. 182, Nol. 6, September 22, 2012. The fact that there are common words for "wheel" and "axle" and related terms suggests that the language arose among a community who had the wheel and carts, invented perhaps 4,000 B.C.E. in the western Eurasian steppes, allowing for highly mobile pastoralism. There is much technical literature on this subject. For example, see D. W. Anthony, *The Horse, the Wheel, and Language* (Princeton, NJ: Princeton Univ. Press, 2007), and numerous articles in journals, such as R. Bouckaert, P. Lemey, M. Dunn, S. J. Greenhill, A. V. Alekseyenko, *et al.*, "Mapping the origins and expansion of the Indo-European language family," *Science* 337:957–60 (2012).

[16] For more details, see the section on "The Proto-Language" in chapter 2 of this textbook.

[17] The Indo-European language families includes the languages of Europe, of Iran, and of northern India. The languages related to Sanskrit include Iranian languages, Greek, Romance languages descended from Latin, Armenian, the Germanic languages (which includes English), the languages of Albania, the Slavic languages, the Celtic languages, and the Baltic languages of Lithuania and Latvia.

[18] In physical geography, a steppe is a high plain similar to a prairie, although dominated by short grasses instead of dominated by tall grasses as in a prairie. The world's largest zone of steppes are found in central Russia and neighboring republics of Central Asia.

correct or supplement Old Testament statements.

Although the Europeans expected the most ancient Indian texts to support the stories of the Old Testament, they were shocked to discover that Indian religion seemed to have little in common with Jewish and Christian religious views, yet seemed to be at least as old, and very probably older than the Old Testament. Christians believed that all religions must have been descended from Jewish religion, descended from Adam and Eve, and then all humans were descendants of Noah and his family who had survived the world-wide flood described in the Old Testament. But the most ancient Hindu scriptures had no similar stories, no mention of a loving God creating the universe out of nothing, no mention of two original humans, Adam and Eve, no concept of Original Sin or free will, no story of a garden of Eden, no tale of a family named Noah surviving a universal flood caused by an angry punishing deity, and no commandments.[19] Could it be that Jewish and Christian claims for the antiquity of the human race were incorrect! Were the first eleven chapters of the Old Testament book of *Genesis* simply myths of certain ancient and local populations? Scholars looked to ancient Indian texts for clues.

There was another complicating issue: ethnocentrism and racism. By contemporary standards many in Europe were profoundly ethnocentric and racist. Many English and European Christians during the 1800s were absolutely opposed to the idea that the darker-skinned people of India could be a common community with the people of Athens and Rome (but they must be if Indian Sanskrit were a sister language of Greek and Latin).

At this time, India was a colony of the British Empire. Many in England were quite certain that Europeans were superior to the native peoples of India which then justified the British colonial domination of India (as early immigrants into north American believed they were superior to the native American peoples). The English world view was one which emphasized the differences between Indian civilization and British culture, stressing the cultural superiority of the Europeans over the inhabitants of India. Considerations of skin color were also relevant, so that these scholars believed that the darker skinned people of India could not possibly have anything in common with the British. But, how to explain the relationship between Indian Sanskrit and the ancient Greek language of Socrates and Plato?

The earliest European scholars created a hypothesis in an attempt to explain the linguistic connection of Sanskrit with European languages. They theorized that a noble group of light-skinned Aryans brought civilization to India from Europe. These Aryans would have been a common group whose origins would be with the northern Europeans, the ancestors of Greek and Roman civilization. Although this was rejected by later historical and linguistic scholarship in the West, some in India adopted this European idea of a great Aryan race and civilization, and this has view influenced popular movements in Indian politics, some of which identify themselves with an ancient Aryan race and an ancient spiritually advanced civilization.

The Nazi Perversion of History

However, this early mistaken hypothesis also led to a twisted Nazi perversion of history. Some German Europeans constructed a false and profoundly racist view of darker-skinned indigenous Indian populations and the later blonde blue-eyed fair-skinned Aryans, so according to this, India would be the product of two original races, one dark and lazy, the others blonde and successful.[20] This view would later lend support to the Nazi claim that an invading group of white-skinned Aryans (originating in or north of Germany) came to India and brought Sanskrit and a sublime higher civilization to a crude dark-skinned native population.[21] In the present time, no scholars accept this German

---

[19] In the Hindu legend, a good god saves the world from an evil flood. See Sukumari Bhattacharji, *The Indian Theogony: A Comparative Study of Indian Mythology from the Vedas to the Puranas* (Cambridge Univerity Press, 1970), p. 289.

[20] Edwin Bryant, *The Quest for the Origins of Vedic Culture: The Indo-Aryan Migration Debate* (London: Oxford University Press, 2001), p. 25.

[21] *Ibid.*, p. 26.

Nazi view, viewed as a perversion of history and a perversion of archaeology to serve a racist political and social agenda. The original Aryans were not blonde or fair-skinned like Scandinavians, and the Aryans did not originate north of Germany. This is discredited Nazi mythology and propaganda.

1.7 THE ANCIENT INDUS VALLEY CIVILIZATION

The Indian subcontinent is vast and has a varied climate. There have been several ancient cultural groups in India, and archaeologists have unearthed enough to indicate that these compose several different groups with very different languages. In the 1800s and early 1900s, the standard view was that these ancient civilizations were primitive and of little significance. The oldest Indian religious texts stressed the only sophisticated culture as the Vedic culture associated with a group who called themselves Aryans.

In the early 1920s, Indian and British archaeologists made a startling discovery. They found that before the Aryan civilization developed in the area called the Indus Valley, there had been a very highly civilized group of inhabitants living there for several thousand years before. This is the Indus Valley civilization, because it seemed centered along the Indus river, but also called the Harappan civilization, named after the ancient town of Harappa which was one of the first excavated by British archaeologists.

We know now that the civilization extended well beyond the Indus river valley, occupying perhaps as much as 300,000 square miles. It appears that before 6000 B.C.E. there was an extensive rural village culture growing wheat, barley, peas, melons, cotton, and goats, sheep, pigs and dogs. The Harappan culture may have started out as a farming society in a rural environment, but later it developed into an exceptionally sophisticated urban culture. The area of the Harappan culture includes northwestern India and Pakistan, paralleling but extending beyond the alluvial plain of the Indus river and its many tributaries.

Some scholars have wondered if perhaps this ancient civilization was simply the result of a much earlier migration of one of the same extended groups who appeared in India around 1500 B.C.E and who called themselves "Aryans." As noted before, some in India who accept the Vedas as inerrant history, believe that the Harappan civilization was not before the Aryans. Rather, it was simply the civilization of Aryans who had always been in India, and the Western story of the migration of Aryans into northern India was a lie told by deceitful imperialistic Western scholars.

Whatever its origins, the Harappan civilization was contemporary with the civilization then emerging in Egypt. The Harappan culture covered an extensive area approximately the size of modern-day France, perhaps 250,000–300,000 square miles of land.[22] The civilization comprised over 1500 settlements, and the largest city may have housed up to 60,000 people. In the excavated archaeological remains, there is no evidence of military barracks or anything related to warfare, such as thick city walls designed to protect citizens from marauding armies. Archaeologists can find no evidence of a cult of individual rulers: there are no fancy burial sites, no monumental displays of wealth. There are no lavish palaces. There are no readily identifiable large temples or grand religious structures.

The Harappans worked in copper and bronze (a copper-tin mixture). Archaeologists have found exquisite jewelry, statuary, and ceramics decorated with real and fanciful animals. Toys, and games like dice and what may be chess, abound. The fully developed Harappan civilization also comprised sophisticated sailors. They measured angles and the positions of the stars for navigational purposes. It is possible that they found the compass. The Indus Valley civilization traded with the Mesopotamian world, with Bahrain (a small island-state connected with Saudi Arabia), Ur (an important city-state in ancient Iraq), and later, with Cyprus, Syria, and with Afghanistan. Indus valley ships traded metals, semi-precious stones, beads and bangles and jewelry up the Persian Gulf to the cities of Mesopotamia.

---

[22] Jonathan M. Kenoyer, "Birth of a Civilization," *Archaeology 51* (January-February 1998).

CHAPTER 1: THE ORIGINS OF INDIAN THOUGHT

Archaeologists have found Harappan artifacts in the Mesopotamian world. Thus Harappan civilization had some influence upon the Sumerian civilization.

___

The Cities of the Indus Valley Civilization

The Harappan civil engineers created the first planned-out cities known to history. The major cities were built of rectangular city blocks following a rigid master plan, with *all* major streets and buildings planned out before any homes or buildings were constructed. They planned a great civic center which surely included something resembling religious activities. There was also a separate large residential area with multi-storied homes. The streets run parallel to one another; and the houses are at right angles to the streets, and accessed via pathways which are perpendicular to the street (like modern cities). There were bathrooms and the household drain systems connected with the tiled sewers underneath the roads.

The engineers devised a sophisticated drainage system to make the city safe from flooding, and provided a means for bringing water to individual homes, and removing human waste from each home. There were sophisticated toilets in each home, leading to tiled sewers underneath the roads, i.e, the sewers were planned before any single house was built; the underground sewers were there from the very beginning of the cities and not added on later.

The homes had tiled baths. All bricks in the city were made with the same length-width-height ratio of 4x2x1. There were public wells and public granaries. The same units of length were used for a thousand miles in all directions. There were standardized weights and potters turned out identical designs throughout the kingdom. This must reflect some sort of centralized control.

An astonishing aspect of the archaeological excavations revealed that the physical buildings in the cities changed very little in a thousand years. There had to be some very rigid form of social control to ensure that as the bricks of each house crumbled, its successor would be reconstructed on the foundation of the previous home, to ensure that all zoning requirements are enforced, and this endured for a thousand years.

In addition to excavations among the ruins of buildings, a major source of information on the Harappan civilization is the many seals and tablets which have been excavated. Archaeologists have found over 3,000 objects inscribed or impressed with Indus Valley writings and images. The Harappans used stone, clay, metal, and probably palm leaf, for writing. Most likely the clay seals were the documents of the ruling powers or successful wealthy merchants. The earliest discovered seals were made of soapstone. On these seals animal images are common including single-horned "unicorns," three-headed bull buffaloes, elephants, snakes, tridents, and fish. Images of trees and plants are also found. The ancient image of a swastika is also found in Indus artifacts.[23] Dice have been discovered in excavations, and the Harappans seem to have played an early form of chess, for archaeologists have found terra cotta chess pieces very similar to modern chess pieces.

Many scholars believe that the Indus civilization utilized a written language with both phonetic and pictorial characters. Translating the language from the seals has been a high priority for many decades. Several teams of scholars have claimed breakthroughs, but it is not yet clear that the language itself has been deciphered. It has also been proposed that this early writing has not been translated yet because it was actually a set of standardized symbols but not a grammatical system. If so, this Harappan set of symbols on seals would not qualify as a written language since it lacks the grammatical sophistication of a true language.

___

[23] The swastika is a cross with four ends bent directed towards the right, to rotate clockwise. Scholars believe it may symbolize the sun which moves symbolically in a clock-wise motion; later it is associated with the Hindu divinity Vishnu who is again associated with the sun. The swastika has been a symbol of good fortune in the art of the India, the Egyptians, Romans, Celts, native Americans, Persians, and Greeks.

CHAPTER 1: THE ORIGINS OF INDIAN THOUGHT

1.8 RELIGION IN THE INDUS CIVILIZATION

In the excavations of these huge cities, there are no clearly identifiable palaces or temples; no monumental religious architecture typical of similar ancient civilizations. Based on excavations of the sites, water was very important to the Indus Valley civilization, not just in terms of watering the fields, but most likely for ritual bathing as well. Homes had baths. In the Indus Valley city of Mohenjo-Daro, the central area of the ancient city is built on a huge platform, and at the center of the platform is a large pool where one would expect to find public rituals enacted. It was 23' × 29' and 8' deep. Could the central public pool and buildings have been designed for bathing? Possibly, but hardly necessary since bathtubs were in the homes. Considering its central location where the offices of power were located, it is not likely a recreational area.

Many scholars think that this large pool must have involved rituals, perhaps formal purification rituals which were regarded as being requisite to a good government and a good relationship with sacred powers. If so, temple rites, ritual purity and ritual cleanliness must have been of great importance to the culture. Ritual purity produces the cleanliness required if one is to approach the sacred realm of the gods. Ritual purity helps to support the order of society, removing those things which were considered impure and therefore disruptive. Was there a separate guild of priests who were in charge of these rituals, who guaranteed ritual purity? Did they imagine that humans were here to serve the many gods? We do not know.

Although the central pool in the city of Mohenjo-Daro may have been used for rituals, archaeologists have not found evidence of a separate class of religious specialists such as priests. Perhaps the family home was the center of religious practice. One possible conclusion would be that for the Indus Valley civilization, the holy realm was not separated from the ordinary world, there was no specific domain recognized as religious and set aside from the secular. It is likely that the realm of plants and animals was not merely in the secular world; it involved the sacred realm as well.

In addition to bathing and purification, archaeologists have found raised platforms, some used for animal sacrifices and others used for some kind of fire ritual or ceremony involving clay-lined pits and ceremonial water wells.[24] There were also fire altars scattered in the houses of the city. Could the fire altars been used for food preparation, or were they involved in religious ritual? Was fire seen as a divinity, or a messenger of the gods? Did the Harappans worship fire, or merely regard it as a personified dangerous force which needed to be pacified to lessen its danger?

Studying the engravings on Indus seals provides additional hints and clues about religion in the Harappan culture. In many of the world's ancient religions, specific animals were associated with specific deities. Lions, tigers, and cats have been divine or associated with divinities in ancient cultures. The strong bull is another common symbol of power, virility and fertility. Impressed on the Harappan seals we find male animals, often with unicorn-like horns. Indus civilization clay seals shows apparent deification of animals, including the elephant, tiger, buffalo, bull, fish and snakes. Some seals seem to depict parades of animals.

There were some statues and statuettes of female figures found in the ruins, suggesting the possibility that Harappans worshiped one or more goddesses or a figure associated with human fertility and the fertility of the soil. The female figures have exaggerated hips and breasts, again suggesting fertility. Perhaps Harappan religion did worship a Great Goddess, or perhaps several goddesses and other female divinities, but their precise function and importance is not clear.

Significantly, several seals show human beings. One has what appears to be a horned human figure surrounded by animals. He is seated in what we call the "full-lotus" posture typical of Yoga and other meditation traditions. Is this a human wearing some sort of headdress, or is it the lord of the animals? One seal depicts a fig tree (a sacred tree in India) with a male seated beneath it in the full-lotus posture of meditation. Also terra cotta human figures depict

---

[24] S. R. Rao, *Dawn and Devolution of the Indus Civilization* (New Delhi, 1991), pp. 284ff.

11

people seated in postures suggestive of yoga. Sometimes the males on the seal have erect sex organs, again symbolic of fertility, fecundity, and perhaps power. The reproductive function, the generative power of sexuality, is important for the Harappan civilization. Carved phalluses were also found among the artifacts, which may have functioned to facilitate fertility of the people and the land. Some scholars believe that some of these images are Harappan deities who later become Aryan Indian gods associated with what became Hinduism[25] a thousand years later.

The Harappans buried their dead. There have been some graves found, with objects buried with the body, and sometimes more than one body in a grave. Sometimes pots filled with food were included in the grave. Normally the bodies were laid with head facing north. Pots have been found with cremated bodies in them. All of this suggests that there was a belief in life after death, but it is difficult to know how important this was. For many early religions, life after death was relatively unimportant. Harappan religion seems to have stressed stability in this world, and not in an afterlife.

The fact that the Indus Valley civilization continued century after century with little change in the physical buildings and structure of the city suggests to scholars that Harppans had some feature of their society which resulted in the minimization of change. The lack of military buildings suggests that it was not military control which imposed order on the Harappan civilization. Besides the military, another way to accomplish this is to impose a rigid social stratification which controls social roles and hereditary occupations.

Did the Harappan society have a caste system? Does this imply that the Indus Valley civilization was identical with the Aryans who arrived much later, and who had a caste system? The problem is that scholars believe that rigid caste distinctions were *not* typical of the Aryans in their early history. This would imply that the Aryans did migrate into India with a flexible occupational system but a thousand years afterwards the indigenous Harappan social arrangements transformed that into a fairly rigid caste system. This suggests that the later Aryans may have utilized an indigenous Harappan class system and combined it with their own social occupations to produce the four rigid social classes which endure in modern India.

1.9 END OF THE INDUS CIVILIZATION

Archaeological excavations reveal that the Indus Valley civilization was falling into disorder between 1900 and 1600 B.C.E. No one knows for sure what caused this, but many scholars believe that the most likely cause was changes in the weather patterns, changes in river beds, and the drying up of important rivers. Some have suggested earthquakes were responsible. Earthquakes might have caused rivers to divert their channels and dry up in the areas of the major cities. Several ancient cities of the Indus were discovered alongside dried up rivers. The most likely hypothesis is that it was extended drought followed by agricultural failures[26] which forced the majority of city inhabitants to flee south in search of water and farming land. Serious flooding is another possibility. Food production would have been disrupted. Some scholars have suggested that a deadly epidemic decimated the major cities.

Whatever the ultimate causes were, the archaeological excavations reveal a breakdown of central authority and municipal regulations during this final period. The large urban city populations in the north may have dispersed southward and eastward into smaller communities. Western scholars believe that it was toward the end of this period of disorder that a series of large migrations of Aryan Indo-Europeans into northern India occurred.

---

[25] Some identify the figure with the popular Hindu deity Shiva because these Harappan images are very similar to those associated with Shiva, associated with creation and known as the Lord of the Animals. Others have identified the figure as Hindu deities including a proto-Varuna or Agni, associated with fire. There is no consensus.

[26] S. R. Rao says that "by the beginning of the first millennium the entire Hakra channel went dry, forcing migration of population to a wetter region." (S. R. Rao, *Dawn and Devolution of the Indus Civilization*, p. 40).

CHAPTER 1: THE ORIGINS OF INDIAN THOUGHT

Indo-European Migration into Northern India

Evidence for Aryan Indo-European migrations comes from several sources. Archaeological evidence and linguistic studies of language families suggest that about 2500 B.C.E. several groups of Indo-European speaking pastoral nomadic peoples slowly migrated from the Anatolian region (Turkey) or the Ukraine. Many think they traveled most probably on horseback using wagons and chariots and spread their language in the process. Over a period of a thousand years, the groups slowly spread to northern Iran and the eastern edges of northern India. These new immigrants, calling themselves Aryans, slowly began to migrate in great numbers into northern India about 1500 B.C.E. These theories were then confirmed by extensive DNA studies within the last few years.

The Aryan migration into the Indus Valley civilization brought an end to the already decaying city life of the Harappans, an end to their high culture and urban planning skills, an end to sophisticated architecture, carefully planned sewers and water development, and an end to the Indus Valley's writing system.

We will discuss the Aryan civilization and its language and religious beliefs in more detail in the next chapter.

1.10 SUMMARY OF THE CHAPTER

We have explained why Western scholars argue for the conclusion that Indian civilization has several different sources, with two sources making the greatest contribution to religion: (1) the more ancient Indus Valley civilization and (2) the later Aryans who came into India around 2000–1500 B.C.E. We have discussed the social engineering skills of the Indus Valley civilization, and have made some attempts at understanding what the culture's religious beliefs and practices might have involved. Those included a stress on water, cleanliness and purification, very probably ritual purification. Fire may have been a divinity. Female figures may symbolize goddesses. Some animals had special significance, and may have been perceived as divine. One or more divinities may have sat in the cross-legged posture typical of meditation in later forms of Yoga.

The Indus Valley civilization was so fixed for so long that some believe there may have been an instrument of social control, such as a social or religious caste system, imposed upon the culture. However, when one goes beyond the actual physical records from archaeology and begins to make guesses about more abstract elements of the civilization, one can no longer discuss these issues with any certainty.

1.11 TECHNICAL TERMS USED IN THIS CHAPTER

Aryans   [Ahr-yuns] Indo-European-speaking peoples who entered the Indus Valley region of India about 1500 B.C.E.

bhakti   [bakh-ti] religious devotion and worship directed towards a deity.

bhakti-marga   [bakh-ti mar-ga] the pathway of devotion

darshana   [dahr-shan] direct seeing reality

dharma [dar-ma] social, religious, and moral duties which uphold the pattern of reality

dhyana-marga   [dyah-nah mar-ga] the pathway of focused concentration

CHAPTER 1: THE ORIGINS OF INDIAN THOUGHT

Harappa   [Ha-rahp-pa] modern name for an ancient city of the Indus valley civilization

karma-marga   [kahr-ma] the pathway of ritual action as a way of being religious

jnana-marga   [NYNAH-na mar-ga] the pathway of liberating wisdom as a way of being religious

Mohenjo-Daro   [Mo-hen-jo Dah-ro] an ancient city of the Indus valley civilization

Vedas   [VAY-daz] the sacred scriptures of the Aryans

1.12 QUESTIONS FOR FURTHER DISCUSSION

1) We discussed four different ways of being religious, but in modern times some scholars have suggested that there are more than four ways of being religious. What other ways of life would you consider to be "religious" that are different from devotion, critical thinking and wisdom, ritual practice, and meditation?

2) What do you think about the fact that there is no single term in Indian thought which carries the same meanings as "religion" does to Western people? Do the Sanskrit terms *dharma* or *darshana* carry the same connotations as "religion" does to those in the West?

3) Religious people in India ask questions about the relationship of the deepest self to ultimate reality. How do Western religions express concern for this question? Do non-Indian religions (such as Judaism and Christianity) put more stress upon different questions not stressed in Indian religion?

4) There is no common list of items which all Hindus are expected to believe or accept. Is there a common list of items which all Christians are expected to accept or believe in?

5) What are the most important religious themes in the Indus Valley civilization?

6) We do not have any successfully translated written records of the Indus Valley civilization, so how reliable are our guesses about the religious practices of the Indus Valley culture?

7) Could the various animals and objects pictured on the seals have non-religious significance? Could the man seated in cross-legged meditation or the elephant depicted on these seals have meaning that was not religious? If so, what meaning would you suggest?

8) We have seen that some in India consider the claim that Indian religion is a mixture of the Indus Valley civilization and later migrating Aryan groups, to be controversial. Westerners might appreciate this controversial aspect better if we were to consider how a Western person would react to non-Christian scholars from a non-Western culture who claimed that Jesus was not the founder of Christianity, but that Christianity was a mixture of the myths and practices a number of earlier more ancient religions originating in the Asian parts of the world. Some people would be offended. Discuss the issue.

9) You might try to do a search on the internet for the Harappan civilization, or the Indus Valley civilization. Who are the authors of the sites? Does the information seem well-researched, or is it perhaps more romantic,

more metaphorical in its intent?

A SELECTED BIBLIOGRAPHY

Ancient India

Bryant, Edwin, *The Quest for the Origins of Vedic Culture: The Indo-Aryan Migration Debate* (London: Oxford University Press, 2001)

Fairservis, Walter A., Jr., *The Roots of Ancient India: The Archaeology of Early Indian Civilization*, 2nd revised edition (Chicago: University of Chicago Press, 1975).

Finegan, Jack, *Archaeological History of Religions of Indian Asia* (1989).

Kenoyer, Jonathan J., *Ancient Cities of the Indus Valley Civilization* (Karachi: Islamabad: Oxford Univeristy Press American Institute of Pakistan Studies, 1998)

Joseph, Tony "How genetics is settling the Aryan migration debate," in *The Hindu*, June 19, 2017, found online at www.thehindu.com/sci-tech/science/how-genetics-is-settling-the-aryan-migration-debate/article19090301.ece

Hinduism

Barua, B. M., *A History of Pre-Buddhistic Indian Philosophy* (Calcutta: University of Calcutta Press, 1921)

de Bary, William T., ed., *Sources of Indian Tradition*, 2nd edition, 2 volumes (New York: Columbia University Press, 1988).

Eck, Diana, *Darsan: Seeing the Divine Image in India* (New York: Columbia University Press, 1998)

Herman, A. L., *A Brief Introduction to Hinduism* (Boulder, CO: Westview Press, 1991)

Knott, Kim, *Hinduism: A Very Short Introduction* (London: Oxford, 2000)

Koller, John, *The Indian Way: An Introduction to the Philosophies and Religions of India*, 2nd edition (New York: Prentice Hall, 20005)

Koller, John and Patricia, *Sourcebook in Asian Philosophy* (New York: Macmillan, 1991)

Michaels, Axel, *Hinduism: Past and Present* (Princeton, 2003)

Mohanty, J. N., *Classical Indian Philosophy* (Lanham, MD: Rowman and Little, 2000)

Moore, Charles A., *The Indian Mind: Essentials of Indian Philosophy and Culture* (Honolulu, HI: University of Hawai'i Press, 1967)

Panikkar, Raimundo, *The Vedic Experience: Mantramanjari* (Los Angeles: The University of California Press, 1977)

Potter, Karl H., *Guide to Indian Philosophy* (Boston: G. K. Hall, 1988) An extensive bibliography.

Potter, Karl H., ed., *The Encyclopedia of Indian Philosophies* (Princeton, NJ: Princeton University Press, 1961-2015)

Radhakrishnan, Sarvepalli, *Indian Philosophy*, 2 volumes (London: Allen and Unwin, 1923)

Shattuck, Cybelle, *Hinduism* (New York: Prentiss-Hall, 1999)

CHAPTER 2: THE ARYANS

CHAPTER 2: THE ARYANS COME TO INDIA:

RITUAL – THE FIRST OF THE FOUR WAYS OF BEING RELIGIOUS

2.1 OVERVIEW OF THE CHAPTER

In this chapter we will discuss the historical background and key ideas of the Aryans, the second group of people who contributed to and helped define the numerous religions of India, and the earliest roots of Aryan religion, which is based in religious ritual. This period ranges from about 1500 B.C.E. to about 600 B.C.E.

In Hindu thought, there are at least four different ways of being religious. One of those ways of being religious is the *karma-marga*, or the action pathway of sacred ritual. Early Aryan religion was based on ritual. Ritual sacrifices were how the universe came into being, and Aryan priests who performed ritual sacrifices provided human assistance to reenact the creation of the universe, and the regular performance of sacrifice ensured the regularity of the universe.

We will also discuss the various sacred books of ritual, called the *Vedas*, and the implications of the world-view embedded in the prayers and hymns of the *Vedas*. The chapter will conclude with other sacred texts, the *Brahmanas* and the *Aranyakas*.

2.2 ARRIVAL OF THE ARYANS

Although some in India believe that the Aryan Vedic civilization is simply a continuous development of the early Indus Valley civilization, as discussed in the previous chapter, recent DNA analyses support a different conclusion. According to recent DNA research combined with nearly two-hundred years of Western scholarship, the Aryan civilization is the result of an extended series of migrations into northern India including a new group of Indo-European peoples around 2000-1500 B.C.E. Recent DNA evidence has confirmed this analysis.[1]

These migrating groups may have been farmers seeking new lands, but many believe they were nomadic peoples who had tamed horses and herded animals, possibly originally from the steppes region north of the Black Sea, in what is now the Ukraine, or the farming regions of Anatolia (Turkey). These groups, calling themselves Aryans[2] were not

---

[1] An excellent summary of the scholarly technical discoveries in DNA research can be found in Tony Joseph, "How genetics is settling the Aryan migration debate," in *The Hindu*, June 19, 2017, which can be found online at www.thehindu.com/sci-tech/science/how-genetics-is-settling-the-aryan-migration-debate/article19090301.ece. There are numerous scholarly studies of these events summarized in this article. DNA studies indicate a group of Ancestral North Indians, and a separate group of Ancestral South Indians. The upper-class Brahmin populations have DNA which shows a shared ancestry with northern Eurasian, European/Mediterranean populations. There were several different groups who migrated into the Indian subcontinent. Scholars agree that India has one of the most genetically diverse populations of anywhere in the world.

[2] "Aryan" means something like Worthy, or Noble ones who inhabit the land; Aryan has the same root as "Iran," and so names a people of the Iranian plateau. The name "Ireland" is also related to Aryan.

a racial or ethnic group, but rather what they shared was a common Indo-European language and culture.

Current evidence supports the conclusion that these groups were not a single tribe or a single migration. Rather, based on DNA, archeology, and linguistics, they seem to have been a collection of different tribes which spread from south Russia and Turkistan through Mesopotamia and Asia Minor.[3] Some of the Aryan groups migrated west and north into what is modern Europe, settling from Ireland to Finland. Others moved south or east and settled in Iran. These diverse groups of people migrated from the steppes of central Asia into Iran and then India. Using wagons and chariots they overwhelmed a series of indigenous cultures, and spread their own language in the process.

The Aryans were very probably nomadic clusters of tribes sharing a common language and common divinities. Many scholars hold that before they arrived in India, the Aryans had developed a male-dominated, warrior society, divided into three principal social groups: warriors, priests, and producers, primarily cattle-herders and breeders.[4] Aryan divinities were the sun, moon, fire, thunder, and other natural forces. Each social group had their own anthropomorphic patron deity but they were not in a fixed locality so they did not have temples. These groups arrived at the central plateau of Iran from central Asia around 2000 B.C.E. Although the majority settled in Iran, other groups continued to expand eastward and south to find new lands and then several centuries later arrived at the edges of northern India (which now is called Pakistan).

These smaller sub-groups from different tribes continued migrating from Iran into northern India, and arrived in large numbers about 1600–1400 B.C.E. The first Aryans entered India from the northwest, followed by Aryan specialists in ritual and cattle-herders. Finding the Indus Valley civilization seriously disintegrated, the Aryans overwhelmed what was left and replaced it with their very different lifestyle.

Over the next thousand years the Aryans spread their spoken language, religion, rituals, and social organization throughout the Indian subcontinent, overwhelming the Indus civilization and submerging Harappan gods and religious practices. The early Aryans did not have the architectural knowledge of the Harappans, or the Indus skills with water management. Although the Aryans did not have the urban or artistic advances of the Harappans, they seem to have been more skilled in weaponry and metallurgy, and in using chariots.

The Proto-language

As discussed in the previous chapter, about two hundred years ago, scholars of linguistics discovered that the Indo-European language family, including English, is descended from a single proto-Indo-European language spoken some 6,000 to 8,000 years ago possibly originating in what is now the eastern Ukraine and Kuban regions of what used to be called Russia, or the Anatolia region between the Black and Caspian Seas, which is modern Turkey.[5] This is known as the Kurgan hypothesis. By the time of Christ, that language spread from Ireland to India. English, Sanskrit, Aramaic, Greek, Latin, German, and Old Icelandic are examples of Indo-European language family descendants. As scholars use the term, "Aryans" are speakers of the Indo-European language, and not one unique ethnic group or race.

---

[3] Although there is agreement among Western scholars that an Aryan migration occurred, there is no consensus on precisely where that group originated. The Caucasus area is one possibility; Anatolian farming communities between the Black Sea and the Caspian sea (modern Turkey) is another popular possibility. Bactria, and the vicinity of the Balkan-Carpathian area are other possibilities. See Edwin Bryant, *The Quest for the Origins of Vedic Culture: The Indo-Aryan Migration Debate*, pp. 38–44. See also Bruce Bower, "New roots for a big language family," *Science News*, Vol. 182, No. 6, September 22, 2012, p. 10. New information from DNA studies has clarified the issues. This general area is described as the Pontic–Caspian steppe, a genuinely vast area from the northern shores of the Black Sea eastward to the Caspian Sea. It stretches from Moldova and western Ukraine to western Kazakhstan, forming part of the larger Eurasian steppes.

[4] There is disagreement. Some scholars argue that the original Aryans may have been migrating farming communities from Anatolia and not warlike nomads. Bruce Bower writes: "A new study adds support to the proposal that the language family expanded out of Anatolia – what's now Turkey – between 8,000 and 9,500 years ago, as early farmers sought new lands to cultivate." Bruce Bower, *ibid.*

[5] See "Mapping the Origin and Expansion of the Indo-European Family of Languages, *Science*, August 24, 2012, pp. 957–960.

CHAPTER 2: THE ARYANS

"Aryan-speaking," like "Latin-speaking," is a cultural term, not a racial group.[6] The Aryans understood the term "Aryans" as meaning "Noble Ones" or perhaps the noble ones of the land.

Groups of migrating Aryans did not have the Harappan skills with urban planning, architecture, tiled sewers and sophisticated bathrooms, and did not have a written language. Over the centuries, the indigenous population in the north adopted the Aryan spoken language. By about 1200 B.C.E., Aryan priests (calling themselves Brahmins[7]) became the leaders of Indian civilization, and the sun-centered Aryan forms of religion superceded Harappan religion. From 1500 B.C.E. (3,500 years ago) to about 500 B.C.E. (2,500 years ago) the Aryan culture solidified its hold on and transformation of India, but surviving elements of the pre-Aryan Harappan religion continued to exist in rural populations and began to emerge and influence Aryan religions as well.[8]

Thus, according to Western scholarship, Hinduism and Indian culture in general has evolved from at least two related competing sources, and not just the Aryan Vedic culture as had been thought previously. These two are: (1) the pre-Aryan civilization in India, especially the Indus Valley civilization, combined with other smaller independent groups indigenous to ancient India; and (2) the Aryan civilization whose sacred scriptures were the Vedas, whose members began migrating into India around 1700–1400 B.C.E.

2.3 THE RELIGIOUS SCRIPTURES OF THE EARLY ARYANS

Upon arriving in northwestern India, most groups settled down although some continued to move further south. The Aryan priests, the Brahmins, were ritual specialists and had an existing tradition of chanting memorized religious hymns (at this time, the Aryans did not have a written language) compiled and memorized by the priests and their sons. The primary function of the Brahmin priests was uttering sacred sounds, chanting prayers aloud while performing traditional rituals and sacrifices. This is called the "pathway of religious action" (*karma-marga*).

Aryan Vedic tradition minimizes the written word. It is the sound that is important, not written words. Holy and sacred scriptures are **heard**, not written. Hearing, one memorizes and chants the sacred sounds. Also coming face-to-face with the holy is of central importance. Thus, **hearing** and **seeing** are what is essential with holy scriptures. The most important sacred works are known as "that which was heard" (*shruti*) and are divinely revealed texts which the earliest sages memorized word-for-word. They are the most sacred of the Hindu scriptures. A text composed by a human being who was divinely inspired are called "remembered" or "handed down" (*smriti*).

Between 1500 and 800 B.C.E. the sacred literature increased in bulk and complexity. Rituals became more elaborate and could last for days. The priests who performed these rituals were endowed with status and prestige, and

---

[6] Adolph Hitler's Nazi philosophers had a theory that the harsh northern climates make for an intelligent race of people, whereas more benign and warmer climates make for a lazy and stupid population. Hitler believed that the Germanic peoples, living in the north, belonged to an older and more racially pure blonde Aryan race. Such prejudices are not unique to Germany. Hitler would have been shocked had he known that the earliest speakers of the Aryan language would not look Scandinavian but would look very much like the people who live in Iran.

[7] The term for a priestly specialist in ritual is "Brahman" but the term Brahman is ambiguous. Brahman can mean (1) the group of priests who specialize in Vedic rituals, (2) the power of prayer, (3) the ultimate creative power which underlies reality and which is the source of all the gods, and (4) the *Brahmanas*, the texts instructing apprentice priests how to perform the rituals of the Vedas. One common strategy to clarify that one is discussing the priests is to use the older spelling, Brahmin. We will employ that strategy in this book.

[8] Sukumari Bhattacharji, *The Indian Theogony: A Comparative Study of Indian Mythology from the Vedas to the Puranas* (Cambridge: Cambridge University Press, 1970), pp. 9ff.

became wealthy performing rituals for rulers and other wealthy supplicants. Different guilds of priests were required to specialize in different aspects of this vast oral sacred literature and ritual.

The Vedas

These earliest collections of memorized sacred hymns of the Aryans are called the **Vedas**. The Vedas are the source for rituals performed by Brahmin priests. The respect for these Vedas was so great that the wording and even the tone accents of ancient Vedic Sanskrit have been very carefully memorized and preserved.[9] The sacred sounds are treated like a living presence and a source of mysterious power. In the Hindu religious view, the sacred is experienced through sound and vision, not writing. Aryan religious literature focuses upon chanted rituals which are dominated by images of fire, rain, thunder, sacred plants, and animals.

It wasn't until about 800 B.C.E. that the Aryans formally organized their oral tradition of religious poetry into three separate collections known as the Vedas (but these are not yet written). When finally put down in script,[10] the Vedas were written in Sanskrit, a written language which some argue may have borrowed from the cursive script of the Harappan written language. By 800 B.C.E. three collections of the wisdom of the Aryans were formed: (1) the *Rig-Veda*; (2) the *Sama-Veda*; (3) the *Yajur-Veda*.

Each of the three Vedas was memorized and preserved by a separate guild of priests whose purpose in life was performing ritual. Over the centuries, a fourth Veda was growing but was not yet sanctified, not yet finalized. The fourth was a collection of spells and incantations, and it would become the *Atharva-Veda*, the last Veda. Hindus categorize the four Vedas as divine revelation (*shruti*).

The Oldest Veda: The Rig-veda

The earliest of all the Vedic Sanskrit texts is the *Rig-Veda*, dating back to perhaps about 1500 B.C.E. or even earlier.[11] It is a collection of 1028 stanzas or verses used in rituals to praise the gods. Each chanted hymn is addressed to a particular *deva* or divinity, such as Varuna, Rudra, and the solar god Vishnu, who later became universal deities in one form or another.[12] The *Rig-Veda* is the chanted words of the original guild of priests who performed rather simple rituals and sacrifices, perhaps alone or with one other priest.

The 1028 hymns of the *Rig-Veda* are organized in nine divisions or books (a tenth book was added very late, long after the other three Vedas had come into existence). These hymns were memorized by the guild of Brahmin priests who specialized in the *Rig-Veda*. The purpose of these hymns is clearly oriented towards material benefits in this world, and not concerned with an afterlife. The *Rig Veda* is concerned with ritual and sacrifice, focused on flattering the gods and giving gifts, thereby receiving back what we need from the gods for a comfortable life in the present. The priests performed the rituals in the hope of worldly rewards. Humans give gifts to the gods; the gods return gifts to humans.

The prayers and hymns in the *Rig-Veda* are directed to divinities who dwell in the heavens, in the sky above,

---

[9] Michael Witzel, "Autochthonous Aryans? The Evidence from Old Indian and Iranian Texts," *Electronic Journal of Vedic Studies*, Volume 7, Issue 3, May 25, 2001, p. 5.

[10] Many different dates are suggested for when the Vedas were first written down. Some believe that the writing may have occurred before the common era, but most scholars put it much later. Perhaps as late as 800 C.E. or 1000 C.E. according to Dr. Witzel, *ibid*.

[11] In scholarly works, the title is *Rg* or *Rk veda*.

[12] However we must note that there are hymns addressed to a great number of divinities who later faded from the sacred firmament, such as Parjanya, Surya, Soma, Matarisvan, Savitr, Usas, Pusan, Bhaga, Aryaman, Daksa, Amsa, Mitra, and even Agni.

CHAPTER 2: THE ARYANS

or in this world.[13] The universe is thought to have eight divisions, and each divinity operates mostly within its own eighth. These divine beings resemble humans, and might be thought of as forces of nature operating by or directed by a divine will. The Hindu divinity (or *deva*) with the greatest number of prayers and hymns directed to him is the war god Indra, the model soldier who led his people into battle. Indra was associated with the powerful forces of nature, especially thunderstorms. Indra carries a scepter which symbolizes his thunderbolt power, a scepter in the shape of an hourglass called a *vajra*.

A Hymn to Indra

> Let me now sing the heroic deeds of Indra, the first that the thunderbolt-wielder performed. He killed the dragon and pierced an opening for the waters; he split open the bellies of mountains. ... Wildly excited like a bull, he took the Soma for himself and drank the extract from the three bowls in the three-day Soma ceremony. Indra the Generous seized his thunderbolt to hurl it as a weapon; he killed the first-born of dragons.
> Indra, when you killed the first-born of dragons and overcame by your own magic, the magic of the magicians, at that very moment you brought forth the sun, the sky, and dawn. Since then you have found no enemy to conquer you.[14]

The deity with the second largest number of prayers and hymns directed to him is Agni, the divinity associated with fire.

A Prayer to Agni, the God of Fire

> I pray to Agni, the household priest who is the god of the sacrifice, the one who chants and invokes and brings the most treasure. ...
> Through Agni one may win wealth, and growth from day to day, glorious and most abounding in heroic sons.
> Agni, the sacrificial ritual that you encompass on all sides — only that one goes to the gods.
> Agni, the priest with the sharp sight of the poet, the true and most brilliant, the god will come with the gods.[15]

The Second Veda: *Sama-veda*

Over the centuries, as the priests settled in and served the needs of the leaders and the wealthy, the rituals became more complex. More priests were needed to perform the ever more complicated rituals for the aristocracy, for the protection of the kingdom, to ensure the crops would grow and the land be fertile. The second of the four Vedas, the *Sama-veda*, reflects this growing complexity. The *Sama-veda* is an anthology of the earlier chants now sung with a melody. These are the songs of those priests who specialized in musical parts of rite and ritual. Most of the content is the prayers of the *Rig-veda* set to music. The verses of the singing priests are called *samans* (or "songs"), and the name

---

[13] Vedic society was patriarchal. Male divinities greatly predominate in the *Rig Veda* with goddesses playing minor roles. Among the female gods is Usas, goddess of dawn, Bharati, Sarasvati, and Aditi. Goddesses begin to be more popular with the later texts called *Brahmanas* and ultimately become powerful and plentiful in post-Vedic Indian religion. Many scholars have argued that in pre-Vedic society, goddesses were very popular and suppressed by the male-dominated Aryan priests when they arrived in India.

[14] Rig-Veda 1.3; James Fieser and John Powers, *Scriptures of the East*, Second edition (New York: McGraw-Hill, 2004), p. 10.

[15] *Ibid.*, p. 11.

Sama-veda thus is the songs of the guild of singing priests. Unfortunately, we have no way of knowing whether any of the original melodies have survived.

The Third Veda: *Yajur-veda*

The third Veda is the *Yajur-veda*. It was the special province of another guild of priests who specialized in physically moving utensils during the ceremonies and while doing this, the ritual required them to murmur various phrases or incantations, called *yajus*. Remember that for the Brahmin priests, accurately reproducing the actual sacred sounds was extremely important.

A *yajus* is a short formulaic phrase in which the meaning and purpose of the ongoing ritual is described, and thereby the murmur gives additional power and effectiveness to the ritual. About half of the *yajus* in the *Yajur-Veda* are extracted from the earlier *Rig-veda*, but the remainder are new materials.

The Fourth Veda: the *Atharva-veda*

Iron makes its appearance in south Asian civilization ca. 1200-1000 B.C.E. and the fourth Veda, the *Atharva-veda*, is the only one which mention iron, so this collection of texts is subsequent to the 1200-1000 B.C.E. time period. In fact, this text is quite late and may not have become part of the official *vedas* until the second century B.C.E.

The *Atharva-veda* is the collected literature of the *atharvan* guild of priests who originally had no part in the aristocratically-oriented rituals of the three higher groups of priests who dominated the urban centers of power. The contents of the *Atharva-veda* are completely independent of the prior three Vedas. The *atharvan* priests started as the country village priests who performed the duties of a village shaman or medicine healer who focused on the more immediate needs of the poorer rural populations. They were the village psychologist or faith-healer, and provided spells and incantations for protection against illness, against demons, and against 'black magic.' They also provided incantations to get a lover, to get children, to increase luck in gambling or battle, or success in business. Here is a prayer which offers protection from fever:

> As if from this Agni [fire], that burns and flashes, the fever comes. Let him pass away like a babbling drunkard! Let him, the impious one, search out another person, not ourselves! Reverence be to the fever with the burning weapon! Reverence be to Rudra, reverence to the fever, reverence to the luminous king Varuna!

Here is a spell from the *Atharva-Veda* to cause a woman to fall in love:
> Desire my body, my feet, my eyes, my thighs! As you lust after me, your eyes and your hair shall be hot with love! I make you cling to my arm, cling to my heart, so that you shall be in my power and shall come to my wish! The cows, the mothers of the sacrificial butter who lick their young, in whose heart love is planted, shall make this woman love me![16]

Those *atharvan* priests who seemed successful at protecting and doing ritual magic became very popular, and as their reputations grew, the ruling nobles in the larger cities brought some of the rural *atharvan* priests in to guarantee the security and prosperity of their rule. The larger more complex aristocratic rituals had priests from each of the three groups (the three *Vedas*), and a fourth, supervising priest whose duty it was to ensure that everything went well. It was

---

[16] Atharva-Veda 6.20 and 6.9, in Robert E. Van Voorst, *Anthology of Asian Scriptures* (Wadsworth, 2001), p. 51.

thought that rituals were very powerful, and if done poorly, could have catastrophic consequences for the person, priest, or community. The *atharvans* became so popular, that they were often appointed to this supervisory role. As a result of this power, their book became officially recognized as the last official Veda, the *Atharva-veda*.

2.4 THE AUTHORITY OF THE VEDAS

Any system of thought in India which accepts the status of the Vedas as eternal sounds of truth, is considered **orthodox** and Hindu. Although Hindus consider the Vedas as holy texts, most Hindus could not read them even if they tried. The Sanskrit language of the Vedas is so ancient that only highly-trained scholars can read it.

As we have discussed, the Vedas were memorized by a handful of Brahmin priests who specialized in the Vedic rituals. In fact, it was considered inappropriate to commit the Vedas to writing because it was the sound which was most important, and was disrespectful to write it down. It could have been as late as the eleventh century in the common era that the Vedas were actually written down for the very first time. Until then, they were an ancient oral tradition known only to the Brahmin priests.

The Vedas are in a very ancient form of Sanskrit and the first two are set in a complicated poetical form (which helps the priests to memorize them). The hymns and verses are not organized under any general structure or principles, and only share a very vague mythological framework. Only the most elite of the Brahmin priests read these, or performed highly intricate rituals intended to propitiate the various gods. Only the Brahmin priests had the authority to study and teach the Vedas; other levels of Hindu society were either not encouraged, or forbidden to read them.

The Vedas have been interpreted, and re-interpreted over the centuries, adapting to time and place. Truths need to be reinterpreted for each time and situation, and adapted to the varying capacities of humanity. Scholars and sages can write explanations which are not of absolute authority, but the authors' words are valuable because they were uttered by wise men learned in the Vedas.

Who is the Author of the Vedas?

Not all Hindus consider the sacred Vedas to be the revelation of gods. For some, the Vedas were originally taught by the god Brahma. However, for many Hindu religions, the Vedas were never spoken by a god, or any sort of divinity; rather, the Vedas arise at the beginning of all things alongside the deities. They are called "author-less."

For those who hold that the Vedas are author-less, the Vedas are manifestations of the power of the ritual incantations, they are a **sound** which reverberates eternally in the celestial realms. At the beginning of each cosmic eon (*kalpa*), the world emerges from cosmic dissolution, certain great sages hear the divine sound, and memorize and then utter it, and thus the Vedas are reborn again into human society. For many Hindus, the Vedas are divine, and infallibly true in every word.

2.5 THE VEDIC WORLD VIEW

The time period from approximately 1200 to 600 B.C.E. is the early Vedic age. During this period, Vedic Hinduism was primarily rituals performed by priests on behalf of their patrons, and not much concerned with answering philosophically or theologically oriented questions. There really wasn't even a standardized group of questions asked in the Vedic literature. Obviously, there were no universally agreed-upon answers to many of the ultimate questions of later Hinduism. However, reading the Vedas we can distinguish a set of presuppositions or world-views that permeate the Vedic literature.

CHAPTER 2: THE ARYANS

The Vedic World View: What is a Human Being?

What is the essence of a living human being? The area of philosophy which attempts to answer this question is called philosophical anthropology, and it attempts to answer questions about human nature which cannot be answered by observation, genetics, archaeology, or biology. For example, stones and trees do not move on their own. Human beings move. But a human being who has died no longer moves. What makes the difference between a living person and one who is not living?

In India the initial answer is that something alive has breath; stones and trees do not breathe. Human beings who are not alive do not breathe. It would seem to follow that the essence of a living human being is breath, because when breath goes, so too goes life. The Sanskrit word for this life-principle was called **atman**. Although initially it probably meant just the idea of the process of breathing air, *atman* came to mean the essential feature of a living thing, rather than just respiration process.[17] Perhaps in the Vedas *atman* can be understood as the subtle essence of life associated with the life-breath.

The Vedas do not have a single vision about what happens after death. In some *Rig Veda* verses, it was thought that at death, the *atman* left the body and could be carried to a heavenly realm by the flames of the crematory funeral pyre. In that heaven, flutes, music, dance, eternal light and ancestors awaited one. This highest heavenly realm was not unlike earthly life. The heavens were achieved via correctly performed ritual, and were not a reward for obeying a god-given moral code, or for faith. If you lived and fulfilled your ritual duties towards the *devas*, faithfully performed the ritual formulas, and then your sons performed the correct cremation rituals, you could go to the heavenly realm and enjoy eternal happiness.

At this early stage, the Vedas reveal that human existence was seen as good and enjoyable, and religious rites could prolong one's physical existence in a world perceived as good. **The heavenly realm was not a reward for being moral; rather, it was the natural conclusion of a life where the human properly fulfilled their ritual duties, called their *dharma*.**

However, not all the Vedas share this view of life after death. In other verses of the Vedas, the vision is that the aspects of the person dissolves and returns to the parts of the earth. Perhaps the cremated body can serve as food for the gods in the heavenly realms. Death was not seen as something to fear. It may be an occasion for grief, but it does not terrify; it simply happens. There is no belief in either karma or reincarnation anywhere in the Vedas. In the early Aryan religion there is no single agreed-upon destiny for a human being after death.

The Vedic View of the Universe

Metaphysics is the branch of human thought which attempts to understand the nature of ultimate reality. Metaphysical questions were of little importance during the earliest ages of Aryan thought. Nothing in the four Vedas reveals any serious concern with the nature of ultimate reality. There really is not any extended discussion on the substance of the universe, its origins or its mode of operation. But, there are some aspects which allow us to make an informed guess about the world view.

The ancient Vedas reveal that people had a feeling of being surrounded by unseen forces, forces which are not a part of the material world we observe. These forces become evident in thunderstorms, in the movement of the sun and moon, but they can also be a presence, or a spirit, or an impersonal power. These forces might reside anywhere: in the sky overhead, in a tribal leader, in plants, rocks, mountains, rivers, or animals. Generally these forces correlate with natural forces, to be associated with wind, sun, sea, stars but they might possess some characteristics similar to

---

[17] In English *atman* is often translated by the Christian term *soul*, corresponding to the Latin *anima* and the Greek *psyche*, that feature which living things possess that makes them alive and animated, and which departs when a living thing dies. However, the Hindu *atman* was not created in the image of a god, and has no relation to Christian religious concepts such as self-consciousness or free will.

those of human beings. These forces did interact with human beings, and it was the role of the Brahmin priest to manipulate this interaction for the benefit of the group.

The *Triloka*

It does not take much to realize that we humans live on the earth, that some living things fly above the earth, and that the lights in the sky including the sun and moon are divinities far beyond the realm where birds fly. This leads to a central concept of the ***triloka***, the Three Realms (the Sanskrit "tri" is same root as words like "tri-cycle" in English, and "loka" literally means "realm," so *triloka* is the three realms).

Humans and animals inhabit the earthly realm, but so do other forces or powers which can be felt and sensed, but not seen. Above the earthly realm was the sky, or atmosphere, in which birds fly and the chariots of the gods were sometimes seen. The realm higher than the highest birds can fly is the realm of mystery, eternal light, the heavenly realm—the most important deities dwell here and later it is thought that dead humans can have their life-essence, their *atman*, carried to this realm with the smoke of the funeral pyre.

The first human being to discover the path to the heavenly realm was named Yama, and as a result he presides over it, but only because he was the discoverer—not because he is divine, or a judge, or a creator.

2.6 REGULARITY AND ORDER IN THE UNIVERSE

The daily lives of people who live in a farming community are regulated by the patterns of nature which are obvious to a farmer, but barely noticeable for someone living in a contemporary big city. For rural people, it seems obvious that something keeps the seasons continuously rotating from summer to fall to winter to spring. Something must keep the sun and stars in their patterns. Something keeps events from being chaotic and random.

It is an easy step to assume that the something that keeps events in their proper order is the **same** something that keeps human beings in their proper social patterns and this ensures peace and order among humans. In other words, there is a correct pattern in everything. The Sanskrit term for this proper ritual and moral pattern is ***rta***, an **impersonal** force which ensures regularity and order everywhere. Even in worship, *rta* is the pattern of correct performance of religious sacrifice. *Rta* was not created by any divinity, and all gods are subject to *rta*.

Early Aryan religion was primarily oriented around rituals, and it was believed that proper performance of rituals by priests helped to maintain harmony in nature, but also harmony between the divine forces overhead and the human world below. When you and I guide our lives by *rta*, we will find ourselves in harmony with nature and with our fellow human beings. The proper performance of rituals was also *rta*. Proper social interaction with our fellow humans was *rta*.

The Ultimate Source of Reality

In the early Vedic times, we know that the problem of the origin of the world was not of concern because the first nine chapters of the *Rig-veda* shown no concern with this metaphysical issue. Where did everything originate? What is the source of all that exists? It is not until perhaps a thousand years later that this issue begins to intrigue the authors of the sacred texts. A tenth chapter was added to the previous nine of the *Rig-veda*, and it reveals some interest in the topic. In *Rig-veda* 10.72, we have a depiction of the gods being born from non-existence, and then the quarters of the sky "were born from her who crouched with legs spread." In a similar manner the earth was born, and then the gods and their children. The first seven children were immortal, but all those who were born of the eighth child would beget offspring and then soon die.[18]

The most popular Vedic tale of creation is found in the "Hymn of Creation" which is the *Rig-veda* 10.129, and it is entirely more speculative and philosophical in its treatment of the topic.

> There was neither non-existence nor existence then; there was neither the realm of space nor the sky which is beyond. What stirred? Where? In whose protection? Was there water, bottomlessly deep? There was neither death nor immortality then. There was no distinguishing sign of night nor of day. That one breathed, windless, by its own impulse. Other than that there was nothing beyond. Darkness was hidden by darkness in the beginning; with no distinguishing sign, all this was water. The life force that was covered with emptiness, that one arose through the power of heat. Desire came upon that one in the beginning; that was the first seed of mind. Poets seeking in their heart with wisdom found the bond of existence in non-existence. Their cord [the bond of existence, extending across the universe] was extended across. Was there below? Was there above? There were seed-placers; there were powers. There was impulse beneath; there was giving-forth above. Who really knows? Who will here proclaim it? Where was it produced? From where is this creation? The gods came afterwards, with the creation of this universe. Who then knows where it has arisen? Where this creation has arisen—perhaps it formed itself, or perhaps it did not—the one who looks down on it, in the highest heaven, only he knows—or perhaps he does not know.[19]

In the Vedas, almost all of the various divinities are associated with some aspect of the physical world, such as sun, thunder, rain, wind or fire. Thus the "Hymn of Creation" explains that the creation was prior to the natural order, i.e., prior to the gods. In the earliest Vedic view, the universe does not have a divine origin; rather the origin of the cosmos is prior to the birth of the gods. The creation was an event so far back into the past that we cannot know any details; all is mystery. It is interesting to note how different this extraordinarily ancient story of creation is from the familiar Western story. For the Hindu, the origin of all things was prior even to the gods, and even the highest god in the highest heaven may not know where it all began.

Notice that in the "Hymn of Creation" the first divinity arises from the power of heat, much as a chicken egg is incubated, that is, is born from the body heat of the mother hen, the method we call "brooding." The next stage involves erotic desire, and consciousness is born.[20] We might also note that in this very early creation tale, there is no concern with reincarnation, with karma, or with liberation, and there is no concept that humans are one with the source. There is no concern with returning to that source.

The Vedic View of Social Divisions

The earliest Vedic hymns reveal that as the early Aryan populations began to settle in India, they comprised three social groups: (1) warriors, administrators and rulers; (2) priests; (3) animal herders or common people. Scholars

---

[18] From Rig-veda 10.72, from Wendy Doniger O'Flaherty, *The Rig Veda, An Anthology* (London: Penguin, 1981).

[19] Rig-Veda 10.129, *ibid*.

[20] The student should realize that there are many quite different creation stories besides the biblical tale of Genesis and Adam and Eve. There are several creation myths in India, and dozens from around the world. A good source describing many of the world's religious creation myths is by Barbara C. Sproul, *Primal Myths: Creation Myths Around the World: A comprehensive collection of creation stories ranging across widely varying times and cultures, including Ancient Egyptian, African, and Native American* (New York: Harper Collins, 1979). There is a good treatment of creation stories in Nina Rosenstand, *The Human Condition: An Introduction to Philosophy of Human Nature* (New York: McGraw-Hill, 2001).

believe that in the early centuries, these divisions were not rigid. Commoners could become priests or warriors. There was flexibility. Not all occupations were hereditary.[21] Before the second century B.C.E., we find various trades and crafts beginning to be ordered in a hierarchy of prestige, value, and dignity. Then later, as we shall see, ultimately Indian society will be broken into four social groups further subdivided into various hereditary occupations. Some scholars believe that the subdivision of the lowest social groups reflects a pre-Aryan Harappan concern. Ultimately, strict hereditary divisions of society will come to dominate Indian society.

2.7 THE *DEVAS*: VEDIC DIVINITIES OF THE ARYANS

The earliest Aryan hymns of the *Rig Veda* are ritual tools used to entreat divinities to do favors for us in this world, or rituals to placate the anger of one or more of the superhuman beings called *devas* in Sanskrit.

The Sanskrit term *deva* shares the same root as the English word "divine" and the Latin word for a divinity, *deus*, or *theos* in Greek. It is very important not to think of Western Christian associations for the term "god" or "gods." In the West, over the centuries the term "god" came to denote a transcendent being of infinite power, infinite knowledge, and creator of all that exists. None of these associations are appropriate for the Sanskrit term *deva*. Like the gods of the Greeks, Romans, and Egyptians, a *deva* is a being of great power, but not infinite power. The most important *devas* reside in a celestial abode of luminous heaven, the highest heavenly realm of mystery and eternal light.

In the *Rig-veda* the forces of nature were personified and deified. Natural forces were vaguely thought of as having human-like forms and human-like characteristics, feelings, desires, and faults. There are divinities of nature, including sun, moon, thunder, wind, rain, water, fire, father heaven, and mother earth.

Most of the *devas* are associated with natural phenomena and natural functions. For example, one of the *devas* most commonly named in the *Rig Veda* is Agni who corresponds to fire.[22] Varuna is the *deva* associated with water. Vata is power of wind, while Surya is the sun which moves across the sky. Usas is the goddess of dawn and there were dawn rituals performed daily in the homes of the Aryans. Rudra the Howler was an archer who gave gifts, but also personified the howling wind-caused destruction of great storms, an angry and destructive *deva* with a very volatile bad temper. The most important of the *devas* in the *Rig Veda* include Agni, the god of fire, and Indra, the god of war. There are divinities which favor moral behavior, and other *devas* for whom morality is irrelevant.

AGNI

Although the Vedic *devas* are associated with natural phenomena, several stand out as particularly important. As mentioned previously, **Agni** is the *deva* of fire, but do not think of Agni as related to something like a cooking fire or a campfire. Agni dwells in many realms. He lives on earth in one's fireplace, and in plants. He dwells in the sky above as lightning. Agni mediates between the *devas* and the humans. Fire and the smoke resulting can carry messages upwards from the earthly realm to the highest celestial realm, and as such Agni is a messenger of the *devas* and a *deva* himself. As we are all aware, fire can burn down a home, a city, or even a countryside and thousands of square miles of forest.

In addition to Agni there is **Rudra**, the gift-giving archer associated with the howling wind, Vishnu associated with sunlight, Indra associated with thunder and rain, and Varuna associated with water.

---

[21] Scholars note that every culture established by these nomadic Aryans (not just in India) set up a social system with three or four divisions, with priests, warriors, and farmers as the top three.

[22] The name "Agni" is related to the English words "igneous" and "ignite."

CHAPTER 2: THE ARYANS

INDRA

Indra is a very ancient *deva*. He is often called the chief of the *devas*, the Supreme Ruler and is mentioned in the *Rig Veda* more often than any other *deva*. Indra personifies not only thunder and rain,[23] but also war, chaos and conflict. Indra ruled over the waters of heaven and brought the monsoons. Indra was the patron *deva* of the Aryan warriors before they arrived in India. As such, Indra was a personification of the ideal powers and virtues of the Aryan warrior class. Indra is big, strong, and he does not need to be particularly intelligent. He's closer to what we might call a force of chaos and disorder.

Large feasts are held in his honor, where intoxicating beverages are consumed. Indra drinks to excess, he eats to excess, and he boasts of his fighting skills to all who are present. Indra is dangerous. But because Indra is big and powerful, with these qualities he helps his people, the Aryans, to win in battle! Indra is not concerned with farms and most likely was the most important *deva* of the Aryans before they settled down.

VARUNA

Varuna is Indra's equal, also referred to as chief of the *devas* and a Supreme Ruler, but Varuna is a force who defends social order and harmony (just the opposite of Indra who is associated with the vigorous and chaotic disorder of battle). Varuna wants speech which is truthful, and rewards moral behavior. Varuna is the patron of those who rule, those who must keep order in society, and thus Varuna is the one who confers legitimacy upon the authority of the king. Varuna's association with water was very significant, for water is life to a farming community. Varuna upholds the balanced patterning of the universe, defending *rta* and thus Varuna supports order, honesty, and a stable world.

VISHNU

There is also the solar god **Vishnu**, a relatively unimportant *deva* in the *Rig-Veda*, who personifies sunlight, and strides through the universe in three steps (the rising of the sun, the culmination of the sunlight at noon, and the setting of the sun). He is referred to as the "unconquerable preserver" and he will become associated with a force for preservation in later Hinduism. Vishnu is associated with sunbeams which ripen crops and beautify the plants and flowers. Stories will associate him with the power of water to preserve our lives, and he is said to sleep on the blue waters on the back of a divine cobra.

From the perspective of the Vedas, the various *devas* and their powers seem to be related, interrelated, interconnected, and interdependent. At this stage in Vedic religion, the *devas* are impersonal powers and aspects of pervasive forces, but they are not personal deities who care about human beings as individuals. They might bestow favors, but only because we humans have bribed them with gifts, not because we humans had a special place in their affections. In addition, like the human realm, all *devas* were subject to the laws of nature and the powerful force of *rta*.

Prayers, rituals and sacrifices directed towards *devas* can be understood to be intimately related to the lives of the rulers and the ordinary people who were mostly farmers. Living on a farm is dangerous, with injuries and potentially life-threatening infections. The *devas* may be able to protect us from the dangers of nature, disease, injury, starvation, and want.

Of course, the huge geographic area we call India was composed of different tribes and groups, and these would engage in armed conflict. Thus, prayers, rituals and sacrifices directed towards supernatural beings request protection from military insecurity, invasion, and battle. Also, your own local *devas* were needed to provide protection from strange and foreign peoples and their (equally real) divinities. Finally, there are the community insecurities, the dangers caused by brigands, thieves in the neighborhood, destructive individuals and people who exhibit other forms of

---

[23] Indra the storm god is also Thor in Scandinavian mythology.

antisocial behavior. Prayers and hymns directed towards local deities of trees, rivers, and other sacred places may help us with these situations as well.

Although Indra, Agni, and Varuna are the most important of the Vedic *devas* for over a thousand years, their importance gradually wanes and by the second century B.C.E., newer *devas* like Krishna and Shiva begin to take their place.

2.8 THE *KARMA-MARGA*: The Vedic Pathway of Ritual

During the Vedic era, the function of the Brahmin priests was to perform rituals as preserved by priestly guilds, whose chanted words were taken from the first three of the Vedas. The Sanskrit term *karma* means "action," and a ritual is clearly a very special sort of important action. Early Vedic religion follows the *marga* ("pathway") of ritual action, or *karma*. Thus, the early Vedic religion can be described as a **karma-marga**, the pathway of ritual action.

Rituals of the Vedic Age

A religious ritual is a form of conducting worship established by tradition, or established by the authority of a religious organization. Early in human history rituals were especially important. A wide variety of behaviors can be ritualized, including sacrifices, prayers, mimetic dances, processions, dramas, ordeals, games, mysteries, and feasts. Later in India, even sexual intimacy came to be ritualized.

Formal rituals are done at prescribed times and most often occur at regular intervals.[24] Rituals are often tied to the seasons, cycles of the moon and cycles of springtime planting and fall harvest. Rituals are essential for important celebrations, such as the coronation of a new ruler, the birth of a prince, and even essential for welcoming in a new year. More personal rituals may be done on the occasions of births, coming of age, marriages, recovery from sickness, and death.

Rituals may also be performed to cleanse people of pollution which is offensive, or to purify people of their offenses against the gods; there are rituals to protect one from one's enemies and there are also rituals for execration, that is, rituals to harm or curse one's enemies. In cultural and political terms, rituals are also done for hunting, planting, harvesting, and during wartime. Political leaders can engage in rituals on behalf of the populace.

An important characteristic of religious ritual is that it is often a symbolic re-enactment of the acts of the divinities. The ritual actions are done in the present time, in history and performed by human beings. But, these actions are interpreted by people as having been initiated by the gods. Human beings may be the ones who perform the ritual act, but humans experience the gods, the *devas*, as the inspiration and the real agents behind what is done.

The role of the Brahmin priests in society was to do the sacred work of society, that is, to preserve ritual knowledge and perform the most important sacred rituals. Rulers, wealthy people, and ordinary people would hire Brahmin priests to perform the larger rituals, to satisfy the needs of the family or the farm or the kingdom. They felt that external forces, or *devas*, were granting favors because the *devas* looked kindly upon the priests who were performing sacrifices to the gods and performing flattering ceremonies. The Brahmins offered gifts and the *devas* responded with favors. The *devas* were cosmic powers and cosmic forces, and the sacred sounds of rituals performed properly, and the properly performed sacrifices were directly accessing cosmic powers and forces, which could be used to the worldly advantage of the person paying for the ritual.

---

[24] The author is indebted to Dr. Robert Doud for many of these observations.

The words in the sacred Vedas were never sounds uttered by humans; the sounds of the Vedas are the most sacred sounds enunciated by sacred reality itself, or the divine gods themselves. It was believed that the Brahmin priests could tap into powers which arise from the priest's proper enunciation of powerful **sounds** which can invoke divinities and perhaps control the forces of nature. These sacred powerful sounds were the sacred words of the Vedas, but their powers were activated only when enunciated properly and chanted with special secret knowledge. There were thousands of prayers that had power. In the same way that when we utter a fellow human being's name, we attract her attention, similarly the names of the *devas* were seen as especially powerful sounds which connected us to powerful forces.[25] Invoking the names of *devas* with sacred sounds was to tap into these powerful forces, but of course, it was also very dangerous. One was dealing with cosmic forces which cannot be controlled and which can cause great harm if not treated with utmost ritual respect!

Chanted *Mantras*

If individual rites, rituals, and sacrifices successfully manipulated particular cosmic forces, there must be some correspondence between the rituals and properly pronounced words, and the ultimate reality. These properly pronounced words are called **mantras** [mahn-tra] and the sounds had to be pronounced at precisely the correct pitch and the inflection must be perfect. Otherwise, they had no effect. Each Brahmin priest spent a lifetime learning the perfect pronunciation of sacred words and phrases. The Sanskrit etymology of the original meaning of *mantra* is that by which one thinks, or an instrument of thought. For the priests, it referred to the sacred and power-filled sounds of the Vedic verses.[26]

In the early period of the Vedas, the rituals were thought to be a tiny representation of the cosmos, with secret symbolic meanings assigned to the shapes of rituals and sacred fire pits, and the sounds of rituals. There are secret correspondences between sacred sounds (*mantras*) and cosmic forces and knowledge of these correspondences gave the priest great power. Understanding those secret correspondences would give the Brahmin priests a deeper understanding of the sacred ultimate.

In the 800–200 B.C.E. period, the attention of the elite Brahmin priests turned from studying correspondences between particular individual rituals to the possible cosmic interconnections of aspects of the sacrifices themselves. How did sacrifices in general connect to the cosmic forces? Understanding these esoteric interconnections was important. The more the priest understood of the patterns of correspondence between the rite and the supernatural realm, the more power the individual priest might wield.

2.9 THREE TYPES OF RITUAL IN VEDIC INDIA

In India during this time period including 600 B.C.E., the great majority of the population were engaged primarily in herding and farming, with a small merchant and artisan classes arising, but truly large cities had not yet developed. During this era, three distinct types of religious rituals can be distinguished.

Family Rituals

The family rituals during this time period are thought to be rather simple and did not require a professional Brahmin priest to perform. The father of the family was required to purify himself (so as not to offend the deity) and

---

[25] Many world religions have similar injunctions. Compare this with the Jewish injunction against uttering or writing the name of the deity, or the Christian commandment against taking the name of the Lord in vain.

[26] Although a popular Tibetan explanation of the term *mantra* is that it is something which protects the mind, Sanskrit etymology does not bear this out. Cf. Agehananda Bharati, *The Tantric Tradition* (New York: Doubleday Anchor Books, 1970), p. 103ff.

greet the dawn with rituals involving milk and food. These are intended to protect the family from harm, and bring blessings down on the sacrificer and his family. There were other rituals involving important family events such as funerals. The sons were required to perform special rituals in the year after the death of the father, designed to ensure that the parent would achieve a heavenly afterlife after an arduous journey. If the person was not obedient to their social, moral, and religious duties (*dharma*), or did not have the proper rituals performed, it was believed that their individual identity would be lost and they would simply dissolve back into the earth.

Rituals of the *Atharvan* Priests

Also, there are magical rituals performed by the village priest, the shaman who has the *atharvan* spells and incantations, usually performed as the need arises. The *atharvans* helped individuals in the rural group with rituals to alleviate personal and family crises. These priests served as therapists, as faith-healers, and as the local pharmacist administering herbal medicines.

Spells and incantations were used to protect the person or his family against illness, against demons, against spells cast by enemies, and incantations to get a lover, to get children, to improve luck in gambling or battle, or in business, and other such concerns. Some of the spells are aimed at harming one's enemies. Probably the most important part of the ritual is the recitation of sacred *mantras* thought to be especially powerful, but as noted above, these rituals could also involve herbs, spells, and other things we would consider magical. Here's an example of a spell powered by the names of two gods intended to improve a business:

> I urge Indra the merchant, come to us and be our foreruner. Ward off the unpaying one, the cutting beast, and let masterful Indra be a bringer of wealth to me. O Gods! That money with which, desiring more money, I conduct my business, let that multiply and never decrease. O Agni, with this sacrifice frustrate those who would ruin my profit.[27]

As should be clear, what the sacrificers hoped to attain via the ritual were very much focused on this world, i.e., wealth, power, health, prosperity, material benefits, success during one's lifetime, and after death, *permanent* immortality in heaven.

The Community Fire Rituals

Finally, there are rites considered essential to the health and welfare of the village or community. Later, these rituals were essential to the kingdom and its citizens. As the cities became larger, these rituals became very intricate and complex. The most important included sacrifices related to the sacred fire and involving animal sacrifices. Many different divinities were worshiped in elaborate rituals, but two who were especially important were Indra and Agni.

The ceremonies grew more and more complicated as the centuries passed. Rulers and nobility would pay for community rituals and feasts that were public and for the benefit of all. It required many priests to perform the community rituals. The biggest annual ceremony is the one performed at New Years, and the ceremonies and rituals would follow the seasons and important events of the year. Some rituals could last for a year and require the full attention of many priests to accomplish satisfactorily.

Agni is the Messenger

The fire divinity **Agni** is central to the fire sacrifice. The fire ceremony could have been used to install a new king, or simply to improve relations with the *devas*. Animals were killed and provided a community meal where the food was offered to and shared with the *devas*, and all sorts of worldly advantages were promised. The various hymns were chanted and sung, while the Brahmin priests offered food to the *devas* by burning it in the ritual fires.

These community rituals were performed in a fixed outdoor setting for the entire village, or town. The

---

[27] Atharva-Veda 3.16, in Robert E. Van Voorst, *Anthology of Asian Scriptures, op. cit.*, p. 51.

fire-flames would carry the offerings to the gods in heaven. Grain, animal flesh, and clarified butter were placed in the flames, transforming them into the smoke that could carry the foods to the heavens where the *deva* would be pleased, and even nourished.

Agni, the *deva* of fire, and the fire itself-as-messenger, delivered these gifts to the gods in the heavens. The *devas* are invited to the offering ground, are seated next to the sacred fires in the place of honor. They are fed with meat or grain cakes and with the intoxicating sacred drink of *soma*. To drink *soma* allowed a person to feel transformed, to feel ecstatically transported to the realm of the divinities.

The *devas* are entertained by poets who recite memorized hymns, but some of whom do improvised verses. They will also praise not only the *devas*, but also the rulers and nobility (and especially the patron who is paying for the food and the rituals and the priests). This ceremony would join together the realm of humans and the divine realm, celebrating a interconnection and unity of the secular and the sacred. The fire ritual was essential to the maintenance of order within the entire universe. If the *deva* were pleased, well-fed, and grateful, the personified natural forces that were the *deva* would sustain creation, and ensure the prosperity of those who paid for the sacrifices.

The earliest fire sacrificial celebrations were not restricted to just priests; householders could and did perform much smaller ceremonies for themselves and their families. It was the bigger, more elaborate ceremonies which required priests, and required wealthy patrons to pay for them.[28] The goals were straightforward: a long life, a happy life, and then permanent happy celestial home after death.

The **Brahmanas** and the Fire Ceremony

As the community fire rituals grew more important and more complex, it became impossible for one priest to perform the ceremony, and by the time four priests were required, it became increasingly difficult for priests to keep all the details correct. Some rituals required weeks to perform; others were only performed so rarely that few living priests would have the details straight. As a result, priests who conducted the fire sacrifices wrote notes for the use of their apprentice priests, most likely sons or nephews.

These notes, called *Brahmanas*, were loose commentaries on the content of the Vedas. Each of the Vedas has many *Brahmanas* attached to it. The *Brahmanas* are useful only for priests. Unlike the hymns of the Vedas, the comments in the *Brahmanas* are straightforward explanations of ritual and the powerful chants and words used in rituals. The *Brahmanas* provide symbolic interpretations of passages, and also cautioned the priest on how to avoid common errors in performance of rituals.

The name of the texts which explain rituals, *Brahmana*, comes from the term *Brahman*, originally a prayer, but the term *Brahman*[29] came to mean all prayers, the power behind all prayer, and then it came to mean all powerful sacred sounds. It is in the *Brahmanas* that the idea first arose that the Vedas were revealed scriptural supreme sources of knowledge, that is, the Vedas were not composed by the early seers, but are instead divine revelation, perhaps even prior to the gods.[30] Scholars believe the earliest of the *Brahmanas* were composed between about 800 B.C.E and 500 B.C.E.[31]

---

[28] Thomas J. Hopkins, *The Hindu Religious Tradition* (Belmont, CA: Wadsworth, 1971), p. 15.

[29] Be careful not to confuse *Brahman*, the impersonal creative force behind sacred sounds, and *Brahmanas*, books of notes for apprentice priests on how to perform the fire sacrifice.

[30] K. N. Jayatilleke, *Early Buddhist Theory of Knowledge* (London: George Allen & Unwin, 1963), p. 29.

[31] Sukumari Bhattacharji, *The Indian Theogony, op. cit.*, p. 18.

CHAPTER 2: THE ARYANS

The Fire Rituals and the Priests

It is important to remember that the Vedic rituals were not just visual spectacles; the priests and householders were certain that there really were *devas* involved and hidden powers could be obtained via each ritual. Everyone believed that rituals were essential. Rituals kept the universe regular, and human priestly performance of ritual aided the return of the new year, the return of spring, and even protected the universe from chaos. Rituals mediated between the human personality and the reality of the external world. To accomplish the goals of the ritual, the priest had to know the hidden symbolism that related ceremonies and rites.[32] The priest who knows the symbolic contents of the Vedas and the secrets in the *Brahmanas*, could perform the fire ritual and be certain of getting the desired result because the various elements are connected, and knowing the secret connections gives power to control. Ordinary people could not preside over this sort of fire ritual; it required a priest to perform the ritual and obtain results.

Over the centuries, the Brahmin priests came to believe that the maintenance of the entire universe depended upon regular performance of the fire sacrifice, but only when performed by priests who knew the esoteric meanings. Without the proper knowledge, the sacrifice was no better than an offering poured on dead ashes.[33] These rituals were quite technical and required priests who had special expertise. The fire ritual might require several days or weeks of preparation. The ritual itself involved sacrificing an animal, cooking it, and offering the food to the gods. But if the priests chanted the sacred words accurately, the results were guaranteed.

This is a complete reorientation of the nature of the sacrifice. Originally, the priests offered gifts and begged favors from *devas*, in an attempt to persuade or bribe the deities to grant favors to the sacrificer. Later, it was thought that the ritual itself controlled the cosmic powers; it all depended upon the secret knowledge of the priests, and a priest who knows the contents of the Vedas and Brahmanas could **compel** the *devas* to produce the desired results. Many rituals required the ingesting of a very powerful intoxicating drink, called *soma*.

Soma: **The Drink of the Gods**

To drink *soma* gave the imbiber a feeling of being transported to the sacred realms, making the person feel immortal. This meant that the person was in communion with the gods, or at least had access to the spirit realm. As a result of the effects of consuming *soma*, the priest believed the experiences confirmed the sacred existence of the *devas*. The power available in the esoteric *soma*[34] sacrifice kept the world working in an orderly fashion, and ultimately gave the priests control over the universe itself; the knowledge of the ultimate source of reality and the acquisition of powers were only for those ritually pure and fit, and these powers raised men to the status of gods and gave them control over the gods.[35]

It is not too difficult to understand the reasoning behind such a claim. All followers of Aryan religion believed that the ritual sacrifices properly performed were effective. The *karma-marga* "action-pathway" of ritual sacrifices were the unquestioned heart of early Vedic religion. Not only did the Aryans consider the sacrifices to *devas* to be effective,

---

[32] Michael Witzel "Autochthonous Aryans?" *op. cit.*, p. 5

[33] Thomas Hopkins, *The Hindu Religious Tradition*, p. 33.

[34] *Soma* is a divine intoxicant of the *devas*. Over the centuries *soma* begins as a plant, and then *soma* named the drink derived from the plant, and eventually *soma* became a *deva*. It was made from a creeping plant combined with milk, and gave the priest ecstatic states of mind, feelings of exaltation, visions of *devas*, and visions of divine realms. The plants were all used up during the Vedic age, and no one today knows for certain which plants were used to create *soma*. Several people have made numerous suggestions involving cactus and mushrooms, but no one knows.

[35] Hopkins, *Hindu Religious Tradition*, p. 32.

but the Aryans also believed that all *devas* are subservient to *rta*, the abstract but active positive force of regularity and order.

If a priest could manipulate these forces using rituals, perhaps it is not the *devas* who were simply responding to the sacrificer's entreaties. Perhaps the priests were controlling hidden connections between the ritual itself, and the cosmic functions and powers which human beings called by the names of gods. The priest uttering the sacred words of the Vedas was able to control the forces which themselves control the universe. The sacred words of the rituals were believed to have power, and priests could control that power. Words and **sounds** with power (*mantras*) could change reality. Words correspond to external realities, and properly manipulated by a priest with secret knowledge, these sacred sounds give power to Brahmin priests.

The most powerful words were the names of the *devas* and the divine words of the Vedic hymns. These were much more powerful than ordinary words. Knowledge of sacred words might give the priests control over reality.

For Aryan religion, the sacrifices were effective, they worked, but now a select group of special priests began to believe that the ritual sacrifices worked because the **rites themselves brought about the desired ends/goals**, independently of the gods. Vedic *devas* were associated with natural forces such as wind, rain, thunder, sun and moon, but for some the priests themselves were controlling the forces of nature, directly, without asking for the intervention of separate gods. The actual words and sounds of the Vedic hymns had the power to affect and direct the universe! This stress on sacred words and the details of sacrificial rituals describes the realm of Aryan Vedic religion before the period where classical Hinduism begins to take its characteristic shape.

2.10 OLDER TRADITIONAL BRAHMIN RITUALS ARE LESS VALUED

Up until about 700-600 B.C.E., the rituals prescribed and transcribed in the Vedas were the single most important aspect of the Aryan spiritual life. Thus, early Vedic religion is the *karma-marga*, the pathway of ritual, protected by and practiced by the Brahmin priests. During the following centuries, traditional Vedic Hindu emphasis upon the pathway of ritual (*karma-marga*) becomes challenged by cultural and economic changes in India, and by religious perspectives that reject much of the Vedic certainties. Those priests who understood their role as protecting and memorizing the scriptural tradition of the Vedas upheld and protected tradition as well. However, not all religion in India involved protecting Aryan tradition.

The effectiveness of these Vedic rituals and ceremonies was beginning to be doubted, and it is entirely possible that the pre-Aryan Harappan religious ideas involving meditation and perhaps karma and reincarnation, were beginning to exert influence upon Aryan religion. During this historical period new forms of religion were arising which minimized the ritual pathway and minimized or rejected the authority of the four Vedas. These include Jainism and Buddhism which arose as independent religions, both of which denied the authority of the Vedas.

In terms of society, major changes were occurring. The old order of tribally oriented social and political structures was breaking down. Central powerful kingdoms run by monarchs were replacing pastoral and agricultural villages. Society was becoming more oriented towards cities and a merchant middle-class. These more cosmopolitan kingdoms were based on territory, not tribe or clan.

In the process, society became more complex, trade and travel increased, bringing exposure to other different native cultures, other gods and other ways of worship. It was a time of wars of conquest, with armies moving across farmlands decimating them as they went. Ancient empires were uprooted, and peoples were thrown into growing urban centers (without their familiar shrines and familiar gods), and people were left to themselves to find images that worked for them, and new religious experiences became convincing and meaningful.

It was during this same period when the religious authority of the traditional priesthood was being challenged. Reliance upon rituals and sacrifices were no longer accepted as effective by all in India. Groups of homeless wandering ascetics or mendicants known as *sramanas* (pronounced shra-ma-na) began to proliferate, claiming religious authority based on personal experience or personal knowledge. There was also the *munis*, the solitary silent sages who lived in the forests and survived by begging. They minimized the rituals of the Brahmin priests, and instead pondered philosophical and religious ideas, and advocated different religious practices such as seated meditation. It is from these groups that the *guru* or personal spiritual guide, arises.

It is a time of spiritual crisis, and many of the major religious and philosophical founders originated and flourished during this time.

Anxiety Concerning the Ritual Sacrifices

The goals of ritual sacrifice included wealth, power, health, prosperity, success during one's lifetime, and after death, *permanent* immortality in heaven. Some new ideas began to undermine the possibility of achieving these goals. The sacrificer paid a Brahmin priest to perform a finite ritual, in hopes of achieving an infinite result—the sacrificer's true self, the eternal unchanging *atman*, could enjoy permanent immortality in the heavenly realm. But, how can one achieve an infinite result from finite causes? If the sacrifices did work and did allow one's *atman* to achieve a heavenly realm, it could only be for a limited amount of time. What would happen when the finite positive results of the sacrifices were exhausted? Would the sacrificer's *atman* return back to this world, when all of the positive consequences of the rituals were exhausted?

In the later *Brahmanas*, fear arose that the effects of ritual sacrifices would run out, and the person's *atman* must leave the heavenly realm and be reborn back into this world. If the finite ritual did not bring permanent satisfaction of desires, and re-birth and re-death brought an end to the benefits of the ritual performance, what is the ultimate value of the sacrifices? Are the benefits just temporary?

Good Karma, Bad Karma

This way of thinking led to new concepts in Vedic culture: the idea of good and bad karma and the endless cycle of birth and rebirth, called *samsara*. These were going to cause a major change in the religious world-view of India.

The idea that the performance of appropriate rituals would generate enough karmic energy to send one to the next life began to be questioned. What happened when the ritual karmic energy ran out? Would one return to this life of pain and suffering again? This idea generated anxiety—how could the causal energy produced by finite rituals produce infinite and eternal happiness as a consequence? Is there any action or wisdom which could bring about eternal life in the heavens? These concepts were especially influential upon the Brahmin priests who manipulated the sacred words and rituals. They began to wonder if one needed to do the actual physical ritual involving lifting, carrying, and a physical altar. Could the rituals be equally effective if performed mentally, privately, internally?

Some Brahmins believed that private mental performance of the ritual was as effective as external public performance. A modern concert violinist or concert classical guitarist might sit quietly on an airplane, while mentally imagining every note of the music and every movement of her fingers. A gymnast may quietly visualize every movement of her routine before the event. This is an intense form of concentration. Priests who began vivid mental rehearsals of the rituals retired to the forests to perform every detail of religious sacrifices mentally, but not physically.

2.11 THE FOREST BOOKS: *Aranyakas*

The priests who performed mental rehearsals of the rituals in the forest are responsible for another kind of Vedic literature which began to appear perhaps beginning around 600-400 B.C.E. This is a new third group of texts in addition to the Vedas and Brahmanas, a new group composed in response to the new questions asked by people with an ascetic inclination, people who left home to meditate in the forests on the outskirts of the towns and villages. These persons were not interested in upholding Vedic ritual and tradition. They were more speculative.

CHAPTER 2: THE ARYANS

Reflecting the interests of this group, the *Aranyakas* or Forest Books, emphasize the meaning of the rituals without assuming that they would be physically practiced. In the *Aranyakas*, it is not the physical ritual which is effective; rather it is the knowledge of the symbolism behind the ritual which is efficacious. For one with the special knowledge, the physical performance of the ritual may be discarded. Each of the four Vedas had *Aranyakas* affiliated with it, treated as commentaries on the Veda.

Recall the Sanskrit term *Brahman*, the term for the power of the sacred prayer. Over the centuries, Brahman[36] comes to mean the source of the power of prayer, the power of the Vedic hymns and the power of the sacrifice (as understood in the Vedas and Brahmanas). Later, *Brahman* is used to name the ultimate source of prayer and power, the absolute reality of the universe, and the ultimate creative origin of all that is sacred, including the universe and all the *devas*.

The Focus is Upon Timeless Reality

The ascetics in the forest engaged in speculation on the nature of *Brahman*, asking how can *Brahman* be known? In this new religious orientation, the forest dwellers searched for the timeless source which is thought to be incomparably superior to the realm of time and change. This timeless reality is transcendent, ineffable, sacred, absolute, and beyond thought. In India, it was believed that anything that changed was less real than things which were immutable, eternal. During this time the *devas* were thought of as being like humans and they too lived, trapped in the realms of time and change. The forest ascetics focused upon a timeless original oneness of all things, prior to all the gods. They concluded that our world of conditioned reality is not the ultimate Reality.

The forest books, or *Aranyakas*, will set the stage for the fourth and last development of the Vedas, the sacred books called the *Upanishads* (to be discussed in the next chapter). The *Upanishads* will reorient some of the Brahmin priests of Vedic religion to sacred knowledge achieved only after great intellectual and meditative effort, rather than relying on chanted quotations from sacred texts. However, this sacred knowledge will provide the solution to the problem of the *karma-marga*. If physical performance of ritual sacrifices cannot possibly result in an infinite life of happiness in a celestial realm, then perhaps esoteric knowledge of the ultimate force underlying all reality can achieve that goal.

The *karma-marga* pathway of ritual action never disappears in India; it will continue to dominate Aryan religions. But alongside of ritual new forms of religion and social institutions will arise, and these provide the foundation for much of classical Hinduism, the Hinduism that dominates India today. Another pathway will develop as well, a pathway of sacred hidden wisdom resulting in liberation from the apparently endless cycle of birth and death. This wisdom pathway is the *jnana-marga*, to be discussed in another chapter. This new orientation begins to emerge with the next group of Aryan religious writings, the *Upanishads* and the *Bhagavad Gita*.

The sacred Vedic literature can be thought of as commentaries appended to the earliest Vedic texts, originally memorized, chanted, and protected by Aryan Brahmin priests. In this manner, we can think of the *Rig Veda* as consisting of (a) the root verses and hymns in praise of divinities,[37] (b) *Brahmanas*, texts which explain the meaning

---

[36] As pointed out previously, the term Brahman is ambiguous. It can mean (1) the group of priests who specialize in Vedic rituals, (2) the power of prayer, (3) the ultimate creative power which underlies reality and which is the source of all reality including the gods, and (4) the *Brahmanas*, the texts instructing apprentice priests how to perform the rituals of the Vedas. In an effort to minimize some of the potential confusion, this text has adopted the spelling "Brahmins" for the priestly group.

[37] These earliest hymns in the Vedas are called the *samhitas*.

of the rituals and how to perform the rituals, (c) Forest books, *Aranyakas*, which explore inner performance of ritual, and (d) the philosophical explorations of key ideas and religious experiences, called *Upanishads*. Western scholars tend to restrict the term "Vedas" to the four collections of earliest hymns (*Rig, Sama, Yajur* and *Atharva*) and treat the *Upanishads* as independent, but in India a Veda is usually thought to include all of the commentaries appended to the earliest verses.

2.12 NON-VEDIC INDIAN THINKERS

Although we have stressed Aryan Vedic religion, the student should not conclude that all Indian religion of this time period was slavishly Aryan or Vedic, or that all Indian thinkers believed that ultimate religious knowledge could be found in scriptural tradition or memorized quotations from scriptures.

In fact there were materialist Indian thinkers who completely rejected the supernatural claims of the Vedas and *Upanishads* and rejected the possibility of knowledge obtained from anything beyond the senses. The materialists stressed sense experience as the only genuine source of knowledge, and the physical realm as the only reality. According to materialist thinkers, the only laws are physical laws and there is no spiritual law of karma (which guarantees that good deeds will return to the doer, and evil deeds will also return to the doer), no immortal *atman*, no afterlife, no cycle of birth-and-death.[38]

There were also people who rejected the Vedas but held that every action produced an inevitable karmic consequence which traps us and which could not be avoided. For this group, one should use extreme ascetic practices to minimize all action. Liberation from the realm of time and change required self-mortification, torture of the flesh, and the least amount of activity possible.

Yet other groups rejected the Vedas, and also rejected the idea that the consequences of karma were inevitable and beyond our ability to influence them. These groups rejected ritual as a means to control reality, and instead stressed personal practice, understanding and knowledge, leading to wisdom which could liberate one from the apparently endless cycles of birth-and-death.

2.13 INFLUENCE OF HARAPPAN CULTURE ON LATER VEDIC RELIGION

The Indian religious tradition as we know it historically has many important characteristics that cannot be traced to the earliest Indo-European Vedic religious sources. Although one cannot speak with certainty, it seems likely that some of the features of the Hindu religion as practiced in contemporary times go back before 1750 B.C.E. to Mohenjo Daro and Harappa, and to the Indus Valley religious traditions.

There is no mention of ritual purification involving water in the four Vedic sacred books. Yet, classical Hinduism stresses ritual purification using water. The Indus Valley culture seems to have stressed water and ritual cleanliness. In the Vedas there is no suggestion that cross-legged meditation is a valuable religious tool, yet classical Hinduism utilizes cross-legged meditation (remember that a man seated in a meditation posture was depicted on the Indus valley seals). Ascetic practices of forest dwellers may well have begun in Harappan religion.

As a result of careful archaeological analysis, it has been discovered that several sacred sites in India which are popular religious sites in modern India were popular religious sites 4,000 years ago, before the Aryan migration into northwest India. It seems likely that at least some of the sacred locations for the Harappan civilization became sacred sites for later Aryan and Hindu religion.

The Harappans had fire altars and most likely fire rituals. Did these have any influence upon the popular fire rituals of the Aryan Brahmin priests?

---

[38] These and other views are discussed in David Kalupahana, *Buddhist Philosophy: A Historical Analysis* (Honolulu: The University Press of Hawaii, 1976), pp. 7-14.

The Vedas place no stress on female divinities, or goddesses, but later Hinduism puts special emphasis upon the goddess.[39] Is this related to goddesses in Harappan religion, as exemplified by the statues of females found in Harappan ruins?

It appears that the Aryans of the *Rig Veda* did not have a rigid caste structure, but rather flexible occupational groups. One cannot be certain, however. Some scholars believe that Harppans may have had a rigid birth social stratification which controlled hereditary occupations, resulting in minimal change over a thousand years. It seems possible that to maintain their own superiority, the Aryans took the social structures of the class system of the Harappans, and elaborated on them, relegating the native inhabitants to a low status within it.[40]

Finally, concepts like karma and reincarnation are not found in the four Vedas, but in the absence of any written records from the Harappan religious realm, we do not know if these sorts of concepts played any role in the Indus Valley civilization.

2.14 SUMMARY OF THE CHAPTER

We have discussed the world-view and the religious views of the Aryans, the Indo-European speaking nomads who immigrated into northern India around 1500 B.C.E., and their early sacred literature. We discussed the contents of the four early Vedas (the *Rig-veda*, the *Sama-veda*, the *Yajur-veda*, and the *Atharva-veda*).

Then we discussed the *Brahmanas*, the books of instruction for apprentice priests. We also discussed the *Aranyakas*, the Forest Books of those who believed that the mental performance of ritual was as effective as physical performance of ritual. Those Indian lineages which accept the authority of the sacred Vedas and their commentaries, and also accept the social position of the Brahmin caste of priests, are called **orthodox**. Those lineages of monks and ascetics which reject the Vedas and the religious authority of the Brahmin priestly caste are **heterodox**.

We then explained the early development of the idea that human beings are trapped in a cycle of birth and death, called *samsara*. The energy of karma was explained as the force which keeps humans trapped in *samsara*. We also suggested that some of the features of classical Hinduism may derive from the earlier Indus valley civilization.

2.15 TECHNICAL TERMS USED IN THIS CHAPTER

Agni   The energy of fire, messenger of the devas, and a deva himself

Aranyakas   The Forest Books, the Vedic books created by the mendicants who had left society and gone to the forests to try to understand the nature of ultimate reality, *Brahman*, and the true self, *atman*.

Atharva Veda   the fourth and last of the four Vedas; a collection of spells and incantations

aryan, aryans   The group who migrated into India about 1800-1400 B.C.E. and created the Vedic sacred texts

Asuras   opponents of the devas who engage in yearly battles

---

[39] The Vedas make reference to Saraswati, where the term names a river and also symbolizes learning, but later in the *Brahmanas* she is identified as a goddess of speech, and as such is the mother of the Vedas.

[40] Gregory L. Possehl, ed., *Harappan Civilization: A Recent Perspective* (New Delhi: Oxford University Press, 3rd ed. , 1993).

atman	the principle of breath and life; the eternal essence of a human which moves from one lifetime to another
Brahmins	The name for the Aryan priestly group who recited prayers and hymns. The term is properly transliterated "Brahmans" but in order to minimize confusion with the other meanings for the term, we use the older spelling "Brahmins."
Brahman	Originally, "Brahman" named the mysterious power present when the prayers and hymns of the sacrifice were uttered or recited. Thus, Brahman was a power or force connecting the rite, ritual, or liturgy, with the supernatural sacred realm of powers, gods, spirits, devas. Over the centuries it comes to mean the name of the source of all reality, the sacred ultimate source of all the gods
Brahmanas	The commentary books on the Rig Veda composed between 1200-600 B.C.E. explaining to apprentice priests how to perform the rituals and the meanings of the rituals.
deva / devas	superhuman beings, divinities, or gods
Indra	deva of war, patron of the warriors and protectors in Aryan culture
karma	literally, "action," and as such, the term can refer to the physical action of ritual and sacrifice, or actions with moral consequences
ksatriyas	the warrior group of the early Aryan society which later includes the protectors and administrators of society.
mantra	words and phrases which contain power and have secret correspondences with our world and divine realms as well. *Om* is a famous mantra.
marga	the Sanskrit term for "pathway"
muni	a "sage" or "wise teacher" who has gone into the forest to discover the secret of life
ric	The Sanskrit term for "praise," from which *Rig* is derived.
rsis	those who see the highest truth, thus "sage" or "seer."
Rig Veda	the earliest of the four sacred books of the Aryans; a collection of 1028 hymns addressed to various devas
rta	the fundamental principle which ensures order and stability in the universe; this impersonal force is prior to the gods and the devas are subject to rta
Rudra the Howler	the deva of destructive storms—very bad temper
Sama Veda	the sacred liturgical verses of the Aryans that were sung
samsara	the ongoing cycle of birth and death, as the true self, the *atman*, moves from life to life, and from realm to realm
Sanskrit	the early Indo-European language of the Aryans, and the language preserved in the Vedic sacred books of India and other technical treatises
soma	intoxicating drink which gave visions; used in early Vedic sacrifices
sramanas	these are people who have rejected the comforts of society for religious reasons, and have chosen to live in the forests, in an attempt to find the ultimate meaning of life
Surya	deva of sun
Triloka	the three realms of earth, sky, and the celestial realm above the sky

CHAPTER 2: THE ARYANS

Usas	deva of dawn
vaishyas	the common people, the herdsmen of the Aryans
Varuna	*deva* associated with water, but also the deva who values truth, morality, and the patron of the rulers and guardian of *rta*.
Vata	*deva* of wind, also generally the same as Vayu
Vishnu	*deva* associated with water and with preservation
Yama	the first human who was able to make his way to the heavenly realm after death, and who is the ruler of this realm just because he was the first to get there
Yajur Veda	the third of the four Vedas, with verses to be muttered while moving physical implements during the performance of ritual
yajus	A *yajus* is a short formulaic phrase murmured during ritual performance, in which the meaning and purpose of the ongoing ritual is described, and thereby gives additional power and effectiveness to the ritual.

2.15 QUESTIONS FOR FURTHER DISCUSSION

1) Many people consider ritual to be a universal feature of religions. Early Aryan religions are based on rituals performed by priests, but is it true that ritual behavior must be religious? Are there rituals which are not religious? Discuss.

2) The term "Aryan" has had a negative connotation to people in the West since the Second World War. What was the original meaning of the term in India? How did "Aryan" come to be associated with racism?

3) The early Aryan religion did not have any concern with an afterlife of reward or punishment, but rather put their energy into rituals. What could be the point or purpose of a ritual if it is not going to bring us a happy life in heaven?

4) Earlier we discussed Shamanism. Do you see any parallels or similarities between the practices and beliefs of the Vedic priests and Shamanism?

5) If you lived in a village with a shaman, what sorts of experiences would lead you to consult a shaman? (for example, would you be likely to visit a shaman to deal with the illness of you child? would you be likely to visit a shaman to purchase firewood?)

6) The Aryan priests had four sacred Vedas. Explain the relevance of each of the four Vedas to early Hinduism. Explain how each of the four texts was used and what the contents were about.

7) An important concept in early Vedic religion was *rta* (rita). Explain how *rta* is related to the universe, how it is related to human social affairs, and how it is relevant to religious rituals.

8) Some scholars believe that Indus Valley religious beliefs and practices may have exerted an influence upon later Hinduism. What features of early Indus Valley religion might have influenced later Hinduism?

CHAPTER 2: THE ARYANS

9) You might consider doing an internet search on the term "Aryan," and seeing what turns up. How many sites actually discuss the ancient Indo-Europeans who migrated into northern India, and how many are involved in political or racist agendas?

==

A SELECTED BIBLIOGRAPHY

Hinduism

Barua, B. M., *A History of Pre-Buddhistic Indian Philosophy* (Calcutta: University of Calcutta Press, 1921)

Bilimora, P., Joseph Prabhu and Renuka Sharma, *Indian Ethics* (Burlington, Vt: Ashgate, 2005)

Bryant, Edwin, *The Quest for the Origins of Vedic Culture: The Indo-Aryan Migration Debate* (London: Oxford University Press, 2001)

Chatterjee, Satischandra, and Dhirendramohan Datta, *An Introduction to Indian Philosophy* (Calcutta: University of Calcutta, 1968)

de Bary, William T., ed., *Sources of Indian Tradition*, 2nd edition, 2 volumes (New York: Columbia University Press, 1988).

Doniger, Wendy, *The Rig Veda: An Anthology* (New York: Penguin Classics, 2000)

Eck, Diana, *Darsan: Seeing the Divine Image in India* (New York: Columbia University Press, 1998)

Hopkins, Thomas J., *The Hindu Religious Tradition* (Belmont, Ca: Wadsworth, 1971)

Grimes, John, *A Concise Dictionary of Indian Philosophy* (Albany, NY: State University of New York Press, 1996)

Halbfass, Wilhelm, *Tradition and Reflection: Explorations in Indian Thought* (Albany, NY: State University of New York Press, 1991)

Herman, A. L., *Brief Introduction to Hinduism* (Boulder, CO: Westview Press, 1991)

Hirayanna, M., *Essentials of Indian Philosophy* (London: Unwin, 1978)

Hirayanna, M., *Outlines of Indian Philosophy* (London: Allen & Unwin, 1970)

Knott, Kim, *Hinduism: A Very Short Introduction* (London: Oxford, 2000)

Koller, John, *The Indian Way: An Introduction to the Philosophies and Religions of India*, 2nd edition (New York: Prentice Hall, 2005)

Koller, John and Patricia, *Sourcebook in Asian Philosophy* (New York: Macmillan, 1991)

Michaels, Axel, *Hinduism: Past and Present* (Princeton, 2003)

Mohanty, J. N., *Classical Indian Philosophy* (Lanham, MD: Rowman and Little, 2000)

Potter, Karl H., *Guide to Indian Philosophy* (Boston, MS: G. K. Hall, 1988) An extensive bibliography.

Potter, Karl H., ed., *The Encyclopedia of Indian Philosophies* (Princeton, NJ: Princeton University Press, 1961-2015)

Radhakrishnan, Sarvepalli, *Indian Philosophy*, 2 volumes (London: Allen and Unwin, 1923)

Shattuck, Cybelle, *Hinduism* (New York: Prentiss-Hall, 1999)

Sharma, I. C., *Ethical Philosophies of India* (Lincoln, NB: Johnsen Publishing Co., 1965)

CHAPTER 2: THE ARYANS

CHAPTER 3: BEGINNINGS OF CLASSICAL HINDUISM

3.1 OVERVIEW OF THE CHAPTER

As the Aryan civilization developed between the period of 1500 B.C.E. and 200 B.C.E. Aryan priests slowly shifted away from the Vedic stress on the fire sacrifice and priestly rituals, and the Aryan stress upon ritual expanded to include many new practices and new ideas as well. Culture and religion were not distinguished. Religious concerns began to dominate all aspects of everyday life including occupation and social obligations.

This chapter will deal with the thousand-year-period of approximately 700 B.C.E. to approximately 300 C.E., the time period when many of the basic features of the religion we call Hinduism were taking recognizable shape. This marks the lessening of the importance of traditional Vedic ritual traditions, and during this period Indian religion expanded to include new concerns and new beliefs which cause dramatic changes in spirituality. Indian religion will never give up rituals, but new philosophical concerns involving death and the sacred supreme ultimate reality bring about new practices.

The earliest roots of many fundamental features of the modern religion we call Hinduism become recognizable during this time period. We will see the religious underpinnings of the caste system, support for hierarchy, stress on innate differences between classes which justify privileges for some and not for others, and other important features of classical Hinduism such as the traditional four stages of life. The third and fourth stages of the four stages of life focus upon the question of death, afterlife, and our relationship to the sacred source of all that is divine. We will see the notions of pollution and contamination, and how upperclass Hindus were taught to avoid certain fluids and meats, and to shun certain people as too impure to interact with because they were contaminating.

The classical Hindu social and religious order from earliest times up until the early twentieth century has been a society which tries not to change, composed of groups of unequal privilege. Many features of classical Hinduism as religion help people to be content while living in a social order in which a few had many special privileges and the majority had few.

As was remarked earlier, it is with Hinduism that we see how very different world religions can be. The Hindus were not asking or answering the questions and concerns that drove the Biblical-Christian religions. There is no single founding figure for Hinduism, no figure corresponding to Moses, Jesus, or Mohammed. There are no tales of an original human couple, Adam, an Eve, or a Noah or a great flood caused by an angry god to eliminate humans. During this period (and into modern times) there was no single belief, no single doctrine that was required to be a Hindu. There was no creed or core belief that was considered essential. Hindus can be monotheists, polytheists, pantheists, monists, agnostics and even atheists. Although ritual purity was important, doctrinal purity was not a feature of Hinduism. There was no sacred truth that all Hindus must believe. Hindu gods did not punish humans for believing the wrong doctrines, or not having faith. There never was a centralized institutional authority for all Hindus. Hinduism does not share a single moral code.

Religious attitudes in the early times embraced differences. Humans are at different stages of religious understanding and spiritual life, and different practices and beliefs are appropriate for one's own stage of development. There is no single set of doctrines and rituals for all humans. We must ask, what is most meaningful for the individual at his or her own level of development? Is it ritual? Is it devotion to a divinity? Is it some sort of special knowledge? Is it meditation?

3.2 EARLY CLASSICAL HINDUISM: THE WAY OF ACTION

During periods of cultural dislocation and crisis, there is a tendency for new developments and trends in society and culture to arise, and in this time in history religion cannot be separated from culture. Thus, new developments in religion are to be expected. Much of the changes have been discussed in the previous chapter.

By 700 B.C.E. the Aryans had dominated the Ganges valley for over eight-hundred years. The Aryans had constructed fortified cities and plowed all easily available lands. Political changes occurred: first there were regional monarchies which then slowly began to give way to vast empires. Small tribes united to become monarchies ruled by kings and alliances and rivalries developed. Social, political, and military life became more rigid. The Aryans were in the process of constructing urban structures in the Ganges valley, and becoming more skilled and powerful as they moved east. The sixth century B.C.E. was a period of great transition for India.

The Karma-marga

Before the eighth century B.C.E., generally the pathway of the ancient Brahmin priests was the path of ritual activity, the *karma-marga*. The priests offered gifts through the rituals, and it was hoped that the deities would reciprocate by giving gifts of health, wealth, long life, and success. The sacrifices and offerings of the Brahmin priests supplied foods which provided the gods with the sustenance they required, and thus priestly rituals helped to keep the universe healthy. The priests also believed that their rituals kept the universe going smoothly, believing that human performance of rituals enhanced the power of the gods to maintain cosmic order, helped them to do things like ensuring that the sun maintained its proper course and the seasons following without chaotic deterioration.

Ritual purity was especially important because the gods are of transcendent purity, so the priests must be extra careful so as not to offend these powerful beings. If either the priest was polluted, or the ritual offering was contaminated, things could go terribly wrong. However, during this 700–200 B.C.E. period something began to develop which would supplement the ancient reliance on ritual. This new development was a deepening sense of selfhood and a heightened awareness of personal spirituality, and many facets of later Indian religions arise as a result.

During this time the Vedic worship of natural forces as deities no longer had as much appeal as in the past. At least some in India were beginning to doubt the efficacy of rituals. Others may have thought that rituals did work, but doubted whether what the rituals could provide was really important. Vedic rituals provide cattle, horses, children, wealth and long life, but were these really what counts as most valuable? Some practitioners of Indian religion wanted more than rituals could promise: how can one obtain infinite and eternal life in heaven with the finite action of rituals performed for an hour, or a day, or a month? Finite rituals may be able to produce a finite existence in heavens, but it can only be finite and then one's eternal unchanging true self, the *atman*, will return to the earth.

In addition, it appears as though the ancient religious beliefs of the Indus Valley civilization may have begun to exert influence over Aryan beliefs. Ancient rituals of the Vedic period were slowly being replaced by new rituals, performed by the Brahmin class of priests who were the specialists in ritual. Hinduism has been male-dominated, and the social and sacred roles of females came to be less important. The sacred hymns and scriptures were inevitably authored by male Brahmins. What we call "classical Hinduism" arises during this period.

3.3 NEW LITERARY FORMS: SUTRAS

The Brahmin priests of this era were literate and were very good at memorizing; this gave them a leading role in creating the standards, and recording those standards for the new society of 700–200 B.C.E. Popular scriptures composed during this period do not have quite the same standing as the Vedas (which are thought to be infallible, although needing constant reinterpretation). Some of these popular scriptures acquired a very high status. We will discuss the most important of these, the codes of ethics, laws, and society, which are the *dharma-sutras* and *dharma-shastras*, "discourses on domestic rites."

Sutras

As used in Hinduism, the Sanskrit term "*sutra*" means "thread," and it is a text which has one common thread, theme, or topic running throughout it. The ancient Vedic classics are not *sutras*; rather they are a compilation of miscellaneous sayings, verses, hymns and brief prose portions which we might call a "miscellany" or an "analect." A *sutra* is different. A *sutra* is a discussion focused on one subject.[1]

However, in a culture which stresses memorization over written records, a *sutra* is not the sort of prose essay that a modern person might compose. Rather, a *sutra* is more like a versified outline where each major point is stated and one or two points underneath are listed. A student would memorize the outline, and the teacher would provide lengthy oral explanations of each point. An outsider without the benefit of the oral explanations would find it very difficult to simply read a *sutra* and comprehend its subtle details.

Shastras

For this reason, over time a *sutra* could come to have numerous supplementary explanatory essays attached to it, called *shastras*. A *shastra* is a commentary and explanation of various points briefly mentioned in the clipped outline of the *sutras*. The earliest *sutras* and *shastras* provided an outline of basic instructions on performing the fire ceremonies. Another kind of *sutra* outlined the ritual responsibilities and ceremonies to be performed by the father of a household. Then, a few hundred years before the common era, a new group of texts began to appear—the *dharma-sutras*.

SOCIAL AND RELIGIOUS RULES: *Dharma-sutras* and *Dharma-shastras*

An exceptionally important category of *sutras* and *shastras* are those relating to one's *dharma*. In Indian thought, the term *dharma* has a cluster of related meanings. Sometimes the term *dharma* is translated as religious, moral, and social duty, but the sense is captured in the phrase "principles of right living." One's *dharma* is the proper way for an Aryan to live, socially and morally as well as religiously. The religious sense includes ceremonies, and rituals. In this sense it is the "pattern of ideal behavior." However, *dharma* also involves social and political responsibilities in addition to the moral and religious dimensions. One's *dharma* includes not only one's caste, but also one's occupation, life stages, diet, rights, duties, political obligations, rules of behavior and rules of morality.

In the previous chapter we discussed the ancient Aryan concept of *rta*, the pattern of the universe, the principle of cosmic order. Originally it included proper behavior for ritual as well as orderly movement of the seasons and planets. Gradually, the term *dharma* comes to absorb the meaning of *rta* and extend it as well.

The manifold meanings of *dharma* comes to suggest that one's social, economic, and political duties are religious duties at the same time. One's social obligations are religious obligations, and one must uphold one's *dharma* if the pattern of the world is to continue in a stable manner.[2] Certainly this is true for Brahmin priests, but it is also true for every other occupation and social role. Correctly performing one's social, occupational and religious duty is to uphold the universe.

---

[1] The topics for *sutras* included (a) codes for community sacrifices, (b) family rituals and ceremonies, (c) codes of conduct governing the four stages of life, (d) ceremonial architecture. Sukumari Bhattacharji, *The Indian Theogony,* p. 18.

[2] The Sanskrit root of *dharma* is usually explained as "to make firm," "to restrain," "to preserve." One's social and religious duties uphold the sacred order. The implication here is that social and moral duties belong to a sacred realm, which is a firm, steady, unwavering world.

CHAPTER 3: CLASSICAL HINDUISM

If the path of *dharma* is religious, then *dharma* cannot change over time because that which is sacred is also eternal. The sacred pattern is blessed, and the follower should never be swayed from that path of righteousness. Duties and obligations which are sacred are not conventional and are not relative to time and culture; sacred duties are not to be changed.

Hinduism Becomes More Resistant to Change

From this point on, classical Hinduism becomes more and more resistant to change. Change is regarded as destructive. One can never claim to have a *new* solution to a problem, because innovation is movement away from the eternal sacred obligations. The pattern of the way things are is fixed, and all obligations and duties are correct, and they can never be changed (including the duties inherent in the social order). Anything new was dangerous, and if something new had to be introduced, it would be explained as a return to some earlier ideal, real or imagined.[3]

The authors of these *dharma-sutras* were Brahmin priests, who gave instruction in ethical matters, moral and social duties. These were reflected in the legal system as well. The authors of the *dharma-sutras* and *dharma-shastras* were solidifying their understanding of sacred moral codes. This means that the Brahmin priests became the general arbiters of correct behavior of all kinds, social, moral, and legal.

A *dharma-shastra* was an expanded verse composition explaining a *sutra*, making it easier to study. A *dharma-shastra* is not as difficult to understand and interpret as the succinct *dharma-sutra*, so the *dharma-shastras* became the most popular sources for guides to ideal social behavior.

The Laws of Manu

The most important and most famous of these *dharma-shastras* is the *Manava-dharma-shastra*, which is "The *Dharma-shastra* of Manu," but in English is best known as "The Laws of Manu" attributed to a sage named Manu.[4] Scholars believe it was probably compiled around 200 C.E., although portions might go back to 200 B.C.E. Certainly, the ideas go back farther into the past than the actual date of composition.

The *Laws of Manu* explains proper relationships between the four basic social groups, lays down religious rules prescribing relationships between men and women, outlines punishments for violations of social and ritual order, and also deals with the organization of the state and the judicial system. Thus the *Laws of Manu* explain religious law and stress social order and the duties of each group within society. The *Laws of Manu* explains reincarnation, the workings of karma, and all aspects of law.[5] The text explains how important it is to avoid ritual pollution and how essential ritual purification is to a Brahmin priest. This text describes the ideal customs of the Brahmins, and how the Brahmin priests thought that all the other groups in society should behave. Over time it became the ideal for public norms of behavior in classical Hindu society.

Manu grounds and justifies his explanations by referring to the sacred Vedas, and declares that the Vedic truths should not be questioned, and anyone who would question the Vedas is outside of the true religion. Those groups which did question Vedic authority and did deny the special role of Brahmin priests to interpret eternal truths, like the Buddhists and Jains, are therefore not orthodox Hindus. These groups are called **heterodox**.

---

[3] We will see the same attitude in Confucian China, but with a different rationale.

[4] This is a human composition, not revelation. These 2,700 verses are also known as the *Manusmriti*, that is, what is *handed down* or *remembered* of Manu's explanations.

[5] See Patrick Olivelle, *The Law Code of Manu* (Oxford: Oxford University Press, 2004) and Patrick Olivelle, *Manu's Code of Law: A Critical Edition and Translation of the Manava-Dharmasastra* (Oxford: Oxford University Press, 2004).

CHAPTER 3: CLASSICAL HINDUISM

Since the *dharma-shastra* of Manu is based upon a sacred text describing sacred relationships, it is eternal and not subject to change. The *Laws of Manu* describe a world which is firmly structured by *dharma*, that which upholds stability. According to Hinduism, the rules of *dharma* were established as the universe unfolded and are *not* supposed to be subject to change, growth, or improvement.[6] The rules set out in the *Laws of Manu* are unalterable. As mentioned previously, the result was a society which became fixed, rigid, and unalterable with the sanction of religion to enforce it.[7] The *Laws of Manu* is the most authoritative and best known legal text of ancient India. Many features of Indian civilization with which westerners feel uncomfortable are justified in the *Laws of Manu*.[8] The primary example of this is the Indian caste system.

3.4 THE CASTE SYSTEM

A strong sense of class consciousness has been typical of India for at least 2,000 years. This is a sense of belonging to a group which provides a social and economic identity, an identity which is a boundary separating this group from other groups nearby. When the Aryans arrived in north-western India, they appear to have had a loose system of social classes, but it is entirely possible that the origins of the more rigid caste system may be found in the pre-Aryan civilization, perhaps the Harappan culture. Ultimately, in actual practice over time, the Aryan four social groups become subdivided into numerous rigidly defined occupational groups.

Jati and *Varna*

There are two terms in Sanskrit which are relevant to the Indian caste system, but which must be distinguished: **jati** and **varna**. The Sanskrit term closest to what we call "caste" is *jati*, whose literal meaning is "birth." One's social identity, social status, and social value were determined by the occupation of one's parents, that is, determined by birth. One's *jati* is one's particular hereditary occupation, whether it be archer, plumber, florist, doctor, priest, or a thousand others.

The *jatis* are hierarchically arranged and each member of society is aware of his or her position within this strict hierarchy of prestige, value, and dignity. One's occupation determines the purity and dignity of one's group, as well as one's economic status. Although precise numbers are difficult to come by, it is estimated that there are between 2,000–3,000 *jati*. The members of a *jati* are governed by rules about who they can marry, what they can eat, wear, and what occupations are available. Those 2,000–3,000 basic *jati* are then divided into approximately 25,000 sub-castes.

On the other hand, *varna* refers to the basic social groups. *Varna* is social classification based upon social needs. During the early period of the *dharma-shastras*, there were four *varnas* (priest, warrior, farm owner, laborer) but only the lowest of the *varna* were further subdivided into various occupations of varying rank and social status.

According to Manu, there are four basic social divisions, or *varna*:
1) *Brahmins*, who do the priestly sacred and ritual work of society;
2) *Ksatriyas*, who guard, protect, and govern;

---

[6] As the reader will see in *Asian Thought*, Volume II, chapter 15, the Confucians also thought that their moral rituals (*li*) were not subject to change, growth, or improvement, because they were grounded in the nature of reality. For the Chinese, cultures which did not recognize and use these same rituals of courtesy were barbaric and uncivilized.

[7] We might note that the *Laws of Manu* only knows the first three Vedas and this is further evidence of how late the *Atharva veda* (the fourth Veda) is.

[8] Manu's verses are quoted in support of the low status of women. Manu's verses justify the unequal social structure whereby the majority lowest social classes are dominated by the small minority of upper classes.

3) *Vaishyas*, who own the farms and engage in trade;
4) *Shudras*, the menial laborers of society who do not own land.

Social Classes Originated when the Giant *Purusha* is Sacrificed

Although the earliest versions of the *Rig Veda* had only nine chapters, much later a tenth chapter was added after the *Sama Veda* and *Yajur Veda* were already completed. In this tenth chapter, *Rig Veda* 10.90, there is the story of a great sacrifice in which the primordial human being, *Purusha* (literally, Person or Human or Man), a giant with thousands of eyes, arms, legs and feet, became a ritual sacrifice performed by the gods. Purusha was dismembered, and all the features of the physical world and the human realm (including social classes) were formed from its bodily parts.

The Man [Purusha] has a thousand heads, a thousand eyes, a thousand feet. He pervaded the earth on all sides and extended beyond it as far as ten fingers. It is the Man who is all this, whatever has been and whatever is to be. He is the ruler of immortality; when he grows beyond everything though food. This is his greatness, and the Man is yet more than this. All creatures are a quarter of him; three quarters are what is immortal in heaven. With three quarters the Man rose upwards, and one quarter of him remains here.[9]

Drawing upon the existing social divisions of his society, the story from the 10th chapter of the *Rig Veda* is used by Manu to explain the ultimate religious origin of the existing social and economic classes and structures. The Brahmin *varna* came from the mouth of Purusha (for the priests speak the sacred sounds). The arms of the giant became the protectors, the *ksatriyas*. The thighs became the *vaishya* (farmers, traders). The feet became the *shudra* (the menial or servant class).

With the *varna* now outlined and justified in the *Rig Veda*, the four traditional social divisions are now a part of religion, they are *dharma*, and they cannot be changed. The groups are sharply different, with different duties proscribed, different rights, different obligations of behavior and ritual, different degrees of purity and impurity, and with different economic and social value or dignity assigned to them, with the Brahmins as the most noble. Over the centuries numerous traditional and newer trades and crafts slowly work their way into the *varna* where they acquire a ranking of prestige, value, and dignity. Within any particular *varna*, there is further distinction between sex and age. The elder have higher status than the younger; the males have higher status than the females.

Some People are Permanently Contaminating

Social group contamination and individual pollution have been important concepts in India since the earliest times. It is believed that people can become polluted by what they eat or drink, and by what they touch. The *Laws of Manu* make clear that some humans are permanently impure. That is, they have ritual pollution attached to them by virtue of their birth, and because of their contamination, they must be avoided by the upper castes. Some forms of pollution are temporary and can be eliminated by rituals performed by Brahmin priests. Pollution can be transmitted from one human to another, and even clothing, food and water can be polluting depending on the form of their preparation and the ritual status of the person who makes or prepares them. Purity and pollution become of obsessive concern for the *Laws of Manu*. An upper class Brahmin cannot drink a glass of water handed to him by a member of the lowest class—it would be contaminated and contaminating.[10]

MANU ON THE DUTIES OF THE SOCIAL CLASSES

---

[9] Rig-Veda, 10.90; Robert E. Van Voorst, *Anthology of Asian Scriptures* (Wadsworth, 2001), p. 37.

[10] Things that are impure include cow meat, dog meat, elephant meat, horse meat, human flesh, feces, urine, blood, semen, and marrow. Each of these is contaminating.

CHAPTER 3: CLASSICAL HINDUISM

The duties of the various classes are spelled out in the *Laws of Manu* which offers an interpretation of the story found in the *Rig-veda*. Manu declares that these four social *varnas* are divinely inspired, are hereditary, they are unequal, and the Brahmins occupy the superior position in society because of their superlative qualifications and rights.

The Brahmins

The Brahmin priests are the caste of ritual specialists. They communicate with the *deva*; they do the sacrifices which guarantee order in the universe and blessings; they do sacred work for the benefit of all of us. The purity of the Brahmin priests is essential; they must avoid contact with anything impure. Through the performance of the fire sacrifice, the Brahmins keep the world revolving, and keep order and pattern instead of chaos. Brahmins are the intermediaries between the sacred realm and the human realm. Memorizing and preserving the hymns of the sacred Vedas is the responsibility of the Brahmins.

Thus the members of the Brahmin caste are associated with communication, recitation, language, and can manipulate the power contained within powerful chants (*mantras*). By birth Brahmins are the most pure and noble, and it is especially bad to injure a Brahmin. The legal penalties are more severe if someone of a lower *varna* injures a Brahmin. In fact, there are punishments for those of the lower *varnas* who merely presume to criticize a Brahmin, and there are also punishments for those of the lower castes who attempt to emulate a Brahmin. By right, the proper social role for Brahmins is priesthood, but if they desire, they can do the jobs of the *ksatriyas* and if they are facing serious economic difficulties, they can even take the jobs of the *vaishyas*. Brahmins are expected to marry within their own social class, and not below.

Early on, there was only one occupational group for Brahmins, but later, the highest *varnas* were subdivided into occupational castes. For example, some Brahmins specialize in the fire rituals, others specialize in rites of childhood, or rites of adulthood, and yet others specialize in very specific areas. An appropriate specialization for a Brahmin can be Sanskrit phonetics or astrology. In society, Brahmins are the only ones allowed to expound on Vedic wisdom. Many Brahmins focused upon herbs and health, and in modern times, they became the medical professions. Often, Brahmins hold academic positions and are counselors or associated with spiritual learning such as spiritual teachers.[11] Ritual purity is essential to the Brahmins, and so Brahmin priests do not perform funerals. Neither do Brahmins perform exorcisms of dangerous spirits.

The Protectors and Guardians

The *ksatriyas* were the original warriors of the Aryans, and later they took over all those roles involving governance and the protection of society. They became the guardians. In addition to warriors and other protectors, politicians and kings generally belonged to the *ksatriya varna*.[12] The duty of a *ksatriya* is to rule justly and protect Aryan society, especially protect the Brahmin class. As a group they are not as pure as the Brahmins. If a Brahmin wishes to offer advice, the protectors must listen. The *ksatriyas* are required to marry within their own social class, and are forbidden to marry anyone of a higher class. Warriors can never move upwards and take over the jobs of the Brahmins, but they can do the work of the *vaishyas* or even *shudras* if economic need arises.

Many of the *ksatriyas* migrated out of military occupations and came to have jobs such as landowners and farmers. However, they maintain their caste status as *ksatriyas*. They can be teachers, but not teachers of Vedic wisdom. The *Laws of Manu* says that these people must work to conquer their senses, and they do this by not engaging in

---

[11] In Chapter 4 on the path of wisdom, we will use the term *guru*, who is a spiritual guide who can lead an individual to liberation from the trap of rebirth. A *guru* need not be a Brahmin, and the great majority of Brahmins simply do rituals and are not concerned with the pathway of liberating knowledge. The authority of a *guru* comes from personal experience, not from education in the Vedas or social standing.

[12] In Chapter 8 we shall see that the Buddha was born into this social group.

hunting, drinking, gambling or falling into a base obsession with women. These people rank second in the social class system because of their courage and valor, according to Manu.

Merchants, Landowners, Farmers, and Providers

The third *varna* is the *vaishya*. These are the middle-class people who work their own land and own their own livestock. They are expected to multiply the wealth of the country. These include traders, herdsmen, and farmers. In more recent times the members of the *vaishya* group are mostly associated with occupations involving trade, the traders of commodities, herdsmen, the mercantile class, and farmers, and in modern times the *vaishya* are now associated with merchants, money, and commercial transactions. The *vaishya* group raised cattle, bought and sold merchandise, raised crops and sold their produce. In addition to farming and trade, proper *vaishya* occupations include those groups who keep official records, moneylenders, goldsmiths, and dealers in grain. The *vaishyas* have their status in Indian society from their commercial abilities and their wealth. Within the *vaishya varna*, there is further distinction between sex and age.

According to Manu, *vaishyas* are not allowed to marry anyone not in their caste, and especially not someone above their class. This group is not as pure as the two *varna* above them. The *vaishyas* are not supposed to move upwards and take over jobs of Brahmins or *ksatryas*, but they can do the jobs of the lower *shudras* if the economic necessity arises. As must be obvious, the *vaishyas* became the wealthiest group, and made almost all the important economic decisions in Indian society, and they were taxed heavily to support the upper two groups, *Brahmins* and *ksatriyas*. These top three *varnas* are called "twice-born," and only twice-born males were entitled to listen to the recitation of the Vedas.

The Laborers and Servants

A great divide exists between the top three *varnas* and the fourth one, the *shudras*. This is the group who performs the labor but they do not own. The *shudras* are regarded as too polluted to study the sacred texts. According to the *Laws of Manu*, *shudras* have no source of status except old age. The proper occupation for *shudras* is service to the higher castes and manual occupations which are *not* impure or morally tainted. Typical occupations include servants, potters, barbers, gardeners, ditch-diggers, carpenters, florists, and tailors. There are also weavers, washerwomen, craftsmen, and singers. According to the *Laws of Manu*, *shudras* are not entitled to be wealthy; they cannot study the Vedas or attend any Vedic religious ceremonies or rituals, and they are not allowed to marry anyone of a higher social caste.

Shudras are entitled to receive the broken furniture, old clothes, and leftover foods of Brahmin households. The three higher castes have an obligation not to allow *shudras* to starve. It is improper for *shudras* to accumulate wealth, however, and under no circumstances may they assume the work of the higher castes. *Shudras* were domestic servants of society; they are the ones who perform manual labor using tools owned by their employer. According to Manu, a *shudra* can never be the absolute owner of property because his riches should be determined by his master's will. As the *vaishya* herders and farmers migrated into the cities, and mastered new occupations which made them wealthy, there were farms available to the lower *varna*. *Shudras* took over many of the farm-related occupations and in this way their position was elevated.

According to the *Laws of Manu*, the *shudras* occupy this low position because in previous lives when they were members of the three higher social groups, *shudras* did not accept and fulfill their social and religious roles properly and thereby created bad karma, they behaved in an impure manner, and the negative consequences of their behavior resulted in their being reborn among the *shudra* rank. It is fair and just that *shudras* are mistreated the way they are. They earned mistreatment by their polluted or immoral behavior in previous lives. It was divine law that some castes should be wealthier, more privileged than others. The *Laws of Manu* explains the punishments to be meted out to the lowest classes if they dare to criticize, emulate, or harm members of the highest classes.

CHAPTER 3: CLASSICAL HINDUISM

The only way to move to a higher socio-economic group is to die and be reincarnated into an upper-caste family. No one is allowed to move up to a higher caste in this life.

The *Laws of Manu* says it is better for a person to do one's own *dharma* imperfectly, than to do another's *dharma* well. Manu makes it clear that a person is never allowed to pretend to be of a higher caste and take over the occupation from someone higher than their *jati*. It was not possible to move to a new village or town and pretend to belong to a higher caste. In the past, occupational roles were very much familial and hereditary; one could not simply go into a new town and seek work as a member of a higher caste. No one would hire a stranger. Even if one might succeed in the pretense, it was believed that they would generate bad karma and consequently be reborn in a very much lower caste in the next life.

In the *Laws of Manu*, one's value and status depend upon one's *varna* and *jati*. Higher-class elites are worth more than lower members of despised and impure classes. There are special privileges for the upperclass. They deserve these benefits because the priests communicate with the gods, and they ensure that the deities will bless us all with a fruitful and non-dangerous environment. Thus, the laws which apply are different depending upon one's *varna*. According to Hindu society, special privileges are fair, because each of us is born into the *varna* and *jati* which we deserve, due to choices and actions made in previous lives. We each have earned whatever comes to us. If we are born into a wealthy upperclass family, it is because we deserve it. If we are born into the lowest and most despised groups, it is because we deserve it due to behavior in previous lives.

The Role of the Wife

In all of these *varnas*, the role of the wife is simple: to serve and support the husband whom her parents have chosen for her. This is her purpose in life. The prestige and worth of a woman is dependent upon her husband. In traditional Hinduism, women do not remarry, and a woman who is without a husband, either as a widow or divorced, has very little value in traditional Hindu society. Manu says that a woman should serve her husband as though he were a *deva*, and devote herself to his memory after he dies.

People without Varna ("Outcastes")

There are thousands of other occupations necessary to society which are thought to be impure, or ritually polluting. Those employed in these occupations come into contact with bodily fluids and other contaminating things in their daily work. These groups are not described in the *Laws of Manu*, and thus the people who perform these have no *varna* (they are *avarna*, "no-varna"). They have no formal place in the hereditary *varnas*. These peoples are outside of the traditional four castes, and are often described as "outcastes" (*dasyus*). These include everyone performing manual tasks which are thought to be ritually polluting or grossly unclean. These people do the demeaning, dirty, impure, ritually polluting tasks, or things which can make one religiously unclean. Because of this, it is polluting to touch one of the members of this lowest class. They are contagious. They are not to be touched. The major sources of pollution involve substances related to death or to bodily fluids. The trades and crafts of the outcastes have no prestige, no dignity, and only utilitarian value. They also have been referred to as "untouchables" or *Dalits*.[13]

Outcaste occupations include toilet cleaners, sweepers of the streets, makers of and sellers of alcohol, people who kill living things like hunters and fishermen, leather workers who kill and scrape flesh from the hide of an animal, executioners, and people who handle the bodies of dead people who are not members of their own family.

Brahmins are forbidden to associate with these. The members of this group were considered so impure that

---

[13] *Dalit* is a popular term for those Indian people who used to be called "untouchables," people who are outside the system of caste, 'avarna'. Contemporary untouchables call themselves *Dalit* which they explain means unfortunates, or "ground down." Like the four higher social groups, they too are organized into birth groups, *jatis*, arranged in a hierarchy among themselves from high to low. The lowest category was those who collected human excrement from houses.

they must live outside the villages and are not allowed to enter the streets at night. They are to be given food in broken dishes placed on the ground. They were not allowed to drink from the same water containers or water sources that the upper classes used. Opportunities for education were non-existent.

Bhimrao Ambedkar (1891-1956), a highly educated and brilliant modern Hindu reformist famous for his vigorous opposition to the entire caste system, wrote:

> To the untouchables, Hinduism is a virtual chamber of horrors. The sanctity and infallibility of the *Vedas, Smritis* and *Shastras*, the iron law of caste, the heartless law of *karma* and the senseless law of status by birth are to the Untouchables veritable instruments of torture which Hinduism has forged against the Untouchables.[14]

Scholars have speculated that the majority of those in the lowest castes may have been descended from the non-Aryan groups in India, including Harappans. Is the outcaste status a way by which Aryans made room for the non-Aryan indigenous people within the Aryan Vedic labels and categories? Did the outcaste status provide a social continuity connecting the bottom of the classes with the highest?

As was suggested previously it is likely that the Aryans brought three *varnas* with them (three social classes), and over the centuries those become mixed with (pre-Aryan?) *jati*, rigid hereditary occupational castes. In 1950 the constitution of modern India outlawed the social system based on untouchables, but such traditions are very slow to change.

3.5 THE FOUR *ASHRAMA*, THE FOUR STAGES OF LIFE

The Laws of Manu also lay out the stages of life expected by duty, by *dharma*. Manu describes four *ashrama* ("stages of spiritual effort") which an individual was encouraged to traverse on the path through life, each stage with an increasing dignity to it. Originally they were simply alternate life-choices, but later they are understood as four consecutive stages. These four *ashrama* apply to the "twice-born" (members of the top three *varna*) who were provided with a guideline for various stages of their lives. However, these stages only apply to males within a group; women were excluded from these four life-stages progression. Excluded also were *shudras*, and people like *Dalits* (outcastes) and murderers.

The First Stage of the Four *Ashrama*: The Student Stage[15]

There is no official age where the student stage begins, although it is usually between age eight and twelve, and before twenty-four. The family of a boy of the upper three *varnas* would make arrangements to indenture their son

---

[14] Bhimrao Ambedkar, *What Congress and Ghandi Have Done to the Untouchables* (Bombay, India: Thacker and Company, 1934), pp. 307–308. Ambedkar was an extraordinary historian, lawyer, philosopher, and economist whose importance in Indian politics rivaled that of Gandhi. He labored for equality, and criticized not only the caste system, but also the Muslim support of the caste system and the Muslim treatment of women. He supported the division of India into two states, but he condemned the practice of child marriage, as well as the mistreatment of women in Muslim society, writing: "No words can adequately express the great and many evils of polygamy and concubinage, and especially as a source of misery to a Muslim woman. Take the caste system. Everybody infers that Islam must be free from slavery and caste. [...] [While slavery existed], much of its support was derived from Islam and Islamic countries. While the prescriptions by the Prophet regarding the just and humane treatment of slaves contained in the Koran are praiseworthy, there is nothing whatever in Islam that lends support to the abolition of this curse. But if slavery has gone, caste among Musalmans [Muslims] has remained." (Ambedkar, Bhimrao Ramji, "Chapter X: Social Stagnation," in *Pakistan or the Partition of India* [Bombay: Thackers Publishers, 1946], pp. 215–219).

[15] In Sanskrit, *Brahmacarya*, studenthood.

to a teacher. Depending on the *varna* and the occupation of the family, the teacher would teach the child to memorize and recite the appropriate Vedic verses, or perhaps to read the other sacred texts. As was appropriate to his *varna*, the teacher might also teach archery, medicine, astrology and music. The child was obligated to render personal services to his teacher, to obey the teacher, and show respect to his teacher–he can never be critical of his teacher, or listen to things critical of this teacher (even if the criticisms are true). During the student stage a young man was expected to be celibate and to devote himself to learning.

Second *Ashrama* Stage: The Householder[16]

When finished with his student stage, the male student would return home, and when the family felt it was the appropriate time, the family would finalize the arrangements for a marriage with an appropriate woman who shared the same caste. Hindu parents would utilize astrologers who would study the birth times for male and female in order to guarantee a harmonious marriage. With his arranged marriage, the young man would now enter the stage of a householder. The householder is obligated to repay his debt to his forefathers, perform the appropriate rituals and rites for his family and for his parents when they died, and his spiritual debt to the *devas*. The householder had been trained in his occupation by his father or uncles, and he may simply have worked in the family occupation, such as farming or the military, or the family business. The householder had a duty to support his family with work appropriate to his *jati*. He also had a duty to beget sons and he had a duty to try to make his wife happy.

The new wife (often quite young) of the householder moves into the house of her mother-in-law, often with a dowry that she brings into her new family, and from now on she will focus her rituals on the family of her husband. She is obligated to devote herself to serving her husband, to show loyalty and subordination to her husband, to not even mention the name of any other male, to do nothing to displease him as long as he lives, to devote herself to his memory after his death. After the death of her husband, she is to be subordinate to her sons. In the vision of Manu, a woman must be dependent upon the proper male at all periods of her life, whether it be her father, her husband, and after her husband's death, she will be dependent upon her sons or her brothers to keep her.

The Third Stage: The Hermit or Forest Dweller[17]

The first two stages were pretty much standard and traditional. The third stage is optional and commences when a householder has fulfilled his duties toward family, and his children are able to support themselves and take over the appropriate social responsibilities. At this stage of life, the man's skin is wrinkled, his hair is grey, and he is a grandfather. While still living at home, gradually he will retreat away from family activities and prepare himself for spiritual matters. He will develop an attitude of non-attachment towards his wife and family, because the new goal is to attain liberation from the world of sensuality and transcend the physical world. At some point he will rid himself of every material possession (usually that means giving everything he owns to his sons) and retreat deeper into the search for his own true nature.

If he wishes, he is allowed to leave home and enter the higher status *ashrama* of spiritual practices in the seclusion of the a wilderness area away from people. He and his wife may go together into the wilderness, and she will care for him living a very simple life, while he recites the Vedas. He will gradually renounce the family life and society. He will renounce sensuality and sex, and will cultivate rituals and attempt to master his body and master focused concentration.

Very few householders went beyond this third stage. However, if he wishes, another stage is possible. In the seclusion of the forest, the forest dweller will sever all remaining social ties and begin to pursue seriously and whole-heartedly the goal of final liberation with practices involving severe asceticism.

---

[16] In Sanskrit, *Grhasthya* or householder's life.

[17] In Sanskrit, *Vanaprastha*, retirement away from society and focus on the forest.

CHAPTER 3: CLASSICAL HINDUISM

The Fourth Stage: The *sadhu, sannyasin* or Ascetic[18]

The distinction between the third forest dweller stage and the fourth, the ascetic stage, is not strictly drawn. When the forest dweller has overcome all spiritual impediments, he may cease all ritual practices, sever all remaining social ties, and enter the final stage of life. He is independent of the social and political systems. He will not observe rituals in court rooms or in throne rooms. Politics and politicians are of no concern to the ascetic. He owns nothing and pays no taxes. He will wander alone, perhaps covered by a loin cloth, perhaps naked. He will never cook any food or sleep on anything except the forest ground. His only source of food is begging. During the fourth *ashrama*, the ascetic is free of society's concerns, but as he wanders he is looking for his own true spiritual teacher who will guide him to ultimate liberation (*moksha*), and when they finally meet face to face, each recognizes the other.

The spiritual guide or teacher (*guru*) administers a rite of ritual rebirth and gives the *sannyasin* (ascetic) a new name free of any caste associations. It is then that the *guru* guides the follower in advanced meditative discipline, abstract philosophical explorations leading to insight, and other spiritual practices. The ascetic chooses to invest complete energy and devotion to the spiritual teacher in the forest, and hopes to attain complete liberation from the cycle of birth and death.

It was believed that severe ascetic practices could generate a spiritual energy, or spiritual heat (*tapas*) which could be directed to produce special powers and ultimately provide the energy needed to propel the ascetic to the final goal of liberation. Every day is spent in the wilderness, far away from centers of power or commerce, quieting all passions, practicing breathing exercises, cultivating detachment, engaging in painful acts such as standing on one foot for months or years, cultivating yogic exercises and developing spiritual powers including such things as reading minds, telepathy, and the ability to walk on water and float through space. Generating spiritual energy (*tapas*) is important but it is not sufficient to achieve liberation. Even more important is insight into the true nature of reality. The primary practice of the ascetic is focused concentration (*dhyana*).

Indian society had an ambivalent attitude toward those in the fourth stage, the *sannyasins*. The ascetics occupy a place higher in respect than even Brahmins. They are treated as superior to all other people, and entitled to unquestioning support and complete respect. Yet, when the ascetic is in the village, he is feared and regarded as a threat to society. The *sannyasin* has rejected everything that keeps the village society stable, everything that determines rank and appropriate ways to respond to a fellow human. As such, he engenders apprehension from villagers. He is a person for whom the rules do not apply, and as such he is a potential source of personal pollution and social corruption, and villagers maintain their distance (on the rare occasions the ascetic comes into the village).[19]

One might assume that, because the ascetic had such high prestige, then the wife who remains behind in society might also have high prestige. This is not the case. A woman's purpose is to serve her husband. The wife of a man who had left home and gone to this fourth stage had lost her purpose and her position in society with it. She becomes like a widow, a person of low esteem. She should shave her head, dress plainly, and serve her sons. If a woman is a widow, or her husband has gone into the forest, and she has no sons, it is her own brothers who are expected to take her in and in their households she would most likely take on a role similar to that of a servant.

Defining "Hinduism" In Terms of Stages of Life

The idea of the four *varna* and the four *ashrama* become one of the common themes for Hinduism, even for those who did not intend to enter the forest and who expected to achieve liberation by some other means. The combination of these are called *varna-ashrama dharma*, that is, one's social class duties and the duty to progress through the four stages of life. In India, one common definition of "Hinduism," is just *varna-ashrama dharma*.

---

[18] In Sanskrit, *Yati*, the state of a hermit isolated from worldly concerns.

[19] John Koller, *Indian Way*, p. 196

3.6 *KARMA* AND REBIRTH IN THE CYCLE OF *SAMSARA*

As we discussed in the previous chapter, the key concept of early Aryan world-view was *rta*, the regular and correct order and pattern of the universe. The belief was that the regular natural patterns of the universe include moral conduct as well. These ideas serve as the basis for the Indian ideas of karma and **reincarnation**. This reflects the intimate connection between Hindu religious doctrine, and Hindu society. As we have seen previously, the Sanskrit term karma means "action," especially a ritual action which is morally important because it is required or prohibited by the rules and social codes of *dharma*. It is an energy generated by the performance of such an action. This becomes another related meaning for karma.

At the risk of oversimplification, karma is understood to operate in the same way that an impersonal law of nature describes the world. There is no reward or punishment associated with karma. The idea is straightforward: one's choices and actions will generate consequences which resemble their causes. Good acts (acts in accord with one's caste and *dharma*) produce good consequences to the agent. Evil acts produce evil consequences to the doer. The energy of the act persists after the action occurs, much as money sits waiting in a bank until it is appropriate to use. The energy, whether good or evil, rebounds back upon the agent (or doer, actor), and this causes the original agent to experience the consequences of that action, consequences which resemble the original causes.

According to popular Hinduism, the performance of correct ritual will generate good karma, and with enough ritual one can be reborn into the heavenly realms. However, no one can avoid the result of his or her actions; therefore if one does not experience the consequences in this life, one will experience them in another life. The moral forces generated by previous choices in previous lives causes our eternal unchanging *atman* or "soul" to be reborn into a new family or a new caste. Accumulated karma will either take effect in this life, or take effect after one's death, which will determine whether the individual will be reborn as a Brahmin, protector and guardian, merchant, servant, or even untouchable or outcaste. It is the correct performance of ritual actions (karma) which determines the quality of the next life in the cycle of life and death.[20] Thus one is trapped, wandering into an endless cycle of birth and death, called *samsara*.

One will be reborn into the group that one has earned by one's life choices. Thus, everyone is reincarnated in the *jati* that they have earned by previous deeds, and the entire social system of *varna* and *jati* is entirely fair and just. *Shudras* can be reborn as Brahmins if they do their duty uncomplainingly, live moral lives, and do nothing to annoy the upper classes and do nothing to upset the existing social and moral order.

From the period when the *dharma-sutras* were outlining the new society that restricted occupational choice, the foundation of Indian society, culture, and religion became the caste system, karma, reincarnation, and the four stages of life.

Originally *atman* was a life force ("breath") that made something alive but slowly it began to be understood as an eternal unchanging substance which reincarnated again and again, wandering through cycles of birth and death.[21] The *atman* was never created; it was permanent, self-existent, and immutable. This raises the question: what controls which next life our *atman* will be born into? The answer is our choices, our actions ("karma" means "action"). If one acted in accord with the social and ritual duties appropriate to one's social group (*varna*), then one had done good deeds and as a result would have a better life in the next reincarnation. Acting in accord with one's dharma would generate good consequences in this life or in the next life. Acting contrary to one's dharma (actions inappropriate to one's caste) would generate bad consequences in this life or in the next life.

---

[20] With karma, the Buddhists in India tended to place less stress on ritual and more stress on morality.

[21] *Atman* is eternal and unchanging; it is identical from one life to the next, and explains how we are identical with the person we were in a previous life. The actions we choose generate either good karma or bad karma.

There is no single agreed-upon explanation for how karma functions in the universe, and there are no arguments attempting to show that karma genuinely exists.[22] Some Hindu systems understand karma to function like a cosmic bank, where the positive or negative karmic energy is stored up in a personal account, resulting in either credits or debits. Some associate karma as directly connected to the eternal unchanging soul, the *atman*, poised to interact with our life at every moment. Some interpret karma as a psychological force which creates good or evil effects by affecting our desires and our drives. Some see karma as a physical substance made of fine which is connected to the *atman*, but most see karma as a non-physical agent. If one believes in the gods, the *devas*, then karma can be understood as implemented by the divine being who keeps tracks of one's moral choices, and then metes out justice during our lives, or after death, sends us on to the appropriate realm we have earned for ourselves.

Five Different Destinations for Reincarnation

Among the followers of the more intellectual tradition, there is a popular view that the eternal unchanging substance called *atman* can be reincarnated in five different karmic destinations, none of which are permanent. If one is good and fulfills the social roles with no complaint, and correctly performs the appropriate rituals, then one will be reborn in the human realm, in one of the four respectable social groups (*varna*) depending on how good one's choices were in the previous life, or reborn as an outcaste if one made relatively poor choices. Certainly one can be born in non-Indian cultures as well, and this is a result of bad karma. Being born as a human being is a rare event, one to be valued and being reborn a human and a Hindu is even more to be treasured. This one human lifetime should not be wasted.

If one was exceptionally good in one's choices, then one can be reincarnated in the heavens for a while. It is even possible to be reincarnated as a *deva*, or in the highest heaven. Some Brahmins understood that every *deva* had been a human being at some previous life in their past, and when the accumulation of good karma runs out, the *deva* will return to the human realm again as a human, and no longer a *deva*. Not only could you have been a male or female, king or slave, in a previous life, but you could also have been a god or goddess.

If behavior is not good enough to merit rebirth in the human realm, then such will be reborn as animals, as horses, lions, elephants, if not too bad; if worse, fishes, snakes, lizards, and spiders. Those who stole meat will become vultures in their next life. Thieves of grain are reborn as rats.

There is another realm for those not good enough to be reborn as an animal. The greedy and envious can be reincarnated as anguished and hungry ghosts who wander the world of humans, seeing happiness everywhere but unable to participate in it. One step lower than anguished spirits are the very evil. These are reincarnated in hellish realms, but remain there only until they exhaust their bad karma. Then they are reborn again.

3.7 THE FOUR LEGITIMATE GOALS OF LIFE

There are four goals or aims for which the upper class Hindu is expected to strive. Three of these apply to the householder stage. The four goals are (1) *dharma*, (2) *artha*, (3) *kama*,[23] and (4) *moksha*.

(1)   The first is *dharma*: fulfilling one's social and religious duty, observing the social duties determined by one's *varna*. A good Hindu should try to live according to the rules of the *Laws of Manu* and other rules, to cultivate a pattern of ideal behavior which certainly includes participating in appropriate rituals and sacrifices.

---

[22] Indeed, some Indian religions deny the existence of karma and deny the belief that the soul endlessly wanders in the cycle of birth-and-death, called *samsara*. Those who accept these ideas of karma and the cycle of life-and-death seem to feel that meditating forest sages have some special insight which allows them to verify personally these concepts. In this sense the forest sage is treated as an "expert" so the evidence supporting karma and reincarnation is testimony by meditating experts.

[23] Do not confuse *kama* (sensual pleasure) with *karma* (action, ritual, moral cause and effect). A popular Indian text known in the West is the *Kama Sutra*, a book devoted to achieving the good life by maximizing *kama*.

(2)   The householder is encouraged to pursue *artha*: wealth, status, material gain, worldly success and power. Monetary and social success and social standing is an appropriate goal for every householder.

(3)   The householder should cultivate *kama*: sensual pleasure, appreciation of beauty, enjoyment of sexuality. This is good, positive, and healthy and appropriate for every householder.

(4)   At some point, after countless lives spent wandering, trapped in the cycle of birth and death, a few householders will begin to realize that despite success, pleasure, and social standing, they are still trapped in an endless cycle of birth and death, rebirth and re-death. Then, when they are ready, the new goal is to attempt to achieve *moksa*: liberation from *samsara*, liberation from endlessly wandering the cycle of birth and death. Clearly, this is where the third and four of the four *ashrama* (hermit, forest dweller, ascetic) fit into the human life cycle.

3.8 THE PROPER ROLE OF WOMEN ACCORDING TO THE LAWS OF MANU

In Hinduism, women had an important role to play in the household, but the proper role of a wife was always subservient to her husband. According to the *Laws of Manu*:

Nothing must be done independently by a girl, by a young woman, or by an old woman, even in her own house. In childhood, a female must be subject to her father, in youth to her husband, and when her husband is dead to her sons. By leaving them she would make both her own and her husband's families contemptible.

     She must always be cheerful, clever in household affairs, careful in cleaning her utensils, and economical in expenditure. She shall obey the man to whom her father may give her ... as long as he lives. When he is dead, she must not insult his memory. For the sake of getting good fortune for brides, the recitation of benedictory texts and the sacrifices to the Lord of creatures are used at weddings, but the betrothal by her father or guardian is the cause of the husband's dominion over his wife. ... Although he may be destitute of virtue, or seek pleasure elsewhere, or lacking good qualities, yet a husband must be constantly worshiped as a god by a faithful wife. ...

     A faithful wife who desires to dwell after death with her husband must never do anything that might displease him, whether he is alive or dead.[24]

3.9 HOW MUCH INFLUENCE DID MANU ACTUALLY HAVE ON INDIAN SOCIETY?

Although the *Laws of Manu* carry the authority of religion, in actual practice the *Laws of Manu* were not strictly followed.[25] In fact, the actual *varnas* and *jati* are considerably more complicated than the simple structure of four described in this chapter. Outside of the family, women had relatively low value in the book of Manu. For example, the laws forbid women from being taught Vedic verses. Nevertheless, there is evidence that most classes of society did not follow Manu's evaluation in a strict manner. Individual extended families developed their own interactions and did not slavishly obey Manu.

     The *Laws of Manu* are only one of many factors in the social and judicial life of traditional India. Marriage between classes was not encouraged, but certain partnerships were more acceptable than others. A marriage between a man of a higher class, and a woman of the next class down, was barely acceptable. A marriage between a man of a

---

[24] The Laws of Manu, 5:147-165, in Robert E. Van Voorst, *An Anthology of Asian Scriptures* (Wadsworth, 2001), pp. 43-44.

[25] This is true for every religious tradition. For example, officially in the Christian religion, unmarried couples are strictly forbidden to engage in sexual behavior. Unofficially, this occurs regularly even if it is not officially permissible.

lower class and a woman of a higher class was socially forbidden—there were severe social sanctions for people who did this.[26]

3.10 THE RITUALS OF CLASSICAL HINDUISM

The religion of the earliest Aryans was *karma-marga*, the pathway of ritual activity and sacrifice. In general the pathway of ritual is not concerned with such things as meditation, as spiritual liberation or realizing the true nature of the self. The importance of sacred rituals focuses upon a mutual exchange of benefits with *devas*. The ancient stress on ritual continues on into the period of classical Hinduism as well, with some changes. Although Brahmins still perform the very expensive large community rituals, the more costly Brahmin priestly-performed rituals became less popular and smaller more personal rites came to be celebrated by family members in a family context.

Although Hindu rituals are performed by human beings, rituals communicate with the gods. In rituals the divine becomes really present to the human as at no other time. Thus, during the ritual sacrifice, gifts such as incense, respect, reverence, devotion, food and drink are given to *devas*. In a process of mutual exchange, the *devas* then give gifts back: protection; support for a stable social order; economic benefits; farming benefits such as rain; success and support for wars; health; long life. As a result, human needs are satisfied.

Family Rituals

During the classical period and into more recent times, many rituals are keyed to the passage of the sun's three phases. Dawn, noon, and twilight are important times in Indian religion as they are in Indian music.[27] The devoted higher-caste Hindu father will rise at the first glimmer of dawn, do ritual cleansing, and will spend a few minutes doing breathing exercises to cleanse mind and body of impurities. Next, he recites lines of sacred text. Many Hindus still recite the Gayatri *mantra*, a verse from the *Rig-Veda*, three times a day.

> Many we attain to the excellent glory of Savitar the god; so may he stimulate our understanding and prayers.[28]

Family Rites Celebrating the Major Events of the Life Cycle

In India, just like the rest of the world, families use rituals to celebrate important transitions in their lives. These sorts of rituals are mostly performed in the home, usually near the family hearth. The head of the household, the father or grandfather will officiate, although the mother also plays a role. In Western civilization, we share many of the rituals in common with Hindus, including ritual recognition of births, marriages, and funerals. In India, traditionally these family rites include rituals to be performed in celebration of the following occasions:

(1) Moment of the child's conception
(2) "Male-producing Rite" about the fourth month of pregnancy.
(3) Ceremony to ensure a safe pregnancy for the mother-to-be.
(4) Ceremony to celebrate the birth.
(5) A ritual where a name is assigned to the child (10 or 12 days after birth).

---

[26] A book discussing more recent information on the role of women in India prior to India achieving independence is Tim Alexander, *Learning Femininity in Colonial India, 1820–1932* (Manchester: Manchester University Press, 2016).

[27] If you are familiar with classical music of India, you will be aware that most *ragas* are religious in nature, and are to be played specifically for dawn, noon, or evening

[28] Rig-Veda 3.62.10, in Robert E. Van Voorst, *Anthology of Asian Scriptures,* p. 45.

(6) Feeding the baby solid food ceremony (6 months).
(7) Ritual celebrating the first haircut (male child's third year).
(8) Male child begins study of Vedas with teacher
(9) Wedding
(10) Funeral and cremation.
(11) Ceremonies to honor the deceased, monthly for a year. If these are not performed properly, the parent may not make it to the heavenly realms.

Puja: RITUALS FOCUSED UPON IMAGES

The Sanskrit term *puja* literally means "devotion" and is ritual devotion and ritual offerings addressed to a particular image of a *deva*. *Puja* establishes and maintains a connection between the human realm and the realm of *devas*. One must remember that there are uncountably many *devas* in the Hindu pantheon.[29] We have discussed a few of the major *devas*, but every location in India had its own local divinities or forces, some of whom might even live in the nearby forest, in the hills, in the rivers, in the farmland or even in one's own home. Each deity will have a festival and procession celebrated by the local community of worshipers. These are occasions for *puja*, feasting, live cultural performances, special food and drink, and rest.

Puja, rituals and ritual offerings focused on an image of a *deva*, became popular and replaced many of the costly Vedic sacrifices, perhaps because people became dissatisfied with the expenses involved. Precisely when and where the *puja* images originally were developed is unknown; but it is thought that some may date back to the period before 200 B.C.E.

A statue of a Hindu deity is not just carved wood or stone; it is concentrated spiritual energy which connects sacred beings and other sacred realms with our universe and even with our home. People who perform *puja* are not just worshiping an image or worshiping a statue. The divinity is fully present before the devotee; the statue is the actual home for the god. So the *puja* rituals are reverence and devotion offered to an actual *deva*, a ritual which confirms the elevated status of the deity and the inferior submissive status of the follower. The *deva* is fully present, listening to the follower, looking at the devotee as the devotee encounters the divinity face-to-face. The follower worships the deity with loving devotion, and hopes that the divinity will respond with gifts. But the statue must be treated with the respect you would give to an actual god sitting in your living room, your room of worship.

The divinities involved in ritual *puja* are very much like we humans, but more powerful. The gods fall in love, they get angry, they offer gifts, they withhold favors. Gods have doubts, they experience regret for actions performed, and like the same kinds of things that we like. We must try to make the gods happy, and we know that we can do that simply because the gods are so much like us. We know what makes us happy; thus we know how to make the gods happy.

Puja is a nearly universal practice among all Hindus, no matter their caste or social status. The rituals of *puja* acknowledge that spiritual beings exist and we have a personal relationship with those deities. Worldly blessings are anticipated by those who offer unconstrained love and adoration. Flowers are offered, holy water, and other gifts. The gifts are offered to specific *devas* and are usually connected to the stories and myths associated with the divinity. Favorite foods for specific deities are often gifts. Special colors are associated with particular *devas*. Devotees can visit a temple which is home to a particular *deva* in the sense that an icon has been empowered by complicated rituals, and place offerings of coins to the deity, which is then kept by the priests who serve at the temple. This respect to a *deva* can be public, but most homage to gods is private, not public, and *puja* offerings are most often made to statues in the home shrine.

With *puja* that is centered in the home shrine, the householder offers ritual respect for a superior deity who has taken up residence in a statue created expressly for the purpose. The householder will hire a sculptor to carve an

---

[29] Some sacred texts say there are 330 million *deva*.

image with all the iconography appropriate for a specific *deva*. An image is created and delivered. Then a Brahmin priest may be hired to perform a rite of installation, inviting the *deva* to descend and reside in the beautifully carved image. The ceremony will include a long series of purification rituals accompanied by the chanting of thousands of hymns, hoping to activate the divine power of the *deva* and imbue the statue with life energy.

A genuine *deva* has the power to dwell anywhere, or to dwell in more than one place. The ritual concludes with a "waking up" ceremony, which includes the opening of the eyes on the statue (which must be done with great care by the priest). If the *deva* can be lured to take up temporary abode within the earthly home, the householder and his family have a *deva* sharing their home, and if treated with reverence and respect, it will be available to protect and interact with the family and its needs. The follower offers food of the very highest quality, very expensive clothing, gentle bathing, and even a foot-rub.

Puja is not the sort of weekly group worship and devotion typical of Western Christian religion. *Puja* is an individual offering for personal reasons, or for the benefit of one's household. Thus, *puja* often occurs in the shrine of a private home. Rites must be performed at least once a day; perhaps more often. Depending on the wealth of the family, there might be a professional Brahmin priest hired to perform the rites, but more often it is a household member.

As long as their needs are cared for, and the images are shown proper respect and devotion involving frequent rituals and offerings, it is believed that the *deva* will remain with the family. If the *deva* is offended for any reason, the *deva* will abandon the image. The family will know that the *deva* is gone because unfortunate events, illness, or even disasters will affect the family. A priest can be hired in an attempt to invite the *deva* to return, but the ritual of return is not always successful.

PUJA IN THE HINDU TEMPLE

A Hindu temple is a place for individual *puja*. Temples do not serve the same functions of Christian churches. Temples are not for public worship, and in a temple there is no preaching, no pulpit, no weekly meetings. The Hindu priests are not there to save someone's soul; if someone wants liberation, it is not to be found in a temple, and no Brahmin priest can offer it.

Hindu temples are usually built by wealthy individuals, and their primary function is not related to public worship, although individuals who are not family members are admitted to the temple to observe, or pray to the deity who occupies the temple. In classical Hinduism, worship is individual and private. There are communal rituals and ceremonies, but they typically do not take place in temples.

PUJA: THE VILLAGE RITES OF APPEASING LOCAL *DEVAS*

Another dimension of *puja* is found in rural villages. As described in previous chapters, the Indian world-view is that of a world filled with unseen powers and forces that can and do affect our lives. Although there are the major *devas* described in the prayers of the Vedas, there are also uncountably many local unseen beings who can harm us. In rural areas, *puja* is a ritual offering of grains and incense, or animals, offered to specific village deities, but these *devas* do not reside in a statue in our homes. These deities reside near the village, interact with villagers, and are often destructive.

The names of these *deva* do not appear in the Vedas. This is because they are local destructive natural forces. In India, the color red is associated with something holy. In this case, it is the typical color of a holy abode for an unseen presence that requires offerings. Insofar as they are destructive, these divinities need to be placated. These *deva* are both male and female. The female spirits are not always understood as kindly or mothering. Some "goddesses" are mother-protectors of the village but other "mothers" inflict diseases, injury, blights, and other forms of harm.

The local village *puja* rituals are communal ceremonies and are not Brahmin rituals and are not sanctioned by the Grand forms of Hinduism. The local destructive *deva* is believed to derive pleasure from the pain and suffering of the villagers, and with these rituals animals are tortured and it is hoped that the divinity will accept the animal's pain instead of exacting it from the humans. Village rituals deal with immediate negative forces to lessen danger. These rituals have nothing to do with Vedic *devas*, and have no concern with *karma* or *samsara*, no concern with the major issues of classical Hinduism. Note that these ceremonies are communal and not individual or private (as is typical of most Hindu religious observances).

3.11 DHARMA: THE PLACE OF RELIGIOUS PRACTICE IN HINDUISM

As we discussed previously, one's duties are *dharma*, and *dharma* includes ritual obligations, caste, religious, social and moral obligations. All the various *dharma* are the requirement of the holy Vedas. In earliest times, observing traditional duties and ritual sacrifices would lead the follower to an immortal life in the celestial realm of the ancestors. Later, the concept of karma brought a change. Karma means "action," and we have been explaining it in terms of ritual actions. However, a new idea slowly develops: actions done in accord with one's *dharma* bring good consequences to the agent; actions not in accord with *dharma* bring bad consequences to the actor. Good karma would cause good consequences, perhaps even a heavenly rebirth, but accumulation of good deeds alone could not get infinite life in heaven, for karma is always finite, and a finite cause cannot generate an infinite consequence.

This doctrine of karma makes it clear that the Brahmin's sacrifices cannot ever deliver a person to the ultimate goal of infinite life.[30] You can never generate enough finite good karma to do anything more than cause a temporary rebirth on a higher plane; thus you can never escape *samsara*, the cycle of birth and death, via the mechanism of karma. Karma works within the field of causal action, but you need to transcend the entire field of karma if you desire to escape.

Around 500 B.C.E., some peoples of India were losing faith in the efficacy of rites and rituals to bring about ultimate freedom (even good karma keeps one bound to the cycle of birth-and-death), and this is when the Indian religion begins to be separated out into four different ways of being religious. Each of these pathways offered a different solution to the problem of being trapped in an eternal round of *samsara*. The old pathway, the pathway of ritual action (*karma-marga*) was losing followers, and some people wanted something more.

As a result, new pathways (*margas*) appeared which focused on the means to attain ultimate liberation, ways which went beyond the limitations of *karma* and karmic action. These paths will be studied in the following chapters, and include the pathway of **knowledge**, the pathway of **meditation**, and the pathway of complete **devotion**.

Some people of India retreated into the forests to follow the pathway of liberating knowledge, but the details of this pathway were secret and often required advanced educational skills because it was so profoundly intellectual. The pathway of focused concentration or meditation was associated with the forest dwellers as well. For other Hindus, the *deva* become personal deities instead of divinely impersonal forces of nature, and devotion to such deities can produce positive results.

3.12 SUMMARY OF THE CHAPTER

In this chapter we have traced the development of Hinduism from its origins in rituals performed by priests, to a more general religious tradition whose characteristics are still recognizable in contemporary India. We have seen the new ideas of karma and *samsara* which expanded the realm of Indian religion beyond the more ancient priestly rituals. We saw the caste system (priests, protectors, merchants, servants, outcastes) take shape under the religious aegis

---

[30] It should be noted that for the majority of Hindus, rebirth in a higher level of status is their primary concern. Most are not seeking liberation from the cycle of *samsara*.

CHAPTER 3: CLASSICAL HINDUISM

of the *Laws of Manu*, and we also came to understand the four traditional stages of life (student, householder, hermit, ascetic), and the four goals of a good Hindu (wealth, pleasure, duty, liberation), according to classical Hinduism. Finally, we discussed *puja*, ritual devotion to *devas* as they occur in family situations as well as in village situations.

3.13 KEY CONCEPTS AND TECHNICAL TERMS IN CLASSICAL HINDUISM

artha   The appropriate goal for a householder: financial success.

ashrama   These are four "stages of spiritual effort" the members of the three higher varnas are supposed to go through, including student, householder, hermit forest dweller, and ascetic

Brahma   A *deva* who presides over the creation cycle of the universe.
Brahmins   The priestly *varna*, or social group (correctly spelled Brah<u>m</u>an, but spelled Brahm<u>i</u>n in order to be specific that the reference is to the priestly caste, not the power behind the gods).
Brahman   The creative power behind all the gods, behind all the universe, the impersonal cosmic power, the absolute ultimate reality.

dhyana   the practice of focused concentration, or meditation

dharma   one's social, moral, and caste duty, but a good translation might be a "principle of right living." One's *dharma* is the proper way for an Aryan to live, morally as well as religiously. The religious sense includes ceremonies, and rituals. It is the "pattern of ideal behavior." However, *dharma* has additional related meanings involving social and political responsibilities in addition to the moral and religious dimensions. One's *dharma* includes one's caste, occupation, life stages, diet, governmental obligations, and rules of morality.

dharma-sutra A text which explains the social, religious, and moral duties, codes, rules and laws which regulate the lives of of the various social groups.
dharma-shastra A commentary text which explains dharma-sutra codes and laws

jati   a term which literally means "birth," and which can be translated into English as "caste;" one's social position, occupation, and other important features of life are determined by one's birth and the status and occupation of one's parents

kama   sensual pleasure; one of the four goals for the householder.
karma   the impersonal law of cause and effect which describes how actions in accord with one's dharma produce good consequences in the present and future, and actions contrary to dharma produce bad consequences.

ksatriya   the protector or warrior social group; the second of the four *varna*

Manava-dharma-shastra the *dharma-shastra* written by a Brahmin named Manu; it could be translated the *Rules of Manu*, or the *Law Codes of Manu*, or the *Laws of Manu*

moksha   liberation from the cycle of birth and death which is the appropriate goal for an upper-class Hindu

puja   rituals and ritual offerings focused on an icon or statue of a *deva*

sannyasi	the fourth, ascetic stage of the four *varna* described in the *Law Codes of Manu*
shastra	A commentary or explanation of a sutra or a part of a sutra.
shudra	the menial laborer social class; lowest of the four *varna*
sutra	A text which focuses upon a single thread or a single topic; the sutras are like a brief outline of important points
vaishya	the social groups including land-owning farmers, businessmen, merchants, traders, etc. It is the third of the four *varnas*.
varna	the basic social groups of India, including priests, protectors, merchants and farmers, and servants and menial workers
varna-ashrama dharma	The duties and obligations arising from the combination of the four basic social classes (*varna*), and the four stages of life (*ashrama*), which are defining ideas of Hinduism.

3.15 QUESTIONS FOR FURTHER DISCUSSION

1) Can you give a brief account of the origins of the world religion called "Hinduism"? How did it develop? What features were most important?

2) Compare the early Aryan and Vedic world views with the later view of classical Hinduism discussed. Where are the similarities? What are the differences?

3) We saw that Hindu culture distinguishes *varna* from *jati*. Both terms have been translated as "caste." Discuss their differences and their similarities.

4) An important text in Indian religion was the *Laws of Manu*. Explain its contents and discuss its influence on Indian society. Do non-Indian religions have comparable books of rules for proper religious behavior? Are those followed closely, or is a certain latitude allowed?

5) Officially, Western societies do not have a caste system. Are there members in Western societies whose social standing is determined by their birth? Is there anything that corresponds to "outcastes" in Western societies? Which occupations have the highest status? Which the lowest status?

6) Are there stages of life in Western societies? Our society does require every child to go to school. Are there other stages expected of everyone?

7) Some people in the west will quote the Christian Bible to the effect that "as you sow, so shall you reap." Is this the same thing as the Indian concept of karma? What are the differences?

8) Many in the west believe that after they die they will be reborn into either a heavenly realm, or a hellish realm. What other possible destinations do the Hindus add to these two?

9) Many in the West believe that after they die they will be reborn into either an eternal heavenly realm or an eternal hellish realm. In Western thought, what determines the ultimate destination? Is it one's moral behavior? Is it one's beliefs? Is it simple faith? Does the religious group that one belongs to have any influence? Does performing rituals have any influence on these destinations?

10)   Indian society endorses four official goals appropriate to one's life. What are those four goals? Would these same four be important in Western societies? Are there other goals that Western religion endorses?

11)   This chapter discussed the origins of the caste system. If you have any friends from an Indian background, you might want to ask them about how the caste system functions in their life, in their family, or their community.

12)   You might want to research the role and function of the caste system in contemporary India. How are the attitudes in the cosmopolitan centers different from rural communities? Which Hindu politicians and political parties support the caste system, and which groups tend to minimize or reject the system?

A SELECTED BIBLIOGRAPHY

Hinduism

Primary Sources

de Bary, William T., ed., *Sources of Indian Tradition*, 2nd edition, 2 volumes (New York: Columbia University Press, 1988).
Hopkins, Thomas J., *The Hindu Religious Tradition* (Belmont, Ca: Wadsworth, 1971)
Koller, John and Patricia, *Sourcebook in Asian Philosophy* (New York: Macmillan, 1991)
Miles, Jack, and Wendy Doniger, *Hinduism* (New York: Norton, 2015)
    This Norton Anthology of World Religions volume is an excellent collection of original sources.

Studies in Hindu Thought

Bilimora, P., Joseph Prabhu and Renuka Sharma, *Indian Ethics* (Burlington, Vt: Ashgate, 2005)
Chatterjee, Satischandra, and Dhirendramohan Datta, *An Introduction to Indian Philosophy* (Calcutta: University of Calcutta, 1968)
Doniger, Wendy, *The Laws of Manu* (New York: Penguin Classics, 1989)
Eck, Diana, *Darsan: Seeing the Divine Image in India* (New York: Columbia University Press, 1998)
Grimes, John, *A Concise Dictionary of Indian Philosophy* (Albany, NY: State University of New York Press, 1996)
Halbfass, Wilhelm, *Tradition and Reflection: Explorations in Indian Thought* (Albany, NY: State University of New York Press, 1991)
Herman, A. L., *Brief Introduction to Hinduism* (Boulder, CO: Westview Press, 1991)
Hirayanna, M., *Essentials of Indian Philosophy* (London: Unwin, 1978)
Hirayanna, M., *Outlines of Indian Philosophy* (London: Allen & Unwin, 1970)
Knott, Kim, *Hinduism: A Very Short Introduction* (London: Oxford, 2000)
Koller, John, *The Indian Way: An Introduction to the Philosophies and Religions of India*, 2nd edition (New York: Prentice Hall, 20005)
Michaels, Axel, *Hinduism: Past and Present* (Princeton, NJ: Princeton University Press, 2003)
Mohanty, J. N., *Classical Indian Philosophy* (Lanham, MD: Rowman and Little, 2000)
Moore, Charles A., *The Indian Mind: Essentials of Indian Philosophy and Culture* (Honolulu, HI: University of Hawai'i Press, 1967)
Potter, Karl H., *Guide to Indian Philosophy* (Boston: G. K. Hall, 1988) An extensive bibliography.

CHAPTER 3: CLASSICAL HINDUISM

Potter, Karl H., ed., *The Encyclopedia of Indian Philosophies* (Princeton, NJ: Princeton University Press, 1961–2015)
Radhakrishnan, Sarvepalli, *Indian Philosophy*, 2 volumes (London: Allen and Unwin, 1923)
Shattuck, Cybelle, *Hinduism* (New York: Prentiss-Hall, 1999)
Sharma, I. C., *Ethical Philosophies of India* (Lincoln, Neb: Johnsen Publishing Co., 1965)

CHAPTER 4: THE TRADITIONS OF LIBERATING WISDOM

4.1 OVERVIEW OF THE CHAPTER

In this chapter, we will cover the traditions of liberating wisdom (*jnana*, pronounced NYA-na) in India which developed from approximately 600 B.C.E. to the fifteenth century in the common era.

In classical Indian thought, there are at least four ways of being religious and they depend upon and correspond to one's personality. Some people seek to express their religious nature in the performance of ritual. We have already discussed the more ancient traditional Vedic pathway of *karma-marga* focused upon sacred rituals whose purpose was to produce a good life in this life, a long life, freedom from illness, material prosperity, good crops, and children. Initially, the way to be religious for the Brahmins was the *karma-marga* based in sacrifice, ritual, and words of power, and the goal was to obtain control of natural forces using the fire sacrifice and magical sounds of power. Then, the goal changed for the forest monks. The goal for the authors of the *Aranyakas* became knowledge of the true self and ultimate reality. Then we have the sacred texts called *Upanishads*, and the goal is transformed again.

In this chapter we will discuss this new and different spiritual pathway, the pathway of liberating knowledge or liberating insight which attempts to make sense out of questions about death, the afterlife, and the relationship between the individual and the supreme sacred ultimate source of all that is real and all that is divine. The pathway focused upon these issues is called the *jnana-marga*. In this chapter we will also discuss a related pathway associated with the *jnana-marga*, and this is the *dhyana-marga*, or the pathway of focused concentration or meditation. The sacred literature most closely associated with these pathways is the *Upanishads*. Several important forms of Hinduism arise out of the *Upanishads*. One is called Vedanta, and it has several varieties. Another wisdom tradition is Yoga. Both of these forms of Hinduism are taught in Western countries and may be familiar to the student. The third system we will discuss is the Samkhya, which has much in common with Yoga.

4.2 THE ORIGINS OF THE PATHWAY OF LIBERATING WISDOM AND MEDITATION

During the time period some scholars have labeled the Axial period, approximately around 800 B.C.E. to 200 B.C.E., several new developments appeared in Indian religious traditions. Indian society was in the process of becoming more complex, and the growth of farming technology was spurred by the use of iron which increased middle class wealth, increased trade and travel, and as a result many new kingdoms arose. Iron provides more wealth and greater crop yields, and also changes the destructiveness of war, with iron-tipped arrows and spears which rip through the armor that protected warriors in earlier eras. It was a time of wars of conquest, with armies marching back and forth across the farmlands. As the more ancient empires were uprooted, the farming people slowly emigrated into growing urban centers (without their familiar villages and familiar local divinities, or *devas*), and in these more urban environments people needed new religious imagery that they could relate to, and religious experiences that could be both convincing and meaningful.

CHAPTER 4: THE WISDOM TRADITIONS

Religion is inseparable from culture, and in India, this time period is the emergence of large-scale literate and historical cultures, kingdoms, empires, and world religions. Alongside the traditional religious practices of ritual action (*karma-marga*), new questions begin to be asked, and new modes of religious activity developed.

One of the major changes in Indian religions is the fading away of the expectation that properly performed rituals guarantee a good earthly life, and the expectation that the cremation fires can carry our individual unchanging *atman* into an eternal life of heavenly bliss. Would it be possible to attain the goal of heaven, but then in heaven one could die again? What power takes us to heaven, and how can we ensure eternal life in heaven? Is it possible that the individual self undergoes a continuing series of birth, death, and re-death? The developing idea of karma as moral cause and effect will produce a great anxiety about these issues. Karma is going to produce a very different world view.

Karma

We have already seen that karma means "action," and as such, it can refer to the pathway of correct ritual action (*karma-marga*), but in this later time period it acquires an enriched new meaning: karma also suggests that a person's social and ritual duties constitute moral actions, or good deeds, and acting in accord with one's social duties will produce good consequences for one's life, and bad deeds, actions contrary to social expectations, generate bad consequences. If one performs a bad deed, and then dies, the negative karma does not disappear; one will experience the consequences of his or her actions—if not in this life then in the next life.

What constitutes "good deeds"? In addition to correct ritual actions, proper and correct deeds are doing the actions appropriate to your social role, or *varna*, and your duties appropriate to your caste, *dharma*. These actions are what is called "good karma" which produces a better life in the next life, and bad karma (caused by not fulfilling the moral, social, and religious duties appropriate to your *varna*) produces rebirth in a lower realm, even a hellish realm. However, either way, our true self, our permanent and immutable *atman*, continues on—trapped in a cycle of birth followed by death, followed by another birth, followed by another death. This new understanding of karma appears in the Vedic literature called the *Upanishads*.

The concept that good deeds produce good consequences for the person, and bad deeds generate bad consequences for the person, has a serious consequence. If one performs enough good deeds and rituals, it should get us to heaven. Karma may guarantee that ritual sacrifices may be able to get one to the heavenly realms, but good karma will be unable to deliver a person to the ultimate goal of *eternity* in a heavenly realm. If rituals produce good karma, we need to realize that these good deeds are not infinite, but only finite. Yet, the goal is infinite bliss in an eternal heavenly realm. Good deeds are always finite. Finite good karma can produce only a finite time in a heavenly realm.

Karma describes how consequences flow from our action. The mechanism connecting karma and the endless cycle of death and re-death, called *samsara* (literally "wandering") is self-centered desires and egoistic attachment, which keeps the eternal *atman* tied to the consequences of action. You desire a specific goal, you desire something or someone; you resolve to acquire the object of your desire; you then act (karma) upon that resolve. As you act, the consequences attach to you. That the consequences will affect you is inevitable. For the majority of Hindus, karmic consequences cannot be avoided. Karma is the fuel that drives the unchanging *atman* from one life to the next.

Reincarnation

Reincarnation is the Western term we give to the process by which the unchanging eternal true self, or *atman*, wanders from one life to another as a result of karmic energy. By constantly trying to satisfy his or her desires, a person continually recreates his or her bodily form; and, as long as the consequences of previous action (karma) persist, the person will persist, to once again feel the pull of desire, and once again act in ways which generate consequences (more karma).

CHAPTER 4: THE WISDOM TRADITIONS

What is the True Self?

The true self, the *atman*, may be trapped in the cycle propelled by karma, but what sort of thing is this *atman*? According to the sacred scriptures and the testimony of the sages, the *atman* is something within us which is permanent and unchanging, an eternal uncreated substance which unifies our mental and physical life, and the decisions of the *atman* control and shape our lives. Each of us possesses a permanent autonomous essence which has no parts, and thus can never be affected by our insecure constantly changing world. It is the inner controller. The *atman* drives the body the way you drive an automobile. It is self-existing, separate and distinct from our physical body. This self-existent eternal unchanging *atman* is in control of our body and in control of our choices and resulting actions. Thus the resulting good karma or bad karma is connected to the unchanging *atman*.

The true self is self-existing and eternal, and thus remains unaffected by this continual passage through life cycle after life cycle, *samsara*. This is the immutable true self that seeks to be liberated from the ongoing cycle of existence. The problem is trying to explain how rituals and good deeds could bring about that liberation. If one thinks about it carefully, no one can ever generate enough finite good karma to do anything more than cause a temporary better rebirth on a higher plane in the next life; thus you can never escape wandering in the cycle of birth and death, the cycle of *samsara*, via the mechanism of karmic good deeds.

For the well-educated Brahmin priest, this newly emerging idea of karma had shattering consequences. If there is a continuing cycle of birth and re-birth, death and re-death, fueled by karma, then we are trapped. Why are we trapped? Because each and every one of us must act, and action (karma) traps us, action is the unavoidable push that propels us to another life. The desire to escape wandering life to life within the prison of karma becomes of great importance for some groups within Indian society.

The ancient rituals, even when done properly, are only able to produce a finite amount of good karma, and thus can only produce a brief but better rebirth in the next life. Good deeds in accord with one's social *dharma* result in a favorable next life; wicked deeds contrary to one's social and religious *dharma* duties result in an unfavorable next life. However, even if the next life is favorable, one is still trapped in *samsara*, the endless cycle of wandering through birth and death. Finite ritual actions cannot produce eternal escape from the cycle; so how is it possible to escape the trap of *samsara*? This is the spiritual crisis dominating the axial era in India, and several new major religious traditions and philosophical founders flourished during this time.

For the Hindu world-view, the ultimate goal of eternal happiness can never be found in this world. The Indian world-view tended to see the world we inhabit as a place of ignorance, misery and suffering, a universe on a downward spiral toward destruction. Such a world was to be escaped from. The world we live in could not be improved.

4.3 A NEW AND IMPORTANT QUESTION ARISES

As a result, the new key question for many in this era became "Is it possible for one to escape the endless cycle and prison of birth-and-death, the cycle of *samsara*?" For those who took the question seriously, the general answer was "yes," but there is no agreement as to precisely how to accomplish this.

To answer the question of how to achieve liberation from the trap of *samsara*, several religious *margas* (pathways), slowly emerged. One *marga* is the *bhakti* or devotional path (pray to the right divinity or *deva* and perhaps you can be free).[1] Another *marga* says that the way out of the endless cycle of *samsara* is neither priestly ritual nor devotion, but rather some special sort of liberating knowledge, referred to as *jnana* (pronounced NYA-na).

---

[1] This *bhakti* pathway develops more slowly than the wisdom pathway, and emerges later, and so the *bhakti-marga* will be discussed in detail in the next chapter.

CHAPTER 4: THE WISDOM TRADITIONS

One who can achieve liberation from the cycle will not be a shaman who communicates with spirits or a Brahmin priest who performs rituals for pay, but rather some special person, utilizing sacred knowledge, who achieves liberation in this very life, perhaps even an awakened person, a savior or a great philosopher. Someone somewhere must have discovered the liberating knowledge of how to escape the trap of karma and the endless rebirth cycle of *samsara*. Such a person would know the secret of how to escape the apparently endless cycle of *samsara*, and this person can reveal to the disciples the special insight, that liberating *jnana*, which brings about liberation from the cycle of *samsara*.

This search for liberation generated a new class of literature: the **Upanishads**, the sacred books recounting the teachings of the ones who had escaped, or nearly escaped the endless cycle of *samsara*, the liberated ones. The liberated person is a sacred person, someone who has attained universal liberating knowledge, knowledge which can bring about freedom for the individual person, but if shared could ultimately bring liberation for all humans. For the followers of this new pathway, forces of nature, fire, water, plants and animals are no longer the central focus of the rituals and temples; now it is the liberated one, the godlike one, who has achieved liberation via the pathway of *supreme insight*.

So, the initial concern about the never-ending cycle of death and re-death led to a new emphasis upon individual liberation. For a minority of followers of Vedic religion, the goal shifted from an emphasis on having a long and successful life in this world to achieving liberation of the eternal *atman* from *samsara* by encountering a timeless realm which undergirds and supports all of reality. The older pathway of the *karma-marga* is the realm of time and change, and history. The new pathway of wisdom offers liberation from the realm of time and change, liberation from the trap of reincarnation and *samsara*, into a timeless transcendent oneness of all things.

4.4 *Jnana-Marga or Jnana-Yoga*

The new pathway of *jnana*, or the method of *jnana*, is the primary focus of this chapter. The term *marga* is "pathway," and here the term *yoga* basically means "method." The key term is *jnana* (pronounced NYA-na), "knowledge" or "liberating insight." Thus we have the pathway of *jnana* (*jnana-marga*) or the method of *jnana* (*jnana-yoga*).

Jnana is usually translated into English as "wisdom" or "knowledge," but there is no word in English which carries the meanings of *jnana*. *Jnana* is not factual knowledge. One could never master *jnana* by sitting in a classroom listening to a lecture, or by reading a book, even a sacred book. Even the stronger English term "wisdom" is not strong enough to translate *jnana*.

Jnana is the liberating insight which reveals the sacred ultimate and transforms one's life. When one achieves *jnana*, one's life changes; nothing remains the same. One's values and perception of reality are transformed. Everything you and I have thought to be true about the world as it appears is now seen to be at best incomplete and mistaken, or at worst, false. *Jnana* is the knowledge of ultimate sacred reality, the knowledge of how things really are, of who you really are, and *jnana* results in the ability to live in accord with that insight (*darshana*). For some followers, this knowledge may also provide mastery or control over reality.

The Six Schools of Hindu Thought

Traditionally there are six different schools which stress liberating knowledge as the key element of liberation. They include the Samkhya and the Yoga, the Nyaya and the Vaisheshika, and the Mimamsa and Vedanta traditions. The Nyaya, Vaisheshika and Mimamsa have faded away throughout the course of Indian history, with many of their concepts continuing on into the Vedanta traditions. The Yoga and the Vedanta remain strong. The Samkhya tradition seems to supply the well-springs of Yoga, and as such, we will discuss it briefly.

4.5 NEW SACRED SCRIPTURES AND SACRED SOUNDS BEGIN TO APPEAR

In the previous chapter we discussed the *Aranyakas*, the forest books authored by those willing to dispense with physical ritual and replace it with knowledge of the symbolism of the ritual. For these forest ascetics, mental performance of the ritual was just as effective, or perhaps even more effective. The *Aranyakas* recount the search by ascetic monks who lived on the edges of society in the forests who were trying to understand the nature of the self, the nature of the sacred ultimate, and to achieve liberation from the endless cycle of *samsara*. Apparently, some of those forest ascetics (*sramana*) achieved their goal, because the forest texts give way to a new class of literature which offers insight and solutions to the ultimate problems motivating the ascetics.

The *Upanishads*

The "pathway of liberating knowledge" (*jnana-marga*) is described in the sacred books produced by the ascetics in the forests, the books called the *Upanishads*. Thirteen of them are considered of greatest importance although there are over a hundred *Upanishads*. The *Upanishads* developed along with the social caste system but devalued society, family, home, marriage, and caste.[2]

The ascetics who had entered the forest in search of liberation were hermits. They did not put any stress on public ritual (karma) and had little interest in the ritual activities of the Brahmin priests, and were unconcerned with social and moral duties determined by one's caste (*dharma*). Instead, these recluses stressed personal experience and severe mental disciplines. However, the sages in the forest did not operate in a vacuum. They brought with them all of their religious background which may have included non-Aryan religious practices and views, as well as the Vedas and the assumptions of the Vedas. During the course of cultural transformation, there were several developments in the understanding of ritual among the Brahmin priests. These help to shape the search that we see reflected in the *Upanishads*.

Mantras

As discussed previously, in the early centuries the people felt that external powers, divinities, or *devas*, were granting favors because the *devas* looked kindly upon the priests who were performing sacrifices and ceremonies, and were flattering the gods so profusely. Then some of the Brahmin priests thought that the sacred *sounds* of rituals performed properly were directly manipulating cosmic powers and forces. The actual vibrations of sound had the magical power to change reality, the power to create and the power to destroy. The priests were no longer asking favors of gods; instead, the priests were controlling these natural or supernatural forces by properly enunciating powerful sounds, the sacred powerful vibrations which were the sacred words of the Vedas. These properly enunciated sounds of power are called *mantras* (pronounced mahn-tra). There were thousands of prayers that were believed to have such power. An example of a Hindu mantra is this:

HRIM SRIM KRIM PARAMESHVARI SVAHA.[3]

---

[2] There is a strong tendency among Indian religious commentators to describe the *Upanishads* as though they all agreed upon a single systematic and coherent philosophy. However, "we find evidence of conflicting theories, of the criticism and replacement of one theory by another and the influence of earlier views on later thinkers, who build on them. All this would not have been possible if there were a single uniform philosophy ... which is unfolded on every page of the Upanishadic texts" (K. N. Jayatilleke, *Early Buddhist Theory of Knowledge* [London: George Allen & Unwin, 1963], p. 32).

[3] Agehananda Bharati, *The Tantric Tradition* (New York: Anchor Books, 1970), pp. 119-120. There are Sanskrit diacritical marks in the original quotation which have been omitted here.

CHAPTER 4: THE WISDOM TRADITIONS

Another popular mantra is:

> HARI KRISHNA HARI KRISHNA
> KRISHNA KRISHNA
> HARI HARI
> HARI RAMA HARI RAMA
> RAMA RAMA
> HARI HARI

Usually the mantras do not have a conceptual meaning, or else the meaning is only barely relevant to the power of the sounds.

OM: THE MOST SACRED SOUND

 One of the most important of the sacred sounds or vibrations is **Om**. It is often referred to as the source of all the other mantras. Om is a common prefix and suffix for Hindu prayers. Why is this the source, the key sound in Hinduism? At the beginning of a cosmic cycle, as reality comes into existence, the sound Om is the primordial vibration, the first manifestation before the cosmos actually appears, the first manifestation of the one sacred ultimate. It is the experience of the infinite within each of us.

> The word that all the Vedas disclose; The word that all austerities proclaim; Seeking which people live student lives; That word now I will tell you in brief—It is OM!
> For this alone is the syllable that's *brahman*. For this alone is the syllable that's supreme! When, indeed, one knows this syllable, he obtains his every wish.[4]

When properly chanted, Om is a combination of the sounds A - U - M, and each of the sounds has a separate symbolic spiritual meaning, ranging from ordinary consciousness to spiritual consciousness, and ultimately consciousness of undifferentiated unity.[5] It is believed that chanting the sound Om can function as a tool to achieve *moksha*, ultimate liberation from the prison of the apparently never-ending cycle of birth and rebirth, the cycle called *samsara*. "Just as a spider climbs up on its thread and gains freedom, so the yogin climbs towards liberation by means of the syllable OM."[6]

There is no single agreed-upon meaning for Om. From Hindu tradition to Hindu tradition, it is variously described as light, as eternity, as absolute peace and bliss. It is divine, infinite power, universal law. It is all-embracing divine love, it is the cosmic rhythm of the perfect, the eternal. It is the unity of duality, it is the oneness of supreme reality. Om is the most sacred sound, and it contains all other sacred sounds. With the mind filled with the sound of Om, the knowledgeable practitioner realizes that all things are not separate, and a oneness pervades all.

> Om is the primordial sound of timeless reality, which vibrates within us from the beginningless past and which reverberates in us, if we have developed our inner sense of hearing by the perfect

[4] Patrick Olivelle, *Upanishads* (Oxford University Press, 1996), p. 237. See also S. Radhakrisnan, *The Principal Upanishads* (New York: Harper & Bros., 1953), *Katha Upanishad* I, ii, 15–17, pp. 615–616.

[5] Lama Govinda, *Foundations of Tibetan Mysticism* (London: Rider & Co., 1960), p. 23.

[6] *Ibid.*, p. 22.

pacification of our mind. It is the transcendental sound of the inborn law of all things, the eternal rhythm of all that moves, a rhythm in which law becomes the expression of perfect freedom.[7]

The sacred sound Om contains all that is sacred. However, there is another sacred sound which focuses upon the source of the power of the *devas* and by extension, the most sacred power. The power of the sacred ultimate of which Om is the first manifestation is called **Brahman**. This sound names the origin of all the gods, and all that exists.

BRAHMAN: The Master Sound Corresponding to the Sacred Ultimate

We know that there are many *devas* and many prayers invoking the *devas*, and each *deva* is associated with a force or power, but what is the common source of these various divinities? From where do gods like Indra, Rudra, Varuna and Agni derive their powers? Whatever that supreme source is, the authors of the Vedas and *Upanishads* believed that there must be a sound that corresponds to it. The stress upon sound was such that the Brahmin priests thought that creation arises out of sound vibrations, some loud, some softer, some deeper than humans can hear, some at a higher pitch than we can hear. All of these give rise to creation.

Originally, the Sanskrit term "Brahman" was used to describe the power behind the prayers and rituals performed by the Brahmin priests. This raises a further issue: there must be some original sound, some deep sound, some supreme sound that would be the key giving the knowledgeable Brahmin priest access to the single source and power behind all the individual particular forces. It is during the 700-200 B.C.E. period that the attention of the elite Brahmin priests turned from individual specific rituals to the understanding of esoteric cosmic interconnections of aspects of the sacred sounds of the sacrifices to the sacred ultimate.

One sound came to be thought of as the power of prayer, the power of ritual, and then the power behind all ritual, and finally the one sound symbolizing the sacred creative ultimate force itself, the timeless eternal source of all reality. The various incantations which were muttered all came together with the master sound, which was *Brahman*.

Brahmin priests were certain that knowledge of how to manipulate this master word should give access to total cosmic power, and provide the solution to the most desperate human problem, being trapped in the endless cycle of *samsara*. Brahman is the eternal substratum, it is the ultimate foundation, the ultimate reality which underlies our changing and decaying realm we mistakenly think of as reality. Brahman is perfect and beyond the imperfections of our changing world.

Brahman is beyond all human thought

Brahman is the absolute, the ultimate, the transcendent, the sublime, the immaterial, the eternal, pure, and unchangingly blissful. Even these terms are inadequate. Brahman is beyond all human categories and concepts. Brahman transcends all qualities and characteristics. Brahman is the sacred ultimate reality which cannot be divided into parts, which cannot be defined by such terms as "spiritual," as "infinite," as "eternal," or anything else. We need to escape this imperfect and relative world and get to the absolute beyond all concepts, Brahman.

It is the sacred words of power, and the mental meditative states of the priests that is the key to liberation. Knowledge of the internalized sounds and actions (mental performance of ritual) was just as effective as ritual action; ritual knowledge does not depend on physical ritual. For these people, it seemed obvious that traditional physical rituals can not bring about liberation from *samsara*.

---

[7] *Ibid.*, p. 47.

CHAPTER 4: THE WISDOM TRADITIONS

This knowledge of the sound of ultimate power, Brahman, must not be allowed to fall into the wrong hands of those who could misuse these keys of control over the universe. These powerful ideas must be protected. This was a secret teaching, an advanced ritual practice, restricted to the elite priesthood.

A New Group of Sacred Texts Appears

Out of these secret teachings, a new fourth group of advanced esoteric oral memorized literature begin to appear. We are already familiar with (1) those Vedic books which emphasize hymns and ritual verses (the four Vedas, i.e. *Rig*, *Sama*, *Yajur*, and *Atharva*). (2) The second group of sacred texts were the *Brahmanas* (priestly commentaries upon the four Vedas explaining the symbolism of rituals). Both of these groups focus on sacred rituals and sacrifices and the goals of the Vedas and Brahmanas were wealth, power, health, prosperity, success during one's lifetime, and after death, permanent immortality in heaven.

Towards the end of the *Brahmanas* period, the fear arose that the good karma generated by sacrifices performed during this life and previous lives would run out, and the person would die and be reborn again . . . and again. If ritual did not bring permanent release, what could?

(3) The third collection of sacred texts, the *Aranyakas*, begins to address this problem. The *Aranyakas* are the literature of forest-dwelling ascetics, called *sramanas*, who believed that an inner private performance of the sacrifices were as effective as physical performance and this group emphasized meditation and an introspective search for the true self. What is the essential enduring nature of a person? What is the *atman*? How can one achieve ultimate liberation from the ongoing cycle of *samsara*?

(4) The fourth and last group of Vedic classic texts are the *Upanishads*, the advanced secret insights of the liberated and nearly liberated ones who live in the wilderness. These provide answers to the questions left by the forest dwelling *sramanas*. The *Upanishads* are the last of, or the end of the Vedas, or the culmination of the Vedas.[8]

4.6 THE *Upanishads* ANSWER THE ULTIMATE QUESTIONS

The Upanishadic teachings begin to arise during this axial age, an era of new thought, free debate, and the willingness to think new ideas and new interpretations and to question older traditions and verities. The *Upanishads* reflect the ideas of those who had no stake in upholding and protecting Vedic ritual tradition, no interest in protecting the position of the priestly caste. Most likely these would be people like the *sramanas* and the *munis*, the ascetics and silent sages of the forest.

"Upa-ni-shad" is usually interpreted to mean "to sit devotedly at the feet of" a teacher, and implies the private teachings of highest wisdom which the spiritual teacher, called the *guru*, imparts to his student on a one-to-one basis, not to a classroom of students. We should note that a *guru* is not the same thing as a member of the Brahmin caste. Although both are teachers who hand down religious knowledge, a *guru* can come from any caste group. The only requirement is that the *guru* have personal experience of and insight into the path that liberates one from *samsara*.

In this sense, the *Upanishads* contain secret teachings intended only for the closest pupil of the *guru*. The *Upanishads* reveal the secret of the ultimate nature of reality. Only very special students who have worked very hard and achieved deep knowledge should be allowed to study and master these insights.

---

[8] As was noted earlier, in India the title *Rg Veda* does not name only the hymns, but also the later commentaries traditionally associated with the *Rig*, namely the *Brahmanas*, the *Arayakas*, and the *Upanishads*. Western scholars use the label *Rg Veda* for only those earliest prayers and hymns.

CHAPTER 4: THE WISDOM TRADITIONS

The *Upanishads* are the culmination of the Vedas

Much of later Hinduism draws upon passages of the *Upanishads* as interpretations of the Vedas. The *Upanishads* are the culmination of the Vedas, the last of the Vedas, and the highest of the Vedas. It is thought that none of the *Upanishads* are earlier than 800 B.C.E. and most likely after 600 B.C.E., and the classic thirteen major *Upanishads* were probably composed before 100 B.C.E., although many *Upanishads* were certainly written a thousand years later than this time.

The Authors of the *Upanishads*

Considering the content of the *Upanishads*, it is seems likely that the authors were forest dwelling *sramanas* of superior education. We do not know whether the authors originally belonged to the Brahmin group or the *ksatriyas*, but the Brahmin priests did preserve the *Upanishads* and the Brahmins treated them as extensions of the first three collections of Vedas.

Meditation

The stress on meditation (*dhyana*) found in some of these new Upanishad texts raises an interesting question for scholars of Indian religion. Focused concentration is one essential tool of the liberated sage, but there is no advocation of *dhyana* meditation in the four basic collections of Vedic literature, the *Rig Veda*, the *Sama Veda*, the *Yajur Veda* and the *Atharva Veda* or their earliest commentaries. Did the early Aryans value and practice *dhyana* meditation but just fail to mention it? That does not seem likely.

One possibility would be that meditation originates somewhere other than with the Aryan Vedic religious traditions. From seals discovered at Harappa and elsewhere, it appears that the pre-Aryan Harappan civilization practiced something like seated meditation. A controversial conclusion could be drawn from these facts: the more ancient non-Aryan religious practices were beginning to exert an influence upon traditional Aryan religion. However one interprets these facts, the ancient Aryan stress on public sacrifices is declining, and the practice of private meditation is increasing.

The Anxiety at the Root of the *Upanishads*

As we saw in a previous chapter, there were those who thought that sacrifices were not effective for ultimate liberation from the apparently endless cycle of *samsara*. Instead of ritual sacrifices which produced a better life in the next life, these people sought the key which would unlock the prison of this realm of endless rebirths.

Throughout history, in the West and in China, many sought the secret of immortality. However, the religious Hindu is not seeking immortality—her soul is eternal and immortal. In the context of karma and *samsara*, the *atman* never dies. It is self-existent, unchanging, permanent, and has no parts, and thus it can never "come apart," that is, disappear. It will be reborn again and again, apparently without end. The problem is that we are condemned to live forever, going round and round in the cycles of birth and death, repeating over and over—and *life does not get any better* except temporarily, because even the divinities are locked into the karmic cycle of *samsara*.

===

Moksha: Ultimate Liberation from *Samsara*

Since we are all trapped in the cycle of *samsara*, the new goal of the followers of the *jnana-marga* is **moksha**, ultimate liberation from karma and reincarnation. *Moksha* is liberation from the bonds of karma and liberation from the endless cycles of *samsara*. Is it possible to achieve *moksha*? The authors of the *Upanishads* claim that understanding the source of all reality, Brahman, is one key to liberation, a key to *moksha*.

As we have seen, originally, Brahman was the sacred power that made prayers effective, the mysterious power present when the *mantras*, hymns and prayers of the sacrifice were uttered or recited. Brahman was an abstract power or force connecting the rite, ritual, or liturgy, with the supernatural sacred realm of powers and *devas*. Brahman was the hidden power, latent in all things, whenever sacred sounds are uttered, the sacred power which the *devas* drew upon for their powers and their very existence. Thus, Brahman was the single unchanging highest and holiest ultimate reality.

Brahman is the fundamental basis of all existence. Brahman is the source from which all material things in the universe evolved or sprung, the deep substratum and essence of reality; it is because of Brahman that everything exists materially. Brahman is not a personal creator God, and not a god at all.[9] Brahman is the trans-personal source, that out of which even God arises. "All things come from Brahman and are supported by Brahman; to know Brahman is to know all, since Brahman is 'this All', this universe."[10]

Because Brahman is the non-physical unchanging inner essence, the underlying truth behind all changing appearances in our world, Brahman cannot be discovered by ordinary sense perception. Brahman is a sort of universal matrix, the sustaining frame or structure upon which is woven all of existence, including space and time.

Atman: The Real Self

The follower of the *jnana-marga* needs to be able to answer these questions:
"Who am I, really?"
"What is the essence of the true self? What is the *atman*?"

Since my physical body does grow old and die, and the common belief was that *atman* was never born and never dies, it follows that the essence of the person cannot belong to the physical body. The *atman* moves from one life, one body, to the next life, to another body. Therefore, it must be a non-physical self-existing substance which unifies our mental life, which organizes perceptions and sensations, and plans, decides, and then gives orders to the physical body. The ordinary self is able to know, to perceive, to sense. These properties must belong to some non-physical substance which is the bearer of these properties.

The Upanishadic teachers thought of the true substance-self as the ultimate knower, seer, hearer. It is the consciousness that allows us to know, to see, to hear. *Atman* is the inner director, the inner self, which occupies and controls the body just like the driver controls an automobile.

Atman is Uncreated and Self-Existing

The true self cannot have parts, because anything which has parts could come apart and die. The *atman* is one, not many. It exists, but nothing created it, so *atman* must be self-existing. Behind all that we think and feel, there must be some unchanging inner essence, something independent and self-existent.

What part of you and me gives directions to the physical body? What part of us makes the arm raise, the legs run, the eyes follow their target? The sacred *Upanishads* do not agree on a single explanation for precisely what this inner director is or how it works. The *Upanishads* offer several different explanations for *atman*. Whatever it is, the inner director *atman* is not physical, so it must be related somehow to our consciousness. *Atman* is spirit, not material. It is a non-physical inner self-existing unchanging essence or substance. It is our true self. *Atman* is beyond concepts, deeper than language, limits, or categories.

---

[9] In the chapter on devotional Hinduism, we will discuss the creator deva, Brahma. But Brahman is a transpersonal force, not a god.

[10] Hopkins, *The Hindu Religious Tradition*, p. 38.

Two Questions

Our ordinary empirical consciousness is focused outwards, and because the *atman* is the part of us that is the inner knower, how can we ever know it? The eye cannot see itself, only a pale reflection of itself. The finger cannot touch itself. How can the knower know itself? We must direct our attention inwardly. The *Upanishads* advise us to use introspection, focused concentration and yogic meditation—using these, we can focus consciousness on the true self, the *atman*. We must allow our consciousness to become illuminated by its own illumination, to realize its own radiant consciousness.

Thus the ascetics, the *sunnyasins*, the *sramanas* and *munis* in the forest, the authors of the *Upanishads*, have two questions:
What is Brahman, what is the sacred ultimate underlying source of the material universe?
What is the eternal unchanging *atman*?

4.7 THE DEEPEST TEACHINGS OF THE *Upanishads*

What is being revealed in the next few paragraphs was never intended to be taught to people who had not devoted their life to wrestling with these deepest questions. These revelations were never to be given to a class, or published in a book. This is not because the teachers did not want ordinary people to know about it. Rather, it is because ordinary people lack the proper spiritual training to comprehend this ultimate truth. Without adequate preparation, the liberating aspect of the deepest teachings will not be understood, will not provide liberation, and will appear less profound than they actually are. In addition, some of these teachers reveal truths and *mantras* that produce great power, and power in the hands of someone immoral would be extremely dangerous.

Let us try to imagine what it would have been like for a student about 200 years before the common era. The student renounces society and enters the wilderness or forest, and wanders until the student finds a spiritual guide, a *guru* with whom a deep spiritual connection is sensed. Finding a *guru* is just the first step. The student must be ready to commit the rest of his or her life to the quest for the answers to the deepest questions of life. The student must follow the teachings of the *guru* with unquestioning total confidence.

The *guru* guides the student through years and years of deepening comprehension with questions that the student must focus upon with complete unwavering concentration. With much careful exploration and prodding, the student begins to realize that this changing world is *not* the ultimate reality. The ultimately real must be eternal and unchanging. With this realization, the student begins to seek the unchanging realm of the truly real. Now the student begins to comprehend the nature of Brahman, the spiritual essence which underlies all of the material world and provides the ground for the realm of the gods, the *devas*. After much meditation, the student begins to glimpse the *atman*, the true self, the single inner controller, the inner director. It is only then that, after many years, the teacher determines that the student has finally achieved the necessary preliminary understanding and is ready to be taught the deepest teaching.

The Final Question and the Ultimate Answer

Now comes the final question:
How is one's true self, one's *atman*, related to the sacred ultimate, Brahman?
The answer to this question is the insight which leads to liberation, leads to *moksha*. The classic source for this deepest teaching is the *Chandogya Upanishad*, 6.8-16 when the ultimate question is raised:

"What is the relationship between Brahman and *atman*?"

The sage Uddalaka Aruna sends his son, Svetaketu, to be taught the Vedas, but when his son returns, the sage finds that Svetaketu has memorized much but has little understanding of the true meaning of the highest teachings. Uddalaka Aruna skillfully asks a number of questions of his son, which he cannot answer. Svetaketu realizes that his understanding is shallow, and asks his father, "Please sir, tell me more." The dialogue turns to the true Self, the *atman*. The last paragraphs of that teaching are as follows:

> "These rivers, my son, run, the eastern like the Ganges, toward the east, the western like the Sindhu, toward the west. They go from sea to sea, that is, the clouds lift up the water from the sea to the sky, and send it back as rain to the sea. They become indeed sea. And as those rivers, when they are in the sea, do not know, I am this or that river, in the same manner, my son, all these creatures, when they have come back from the True, know not that they have come back from the True. Whatever these creatures are here, whether a lion, or a wolf, or a boar, or a worm, or a midge, or a gnat, or a mosquito, that they become again and again.
>
> "That which is the subtle essence, in it all that exists has its self. It is the True. It is the Self, and that, Svetaketu, you are."
>
> "Please, Sir, inform me still more," said the son.
>
> "Be it so, my child," the father replied.
>
> "If someone were to strike at the root of this large tree here, it would bleed, but live. If he were to strike at its stem, it would bleed, but live. If he were to strike at its top, it would bleed, but live. Pervaded by the living Self that tree stands firm, drinking in its nourishment and rejoicing, but if the life (the living Self) leaves one of its branches, that branch withers; if it leaves a second, that branch withers; if it leaves a third, that branch withers.
>
> "In exactly the same manner, my son, know this. This body indeed withers and dies when the living Self has left it; the living Self dies not.
>
> "That subtle essence is the self of all that exists. It is the True [Brahman]. It is the Self [*atman*], and that, Svetaketu, you are."[11]

The sage Uddalaka Aruna taught his son, Svetaketu, "*Tat tvam asi, Svetaketu!*" "That is *Brahman*, That is *Atman*, That thou art, O Svetaketu!"

You already knew that your deepest truest self is the *atman*, but you did not know that you are Brahman. *Atman* and *Brahman* are not two different things. Brahman is identical with *atman*. The liberating illumination: in their essence, the two are not different. That Brahman is what you are in your deepest true self. There is no difference; you are Brahman. That which sustains the universe, beyond thought and beyond language, and that true self which is at the core of us and struggles for our recognition, is the same thing. The finite is within the infinite; the infinite is within the finite. The sacred ultimate is identical with our true self. Only Brahman is truly real. Brahman is the eternal behind all appearances. Brahman is One, eternal, and unchanging.

Before achieving this final understanding, the student mistakenly believed that his empirical changing individual personality is his true self, and that his self was trapped in the cycle of *samsara*. However, the liberating insight reveals that this perception is a mistake and has always been a mistake. The empirical personality is not the true self, it is not one's *atman*.[12]

---

[11] Chandogya Upanishad 6:9-11; in Robert E. Van Voorst, *Anthology of Asian Scriptures,* pp. 34–35.

[12] It is interesting to note that in this very important Upanishadic passage, there is no indication that the youth needs to practice meditation to achieve this insight. Rational understanding is sufficient for liberation.

For the follower of the Hindu school of Vedanta, spiritual liberation (*moksha*) results in dissolving one's individual personality (which was only temporary) into the sacred Brahman/*atman* which is one, eternal, self-existent, and unchanging. With liberating knowledge, *jnana*, we realize that our *atman* has never been trapped. It could never be trapped. In fact, it has never been separate from the sacred ultimate, Brahman. With the dissolving of the empirical personality, all restrictions (caste, purity and impurity, pain, frustration, separateness, suffering) disappear and the person disappears into unity with the divine source of all the gods, the source of all that exists. The empirical ego is gone and the result is spiritual joy and serenity. You finally know who you really are and become what you have always been. The ultimate essence of all external reality, and the force behind all the *devas*, is **identical** with the inner essence—you are God and the source of all gods.

There are several versions of an Indian folk story which illustrates this. The story is that the student studied with his *guru* and finally achieves the liberating insight of *Tat tvam asi*, ("That Thou Art") and comes to the deep realization that he is not different from Brahman itself. He is elated and walking serenely down an overgrown narrow jungle pathway when he sees in the distance a man on an elephant and it is trotting down the pathway towards him. The man on the elephant yells, "Get out of the way!" but the student thinks "I am Brahman; I don't have to get out of the way." The elephant is nearly on him and the driver shouts "Get out of the way, you fool!" The Brahmin stands before the elephant and does not move. A second later the elephant has knocked him aside. Confused, he picks himself out of the bushes and brambles, and makes his way back to his *guru*. He tells his teacher "I thought I was Brahman. Why did I have to get out of the way?" The *guru* responds, "Of course you are Brahman. But didn't you hear Brahman telling you to get out of the way? Why didn't you listen?"[13]

The *Upanishads* which stress the identity of *atman* and Brahman are not teaching **monotheism**, not teaching worship of one divine god separate from the world and separate from humans. Rather, a religion grounded in the oneness of all reality is properly described as **monism**. Ultimate reality is just one, eternal, and unchanging. You and I are not separate from this one.

At this point in Indian religious history, the religious practice of the great majority was still the *karma-marga*, reliance upon Brahmin priests to manipulate the forces and the *devas* with *mantras* of power, with fire sacrifices and numerous other rituals. The concept of wandering through realms of *samsara*, of good and bad karma fueling unceasing reincarnation was becoming a major source of anxiety, yet the performance of traditional Vedic rituals by Brahmin priests could not solve the problem. Although the *Upanishads* offered solutions to these problems, the difficulty is that the *Upanishads* were a secret teaching, which required leaving one's home and practicing focused concentration, and thus not widely available.

Over the centuries the liberating insight of the *Upanishads* began to permeate the ordinary lives of farmers and merchants. The concepts became more and better known. Hindus sensitive to the problem began to study the *Upanishads*, even before they left home to enter the forest. Wise teachers prepared their students for the ultimate realization, but there was a nagging problem that was fairly obvious to all those who were familiar with the *Upanishads*.

A TROUBLING INCONSISTENCY IN UPANISHADIC TEACHINGS

The problem with the *Upanishads* and the problem for the philosophers and the mystics: the *Upanishads* say that reality is One, eternal, and unchanging, and yet the world that I experience is not one, it is constantly changing, and in fact is a world of multiplicity. How can reality be One and many simultaneously? The *Upanishads* make no effort to explain this apparent contradiction.

---

[13] I heard this story from a teacher from India long ago, but have not been able to track it down in precisely the form I learned. A slightly different and more modern version, with the same point, is found in A. K. Ramanujan, *Folktales from India* (New Delhi: Penguin Books India, 1993), p. 175.

CHAPTER 4: THE WISDOM TRADITIONS

The sacred *Upanishads* say that in our essence we are not individuals, but rather eternally one with the universal and immortal Brahman, which is the only reality. Yet, according to my sense organs and perceptions, there seem to be many different people in the world, and separate and distinct buildings and highways. My universe is a realm of cause and effect, and cause and effect are the engine of change. The holy books say that reality is One and unchanging, but that's not what we perceive: we perceive change and multiplicity, we perceive cause and effect. Are the sacred *Upanishads* wrong? They contradict our experience. How can we believe the *Upanishads*?

There seems to be just two choices. Either (a) the world of everyday cause-and-effect, the realm of multiplicities does not exist (because reality is ONE, not multiple), or else (b) the sacred ultimate Brahman itself does not exist, is a fiction (if the world of multiplicities is what is REAL then the *Upanishads* must be wrong).

This troubling and obvious inconsistency remained in the background of Upanishadic thought until the late eighth century in the common era. An Upanishadic tradition called Vedanta provided one way to resolve this problem.

4.8 THE VEDANTA TRADITION

A new religious tradition arose basing itself upon the *Upanishads*, and it is known by the name Vedanta. "Veda-anta" means "the end/culmination of the Vedas," and this means that the Vedanta school saw itself as based upon the highest development of the Vedas. Of course, the end and culmination of the Vedas was the sacred scriptures of the *Upanishads*, the fourth and last great collection of Vedic texts. The *Upanishads* are the source for the religious insights of the school of Vedanta.

The Vedanta tradition quietly grew for 1,000 years. In its earliest forms, the poetic visions and intuitions of the sages who inspired the *Upanishads* were the sources for the ideas of the Vedanta. The second step in the development of Vedanta was a collection of aphoristic writings called the *Brahma-sutra* of Badarayana (circa 200 C.E.), which gather and arrange the ideas about the nature of Brahman. Then Vedanta entered the stage of elaboration, beginning with the commentaries on the earliest texts by the religious genius named Adi Shankara and later thinkers named Ramanuja and Madhva

The Advaita Vedanta Tradition Founded by Shankara (c. 788–820 C.E.).

Adi Shankara is famous in Indian religion, but, despite his fame, there are not very many authentic facts known about his life. What we do know is that he engaged in numerous debates with followers of other schools of Hinduism, with Buddhists, and Jains, traveled extensively, founded several monastic orders, and died at age 32, after creating the first full presentation of the Vedanta system in his famous commentary on the *Brahma-sutra* of Badarayana (c. 200 C.E.). Shankara takes the relationship between Brahman and *atman* quite seriously. He asserts that *atman* and Brahman are "not two." In fact, the tradition associated with Shankara is called "Not-Two" Vedanta, or **Advaita Vedanta**. The initial "a-" of "Advaita" is a negative and means "not," just as an initial a- does in English (an amoral person is not-moral). The second half of the word, -*dvai*, is related to the English word "dual" or "two." Thus, Advaita Vedanta is "Non-Dualistic Vedanta." *Atman* and Brahman are *not two* different things.

With Advaita Vedanta, Shankara provided a complete resolution to the problem: how can we believe the Upanishad's statements about reality, that reality is One, when all we experience is causal change and multiplicity? If reality is one, eternal, and unchanging, then why does it appear that I exist, that I am changing, and that I am different from you? If I am one with Brahman, how can I be undergoing the continual cycle of *samsara* caused by karma? The *Upanishads* say we are One with Brahman, perfect reality, but it sure doesn't seem so. The *Upanishads* say that Reality is One and Unchanging; so what are we seeing or experiencing if we are not seeing or experiencing Reality? How can the *Upanishads* be true?

Shankara's Solution to the Troubling Inconsistency

Shankara begins by asking abut the nature of the self and how we get knowledge of the self and of the world. If we ask, "What am I?" the ordinary person answers in terms of his or her body, or perhaps his or her occupation. We mistakenly believe that we have a separate body which is a real and lasting part of ourselves. We associate ourselves with the history of our changing bodies, thinking that our real selves can grow old and die. Seeing ourselves as separate from each other, we think in terms of "I" and "mine" and "me" (ego). As a result, we believe happiness comes from making the body happy, and we seek pleasure, comfort, wealth. We are never satisfied, we remain miserable, and we are unaware of the reason for our misery. The reason is that we are **ignorant** of something very important. We want to be liberated from the apparently endless cycle of birth and death, but we are ignorant of what is causing us to remain trapped in *samsara*.

Shankara's solution begins with a careful analysis of the nature of knowledge. What sorts of things are known? How do we know that we are separate and individuals? How do we know the world is multiple? We can also ask: what is real? It seems to Shankara and people in India that some things are **more real** than other things.[14] To explore these issues, Shankara provides an analysis four objects of knowledge that correspond to four levels of reality, from the least real to the most supreme reality.

Four Levels of Knowledge and Four Levels of Reality

The first and lowest level of knowledge: verbal knowledge.
This corresponds to the lowest level of reality: **the forever unreal.**

By calling this "verbal knowledge," we see that we can use language in ways that seem to be describing something, but there is nothing that corresponds to the words. For example, suppose I ask you to get a sharp pencil and a piece of paper, and draw a square circle and bring it to me. There is something seriously wrong with my request. It is not just difficult; it is impossible for you to draw a square circle. I am asking you to draw a shape that (a) has no corners, and at the same time (b) has four corners. A square circle is a self-contradiction and is impossible.

This first level of knowledge, verbal knowledge, relates to phrases which seem to describe things, but those things are logically contradictory and impossible. We can talk about a "square circle," so a square circle has a verbal status, a conceptual status, but its conceptual status exists only as contradiction. Corresponding to verbal knowledge is the forever unreal. The Unreal is that which, in principle, cannot have an objective counterpart. A "married-bachelor" has a verbal reality, but no human being can be a "married-not-married" person.

The second level of knowledge: deluded knowledge.
This corresponds to the second level of what is real, those things which are **illusory existent**.

This category corresponds to things we experience, but misconstrue. We misinterpret our initial experience of something, and a later subsequent experience shows us that we were mistaken; we have a new experience which contradicts our previous experience, and as a result we no longer trust or believe the previous experience. Our judgment is radically changed by a later experience.

---

[14] In the Western philosophical tradition, the same view was accepted by Plato and the Christian churches. It was common to argue that God is **more real** than the world that God created. An infinite eternal God must be more real than finite and fallen creatures. Nevertheless, for Christians humans are the special creation of God, created for fellowship with God, and thus humans must be more real than insects and plants.

For example, we are dreaming that we are in danger of falling, and then we awaken to find ourselves in bed, flailing about—our subsequent waking experience has shown us that falling was a misperception, a misunderstanding. We are driving on the highway on a hot summer day. We experience what appears to be a pool of water on the highway ahead, but when we get to that place in the road, there is no water there, and our subsequent experience has overridden our previous judgment that there was a pool of water on the road. Whenever we seem to experience something, and then subsequent experience reveals that we were mistaken, we have had this second level of knowledge, "deluded knowledge," based on an illusory experience. Our first experience did not give us genuine knowledge. This is deluded knowledge and the level of reality that corresponds to deluded knowledge is illusion. This realm includes illusions, mirages, hallucinations, dreams with no basis in reality, and things which could exist but do not exist as perceived (hobbits, Pegasus, Superman, trolls, Tarzan, unicorns, and so forth).

The third level of knowledge: empirical knowledge.
The level of reality corresponding to empirical knowledge is called **appearance**.

The term "empirical" refers to all that we see, hear, touch, taste, and smell. Empirical knowledge is knowledge gained by sense experience. It corresponds to things we experience while awake, things that are not mirages, not hallucinations. Empirical knowledge is the way things **appear** to us when we are awake and carefully observing our world. Empirical knowledge is the basis of science and scientific observation. The level of reality that corresponds to empirical knowledge is appearances.

The realm of appearances is what we call reality—and in our empirical experience we do not see oneness, we do not experience that which the *Upanishads* claim to be ultimate reality, i.e., the one eternal unchanging Brahman. What is more, we do not expect future experiences to override or sublate our empirical waking experiences. Is it conceivable that any future experience could sublate these waking experiences which comprise our life?

I suspect that most of us are aware that at least some people, some famous people, some religious and philosophical leaders, have claimed that they have had profound transforming experiences which led them to devalue their prior ordinary everyday lives. These people seem to have experienced something which causes them to reevaluate what they used to think was important. There are people who "drop out" of their expected social roles to become wanderers or maybe monks, apparently because they have found (or are searching for) a level of experience which renders our ordinary experiences to be of less value or less reality.

This suggests that there might be one level of knowledge which overrides or sublates our empirical experiences. There might be a level of knowledge which gives us knowledge of something which is more real than empirical appearances. Shankara argues that there such a level of reality. There is a higher level of reality, a higher realm which can be the object of a higher knowledge, called Ultimate Reality.

The highest knowledge: Supreme Knowledge.
The object which is known corresponds to the level of **Ultimate Reality**, which is Brahman.

Many *Upanishads* teach that there is a liberating experience where all distinctions, contradictions, and multiplicities, are transcended. The empirical consciousness slows, stops and then we have the silence of the true mind. The result is a much deeper understanding of what is fully real. If this is so, then our empirical perception of an independent, substantial world of uncountably many real objects, persons, and processes must have been grounded in some pervasive error.

We can distinguish two levels of insight. (1) The first is the fully liberated sage, someone who has embodied the original complete unity of Brahman and *atman*. The liberated sage has taken the ultimate step of entering into Ultimate Reality. (2) Then there is the second level, the spiritual vision of the advanced *sramana*, a person of extraordinarily deep insight into the nature of ultimate reality, but lacking the ultimate step.

Shankara writes:

Then let him meditate upon the identity of Brahman and Atman, and so realize the truth. Through spiritual discrimination, let him understand the true inner meaning of the terms "Brahman" and

"Atman," thus realizing their absolute identity. See the reality in both, and you will find there is but one ...

Just as a clay jar or vessel is understood to be nothing but clay, so this whole universe, born of Brahman, essentially Brahman, is Brahman only — for there is nothing else but Brahman, nothing beyond That. That is the reality. That is our Atman. Therefore, "that is you" [*tat tvam asi*] — pure, blissful, supreme Brahman, the one without a second.[15]

This is an echo of the *Upanishads*, "that thou art." Truly, you are Brahman, your *atman* is identical with Brahman. The realization that your deepest self is nothing but Brahman is the insight that leads to immediate liberation, *moksha*.

THE TWO ASPECTS OF BRAHMAN

We can discuss Brahman from two perspectives. The first is Brahman as perceived by us, *saguna Brahman* or **Brahman with qualities**. From this perspective we can describe Brahman as a divinity, as Govinda, as Vishnu, as Shiva, as Ishvara, as Krishna, as Shakti. We can describe *saguna Brahman* as loving, merciful, or frightening, and we can have a relationship with *saguna Brahman*. From the perspective of *saguna Brahman*, it is correct to say that everything has a trace of the divine in it. It is correct to describe *saguna Brahman* as pure, as ultimate reality. This is Brahman as perceived by the advanced sage in the forest.

The second perspective is Brahman itself, *nirguna Brahman* or **Brahman without qualities**. This is not the conceptual understanding of humans; rather, it is the vision when one has gone beyond understanding, beyond description, beyond language, beyond conceptualization. Everything we say about *nirguna Brahman* is trapped within the limited net of human concepts and is therefore inadequate.

Sat, Cit, Ananda

Brahman without qualities, *nirguna Brahman*, is the ultimately real, and is just pure Existence (*sat*, pronounced "sut"), pure Consciousness (*cit*, pronounced like "chit"), and pure Bliss or pure Ecstacy (*ananda*). All that can be said meaningfully about Ultimate Reality is *sat, cit*, and *ananda*. Anything else is wrong. In the deepest Brahman experience there is awareness of just *sat, cit, ananda*, and the awareness that anything else lacks full reality.[16]

Reality and Change

The Ultimate Absolutely Real cannot change, for this would mean it could change into something else, something not-so-ultimate, not-so-absolute, not-so-real. Ultimate reality must be beyond the possibility of undergoing change. This is the fundamental assumption of Vedantic thought: **any thing that changes cannot be absolutely real**.

In the realm of empirical reality, the realm of sense experience, everything we see is changing due to the process of cause and effect—and things that change cannot be absolutely real. What we call "the world" is a realm of illusory appearances. Any talk about illusory appearances provides a realm of opinion and belief, but *not* knowledge.

---

[15] From Shankara's Crest-Jewel of Discrimination, quoted in James Fieser and John Powers, *Scriptures of the East*, Second edition (New York: McGraw-Hill, 2004), p. 25.

[16] Some of Shankara's Brahmin opponents accused him of being a Buddhist, because his understanding of Brahman was so abstract and depersonalized that it reminded them of the Mahayana Buddhist idea of "empty of essence" discussed in *Asian Thought*, Volume I, chapter 10, on Mahayana Buddhism.

Maya: **The Veil of Illusion**

Maya means "illusory" and is one of the most important concepts of Vedanta thought. The empirical world of cause and effect, and change, is all *maya*, is all illusory. *Maya* is what makes oneness appear as many. *Maya* exists every time we use concepts and ideas to break up reality into artificial discriminations. *Maya* is whenever we fail to realize the oneness of the real.

> Whenever the "I," "me," or "mine" is present, there also is *maya*. *Maya* is all experience that is constituted by, and follows from, the distinction between subject and object, between self and non-self.[17]

Ignorance of the nature of reality is the explanation for why we do not perceive ultimate reality as one, eternal, self-existing and unchanging. Change belongs to appearances only; change is not ultimately real. We fail to realize that our empirical world is not ultimately real; it is the effect of *maya*.

To say that the world is *maya* does **not** mean that the world is unreal. Rather, it means that the world is **less real** than Brahman, but it is more real than hallucinations, more real than illusions, dreams, or fantasies.

Shankara is arguing that there are degrees and levels of reality. The highest level of reality is Brahman, One, eternal, unchanging, precisely what is described in the *Upanishads*, and accessible to the spiritual vision of the liberated sage and the advanced *sramana*. To know this is to know the ultimately real, and one has the highest supreme knowledge. The next highest level of reality is what we ordinarily consider reality, the empirical world, the realm of appearances, but it is less real than it appears. Its apparent reality is a product of our ignorance. We are not perceiving reality; we are perceiving an illusory realm created by *maya*.

Then there are things even less real than empirical reality. There are illusions, and mirages, where we see something, but we misunderstand what we perceive. I see a coiled up piece of rope in the twilight, and mistake it for a snake. We see a store mannequin or a wax figure of a person, and we mistakenly believe it is a living person. These are less real than empirical reality, but they are grounded in empirical reality.

Then there are hallucinations and dreams with even less basis in reality. Less real than dreams and hallucinations are things which do not exist, things like hobbits, like Tarzan, like wizards and witches, things like Batman, like flying horses (Pegasus), trolls, or unicorns. These things are what Sankara described as deluded knowledge

There is one step lower than non-existent things. It is things which cannot exist, things which are self-contradictory, things like square circles, or married bachelors. Shankara described these as purely verbal knowledge which corresponds to spoken words which only seem to name things, things that are forever unreal and can never become real.

SHANKARA'S SOLUTION SUMMARIZED

Shankara's solution to the problem of the apparent conflict between the teachings of the *Upanishads* (reality is one, eternal, unchanging) and human experience (reality is constantly changing) is now clear. According to Shankara's analysis, what the *Upanishads* are describing is correct, because the *Upanishads* are describing ultimate reality, not appearances contained within *maya*. The realm of appearances is less than completely real, and we have been taking

---

[17] Eliot Deutsch, *Advaita Vedanta: A Philosophical Reconstruction* (Honolulu: University of Hawaii Press, 1969), p. 28.

our empirical experiences as reality. We have confused mere appearances with the ultimately real.[18] Therefore, from the higher perspective of liberation, the apparent contradiction is resolved.

According to Shankara's school of Advaita Vedanta, we mistakenly consider the limitations of our empirical existence as limitations of Reality. All the misery of life is *maya*. All attachments, aversions, and fears, are based in *maya*. All memories, cognitions, and empirical awareness are grounded in *maya*. *Maya* is whenever we fail to realize the oneness of the real. Because time arises only within it, *maya* itself is beginningless.

Maya cannot be thought about, for all thought occurs within it. It is indescribable, for all language results from *maya*. The level of empirical reality and appearance is just *maya*.[19] The highest truth is that *atman* and Brahman are not-two, are non-dual. We have been ignorant of this, and our ignorance has caused us much grief. The wisdom that makes the ultimate truth real to us is the liberating *jnana*.

A Fundamental Problem with the Doctrine of *Maya*

According to Shankara, the only thing truly real is Brahman. All else is illusory, and less real, caused by *maya*. So, what is the status of *maya*? Is *maya* real?

If *maya* is real, then *maya* must be Brahman because Brahman is the only reality. But *maya* is the opposite of Brahman. Brahman is the unchanging, but *maya* is a principle of change. *Maya* falsifies reality. *Maya* cannot be in the realm of appearances because *maya* creates appearances, creates non-reality, and is the source of ignorance and the cause of human suffering. Therefore *maya* cannot be Brahman. *Maya* cannot be a part of Brahman, because reality does not come in parts. However, if *maya* is unreal, it could not produce any real effects. But *maya* certainly produces effects! It explains *samsara* and reincarnation. Our empirical world is the effect of *maya*.

Yet these effects exist in the realm which is not completely real, but more real than dreams, illusions, or fantasies. So, *maya* is neither real nor unreal, neither Brahman nor not-Brahman, not within Brahman nor without Brahman. Clearly there is a major problem to understand what *maya* is and where it exists

---

Duties of a Vedanta householder within the Vedanta framework.

This vision of ultimate liberation had a great attraction for many in Indian society. In the earlier centuries many young men were abandoning society and their family responsibilities, and entering wilderness areas seeking to achieve the liberating knowledge of the identity of Brahman and *atman*, but this was causing a severe problem for Hindu society. If the young men were entering the forest, then they were not staying home to take over the family business, or to farm the land. The young men were not marrying, and were not having children or grandchildren.

Followers of Vedanta are not required to leave home and enter the forest, although that is allowed. There is an endless cycle of lives wherein one can begin this difficult journey. It doesn't have to be this very life. A person must be prepared for such a momentous decision. Renouncing the world is not to be undertaken unless one feels a profound disillusion with worldly goals and pleasures and a deep longing for liberation from *samsara*.

While still a householder, and a deeply disillusioned person, the Vedanta follower begins to prepare himself for leaving society and the world of *maya*. He begins with cultivating and perfecting moral requirements, including (a) avoiding bad conduct (b) curbing the ego and calming the mind by selfless performance of duty, and (c) observation of basic ethical virtues including non-injury, non-hurting (*ahimsa*), truthfulness in speech, honesty, sexual restraint,

---

[18] *Ibid.*

[19] *Ibid.*, p. 29.

and freedom from grasping or holding to possessions.[20]

The householder should also practice purity, cleanliness of body and diet, making sure that all forms of pollution (social or ritual) are avoided. The householder should practice contentment and austerity to break free from the desires of the body.[21] The householder may share his home with his wife, but not her bed. Sexual restraint will become celibacy. Not yet ready to leave home and become a beggar, the householder still lives at home, somewhat as a hermit.

He should study sacred texts and doctrines, including the Vedas, *Upanishads*, and texts on Yoga. He meditates on the divine Lord Ishvara, because devotion to the god Ishvara is regarded as useful for those who have not yet experienced the non-duality of *atman* and Brahman. To achieve liberation, one must leave society and wander on the edges of civilization, begging for each meal. To have a wife and children would make such a life impossible.

After many lifetimes of such preparation, the householder will become aware of the proper time to renounce the world. He has already separated himself from his wife and his family duties, and lived as a hermit in his own home. If he is certain that the time has arrived, he leaves the village life. He gives away everything he has ever owned, every object he has ever valued, everything that could ever remind him of his old life as a family man. He gives away all his possessions, holding nothing back. He makes arrangements for his wife to be taken care of by sons or perhaps by her brothers. He leave the village on foot accompanied only by his son. At certain spot, father and son take a back-to-back position, the son facing towards the village and the father facing the forest. Both stride off resolutely without looking back. The father then must walk straight ahead until the end of the day without stopping. He is now a wandering beggar. He will never mention the name of his village. Ideally he should not even think of it. He will not cook any food or even make a fire to keep warm. Beggars are people who eat whatever scraps may be given. He sleeps wherever night overtakes him (often under a temple or shelter for monks).

India has a living tradition of these solitary forest dwelling wanderers and beggars. A wandering "holy man" need not be a follower of Vedanta, or even the *Upanishads*. The term *sadhu* ("good man") is applied to all religious wanderers, whether they are learned scholars, wanderers reciting the name of their deity over and over, or psychologically disturbed individuals. We previously encountered the term *sannyasi* or ascetic, and this is reserved for persons presumed to be learned in the spiritual traditions of the Way of Knowledge, and to be serious seekers of liberation.

The wanderer is no longer involved in the rigid caste structure. He roams free of all the concerns of society, no longer concerned with politics or taxes, no longer concerned with social politeness or rituals, and no longer concerned with his village or his family. The wanderer cannot achieve the goal by himself alone. The pathway ahead is long and difficult, and the wanderer needs to find someone ahead of him who has traveled the path. He needs to find that one spiritual guide who can lead him to ultimate liberation. He continues begging until some day he will encounter his own true spiritual teacher, his *guru*. The teacher and the student both recognize that they have a deep spiritual connection. The *guru* administers a rite of ritual rebirth and gives the *sannyasin* a new name free of any caste associations (in theory, caste strictures are forgotten). Then the *guru* guides the follower in the guru's style of advanced meditation-based discipline. This is the ideal goal in life for the follower of Adi Shankara, the follower of Advaita Vedanta.

Shankara's Advaita Vedanta is not the only tradition of Vedanta. Another form of Vedanta arose about three hundred years later which stressed devotion to a *deva*. Despite the fact that Shankara taught that "worship of the personal God is based on a half-truth and is suitable only for the preliminary instruction of immature minds,"[22] a teacher named Ramanuja worked out a form called the "Qualified non-dualism of Ramanuja." For Ramanuja,

---

[20] In the forest one's needs are very few. The *sramana* begs for food, and sleeps in the forest, under the trees.

[21] Hiriyanna, *Essentials of Indian Philosophy* (London: Unwin, 1978), p. 123.

[22] Fenton, *et. al.*, *Religions of Asia*, 2nd edition, p. 110.

Brahman is another name for Vishnu, Ishvara, or Krishna Vasudeva. *Jnana*-wisdom as taught by Adi Shankara is not enough. For Ramanuja, loving worship and devotion to a god (in Sanskrit, *bhakti*) is the essential requirement for full liberation.

4.10 SAMKHYA: A DIFFERENT FORM OF THE *Jnana-marga*

As we have seen, the books of the *Upanishads* raise questions about the eternal unchanging essence of living things, the part of us which is pure subject, pure awareness. However, another part of us is the self rooted in society, rooted in social relations, a self which sees, hears, touches, tastes, and smells. In Sanskrit, it is called the *jiva*. It is this *jiva*, the empirical self, which is active seeking liberation and which brings about the realization of the eternal self.

The *Upanishads* focus on the true self and the nature of reality, and do not concern themselves with an analysis of the relationship between the eternal true self, and the temporary, changing empirical self. The Samkhya ("Analysis") tradition explores this relationship, but in a way which is importantly different from the Vedanta tradition which draws so heavily upon the *Upanishads*.[23]

The two traditions of Samkhya and Yoga are often treated as a pair of religious traditions which explore similar related questions, which they answer in similar ways. For example, how is the self in bondage, and how can it be untangled? Samkhya often treats the philosophical underpinnings of the nature of the self and its relationship to the non-self. Samkhya analyzes human nature, enumerating its elements, analyzing how human nature is trapped. The person thinks of herself or himself as the collection of inclinations, desires, habits, tendencies and memories which seem to make up the self. However, how can this be the true self? And if it is not, then how is it related to my true self?

Samkhya is Non-Theistic

The Samkhya tradition does not invoke any sort of divine being or divine causation; gods are irrelevant. Samkhya is non-theistic. Liberation of each true self (called the *purusha*), is brought about by self-control and mental discipline; there is no need for a special agency by some divinity to do this. The *devas* play no role in Samkhya. In contrast, the related Yoga tradition is monotheistic and worships the *deva* named Ishvara. However, Ishvara is not creator of matter; rather, Ishvara is the instigator of the evolution of the universe from pre-existing matter.[24]

The World is Not *Maya*

In the Samkhya and Yoga schools, the world is real, it is not *maya* and this is consistent with some of the *Upanishads*. There is a wide variety of views expressed in the various *Upanishads*. In some of them, Brahman is said to have created the universe, and then entered into it.[25] Samkhya concludes that the holy Upanishad makes it clear that the world must be real because Brahman is its source, and thus there are two different realities: (a) Brahman and (b) the real objective world of things we experience. Brahman is *more real* than the empirical world, although ordinary

---

[23] We do not find much discussion of the key terms, Brahman and *atman* in Samkhya literature and Yoga until much later, perhaps the fourteenth century C.E.

[24] There is another Indian tradition that has much in common with the Samkhya and the Yoga schools, and that is the Jain religion. Jainism accepts the duality of *jiva* (soul) and matter, and adopts methods of serious ascetic practice to liberate the soul from the trap of matter. The early Jains also considered the gods irrelevant. See *Asian Thought*, chapter 6 of this book, which is devoted to the Jain religion.

[25] In the *Brihadaranyaka Upanishad*, *atman* is said to have entered into the universe.

means of knowing cannot reveal Brahman; ordinary means of knowing reveal only a world of objects.

If we wish to put an end to suffering and find our true nature, there is only one place we can begin our search. That is within this empirical and ever-changing universe. We must begin with the world of human experience, things seen, heard, touched, tasted and smelled.

Samkhya philosophers and theologians argue that everything that we can experience is all made of the same fundamental stuff. Rocks, trees, odors, colors, feelings, consciousness, desires, and intelligence, are all the content of experience; all of it can be experienced. All the things we experience are real, but somehow we are experiencing it all. However, that which is doing the experiencing cannot experience itself; the finger cannot touch itself, the eye cannot see itself (but only a reflection of itself). What is doing the seeing? What is doing the feeling? It is the self, the ultimate subject.

The Samkhya Theory of Causality

The Samkhya argument for the nature of ultimate reality (metaphysics) is grounded in an analysis of the causal connections between things. This analysis of how causality works is based on analogies. There is stuff, and this stuff is shaped into the forms we recognize in this world. The model is the relation between clay and jug, seed and plant, the wood or marble, and the statue; the lumber and the building; that is, the transformation of one thing into another.

There are two sorts of causes. One is like the potter who shapes the clay, the carpenter who works the wood, the sculptor who shapes the marble. These are the efficient cause which initiates the transformation, but what they transform is the pre-existing matter. The second is the material cause, the matter itself. This corresponds to the clay underlying the pot, the lumber itself, or the marble.

When there is change, some **thing** is changing. A pile of clay is changing from a lump into a pot, raw lumber is changing into a table or building, a piece of marble is changing into a statue of a god or goddess. Things do not just pop up out of nothing (if they did, a cow could appear right on this book).

If something never existed, how could non-existence be brought into existence? A pot does not appear out of nothing; it appears out of a transformation of clay. The clay changes its form; it goes from the form of amorphous clay to the determinate pot or dish. From gold we can make a statue of a lion; the form of the gold has changed, but no new matter has appeared. The golden lion resembles the gold it was made from. It is clear that the cause resembles its effects; the effects are not brand new, they do not pop into existence out of non-existence. Based on these examples, the Samkhya school concludes that every effect already pre-exists in the cause, the way the lion-shape pre-exists within the clump of gold waiting to be shaped.

Samkhya Metaphysics: On the Nature of Reality

Samkhya philosophers argue that material does not change, but only the form of the material changes. Therefore no new matter comes into existence, since the form is the only thing which changes. Nothing radically new is ever produced through causality; it is always a transformation of what existed before. So, everything that exists is caused; all things that are caused are effects; all effects pre-existed in their causes; all effects are transformations of their causes. From this Samkhya asserts that all of reality, all that exists, is a transformation of some one original cause![26]

There must be one Ultimate Principle out of which all things that exist are transformations. The Samkhya people give the name *prakriti* for this original single stuff. All matter and all forces are transformations (or effects) of one basic material cause: *prakriti*. Even your ordinary awareness and waking consciousness is *praktiti*.

---

[26] In Sanskrit, this causal principle that effects pre-exist within causes is *satkaryavada*.

88

CHAPTER 4: THE WISDOM TRADITIONS

Prakriti: The First Component of Reality

Everything that exists must have pre-existed in *prakriti*; but how to account for all the many different varieties of things which we experience? How could it all have come from one stuff? The answer: *praktiti* contains within itself three different tendencies — all of reality has these three in differing proportions, and the relative proportions determine the kind of characteristics any thing possesses. These three are called *gunas*. The combining of these three *gunas* in various proportions creates the basic elements, which recombine and account for all that exists in the world.

The Three Tendencies Create the Physical World

(1)   The first of the three tendencies is experienced by human beings as positive upwards motion, as **elevating**, as pleasurable. It is whatever is fine, light, uplifting, illuminating; that which is the source of happiness or pleasure. It is potential consciousness. It is associated with purity, with goodness, and with subtlety.

(2)   The second is the tendency to **action**; it is experienced by human beings as pain. This is things which are heavy, coarse, in motion, active, things which are transient, changing, impermanent, it is a principle of activity, energy, and motion, and when activity increases, pain results. It is associated with bad habits or tendencies which keep us in an ignorant or low (heavy) position.

(3)   The third tendency which constitutes all that exists is the tendency of **indifference**, inertia, non-action, sloth. Objects for which this strand dominate will obstruct activity, obstruct illumination and instead produce darkness, ignorance, inertia, and indifference. It is experienced by human beings as indifference because it is neither pleasurable nor painful; it is neutral.

Human Nature According to Samkhya

All things, including human beings, are composed of varying amounts of these three basic characteristics, although in each of us one of them dominates and the other two are recessive. We get a theory of human personality out of these three tendencies. A person dominated by the first tendency would be cool, detached, withdrawn, reflective, precise, intellectual, introspective, shy, extra-sensitive, gentle but aloof, indifferent to success and failure, mindful of moral duty, unwavering, attached to knowledge, self-controlling, firmly in control of mind and senses, patient.

A personality dominated by the second tendency would be active, energetic, impetuous, hot-tempered, domineering, assertive, competitive, talkative, forceful, passionate, restless, attached, violent, envious, combative, ambitious, capable of strong emotions, strong hatreds, and so forth.

Humans dominated by the third would tend to be lazy, procrastinating, sleepy, lethargic, sluggish, subservient, tending to be ignorant, slow, soft-tempered, relaxed, calm, dependent, friendly.

This Samkhya doctrine of the three tendencies is then correlated with the Hindu analysis of *varna*, one's social class. The Brahmin caste (the priests, teachers) has the first neutral intellectual tendency dominating, and the ideal Brahmin spiritual pathway would correspond to *jnana*. The *ksatriya* (protectors, rulers and administrators) have activity dominant, and the religious pathway which corresponds is the path of action, *karma marga*. If you are a *vaishya* or a *shudra* it is the third subservient tendency which dominates in your personality, in which case the most appropriate path is *bhakti*, or worship and devotion to *devas*.

Purusha: The Second Component of Reality

Pleasure, pain, and indifference cannot exist unless they are experienced. There must be some intelligence to experience them. Experiences do not exist by themselves waiting to be experienced. Pain does not exist unless there is some intelligence or sensation to experience it. Also, human beings have a profound desire for ultimate liberation, so

89

the Samkhya thinkers conclude that there must be some principle of intelligence which makes *moksha* possible.

In addition, the three original tendencies of uplifting, heavy, and indifferent, must have existed in a state of harmony, balance, or equilibrium, and if there are only these three, then they must still be in unchanging static equilibrium. There must be a fourth feature which caused the original harmony of these three tendencies to become unstable. Samkhya people call this destabilizing factor *purusha*, pure consciousness, as opposed to ordinary worldly consciousness. The mere existence of *purusha* caused the harmony of the tension between the three tendencies to become unbalanced.[27]

Purusha, pure consciousness, is changeless; it has no parts; it is eternal, always existing; and it is entirely passive. Anything which changes or involves activity is not *purusha*. Human thought and human experience is constantly changing, so it cannot be *purusha*. Ordinary daily mental activity belongs to the realm of changing matter, *prakriti*, not in the realm of *purusha*. *Purusha* is separate from and independent of *prakriti*. *Prakriti* accounts for all that we experience, the empirical world of active matter. On the other hand, *purusha* accounts for the intelligence and awareness and purposes we know exists in the world.

Our Ignorance Has Trapped Us

According to Samkhya, the stuff of our true intelligence or mind becomes trapped in *prakriti*. Consciousness is clouded so that we are unable to realize our true nature, which is *purusha*. It is human ignorance which (a) confuses ordinary active mind, ordinary consciousness with the pure consciousness of *purusha* and (b) we confuse *purusha* with *prakriti*, and (c) we mistakenly believe that our everyday experience is ultimate reality. Our physically active minds are turbulent, confused, disturbed, ignorant, distracted. We are ignorant of the fact that our true nature is pure passive *purusha*, not ordinary waking consciousness. We ignorantly think we are just varying states of *prakriti*. Our true nature is neither our temporary physical body nor our constantly-changing states of mind, but we do not realize this.

The Goal of Samkhya

The goal of the Samkhya school: use wisdom to release our own individual *purusha* from the prison of *prakriti*. This is not the Vedanta goal of realizing identity of self and the non-dual divine. The goal of Samkhya is **not** to realize the identity of *purusha* and *praktiti*. The goal is to liberate the true self (*purusha*) from *praktiti*. The goal is to separate *purusha* from *praktiti*.

The method or technique to accomplish this is to bring the active worldly *prakriti* mind to rest, and then one can behold one's true nature apart from the animated whirling physical world. The true self remains forever tranquil, serene, and apart. This puts an end to suffering, for the true self no longer confused with the empirical self/body, which is *prakriti*. This is a state of eternal bliss.

Samkhya is Pluralistic, Dualistic, and Non-Theistic

In Samkhya, there are an infinite number of selves or *purushas*, each eternally distinct from the others and eternally distinct from active changing matter, *prakriti*.[28] Thus Samkhya is *pluralistic* (the number of selves is many, is

---

[27] Note that for Yoga, it is the *deva* Isvara that pushes everything out of balance.

[28] Hopkins, *The Hindu Religious Tradition*, p. 68.

plural). Liberation of each *purusha* is brought about by mental discipline; there is no need for a special agency by some divinity to do this. Salvation is not a gift from a god. The *devas* play no role in Samkhya When *moksa* liberation occurs, *prakriti* remains but the *purusha* is free from its effects. *Purusha* is plural, is many, not one. However, there are just two basic principles of reality: *purusha* and *prakriti*. Reality is not one, it is two, it is *dual*.

4.11 YOGA: A DIFFERENT FORM OF THE *Jnana-marga*

Yoga could be described as the attainment of liberation from the endless cycle of birth and death (*moksa*) by disciplined activity, including liberating knowledge. Thus it belongs to the *jnana-marga* traditions. It is also a working out of the implications of the Samkhya philosophical positions.

Yoga is taught in many places in the West. In general Western Yoga teachers stress using breathing, concentration, and movement to create balance and strength in body, mind, and spirit. Yoga is treated as a sort of physical culture involving bodily postures, breathing techniques, and stretching exercises, all of which are intended to improve health and physical and mental well-being. It is pretty obvious that people in normal health will benefit from such sensible health measures. Some aspects of Yoga have been related to Western Christian religions as well.[29]

This physical exercise aspect of Yoga is known as *hatha yoga*, the Yoga of physical postures and physical exercises, but this is only a small part of the Indian philosophical and religious system of Yoga.[30] As we shall see, modern postural yoga is a very recent phenomenon. In ancient India, Yoga was not just physical exercises and breath control. It was a genuine alternative monotheistic religious tradition with a metaphysical view of the nature of reality and a search for the sacred ultimate. In fact, that monotheistic metaphysical view of early Yoga does not seem derived from the Vedic world view described in the previous chapter. Its origins might be traced from somewhere else.

Yoga and Supernatural Powers

Some techniques of Yoga stress the development of mental skills. In India, this form is known as *raja yoga*. Practitioners of Yoga are sometimes thought to be able to develop special paranormal mental powers, such as the ability to read another's mind, or fly through the air, to stop their heartbeat, to walk through walls, or levitate things using only mental powers. These sorts of paranormal powers are referred to as *siddhis* in Sanskrit. Although popular, not all people in India accept these sorts of claims. In his *Practical Lessons of Yoga*, Swami Sivananda writes, "There is no such thing as miracle or Siddhi."[31] However, many within the tradition do accept the existence of *siddhis*. The sage Vasu accepts the existence of powers, but argues that the genuine student of Yoga will not seek these *siddhis*.

Siddhis are no ambition of their [the true yogi] souls; they do not court them; nor are they elated if they produce some phenomena now and then. Their eyes are bent upon *moksha* ; these students of Yoga do not tarry in their course to pick up these baubles of Siddhis.[32]

---

[29] There are many books on this topic. For example, Dechanet, *Christian Yoga*; Goswami, *Jesus Christ and Yoga*; Graham, *Zen Catholicism*.

[30] Western misconceptions of Yoga are described most interestingly in Troy Organ, *Hindu Quest for the Perfection of Man*, p. 298ff.

[31] *Ibid.*, p. 300

[32] *Loc cit.*

CHAPTER 4: THE WISDOM TRADITIONS

Most westerners adopt yoga exercises without being bothered by its overtly religious metaphysics. Some Western people have studied these physical exercises and then call themselves teachers of Yoga. The problem is that the religious tradition of Yoga is much broader than physical exercises.[33]

The Religious Tradition of Yoga

The ancient origins of Yoga are difficult to ascertain. It has much in common with the Samkhya tradition, but also there are differences. Unlike atheistic Samkhya, Yoga is monotheistic, with the *deva* Ishvara as the one supreme divinity, the force which ultimately disrupts the harmony of the three tendencies discussed in Samkhya.

The early *Upanishads* seem to make references to yoga practices and techniques, and Buddhist texts from the fifth century B.C.E. also describe people who seem to be practicing something similar to what we know as Yoga. The first textual evidence for a religious school of Yoga is found in a volume entitled the *Yoga sutra*, or the *Patanjala-sutra*. The author of this text is a sage named Patanjali.[34] Scholars assign a date of somewhere near the end of the fifth century C.E. for this Patanjali.[35]

Yoga is a *jnana* system which attempts to eliminate the ignorance wherein what is the true self (*purusha*) has been confused with what is not the true self (*prakriti*). Ending this ignorance puts an end to all suffering, for the true self no longer confuses itself with the empirical self and the physical body which suffers. Yoga constitutes techniques for separating the true self from what is not the true self, and replacing it with a state of pure consciousness. This is *moksha*, this is liberation from the cycle of *samsara*, and is a state of eternal bliss.

The German scholar G. W. Briggs summarized Yoga as follows:
Yoga finds its classical expression in the Sutras of Patanjali, written somewhere between A.D. 300 and 500. The author was a compiler, a systematizer, rather than an original thinker. While the Sutras may be interested in speculation as such, still, they are based upon methods of action, disciplined actions, with their concomitant supernatural powers associated with self-hypnotism and the like. The superior powers of the Yogi are simply those of attaining the highest goal, release; such powers *as such* being viewed as unworthy of the struggle.
The aims of yoga, in Patanjali's sense, may be spoken of as controls of various kinds, a graded series of disciplines, directed towards steadying the mind; gradually advancing stages of rigid control of body and mind; the stoppage of all movement and all thought—that the soul be absorbed in itself, losing the sense of duality, of subject and object; immediate perception; ultimately, prolonged, fixed attention to the point where the mental processes are stopped absolutely.
But there is ancillary to the mental discipline, a long period of preparatory action, organized according to a well-developed, progressive plan. In the preliminary stages of the preparation for the fixing of the attention, there are purifying processes to be carried out, first with stress laid upon

---

[33] For more about contemporary Yoga in India see Joseph S. Alter, *Yoga in Modern India: The Body Between Science and Philosophy* (New York: Princeton University Press, 2004). There are many other valuable books on this topic. See the remarks in footnote on page 95, later in this chapter.

[34] There was more than one Patanjali in Indian history. We must be careful not to confuse them. There was a celebrated grammarian named Patanjali, belonging to the second century B.C.E., but the Patanjali who wrote the Yoga sutras lived much later, in the fifth or sixth century C.E.

[35] Hiriyanna, *Outlines of Indian Philosophy* (London: George Allen & Unwin, 1932), page 270.

external means, then, after these have been mastered, with recourse to the internal controls.[36]

Most commonly the term "yoga" is used simply to mean "technique" or "method" as in the "method of meditation" for *dhyana-yoga*. The Sanskrit scholar Hiriyanna interprets "yoga" as "shaking off the yoke of matter [from the Self]."[37] Some gloss "yoga" as "union," but that is not the understanding of the *Yoga sutra*. In Patanjali, Yoga does not mean "union" but rather "effort," "exertion," or "strenuous behavior."[38]

The Yoga helps us to reach a higher level of consciousness, through a transformation of the psychic organism, which enables it to get beyond the limits set to ordinary human experience. We discern in the Yoga those cardinal conceptions of Hindu thought, such as the supremacy of the psychic over the physical, the exaltation of silence and solitude, meditation and ecstasy, and the indifference to outer conditions, which make the traditional Hindu attitude to life appear so strange and fantastic to the modern mind.[39]

The Special Goal of Yoga.

As we have already seen, the goal in the Advaita Vedanta school of Shankara, based on the *Upanishads*, is union of the *atman* with Brahman, but in Yoga, the goal is not union, but rather separation of *purusha* from matter, from *prakriti*. The goal of liberation is dis-union, not union.[40] Concepts of *atman* and *Brahman* are not used in the earliest forms of Yoga.[41]

Yoga is Dualistic and Pluralistic

Like the Samkhya position discussed previously, the metaphysical position of Yoga is grounded in absolute and ultimate duality. In both Samkhya and Yoga, reality is dual, made up of two ultimate principles, *purusha* and *prakriti*. *Purusha* is the true self, different from the everyday ordinary conscious mind, and the *purusha* of each of us is separate and distinct from every other *purusha*. There are an infinite number of *purusha*. Thus the position is pluralistic. Pluralism is very much unlike Advaita Vedanta, which asserts that *atman* and Brahman are not-two, are non-dual. Vedanta is non-dualism or perhaps monism, but not pluralism.

Prakriti is everything that is not eternal unchanging true self. *Prakriti* includes the physical stuff of the world, but also the animated consciousness typical of our ordinary mental lives. *Prakriti* is matter and all modifications of matter including our active mind. Our physical body and our empirical personality and empirical consciousness belong to the realm of *prakriti*. One's *purusha* is trapped in the realm of *prakriti*, but it is unaffected by *prakriti*. Yoga accepts this dualistic view.

The goal of Yoga is liberation, but this is to liberate *purusha* from the restraint of *prakriti*. We have confused

---

[36] Translated from the 1938 German book and included in David Snellgrove, *Indo-Tibetan Buddhism* (Boston: Shambhala, 2002), pp. 124–125.

[37] M. Hiriyanna, *Outlines of Indian Philosophy*, p. 295.

[38] Radhakrishnan, *Indian Philosophies*, vol. 2 (New York: Macmillan and Company, 1958), p. 337

[39] *Ibid.*

[40] M. Hiriyanna, *Essentials of Indian Philosophy* (London: Unwin Paperbacks, 1978), p. 122.

[41] As was mentioned previously, there is little discussion of Brahman and *atman* in Samkhya literature and Yoga until perhaps the fourteenth century C.E.

our true self (*purusha*) with our empirical personality, we believe that we are young, old, healthy, ill, male, female, wealthy, or poor. We confuse our true *purusha* self with the ideas, feelings, beliefs, sensations and contents of our everyday minds (*citta*). We think that the pains and misery of our life are really affecting us, and we suffer as a result. Liberation or *moksha* is the release of *purusa* from *prakriti* by eliminating this misunderstanding, and this is achieved by the mental discipline of yoga. Practice of yoga leads to the restraint of the senses and the mind, which leads to the ultimate attainment of pure consciousness.

Samadhi

In the Yoga school, the term for this perfect state of liberation, of pure consciousness, is *samadhi*. In *samadhi*, the Yogin (expert practitioner of Yoga) stops all mental activity, becomes oblivious of the world and even oblivious of his or her own existence as an empirical individual. All operations of the internal mind-stuff ceases, empirical consciousness vanishes completely, leaving the *purusha* apart and alone. In Patanjali's system, Yoga is very precisely defined as *citta-vrtti-nirodha*, literally translated as the "cessation of all mental functioning," or "suppression of the modifications of the mind (*citta*)."[42] The empirical consciousness has been brought to a halt.

The goal is a state of pure consciousness in *samadhi*, undisturbed by psycho-mental processes or by any object of awareness. This is the purified consciousness of the self (the *purusa* in Patanjali's terminology), freed of the influence of the *gunas* [three empirical modifications of up, down, and neutral] of *Prakriti*. It can be reached only by controlling and finally suppressing altogether the modifications of *Prakriti* that constitute mental activity.[43]

Yoga attempts to eliminate the ignorance wherein *purusha* is confused with *prakriti*. Ending this ignorance puts an end to all suffering, for the true self no longer confuses itself with the empirical self and the physical body (*prakriti*). The empirical self and the physical body may continue to suffer, but we no longer confuse that with our true self. This is liberation, this is *moksha*, this is a state of eternal bliss.

The techniques to achieve this involves moral behavior, seated postures, and breathing exercises, sometimes involving the recitation of the mantra, *Om*. It also involves removing the senses from the world and focusing one's mental powers inwardly. Then there is steadying the power of attention so one can focus for extended periods of time on any chosen object. We can recognize this focused concentration as deep and powerful meditation, called *dhyana*.

THE EIGHT LIMBS (TECHNIQUES) OF YOGA

In India, Yoga is associated with the Eight Limbs, which are eight techniques for deconditioning the self of consciousness associated with the physical body and empirical mind (both of which are *prakriti*) and replacing ordinary consciousness with pure awareness without content, the true self, *purusha*. The techniques constituting the Eight Limbs are like a ladder, with each succeeding step based on the solid foundation of prior steps. The Eight Limbs can be broken down into the two groups of morality and meditation.

Item 1: Five Moral restraints

The first limb of Yoga is morality. Moral requirements begin with avoiding bad conduct, curbing the ego and calming the mind by selfless performance of duty. In addition one must begin cultivation of the five ethical virtues. The most important virtue is non-harm or non-injury (*ahimsa*), commonly rendered non-violence. In addition to non-

---

[42] Thomas Hopkins, *Hindu Religious Tradition*, p. 67–68.

[43] *Ibid.*

harm, one should cultivate truthfulness in speech, honesty and sexual celibacy or sexual restraint. Sexual behavior is not considered immoral or wrong in Indian thought. Sexuality is appropriate for a householder. But one is beginning a new phase in life. One has now chosen to enter a new realm where spouse and family are no longer relevant. One is now pursuing a solitary life of mind and meditation, so we must give up the pleasures of family and marriage. Now it is time to channel one's sexual energies solely towards liberation, towards *moksha*. Sexual desire is a very powerful form of bondage to the physical realm of *prakriti*, so celibacy is the path followed by the Yogin.

In addition it was believed that the loss of male semen was like the loss of blood, a loss of essential psychic energy, and instead followers of Yoga wanted to take the sexual energy of the semen and redirect it, to draw it up the spine to the brain producing a spiritual ecstacy. Finally, the Yogin cultivates eliminating the desire to possess anything, practicing non-grasping, disowning possessions. The Yogin's needs are very few. The Yogin begs for his or her meals, eats whatever is offered, and sleeps wherever he is, in the forest, under the trees.

Item 2: Five Spiritual Observances

The second limb of spiritual observations are concerned with purity and rites of purification. Purity includes cleanliness of body and diet. All forms of pollution (social or ritual) must be avoided scrupulously. Ritual purification must be used to de-contaminate.

In addition, the mind must be purified. The student must develop contentment, or satisfaction with whatever life provides. The student will practice asceticism and develop a sense of austerity, and develop powers of self-denial and endurance. It is also required that the student study religious texts and doctrines under the guidance of a *guru*, especially the Vedas, *Upanishads*, and texts on Yoga. One must devote oneself to the supreme *deva* Ishvara, and devote oneself to one's *guru* as though he were a god.

The first two limbs of Yoga constitute the morality group, and provide the absolutely necessary foundation upon which the remainder of yogic training rests, if it is to be successful. The remaining six limbs constitute the discipline component of Yoga, specifically cultivating the power of focused mental concentration.

Item 3: Physical Posture

Because we are trapped by the physical world, teachers of Yoga used postures designed to bring the body under control in order to free *purusha* (the true self) from the realms of physical matter and ordinary consciousness (*prakriti*). In addition, control over the physical body brings increased control over the contents of consciousness. We might note that in recent decades there have been numerous scholarly findings that a great many of the physical poses taught in Yoga classes are not as ancient as previously claimed.[44]

Item 4: Breath control

The fourth limb of Yoga focuses on breathing. The Sanskrit term for **breath**, the air entering and exiting the nostrils, is *prana*, which is the vital energy that separates life from death. Teachers of Yoga believe that proper inhalation and exhalation brings more vital energy and clears the body of impurities. Special meditative attention is

---

[44] Recent scholarship has revealed that contemporary postural Yoga in India and in the West is quite different from its earliest roots. The yoga of postures has been profoundly influenced by colonial British military physical calisthenics and exercises taught to Indian troops. Yoga postures are clearly the product of colonial and post-colonial globalization. In addition, the influence of exercises for dancers are also responsible for many new yoga postures which are popular in modern yoga. A highly regarded meticulously researched scholarly book on the subject is Mark Singleton, *Yoga Body: The Origins of Modern Posture Practice* (New York: Oxford University Press, 2010). A review of this book remarks, "as Singleton clearly and convincingly demonstrates, the physical practice of today is less than 100 years old, and it has very little to do with either Patanjali's or Krishna's teaching. Instead, it's the product of such disparate elements as British colonialist policies in India, 19th century physical health movements in Europe and India, the invention of the camera, and the reformist programs of Indian yoga teachers . . ." See also Joseph S. Alter, *Yoga in Modern India: The Body Between Science and Philosophy* (New York: Princeton University Press, 2004) and N. E. Sjoman, *The Yoga Tradition of the Mysore Palace*, 2nd ed. (Abhinav Publications, June 1999). Another valuable book is Elizabeth De Michelis, *A History of Modern Yoga* (London: Continuum, 2004).

spent on breathing slowly, and focusing on the point between inhalation and exhalation. It is the calm between the in-breath and the out-breath which reveals the deepest levels of consciousness. Finally, extending the amount of time that one can hold one's breath is an element in breath exercises.

Item 5: Withdrawal of attention from sense objects.

The goal is to free the true self, or *purusha*, from the physical world which is *prakriti*. To accomplish this, we must separate ourselves from the objects of the senses of sight, hearing, touching, tasting, and smelling, all of which are *prakriti*. The Yogin works to achieve no sensory input to consciousness, because true consciousness is independent of *prakriti* and is self-sustaining.

Item 6: Steadying the mind, developing concentration.

The true self is *purusha*, and we confuse our true self with our ordinary mind, the *prakriti* mind. The *prakriti* mind is constantly wandering, distracted. It must be slowed down. One way to accomplish this is to focus on an object, sometimes a visual object, sometimes a sound (*om*), sometimes a geometric design (*mandala*), focusing upon the breath, focusing on sacred concepts of Brahman and feminine cosmic energy (*shakti*), and sometimes focus on a *deva*. Then *purusha* can be glimpsed in its own illumination.

Item 7: Meditation on religious insights (*dhyana*)

This is concentration without utilizing the objects recommended in the sixth limb above. One uses thought to silence thought. The meditator does not use sounds, visual designs, or concepts. If human beings will meditate upon Lord Ishvara and have trust in him, then Ishvara, out of his abundant mercy which is one of his perfections, will help humans to achieve spiritual freedom.[45]

Item 8: Attainment of *samadhi*.

When control over the mind has finally been achieved, one can directly meditate upon the ultimate awareness of one's self as *purusha*. The goal is *samadhi*, which is simply the illumination of *purusha* without any content whatsoever. It is the cessation of active thinking, the cessation of ordinary changing *prakriti* consciousness. All mental activity ceases, for all mental activity is just *prakriti* and not part of the true self. All awareness is gone, all emotions and feelings are gone, all memories are gone, all sensations are gone, all subject-object knowledge is forgotten. We are free from all concepts. The mind is silent.

When *samadhi* is achieved, the Yogin becomes non-responsive to the world and unaware of his or her own existence as an individual. Plurality and multiplicity are no longer related to the self. The ultimate attainment is the cessation of all mental functions.[46] When all mind activity stops, *purusha* stands apart and alone. The follower of Yoga who achieves this has achieved liberation from *samsara* in this very life with only a small amount of physical energy acting as an anchor, connecting him or her to the world of *prakriti*. When this life ends, the Yogin attains the final goal of Yoga; this is ultimate *moksha*. The Yogin will never be reborn again.

In later centuries, the practice of Yoga was brought into accord with the teachings of the *Upanishads*, and so followers of Yoga can be described as having achieved the state of identity with Brahman. The mind freed from concepts becomes non-dual, undivided from itself and undivided from the sacred ultimate.

4.12 SUMMARY OF THE CHAPTER

---

[45] Hiriyanna, *Essentials of Indian Philosophy*, p. 126.

[46] Chatterjee & Datta, *Introduction to Indian Philosophy*, p. 43

CHAPTER 4: THE WISDOM TRADITIONS

The path of liberating insight or wisdom (*jnana-marga*) is an ancient tradition in India. The wisdom pathway is one of four *margas* which include wisdom, meditation, devotion, and action (ritual action, social duty).

Over many centuries religious concepts of *karma* and *samsara* developed, although these ideas are not found in the earliest verses of the Vedas. Karmic actions generate energy that results in consequences similar to the original action. Good actions produce good karmic consequences for the doer, including a better life in one's next reincarnation. Evil actions produce similar evil consequences to the doer. The unwelcome consequence of these ideas is that karmic energy pushes us from one life to the next, endlessly. The next life may be a better one than this one, if we do our social duties properly, but it is only temporary.

For some spiritual seekers, a better life in the next life-cycle is not enough. Those Hindus seek eternal bliss, they seek a true self freed from the apparently endless cycle of *samsara*, the cycle of birth and death. The goal of the wisdom systems is *moksha*, or liberation from the cycle of *samsara*. Most forms of *jnana-marga* are grounded in the *Upanishads*, the fourth and last collection of texts which make up the Vedas.

One of the most influential of the *jnana-marga* systems is Non-dualistic Vedanta (Advaita Vedanta) as worked out by the eighth century sage, Adi Shankara. Shankara took the central insights of several *Upanishads* and using those, he taught the ultimate identity of the *atman* (self-existent true self) and Brahman (the sacred ultimate source of all). *Atman* and Brahman are non-dual, are "not-two." Shankara analyzed knowledge and concluded that what we think of as "reality" is actually just appearance, it is *maya* (illusory), it is less real than Brahman. Any time our experience is of anything other than unchanging eternal unity, then we are experiencing *maya*. A deeper level of knowledge is achievable, in which Brahman is realized as one, eternal, and unchanging. When we experience Brahman, ignorance is eliminated and we have achieved *moksha*, where the illusion of a separate self is dissolved, and all that exists is the one eternal unchanging *atman* which is identical with Brahman.

An ancient *jnana* tradition of India is the Samkhya school, which seems not to be connected historically to the teachings and insights of the Vedic Aryan religions. The Samkhya tradition is non-theistic. Samkhya pays no attention to *devas*. It stresses an ultimate duality between the true self, *purusha* and the world of matter, *prakriti*. Each self is distinct from every other self, and the goal is to free the true self from the bondage of matter.

Yoga is another of the *jnana-marga* traditions. Although Yoga is monotheistic, it is a system which shares much in common with Samkhya. Using the system of Eight Limbs, Yoga attempts to eliminate the ignorance wherein what is the true self, *purusha*, has been confused with what is not the true self, *prakriti*. Ending this ignorance is achieved by stopping all mental activity, which puts an end to all suffering, for the true self no longer confuses itself with the mental activities of the empirical self and the actions of the physical body. Each individual self is ultimately separate and alone, unrelated to the physical world. Putting an end to all mental activity allowing the true self to stand illuminated by its own illumination, is *moksha*, this is a state of eternal bliss.

4.13 TECHNICAL TERMS

advaita	Literally, "not-two" usually translated "Non-dual." Advaita Vedanta is one of the major Vedanta traditions, this one founded by Shankara
ahimsa	Non-hurting, non-violence. Do no harm.
ananda	Pure Bliss, a description of Brahman.
Aranyakas	The forest books of those who began to practice internal rehersal of rituals, in an attempt to understand the nature of ultimate reality.
ashrama	In contemporary times this refers to a spiritual community, but in the past this referred to the Four Stages of life or "stages of spiritual effort" as explained in the *Manava-dharma-shastra*.
atman	The eternal unchanging True Self which moves from lifetime to lifetime trapped in the cycle of birth and death.

CHAPTER 4: THE WISDOM TRADITIONS

bhakti	Loving devotion to a deva.
Brahma	The creator *deva*; one of the divine trinity of *devas*.
Brahman	The term of power which names the impersonal sacred ultimate source of all that exists, even the source of the *devas*.
Brahmins	The social group made up of priests who specialize in religious ritual
Brahmanas	Vedic books which provide instructions to apprentice priests on how to perform the fire sacrifice.
cit	Pure Consciousness, a description of Brahman (pronounced "chit").
citta	The empirical consciousness which is made of matter, or *prakriti*, and according to the Yoga and Samkhya traditions, we confuse *citta* (pronounced "chee-ta") with our true Self, *purusha*.
devas	spirits, gods, divinities, forces, powers
dhyana	Focused concentration, deep meditation
gunas	The three aspects of ultimate matter, *prakriti*. Applied to humans, pleasure, pain, and indifference constitute the three *gunas*.
guru	A spiritual teacher who is supposed to have deep insight into the nature of reality, and the ability to guide others to similar deep insight.
Ishvara	An important god or *deva*, especially important to the tradition of Yoga
jnana	The liberating knowledge, wisdom or insight (pronounced NYA-na) which frees us from *samsara*
jnana-marga	The pathway of liberating insight
jnana-yoga	The technique or method of liberating insight
karma	The term means "action" and can be (1) ritual action, or (2) the actions which generate a moral effect, providing the energy that propels us from one life to the next.
karma-marga	The pathway of ritual action, the dominant Aryan religious practice in the earliest times.
mantra	words and phrases which contain power and have secret correspondences with our world and divine realms as well. *Om* (pronounced "ah-uu-mm") is a famous mantra.
maya	The veil of illusion that obscures the Oneness of ultimate reality and makes it appear to be multiple, thereby causing misery.
nirguna Brahman	Brahman as it is, the ultimate reality to which no human concepts can apply; Brahman without qualities.
sadhu	The term *sadhu* ("good man") is applied to religious wanderers, whether they are learned scholars, wanderers reciting the name of their god over and over, or psychologically disturbed individuals.
saguna Brahman	Brahman as understood by minds still trapped in concepts, so this is Brahman with qualities
samsara	The cycle of continuing birth and death in which our *atman* is trapped
sat	Pure Existence, a characteristic of Brahman (pronounced "sut").
sannyasin	The fourth ascetic stage of the four *ashrama*.
sannyasi	The ascetic who is in the forest seeking liberation
Shankara	The founder of the Advaita (Non-dual) tradition of Vedanta, who lived approximately 788-820.
sramanas	People who have rejected the comforts of society for religious reasons, and have chosen to live in the forests, in an attempt to find the ultimate meaning of life

CHAPTER 4: THE WISDOM TRADITIONS

tat tvam asi	"That thou art," or "that is what you are." This famous phrase from the *Upanishads* indicates the liberating insight that "that" (Brahman) "is what you are," that Brahman is identical with *atman*.
Upanishads	The sacred books of forest monks which offer the liberating insights which can free humans from the cycle of *samsara*, birth and rebirth.
yoga	the word "yoga" is related to the English word "yoke" and might be interpreted as "shaking off the yoke of matter [from the true self]." "Yoga" can mean "technique" or "method." Some gloss "yoga" as "union." In the *Yoga sutra* of Patanjali, yoga means "effort," "exertion," or "strenuous behavior."
Yoga	the *jnana* tradition which teaches how to achieve moksha by separating the true self (*purusha*) from all of empirical reality (*praktiti*).
Yogin	A serious practitioner of Yoga, usually one who lives as a forest monk
Yogini	A serious practitioner of Yoga who is female.

4.14 QUESTIONS FOR FURTHER DISCUSSION

1) Some people in the West will quote the Christian Bible to the effect that "as you sow, so shall you reap." Is this the same thing as the Indian concept of karma? What differences can you find?

2) We have seen that a key problem for Indian religion is how to free the immortal soul from the trap of reincarnation. The concept of reincarnation was known by the Greeks (Plato) and early Christian church. Is there any equivalent problem for Western religions? Is the soul trapped in any sense? Does the soul need to be freed?

3) The idea that some special and sacred words are powerful is not unique to Indian thought. In the West followers are advised not to take the name of the Lord in vain, and some people write the word "god" as "g_d" because the word is thought to be too sacred and should not be uttered by ordinary mortals. Some believe that the name of god, YHWH, should never be pronounced aloud by anyone except the high priest. Magicians must wave a wand and say the magic words "abra kadabra" in order to make the rabbit pop out of the hat. Are there any other examples of sounds that are especially powerful? Are vulgar words especially powerful? Have you ever heard of someone saying "Gol durn it"? Discuss.

4) There does seem to be a concept in the West of sacred and powerful knowledge which is too dangerous to share with ordinary people. Many of the early translators of the Bible were condemned to death by church authorities for daring to translate the sacred Greek text into common English, French, or German. Does Hindu esoteric wisdom have anything in common with the earlier Western religious prohibition on translating the Christian bible into ordinary languages spoken by everyday people?

5) It is interesting that the major Western religions insist upon the absolute separation and difference of humans and god, whereas the *Upanishads* insist that, in their essence, humans and god are not two different things. Why aren't followers of the *Upanishads* more ego-centered, if they believe they are divine?

99

6)   The Samkhya religious tradition finds no use for any god or gods, yet it sits firmly within the Indian religious world view. If one assumes that all religions must accept a god, then Samkhya would not be a religion. However, Samkhya is one of several non-Western religions for whom deities are irrelevant, and this suggests that it is a mistake to assume that a divinity is necessary for religion. Are there any forms of Western religions which minimize gods? Some Christians seem to believe that there is a religion they call "secular humanism."

7)   How authentic is the Yoga tradition in the West which places stress upon postures, stretching, diet, and breathing exercises? Do such practices automatically lead to the religious ideas of monotheistic Yoga, or can they be separated?

8)   Explain the goal of *samadhi* in Yoga. To the Western mind, it sometimes seems indistinguishable from coma or death. What is it about *samadhi* that followers of Yoga find so valuable?

9)   What are the central techniques of Yoga which lead to *samadhi*?

10)   In Vedanta of Shankara, the only thing that can be truly said of Brahman is *sat*, *cit*, and *ananda*. What do these mean and why are these the only accurate description of Brahman?

11)   Shankara's analysis provides four kinds of knowledge, and four sorts of levels of reality which are known. Explain each of these four kinds of knowledge and four levels of reality which correspond to them, and explain why Shankara thought it was valuable to make such distinctions. What was the point?

12)   The Hindu traditions insist that the *atman* is eternal and unchanging, but in the world we inhabit daily, there is only change. If the *atman* never changes, then the *atman* will have no memories of this world or this life (because memories require changes). So then, what is the value of liberation if no memories of this world endure? How would Shankara answer this?

13)   Do some research. Are there any Vedanta temples in your area? You might consider visiting such a temple and asking questions to help you understand the modern teachings of Vedanta. Are the teachers from India, or were they born in the West? Should this make any difference?

14)   There are many Yoga centers in the West, but the majority put stress on the physical body and stretching and breathing exercises. You might want to compare contemporary Western Yoga with the roots of monotheistic Yoga in the past. Do any Western yoga teachers claim to have achieved liberation in this very body by stopping the mind of *prakriti*?

15)   There are recordings of Brahmans reciting and chanting verses from the Vedas. You might want to visit a library or go on-line to see if you can hear these sacred sounds for yourself. What is your reaction to these chants?

A SELECTED BIBLIOGRAPHY

Primary Sources

de Bary, William T., ed., *Sources of Indian Tradition*, 2nd edition, 2 volumes (New York: Columbia University Press, 1988).

CHAPTER 4: THE WISDOM TRADITIONS

Deutsch, Eliot, and Rohit Dalvi, *The Essential Vedanta: A New Source Book of Advaita Vedanta* (World Wisdom, 2004)

Easwaran, Eknath & Barbara S. Miller, *Bhagavad Gita* (New York: Random House, 2000)

Eliade, Mircea, *Yoga: Immortality and Freedom*

Flood, Gavin & Charles Martin, trans., *Bhagavad Gita: A New Translation* (New York: W. W. Norton, 2013)

Hopkins, Thomas J., *The Hindu Religious Tradition* (Belmont, Ca: Wadsworth, 1971)

Koller, John and Patricia, *Sourcebook in Asian Philosophy* (New York: Macmillan, 1991)

Mascaro, Juan, *The Bhagavad Gita* (New York: Penguin Classics, 19)

Miles, Jack, and Wendy Doniger, *Hinduism* (New York: Norton, 2015)
     This Norton Anthology of World Religions volume is an excellent collection of original sources.

Olivelle, Patrick, trans., *Upanisads* (New York: Oxford, 2008)

Radhakrishnan, Sarvepalli, *The Principal Upanishads* (Boston: Unwin Hyman, 1989)

Roebuck, Valerie J., *The Upanishads* (New York: Penguin Classics,   )

Thibaut, George, *The Vedanta-Sutras with the Commentary by Sankaracarya* (Qontro Classic Books, 2010)

Wyatt, Thomas & Juan Mascaro, ed., *Upanishads* (New York: Penguin, 1965)

Studies of Hindu Wisdom Traditions

Adiswarananda, Swami, *The Four Yogas: A Guide to the Spiritual Paths of Action, Devotion, Meditation and Knowledge* (N.Y.: Skylight Paths, 2007)

Adiswarananda, Swami, *The Spiritual Quest and the Way of Yoga* (N.Y.: Skylight Paths, 2005)

Adiswarananda, Swami, *The Vedanta Way to Peace and Happiness* (Skylight Paths, 2007)

Alter, Joseph S., *Yoga in Modern India: The Body Between Science and Philosophy* (New York: Princeton University Press, 2004)

Bilimora, P., Joseph Prabhu and Renuka Sharma, *Indian Ethics* (Burlington, Vt: Ashgate, 2005)

Chatterjee, Satischandra, and Dhirendramohan Datta, *An Introduction to Indian Philosophy* (Calcutta: University of Calcutta, 1968)

Dayananda, Swami, *Introduction to Vedanta* (Orient Paperbacks, 1998)

De Michelis, Elizabeth, *A History of Modern Yoga* (London: Continuum, 2004)

Deutsch, Eliot, *Advaita Vedanta: A Philosophical Reconstruction* (Honolulu: University of Hawai'i Press, 1980)

Eck, Diana, *Darsan: Seeing the Divine Image in India* (New York: Columbia University Press, 1998)

Easwaran, Eknath & Barbara S. Miller, *Bhagavad Gita* (New York: Random House, 2000)

Eliade, Mircea, *Yoga: Immortality and Freedom* (   )

Flood, Gavin & Charles Martin, trans., *Bhagavad Gita: A New Translation* (New York: W. W. Norton, 2013)

Hawley, Jack, *Bhagavad Gita: A Walkthrough for Westerners* (New York: New World Library, 2011)

Hopkins, Thomas J., *The Hindu Religious Tradition* (Belmont, Ca: Wadsworth, 1971)

Grimes, John, *A Concise Dictionary of Indian Philosophy* (Albany, NY: State University of New York Press, 1996)

Halbfass, Wilhelm, *Tradition and Reflection: Explorations in Indian Thought* (Albany, NY: State University of New York Press, 1991)

Herman, A. L., *Brief Introduction to Hinduism* (Boulder, CO: Westview Press, 1991)

Hirayanna, M., *Essentials of Indian Philosophy* (London: Unwin, 1978)

Hirayanna, M., *Outlines of Indian Philosophy* (London: Allen & Unwin, 1970)

Keyes, Charles F. and E. Valentine Daniel, eds., *Karma: An Anthropological Inquiry* (Berkeley: University of California Press, 1983).

Knott, Kim, *Hinduism: A Very Short Introduction* (London: Oxford, 2000)

Koller, John, *The Indian Way: An Introduction to the Philosophies and Religions of India*, 2nd edition (New York: Prentice Hall, 20005)

Koller, John and Patricia, *Sourcebook in Asian Philosophy* (New York: Macmillan, 1991)

Malhotra, Ashok Kumar, *An Introduction to Yoga Philosophy: An Annotated Translation of the Yoga Sutras* (Burlington, Vt.: Ashgate Publishing, 2001)

Michaels, Axel, *Hinduism: Past and Present* (Princeton, NJ: Princeton Press, 2003)

Mohanty, J. N., *Classical Indian Philosophy* (Lanham, MD: Rowman and Little, 2000)

Moore, Charles A., *The Indian Mind: Essentials of Indian Philosophy and Culture* (Honolulu, HI: University of Hawai'i Press, 1967)

Panikkar, Raimundo, *The Vedic Experience: Mantramanjari* (Los Angeles: The University of California Press, 1977)

Potter, Karl H., *Guide to Indian Philosophy* (Boston: G. K. Hall, 1988) An extensive bibliography.

Potter, Karl H., ed., *The Encyclopedia of Indian Philosophies* (Princeton, NJ: Princeton University Press, 1961-2015)

Radhakrishnan, Sarvepalli, *Indian Philosophy*, 2 volumes (London: Allen and Unwin, 1923)

Roebuck, Valerie J., *The Upanishads* (New York: Penguin Classics,)

Shattuck, Cybelle, *Hinduism* (New York: Prentiss-Hall, 1999)

Sharma, I. C., *Ethical Philosophies of India* (Lincoln, Neb: Johnsen Publishing Co., 1965)

Singleton, Mark, *Yoga Body: The Origins of Modern Posture Practice* (New York: Oxford University Press, 2010)

Sjoman, N. E., *The Yoga Tradition of the Mysore Palace*, 2nd ed. (Abhinav Publications, June 1999)

Studholme, Alexander, *The Origins of Om Manipadme Hum: A Study of the Karandavyuha Sutra* (SUNY Press, 2002)

Thibaut, George, *The Vedanta-Sutras with the Commentary by Sankaracarya* (Qontro Classic Books, 2010)

Torwestern, Hans, and Loly Rosset (adapter), *Vedanta: The Heart of Hinduism* (N.Y.: Grove Press, 1994)

Wyatt, Thomas & Juan Mascaro, ed., *Upanishads* (New York: Penguin, 1965)

Vajraprana, Pravajika, *Vedanta: A Simple Introduction* (Vedanta Press, 1999). The author is a Western nun writing for Westerners.

CHAPTER 5: THE PATHWAY OF DEVOTION

5.1 OVERVIEW OF THE CHAPTER

Devotion to and love for various Hindu deities has been the dominant form of religion in India for at least two thousand years. Loving devotion directed to divine beings (*devas*) who can return that love is clearly existent by the second century C.E., and sets the tone for later Hinduism and the great Hindu religious texts, including the later *Upanishads* and the classic text, the *Bhagavad Gita*. The devotional religions are rooted in the unconditional and unrestrained love of the great *devas* of salvation, who include such deities as Vishnu, Krishna, and Shiva. It is during this early period that the ancient divinities acquire much of the imagery and symbols that will be associated with them in later times.

After 400 C.E., traditional rituals of Vedic religion had been pretty well assimilated into popular devotional traditions. From the fifth century of the common era on, devotion to deities is everywhere in India: it is an age of statues, temples, pageantry, brilliant colors, sacred dance, sacred music, pilgrimage, and prayer. The path of devotion, faith, total surrender of the follower of the will of God for the love of God, comes to dominate Hindu thought. The worship of a large number of goddesses also becomes important. Many goddesses are incorporated into Vedic religion by treating them as the *Shaktis*, the feminine aspect of or consort of Shiva, including Uma, Durga, Parvati and Kali among others. The devotional pathway is an intensely personal approach to the sacred ultimate reality. Even the wisdom pathway of Advaita Vedanta modulates into a version which offered a devotional reconceptualization of the relationship between the true self and the sacred ultimate.

The core belief is that various *deva* will extend their loving kindness to human beings, in return for the worshiper's unselfish love and devotion to the deity. The goal of the *bhakti* pathway is a long life, health, wealth, sons, and then rebirth in heavens. The pathway includes praising the relevant *deva* by their names, their forms, their actions, and even their friends. This ideal of unselfish love and devotion directed towards one's special *deva* has become the most significant form of Hindu religion throughout the centuries including the twenty-first century.

Although we will make many artificial distinctions in this chapter, trying to separate out one strand of Hinduism from another, be aware that the actual lines are much more blurred than one might think. As indicated before, Asian religions are not exclusive the way Western religions are. It is quite common for people whom we might categorize as belonging to one Asian religion to revere or worship the gods that we associate with an entirely different strand.[1] Although Buddhists are supposed to worship Buddhas, and Hindus worship Hindu deities, in the popular religions of India, these lines were never as rigid as one might suppose. Many temples offer monks proficient in performing rituals to many spirits, and the believers are certain that paying these monks to perform these rituals will ensure wealth and success in business or in love. Monks will calculate auspicious days for weddings or for ceremonies, using astrology. Temples manufacture and sell fancy charms and amulets to ward off the black magic of the patron's competitors. It is not only Hindu gods who are prayed to and worshiped. Contemporary devotional Hinduism has long encouraged the worship of spirits, culture heroes, animals, and even snakes, and popular religion encourages this and encourages the follower's enthusiastic participation in these practices.

---

[1] As we will see in a later chapter, even today many Buddhists in Buddhist countries engage in rituals in honor of a variety of Hindu gods, in addition to a wide range of Buddhas and bodhisattvas who are indistinguishable from gods.

CHAPTER 5: THE PATHWAY OF DEVOTION

Around the sixth or seventh century C.E. in India, some secretive forms of Hindu devotional practices, called Tantric practices, begin to appear, These move into a new direction when compared to the older rituals. These Tantric ascetics sought to emulate the deity Shiva, by living their lives the same way the stories depict the life and actions of Shiva. They will focus upon spiritual discipline to attain supernatural magical powers. The Tantric rituals will combine the devotional ritual practices of the past with goddess worship but will include sexuality and sexual symbolism as tools leading to the ultimate goal of *moksha* (liberation from the cycle of birth and death). These aspects are particularly strong in Kashmir, Bengal, and Nepal. According to contemporary scholars, these wide variety of Tantric practices have been profoundly misunderstood by westerners.

As in the earlier forms of Hindu religion, Hindu devotionalism does not have any central core of elite priests who control and regulate the fundamental beliefs and practices of followers. A wide variety of different practices focused on different supernatural beings and gods (including snakes, bulls, elephants, buffalo, and cow) and all of them fit under the umbrella of Hinduism. In this respect, devotionalism is like the other pathways of Hindu religion. There is no elite core who determine what is orthodox and what is heterodox for any of the four pathways of religious practice in India: ritual, meditation, wisdom, and devotion.

5.2 A BIT OF HISTORY

Although in the first chapters of this book we discussed what little is known about the Indus Valley religion and the early Aryan forms of Hinduism, these two were not the only form of spiritual tradition in India. Buddhism (to be discussed in later chapters) had been supported by Indian royalty from about 200 B.C.E. to about 200 C.E. Hindu priests reasserted their authority around 320 C.E., when the new ruling dynasty authorized and utilized Hindu rituals that had been suppressed by the Buddhists (involving Vedic animal sacrifices such as the horse-sacrifice). Hinduism was once again the dominant political and religious system.

During this period of Brahmin dominance, the caste system was reinforced and several important developments in science occurred. Buddhist and Hindu interest in astronomy and mathematics led to the discovery of zero and the use of mathematical decimals long before they were introduced into European mathematics by Arabs who learned these ideas when they came to dominate India.

The earlier forms of priest-centered Hinduism stressing ritual, mantras, and sacrifice, were giving way to the pathway of *bhakti*. *Bhakti* is usually rendered as devotion, but it is more than that. It also includes having complete loyalty to one's *deva* with nothing held back. It includes a willingness to serve, combined with unhesitating gratitude for the opportunity and complete trust in the *deva*. The great majority of the population in India were illiterate, and because *bhakti* religion does not require the ability to read or memorize sacred scriptures or sacred words, it is an ideal form of religious practice for most followers of folk traditions. This form of religion utilizes visual aids including art, pictures, statues, and even physically tactile actions to complement oral teachings which communicate with those who cannot read or write.

For the majority of rural and village people, travel was infrequent, mostly linked to war or religious pilgrimage. The great majority of the population did not wander far from their place of birth. They lived in smaller villages and farms, and their spiritual lives were intimately connected to the local temple, local deities and the local village. For these worshipers, the sacred is pictured primarily in human form, although it also includes supernatural spirits, a variety of animals, and snakes.

For the majority of Hindus, the gods, goddesses, immortals, saviors, and angels are all essentially human, often garbed in bright colors not found in daily life. Temples filled with brilliant colors and ritual pageantry grew to become of central importance during this time.

CHAPTER 5: THE PATHWAY OF DEVOTION

5.3 THE RELIGIOUS PATHWAY OF DEVOTION

Bhakti-marga, the pathway of devotion, is also known as *bhakti-yoga*, where the term "yoga" means "method." The method of *bhakti* is the method of devotion, faith, and total surrender of the follower to the will of God for the love of God. This is not an intellectual, conceptual, literary approach to the sacred; rather it is an intensely personal approach to the sacred ultimate. The follower wants to cultivate a relationship with a divinity.

With *bhakti*, the stress is upon the subjective and personal spirit of worship, not upon specific beliefs, specific insights, or the specific actions themselves (unlike *karma yoga*, where the stress is upon rites and rituals required by the devout Hindu).[2] For some Hindus, *moksha* (liberation) can be attained by worship of a personal divinity, so this too can be the *bhakti-marga* path. The *bhakti* pathway reflects the approach of the majority of Hindus—the *jnana* (pronounced like NYA-na) path of insight and knowledge is for the minority; but the three paths of wisdom, ritual, and devotion, are clearly interrelated.

The *bhakti* followers accept the earlier ideas of *karma*, *samsara* and *moksha*, but they build upon it by claiming that Krishna, Shiva, Vishnu, Kali, Durga and other major *devas* have the power to change one's karmic destiny and will do so if one has enough faith and unselfish loving devotion, thereby making it possible to achieve *moksha* even though one has not worked through all of one's previous karmic energies. This provides a new "trap-door" to allow the worshiper to escape from the seemingly eternal cycle of birth and death (*samsara*).

The *bhakti* pathway generated a deeply emotional response from the rural farmer devotee when she or he encountered a statue decorated in bright hues, and a gleaming altar, a solemn procession with incense and drums. The emotional reaction to such sights and sounds could be quite profound. For those who follow the devotional path, the focus is upon a personal deity eternally distinct from our selves. In general, the *bhakti* follower has a religious outlook based in a duality, always a subject-object or what some Western theologians call an "I-Thou" relationship. In general the *bhakti* follower does not hope to become a deity; the follower basks in the glory of the divine, but is not equal to or identical with the creator deity. For most, the goal is rebirth in the heavenly realm presided over by one's *deva*.

With the pathway of devotion, the *bhakti-marga*, in general there is no oneness with the god or goddess. Instead of unity, there is duality. There is no possibility of communication with a deity unless the deity is separate and other. Blessings must originate from the divinity outside of one's self. The means of communication is dialogue (which includes prayer), gift-giving, ritual sacrifice and action. Humans envision the divine persons with statues; they envision temples as the home of the *devas*. Religious ceremonies become glorious ritual pageantry, awash with bright colors, sacred dances, and prayers sung to music and drumming. With these developments the more ancient public religion of Brahmin priests performing rituals for pay weakened even further. After 400 C.E., traditional Vedic ritual religion became assimilated into popular cults[3] of various *devas*.

There are so many divinities[4] that it is possible for each and every one of us to find, choose and focus on the one *deva* whose form is most appropriate for us as an individual, whose teaching is appropriate for our own level of spiritual insight, and who can become the focus of our religious life. There are numerous regional and rural divinities which are unique to only one village, and they need not be in human forms. There are disease gods, and gods who enjoy and feed upon the human pain and suffering they cause, as well as local *deva* who need to be contacted only at

---

[2] Karl Potter, *Presuppositions of India's Philosophies*, pp. 40ff

[3] A cult is a group of people who understand themselves as actively engaged in an attempt to **cultivate** a relationship with a particular *deva*.

[4] "By the classical era *purana* texts asserted the existence of 330 million deities." John Espositio, Darrell Fasching, Todd Lewis, *World Religions Today,* p. 291.

specific occasions in one's life. There are mother-goddesses, tree spirits, animal spirits, and spirits of cremation grounds.[5]

The worshiper makes offerings (*puja*) to a particular *deva*, offers selfless devotion to that *deva*, and studies the stories told about the deity so that one can have spiritual insight into the divine personality of the *deva* and ultimately surrender the worshiper's own self to the divinity. One might devote onself to any of the major Grand Tradition deities, such as Shiva, Vishnu, and Krishna, or the innumerable Little Tradition deities of trees, rivers, snakes, bulls and other animal spirits. In this chapter, we will focus on just a few of the major *devas*.[6]

In previous chapters we discussed the change in attitudes as the Indians lost hope of rites and rituals bringing about liberation (even good karma keeps one bound to the cycle of birth-and-death). As the ancient path of ritual action (*karma-marga*) lessened in importance, the four *margas* separated out, each offering a different solution to the problem of the self trapped in eternal *samsara*.

The path of liberating insight or knowledge (*jnana-marga*) was restricted to ascetic forest dwellers who had left society, and thus their pathway was secret, difficult, meditative, and often intellectual. Sometimes these ascetic beggars would engage in behavior that was shocking to Hindu moral rules of social purity and contamination. In addition, the result of the wisdom path was a complete loss of the individual self. With the *jnana-marga*, there is no communication with the divine, or with departed ancestors and there is no heavenly life after death; instead the individual *atman* is swallowed in the great sea of the universal oneness or Brahman. The individual disappeared. For those whose personality gravitated toward devotion and love of a god outside of themselves, this was not a goal that they could accept.

In the older Vedas before the development of the pathway of devotion, the *devas* were human-like personifications of impersonal forces but they were not personal, and did not care about us as individuals. Even for those who lived in rural areas, the majority of *devas* were local to one's community. If something catastrophic happened to a community, it must have been because some divinity was annoyed. Vedic religion was not monotheistic; the numerous *devas* were limited in power and function, and inhabited only a part of the three realms which constitute reality (earth, sky, heavens). Even Indra and Vishnu, the two greatest of the *devas* in the early period, controlled only a part of reality.

In the developing *bhakti-marga*, several of the older Vedic gods faded away, and others gradually transformed and came to assume a new personal status, in some ways like the God of Christianity. However, for most Hindus the *devas* are not infinite, not the source of morality, and do not transcend everything human. In fact, most often the *devas* are not so different from humans.

It is easier to feel close to a divinity when the divinity is much like us, but more beautiful, more powerful. Hindus feel awe, wonder, and admiration for these divine beings who are not so very different from humans. The *devas* are not perfect. Like the Greek and Roman gods, the Hindu gods share many human traits such as jealousy, anger, lust, and boastfulness. Some of the *deva* have wives and consorts, and others can appear in feminine forms as both gods and goddesses.

Sometime after the fourth century B.C.E., the oldest divinities began to be supplemented by a conception of a universal *deva*, comparable to the abstract Brahman, but personal. By about 500 in the common era one finds a

---

[5] For more on the early goddesses and how they influenced later Indian religion, see Sree Padma, *Vicissitudes of the Goddess: Reconstructions of the Gramadevata in India's Religious Traditions* (New York: Oxford University Press, 2013).

[6] An excellent study of the dominant divinities is Sukumari Bhattacharji, *The Indian Theogony: A Comparative Study of Indian Mythology from the Vedas to the Puranas* (Cambridge: Cambridge University Press, 1970).

pantheon of divinities which are recognized by most Hindus.[7] This is seen completely developed in the classic scripture entitled the *Bhagavad Gita*, a great religious text where a monotheistic theology is fully worked out.

Many in India resisted the Hindu caste system, including non-Hindu Buddhists, forest ascetics and the foreign dynasties which had conquered India. This weakened the Hindu social order's stability. When Buddhist power waned, the political and religious authorities again supported the caste structure, and society moved towards establishing a thoroughly Hindu social order dominated by a small minority of Brahmins. Hinduism as a political religion devoted itself to helping people to be content while living in a social order which accommodated itself very little to individual's desires and personal needs. As part of this process, two great *bhakti* traditions come to dominate Indian religion. One involves worship and devotion to Shiva and the other worship and devotion to Vishnu.

5.4 THE HINDU TRINITY: BRAHMA, VISHNU, SHIVA

In the early centuries, there were three *devas* who provided an explanation for the universe and its functioning. **Brahma** became the *deva* who is the personification of the impersonal creative force of Brahman, the sacred ultimate. The *deva* Brahma is associated with creation, the force that brings novelty into existence, an important aspect of reality.[8]

In accordance with his role in the Vedas, **Vishnu** became the force that sustains reality. Vishnu is identified with the sun, warmth and growth, providing food and crops, as well as protecting unborn babies in the womb. Under the rule of Vishnu the universe is friendly and good, supportive of human beings. The sacred text for the followers of Vishnu is the *Bhagavad Gita*, one of the great religious scriptures of India.

In the world, there is creation, and things do persist and endure for a while. But, in our world, things also decay and are destroyed; they go out of existence. The *deva* **Shiva** became the deity who presides over destruction, the personification of destruction. In the same way that night is the destroyer of sunlit day, Shiva is the destroyer, dissolver, and ender of creation.

5.5 THE WORSHIP OF SHIVA

It might seem strange to seek a loving devotional relationship with Shiva, the *deva* who is the destroyer. After all, an essential feature of the *bhakti-marga* is the cultivation of a relationship with a personal *deva* capable of giving and receiving love. Unqualified love becomes the supreme symbol of the divine, and the locus of the human relationship with ultimate reality.[9] Similarly, it is the person who is capable of giving and receiving love who is best at worshiping a personal loving God. What God treasures most in those who love God is the spontaneous gesture of unconditional love. These features would not seem to be associated with Shiva, for Shiva is the destroyer.

Shiva is Not Mentioned in the Vedas

Vedic religion derives from the oral traditions which culminated in the various sacred Vedic scriptures. The name Shiva does not appear anywhere in the Vedas. This would seem to be a problem. How could Brahmin priests

---

[7] Bhattacharji, *The Indian Theogony*, p. 13.

[8] Brahma never developed into the center of a cult so there are no followers, no art, and no devotional literature. Brahma the divinity was absorbed into the philosophy of the impersonal Brahman. Cf. Bhattacharji, *op. cit.*, p. 15.

[9] Robert Ellwood, *Cycles of Faith*, p. 108.

encourage the worship of a god whose name is not found in their sacred literature? There is a rather standard solution to this problem, and it is found and utilized in many religious traditions. You simply discover that your god is mentioned, but by a different name.

If Shiva is a destroyer, then Shiva must be the same divinity as the destroyer mentioned in the Vedas. Originally, Rudra the Howler was the gift-giving archer and at the same time the destroyer, the *deva* with a horrible temper, capriciously violent, and a *deva* to be feared. However, in the Vedas Rudra was just one *deva* among many. His importance grew as it became obvious to priests and other religious figures that because of his horrible disposition, it was most important to appease him in order to ensure safety of people. Safety from death and danger is only attainable by dealing directly with the divinity who presides over such dangers. Brahmins performed fire rituals to appease Rudra.

At this stage Shiva becomes identified with the earlier Vedic *deva* Rudra the Howler. In the early centuries, the followers did not treat Shiva as the monotheistic god of all, but gradually Shiva begins to absorb the creator qualities of Brahma, and thereby became the one god, the ruler over all. The deity Shiva contains and manifests opposites. The new *deva* was ascetic, vicious, violent, and destructive, and simultaneously, lustful, creator, creative, merciful and loving.[10]

Many scholars feel that the major symbols of Shiva result from a merging of unique aspects of both Harappan and Aryan civilizations, for the Aryan Vedic *deva* Rudra is associated with violence and destruction whereas Shiva may be a descendant of a Harappan equivalent portrayed on the Harappan seals (in cross-legged meditation sometimes with an erect sex organ). Shiva has a wife, Uma or Parvati, and he has sons, including the elephant headed Ganesha, and daughters Laksmi and Saravati. But Shiva is also the ascetic in the forest with no ties to the world. Shiva has many sides, including the calm and tranquil side.[11]

Shaiva Religious Thought

The theology of Shiva is referred to as **Shaiva** religious thought. About 50 B.C.E., shrines dedicated to Shiva as one of the supreme *devas*, began to be built. In the context of the Vedic ritual pathway (*karma-marga*), the fury of Rudra-Shiva is uncontrollable, and can only be appeased by the Brahmin fire sacrifice; thus the fire sacrifice became especially important and resulted in Shiva's association with both fire and with Brahmins. The early worship of Shiva was ritual and sacrifices, presided over by Brahmin priests. Shiva is also associated with water, with the sacred river Ganges, which was interpreted as the liquid form of Shiva. As such, even in contemporary times millions make the pilgrimage each year to bathe in its sacred waters.

The *deva* Shiva is famous for wandering as a forest ascetic, and many images of Shiva show the very thin naked ascetic seated in cross-legged meditation.[12] Another image associated with Shiva is the bull (and scholars point out that images of a sacred bull appear on Harappan seals).

Although Shiva begins as Rudra and destruction, eventually the positive images dominate, and for his followers, Shiva becomes the only god instead of simply one among many. Non-Shiva devotional practices like prayers offered to images (*puja*) and meditative yoga become incorporated into Shiva worship as well. If you offer unconditional love to Shiva, he will respond. If you practice yogic meditation you can perceive the radiance of Shiva within yourself. Shiva is the world's central power. Although positive associations dominate, Shiva is still the destroyer

---

[10] As is true for the majority of gods, the deity Shiva absorbed qualities from many prior divinities. "Some of these gods fade out, leaving one or two traits for Siva, others are transmuted to form important and abiding factors of the Siva-complex. Still others rise out of insignificance and become vital aspects of this hierophany. The resultant figure of Siva is that of a sectarian god who stands for different things and is worshiped in a different manner." S. Bhattacharji, *The Indian Theogony*, op. cit., p. 3.

[11] One book devoted to Shiva is Thomas Wyatt, *Speaking of Shiva* (New York: Penguin Group, 1973).

[12] This ascetic Shiva becomes the model for much of Tantric Hindu forest dwellers, as discussed below.

and for people who are sensitive to the brevity of human life, Shiva is the *deva* who most closely fulfills their needs.

Followers of Shiva also come up with a solution to the problem of being trapped in the apparently endless cycle of birth and rebirth. If Shiva is Brahma, then Shiva must be the origin and creator of karma, and if he created karmic chains, then Shiva can also break them!

The *Lingam* and *Yoni* Emblem as Symbolic of Shiva

Over time, Shiva is not merely destruction but also becomes identified with creation. In human terms, creation is connected in its essence with sexuality. In pre-Aryan seals from the Harappan culture, we find the image of a seated man with erect sex organ, a powerful universal symbol of procreation. Later we find similar images used to represent Shiva.

Beginning in the early Shiva shrines, and continuing to the present, one can find a phallic symbol as the object of worship, that is, a stone column shaped to resemble the erect male sex organ (in Sanskrit *lingam*). The *lingam* is the classic symbol of creation and procreation—implying that Shiva was no longer merely thought of as just a destructive power, but now Shiva is also associated with creation and procreation. Later on, the resemblance of the column to the male sex organ lessens, and the more obviously symbolic content is stressed. For example, often one will find four faces on the column, representing the omniscience of the *deva* who faces all directions, past, present, and future. The symbolism of the *lingam* can also include the idea that the erect pillar is the cosmic center of the universe, or that the pillar is the divine universal presence which emerges from the world of mountain peaks which surround the worshiper in India.

The Shiva lingam

Sometimes it is difficult for students to understand and deal with the explicit sexual images which are found in so many non-Western cultures. Sexual imagery, especially in a religious context, has a tendency to make some Western Christian people uncomfortable.[13] Even in the present, among many westerners simple nudity and sexual expression are considered offensive and for some, even pornographic. For many in the West, sexuality is the antithesis of spirituality.[14]

It is important to note that for most of the world, the ancient Indian associations with human sexual organs and sexuality are *not* the same as those of the Christian West. There is nothing sinful, or shameful, or evil, or disgraceful, in sexuality. There is nothing impure, nothing unwholesome, nothing "dirty" in human sexual organs. Sexuality is not at war with spirituality.

For the followers of Shiva, human sexuality is symbolic of the eternal creative energy of the divine source of the universe, that is, God. In Indian religious symbolism, procreation is symbolic of God's divine creation.[15] Not so in the West. For many Western people, procreation is associated with sexuality, which in turn is perceived as the opposite of spirituality.

Yet, in India, if we want a powerful symbol for the divine creative act, the fundamental act of human

---

[13] The explicit sexual imagery of the Old Testament "Song of Songs" and the explicit sexual imagery of the religious mystic poetry of Catholic nuns during the Middle Ages, tends to be ignored or minimized and Church authorities offer complex reinterpretations of these passages in an attempt to deny the obvious connection between sexual imagery and the sacred impulse.

[14] At this time in human history, the primary meaning of sexuality was about procreation and reproduction within a structure of arranged marriages. It is only in more modern times that the association of sexuality with emotional intimacy and bonding provided by physical pleasure for individuals has become primary.

[15] See Wendy Doniger O'Flaherty, *Śiva: The Erotic Ascetic* (Oxford: Oxford University Press, 1980).

procreation is very meaningful. Sexuality is an especially important and powerful symbol of God's divine creative and loving energies.

In temples devoted to the divine creative activity of Shiva, liquids were poured over the phallic column during sacred ceremonies. To keep the liquids from spilling onto the floor, the column was placed in a shallow dish with a spout for the liquids to pour out. However, after a while, that shallow dish was thought of as symbolic of the female sexual organ as well, and called the *yoni* (the vagina). This adds a more profound dimension to the religious ritual, for it serves as a recognition of the role of the female in procreation and reproduction, which are also symbols of creativity. In this way, Shiva combined both dimensions in his special symbol, combining both the male and the female in all divine activity in the cosmos.

The worship of the *lingam* is found in several world religions and has never been pornographic. It is not about gratuitous erotic imagery, and most certainly it is not orgiastic: rather it simply makes a statement about reality. Shiva is the creator god, and Shiva's potent generative power is always obvious before us. New lives are coming into existence continually. Everything new is evidence of Shiva's potency. The sacred creative energy of Shiva is feminine as well as masculine, and the creation of life and the destruction of life are both contained with the force of Shiva.

Although Shiva is famous for wandering as an ascetic, his imagery also includes creative bliss and delight. In many tales, Shiva wanders into villages and as the symbol of divine ecstacy, he seduces the wives and daughters. The imagery is a loving deity worshiped by loving followers. Shiva's explicitly lustful behavior constitute important symbols of this divine love. When Shiva appears, women lose control and go wild, ripping their clothes and making wanton gestures to him. In this case, divine ecstacy is symbolized as sexual ecstacy, without the "dirty" associations that Western people sometimes tend to have. The sexual image is intended to be pure and natural.

Shiva's Dual Nature: Construction and Destruction

As the Vedic *deva* Rudra the Howler, Shiva is originally the source of natural destruction, sometimes quite violent. Later Shiva has a kinder side, showing a constructive side to actions which seem destructive. However, the polarity is both masculine and feminine, with the destructive side associated with the masculine side of Shiva. Religious imagery contains this duality as well.

There are statues of Shiva in which the right half is male and the left half is female. The left half is full-breasted and wearing woman's clothing and ornaments, while right half is male. The feminine side is the active creative side of Shiva, the part that creates the world and controls everything that happens in the natural world. This is birth and novelty. This feminine aspect stresses the protective and loving side of Shiva's nature. Nevertheless, Shiva is also the destroyer. Especially in the earlier times, the male side was clearly destructive. The right half, the male body, was smeared with ashes of cremated bodies, and wears a necklace of the skulls of past *devas* whom he has outlived.[16]

Consider the implications of the worship of Shiva. The world is not just creative goodness. Neither is this world a battleground between good forces of a perfectly god and evil forces of an evil god or devil. It is clear that creation and destruction are both the divine activity of god, both the ecstatic divine activity of Shiva.

Shiva as the Supreme Dancer

A pervasive icon of the divine activity of Shiva is Shiva as "King of Dancers." The dance is the creative activity of god, spiritual, religious, spontaneous, free, divine, whirling in rapture and bliss (*ananda*), the domain of ecstacy. For

---

[16] We shall see that the ascetic Hindu Tantric *sannyasin* followers will emulate these images of Shiva, rubbing their bodies with ashes of cremated bodies, wearing items from corpses, and having necklaces of human bones.

those with sufficient insight, all of that activity happens within one's own heart.[17]

Shiva dances in a circle of fire, which symbolizes change, destruction, and illusion (*maya*). The arch is also the action of material and individual matter and energy, the world, nature, all the things which are changing. The arched semi-circle suggests completeness and wholeness. The arch and circle is time. The shape of the surrounding circle shares its shape with the Sanskrit symbol for the *mantra* of *Om*.

If outside the arch is change and time, inside that arch is the dancing Shiva which is timeless eternity. The completeness of the circle is the unity of time and eternity. The dance of Shiva is the activity of the divine, the activity of god, the activity of bliss and delight.

Shiva dances the universe into existence; by his primordial rhythmic energy, Shiva engenders the numerous natural rhythms of the seasons and the universe which are obvious to all of us. By the dance, Shiva continually creates, preserves and changes. Change destroys all things. Shiva and his drumming create from the sacred syllable *Om* all musical notes in the scale. The musical scales and music in general is a sacred activity. The strings on the sitar, the harp or guitar are plucked, and new musical notes arise. This is creation. However, soon they fade and are gone, and this is destruction. The process does not end here. The notes which have faded are replaced by new notes and chords, and these pulsing energies are the melodies behind the dance of Shiva.

Typically the dancing Shiva has four arms. Often, one right hand holds a drum, the other is uplifted in the sign "do not fear." Creation arises from the beat of the drum; heaven and earth, all worlds are put into order by the alternating beats which constitute the drumming of time. The uplifted right hand points upwards to liberation while it makes the gesture of protection and the sign of hope. One left hand holds a fire, and the other left hand points down on a demon being trampled, who symbolizes ignorance and evil. Fire symbolizes destruction, but that power of destruction is not evil; it is also the destruction of one's bad karma. The destruction of bad karma is liberation

Shiva's hair is braided, which indicates that he is an ascetic, a *sannyasi*. Shiva is located in the center of creation, and the center of creation is everywhere. In Shiva's hair can be seen a cobra, and a skull. In his right ear he wears a man's earring, a woman's earring in his left. Shiva is adorned with necklaces and amulets, bracelets, finger and toe rings.

Shiva's left foot is raised. The *atman*, the eternal unchanging and self-existent true self, can be free of the world, as the lifted foot is free of the world. The raised foot promises eternal bliss (*ananda*) to those who approach Shiva with loving devotion (*bhakti*). He stands upon a lotus pedestal, from which springs an encircling fringe of flame, and touched by the hands holding the drum and fire. The foot on the ground is the sacred divine touching the earth, giving a place to rest in a world of the cycle of birth and death, the cycle of cause-and-effect.

The dance of Shiva is the dance of delight, the union of male and female, dancing in time and uniting all dualities, uniting creation and destruction. Those who behold the dance of Shiva within themselves can escape *samsara*, the cycle of birth and death. Shiva's essence is found in all creative energies that are seen everywhere we look.[18]

The end of the dance is the end of the universe. As Shiva slows down and stops dancing, the heavens and the

---

[17] Classical Indian dancers have statues and images of the dancing Shiva in the same way Western musicians, violinists, cellists, or pianists may have a bust of Johann Sebastian Bach or Beethoven on their piano.

[18] A beautiful art book filled with images and analysis of the dancing Shiva is C. Shivamurti, *Nataraja in Art, Thought, and Literature* (Delhi: Publications of Government of India, 1994).

earth disappear. Shiva even devours time itself. Symbolically Shiva destroys the things which tie one's *atman* to the world, and thereby sets us free. The empirical ego is destroyed, and illusion and karma are burned away—this is the "burning ground" where Shiva dances.

The dance of Shiva takes place in the center of creation. Where is the center of creation? It is the center of one's own heart—everywhere is god, and that "everywhere" is your own heart. You can find your own divine nature by offering selfless love and devotion to Shiva. The dance of Shiva is spontaneous divine play. The dance of Shiva is the playful bliss of divine love. You must cast out all thoughts but the thought of Shiva, and then Shiva abides in your heart and dances in your mind.

> In the night of Brahma, Nature is inert and cannot dance till Shiva wills it; He rises from His rapture, and dancing sends through inert matter pulsing waves of awakening sound, and lo! matter also dances appearing as a glory round about Him. Dancing, He sustains its manifold phenomena. In the fullness of time, still dancing, he destroys all forms and names by fire and gives new rest.[19]

Why Does the Universe Exist? Why is there Something Rather than Nothing?

The universe is danced into existence. Why does the universe exist? Why does Shiva create the world? The answer is simple. Consider the question: why do we dance? The answer: for the fun of it. Like us, the dance of Shiva is *lila*, play, amusement. Shiva creates the universe for the sheer fun of it, and when Shiva stops dancing, the universe comes to an end as well. All of creation is the theater for Shiva. For the followers of Shiva, the answer to the question "Why is there anything at all?" is simply *lila*.

Shiva as the Supreme God.

In earlier times Shiva is merely one *deva* among many who symbolize aspects of natural forces. Vishnu was associated with sun, sunlight and growth, and Shiva associated with moon, darkness, and destruction. However, after the third century in the common era, groups appeared who worshiped Shiva as the Supreme God, the ruler god. By 800-1200 C.E., books of Shaiva religious philosophy were composed, but in following centuries worship of Shiva declined in north India. Worship of Shiva is still the main religious practice of the Tamils in the south of India, who worship Shiva as the One God. There is a series of remarkable devotional religious poetry written in the Tamil language.

The Goal of the Followers of Shiva

It is important to note that the ultimate goal of the followers of Shiva is *not* the Upanishadic goal of union with Brahman. Shiva dances to maintain the cosmos, but also Shiva dances to give liberation to those who seek him with devotion, *bhakti*. Shiva's powers can secure reward in this world, and the bliss of liberation. The liberated one does not become one with Shiva. The one who achieves liberation exists fully in the presence of Shiva, but exists with awareness of ultimate separateness. According to Shaiva theology, for the liberated one, there is no loss of individuality, and the worshiper does not become divine. Rather, Shiva supports the individual, and can set the follower free.

THE SHAKTAS and SHAKTISM: THE FEMININE ASPECT OF SHIVA

Recall that Shiva has dual aspects of male and female: the eternal male associated with the timeless but also destruction; the transforming active creative female energy. The term **Shaktism** focuses our attention upon the *shakti*,

---

[19] Ananda K. Coomaraswamy, *The Dance of Shiva* (NY: Noonday, 1957), p. 78. Much of the above discussion was freely adapted from this book.

CHAPTER 5: THE PATHWAY OF DEVOTION

the power to transform, the feminine creative energy of Shiva. The term *shakti* simply means force or transformative energy. Shiva is not only male destructiveness; Shiva is also female creativity.

The follower can cultivate a relationship with and worship the feminine *shakti* dimension of Shiva as well as the masculine aspect. The feminine *shakti* is the *devi*, the Great Goddess, symbolic of the feminine side of the divine polarity, symbolic of the **active creative** natural processes in the universe.[20]

The male image is static eternity, timeless, passive, and silent wisdom. The female half is active and creative and brings the world into existence as well as everything alive. In India, all rivers are goddesses, or *devi*, for the flowing river is ever active.

Those who worship the goddess are called *Shaktas*. Some of these followers saw the male half as deriving from and secondary to the *shakti* power, and thus the feminine energy is supreme. In Indian religion there is no single group which can define or limit the beliefs of a special religious group. A wide range of possibilities are included under *Shaktism*.

Once again, the dual nature of creation is stressed. As is obvious, for creation to occur, destruction must also occur. You cannot have one without the other. This divine polarity is also found in the feminine goddesses; these goddesses are sweet, motherly, protecting, but the divine feminine can also be dangerous and destructive. The Mother of the World brings suffering and death as well as joy and life, and both suffering and death are as divine as creation, and if one is to love god, suffering and death must be endured.[21]

Durga and Parvati: the Consort of Shiva

Scholars can find no evidence of Shaktism (the divine feminine consort) in any Vedic texts or feminine images in the worship of Shiva in the early times. Apparently the worship of the divine feminine first appears about two-thousand years ago (between 50 B.C.E. and 50 C.E.) in the northern rural, unorganized areas which were still heavily influenced by the pre-Aryan Indus Valley Harappan civilization.[22] Originally, the divine female, *devi*, was ignored by the Vedic Aryans who have only a few hymns for female divinities.

The great Indian epic text, the *Mahabarata*, mentions a *devi* goddess Durga as receiving offerings from some tribes. All the various disparate feminine powers seem to be combined into Durga by the second or third century C.E., and she is accommodated within Vedic religion by transforming her into the wife of Shiva.

Durga is worshiped throughout India.[23] Originally Durga was a warrior goddess and is often portrayed as riding on a tiger. However, note that in Grand Tradition religion, Durga is only an aspect of a supreme *deva* with both male and female characteristics. Durga controls the natural active creative universe. Durga is the active power that determines the flow and nature of events in the universe Shiva, the other half (the masculine half), controls the unchanging, inactive, transcendent, and changeless realm of eternity. Note that the changeless realm of eternity is the truly Real—and this is the goal of liberation.

Durga is not the only female aspect or partner of Shiva. Perhaps there is just one feminine consort who has many different names and appearances. For example, another wife or consort of Shiva is the beautiful and loving Parvati. After being roused by the deity of desire, *Kama*, Shiva makes love with the beautiful goddess of the snow mountains, Parvati, and with her he fathers several divine sons. But the divinely beautiful Parvati is only one of many

---

[20] See David R. Kinsley, *Hindu Goddesses: Visions of the Divine Feminine in the Hindu Religious Tradition* (Berkeley: University of California, 1998).

[21] Fenton, et. al, *Religions of Asia*, Second ed., p. 102.

[22] As noted before, many scholars believe the worship of goddesses originated in the pre-Aryan Harappan civilization, and perhaps among other non-Aryan groups in India.

[23] Laura Amazzone, *Goddess Durga and Sacred Female Power* (New York: Hamilton Books, 2012).

CHAPTER 5: THE PATHWAY OF DEVOTION

consorts. Another wife or *shakti* of Shiva is Uma (perhaps Uma is another name for Durga[24]) who is said to have understood the ultimate mystery when the other *devas* were not able to realize it.[25] One of the most famous *shakti* is the goddess Kali.

Kali—A Wrathful Manifestation of Durga

Kali does not appear in Vedic texts, but she is incorporated into the Vedic pantheon by asserting that she is one of Durga's most dreadful and powerful manifestations.[26] Kali first appears in seventh century Purana texts.[27] There are a wide variety of bloody goddesses worshiped in the history of India, and it seems as though the characteristics of many of them coalesced into Kali over the centuries. Kali is a blood-loving battle queen whose help guarantees victory over enemies. In the ancient texts Kali is not kindly; she is terrifying. She is a goddess who roams battlefields, devouring human flesh and drinking the blood of the killed. Blood trickles from her mouth, and she holds a severed human head. Although Kali is sometimes motherly and protective, Kali has horrible fangs and is very dangerous.

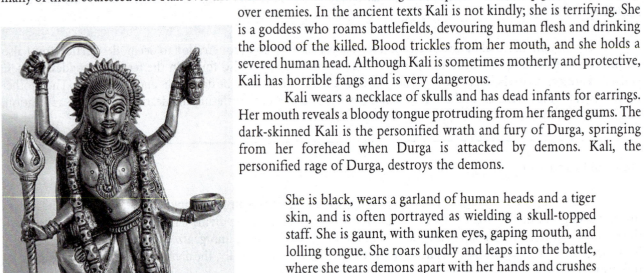

Kali wears a necklace of skulls and has dead infants for earrings. Her mouth reveals a bloody tongue protruding from her fanged gums. The dark-skinned Kali is the personified wrath and fury of Durga, springing from her forehead when Durga is attacked by demons. Kali, the personified rage of Durga, destroys the demons.

She is black, wears a garland of human heads and a tiger skin, and is often portrayed as wielding a skull-topped staff. She is gaunt, with sunken eyes, gaping mouth, and lolling tongue. She roars loudly and leaps into the battle, where she tears demons apart with her hands and crushes them in her jaws. She grasps the two demon generals and in one furious blow decapitates them both with her sword.[28]

Kali is not only a projection of Durga; she is also portrayed as the rage of Parvati, Shiva's wife and consort. In this aspect, Kali becomes so intoxicated by the blood and battle that her uncontrolled anger threatens to destroy all the world. Only Shiva can calm her. Kali is outside the moral order of the world, she is antisocial and unimaginably dangerous.

---

[24] Both Durga and Uma are called the "Mother of the World" by worshipers.

[25] Sukumari Bhattacharji, *The Indian Theogony*, ch. 8: "Rudra-Siva's Consort: The Mother-Goddess," pp. 158ff.

[26] There are numerous scholarly works on Kali, especially David Kinsley, *The Sword and the Flute: Kali and Krsna: Visions of the Terrible and the Sublime in Hindu Mythology* (Berkeley: University of California Press, 1975). An extensive more recent bibliography can be found in Rachel Fell McDermott and Jeffrey J. Kripal, eds., *Encountering Kali* (Berkeley: University of California Press, 2003).

[27] Puranas are ancient tales of the history of the universe from creation to destruction, genealogies of kings, heroes, sages, and demigods, and descriptions of Hindu cosmology, philosophy, and geography. They tend to be stories told by a sage to a willing helper.

[28] David R. Kinsley, "Kali" in McDermott and Kripal, eds., *Encountering Kali, op. cit.*, p. 25.

CHAPTER 5: THE PATHWAY OF DEVOTION

Kali Is Not A Symbol of Evil.

It is very clear that Kali is central to the Little Tradition of goddess worship, but there is also a Grand Tradition understanding of Kali and her role. If one offers a more psychological interpretation, Kali is a personification of those dimensions of reality which terrify human beings. By transforming these overwhelming aspects of reality into a human form, into a person, devotees will find it easier to deal with things like instability, disorder, chaos, violence, suffering, and death—things which are a part of the life of every single human being.

Kali is pain and death personified, but Kali does not symbolize evil. Death and destruction are *not* evil. While in the midst of death and destruction, Kali symbolizes the Great Mother who rescues her children from the terrors of the world, and affirms that love is more fundamental than violence, providing a way out of life's terrors.[29] Kali defeats demons in a most bloodthirsty manner, and inflicts diseases. But Kali also cures diseases. Kali is the feminine energy; Kali's terrible power can defeat and overcome evil. Kali has the power to come to the rescue of those who call upon her. She too is the Mother Goddess.

As with Shiva, there is an explicit duality in the persona of Kali. Goodness takes the form as the terrifying Kali precisely so that we can overcome our fear of death, thereby making room for life, delight, and joy. When you deal with Kali in her most terrible form, it is a chance for you to confront your own fears of death and loneliness, and recognize that all of existence is trapped in change, in pain, and in suffering. Life feeds on death, and time will destroy every one and every thing you have ever loved.

The follower of Kali cannot pretend that these things are not in the world; they are directly before us. Pain, suffering, death and destruction cannot be eliminated. One way for human beings to conquer fear is to stand up and face it. The goddess Kali transcends the oppositions which life presents, but she also encompasses these oppositions. Kali is not there to terrorize you. Kali presents the divine aspect as both creation and destruction. Kali is power, she is sexuality, and she is violence. Beauty and ugliness are divine. Violence and sorrow are as divine as is peace and joy. For those who approach Kali with love and devotion, what was menacing is transformed; what was terrifying becomes delight. Whether confronting Kali fearlessly, or hesitantly as a small child filled with fear, the devotee becomes reconciled to death and accepts the way the world is. Kali frees us from fear itself.

Kali permits individuals to see their overall roles in the cosmic drama. She invites a wider, more mature, more realistic reflection on where one has come from and where one is going. She allows the individual to see himself or herself as merely one being in an endless series of permutations arising from the ever-recurring cycles of life and death that constitute the inner rhythms of the divine mother.[30]

In later eighteenth century iconography, Kali is young, beautiful with a gently smiling face, and makes hand gestures that dispel fears and grants wishes. In its various manifestations, the path of Kali is also the *bhakti-marga*. Kali is a goddess worshiped especially in Bengal, Nepal, Kashmir, and even Sri Lanka.

Kali is also well known in the British Empire, because sensationalist colonial writings depicted Kali as a goddess of the Thuggees, a group of criminal Indians who robbed and strangled natives, and then later attacked British soldiers in the nineteenth century, undermining British rule.[31] Kali became a central image for those trying to overthrow the British colonial powers.

---

[29] John Koller, *Oriental Philosophies*, 2nd., p. 108

[30] David R. Kinsley, "Kali," *op. cit.*, p. 35.

[31] Summaries of this interesting aspect of British rule of India can be found in Cynthia Ann Humes, "Wrestling with Kali: South Asian and British Constructions of the Dark Goddess," and Hugh B. Urban, "India's Darkest Heart: Kali in the Colonial Imagination," in Rachel Fell McDermott and Jeffrey J. Kripal, eds., *Encountering Kali* (Berkeley: University of California Press, 2003).

CHAPTER 5: THE PATHWAY OF DEVOTION

In British newspapers, Kali was portrayed as a dark and terrifying imagery of violence and sexual perversion, which had an erotic appeal to the colonial Europeans in India. As British newspapers wrote about India, tales of the frightening and erotic Kali were told. Kali appeared in Victorian novels and popular culture, and is occasionally utilized in British and Hollywood adventure films such as the 1939 film, *Gunga Din*, the 1965 Beatles *Help!*, the 1974 *Golden Voyage of Sinbad*, the 1984 *Indiana Jones and the Temple of Doom*, and there are characters symbolically named Kali in many films including the 1996 *The Crow* and the 2003 *Matrix Reloaded*.

5.7 HINDU TANTRISM AND GODDESS WORSHIP

Many students will have heard of Tantra or may be familiar with sexually explicit Tantric iconography. Tantra has been popular in various segments of Western civilizations, and many widely varied claims have been made about the religious practices called Tantra. However, in our pop culture there is a great deal of misinformation and popular myth all mixed together, and much of what people in the West call "Tantra" or "Tantric" is actually the projection of Western fantasies upon a poorly understood religious orientation.

Western sources have portrayed Tantric practice as a cult of sexual ecstacy leading to a god-consciousness, fueled by secret erotic massage techniques. In ancient and medieval India there never was such a monolithic "cult of ecstacy" which practiced hidden sexual massage methods. This is the product of sexual fantasies catering to the popular Western imagination.[32] What westerners call "Tantra" is what some scholars describe as "New Age Tantra." David Gordon White writes "New Age Tantra is to medieval Tantra [in India] what finger painting is to fine art ..."[33]

Because of the popularity of Tantra in aspects of Western culture, this section of the chapter will attempt to discuss historical background and some of the actual practices and doctrines of the wide variety of Tantric Hinduism.

The Historical Background for Tantric Hinduism

New developments occurred in religion in India from the fifth century C.E. to the eleventh century. These developments affected all Indian religions including Buddhism; it was not just Hinduism. The earlier forest-dwelling stress on achieving liberation through abstract meditations was modified by a strong devotional trend to substitute a tangible and popular ritual for the earlier solitary meditations. The more ancient approaches were modified to include richly decorative settings and utilized all the arts, including painting, music, sculpture, dance, and drama. In addition to the color and pageantry, wandering ascetics adopted the characteristics of Shiva and were purported to practice secret rituals which gave power over gods and demons. Sexual imagery, bright colors and pageantry become more and more important. The scriptures relating to this religious approach are called *Tantras*, which began appearing in the fourth or fifth centuries in the common era. Thus, Tantras are books.

Think of people living in India during the fifth, sixth or seventh century of the common era. Ordinary people lived in farmhouses and homes made of dirt, wood and straw. Everyday utensils were made of unfinished wood or stone. The clothing was not brightly colored, or decorative; it was earth-colored and practical. Splendid paints and dyes were rare and expensive, and even the monarchs and rulers had few paintings, few tapestries, few brocades decorated with gold or silver.

Someone living such an ordinary life then encounters a brightly hued statue, a gleaming altar, complex and colorful rituals, a solemn procession with tapers and incense, ritual chanting or singing accompanied by the beat of drumming. This can cause a profound emotional reaction, a religious experience. These sorts of sounds and colors and images can be profoundly transforming.

---

[32] See David Gordon White, *Kiss of the Yogini: Tantric Sex in its South Asian Contexts* (Chicago: University of Chicago Press, 2003).

[33] *Ibid.*, p. xiii.

CHAPTER 5: THE PATHWAY OF DEVOTION

The performance of ritual itself is the way to liberation

Rituals are no longer merely done to ask favors of *devas* or to popularize or propagandize religions. In this later time period it was believed that by itself, continuing performance of ritual alone could bring liberation. The tendency was for the rituals themselves to become the pathway, and out of this new religious matrix we find the origins of Tantric Hinduism.[34]

Tantric Hinduism combined the earlier tendencies of Shiva worship and especially the goddess worship of his consort, Parvati, Durga and Kali, and combined numerous diverse elements into a cluster of mystery cults with new practices and approaches. Discernable schools of Tantric Hinduism arose, basing themselves on liberated ascetics who claimed to have acquired special powers as a result of their secret practices.[35]

There is no single religion or religious practice which defines Tantric Hinduism.

There is no single deity, no single teacher, no single text common to Tantric Hinduism. Tantrism arose out of clusters of practices including behaviors which contradicted one's social duties and were considered profoundly contaminating, shocking, and immoral, such as eating meat and fish, or drinking alcohol. Even death (symbolized by Kali) is faced and transformed into an instrument of liberation. The claim is that the duality of life versus death can be transcended. In fact, finding the underlying unity or oneness behind all dualisms is a central theme in Tantric Hinduism.

Tantric ascetics will wear a necklace of human bones, and will wear a sacred thread made from the hair of a corpse. They will drink from a human skull. In addition to socially unacceptable practices there was also seated meditation and goddess worship, with similar colorful rites and rituals like those which appear in the *shaktism* of Shiva-worship.

The Goal of Tantric Hinduism is Liberation

Although the symbols of Hindu Tantric practice are similar to those of Shiva and the female *shakti* energy, the goal of Hindu Tantrism is the goal of the *Upanishads*, namely *moksha* and realization of ultimate non-duality. This is not the goal of the other forms of devotion. The goal of the non-Tantric devotional *bhakti-marga* is dualistic, that is, one's self is separate and apart from the divinity. The worshiper and the god are two, never one. That separate self desires to worship and love and be in the loving presence of the divine. For Tantra, the ultimate truth is non-dual, with no separate divinity. The ascetics of Tantra seek to emulate the behavior of Shiva as part of the devotion to Shiva. The Grand Tradition of Hindu Tantric religion has the goal of non-dual *moksha* liberation, freedom from the endless cycle of *samsara*.

Tantric Hinduism will stress chanted phrases of power, secret and symbolic diagrams, but especially will place stress on the two aspects of the divine (both male and female) in order to become liberated from duality. Tantric Hinduism combines these and others and in the process, new symbols appear.[36] The most famous of these are the

---

[34] "... the Shakta began as an offshoot of the Shaiva but very soon started developing as a separate sect. It became a focus for all the different mother-goddess eiphanies. Assimilation with Tantrism changed its orientation, and a complex cult emerged as Shaktism." S. Bhattacharji, *The Indian Theogony*, op. cit., p. 15.

[35] "The category 'Tantra' is a basic and familiar one today in the vocabulary of most scholars of religions and generally considered one of the most important and controversial forms of Asian religion. In academic discourse, Tantra usually refers to a specific brand of religious practice common to the Hindu, Buddhist, and Jain traditions since at least the seventh century ..." Hugh B. Urban, *Tantra: Sex, Secrecy, Politics, and Power in the Study of Religion* (Berkeley: University of California Press, 2003), p. 1.

[36] Douglas R. Brooks lists ten characteristics which he finds in various forms of Tantric religion: (1) practices which are not justified in the Aryan Vedas; (2) they involve meditation techniques like kundalini yoga; (3) Tantra accepts divinities yet the goal is non-dual liberation; (4) reliance on *mantras* and sounds of power; (5) symbolic *mandala* are used as sacred guides; (6) reliance on a sacred teacher

CHAPTER 5: THE PATHWAY OF DEVOTION

overtly sexual images of the male Shiva and his female consort, locked in sexual embrace.[37] Tantric Hinduism worships gods and goddesses depicted as locked in sexual union with their consorts. This is not just *lingam* and *yoni* imagery, this is explicit sexuality. The rituals of goddess worship become sexualized. However, these religious images are not suggestive of egotistic lust. If the mind is pure, all things are pure.

In its most abstract and theoretical forms, Tantric Hinduism wants to escape the trap of duality, of dividing reality up into separate items each interpreted as valuable or not-valuable, as pure or not pure. The Tantric ascetic no longer wants to see things in terms of good versus evil, of sacred versus profane, superior and subordinate, of pure versus polluted (which is a dominant image in traditional Indian culture). To overcome the trap of duality, Tantric Hinduism draws upon an image of original primal unity, or oneness.

A Hindu Creation Story

In the ancient tales, the original primordial oneness transforms by self-division into two, into a dualism. One divides and becomes two. Unity becomes duality. The classic image of dualism is the male-female bi-polar dualism. The two complement each other, and can be thought of as an original unity which is now dual. The classic expression of this comes from the creation story found in the *Brihad-Aranyaka Upanishad* 1.4.1-7:

> In the beginning the world was *Atman* alone, in the shape of a Person (*purusha*). He looked around and saw nothing but himself. He first said, "This is I." Therefore, he became I by name. Therefore even now, if a man is asked he first says, "This is I," and then pronounces his other name. Before all this he burned down all evils; therefore he was a Person [*purusha*]. Truly he who knows this burns down everyone who tries to be before him.
>
> He feared, and therefore anyone who is lonely fears. He thought, "As there is nothing but myself, what should I fear?" Then his fear passed away. For what should he have feared? But he felt no delight. Therefore a man who is lonely feels no delight. He longed for a second person. As he was large as a man and woman together, he made his Self to fall in two, and there came husband and wife. Therefore Yajnavalkya said: "We two are thus like half a shell." Therefore the void that was there [in the male] is filled by the wife. He had sexual intercourse with her, and humans were born.
>
> She thought, "How can he have sexual intercourse with me, after having produced me from himself? I shall hide myself." She then became a cow. But he became a bull and had sex with her, and therefore cows were born. Then she became a mare, and he a stallion; then he a male ass, and she a female ass. He had sex with her [in both forms], and therefore one-hoofed animals were born. He became a she-goat, she a he-goat; she became a ewe, he a ram. He had sex with her, and therefore goats and sheep were born. In this way he created everything that exists in pairs, down to the ants. [5] He knew this: "I indeed am this creation, for I created all this." Therefore he became the creation, and he who knows this lives in this his creation.[38]

As we can see, the divine original oneness becomes duality, and the interaction of the two poles of male and female produces all the things in the world. In Tantric practice, by reversing that process of creation, we bring about

---

or *guru*; (7) male and female divinities are essential to Tantric symbolism; (8) the teachings are secret and not to be shared; (9) they prescribe socially prohibited activities such as eating fish or meat, drinking alcohol, and engaging in sexual intercourse; (10) they require the student to undergo initiation rituals. Hugh Urban points out that many religions share some of these characteristics and would not consider themselves to be Tantra. See Urban, *Tantra* (Berkeley: University of California Press, 2003), pp. 6–7.

[37] "Although Parvati is usually said to be the recipient of Siva's wisdom in the form of the Tantras, it is Kali who seems to dominate Tantric iconography, texts, and rituals, especially in left-handed Tantra." David R. Kinsley, "Kali," *op. cit.*, p. 29.

[38] Max Muller, trans., *The Upanishads, Sacred Books of the East*, vols. 1 and 15 (Oxford University Press, 1878, 1884). I have substituted *atman* where Muller used "Soul."

a conscious return to unity, to oneness. Using the body in rituals, the polarized world of male and female, static and active, eternity and time, life and death, sacred and profane, pure and impure, are returned to wholeness and unity.[39] The sexual union of male and female can be understood as these dualities returning to original primal unity. The world is no longer fragmented.

The sexual act can also be symbolic of the union of wisdom and compassion, the two becoming one.[40] In meditation, one can imagine the static unchanging wisdom (male energy) uniting with active and creative compassion (female energy) in a sexual symbol of one-ness. Pure wisdom without compassion is cold and hard, empathy with other living things is difficult or impossible. Pure compassion without wisdom is misdirected and can lead to harm. Thus, spiritual practice involves a male-female duality which become one — non-duality.

The Five Forbidden Things

Traditional Hinduism has five forbidden things: drinking wine, eating meat, eating fish, eating parched grain, and sexual intercourse as religious practice. It is important to note that Hindu Tantric symbolic use of sexual intercourse as religious ritual is not considered important in traditional religious Hindu practices. In fact, this is a minimal side of Hinduism, and most Hindus are disdainful of Tantrism because they perceive it as contrary to *dharma*-based morality. Artistic sexual symbolism involving the union of the male and female aspects of Shiva are perfectly fine, but for male and female devotees to perform sexual acts as religious practice is thought to be a perversion of Hinduism by the majority of Hindus.

Nevertheless, it is clear that male and female Tantric followers may practice their religion with sexualized ritual, utilized as a part of an elaborate ceremony.[41] Each partner visualizes himself or herself as a male *deva* or female *devi* in order to cultivate the primordial energy which transforms each. Tantric Hinduism utilizes an image of a serpent coiled along the base of the spine for this primal power or energy, and the ritual sexual union is intended to arouse this energy to travel up the spine to the top of the head.[42] The goal is not just sexual release of tension; the goal is realization of the primordial unity which transcends male-female duality, a unity which is ecstatic bliss. The sacred ultimate transcends all traditional community-based social rules, and thus Tantric practice must also free the practitioner from being trapped in social law and caste-determined rules of *dharma*, ritual purification, or duty.

There are other activities found in Tantra which offended the majority of Hindus. The ascetic beggars of Tantra would rub the ashes of a cremation funeral pyre on their naked bodies, they would carry a walking staff with a human skull on the top, and would hold out a human skull to receive offerings of food, or drink from a skull. They would wear inappropriate jewelry, would share a meal with a family of a social caste considered impure or polluted (forbidden by Hindu rules), and say and do things which scandalized the ordinary people. Alex Sanderson describes a Shavite Tantric ascetic as follows:

> Wearing earrings, armlets, anklets, and girdle [of human bone] with a sacred thread made of twisted corpse hair; smeared with ashes from the cremation-pyres, carrying the skull-bowl, the skull-staff and rattle-drum, intoxicated with alcohol, he alternated periods of night wandering with worship in which

---

[39] Paraphrased from David R. Kinsley, "Kali," *op. cit.*, p. 30.

[40] It is interesting to note that religious Taoism in China places great emphasis upon sexual intercourse, but not in ways which resemble Hindu Tantrism. In China the belief was that when a female achieves orgasm, the male sex organ could absorb her emitted *yang* energy, and thereby prolong the life of the male (sex with 1200 girls could give immortality) and even cure illness. See *Asian Thought*, Volume II, section 18.7, "Techniques of Inner Alchemy."

[41] Tantric Hinduism has two forms: Right-handed and Left-handed Tantra. Right-handed Tantra involves worship of Great Goddess in the approved Vedic manner: ritual devotion to a *deva* or a *devi* were pretty much similar. Left-handed Tantra was worship of the Goddess using sexual symbolism and taboo materials including consuming meat and wine. In meditation, one can imagine the wisdom (male energy) uniting with compassion (female energy) in a sexual symbol of one-ness. The goal is to awaken the *kundalini* energy at the base of the spine, raise it through seven *chakras*/energy centers, and the result would be *moksha*.

[42] This is called *kundalini yoga*.

he invoked and gratified the deities of the *mandala* into which he had been initiated. This gratification required the participation of a ... consecrated consort with whom he was to copulate.[43]

Because traditional Hinduism forbids drinking wine, eating meat, eating fish, eating parched grain, and sexual intercourse as religious practice, the sexualized rituals of Tantric Hinduism cannot be accepted by the majority. This does create a problem; it can be dangerous if outsiders know about these practices. The Tantric sexualized rituals became secrets to be shared only within the membership.

It is not clear how often actual physical intercourse occurred in the Tantric pathway. Often, it is thought that the sexual elements were primarily visualization and meditation rather than actual physical sexual contact. It has been suggested that these behaviors which went against social rules were restricted to the most senior of ascetics and engaged in only rarely. Many argue that such practices were ritual and performed only a few times a year.

However frequent or infrequent, Tantric practices can be defended by asserting that if the mind is pure, then there is nothing impure in one's behavior. It is human ignorance which impels us to categorize things in the world as either "pure" or "impure." If pure versus impure is a distinction which reflects human ignorance, and the Tantric adept is no longer ignorant, then his behavior transcends our ordinary rules of human interaction.

Although sexual intercourse, eating meat, and drinking wine may intrigue us, these are not the dominant practice of Tantric Hinduism. There are many other important techniques such as the use of *mantras* and *mandalas*.

Mantras: Sacred Words of Power

Mantra are one of the defining characteristics of Tantric Hinduism. As explained earlier, *mantras* are highly compressed, power-packed words, phrases, or formulas, usually of classical Vedic Sanskrit origin, charged with deep meaning and magical potency. These sounds were supposed to be present as the universe began, and were heard by the first human sages.

Mantras can be used in several ways. *Mantras* can be recited aloud, but they can also be visualized as part of meditative efforts, or written down repeatedly. Each Tantric *deva* has his or her own special *mantra*, and the student of Tantra will learn appropriate *mantras* from the *guru*, the teacher. The *mantra* are the magic spells or magic sounds that the ascetic or shaman can use for many purposes. The precise symbolism of a *mantra* depends upon the situation, the student's attainment, and the teacher's goal.

The origins of *mantra* are very ancient, and it is possible that they go back to the earliest ritual practices of the Vedic texts. The scholarly etymology of *mantra* interprets the term to be a combination of the root *man-* ("to think") and the suffix *-tra* ("tool"). Literally a *mantra* is a tool of thought, or an instrument of thought.[44] *Mantras* are tools of thinking which are believed to affect the world in the same way a magic spell is supposed to affect the world. In the ancient past the effective part of the *mantra* was the actual vibration or sound, so it followed that correct pronunciation was essential for the person reciting the *mantra* to actually have an effect upon the world. The Brahmin priests understood the sacred Vedas to be manifestations of the power of the ritual *mantras*. *Mantras* are the sounds which the most ancient sages heard which reverberate eternally in the celestial realms.

For a student of sacred ritual, the sacred sounds can be recited aloud as a daily practice which purifies speech and can protect the mind by maintaining a constant spiritual connection with one's personal Tantric *deva*. Another function of *mantra* is that it helps to bring about focused concentration by dispersing the mental chatter in which we carry on an internal conversation with ourselves. In order to serve this function, *mantras* do not need to be uttered aloud. They can be recited silently, sub-vocalized or visualized, or written repeatedly. It is not the meaning of the words that gives *mantras* their power. Many Tantric followers believe that a *mantra* gains efficacy only if given by one's *guru*.

---

[43] Quoted in Christian Wedemeyer, *Making Sense of Tantric Buddhism: History, Semiology, and Transgression in the Indian Traditions* (New York: Columbia University Press, 2012), p. 158. Sanskrit technical terms have been omitted.

[44] The much later Tibetan tradition of *mantras* interprets the suffix differently, and so understands the term to mean "to protect the mind."

CHAPTER 5: THE PATHWAY OF DEVOTION

Simply reciting the sounds without the authority of the *guru* makes them useless. Here are two examples of Tantric Hindu mantras:

HRIM HRIM HAM MAHAISAYA HAM HRIM HRIM

or

OM KITI KITI VAJRA HUM HUM HUM PHAT SVAHA.[45]

Consulting a Sanskrit dictionary will not give the reader any useful insight into a special meaning to these sounds. They are sounds, not words, and although they can be associated with secret meanings (secrets which the *guru* will explain to the student when the student is ready), their primary value is in the sound and not the secret meaning.

Mandalas: Circular diagrams or patterns

A *mandala* is a map of sacred space, usually the sacred space surrounding a divinity. According to the Tantric teachers, a *mandala* is a complex intricate model of both the sacred cosmos and of the total human being who reflects the features of the universe in her or his own physical body. Tantrism asserts that there is an equivalence between the individual, the microcosm, and the totality, the macrocosm. *Mandala* are maps of a spiritual journey which the student undertakes to explore reality by exploring within, under the guidance of a *guru*. Tantric practitioners believe that with the aid of the *guru*, the student can awaken and explore spiritual potentials buried in the levels of consciousness which are deeper than we ordinarily encounter. This path is not to be undertaken lightly, for there are dangers lurking in the unconscious. *Mandala* imagery reveals that within a human being there is a center, guarded by dreaded guards, where some ultimate deity resides. The Tantric student who can use *mantras* and *mandalas* is undertaking a lengthy journey whose ultimate destination is *moksha*, liberation from duality, and liberation from *samsara*.

The need to achieve liberation must also include liberation from social conventions, liberation from society itself and socially determined morality, and the means to accomplish this can often be perceived as shocking. Thus, Tantric yoga may involve the five forbidden things, like eating fish and meat and drinking alcohol, as well as other things unacceptable to Hindu *dharma*. It can also include things such as practicing meditation alongside a decaying corpse or using rituals implements made of human skulls and human bones, both of which are used to help the student achieve liberation.

The Tantric pathway was not an open public path to liberation because some forms utilized socially offensive devices. It was a secret teaching, given to a student only when the spiritual teacher has guided and tested the student, and believes the student is ready for the advanced teachings. Vows are taken by the student to never reveal the content of the esoteric teachings. This also included a prohibition against revealing the symbolism that so obviously contradict the standard *dharma* morality of the higher levels of Indian society.

The *Kali Yuga* and Tantric Devotionalism (*Puja*).

According to Indian tradition, time is cyclical and a universe will arise, endure for a while, and then end. Then another universe will begin and the process has been going on without beginning. A single universal cycle involves four periods. The first period is the time of the creation of the universe presided over by Brahma, a golden age without pain or suffering. All beings find it natural and easy to meditate and live virtuous lives. Vishnu presides over the second and third periods which are the enduring and sustaining periods. At the beginning there are no castes. People are naturally inclined to do their proper *dharma* duty, but this weakens and finally, in the third period, the *varna* and castes need to be formed to ensure order.

The fourth period corresponds to the destruction or dissolution of the universe by Shiva. Following the

---

[45] Agehananda Bharati, *The Tantric Tradition,* p. 130. Sanskrit diacritical marks have been omitted.

destruction, the entire cycle begins again, and once again the sages hear the eternal sounds of the sacred words of the Vedas. This ancient notion reflects the Indian world-view which tended to see the world as a place of ignorance and suffering, a universe on a downward spiral toward destruction, getting worse and worse with each century. It cannot be improved. Such a world was to be escaped from and not to be changed.

The fourth and last of the four periods is called the *Kali Yuga*, the period of the deterioration of the universe as it spirals down to final destruction.[46] As the universe deteriorates, there is a corresponding deterioration of the abilities of human beings to attain *moksha* by means of their own powers. During the *Kali Yuga* Brahmin priests become less worthy, caste members ignore their *dharma* and intermarry improperly, life spans decrease, and finally there will be great destructive natural disasters with a great flood bringing about the final destruction.[47]

In ancient days of the earlier eras, natural human abilities were sufficient to attain liberation, but not during the *Kali Yuga*[48] which began five thousand years ago. The wisdom pathway of *jnana-marga* requires the power of rare insight generated by difficult introspective meditations. To achieve liberation by means of sacred and liberating knowledge or yoga-meditation, is to achieve *moksha* by oneself. But the Tantric followers believe that in our time period, the *Kali Yuga*, the natural human powers are weakened and deteriorating. If one's own wisdom and knowledge and yogic abilities were not able to get one liberated from *samsara*, what could a person do?[49] There was another path for those trapped in the *Kali Yuga*. It is the *bhakti-marga* which is the appropriate pathway for the times of the *Kali Yuga*.

Devotion to a goddess or a Supreme Lord, combined with the use of *mantras* for purification, was available to everyone who sought out a Tantric *guru*. In this case, it is the supernatural power and loving response of the *deva* which frees us from *samsara*, not our own power or our own self. This is because our own power is inadequate. Whether one can read or write, or not, one can seek refuge in any of the various forms of divinities, and worship them, and call out their name in devotion. Following the sixth century C.E., powerful faith in the liberating power of devotion to a *deva* was especially strong in the Tamil-speaking area of South India.[50]

5.8 THE HINDU EPICS: The *Ramayana* and the *Mahabharata*

There is a category of ancient Indian literature referred to as the Epics. Epics belong to a group of Indian religious literature composed by human beings, and thus their sounds are not sacred and their words are not words of power. Although human-created, nevertheless these are divinely inspired and therefore very important. In theory, the most ancient Vedas, Brahmanas, and Aranyakas are much more important but ordinary well-educated people

---

[46] Hindus date the beginning of the *Kali Yuga* as occurring with the horrific carnage which occurred in the great battle told of in the *Bhagavad Gita*. The date 3102 B.C.E. is assigned to this event, and the beginning of the final period. See below.

[47] Vishnu sleeps on the waters of this great flood, and awakens to create Brahma, who starts the entire cycle over again.

[48] As was pointed out previously, India never had the Western view that things can be made better, society can be improved, and that the future in this very life can be better than the past. The *Kali Yuga* view understands the world as a place of ignorance and suffering, a universe on a downward spiral toward destruction, getting worse and worse with each decade. Such a world was to be escaped from and not to be changed.

[49] The later Mahayana Buddhist tradition has a similar aspect: the period when the teachings of the Buddha were easily understood and people achieved nirvana; the second period when fewer and fewer could achieve nirvana on their own; the third degenerate period when humans were no longer to achieve nirvana except by divine grace. These ideas were important in the Buddhist *Lotus Sutra* and were important in Chinese, Japanese, and Tibetan Buddhism.

[50] Hopkins, *The Hindu Religious Tradition*, p. 117.

cannot read these ancient texts, but they can read the epics.

The Epics are much more popular for Indian religion than the ancient Vedas. Epics tell great tales of battle, of loss, of courage, bravery, and the overcoming of great odds. The two most important Epics are the *Ramayana* and the *Mahabharata* and are usually dated between 200 B.C.E. and 200 C.E. The *Ramayana* tells the story of Rama, a great prince who is thought to be an incarnation of the *deva* Vishnu. Rama saves his wife, slays the demon Ravana and displays proper behavior to parents, brothers, and rulers.

The *Mahaabharata* is the great epic poem of India which constitutes a virtual encyclopedia of tales of forgotten history, myths and legends of early India. The earliest oral forms of the poems in the *Mahabharata* may go as far back as 500 B.C.E. but in the form that we have today, it dates to about 200 C.E. Modern scholars are inclined to think of it as a composite work, composed between 500 and 100 B.C.E.

According to tradition, a sage named Vyasa told the tale of the *Mahabharata* to the elephant-headed *deva* Ganesha, and Ganesha then wrote the story down in verse form. The poem is quite immense, composed of nearly 100,000 verses. The most important chapter of the *Mahabharata* is the one which contains the *Bhagavad Gita*, which will become the single most important religious text in all of India, and the text which provides the foundation for the second great *bhakti* tradition, devotion to Vishnu.

5.9 THE WORSHIP OF VISHNU

We have previously discussed Vishnu in the context of the great Hindu trinity which included Brahma, associated with creation, and Shiva, the personification of destruction. The third member of the trinity, the solar divinity Vishnu, sustains reality as the sunlight[51] sustains the crops and provides food, as well as protecting unborn babies in the womb. Vishnu cares about our welfare and happiness. With Vishnu watching over us and protecting us, the universe is friendly and good, supportive of human beings. Vishnu was also associated with water. As water is commonly seen as being blue, and Vishnu is said to sleep on the back of the snake-god Adi Shesha who floats on cosmic waters, it is only natural that Vishnu's representations are often blue-skinned. Vishnu was not the most important deity in the Vedic age, but his importance increases over the centuries because of the myths which tell of his good deeds on behalf of human beings.

Vishnu, the Supreme Being, is the preserver, the protector of the good and the guardian of dharma. Seated on Adi Shesha, the many-hooded serpent, in the primeval waters, he watches over his devotees and rewards the pious. And whenever dharma is in danger, he incarnates himself on earth to rid it of evil.[52]

Those people who were especially concerned about immortality were attracted to the worship of Vishnu. Considering how caring Vishnu was, it is not surprising that those who were followers of Vishnu tended to be people who saw the cosmos as fundamentally friendly and good. The several *bhakti* religions devoted to Vishnu are referred to as the **Vaishnava** traditions. For these worshipers, the sacred seed syllable *Om* is identified with Vishnu.

Vaishnavites understand Vishnu to sleep atop the cosmic ocean during the final destruction of the universe, and then awake and beget Brahma, who in turn creates the universe all over again, beginning another cycle (*kalpa*). In this sense, Vishnu is the one who truly underlies all that exists. Like Shiva, Vishnu has his feminine consort, the beautiful goddess Lakshmi, patron of wealth.

---

[51] The swastika is a very ancient symbol in India and it is auspicious, or lucky, and is the cross with four ends usually bent towards the right, is often seen on the chest of images of Vishnu, where it symbolizes the solar disc, and it also symbolizes good fortune. The image is also found on images of Shiva, perhaps because the swastika symbol resembles markings found on the hoods of cobras, also associated with Shiva. The German Nazis adopted the swastika (primarily right-facing although left-facing swastikas are found on Nazi flags and clothing) for their symbol, thereby associating the ancient religious symbol with their racist white-supremacy agenda.

[52] Krishna, Nanditha, *The Book of Vishnu* (New York: Penguin Group, 2003), cover.

CHAPTER 5: THE PATHWAY OF DEVOTION

THE *BHAGAVAD-GITA*

The ancient epic of history, the *Mahabharata*, has scattered references to a non-Vedic tribe called the Satvatas, a warrior group who were fighters famed for their bravery and loyalty. As the Satvatas began to distinguish themselves in battle, the Aryans respected them and treated them as *ksatriyas*.

However, the religion of the Satvatas was separate from the Aryan Vedic heritage. They did not practice Vedic rituals and Brahmins were not their priests. The Satvatas did not practice meditation, did not feel trapped by *karma*, and were not trying to escape a cycle of birth and death. They did not feel constrained by the caste system, for they had the status of *ksatriyas*, protectors, administrators, rulers and confidants of rulers. Their religion was not affected by the Vedic Hindu pathway of ritual, the *karma-marga*. The secret monist forest teachings of the *Upanishads* were unknown to the Satvatas.

Unlike Vedic Hindus, the Satvatas were monotheistic, not polytheistic. They worshiped a single god they called Krishna Vasudeva, also called the "Bhagavat," "Lord," or "Bounteous One." Thus the title of the sacred *Bhagavad gita* means the "Song of the Lord," or "Song Celestial." This scripture suggests answers to such important questions as "Who am I?" and "What should I do?" and the even more basic question, "How can I know what is morally right?"

Although appealing, the *Bhagavad gita* had a serious problem. There is no mention of a *deva* named Krishna Vasudeva anywhere in the Vedas.[53] If Krishna is not a Vedic *deva*, then any religion based on Krishna could not be orthodox. No Brahmin or Hindu might adhere to it without giving up all the Aryan traditions and losing his rich historical grounding. Also, any text talking about a non-Vedic god could not be sacred revelation because only the Vedas are revelation. Thus the monotheism of the Satvatas could not be accepted by the followers of traditional Vedic religions.

However, there is a common solution to that sort of problem. The solution is that Krishna **is** in the Vedas, but under a different name. The Brahmin followers of Krishna Vasudeva declared that Krishna in the Vedas is the same divinity as the one called Vishnu Narayana (Vishnu Born of Water). In Vedic Hinduism there are many tales of Vishnu, including tales of Vishnu coming down to earth to help preserve and protect the *dharma*. Remember that Vishnu was the protector of the Brahmins and protector of social order. Vishnu is said to sleep floating on cosmic waters, so many artistic representations of Vishnu portray him with skin that is blue. In art, Krishna is portrayed as dark skinned, so he may be blue too. If the Vedic *deva* Vishnu is the same as the deity of the Satvatas, Krishna, then a Hindu may worship Krishna.

The result of all of this is the *Bhagavad Gita* that we know, which is a creative combination of monotheistic religion, combined with the monistic religion of the *Upanishads*. The *Gita* explains the various keys to a good life if one is a Hindu. It explains the nature of the soul, it explains how to live your life when you are not sure what to do, it explains the nature of divinity, and it explains how we ought to respond to divinity.

The story of the *Bhagavad Gita* is an exciting tale of morality, religion, civil war, treachery, and victory. It is about karma and victory over the cycle of birth and death. As such it is exciting to hear, recite, and read, and it was so popular that the editors of the *Mahabharata* decided that it was an important part of the history of India, so they included it as the sixth book of the *Mahabharata*. Once it was contained within the great Indian epic of the *Mahabharata*, the *Bhagavad Gita* was acceptable as official Hindu religion. It is difficult to underestimate the historical importance of the *Gita*. Modern commentators frequently compare the importance of the *Gita* in Hinduism to the Greek books of the New Testament in Christianity.

In Indian society, a conflict developed around the practice of leaving home, renouncing all action, and entering the forest, the ancient path outlined in the *Manava-dharma-shastra* (the *Laws of Manu*). One's social and moral *dharma*

---

[53] The name "Krishna" appears in the Rg Veda, but it has no relation to the great deity who we are discussing. In a Vedic hymn, darker skinned aboriginal inhabitants of India were referred to as "Krishnas" and they and their wives were all killed by the Aryans. The first mention of the deity Krishna is found in the *Bhagavad Gita*.

is determined by one's caste, and in the newer path of *jnana* (liberating knowledge), one must renounce one's social and ritual *dharma* to achieve *moksha*. This creates a problem: the *Upanishads* teach renunciation of all action and of social duty, and young men were renouncing the world before marriage or early in their marriage, without fulfilling their family responsibilities. They did not remain to take over the family occupation, or help their parents when they got older. This was becoming a critical social problem. The *Gita* will offer a solution to this problem.

THE ADVENTURE TOLD IN THE *BHAGAVAD GITA*

The *Gita* is an exciting adventure story telling of a battle between two armies, but it is also the tale of one family fighting its own relatives and cousins to regain the throne that is rightfully theirs. The rival families, the Kurus and Pandavas, belong to the same clan, but they fought each other for control of the northern plains. The Pandavas win the battle, but the battle engendered such carnage to both sides that Hindu tradition says that this battle ushers in the final age of destruction. Hindu mythology assigns the date 3102 B.C.E. to this cosmic battle, which marks the beginning of the final *Kali yuga* period, the end of the universe.

The tale revolves around the question, what is our *dharma*, what is our religious duty, our duty to our caste and clan, our moral duty? The question is a question for everyone, but the *Gita* focuses our attention on one person, who is a stand-in for every human.

There are two main characters in this tale. One is Arjuna (pronounced AR-jun), the middle son of the Pandeva five brothers, and he is a spectacularly good archer and a mighty warrior. The other is Krishna Vasudeva, the chariot driver who guides the horses and drives the archer into battle. It is early morning and the sun is just beginning to illuminate the battlefield, with two huge contending armies lined up viewing one another across a great field. The battle is about to commence.

Arjuna is the greatest fighter on the battlefield. He is a good man, genuinely courageous and a mighty warrior of extraordinary valor and skill, contemplating a battle in which the army of the enemy is composed of relatives, cousins and teachers. It is contrary to his social and moral *dharma* to kill family members and teachers, most of whom are friends from childhood, but if he doesn't fight, others on his side will be killed by those same cousins and teachers.

Arjuna is a warrior of the *ksatriya* caste, and thus his caste duty is to fight but he is sickened at the thought of what his duty compels him to do. How could it be sacred duty to kill members of one's own extended family? What is his duty, his *dharma*? Should he go into battle and kill his own clan members whom he can see clearly on the opposite side of the battlefield, bringing one half of his own family to ruin or should he refuse to fight, thereby still bringing the other half of the family to ruin? Should Arjuna kill members of his own clan, which he swore to defend, or should he run from battle and family responsibilities, thereby not fulfilling his duty as a *ksatriya*?

Arjuna's Dilemma

He has two choices. To fight, or not fight. There seems no third possibility. Whichever he chooses, he will generate bad *karma* and he and others will suffer for it, not only in this life but in future lives as well. Not to perform his duty as a warrior is clearly wrong, but performing this duty seems fully as wrong. This is a terrible dilemma. This is not a battle between right and wrong; whatever he chooses will be wrong. He has to try to figure out which of the two options will be the lesser of two evils.

As the beginning of the battle draws near, Arjuna surveys the battle scene and falls into despair, and loses his will to fight. He decides to give up his weapons, abandon the world, renounce his warrior status, and live by begging. Arjuna thinks that possibly by doing nothing, by renouncing the duty of his caste, he can minimize or avoid bad *karma*.

Krishna Teaches Arjuna

The blue-skinned Krishna, the good friend of Arjuna and the driver of Arjuna's chariot, attempts to show Arjuna a new way of understanding his situation. He talks to Arjuna, but Arjuna simply will not understand what he is trying to explain. Krishna shames Arjuna, telling him he must fight. It is his caste duty, his *dharma*, to go into battle, and not fighting will be perceived as shameful. Arjuna will not change his mind. He wants to do nothing, he wants to quit. More discussion follows, and Arjuna explains that he will be forced to kill teachers, elders, relatives, childhood friends. This cannot be morally right. None of it makes any sense. Arjuna cannot see any way out except to do abandon the battle and become a forest ascetic.

संजय उवाच ।
एवमुक्त्वा ततो राजन्महायोगेश्वरो हरिः ।
दर्शयामास पार्थाय परमं रूपमैश्वरम् ॥ ९
अनेकवक्त्रनयनमनेकाद्भुतदर्शनम् ।
अनेकदिव्याभरणं दिव्यानेकोद्यतायुधम् ॥ १०
दिव्यमाल्याम्बरधरं दिव्यगन्धानुलेपनम् ।
सर्वाश्चर्यमयं देवमनन्तं विश्वतोमुखम् ॥ ११
दिवि सूर्यसहस्रस्य भवेद्युगपदुत्थिता ।
यदि भाः सदृशी सा स्याद्भासस्तस्य महात्मनः ॥ १२
तत्रैकस्थं जगत्कृत्स्नं प्रविभक्तमनेकधा ।
अपश्यद्देवदेवस्य शरीरे पाण्डवस्तदा ॥ १३
ततः स विस्मयाविष्टो हृष्टरोमा धनञ्जयः ।
प्रणम्य शिरसा देवं कृताञ्जलिरभाषत ॥ १४
अर्जुन उवाच ।
पश्यामि देवांस्तव देव देहे
सर्वांस्तथा भूतविशेषसंघान् ।
ब्रह्माणमीशं कमलासनस्थ-
मृषींश्च सर्वानुरगांश्च दिव्यान् ॥ १५
अनेकबाहूदरवक्त्रनेत्रं
पश्यामि त्वा सर्वतोऽनन्तरूपम् ।
नान्तं न मध्यं न पुनस्तवादिं
पश्यामि विश्वेश्वर विश्वरूप ॥ १६
किरीटिनं गदिनं चक्रिणं च
तेजोराशिं सर्वतो दीप्तिमन्तम् ।
पश्यामि त्वां दुर्निरीक्ष्यं समन्ता-
द्दीप्तानलार्ककद्युतिमप्रमेयम् ॥ १७

Finally, Krishna Vasudeva, the chariot driver, stands up and reveals to Arjuna who he really is: the *avatar* (earthly manifestation) of the Lord,[54] the Supreme God Vishnu incarnate, who has descended into the human realm, and taken a human form, in order to help human beings. This is no ordinary driver of a military chariot. This is not even a god. This is the god behind all gods, more than a mere divine being, grim, awesome, filled with might and splendor, unimaginably powerful. Lord Krishna says:

"Here, in Me living as one, O Arjuna, behold the whole universe, movable and immovable, and anything else that thou wouldst see.

"Yet since with mortal eyes thou canst not see Me, lo! I give thee the divine sight. See now the glory of My sovereignty."

"There were countless eyes and mouths, the mystic forms innumerable, with shining ornaments and flaming celestial weapons.

Crowned with heavenly garlands, clothed in shining garments, anointed with divine unctions, He showed Himself as the resplendent one, marvelous, boundless, omnipresent.

Could a thousand suns blaze forth together it would be but a faint reflection of the radiance of the Lord God.

In that vision Arjuna saw the universe, with its manifold shapes, all embraced in One, its Supreme Lord.

Thereupon, Arjuna, dumb with awe, his hair on end, his head bowed, his hands clasped in salutation, addressed the Lord thus:

Arjuna said, "O Almighty God! I see in Thee the powers of nature, the various creatures of the world, the progenitor on his lotus throne, the sages, and the shining angels.

"I see Thee, infinite in form, with as it were, faces, eyes, and limbs everywhere; no beginning, no middle, no end; O Thou Lord of the Universe, Whose form is universal."[55]

The ascetics in India practiced renunciation, doing the least amount possible. Arjuna assumes that this will be the ultimate solution to his own problem. If he drops his weapons and does not act, won't he be able to avoid or minimize the bad karmic consequences of his actions? Lord Krishna explains: One cannot escape action through non-action,

---

[54] In Indian religion, whenever a divinity comes to earth and takes on a material or human form, it is called an *avatara*, pronounced *avatar*.

[55] Chapter 11, Sri Purohit Swami, *Bhagavad Gita*, pp. 99–101. Krishna is universal; Krishna is every god worshiped in the world, no matter what the religion. Another translation:
"If the light of a thousand suns were to rise in the sky at once, it would be like the light of the great spirit. Arjuna saw all the universe in its many ways and parts, standing as one in the body of the god of gods. Then, filled with amazement, his hair bristling on his flesh, Arjuna bowed his head to the god, and joined his hands in homage"
"I see no beginning or middle or end to you, only boundless strength in your endless arms; the moon and the sun in your eyes, your mouths of consuming flames, your own brilliance scorching the universe. You alone fill the space between heaven and Earth and all directions. Seeing this awesome, terrible form of yours, Great Soul, the three worlds tremble. Seeing the many mouths and eyes of your great form, its many arms, thighs, feet, bellies, and things, the worlds tremble, and so do I."

for not-acting is itself an action; it is a moral choice, and carries with it the resulting bad karmic consequences.

Lord Krishna teaches Arjuna that to run away from objects of attachment, as Arjuna wanted to do, does not lessen karmic consequences because to run away does not destroy attachments to things of this world. Karma is caused by ego-centered attachment, caused by one's state of mind, not by one's physical actions.

Krishna reveals to Arjuna the liberating truth that **attachments are in the mind, not in things**. Real detachment is not to renounce objects, but to **renounce the desire** for objects, renounce the emotional push and pull focused on objects. The problem is not action, but rather our attachment to the fruits of action. Non-action is not a solution; in choosing non-action, one is attached to the non-action, and this generates negative karma.

Arjuna must act but must also give up his attachment to the outcome of the battle. He is a warrior and essential to a warrior is to fulfil his *dharma* of action and duty; hence Krishna's teaching to Arjuna places the emphasis upon *karma yoga*, the path of action. Krishna insists upon complete dedication to one's *dharma*, which for a warrior is action, relentless performance of one's military duties. It is the state of mind that makes the act good or bad. It is not the consequences.

Krishna teaches Arjuna that the key is all activity must be done with no thought of self-interest. We must do our best, but act with an attitude of absolute and utter detachment; one's activities are not a means to something else, but instead actions performed without attachment become an end in themselves and generate no *karma*.

Krishna's Solution: "Actionless Action."

Krishna teaches Arjuna the liberating wisdom, or *jnana*. It is to **simply act** (*karma yoga*), simply do your duty completely and fully, and be totally indifferent to the consequences of actions. Be indifferent to success or failure, to reward or punishment. Do not seek glory or recognition. Get the ego out of the action process. If you can do this, then no *karma* is created. Be genuinely non-attached to the consequences of doing one's *dharma*, renounce the fruits of the actions.

This seems almost impossible, but Krishna explains to Arjuna how it is possible. To have the correct mental attitude, Arjuna can do his duty as a service to Krishna, do it for the love of Krishna and no other reason—then this is *karma*-less action, or *karma*-less *karma*, this is actionless action, this is action (*karma*) in inaction, or inaction in the middle of action (*karma*).

Arjuna trembles at the thought of killing. Krishna explains that the *atman*, the eternal self-existent immaterial soul, cannot be killed. When Arjuna goes into battle and shoots his arrows, he cannot really kill because every soul is immortal and continues to transmigrate. Death is an illusion. Do your best in battle, with not a thought about consequences. Devote the fruits of battle to god. Arjuna is a warrior, and the *dharma* of a warrior is to fight.

"One who can see inaction in action, and action in inaction, is the wisest among men. He is a saint, even though he still acts.

"The wise call him a sage; for whatever he undertakes is free from the motive of desire, and his deeds are purified by the fire of wisdom.

"Having surrendered all claim to the results of his actions, always contented and independent, in reality he does nothing, even though he is apparently acting.

"Expecting nothing, his mind and personality controlled, without greed, doing bodily actions only; though he acts, yet he remains untainted.

"Content with what comes to him without effort of his own, mounting above the pairs of opposites; free from envy, his mind balanced both in success and failure, thou he acts, yet the consequences do not bind him.

"One who is without attachment, free, his mind centered in wisdom, his actions, being done as a sacrifice, leave no trace behind."[56]

---

[56] Sri Purohit Swami, *Bhagavad Gita*, ch. 4, pp. 40–42.

CHAPTER 5: THE PATHWAY OF DEVOTION

Doing your duty (*karma yoga*) also involves **knowing why you do your duty** (*jnana yoga*) which is the knowledge of liberation—and so *karma yoga* also encompasses the path of wisdom, the technique of *jnana yoga*. Wisdom includes the realization that one's actions are not the cause of *karma*. It is the state of mind while one acts that causes *karma*.

One's *dharma* is one's duty, determined by one's caste, one's position in the family, and other such concerns. Doing one's duty, action, work or activity is the best worship of god—act for the love of god, dedicate all one's accomplishments to god—and so *karma yoga* is also the pathway of devotion, *bhakti yoga*.

One does not need to leave home to achieve liberation

The implication of actionless action is startling. You do not need to renounce society and enter the forest to achieve *moksha*. **You can live your life in society, following your social role (your *dharma*) merely because it is your duty, and still achieve liberation!** Marry, raise children, work in the family business, do your social duty and dedicate all consequences to god, and the result is karma-less action.

Karma is what traps us in the continuing cycle of birth and death, the cycle of *samsara*; karma-less action is liberation from *samsara*. Thus the *Gita* presents a unique blend of knowledge, devotion, and action, as the way(s) to realize *moksa*.

This strategy applies to other pathways as well. There is not just one way to pursue libation, There are many pathways. One must find the path that is appropriate for one's *varna*, one's temperament. As a warrior, Arjuna's path was that of duty and action, but what about the Brahmin whose pathway is ritual and sacrifice? It is the same scheme: the result of the ritual depends upon the attitude of the doer — a selfish performance leads one to suffering, a dispassionate performance free from desire, detached, and performed for no other reason than the love of god, leads one to the cessation of *karma* and that is *moksa*.

Everyone of us has a *dharma*, a duty, and our duty is determined by the social group into which we were born. In turn, our social class is the right one for us because in previous lives we made choices which caused us to be born as a warrior, a priest, a merchant, or a menial servant in this life. If you are a toilet cleaner, then clean those toilets with all your energy, and do it for the love of god. Following one's nature, one can achieve happiness. The *varna* (social class) into which one was born is the best indicator of what one's dominant nature is. Following the yoga (method) which corresponds to one's *varna* is the best way to achieve *moksa*. Even those traditionally excluded by Vedic religious practice can be included. Women and *shudras* can offer gifts to Krishna like water, or a leaf of a flower, or a fruit. All offerings are valuable.

The strength and power of the *Gita* is that it makes room for all the various personality types, and accommodates all the occupations. The pluralism of the *Gita* allows us to realize our True Self by following any one of the pathways, *bhakti*, *jnana*, *karma*, or *dhyana*.

(1) **Bhakti Yoga** or **Bhakti Marga**: the method or pathway of devotion, faith, total surrender of the follower of the will of God for love of God. Love Krishna and surrender one's will and all concerns to the love of god. One need not worship only Krishna/Vishnu. **Complete faith in any divinity is equivalent and is successful**. Whatever name or image you choose to have complete faith in, it will still be accepted by Krishna; indeed, it will be an aspect of Krishna.

(2) **Karma Yoga** or **Karma Marga**: the path of work, of social and religious duty, of ritual, of action. This is the method specific to Arjuna's dilemma. The solution appropriate for Arjuna to allow him to avoid karmic consequences is **simply act** and do one's duty as a warrior, and be completely indifferent to the consequences, indifferent to success or failure, to reward or punishment. In doing so, one does not generate any karmic consequences at all—it is action which generates no karma, it is actionless action. In addition the rituals of the Brahmins are honored, for they have the possibility of bringing liberation, as long as they are performed with total devotion to god for the love of god.

CHAPTER 5: THE PATHWAY OF DEVOTION

(3) **Jnana Yoga** or **Jnana Marga**: the *Bhagavad Gita* does reveal knowledge of how to escape the trap of karma. The liberating wisdom is that it is not action that generates karma, but rather attachment is what traps us in the cycle of birth and death. Attachments are in the mind, not in things. It is not the action, but it is the state of mind of the person performing the action, that causes karmic consequences and keeps one trapped, revolving in the cycle of *samsara*. Thus doing your duty (*karma yoga*) is also the path of liberating wisdom. One comes to liberation via the intellect, via knowledge, via profound understanding. One comes to know that the true self is identical with the sacred ultimate that created yet transcends the universe. By apprehending the true nature of the self, one comes to the attainment of *moksa*.

(4) **Dhyana Yoga** or **Dhyana Marga**: the yoga or method of meditation. In chapter 6 of the *Bhagavad Gita*, Krishna explains that the yoga of meditation is difficult, and only for those who have great determination, great self-control. One sits, one controls one's desires, brings passions under control, and learns to focus one's attention on the divine, concentrates on loving God. By doing so, one does not stimulate ego-centered desires, so one masters an attitude of focused non-attachment in all things. The result is that one becomes stronger and more disciplined in meditative states of mind. This functions to calm the mind, and increases one's ability to concentrate. With focused concentration, single-pointed attention on things which will not arouse desires, attachments, and bondage, one realizes the ultimate self in an act of immediate intuition, realizing one's true nature.[57] As one moves beyond the normal routine of pleasures and pains, one will rethink one's actions, one's motivations, and becomes less trapped. The resulting detachment does not mean feeling nothing. To be detached is to be concerned without being ego-involved, without being attached.[58] This applies to the ascetics in the forest, and the householder as well.

All Are Welcome

The *Bhagavad Gita* accommodates all forms of Hinduism as aspects of the worship of Krishna without requiring one to be a devotee of Krishna. There is no opposition to non-Vaishnava forms of religion; all pathways can be subsumed under the *Gita*. In other words, you do not have to be a devotee of Krishna to honor and appreciate the *Gita*.[59] One can worship other gods, as long as the worship is done with complete devotion. "When devoted men sacrifice to other deities with faith, they sacrifice to me, Arjuna, however aberrant the rites." All spiritual paths lead to Lord Krishna, if they are performed selflessly and with devotion. All spiritual seekers are honored within the *Gita*; there are many paths to the divine.[60]

THE LATER VAISNAVA TRADITION

Those aspects of Indian devotional religion which focus upon Vishnu are referred to as the **Vaishnava** traditions. However, just because Vishnu is at the center does not mean that Vaishnavism is one religion. Over the centuries many different devotionally-oriented religious groups developed, which focused on several forms of Vishnu, or his *avatar* Krishna in the *Bhagavad Gita*. During the 2,000 years from the creation of the *Gita* to the present, there are what Fenton calls "a great family of religions bound together by the common possession of the *Bhagavadgita* and a few other universally accepted scriptures."[61] When it was decided that Krishna is in the Vedas, where he is called

---

[57] Potter, *Presuppositions of India's Philosophies*, pp. 40ff

[58] *Ibid.*,

[59] Fenton, *et. al.*, *Religions of Asia*, Second ed., p. 105a.

[60] A careful study of the complexity of the text is Gurcharan Das, *The Difficulty of Being Good: On the Subtle Art of Dharma* (London: Allen Lane, 2010).

[61] Fenton, *et. al.*, *Religions of Asia*, third edition, p. 73.

Vishnu, then Krishna-worship is in accord with the Vedas. As a consequence, the religion of the *Bhagavad-gita* is official revealed Hindu orthodoxy.

5.10 THE AVATARAS.

The story of the *Bhagavad Gita* offers the vision of the divinity who takes on a material form, called the *avatara* (pronounced *avatar*). Vishnu chooses to descend to earth, take an earthly body, and help humans. Most Western students are already familiar with the concept of an *avatar*, an incarnation of the supreme divinity. In the world of the Mediterranean and Israel, there was also a literary tradition of divine saviors, who came to earth as incarnations and preached a gospel or "good news." For example, Augustus Caesar was described as a divine savior (*avatar*) by the Provincial Assembly of Asia Minor:

> Whereas the Providence which has guided our whole existence and which has shown such care and liberality, has brought our life to the peak of perfection in giving us Augustus Caesar, whom it [Providence] filled with virtue for the welfare of mankind, and who, being sent to us and our descendants as a savior, has put an end to war, and has set all things in order; and whereas, having become visible [a god has become visible] . . . and whereas, finally that the birthday of the God [Augustus Caesar] has been for the whole world the beginning of the gospel "good news" concerning him, . . . [62]

Vaishnavite Hindus recognize ten different occasions when Vishnu incarnated and descended into the physical realm to help human beings, so there are at least ten *avatars*. They include the eighth *avatar* of Vishnu, Krishna (the *deva* in the *Gita*) and Rama (the hero of the epic called the *Ramayana*). Later, the followers of Vishnu considered the founder of Buddhism to be another *avatar*, even though the Buddha's actual teachings were rejected by Hindus.[63] There is also a future *avatar* waiting for the appropriate time to descend. He is Kalki, who is portrayed as a swordsman mounted on a white horse, who will come to guide human beings in the last times of the *Kali Yuga*. Although in general Hindus accept the ten *avataras*, only the Vaishnavas feel obligated to actually worship any of them.

Another Understanding of an *Avatar*

In the description above, we treated the *avatar* story in a very literal way. The *deva* crosses over from the heavenly realm, descends, and enters our world in order to teach something important to human beings. Although the majority of Hindus understand the concept of *avatar* literally, this is not the only possible way to understand it. A more psychological interpretation is possible: "Descending" or "crossing over" can be taken as a movement of one's higher spiritual consciousness into one's lower state of consciousness. Our superior spiritual nature becomes manifest to our lower worldly consciousness. The divine true self is always present in one's consciousness, and it "crosses over" and brings liberating knowledge. In this interpretation, it is Arjuna himself who moves from a lower level of awareness to a higher level of awareness, or the higher part of himself becomes available to him; he achieves a more profound level of understanding. The great battle between opposing armies occurs in the mind of Arjuna. The enemies are the confused emotional states such as ego, anger, confusion, hatred, and ignorance. In conquering these, Arjuna achieves liberation.

---

[62] Randal Helms, *Gospel Fictions* (New York: Prometheus Books, 1988) p. 24.

[63] Although some regard the Buddha as a valued teacher of the ascetic forest life, others see his divine function as fooling those with bad karma to follow his false teachings, thereby hastening their rebirth into the lower hells. Esposito, *et. al.*, *World Religions Today*, p. 295.

5.11 RAMANUJA'S QUALIFIED NON-DUALISTIC VEDANTA

Vaishnava worship of Vishnu exerted a significant influence over a form of Vedanta. As you recall from the Chapter Four discussion of the Non-dualistic Advaita Vedanta of Shankara (788–820 C.E.), worshiping a personal *deva* is appropriate for those who are spiritually immature, but a personal divine being is not the deepest religious insight. For Shankara, *atman* is Brahman. There are no personal divinities who love us, care for us, reward or punish us, or interact with us. What we think of as reality is actually *maya* (illusory). There is only Brahman, which can be described as *sat* (pure existence), *cit* (pure consciousness) and *ananda* (pure bliss). The monism of Shankara's Non-dualistic Vedanta is only slightly compatible with devotionalism.

Vaishnavite devotionalism (*bhakti*) generated another form of Vedanta, the Qualified Non-Dualistic Vedanta of Ramanuja. For Ramanuja (who lived approximately 300 years after Shankara, i.e. ca. 1020–1137 C.E.), Vedanta is still about *atman* and Brahman, and their relationship, however Brahman is not merely an impersonal force describable as *sat, cit, ananda*. For Ramanuja, we should worship Brahman, and Vishnu is the form of Brahman which is most effective to worship. We still have *atman* and Brahman, but now knowledge alone will not achieve *moksha*. Instead, we need to worship the divine form of Brahman, that is, Vishnu. As such it is *bhakti* that is required for full liberation.

In Qualified Non-dualistic Vedanta, your *atman* is a part of the ultimate sacred oneness, but *atman* is not completely identical with Brahman and god. *Atman* and Brahman are still not-two, but they are not identical. The relationship is **qualified non-dualism**. Ramanuja asserts the reality of separate selves and a pluralistic reality, plus a divine god. Our selves are trapped in ignorance as a result of karma and do not recognize their essential nature. Selves can be released from bondage only by knowledge of Brahman, a god endowed with all auspicious qualities, and the knowledge is of the nature of meditation.

In Qualified Non-Dualism, the *atman* is a fragment of Vishnu, but none of us are Vishnu. The true self realizes itself to be a part of Brahman, like Brahman, in constant communion with Brahman. But, the *atman* retains its own individual identity.

Contrary to Shankara, Ramanuja holds that bondage is not *maya* but is real, and cannot be eliminated by mere *jnana* alone. The cessation of bondage can come only through the grace of god, who is pleased by the devout meditation of the worshiper. No one can achieve liberation on their own. Ultimate liberation is the reward for devout prayer and worship. The final outcome is that the *atman* perpetually enjoys the bliss of constant communion with and devotion to god.

5.12 THE CULT OF GOPALA KRISHNA, THE COWHERD

A new form of Krishna worship arose later and became fully mature around 1000 C.E. These worshipers cultivate a personal relationship with Krishna. Although worshipers are devoted to Krishna, this is a vastly different Krishna from the one who is central to the *Bhagavad Gita*. This Krishna is worshiped as a child and also worshiped as a young cowherder, and both are forms of Vaishnava religion only peripherally connected to the story of Krishna in the *Gita*. These cowherding stories are based on tales found in later texts, called the Vishnu Puranas,[64] which tell of the various *avatars* of Vishnu, including Krishna the youthful cowherder.

---

[64] The Puranas are stories of the history of the universe from beginning to end, cycle after cycle. The Puranas tell of the origins of humans, but stress genealogies of the kings, heroes, sages, and demigods, and descriptions of the nature of and structure of the universe according to the Hindu world-view. The earliest written versions of the Puranas date from 200–700 C.E. which is the time that devotion to divinities was growing and flourishing. The process of adding to the corpus continued on for at least another thousand years. The Puranas present pictures of competing sectarian cults focused upon different *devas*. The Vishnu Puranas telling stories about the cowherding Krishna are among the later texts.

CHAPTER 5: THE PATHWAY OF DEVOTION

The Krishna who lectures Arjuna in the *Bhagavad Gita* is grim, is awesome, is frightening, filled with might, overwhelming power and glorious splendor. The Krishna in the *Gita* fills us with fear and we tremble before him, humbled. The spiritual gulf between the Krishna of the *Gita* and humans is much too huge for any human to relate to; we cannot bridge that gap. We cannot walk up to this Krishna and pat him on the back. We cannot imagine sharing a lunch or a joke with this Krishna. We cannot be friends with the Krishna of the *Gita*.

In later times Puranic tales appear which purport to tell us stories of Krishna before he appeared to Arjuna on the battlefield. There are many names and titles for this youthful Krishna. This Krishna is Gopala (protector of cows), Govinda (finder of cows), Madhava (bringer of springtime), and is also referred to as a charioteer, a reference to his role with regard to Arjuna in the great battle.

One form of this worships Krishna as a child and a different form worships Krishna the youth, when he was a cowherder. The *Gita* makes no mention of these Krishnas. So, entirely new stories fill in the "omissions" of the *Gita*. None of these stories is as ancient as the *Bhagavad Gita* itself. Devotion to the child Krishna is most popular after 1000 C.E. Thus, for devotees of this deity, we have devotion to (a) Krishna the child, and (b) Krishna the youthful cowherder.[65]

The Divine Playful Child

If the spiritual distance between the Krishna of the *Gita* and humans is much too huge for any human to relate to, the spiritual distance between the Gopala Krishna and humans is barely there; the divine Gopala Krishna is childlike and in being childlike, he is irresistibly approachable. The Gopala Krishna is the embodiment of divine childhood, divine beauty, joy, playfulness, and tender love. Krishna is the charming and irrepressible divine child, but some followers worship the slightly older youth, Krishna, who is God as divine dancer and divine lover. Both forms of Krishna demonstrate sacred love, the beauty of God manifested in human form, and the fascinating, creative, purposeless divine play (*lila*) by which Krishna created the universe.[66]

In Gopala Krishna, the child Krishna, God is not approached as a servant to a master; we join him in play and interact with him as an equal, as a playmate. As a cowherder, this Krishna reveals a humble boy, who reveals divine beauty, joy and love of ultimate reality; the youth expresses the divine nature as carefree, exuberant, playful, beautiful. Krishna as the cowherd represents a carefree life, filled with divine pranks. The world was created through play and through play all things are fulfilled. Children are godlike, and the child Krishna is god.

The worship of Krishna in the last 500 years has stressed the loving chanting or singing the names of Krishna, accompanied by drums, cymbals, and often ecstatic dance. These events can happen in private homes, in temples, or street processions. Any devotee can take part. One can be a mother to baby Krishna, rocking him, singing to him.

The message of and appeal of Gopala Krishna is easy to understand. Come to the sacred God, come to the divine through laughter, play, and love (do not attempt to suppress these–glory in them). You too can be drawn into the loving embrace of the supreme God, and taste the divine ecstacy of divine bliss through loving surrender to Krishna.[67]

Life is not meant to be endured and suffered through; it is to be celebrated and enjoyed! The stories told of this Gopala Krishna are tales of *lila* (playfulness): some take the form of the mischievous, impish, fun-loving child, and others tell of the flirtatious, amorous, naughty cowherd who is God. Even when Krishna conquers evil demons,

---

[65] See Edwin F. Bryant, ed., *Krishna: A Sourcebook* (London and New York: Oxford University, 2007).

[66] A paraphrase from Robert Ellwood, *Cycles of Faith*, p. 112.

[67] John Koller, *The Indian Way*, p. 216.

it is play—whatever he does he does only as play. Krishna rescues villagers from evil serpent demons, and saves them from the cruel rains sent by Indra.

Unlike the Hindu locked into a rigid social caste system, Krishna's youthful life is not severe and restricted. He plays as a child and as a youth. He is never concerned with anything serious, and never works. As a baby he tries to catch his own shadow, and giggles in glee as it eludes his grasp. He unties the village calves and cows, and pulls their tails. He makes fun of village adults, he teases other children until they cry. He steals butter and sweets from the kitchens of the neighbors. He is a mischievous child.

Krishna, the Youthful Cowherder

As indicated previously, there was a separate religious tradition of the approachable Krishna which later becomes associated with the young man who is also a cowherd. There is the aspect of God as the embodiment of love, and in the Indian world-view, an image of God's divine love is the loving desire of and union of male and female. The young man, Gopala Krishna, plays the flute, and the music of his flute enters the ears and hearts of the women, summoning them to an erotic rendevous. The call of his flute is the irresistible sweet music of divine love. The sexual symbolism of the flute is obvious.

Gopala Krishna introduces the women of the district to the ecstasy of divine love, through his divine love-play. All the women approach him, and are engulfed in the warm embrace of his divine love. The Lord can satisfy anyone who comes to him in loving devotion, and the lover achieves the ecstatic fulfillment of the deepest human longings in the loving embrace of the beloved Lord. Moreover, he is viewed by his devotees, from ancient times till the present day, as reflecting the intense beauty of God in his physical aspect.

The stories of Krishna are stories of sacred love. Surrounded by hundreds of cowherd women in the forest, Krishna initiates them into the joys of divine love, teaching them the carefree play of love as an expression of their own divinity, awakened by surrender to Krishna's embrace. One should love Krishna, but do not be possessive, do not cling to Krishna. Krishna does not belong to you alone. It is clear that devotion to Gopala Krishna is a form of the path of *bhakti*; liberation achieved through loving devotion to the Divine.

The lover is God as Divine Lover, and the erotic images are just imagery—the vivid sensuousness of the south Indian Tamil language poetry give symbolic power to the images, and sensuous feelings are transformed into spiritual love, the fullest and most joyous expression of life. The divine love that God offers is perfectly symbolized in the erotic love that Krishna offers.[68]

Some interpret the appeal of Gopala Krishna as an outlet for those who feel oppressed by the very firm inflexible social restraints of Hindu caste social order. The Krishna of the *Bhagavad Gita* who is stern and who lectures on duty, becomes less and less important, until it is the child Gopala Krishna who is the primary focus of worship for the Vishnava sect. We can contrast the playful child Krishna with the austere ascetic sages in the forest. These forest-dwelling sages struggle with the hard discipline of yoga. They reject joy and pleasure in their mastery of the ascetic life. This ascetic pathway of pain and suffering is ignored by the followers of Gopala Krishna.

If you see an image of the child Gopala Krishna, you will notice that the skin color is often blue, the color of a blue lotus. Krishna's dark blue skin signifies that he is the *avatar* of Vishnu, who is "Born of Water." As you recall, Vishnu is the *deva* who sustains and preserves, and water is the nourisher of plants and animals alike, the very substance of cyclic existence, and is essential to preservation. As water is commonly seen as being blue, and Vishnu is said to sleep floating on cosmic waters, it is only natural that Vishnu's representations are often shown as blue skinned.

---

[68] John Koller, *The Indian Way*, p. 224:

In the West, the present-day Hare Krishna sect (ISKON, International Society for Krishna Consciousness, founded in 1966) is a Western variant of the cult of worship of Krishna as the roguish young cowherd who uses his divine powers to live in joyful freedom Followers chant, or sing the names of Krishna, accompanied by drums, cymbals, and ecstatic dance. They sing what they call the Great *mantra* which utilizes the names of god:

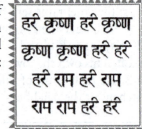

> Hare Krishna Hare Krishna
> Krishna Krishna Hare Hare
> Hare Rama Hare Rama
> Rama Rama Hare Hare

5.13 THE WORSHIP OF RAMA: THE *RAMAYANA*

Connected with the worship of Vishnu is the first-century C.E. worship of Rama, historical person and hero of the epic *Ramayana*. A thousand years after his death, Rama is identified as the eighth *avatar* of Vishnu.

The *Ramayana* is a tale of an illustrious northern India royal family. It tells the heroic story of Prince Rama who, with the help of the monkey god Hanuman, rescues his wife Shita from a demon. Like the European medieval romances, the *Ramayana* manifests the Hindu ideals of exemplary behavior in the performance of *dharma*, one's social, moral and political duty. Each person's life is determined by his and her own *dharma* according to social class, *varna*, and their stage of life, their *ashrama*. Obedience to these, and truthfulness, guarantees social order, highly valued in India.

Ultimately, Prince Rama and his wife serve as models for the duties of each son to father, each husband to his wife, and the duty of wife to husband. As such it also reinforced the rather rigid codes of behavior found in the *Laws of Manu*. Social responsibilities have the highest priority, much higher than personal happiness. The earliest versions of the *Ramayana* show it to be a text which is purely polytheistic and there is no identification with Vishnu or with any form of monotheism. Later, a first chapter and a last chapter were added to the *Ramayana*, which made this identification of the hero Rama with an *avatar* of Vishnu.[69]

5.14 GANESHA, THE ELEPHANT-HEADED DEVA

Ganesha is the happy *deva* of good luck and auspicious blessings, and has an elephant's head with only one tusk. He is careful to fulfill the requests of devotees. Ganesha is a happy *deva*, usually depicted as being rosy-colored, pot-bellied, and adorned with a crown. He has four arms, and in his hands, Ganesha holds various objects (shell, discus, club, water-lily), with one hand stretched out towards us offering greetings, blessings and good fortune.[70] Ganesha enjoys sweets, and this accounts for his substantial girth.

Ganesha is the Lord who Overcomes Obstacles, the *deva* of good luck, the *deva* of wisdom, the patron of learning and scholarship. As such, Ganesha is learned, a good scribe, and very knowledgeable in the sacred scriptures. Ancient tales reveal that a wise sage told the tale of the *Mahabharata* to Ganesha, who then wrote it down for the very first time.

At the beginning of any project, or travel, when the follower wishes good luck and success, Ganesha is invoked and it is hoped that he will provide good fortune and ensure a successful outcome for any enterprise. When the portly Ganesha travels, he travels standing atop a rodent [rat mole]. A very popular and comical image depicts the very large

---

[69] In 1987 the *Ramayana* was shown in India as a television epic of 78 chapters, and it became the most watched television show ever. Actors included Sikhs and Muslims as well as Hindus. The tale is also celebrated in the annual festival of *Divali*.

[70] A good collection of studies on Ganesha is Pratapaditya Pal, ed. *Ganesh, the Benevolent* (India: Marg Publications, 1995).

smiling Ganesha, with a generous pot-belly and elephant head, standing atop a rat, who carries him wherever he wishes to go. For this reason, there is often a rodent at the foot of an image of Ganesha.

There are several different myths about the origins of Ganesha: in one he is the child of Parvati and Shiva; or perhaps created by Parvati (there are many different tales about Ganesha's origins in the *Puranas*). Other myths have Shiva as the creator of Ganesha. For example, in one story it is the beauty of the child Ganesha that is responsible for him having the head of an elephant. It is told that the supremely graceful and fabulously beautiful Parvati was jealous of her own child's exceptional beauty, and cursed the child and as a result of the curse, Ganesha had an elephant head and a pot belly.[71] In another tale, his mother, Parvati, created him in order to stand guard over her while she bathed. Ganesha tried to stop Shiva from entering the bathing area, and in anger, Shiva decapitated him. Parvati revealed the truth that Ganesha was his own son, and so Shiva promised to restore his missing head with the head of the first living thing who came into view. An elephant came into view. Thus, Ganesha has the head of an elephant.

5.15 SUMMARY OF THE CHAPTER

The desire for *moksha* is common for followers of the *jnana-marga* and also for some of the followers of the *bhakti-marga*. In general, those who practice the Way of Action (*karma-yoga*) say little or nothing about liberation. Nevertheless, the four *margas* agree: this everyday world we inhabit could never be the locus of life's final blessedness. We must escape and transcend this world, whether it be identity with the sacred ultimate or basking in the infinite love of a god. We have noted significant differences in how these *margas* pursue their spiritual goals.

Bhakti-marga seeks liberation through overwhelming devotion and worship. This is a pathway which seeks to establish intimacy with a God of cosmic power who can release humans from the bondage of *karma* which keeps them trapped in the apparently endless cycle of *samsara*. Rather than seeking the isolation of the forest, *bhakti* devotees seek emotional release. Those who follow the *bhakti* pathway seek emotional gatherings for worship in song and in story. They seek to be engulfed in the divine love. Devotional followers seek a life of fellowship in which the love between the deity and worshipers can be sustained in a most powerful manner. Devotees seek God's realm or God's presence.

The *devas* of the ancient Vedas were not personal gods. They were local and the personification of natural forces and powers. Somewhere after 500 B.C.E., new *devas* and new approaches arise as personal gods. There are several significant deities, including Shiva (the destroyer) and his female consorts Durga and Kali. Other deities include Vishnu (the sustainer) in several forms including Krishna and Gopala Krishna. There is also Ganesha, the *deva* with the head of an elephant.

Sexual symbolism plays a religious role in the followers of Shiva, and also in Tantric Hinduism, which uses the feminine aspect of reality but puts the stress on liberation to a state of unity with the ultimate reality. In additional to sexual imagery, the Tantric pathway also uses *mantras* and *mandalas*.

The Epics of India include the *Mahabharata* and the *Ramayana*. The *Bhagavad Gita*, chapter 6 of the *Mahabharata*, taught the monotheistic worship of Krishna. The *Gita* was able to include all four pathways, and whether one was a devotee of Krishna or not, the *Gita*'s teachings could apply. The teaching of "actionless action" permitted people to seek and achieve liberation without having to reject society and social rules. If one does one's *dharma* completely for the love of Krishna, then no karma is generated. Karma is what keeps us trapped in the cycle of birth and death. No karma means that one can achieve *moksha*, liberation from the cycle.

When a *deva* assumes human form, descends to the human realm to offer teachings, that is called an *avatara* or *avatar*. Krishna in the *Bhagavad Gita* and the cowherding Gopala Krishna are understood to be an *avatar* of Vishnu. There are others who are also aspects of Vishnu, including Rama, the hero of the *Ramayana*. The deity who offers success and good luck is Ganesha, with the head of an elephant. Ganesha is not an *avatar*.

Shankara's spiritual pathway of Non-Dualistic Vedanta is the wisdom pathway, but a devotional form of

---

[71] More stories of Ganesha can be found in any book on the myths of India. For example, Veronica Ions, *Indian Mythology*, (New York: Hamlyn 1967), pp. 100–101.

CHAPTER 5: THE PATHWAY OF DEVOTION

Vedanta appears around 1100 C.E. called Qualified Non-Dualistic Vedanta. For the Qualified non-dualistic school, Brahman is no longer an impersonal principle of sacred ultimacy, but is now identified as a god. Instead of ascetic focused concentration leading to liberating insight, the Qualified version stresses devotion to god as the key to ultimate liberation. The ultimate self (*atman*) is divine, but it is not identical with Brahman. The *atman* is merely a tiny part of the divine.

As in the other pathways, there is no central institution or core group of elite priests who determine which *deva* is officially Hindu, or which practice is not orthodox. The devotional pathway is a multiplicity of pathways, and not one single approach to the sacred divinities.

5.16 TECHNICAL TERMS

avatar	An *avatara* or *avatar* is the material (most often human) form of a *deva* who has chosen to come to earth in response to the needs of humans, and teach humans important spiritual truths. As an earthly manifestation or incarnation of the divine, the avatar is simultaneously human and god.
Bhagavat	"Lord" or "Bounteous One."
Bhagavad Gita	The *Bhagavad Gita*, the Song of the Lord. The sacred text which teaches monotheism, devotion to Krishna, and monism, the unity of all that exists. One of the most important of all Indian religious texts.
bhakti	love and devotion, devotion, faith, total surrender of the follower of the will of God, love of God.
bhakti-maga	The **pathway** of love and devotion, devotion, faith, total surrender of the follower of the will of God, love of God. Intensely personal approach to the ultimate Reality.
bhakti-yoga	The **method** of love and devotion, devotion, faith, total surrender of the follower of the will of God, love of God. Intensely personal approach to the ultimate Reality.
Brahma	The creator *deva*, one of the trinity composed of Brahma, the creator, Vishnu, the sustainer, and Shiva, the destroyer
Ganesha	The elephant-headed deity of success and good fortune.
Gopala	Gopala is an epithet of the child Krishna, and means protector of cows.
Govinda	An epithet of the child Krishna, and Govinda means finder of cows.
Ishvara	The form of Vishnu worshiped by Yoga and Qualified Non-Dualistic Vedanta.
Kali	One of Durgaa's most dreadful and powerful manifestations, the goddess who roams battlefields, devouring human flesh and drinking the blood of the killed. Although sometimes motherly and protective, Kali has bloody fangs, wears a necklace of skulls and is most certainly dangerous.
Kali Yuga	The fourth and last period of the universe, the time of decline leading to ultimate destruction of all that exists. The *deva* Shiva presides over this time period.
lila	Play, as in playful activity. Divine activity is often *lila*.

CHAPTER 5: THE PATHWAY OF DEVOTION

lingam   The male sex organ, used as symbolic of creation, procreation and Shiva's divine and loving creative energy. This image is especially important in the worship of Shiva.

Madhava   Madhava (bringer of springtime), an epithet of Gopala Krishna.

Mahabharata   The ancient and immense epic which collects history and legends of ancient India. The *Bhagavad Gita* is included as chapter six of this text.

mandala   A diagram, often circular, which provides a spiritual map for a meditator, providing correspondences between the individual human mind and body, and the cosmos.

mantra Highly compressed, power-packed words, phrases, or formulas, usually of classical Vedic Sanskrit origin, charged with deep meaning and magical potency. Sacred sounds of power. Brahmin priests felt that these mantras had power only if pronounced with the right pitch and the precise inflection.

moksha Liberation from the apparently endless cycle of *samsara* (the cycle of birth and death, fueled by karmic choices and karmic energy).

Puranas Ancient tales and stories, myths, lore, legends. Part of the classic literature of Hinduism; the Puranas tell tales of *devas* and more.

Ramayana   An ancient epic which tells the story of Prince Rama and his battles with a demon to rescue his wife. Later, Rama is considered an *avatar* of Vishnu.

Satvatas   A non-Aryan tribe whose monotheistic non-Vedic religion provided the basis for the *Bhagavad Gita* and devotion to the *deva*, Krishna Vasudeva.

shakti   A force, the female energy of creation, which, when combined with the male force of the eternal, is the omnipotent energy of the divine. *Shakti* is the wife, partner, consort, or Great Goddess, symbolic of the feminine side of Shiva as a divine polarity, symbolic of the active creative natural processes in the universe.

Shiva   The personification of destruction as one of the trinity of creator, sustainer, and destroyer. Shiva begins as the destroyer, but ultimately becomes the single god who contains all three aspects in himself. Shiva is both male and female, and sexual imagery plays a role in the iconography of Shiva and his shaktis.

Tantras   Tantras are books which give instructions on how to achieve *moksa*, but the context is devotion, sexual energy, *mantras*, and *mandalas*.

Vaishnava   The several *bhakti* religions devoted to Vishnu are referred to as the Vaishnava traditions.

Vishnu   One of the three deities in the Hindu trinity, the one who sustains existence. Vishnu is worshiped in many forms in India, including his incarnation as Krishna in the *Bhagavad Gita* and Gopala Krishna, the cowherding child and youth who is the personification of divine playfulness.

Vishnu Narayana   Vishnu Narayana means "Vishnu Born of Water" and is a Vedic title of Vishnu, the sustainer.

yoni   The female sex organ, symbolic of birth and divine creation. The yoni imagery is used in the worship of Shiva and in Tantric Hinduism.

5.17 QUESTIONS FOR FURTHER DISCUSSION

1) The concept of a *shakti* female energy component to the divine is not unique to Hindu thought. Some early Christians seem to have worshiped wisdom as a goddess, and many Hindu scholars perceive some Christians as praying to and worshiping a goddess named Mary. Should the sacred ultimate be thought of as primarily male, primarily female, a sacred union of both, or neither?

2) Is destruction a force of evil, or can destruction be understood as the divine activity of the creator as well? Is the capacity to destroy primarily a male characteristic, or can it be a female characteristic as well? Discuss.

3) There are several different ways that followers of Shiva express their devotion to their deity. Explain at least three different techniques that followers use in their religious practices. Are similar methods used in Western religions?

4) How would followers of Shiva the Dancer answer the question, "Why is there anything at all instead of nothing?" How many different answers to this question are found in Western religions?

5) Some people have difficulty perceiving overt sexual symbolism as being religious. What deeply **religious** meanings are present in the *lingam* and *yoni* symbolism of followers of Shiva?

6) In Persian religions and later in the Judeo-Christian traditions, this world is sometimes perceived as a battleground between the forces of ultimate good and the army of evil. This battle will terminate with a final battle at the end of time. However, worshipers of Shiva seem to have no need to explain evil in this world as the product of an evil god. How do Shaivites explain the destructive forces of our human realm?

7) Some Hindus worship a goddess who has fangs which drip blood, carries severed human heads, wears a necklace of human skulls, and drinks human blood. What is it about this terrifying divinity which could inspire love and devotion among her followers?

8) The authors of the *Bhagavad Gita* seem to have resolved this dilemma: Arjuna the archer will generate bad karma no matter what choice he makes. To fight against family members will generate bad karma and a bad reincarnation. Not to fight will mean that he does not do his duty as a warrior, and it will ensure that other family members will perish, and this too will generate bad karma and a bad reincarnation. How does the *Bhagavad Gita* solve this problem?

9) Scholars sometimes claim that all four ways of being religious (ritual action, wisdom, meditation, devotion) are taught in the *Bhagavad Gita*, so Hindu followers can find an appropriate religious pathway no matter what their personality characteristics might be. Explain how these four pathways are included in the teachings of the *Gita*.

10) Some claim that "actionless action" is the central teaching of the *Bhagavad Gita*. What is "actionless action" and how does it solve Arjuna's problem?

11) Tantric Hinduism uses several techniques to achieve *moksha*, including *mantras, mandalas*, goddesses and sexual imagery. Explain how the Tantric followers felt that these techniques could lead to ultimate liberation. Explain why some Tantric methods were shocking to the majority of Hindus.

12) Ganesha is one of the most popular of all the Hindu deities. Why is the god with the head of an elephant so popular in Hinduism? How can we account for Ganesha's popularity? Are there any supernatural beings who might play a similar role in Western religions?

A SELECTED BIBLIOGRAPHY

Primary Sources

de Bary, William T., ed., *Sources of Indian Tradition*, 2nd edition, 2 volumes (New York: Columbia University Press, 1988).
Deutsch, Eliot, and Rohit Dalvi, *The Essential Vedanta: A New Source Book of Advaita Vedanta* (World Wisdom, 2004)
Easwaran, Eknath & Barbara S. Miller, *Bhagavad Gita* (New York: Random House, 2000)
Flood, Gavin & Charles Martin, trans., *Bhagavad Gita: A New Translation* (New York: W. W. Norton, 2013)
Hopkins, Thomas J., *The Hindu Religious Tradition* (Belmont, Ca: Wadsworth, 1971)
Koller, John and Patricia, *Sourcebook in Asian Philosophy* (New York: Macmillan, 1991)
Miles, Jack, and Wendy Doniger, *Hinduism* (New York: Norton, 2015)
    This Norton Anthology of World Religions volume is an excellent collection of original sources.

Studies in Hinduism

Bilimora, P., Joseph Prabhu and Renuka Sharma, *Indian Ethics* (Burlington, Vt: Ashgate, 2005)
Chatterjee, Satischandra, and Dhirendramohan Datta, *An Introduction to Indian Philosophy* (Calcutta: University of Calcutta, 1968)
Das, Gurcharan *The Difficulty of Being Good: On the Subtle Art of Dharma* (London: Allen Lane, 2010)
de Bary, William T., ed., *Sources of Indian Tradition*, 2nd edition, 2 volumes (New York: Columbia University Press, 1988).
Eck, Diana, *Darsan: Seeing the Divine Image in India* (New York: Columbia University Press, 1998)
Easwaran, Eknath & Barbara S. Miller, *Bhagavad Gita* (New York: Random House, 2000)
Eliade, Mircea, *Yoga: Immortality and Freedom*
Flood, Gavin & Charles Martin, trans., *Bhagavad Gita: A New Translation* (New York: W. W. Norton, 2013)
Hawley, Jack, *Bhagavad Gita: A Walkthrough for Westerners* (New York: New World Library, 2011)
Hopkins, Thomas J., *The Hindu Religious Tradition* (Belmont, Ca: Wadsworth, 1971)
Grimes, John, *A Concise Dictionary of Indian Philosophy* (Albany, NY: State University of New York Press, 1996)
Halbfass, Wilhelm, *Tradition and Reflection: Explorations in Indian Thought* (Albany, NY: State University of New York Press, 1991)
Herman, A. L., *Brief Introduction to Hinduism* (Boulder, CO: Westview Press, 1991)
Hirayanna, M., *Essentials of Indian Philosophy* (London: Unwin, 1978)

CHAPTER 5: THE PATHWAY OF DEVOTION

Hirayanna, M., *Outlines of Indian Philosophy* (London: Allen & Unwin, 1970)

Kinsley, David R., *The Sword and the Flute: Kali and Krsna–Dark Visions of the Terrible and the Sublime in Hindu Mythology* (Berkeley: University of California Press, 1977)

Knott, Kim, *Hinduism: A Very Short Introduction* (London: Oxford, 2000)

Koller, John, *The Indian Way: An Introduction to the Philosophies and Religions of India*, 2nd edition (New York: Prentice Hall, 20005)

Koller, John and Patricia, *Sourcebook in Asian Philosophy* (New York: Macmillan, 1991)

Krishna, Nanditha, *Book of Vishnu* (New York: Penguin Group, 2003)

Mascaro, Juan, *The Bhagavad Gita* (New York: Penguin Classics, 19)

Michaels, Axel, *Hinduism: Past and Present* (Princeton, NJ: Princeton University Press, 2003)

Mohanty, J. N., *Classical Indian Philosophy* (Lanham, MD: Rowman and Little, 2000)

Moore, Charles A., *The Indian Mind: Essentials of Indian Philosophy and Culture* (Honolulu, HI: University of Hawai'i Press, 1967)

Potter, Karl H., *Guide to Indian Philosophy* (Boston: G. K. Hall, 1988) An extensive bibliography.

Potter, Karl H., ed., *The Encyclopedia of Indian Philosophies* (Princeton, NJ: Princeton University Press, 1961-2015)

Radhakrishnan, Sarvepalli, *Indian Philosophy*, 2 volumes (London: Allen and Unwin, 1923)

Radhakrishnan, Sarvepalli, *The Principal Upanishads* (Boston: Unwin Hyman, 1989)

Roebuck, Valerie J., *The Upanishads* (New York: Penguin Classics,   )

Shattuck, Cybelle, *Hinduism* (New York: Prentiss-Hall, 1999)

Sharma, I. C., *Ethical Philosophies of India* (Lincoln, NB: Johnsen Publishing Co., 1965)

Studholme, Alexander, *The Origins of Om Manipadme Hum: A Study of the Karandavyuha Sutra* (SUNY Press, 2002)

Wyatt, Thomas, *Speaking of Shiva* (New York: Penguin Group, 1973).

Wyatt, Thomas & Juan Mascaro, ed., *Upanishads* (New York: Penguin, 1965)

Zimmer, Heinrich, *Philosophies of India* (Cleveland, OH: World, 1961)

CHAPTER 6: THE JAIN RELIGION

6.1 OVERVIEW OF THE CHAPTER

In ancient India, there were numerous religious thinkers who were not willing to grant special status and authority to the Brahmin priests, and were not content to merely perform the customary rituals. These were groups in India who preferred to rely on individual religious experience for their access to the sacred. We have previously used the term *sramana* (recluse, ascetic) to describe these people, or *muni* meaning "silent sage." Some *sramanas* accepted the Vedic texts as divinely inspired and this group is considered orthodox. Other groups treated the Vedic literature as of interest, but not divinely inspired. If a group asserts that the Vedas are not divine and merely the work of human beings, then it is called heterodox.[1]

The Jain (pronounced "Jane") religion became important during the sixth and fifth century B.C.E. which was a flourishing period for much of Indian thought. For example this time period included the early forest-dwelling ascetics who recorded their insights into *atman* and *Brahman* in the *Upanishads*. This time was also a fertile period for many religions that were not based on the sacred Vedic literature. Two of the heterodox religions of India appeared at approximately the same time; Jainism founded by Mahavira and Buddhism founded by the Buddha.[2] Jainism and Buddhism both reject the authority of the Vedas, yet both draw upon common ideas in India prevalent at that time such as the interconnected ideas of rebirth and karma.

The Jain religion can be understood as a rejection of the Aryan religious claims of superiority for the Brahmin priests, and a rejection of the divine origins of Aryan religious books. Jainism also rejects the non-dualism of the principal *Upanishads*. Instead it insists that the world is real, that each individual soul is real, and thus the world is a duality of two different fundamental substances. The most important concept for the Jain religion is *ahimsa*, non-harm to all living things. For the Jains, the highest form of religious conduct can be summarized in the term *ahimsa*. The attitude of non-harm for any living thing can be extended to a commitment to preserving all life on earth, and a religious commitment to protecting our ecological systems and environment. The primary goal of the Jain is to desist completely from harming others.

Although Jainism was a powerful force in the past, in contemporary times Jains composes less than one-half of one percent of the Indian population.

---

[1] Those Indian lineages which accept the authority of the sacred Vedas and the social position of the Brahmin caste of priests, are orthodox, or *astikas*. Those lineages which reject the Vedas and the religious authority of the Brahmin caste are heterodox, or *nastikas*. Scholars have wondered whether the *nastika* traditions might represent pre-Aryan religious influences in India.

[2] This time period is approximately the period of Confucius and Lao-tzu in China, and the Hebrew prophets and Old Testament heros Jeremiah and Ezekiel.

6.2 MAHAVIRA AND THE ORIGINS OF JAINISM

Although the Jains date the origins of their religion into the far distant past, the recent historical hero of Jainism is called Mahavira, the Great Hero. As with so many people who lived thousands of years ago (approximately 2,500 years ago), biographical details are less than precise. The Jain religion does not consider Mahavira[3] the founder of the religion, and Jain followers do not consider him to be the first to achieve victory over the cycle of birth and death. Rather, Mahavira is the twenty-fourth in a long line of twenty-four special teachers who forged a bridge crossing over from the world of *samsara* into that realm free from the cycle of birth and death.[4] Each of these twenty-four teachers lived in the ages of the past. Each had a noble birth, each of these renounced the world for the life of a religious ascetic in the forest, each achieved liberation, and finally, each one established a religious community of followers.

Scholars are not sure of the precise dates for Mahavira, but it is believed that he lived between 599 and 467 B.C.E. Mahavira was the second son in a wealthy aristocratic family (perhaps his father was a king) who belonged to a noble caste.[5] At the proper age, a marriage was arranged for him, and a daughter was born. Living in luxury and with high social status should have made Mahavira very happy, but in fact it did not. Feeling trapped in a miserable cycle of birth-and-death, he began to search out religious solutions. He encountered a group of forest ascetics which inspired in Mahavira the desire to leave home and practice the ascetic lifestyle. However, his *dharma* (social and religious duties) required him to live up to his family's social expectations. He stayed home until after his parents had passed away, and his brother no longer needed him to fulfil family responsibilities. Then, at approximately age 30, Mahavira gave away all of his possessions and left his family and entered the forest.[6]

Although Mahavira joined a community of ascetics who meditated continuously and survived by begging, he did not make satisfactory progress. He believed that he needed to practice even more severe ascetic techniques which tortured his body in order to achieve liberation from the cycle of *samsara*. He traveled continuously so that he would not become attached to any place, never sleeping twice under the same tree. He went about naked all year round, intentionally seeking out the coldest places in the winter and the hottest places in the summer.[7]

He came to believe that if he was the cause of even an accidental death of any living thing, it would cause bad karma, so he became very punctilious about not harming a single sentient being, not even an insect. The practice of *ahimsa* (non-harm) to all living things became the cornerstone of his ascetic life. As he wandered he carried a small broom which he would use to sweep the path ahead of him so that he did not accidentally step on any creature. He carefully strained all drinking water so that he would not accidentally swallow any living things. He would eat leftover food, but would not eat food that had been killed in order to feed him.

After twelve years of the most severe ascetic practices, Jains believe that at age forty-two he achieved the insight which produced liberation from the cycle of birth and death, a state the Jains call **Kevala**. He was then known to his

---

[3] "Mahavira" is a title meaning "Great Man" or "Great Hero"; the man's actual name was Nataputta Vardhamana.

[4] Each of these "ford-makers" chose to live out his life teaching others how to achieve liberation, rather than just freeing themselves from the world immediately.

[5] Some biographies make his family members of the *kshatriya* social class and others treat him as belonging to the Brahmin caste.

[6] The earliest Jain biography of Mahavira is almost a thousand years after his death.

[7] Does one have to renounce even clothing to achieve liberation? Does clothing reveal an attachment to possessions? Then one must give up wearing clothes. Does it encourage a sense of ego? One must renounce ego. Then one must give up clothes. Does it reveal a self-centered sense of modesty or shame? One must renounce even modesty and shame. These are obstacles to spiritual progress and one must give up clothes.

followers as a Jina (victor, conqueror)[8] who had overcome all the misery of life and a "Great Hero" (Mahavira).

The Venerable Ascetic Mahavira spent twelve years in this way of life. During the thirteenth year in the second month of summer . . . on its tenth day, on the northern bank of the river Rigupalika, in the field of the householder Samaga, in a north-eastern direction from an old temple, not far from a Sal tree, in a squatting position with joined hands exposing himself to the heat of the sun, with the knees high and the head low, in deep meditation, in the midst of abstract meditation, he reached Nirvana. He reached the full, unobstructed, unimpeded, infinite, and supreme knowledge and intuition called Kevala [knowledge that liberates one from samsara].

When the Venerable One had become an Arhat and Jina, he was a Kevalin, omniscient and comprehending all objects. He knew all conditions of the world, of gods, men, and demons. He knew from where they come, where they go, whether they are born as men or animals, or become gods or demons. He knew their food, drink, doings, desires, open and secret deeds, their conversation and gossip, and the thoughts of their minds. He saw and knew all conditions in the whole world of all living beings ... On the day when the Venerable Ascetic Mahavira had reached the highest knowledge and intuition, he reflected on himself and the world. First he taught the Law to the gods, and then to men.[9]

Mahavira spent the remaining thirty years of his life as a teacher and died of starvation at age seventy-two.

6.3 THE TEACHINGS OF JAINISM

Although the Jains reject the sacred authority of the *Upanishads*, they accept the same world view that drove the authors of the *Upanishads* to enter the forest. That is, the Jains accept the belief that we have eternal souls which are apparently trapped by matter in an endless cycle of reincarnation. The goal of Jainism is to escape the cycle and achieve liberation. As with the other Indian religions, the idea of karma ("action") is the explanation for why we are trapped in a cycle of pain, old age, suffering, and death after death. Every action and deed we perform creates karmic energy, and this karmic energy pushes us into the next life, and the life after that.

Karma in the Jain religion is not identical with karma in most Hindu texts. For the Jains, karma is composed of physical matter. The karmic consequences of our choices and actions accumulate fine material which encrust in layers which cover our souls. This karmic stuff is very fine and is spiritually poisonous, and it is essential that we eliminate this karmic material by generating the least amount of karmic energy. Every time we do something harmful, or even have an evil thought, more karmic matter accumulates on our souls, and weighs us down so that we sink into lower and lower levels of existence.

We generate less karmic stuff by having the very least effect possible—we do that by not harming any living thing and not having any thoughts controlled by ego or desire. The Jain liberating insight is that if karmic energy is what keeps us in bondage, then the less karmic energy we create, the weaker are the bonds. The soul rises upwards into the heavens if the layer of karmic matter is not dense. If our karmic material is very finely deposited on our souls, we can be reborn in the heavens. If the weight of karmic matter is nearly non-existent, the soul can rise up so high that we become liberated from the entire cycle of birth-and-death.

Although every soul is of infinite value, the liberated souls become perfect, attain infinite perception, infinite power, infinite knowledge, and infinite bliss. Such a being has no qualities and no relationship with other entities, yet consciousness does not cease.

---

[8] The name Jain is derived from the epithet *Jina* (victor, conqueror).

[9] Robert E. Van Voorst, *Anthology of World Scriptures* (Belmont, Ca.: Thomson Wadsworth, 2008), p. 114.

6.4 THE JAIN METAPHYSICS: WHAT IS ULTIMATE REALITY

We have previously discussed world-views which are quite similar to the Jain view of the universe. The Jains are realists. That is, they accept the ultimate reality of the world, of matter, of space and time, and the reality of each individual soul. The Jains reject the Vedanta analysis of the world as *maya* (illusory).

The Jain position is that the universe is composed of two radically different substances. We live in a world composed of lifeless matter composed of atoms (*ajiva*) and living souls (*jiva*). In addition to the realm of matter are things which are neither material nor sentient: space, time, motion and rest. Some material is dense like iron, and other material is light and fine like oxygen. Even finer than oxygen is the karmic matter encrusting our souls. But it is all matter. Lifeless matter is eternal; it has always existed. There never was a beginning to the universe, but the universe does go through repeated cycles of happiness and unhappiness. We are presently in the era of unhappiness.

There are three realms to our universe: (a) the underworld occupied by demons and lesser *devas*; (b) the surface of our earth which contains uncountably many worlds, each surrounded by water; (c) the heavenly realms overhead composed of thirty layers. The highest layer is the home of those Jain heroes who have achieved liberation.

6.5 THE FOUR REALMS OF TRANSMIGRATION OF SOULS

The soul (*jiva*) is eternal and good, but there never was a time when souls were originally pure and free of matter. Souls have always been trapped by evil matter and they transmigrate through four realms. Human souls can be reborn in:

(1) the realm of a heavenly *deva*,
(2) the realm of human beings,
(3) the realm of the underworld,
(4) as an animal or plant (including single-celled life-forms).

Matter traps the *jiva* the way a prison cell can trap a person. As long as we are in the realm of matter, we will be trapped in the cycle of birth-and-death.

Our physical body is matter, so our flesh is evil. To torment the flesh is a necessary tool to break the soul free from matter. The fundamental practice of Jainism is severe asceticism. Not all Jains live the difficult life of an ascetic; many marry and live a life devoted to business, but they acknowledge that they are not living the highest quality of lifestyle. Those Jains who are able to escape family responsibilities and subject themselves to painful tormenting practices are closest to *moksha*. The goal is to free the soul from the trap of matter.

This pathway to liberation is solitary. No one can help another succeed in these practices. No one can suffer for another. No one else's pains can lessen one's own misery. No one can save you but yourself.

6.6 THE GODS

The early followers of the Jain religion put little emphasis on divinities (*devas*). As with many other Indian religions, the Jains believe that matter has always existed so there never was a creator god or any need of a creator. There is no final destruction of matter either. *Devas* exist, and although they live in heavenly realms, they are still trapped by the cycle of *samsara* and have not achieved the highest spiritual goal, liberation. The goal, liberation of the soul from the body, cannot be achieved with the aid of the gods. Prayer and worship are of no value whatsoever to achieve the goal. No one can liberate you but yourself.

Despite this attitude of the irrelevance of the *devas*, there is a *bhakti* aspect of Jainism. The twenty-four master teachers are honored as divinities in over 40,000 different Jain temples in contemporary India.[10] There are also rituals involving reciting the names of the saints, rituals in which idols are bathed, and religious icons which have flowers and perfumes offered to them. Some Jains believe that devotion to icons can decrease one's own karmic deposits.

The Jain sacred scriptures are treated with extreme devotion and reverence. Singing hymns is also a powerful tool for some sects. In addition to veneration of the twenty-four Jain teachers, heroes and saints, some worship *yakshas* (demi-gods who live in celestial realms and have limited powers). Thus devotion and ritual worship have been part of Jain religious practice for at least 1500 years.[11] Some Jains openly worship statues and other symbols, and other Jains point out that these are merely important symbols which should remind us that with the right attitude and practices, liberation is possible.

Meditation and Mantras

But not all Jain practice is devotional. Meditation is another common practice among the Jains. The swastika is an important symbol to meditate upon, for its four arms represent the four realms into which human souls can be reborn, and a crescent shape above the swastika symbolizes the realm of liberation from the cycle of birth and death. The Jains also chant *mantras*, phrases which have the power to lessen and even destroy one's karmic matter.

6.7 THE FIVE VOWS

There are five vows that Jains are expected to follow, but the degree to which they apply will be different for Jain householders as opposed to those followers of Jainism who can actually leave their homes and pursue the ascetic life.

1. The vow of *ahimsa* (non-injury and non-harm to all living things).
   This vow applies to both forest-dwelling ascetics and those who follow worldly occupations. *Ahimsa* is the most important of Jain practices. Jains are vegetarians. Jains will not eat meat, fish or fowl. Even killing plant life to survive must be done to cause the least amount of harm, as gently and sparingly as possible. Jains avoid all leather products. Some Jains will not eat food if it was cooked in the same pan that had previously cooked meat. Alcohol, honey, potatoes, radishes, onions, and garlic are also prohibited because there may be micro-organisms living upon or within them. Water must be strained before consuming it. Occupations which are likely to result in harming living things are not open to the Jains. Jain householders are allowed to fight in self-defense, but anyone who lived or died in a hostile manner generated bad karma and was condemned to lower life forms.

2. The vow to speak the truth always.
   Jain ascetics and householders are taught to never hide the truth, and never to lie. If speaking the truth will result in violence, then one is allowed to avoid truthfulness by remaining silent. This applies to all Jains and the result is that Jains are widely respected for their truthfulness.

3. The vow to refrain from taking anything that is not given to them.
   This too applies to all Jains, enhancing their reputation for honesty.

---

[10] Lewis M. Hopfe, Mark R. Woodward, *Religions of the World, 10th Edition* (New Jersey: Pearson/Prentice-Hall, 2007), p. 118.

[11] Vasudha Narayanan, "The Jain Tradition," in Willard G. Oxtoby, ed., *World Religions: Eastern Traditions, Second Edition* (London: Oxford University Press, 2002), p. 184.

4. The vow to renounce sensual and sexual pleasures.

   This vow applies to the ascetics, but it does not pertain rigorously to the Jains who have occupations in the worldly life. For the householder, self-control is the key; one should live as celibate a life as is possible, or at least limit one's sensual activities to what is socially acceptable. In India polygamy was acceptable, and Jain males were permitted to have more than one wife. However, one is not to engage in sensual activities with a woman who is not one of one's wives.

5. The vow to renounce all attachments and possessions.

   The desire to own and possess is one of the major sources of human suffering. Jain householders should own as little as possible and should not desire what others possess. This is embodied in donating one's riches, as part of elaborate rituals. Philanthropy is an important virtue for the Jain community. For ascetics, one gives away everything one has ever owned, before going to live an ascetic life in the forest.

Because all Jains take a vow of non-harm to all living creatures, many popular occupations were unavailable to them. Jains could not be fisherman, or butchers, they could not work in leather or sell poisons. Most importantly, Jains could not farm because a plow could easily kill worms and other living things. Consequently, the Jains tended to have occupations in the commercial world, especially business and banking. The Jain reputation for morality and truthfulness has served them well in commercial occupations, and the Jain followers are often among the wealthiest and most successful of all the occupational groups.

FASTING

Jains are encouraged to eat only what is necessary and to not be trapped by the pleasures of dining. This was to discourage desires and excess. However, in the past, there was an ultimate form of withdrawal from life. It is the practice of fasting until one died (called *sallekhana*). This was done for spiritual reasons and is not suicide. This ultimate fast was done out of the desire to never cause violence to any living thing. This practice was restricted to those of the highest attainment, and it was not considered to be contrary to the vow of *ahimsa*. A holy person was to remain in complete control of her mind and faculties and while in a meditative state slowly withdraw from the world, eating less and less. In a balanced and peaceful state of mind, with the approval of one's family and spiritual teachers, a person slowly starves to death. In the Jain tradition, this was considered the ideal death.

6.8 THE JAIN SECTS

Followers of Mahavira disagreed over several features of his teaching. Mahavira went about naked all year long. The followers asked whether nakedness is necessary to achieve *moksha*. One group, the Digambaras (the "sky clad") said "yes," and the other group, the Svetambara ("the white clad") permitted ascetics to wear white garments.[12]

Mahavira rejected all attachments and considered women to be a major temptation causing men to break away from the path to liberation. The more conservative group that insisted upon nakedness for the most advanced followers also rejected any possibility that a woman could achieve enlightenment, and rejected any role for women in the religion. However, the more liberal "white-clad" sect claims that the nineteenth enlightened teacher in the Jain lineage (Mahavira was the twenty-fourth) was a woman, and also permits women to be members, and even accepts the possibility that a woman might achieve ultimate liberation from the cycle of birth-and-death.

---

[12] The term "sky-clad" (Digambara) is a poetic description of wearing the sky for a garment. Not all "sky-clad" followers go naked; complete nudity is reserved for those who are most holy and closest to the ultimate goal of *moksha*. The Svetambara group is "white-clad."

In addition to the "sky-clad" Digambara sect, and the "white-clad" Svetambara sect, there is also the Sthanakavasi branch of the more liberal Svetambara. This group adopts the attitude of Mahavira about the irrelevance of gods, so it rejects all statues and temples as part of the Jain religion.

The more liberal "white-clad" sect has the most followers in the northern areas of India, whereas the conservative followers dominate in the southern areas.

6.9 THE JAIN SCRIPTURES

The various Jain sects do not share the same set of sacred books. It is believed that there were fourteen earliest texts, but they were lost almost two thousand years ago. Jain teachings are based on later texts which are supposed to preserve the earliest texts. The earliest existing Jain texts date from perhaps as early as the fifth century B.C.E.[13]

The sacred texts themselves are often objects of veneration among Jain followers. As with so many other Hindu traditions, the Jains believe that a student must have the guidance of a teacher of advanced attainment who can explain the passages correctly. Although the sacred texts are essential, scriptural knowledge alone cannot bring liberation; one needs to emulate the severe ascetic practices of Mahavira himself. Two of the most important Jain texts are the *Tattvartha sutra*, composed in the second century C.E., and the *Adi purana* of Jinasena (perhaps the ninth century C.E.).

6.10 JAINISM IN THE WEST

There are Jain centers in Europe, England, and north America. For the most part, the naked or nearly naked male and female ascetics have not left India, so in the West the followers are business people and householders. The Jains and the Hindus share several *devas* and have overlapping tales, so from time to time the Jain community will join with the Hindu communities to share facilities. However, the Jains are especially vigilant to ensure that their distinctive religious attitudes and practices will not become absorbed by Hinduism and then disappear. Much of Jain family practice is similar to the Hindus. For example, in 2015 the author interviewed a Jain follower in Wisconsin whose marriage had been arranged by his parents, following a lengthy analysis of birth-dates by an astrologer (who used a computer to perform his divination) to ensure the life-long compatibility of the young couple.

6.11 SUMMARY

Although the Jain religion is very ancient and developed in India, it is not a form of Hinduism. Like Mahavira (c. 599-467 B.C.E.), the most recent teacher in a long line of teachers, Jain followers seek liberation from the cycle of birth and death, however the Jains reject the religious authority of the Brahmin priests and they reject the claim of divine origins for the Hindu sacred literature. Thus Jainism is considered heterodox. Like Hindus, Jains practice meditation and chant *mantras*. Although the Hindus have a long tradition of asceticism, the severe Jain ascetic path puts greater stress on non-harm to all living things.

Unlike the Hindus, the Jains understand karma to be physical matter deposited on one's soul (*jiva*), darkening it and pulling one downward into a lower life form in one's next life. By practicing non-harm towards all sentient creatures, the Jains hope to lessen the negative karmic matter sticking to their souls, and allow the soul to rise upwards into the heavens. In addition to non-violence, the majority of Jains practice devotional rituals focused on Jain saints and heroes, but also incorporate some aspects of the Hindu divine pantheon.

---

[13] Vasudha Narayanan, "The Jain Tradition," p. 172.

6.12 TECHNICAL TERMS

ahimsa   Non-harm to any living creature; non-violence

Jina   Victor, conqueror. One who has liberated the soul from matter.
jiva (and ajiva)   Alive, and not-alive.

Kevala   knowledge that liberates one from the cycle of birth and death (*samsara*).

Mahavira   the Great Hero

sallekhana   fasting until one died

yakshas demi-gods who live in celestial realms and have limited powers

6.13 QUESTIONS FOR FURTHER DISCUSSION

1) The Jain religion is not a form of Hinduism, yet it originated in India. What are three significant features which distinguish the Jains from their fellow Hindus?

2) The Jains are treated with respect and have an especially high reputation in India. What features of the Jain religion account for that reputation?

3) A student might think that fasting until one has died would be against the vow of non-harm that is essential to the Jain religion. Yet, fasting until death is not considered a form of suicide in the Jain religion. What accounts for the fact that this is not considered harm or suicide?

4) Discuss the Jain understanding of liberation. What is it, and why is it considered a valuable goal?

A SELECTED BIBLIOGRAPHY

Jain Thought

Dundas, Paul, *The Jains* (London: Routledge, 1992)
Jaini, Padmanabh S., *Collected Papers on Jaina Studies* (Delhi: Motilal Banarsidass, 2000)
Jaini, Padmanabh S., *The Jaina Path of Purification* (Berkeley: University of California Press, 1979) This is one of the best books on the Jain religion.
Long, Jeffrey, *Jainism: An Introduction* (I. B. Taurus, 2009)
Paniker, Augustin, *Jainism: History, Society, Philosophy and Practice* (Delhi: Motilal Banarsidass, 2010)
Sethia, Tara, ed., *Ahimsa: Anekanta and Jainism* (Delhi: Motilal Banarsidass, 2004) deals with contemporary Jain thought.
Shah, Bharat S., *An Introduction to Jainism* (India: Setubandh Publications, 2002)
Tatia, Nathmal, tr., *Umsvati: Tattvartha Sutra: That Which Is* (San Francisco, CA: Harper Collins 1994)
Zimmer, Heinrich, *Philosophies of India* (Cleveland, OH: World, 1961) has an excellent chapter on the Jain philosophy.

CHAPTER 7: MODERN INDIAN THOUGHT

7.1 OVERVIEW OF THE CHAPTER

In previous chapters we discussed the numerous strands which weave together to produce the wide variety of religious practices which gradually came to be called Hinduism. We discussed the most ancient practices involving images of males who seem to be meditating, ancient stress on water to purify, and the stress on the feminine apparent in the Indus valley civilization religion. We discussed the polytheism of the Vedas, and the stress on ritual. We followed that with an analysis of the wisdom and insight traditions in India, especially the *Upanishads*, Advaita Vedanta and Yoga. We concluded with the devotional basis for Indian religions, placing the most stress on Krishna, Vishnu, Ganesha, Shiva, Durga, and Kali.

All of these threads are observable in modern Hinduism. The one strand we have not discussed is Islam. The reason for this is that Islam is not an Indian religion at all. Its origins are in the Arab world, and its religious traditions spring from the same sources as do Judaism and Christianity. In fact, Judaism, Christianity and Islam all are grounded in the same Bible and are referred to as the "religions of the Book."

Even if Islam did not originate in India and does not share its origins with the Vedas or Epics, nevertheless Muslim armies expanded their empire into northern India and converted the Hindus living in that region to the Muslim religion. The Muslims ruled northern India for almost eight hundred years, and this influence remains today in the clear division of ancient India into two nations on the brink of war with each other: modern Hindu India and modern Muslim Pakistan.

Islamic rule weakened in the early 1700s and European influences began to overwhelm local Indian rule. In the 1800s the British defeated their rivals and controlled the country until 1947. This was a period of colonial rule. Then India achieved independence from Great Britain, bringing many changes in Indian culture, society, and religion. Seventy-five percent of the people of India still live in rural settings, and most continue the rituals that have been performed for centuries. Nevertheless, modern India was established as a secular democracy, not a Hindu theocracy. Many politicians in India have drawn on divisive religious discourse to gain power, and often advocate a Hindu theocracy. Of course, science-based rationalism also exists among the well-educated in modern India as it does in the Western world. The general purpose of these science-based groups is to help lessen the profound social injustice in India by lessening superstition and ignorance.[1]

Contemporary Indian religions tend to focus around particular individuals, either as charismatic spiritual *gurus* who combine ancient and modern ideas, or as more politically involved leaders of movements to restore India to what they believe is the original traditions of the ancient Aryan and Vedic civilization.

Since Indian independence in 1947, political tensions have exacerbated conflict among the various religious and political movements, and religion is often employed as a political tool to influence Indian society. Many Hindu fundamentalists wish to install a just Hindu king, who is believed to be essential to sustaining the sacred order of a brahmanical society based on the caste system and ensuring that the *devas* (gods) reward that society with success and prosperity.

---

[1] For example, see Johannes Quack, *Disenchanting India: Organized Rationalism and Criticism of Religion in India*. (New York Oxford University Press, 2012).

CHAPTER 7: MODERN INDIAN THOUGHT

Just as we saw in previous chapters, modern Hinduism does not have any central core of elite priests who control and regulate the fundamental beliefs and practices of followers any more than the early centuries of its development. A wide variety of different practices focused on different pathways all fit under the umbrella of Hinduism.[2] There is no elite group who determine what is orthodox and what is heterodox for any of the four pathways of religious practice in India.

Education, technology, medicine and science continue to affect the various forms of Hinduism, both those grounded in classical Hinduism, and those who have struggled to reform Hindu religion to bring it into accord with the best science. Classical Hinduism has versions which are critical of superstition, which are even atheistic (i.e., the Samkhya school and the non-theistic forms of Vedanta by Shankara, discussed in chapter 4), so one can claim to be a cultural Hindu and still be a sceptic or an atheist.

7.2 INTRODUCTION

SOME HISTORY

In previous chapters we observed the development of many loose strands of thought systems in India loosely connected to the Vedas and *Upanishads*. There never was one single Hinduism, but it has always been a large collection of assorted practices. These includes the Brahmins and their Vedic rituals, but it also included those atheistic yogins who practiced seated meditation. Undoubtedly there were other religious practices like the practices of those who composed the *Bhagavad Gita* and others whose origins and details remain obscure. Over the centuries, non-violence and vegetarian meals became adopted into Brahmin practices. Ancient Buddhist monasteries inspired Hindu monasteries for training in meditation.

The wide variety of theistic variations upon Hindu *devas* drew upon many of these same strands, and recombined them in new and interesting ways, including Tantric Hinduism after 600 C.E. We will see that Buddhist influences faded in India after about 1200 C.E., and Hindu upper-class religious practices achieved a sort of unity by focusing on the religious *dharma* duties of all. An unstated goal seems to have been to inhibit change, and try to make all members of society willing to remain in their hereditary social position, no matter how socially unjust the caste system (*varna*) appeared to be. The belief in reincarnation and karma were the tools that supported an apparent unity among the various philosophical, religious and spiritual practices.

Northwestern India was an area particularly prone to invasions by foreign armies. In the sixth century, a military group of nomads described as the "White Huns" swept into northwestern India and caused much social destruction. Islam developed in Central Asian countries in the centuries following the death of Prophet Muhammad (632 C.E.), and Muslim traders slowly expanded Islam into India. In the eighth century, Muslim Arabs arrived at the Indus River, and by the thirteenth century, they had all of northern India under their control. The Muslim Turks arrived later with an especially violent and destructive brand of Turkish Islam in 1192 C.E., and they vigorously persecuted and destroyed Hindu temples and Buddhist universities, ruthlessly executing entire communities of nuns and monks who refused to convert to Islam, and taking huge numbers of Hindus away as slaves.

Following the initial violent domination of India, five hundred years of Muslim rule followed, displacing *ksatriyas* as rulers and governors. Hindus were often allowed to serve as vassals to the Muslim state. In 1699, a Muslim ruler ordered all Hindu temples and schools demolished, and many people were killed in the resulting violence.

However, Muslim persecution was not continuous. As Islamic rule settled in, in some parts of the country a

---

[2] A good introductory text on the variety of Indian religions is Axel Michaels, *Hinduism: Past and Present* (Princeton, NJ: Princeton University Press, 2003).

more relaxed attitude toward non-Muslim religions replaced the persecution. Hindu traditions continued, although high-caste domination and Brahmin *dharma* and law were weakened. Islamic rule was strongest in the north and weakest in the south of India, and in the south we find new teachers appearing including women and teachers from the lower despised *varna* social classes, including untouchables. The sacred language was no longer Sanskrit; Tamil and other regional languages were used, and hymns and songs were sung in religious practices outside of high-caste Brahmin and *ksatriya* control.

Devotional Hinduism stressing dualistic theism and personal salvific intense experiences of the divine continued to grow in strength. Impersonal non-dualism and monism continue as living traditions as well, although the popularity of these more abstract forms of Hinduism never matched that of the devotional forms of Hinduism. In the 1500s a new religion was founded by Guru Nanak (1469-1539) and his followers (*Sikhs*, "disciples,"pronounced "sick") which reveals both Hindu and Islamic origins.

7.3 GURU NANAK AND THE SIKH MOVEMENT

Guru Nanak was a civil servant who, at age 30, underwent a transforming religious experience during a three-day period. As a result of his experience he began teaching. His basic insight was simple: "There is neither Hindu nor Muslim, so whose path shall I follow? I shall follow God's path. God is neither Hindu nor Muslim, and the path that I follow is God's."[3] Followers see Nanak's mission as revealing the full and complete spiritual truth, and the proper manner in which to realize it. Thus, Nanak saw himself as correcting the mistaken practices and partial truths of both Hinduism and Islam.

He taught that there is only one God, who never walked the earth in human form (there were no *avatars*). God is beyond form and all human categories. One does not need to enter the forest or lead an ascetic lifestyle. Householders can achieve the highest goals of liberation. Karma and reincarnation are ended by the grace of God. The tool for salvation is the divine sound heard within one's own consciousness, so Sikh practices involve listening to and singing hymns composed by Nanak and other saints. Sikhs reject the value of Brahmanic ritual acts and pilgrimages, and reject the authority of the Vedas, reject the authority of the Brahmins and reject the caste system, and thus higher-caste Hindus respond quite negatively to the Sikhs.

Following the death of Guru Nanak, nine succeeding gurus followed. The songs and sermons of Nanak, plus additional materials composed by inspired disciples, were collected in a 1430 page sacred text called the *Adi Granth* or *Guru Granth Sahib*. The *Sikhs* remained separate from Hinduism and from Islam, and appealed to many in both religions. The Sikhs are led by the *Khalsa*, an elite group who adopted a strict lifestyle and remain as guardians of the purity of the religion and its teachings.

The Sikhs essentially eliminated class and caste distinctions, and are recognized by uncut hair covered by a turban, short trousers, steel wristlet, comb, and sword. Of the approximately one billion people who live in India, about twenty-million of them are Sikhs in India today (approximately 2%).

7.4 EUROPEAN INFLUENCES

Although the first Europeans to settle in India were missionaries who arrived in the 1500s, followed by traders, the Muslims dominated India until early 1700s. The European powers traded for spices, and later, silks, indigo, and saltpeter; still later it was cotton and hemp. The Portugese came in the 16th century at Goa; followed by the Dutch.

With death of last Muslim emperor (1707), the Muslim empire declined rapidly, and India lay in a state of anarchy. The result was a political vacuum. European merchants began to gain control over many of India's most prosperous provinces. British garrisons were dispatched to protect trade and trade missions, and these were drawn into

---

[3] W. Owen Cole, "Sikhism," in *A Handbook of Living Religions*, John R. Hinnells, ed. (New York: Penguin, 1984), p. 240.

local conflicts. As British soldiers defeated local forces, England began to control various parts of India.

In 1757, Major-General Robert Clive secured a British victory over the French, and defeated the Indian armies. The British had come for trade, but their experience in America convinced them that trade could be secured only if they had firm political control as well. They also brought Christian missionaries into India and supported them militarily. By 1818, the British had eliminated all other European rivals for control of India. Britain then ruled India until 1947, with only one unsuccessful revolt during 1857. What the British called a "revolt" was called the "First War of Independence" in India.

> Powerful outsiders were arriving in significant numbers, proclaiming new truths and boldly denouncing the eternal Hindu verities. This ideological challenge occurred on several fronts simultaneously: the materialist scientific world view of the European Enlightenment, humanistic critiques of religion, proponents of racial theories of European superiority, and the outspoken Christian missionaries with triumphalist Gospel teachings.[4]

In India under British control, all high-ranking officers in the army were non-Indian. All civil service officials were non-Indian except those having a rank entitling them to less than 500 pounds a year. British laws established private ownership of land. Before then, the ruler owned the land and leased it to persons in return for services and favors. It was implicitly understood that the rulers and the persons to whom the land had been leased, were to hold the land in trust for the farmers and the whole community. The British replaced this system with laws supporting land as private property.

The Importance of Religious Labeling

In order to govern, the British authorities needed to break the population into smaller groups with which they could deal. In Europe there had been a long history of groups identifying themselves as Catholics, Anglicans, Baptists, Lutherans, and so forth. It seemed natural to the British to use religious identities in India as well, and they needed some broad categories that fit neatly into their own Western preconceptions. As a result, some natives were classified as "Hindu," some "Muslim," some "Buddhist," and some "Sikh."

British Time Line For Rule in India[5]

1600	Queen Elizabeth granted charters to traders of the East Indies.
1690	Calcutta founded by an agent of the English East India Company.
1757	General Clive gains control of Bengal.
1785	Cornwallis made governor and commander-in-chief of Bengal army, designed the rules that were to govern India for the next 150 years.
1806	An uprising against British control and the East India Company and its missionary efforts.[6]
1818	Military victories ends effective Indian resistance to British rule.
1835	British/English system of education introduced into India.

---

[4] John Esposito, Darrell Fasching, Todd Lewis, *World Religions Today* (New York: Oxford University Press, 2002), p. 313.

[5] Dates and remarks paraphrased from William Theodore de Bary, ed., *Sources of Indian Tradition*, vol. II, p. xv

[6] There are several excellent books detailing the economic and religious activities of the East India Company. One good book is by Penelope Carson, *The East India Company and Religion*, 1698–1858 (Woodbridge, Suffolk: Boydell Press, 2012).

CHAPTER 7: MODERN INDIAN THOUGHT

1857-58	Mutiny of Sepoy troops and widespread rebellion in Northern India, called the "First War of Independence" in India.
1858	East India Company's rule replaced by that of a viceroy appointed by British crown.
1877	Queen Victoria is proclaimed Empress of India.
1893	Mohandas K. Gandhi (1869–1948) begins twenty year's work as a lawyer in South Africa.
1916	Indian Moderates, Extremists, and Muslim League leaders agree on demand for a national legislative assembly to be elected on a communal basis.
1920	Gandhi starts first nation-wide civil disobedience movement (suspended in 1922 after outbreaks of violence).
1930	Proposal of a separate state for India's Muslims.
1930–34	Second nation-wide civil disobedience movement.
1935	"Government of India Act" grants provincial self-government.
1940	Muslim League demands creation of sovereign Muslim state.
1942	Indian Congress demands British quit India.
1945–47	British Labor government prepares to grant India complete self-government.
1947	India, under Prime Minister Nehru (1889–1964) and Pakistan, become separate independent dominions of England.
1948	Gandhi assassinated in New Delhi.
1950	India becomes a republic within the Commonwealth.

7.5 THE RENEWAL OF INDIAN THOUGHT

Even though British forces controlled India for nearly two-hundred years, and tried to impose Christianity on the population, Hindu religious traditions dominated in India for the great majority. Because India was so vital to European trade, India was drawn into a world-wide network of economic relations by the British, which caused British rule to have more influence than previous centuries of Muslim domination.

Social changes occurred as well. Indian merchants generated enough new jobs that the caste system was seriously threatened for the first time since the period of Buddhist rule. In the past, the caste system was a means of control as well as imposing what surely appears to be an unjust structure on India. For any person within the community to challenge the caste system would result in being forced out of the community. Traditionally, if members of groups challenged the caste structure, they were ostracized and could no longer earn a living because moving to a new community would mean that one is a stranger. Strangers are not trusted, and are certainly not hired into new jobs.

However, now there were many new occupations, many of which provided a decent wage. When there are more jobs than the local community can supply, this old system of rigid caste occupations was no longer tenable. Changes in business allowed for people to move elsewhere and find a job. Community pressure no longer had the power it used to have. This had a profound effect on the rigidity of the caste system. A community could no longer rigidly control the occupations of its members. So many new jobs among the merchants (who were the most religiously liberal) rendered significant population in India relatively immune to social/economic pressures for conformity. As a result, millions of Hindus felt free to follow religious leaders of their own personal choice, or even become less religious.

In addition, the British promoted education much more than under Hindu and Muslim rulers, and especially Western learning (taught in English), Western art and ethics, and Christianity was taught in the schools and universities. Western printing presses made English material available to those who could read English. Science, history, economics, and Western medicine were available to the better educated. Many in India traveled to European capitals, especially to London, to Oxford, to Cambridge, and received their graduate training there. This had much greater influence upon the population than Hindu or Muslim rulers ever had.

The British brought something quite new into India. They brought a Western view that things can be made better, society can be improved, and that the future in this very life can be better than the past. The Indian world-view tended to see the world as a place of ignorance and suffering, a universe on a downward spiral toward destruction, getting worse and worse with each decade. Such a world was to be escaped from and not to be changed.

Promises of freedom from disease was made possible by British scientific medicine. The possibility of freedom from poverty and social injustice seemed possible with the new wealth occurring in Indian business. Indians could be proud of their accomplishments, and belong to one socio-political unit. This very world could be made a positive place.

INDIA RESPONDS TO WESTERN THOUGHT

In general, early Indian responses to English civilization tended towards indifference, but over time, two major reactions occurred. There was a tendency for Hindus to respond to Western thought with either hostility or curiosity.

India Responds to Western Thought with Curiosity:

Everything British or Western is superior and the people of India must imitate Western ways. The power of Western learning seemed obviously superior. Western science provided transportation and steamboats for trade and commerce, provided vaccination for medicine. Western vaccinations were obviously superior to the tradition of making offerings to a smallpox goddess. The proper response is to study European civilization, and so many Hindus traveled to England and other European countries to be educated.

India Responds to Western Thought with Hostility:

The more religiously devout claimed that India is the land of gods, the realm of profound spirituality, and in the ancient Aryan past, India was almost perfect. As such India is far superior to the West. The people of India must stress the superiority and grandeur of ancient Indian thought and society. The proper course was to return to the values of Indian civilization of the ancient past, where each occupational group had a place and knew its proper place. British values were crass, materialistic, superficial, and therefore inferior to the deep spirituality of India's golden past. The people of India must reject the materialist challenge of Western science and Western culture, and embrace the superior ancient spiritual Indian civilization. India itself is not just a place or a country. Rather, India is to be identified as the "divine Mother," sometimes identified with Kali, but more often simply identified with "Mother India." Those who stressed the superiority of ancient Indian beliefs and practices often describe the traditional high-caste religion dominated by Brahmin priests as the "true Hinduism," or refer to it as the *Sanatana dharma*, the "eternal duty" or "eternal teachings." Some Hindus claimed that before Muslim rule, India was a land that practiced social equality, was wealthy and prosperous, was governed by just rulers, and numerous awakened *gurus* were found everywhere. They claimed that it was only following the Muslim conquest that Hindu spiritual culture declined, and the later British domination made the decline even worse. These people wanted a return to a government based on "Vedic Spirituality."[7] It was very unclear exactly what "Vedic Spirituality" was, but it included lessening the influence of or eliminating Christianity, treating the Vedas as absolutely true, reimposing and enforcing the *varna*-caste system, and returning to the ancient rituals performed by Brahmins who ought to be restored to their rightful place at the top of the power apex.

Although in 1947 India was established as a secular democracy, there has been much political pressure applied by the wealthy and powerful to make India a Hindu theocracy dominated by the tradition of the two upper castes, the Brahmins and the *ksatriyas*. In India today, there are revivalist and conservative groups that demand that India become a Hindu state, and the official religion be devotion to "Mother India."

---

[7] Esposito, Fasching, Lewis, *World Religions Today*, p. 343–344.

CHAPTER 7: MODERN INDIAN THOUGHT

In either case, the rich, the powerful, and the glorious (whether of India's past, or the West) was held up as the ideal for which India should strive. Of course the British were quite certain that their culture and system was far superior to what they perceived as the ignorance and barbarism of traditional India. In English-language schools, teachers reflected this view. British-educated Indians tended to adopt the British view and devalue the traditional Indian religious and philosophical systems. Study of Greek and European philosophy, and especially English philosophers became the standard in Indian university education.

During the late nineteenth and twentieth centuries, Indian thinkers and *gurus* were active in many realms. Indian thinkers were taught Greek and European history, philosophy and religion in their college courses, and they began to respond to Western philosophy, Western science and technology, and a renewal of philosophical activity ensued. Western ideas of rationality, liberty, progress, education, individualism, nationalism, humanitarian ethics, and social reform were introduced to the well-educated upper classes. The response, from some Indians, was a creative synthesis, incorporating both traditional and Western ideas and values.

7.6 SOME IMPORTANT PEOPLE

Ram Mohan Roy (1774-1833): the first great English-educated reformer.

Ram Mohan Roy was a member of the upper Brahmin class, and he responded to India's domination by England by asserting that India was defeated by Europeans because the Hindus had lost belief in "true Hinduism," that they no longer practiced the ancient rituals and had lost faith in the *Upanishads*. In this sense he is sometimes referred to as the father of modern Hinduism. For Roy, true Hinduism was strictly monotheistic, and he was opposed to popular ritual *puja* as "idol worship" and rejected the polytheism typical of the great majority of Indians.

Roy had learned Christianity from priests and teachers, but found Christianity to be irrational and self-contradictory. He engaged in debates with Christian Protestant missionaries. He argued that the Christian doctrine that one's own misdeeds could be redeemed by another person to be nonsensical. He also argued that the Christian trinity is not monotheism at all, but is clearly polytheism, with three major gods (the Christian Trinity), a goddess (Mary) and numerous lesser divinities ("saints" as beings with supernatural powers able to perform miracles and help those who call for help) including "guardian angels." European communities would celebrate one saint or another, pray to their saints, and attribute miracles to these saints. This seemed no different from Hindu polythism. Thus Western Christianity was not a true monotheism but rather a thinly disguised polytheism.

Roy founded a society, the Brahmo Samaj, whose function was to reform Hindu practices which put what he considered excessive stress on ritual. He strongly opposed the ritual of *sati*, where a widow would burn to death as her husband's body was cremated. Many of his ideas serve as a bridge between Christian thought and forms of Hinduism.

Dayananda Sarasvati (1824–1883)

Dayananda Sarasvati was a member of the Brahmin class. Although he was profoundly influenced by Western ideas, nevertheless he argued that the four Vedas were infallible, and contained the root of all knowledge and all science. He held to monotheistic devotion, and thus, like Ram Mohan Roy, he rejected Hindu polytheism and Christian polytheism. There was only one true god, and it was the god of Hinduism. He asserted that the Hindu god allowed India to be defeated by Western forces as punishment for immoral Hindu practices such as child marriage, the caste system of untouchables and outcastes, and the unjustified subjugation of women by rules of Hindu duty, or *dharma*.

Dayananda was not tolerant of non-Hindu religions. In fact, he was a strong critic of both Christian Protestantism and Islam, and asserted that these were impure and alien, and no true Hindu could follow either one. Swami Dayananda's successors established village institutions, schools, and even a political party which exists today.

CHAPTER 7: MODERN INDIAN THOUGHT

Ramakrishna (1834/6-1886)

One of the most influential of the modern Indian thinkers was the a charismatic *guru* named Ramakrishna whose influence was strongest among Hindus who were open to the reform of Hinduism. Ramakrishna was of a humble Brahmin family, but apparently he had experienced numerous profound mystical experiences, during which he reported being possessed by Kali, Sita, Rama, Krishna, Muhammad and Jesus. He began to look upon the image of the goddess Kali as his mother and the mother of the universe. Ramakrishna reportedly had a vision of the goddess Kali as the universal Mother, which he described as "... houses, doors, temples and everything else vanished altogether; as if there was nothing anywhere! And what I saw was an infinite shoreless sea of light; a sea that was consciousness. However far and in whatever direction I looked, I saw shining waves, one after another, coming towards me." He argued that one divine sacred presence exists in the universe, but different religions give it different names.

He put special emphasis on the Vedanta approach to Hinduism. In contemporary times the missions of the Ramakrishna tradition work to demonstrate that Hindu religion properly interpreted is compatible with modern science.

Vivekananda (1863-1902): the closest disciple of Ramakrishna.

Ramakrishna had many followers, including Vivekananda. Vivekananda went on to become a powerful *guru* himself. He defended the Vedanta religious world-view. He was quite critical of Christianity, which he described as narrow-minded and dogmatic. He pointed out that Christian churches in India supported overt racism, and had never objected to racist British practices and policies. Many Christian groups in India had supported and even justified the mistreatment of native Hindus. The institutions established by Vivekananda became a global Hindu organization with the goal of saving the world. Even today it supports many thousands of hospitals and educational centers in India.

7.7 TWO WORLD WARS ENCOURAGE HINDU NATIONALISM

The two terrible world wars fought by Christians against Christians served to weaken the attraction of European influence and Christian teachings in India, and strengthen Hindu nationalism. Despite its idealistic rhetoric, Christian religion, Western science, and democratic political systems had all failed to stop the slaughter as Christian Europeans and Christian north Americans killed fellow Christian civilians and enemy Christian soldiers alike.

In fact, from the perspective of British India, Christian religion, Western science and democratic governments were handmaidens for death and destruction. Christian politicians used science to build new killing technologies, and Christian priests blessed the bombs and bombers as they flew away to bomb civilian populations. The civilizations of England and Europe could no longer be considered the most advanced and most civilized in the world after all; rather, it was now clear that so-called European civilization was nothing more than a thin veneer over barbarism. What had two world wars revealed? Selfishness, cruelty, slaughter, shamelessness, and corruption.[8]

The Hindu Nationalist movement, which had begun to appear in the nineteenth century, used this new realization of the moral limits of European civilization to grow as an ideology in the period in the 1920s, 1930s, and then in the 1940s. As Hindu Nationalists extolled the virtues of Hinduism, there were increasing tensions between Hindu nationalists and the Muslims, who were predominant in northern India. Ultimately this would help lead in part to India's partition between Hindu India and Muslim Pakistan, and the terrible violence which followed. The 1950s was a period when the newly born India struggled with a variety of social conflicts centered on caste, language, class, and religion. Not only was the tension between Hindus and Muslims causing massive rioting, there was also the problem of how India should relate to European power and American capitalism on the one hand, and the socialism of China and the Soviet Union on the other

---

[8] An excellent book on the issues involved in India's participation in the world wars is Srinath Raghavan, *India's War: World War II and the Making of Modern South Asia* (New York: Basic Books, 2016).

.

This new stress upon classical India, fueled by Hindu religious nationalism, brought about a new pride in the accomplishments of ancient Indian civilization. A common claim was that India must be preserved in a five-fold unity.

(1) One land (reunite Bangladesh and Pakistan with India under the banner of Hinduism).
(2) One race.
(3) One religion.
(4) One culture.
(5) One language.

The single most significant religious and political leader in India who guided south Asia to independence was the man known to the west as Gandhi.

7.8 MOHANDAS KARAMCHAND GANDHI (1869-1948).

Mohandas Gandhi was not born into the Brahmin class, but rather was born to the *vaishya* (merchant and trading) class. He was educated in London and became a lawyer working in South Africa (which had a large Indian minority population) until 1915. He returned to India where he became one of the most important social reformers of his era, and finally he was the political leader of the Indian Congress party during the 1920s and later. His political power came from his personality and his spirituality. He appealed directly to the consciences of human beings: he had no material assets, had no rich friends to give money so he could gain political influence, he held no office, and led no legislature. He was a lawyer, not a diplomat, and not a trained philosopher or an artist.

Certainly, one of the reasons for Gandhi's fame is that he never resorted to force to gain his way. He utilized hunger strikes as a moral tool to move British officials, or to move Indian leaders. Gandhi believed that devotion to truth and love (expressed in non-violent resistence to injustice and wrongdoing) would convince the wrongdoer of the hurtfulness of his or her wrong-doing, bringing about a change in heart to replace evil with good.

His spiritual integrity was legendary, and was what enabled him to triumph over the opposition of the political state. His education and training, and personality, made him open to any ideas that seemed to value the human spirit and contributed to human dignity and social reform, no matter what the source. He worked to reform traditional Hinduism, including a rejection of the high-caste discrimination against the lower classes. He worked to improve the position of the outcastes, although many believed that Gandhi had not done enough.

Although open to all religious ideas which supported social reform, his personal religious attitude was monotheism focused on Vishnu. His family shaped his life-long religious attitudes—faith, devotion and self-surrender to Vishnu, piety and love of Vishnu conceived of as a benevolent and personal god. In this sense, his religion was a traditional Vaishnavite means to self-fulfillment.

There were a cluster of values that Gandhi emphasized in his teachings. He encouraged spontaneity, faith and devotion, and acceptance of love as the supreme value. Gandhi demanded that we serve and sacrifice, and he believed that there existed something called Truth itself which should be treated as divine. Gandhi believed that in their core, all great religions are one, but precepts vary in externals because of languages and cultural institutions. All religions are equal in value, but they are not equal in all lands. Responding to the ongoing Christian attempt to Christianize India, Gandhi said that a foreign religion is not as good as one's own native tradition. He felt that conversion to a foreign religion does not produce a vital and well-functioning faith. Thus, Indians should *not* convert to Christianity. He particularly loved devotional stories and valued especially the Christian *Sermon on the Mount*, and the *Bhagavad Gita*. Gandhi is quoted as having said "When disappointment stares me in the face and all alone I see not one ray of light, I go back to the *Bhagavadgita*."[9]

Gandhi repelled by institutional Christianity

---

[9] S. Radhakrishnan, *The Bhagavadgita*, quoted on the dust jacket of *The Principal Upanishads*.

CHAPTER 7: MODERN INDIAN THOUGHT

Some have found Gandhi's positive writings about Jesus to mean that he loved Christianity, but this is not supported in all of his writings. Jesus's admonitions about feeding the poor and "love thy enemy" and "turn the other cheek" resonated with Gandhi, but he thought that institutional Christianity did not embody the teachings of the founder. It has been said that Gandhi embraced Christ but was repelled by organized Christianity. Gandhi wrote:

> Much of what passes as Christianity is a negation of the Sermon on the Mount . . . . Paul was not a Jew. He was a Greek, had an oratorical mind, a dialectical mind, and he distorted [the original teachings of] Jesus. Christ possessed a great force—the Love force—but Christianity became disfigured when it went to the West. It became the religion of Kings.[10]

Although a popular and influential leader, Gandhi voluntarily embraced poverty including wearing the simple loincloth of an Indian peasant, and by doing so he enabled the ordinary people to identify with the Nationalist movement and with social reform movements. He encouraged small-scale cottage industries, and was famous for using a spinning wheel to make cotton thread, instead of buying clothing made in Europe from Indian cotton. He fought against official persecution using non-violent love (*ahimsa*, non-harm).

Gandhi's stress upon personal purity and simplicity, and his insistence on strict morality grounded in the love for others, showed that he did not only make speeches but that he lived the life he urged others to pursue. The majority of India's poor and illiterate loved and admired Gandhi, as did many others who were not poor. Gandhi's influence upon the image of India was immense.[11] He was a nationally venerated *guru* and as such his deeply principled positions on issues had deep resonance especially with the poorer population. The lasting influence of Gandhi and his great contribution was his ability to combine two apparently opposed positions: political protest against the official powers combined with Hindu religious ideals of love of Truth and love of simplicity.

Gandhi's Message to the Poor

Gandhi's message to India's poor might be summarized as this: we Indians are poor but we have a great capacity for hard work, a spiritual strength, and a morality that will enable us to feed and clothe and educate ourselves, and ultimately to rule ourselves—without giving up the moral and spiritual traditions that have nourished India over the millennia.

Unlike many politicians who say one thing but whose personal lives contradict their speeches, Gandhi's message was followed personally by Gandhi—he was poor and he worked hard, cultivating the traditional spirituality of India, but not excluding other religions. He proceeded to act on his claim, trying to change the world and to perfect himself with great inward strength and passion. The perceptive student will recognize that Gandhi is working out and applying the ancient path of *karma-yoga* drawing upon much in the *Bhagavad Gita* as guide. In India Gandhi was widely regarded as a saint, and the title "Mahatma" which means "Great-Atman," or "Great-Souled One," was commonly applied to him.

General features of Gandhi's thought

As we have seen, Gandhi strongly preferred simplicity over complexity. For him, life need not be as complex as we make it, and it is possible to live simply, which will bring our life in accordance with nature which is spiritual at its base. For Gandhi, reality is not merely a natural order of matter as studied by modern science, but reality contains a moral order as well. Reality is not merely material; it is inherently spiritual, it is moral.

Gandhi believed that no social, political or military power is greater than Truth. Truth should be sought not merely in our spoken words, but in all things. Truth itself is like a deity, and must be served. To realize Truth is to

---

[10] Louis Fischer, *The Life of Mahatama Gandhi* (Bharatiya Vidya Bhavan: 1998), p. 132; originally published in 1948 shortly after the death of Gandhi.

[11] John Koller, *The Indian Way*, p. 364.

CHAPTER 7: MODERN INDIAN THOUGHT

realize purity, to realize one's own true nature, and to realize God. We finally know the Truth that resides at the center of all existence and which brings the fulfillment of human life and liberation. To realize Truth is to fulfill the inner law of one's own being.[12]

Gandhi taught that the basis for social order and law is simply the Truth-force called God. God is the force that encourages and supports moral righteousness in the world. One of the *Upanishads*, the *Isha Upanishad*, explains the identity of God, Truth, and Existence or Being. Gandhi utilizes this to support his own understanding. He writes that all of reality is pervaded by Isha (God, Creator, Lord, Ruler), and the rule of the Lord is the divine law of all creation. In this law all things have their being, and when in accord with the Truth of this pattern, they are fulfilled.

The Truth, from which all things issue, unites all beings into one family, even though each individual thing has its inner rule and inner purpose. However, the Truth is realized by vigorous action—you must act, you must DO something, because ignorance and vice obscure the Truth, confusing each one of us. Vigorous action must be employed to achieve purity and self-knowledge.

Non-violence

What kind of "vigorous action"? Loving non-harm to all creatures (*ahimsa*). *Ahimsa* is the highest *dharma* (duty, requirement) of action. Truth is the God that dwells in all beings (all reality); to love God is to love the beings in whom God dwells.

It is through *ahimsa* that the self is purified and inner Truth is revealed. *Ahimsa* is usually translated "non-harm" or "non-violence," but for Gandhi, it meant a pure and perfect love proceeding from the depths of one's being, and expressing itself in kindness, compassion, and tireless service to others. It is an ethics of compassion, or neighborliness, it is enduring friendship with the world.

Gandhi believed that the Truth-force which is God is everywhere. No one's heart is without the divine spark. God must be in the heart even of those who are doing wrong. Violence is an expression of fear, growing out of inner weakness; non-violence is an expression of love, growing out of the central core of one's inner being and the unity of all that exists. To practice loving non-harm is to exemplify kindness, compassion, and helpfulness. For anyone whose heart is filled with such love, there is no room for hatred or violence. Violence only calls forth more violence, and this weakens the individual and the society.

The ideas of the transforming power of truth, and *ahimsa* or non-violent love-force were then used in the interests of social reform to bring about freedom and justice for all Hindus. In the service of *ahimsa*, Gandhi encouraged and practiced civil disobedience, passive resistance, and even hunger strikes. All of these were weapons which he employed against injustice and evil, whether it be from the British or from Indian political rulers.

Gandhi was well-aware that our world is filled with injustice and filled with humans who oppress others for power or wealth. Gandhi felt that the spiritual love (*ahimsa*, non-violence) which he advocated would bypass greed, logic and rationality, and instead go straight from the heart of the loving follower to the heart of the oppressor. Thus love would be a much more effective means of social reform and human fulfillment. Gandhi believed that only through the active forces of holding tightly to the ultimate truth, and encompassing non-violent love could human dignity, justice and freedom be achieved—and these required personal purification, sacrifice, and faith, on the part of every individual.

7.8 OTHER MODERN INDIAN THINKERS

The following persons are very important to the history of modern India, and are well-known in India. In fact, several are also famous in Western countries. There are many books available on each of these, should the reader care to explore more than the very brief introductions supplied here.

---

[12] *Ibid.*, p. 365.

CHAPTER 7: MODERN INDIAN THOUGHT

Sri Ramana Maharshi (1879-1950)

In 1896, at the age of sixteen, Ramana Maharshi experienced a life-changing experience which followers refer to as his enlightenment. Shortly after this experience, he traveled to a famous holy mountain and never left. He lived a quiet life as an ascetic (*sannyasin*) and slowly a community of followers took root around him. He insisted that silence was the purest teaching, although he would answer questions when asked. His major influence was the Vedanta traditions of the identity of the *atman*-soul and the divine (Brahman). He welcomed everyone, no matter their religious background or attitudes. His followers tried to treat him as a divinity, but he rejected their behavior. He never allowed anyone to treat him as special, and he would not accept private gifts. He told students that the answers to questions were to be found within. Like the Vedanta philosopher Ramanuja, Ramana Maharshi recommended devotion, but he did accept a variety of paths and practices.

Maharishi Mahesh Yogi (1918-2008)

The early details of Maharishi Mahesh Yogi's life are unclear. He earned a bachelors degree in physics in 1942, and then found his own personal guru, Brahmananda Saraswati. In 1955, the Maharishi began to introduce Transcendental Meditation to followers. In 1958 he launched an international tour, and after about ten years, in the late 1960s and early 1970s, the Maharishi became a celebrity because he was the *guru* to many famous entertainers of the time, including the Beatles and the Beach Boys. In the late 1970s, he started a program that claimed that followers possessed powers—they could fly through the air and they could create world peace. Later he moved to the Netherlands. In 2008, the Maharishi announced his retirement from all administrative activities and went into silence until his death three weeks later.

The Maharishi and his immediate followers created charitable organizations and some very successful for-profit businesses including health clinics, mail-order health supplements and organic farms. In 2008, it was reported that the Maharishi organization in the United States valued their assets at about $300 million.

Sri Aurobindo (1872-1950)

Sri Aurobindo studied in London at Cambridge University, and after his return to India, became an Indian nationalist. He was also known as a philosopher, a poet, a practitioner of meditation, and was treated as a guru. He wrote on the Vedas, the *Upanishads*, and the *Bhagavad-Gita*. He was a leader in the Indian movement for independence from British rule. He was imprisoned by the British for opposing British rule in India in his writings. During his stay in the jail he had mystical and spiritual experiences, after which he quit politics and began a life of spiritual exploration. Sri Aurobindo developed a method of spiritual practice he called Integral Yoga. He told followers that human life can evolve into a life that was divine. One's own personal spiritual realization could lead to liberation, but also transform human nature, enabling a divine life on earth.[13]

Rabindranath Tagore (1861-1941)

Rabindranath Tagore, born into the Brahmin caste, was one of the most important and talented of the Indian scholars and poets. He was born in and lived in Bengal (the city of Calcutta is in this region). He is famous as a humanist, but he also was involved in politics and urged independence from the British empire. He is credited with reshaping Bengali literature and music, as well as Indian art. He painted, he wrote poetry and novels, essays, texts, and perhaps two thousand songs. He became the first non-European to win the Nobel Prize in Literature in 1913. He was famous for "elegant prose and magical poetry." He remains very popular in India and Bangladesh, as well as in Sri Lanka, Nepal and Pakistan.

---

[13] A well-regarded biography of Auribindo is Peter Heehs, *The Lives of Sri Aurobindo* (New York Columbia University Press, 2008).

CHAPTER 7: MODERN INDIAN THOUGHT

Dr. Bhimrao R. Ambedkar (1891–1956)

The importance of Dr. Ambedkar in India ranks alongside of Gandhi when it comes to anti-colonial political philosophy. He certainly counts as one of India's most important intellectuals dealing with state-centered politics. He has been described as an extraordinary Indian politician, economist, lawyer, jurist, philosopher, anthropologist, and historian. His importance to the ultimate democracy within India is clear and has been studied.[14] Dr. Ambedkar argued that equality was important to India, but all must be able to share freedom, not merely the upper castes. All must show fellowship, fraternity, and even reverence towards neighbors, including the so-called "outcastes." Dr. Ambedkar criticized Gandhi's positions, especially on the so-called untouchables. Ambedkar is most famous for encouraging the untouchables to reject Hindu castes, and instead adopt the early Buddhist ideals of the Buddha (the Buddha rejected the castes).

7.9 CONTEMPORARY POST-COLONIAL HINDUISM

The influence of the British educational system on Indian students, combined with the general European disregard of the ancient history and glory of India, had made many of the best-educated Indians indifferent to and even despising of their own ancient Hindu traditions; Hindu ideas were not important to the lives of those educated in the British school system. For the well-educated person in India, ancient Indian thought symbolized ancient superstition which subscribed to a medieval cosmology, astrology, many forms of fortune-telling, and especially a pre-scientific approach to nature. Ancient India had supported the profoundly unequal privileges of an ancient aristocracy of Brahmins and *ksatriyas*.

However, as noted above, in modern times there has been a backlash against the British education which minimized ancient India. There has been a strong revival of the more ancient Vedic Brahmanical ideas and influences, and most younger Indians identify themselves as Hindu without hesitation. Despite a good education in Western science and the Western world-view, many younger Hindus feel that there is something divine, some cosmic spirit which interpenetrates our world and can be seen within ourselves as our *atman*. Many Indian politicians encourage this religious view of India as one religion and its people as one race.

Attendance at a wide variety of Hindu temples is high, and new temples and monasteries are being built. The ancient practice of men leaving home and entering the wilderness continues. In the family home, rituals are done in honor of the rising and setting sun. Families still perform the important life-cycle ceremonies which honor birth, coming of age, marriage and death. These rituals provide a unity to Hindu practice that is not obvious when one merely studies beliefs and doctrines.

Throughout India there are shrines to guardian divinities (*devas*) to protect the village and countryside. Stars in the night sky are often considered *devas* and are believed to influence human lives. Astrology and fortune-telling are important in the daily life of many Hindus. For many contemporary Indians, divine forces surround us everywhere we go, and are present in our homes and in our places of work. Ascetics in religious communities train in yogic meditation and meditative breathing, and participate in meditative retreats.

Many new charismatic religious leaders are appearing and becoming spiritual teachers and spiritual guides.[15] These gurus are treated as incarnations of *devas*. Miracles are observed in Hindu temples, including statues and icons

---

[14] Dr. Ambedkar's importance has been ranked alongside Gandhi. A book analyzing his political importance in relation to Gandhi is Aishwary Kumar, *Radial Equality: Ambedkar, Gandhi, and the Risk of Democracy* (Stanford: Stanford University Press, 2015).

[15] One such guru is known as Bhagwan Shree Rajneesh (1931–1990), and also as Osho, who presented himself as self-enlightened and his teachings as radical, iconoclastic, and dangerous. There are several books written by Osho and his devoted followers. A recent scholarly and objective biography of Osho is Hugh B. Urban, *Zorba the Buddha: Sex, Spirituality, and Capitalism in the Global Osho Movement* (Berkeley: University of California Press, 2016).

which drink milk, temple images sweating, and other such "Little Tradition" events. These are reported in daily newspapers with much enthusiasm.

Ganesha was described in the previous chapter on Hindu devotionalism. Ganesha continues in popularity in modern India, mostly because Ganesha is the *deva* who removes all obstacles. A temple in North India claimed that the statues of Ganesha in the temple had actually begun to drink the milk that had been offered during *puja* rituals by devout worshipers. The media in India confirmed the miraculous event and saw it as evidence that traditional Hindu belief was both correct and strong.[16]

7.10 POLITICS AND INDIAN RELIGIONS

Indian religions have had some influence in the West. However, Western approaches to Indian religion are having an influence on India as well. Middle-class Indians use the internet daily and are well aware of British and European television, Western education, and Western interpretations of yoga. British and American style yoga practices have become important in modern India.[17]

In addition, it is very probable that Hinduism will become even more political and nationalistic, because the problem of uniting and preserving the nation is an acute one. Religion is a powerful political force, and it can be manipulated to become a force for unification. We can feel a sense of unity with those who are members of the same general religious community and who worship the same gods that we do.

Traditionally, the large variety of Hinduisms tends to hold that no religious or philosophical system contains the entire ultimate truth, but is merely a perspective on the truth, and the result has been a historical toleration of many competing and even contradictory viewpoints. But the virtue of toleration does not imply that all religions are equal. To tolerate a view is not the same as thinking that the view is valuable. In fact, those who subscribed to this toleration view did not usually hold that opposing disagreeing views were equal in value; most often it was felt that those who disagreed had a more ignorant or less spiritual perspective and would ultimately come around to the higher view.

However it must be noted that political parties and political forces often encourage and support a less tolerant attitude because encouraging blind prejudice can be a very useful tool for manipulating the population. Some politicians have fanned religious intolerance and questioned the loyalty and patriotism of any Indian person who is not a Hindu, who is instead a Muslim or a Christian.

In recent times, Hindu revivalist groups have tried to overthrow the secular democracy and establish a Hindu religious government, a theocracy governed by the upper castes as rulers, as taught in the *Laws of Manu*. In 1923 a group calling itself the "National Union of [Hindu] Volunteers" (the RSS) called for the constitution to be revised to reflect a country devoted to "Mother India." In 1995, an allied "fundamentalist nationalist" party, the Bharatiya Janata party (BJP), appealed to old prejudices, tensions and hatreds and won more seats in congress than any other party in the national Parliament, and in 1998 the BJP party became the ruling party. This group and others reflect the ancient tradition that India should be ruled by upper-caste politicians as it has always done in the past, not by members of lower castes. This appeal to the past has drawn the votes of many in the successful middle classes, who actively discourage members of the lower castes from getting an education and voting. The BJP has reworked traditional rituals and tried to establish a unity among Hindus, often by manipulating religious legends.

The previous democratic and secular political party had tried to weaken the control of the Brahmins and upper classes over the nation's civil service and educational institutions, and the Bharatiya Janata party (BJP) did its best to support the old ways, and fanned resentment against this secular government. The BJP has encouraged Hindus to

---

[16] Esposito notes that there is a substantial community of skeptics in India who claimed to expose such miracles as fake. Cf. Esposito, Fasching, Lewis, *World Religions Today*, p. 336–337.

[17] *Ibid.*, p. 335.

respect what it describes as the venerable traditions of the ancient past which they call "true Hinduism." The BJP has intentionally encouraged those Indians who want a return to the glorious past of Mother India, to have strongly negative feelings directed against those who disagreed with the BJP political party. The BJP has also encouraged disrespect toward Muslims and even sponsored popular events staged to encourage lower-class Hindus to attack Muslims for actions in the past centuries. Claiming that the *deva* Rama had approved of violence against Muslims, the BJP rallied "volunteers" to attack an ancient Muslim mosque because they were told that Rama had been born on that site. Rioting broke out between Muslims and Hindus in many towns in India and in Pakistan.

Although these religious and political groups have made a rallying cry to return to true Hinduism, they are necessarily vague on what this means. They are not precise because at no time in Indian history have the Hindus ever agreed upon what is the central core of Hindu beliefs, beyond loyalty to "Mother India."

In addition, although the ruling political parties were supposed to be neutral in the context of religion, most feel that the modern Indian state has tended to ally itself with the higher castes, leading to the charge that the state is not really secular, but rather a rather "neo-Brahmin" political system. Although the Brahmin caste comprises about 3% of the population, in 1990 their proportion in the Indian civil service was as high as 70%.

Despite the fact that the two upper classes completely dominate the government, they have portrayed themselves as having been persecuted by or discriminated against by the laws and policies of the politicians of secular India. When the secular government encouraged education of the lower castes and tried to get these groups involved in the political processes, Brahmins claimed this was discrimination against them. The fundamentalist-nationalist Bharatiya Janata party (BJP) and its high-caste supporters have attempted to reverse the secular state's successful efforts to include the lower castes, and have successfully slowed the introduction of genuinely democratic elections in the rural villages.

As you can see, the political system of India has several apparently incompatible tensions built into it. Traditional India has a foundation built upon hierarchy, difference, purity, poverty and privilege. On the other hand, modern politics has ideals of equality and democracy. Is it possible to weave together these strands of ancient religion and culture, the legacy of British colonialism, and modern experience? Only time will tell.[18]

7.11 SUMMARY OF THE CHAPTER

The 2011 census recorded a population of 1.21 billion in India (in comparison, the USA population in 2015 is approximately 317 million). The extreme poverty and extensive caste discrimination continue, and several forms of contemporary Hinduism attempt to mitigate the vast inequities. Other forms of Hinduism oppose any attempt to liberalize the old traditions.

The influence of England upon India and Indian values has been immense. Class-conscious British civil servants took control of India, and the British educational system imposed on India taught Shakespeare and British philosophers like David Hume, and minimized the long tradition of Indian thought systems like Vedanta, Yoga, and the many devotional traditions. After many decades of political and non-violent struggle, India broke free of British control, and in 1947 established a secular government.

There has never been one single form of official Hinduism, even in modern times. However, for political reasons many politicians encourage Indians to reject Western values and Western civilization, and return to the ancient traditions and values of "Mother India." Many influential Hindus want to make India into a religious state, governed by religious leaders of the Brahmin caste. Much violence has occurred as a result.

Despite the political instability, most Hindus continue to accept the claim that the world is filled with numerous *deva*, and sacrifices and *puja* directed towards divinities is practiced daily by the majority of Hindus. In

[18] A fine introductory treatment of modern India and these tensions is Maria Misra, *Vishnu's Crowded Temple: India Since the Great Rebellion* (Yale, 2008).

addition, yogic meditation remains important to many. The presence of ascetics and *guru* continue to show the influence of trust in the ancient practices. In modern Hinduism, Hindus can choose from a wide variety of Hinduisms, and can make choices about their own religious path instead of being locked into specific practices controlled by their *varna* or their *jati*. In modern India, *gurus* appear on television and use social media and the internet to communicate with devotees, and spread their teachings outside of India to Indian communities around the world. As citizens from India move into the European and American worlds, their religious traditions accompany them.

7.12 TECHNICAL TERMS

Adi Granth   a Sikh sacred text also called the *Guru Granth Sahib*

ahimsa   translated "non-harm" or "non-violence," but in Gandhi's thought, it meant a pure and perfect love proceeding from the depths of one's being, and expressing itself in kindness, compassion, and tireless service to one's neighbors.

puja   rituals and ritual offerings focused on an icon or statue of a *deva*

7.13 QUESTIONS FOR FURTHER DISCUSSION

(1)   Some Hindus feel that the influence of Europe and England has been pernicious, damaging faith in "Mother India." Other Hindus have valued contributions of Europeans in science, medicine, and technology. Where do you stand on this issue? Would India have been better without Western influences? Consider what you mean when you say "better."

(2)   What was the appeal of Gandhi to the people of India? Why did the poor people love and venerate him?

(3)   It seems as though many of the upper classes of India loved and venerated Gandhi, not just the poor. What was it about him or his message which inspired this affection?

(4)   Not all Hindus valued Gandhi or his message. Why were some Hindus opposed to Gandhi and his ideas?

(5)   This chapter discussed the role of the caste system as understood by many recent Indian thinkers. If you have any friends from an Indian background, you might want to ask them about how the caste system functions in their life, in their family, or their community.

(6)   You might want to research the role and function of the caste system in contemporary India. How are the attitudes in the cosmopolitan centers different from rural communities? How popular are the Hindu politicians and political parties which support the caste system? Are the groups which tend to minimize or reject the system as popular? Why or why not?

(7)   It has been pointed out that Hindu religion can be used to bring about a unity to the political realm. Is there any similarities between India and North America using religion for political reasons?

(8)   Have any Indian thinkers or religious traditions influenced Europe, England, or North America? Which ones? Do you think the people who live in the Western world have a deep understanding of the Indian religious world-view? Discuss.

A SELECTED BIBLIOGRAPHY

Contemporary Indian Thought

Babb, Lawrence, *Redemptive Encounters: Three Modern Styles in the Hindu Tradition* (Berkeley: University of California Press, 1986).

_____, *The Divine Hierarchy* (New York: Columbia University Press, 1975).

Hawley, John and Mark Juergensmeyer, *Songs of the Saints of India* (New York: Oxford University Press, 1988).

Jaffrelot, Christophe, *The Hindu Nationalist Movement in India* (New York: Columbia University Press, 1996).

Jones, Kenneth W., *Socio-Religious Reform Movements in British India* (Cambridge: Cambridge University Press, 1994).

Keyes, Charles F. and E. Valentine Daniel, eds., *Karma: An Anthropological Inquiry* (Berkeley: University of California Press, 1983).

Larson, Gerald James, *India's Agony over Religion* (Albany: State University of New York Press, 1995).

Misra, Maria, *Vishnu's Crowded Temple: India Since the Great Rebellion* (Yale, 2008)

Vanita, Ruth, *Love's Rite: Same-Sex Marriage in India and the West* (New York: Palgrave-Macmillan, 2005).

CHAPTER 8: BACKGROUND FOR EARLY BUDDHISM

HISTORICAL AND PHILOSOPHICAL BACKGROUND FOR INDIAN BUDDHISM

If you have already studied the wide range of spiritual traditions called "Hinduism" which ground themselves in the ancient Vedic literature, then you have the background for Indian Buddhism of the fifth to fourth century B.C.E. If you have not yet become acquainted with the ancient pre-Buddhist religions of India, this will be a very brief introduction.

Orthodox and Heterodox

The religions of India have their origins in at least two sources, the indigenous traditions associated with the Indus Valley civilization which goes back at least 5,000 years, and the later Vedic tradition of the Aryans who migrated into India about 1500 B.C.E., about 3,500 years ago. Based on archaeological evidence, the religious views of the Indus Valley civilization may have influenced later Hinduism in several possible ways including seated meditation, and may have had goddess-worship in addition to deification of trees and animals including snakes, elephants, and bulls.

The early sacred texts of ancient Indian religions are the Vedas, the memorized oral hymns of the priests of the Aryan groups who immigrated into India. Those who regard the Vedic texts as sacred are called "Hindus," but there are a wide variety of Hindu religions, and Hinduism is *not* defined by any special or particular belief—Hindus can be polytheistic, monotheistic, monist, atheistic, and materialists who deny the existence of non-physical spirit. It is interesting that key Hindu ideas like meditation and reincarnation are never mentioned in the ancient religious scriptures of the Aryans, the Vedas. Those in India who regard the Vedas as sacred are called the **orthodox** traditions. Those who reject the Vedas as sacred scriptures are called **heterodox**.

The *Upanishads*

The *Upanishads*, the secret teachings of the forest sages, are a later development of the Vedas. The earliest *Upanishads* are dated to around 600 B.C.E. and a wide variety of Upanishadic texts continue to appear until approximately 1500 C.E. The earliest of the *Upanishads* were taking shape about the same time that Buddhism was developing in the Ganges river area of northern India. The *Upanishads* offer many different teachings on spiritual development, but a primary focus is upon an immaterial immortal unchanging soul (called the *atman*) and its relationship to the ultimate impersonal source and force behind all the gods, a sacred ultimate (called Brahman). These teachings include the idea that our immortal souls (*atman*) are trapped in an unending cycle of continuing reincarnation and the goal of life is to achieve *moksha*, liberation from the continuous cycle of birth-and-death. Meditation is associated with the Yoga traditions of India, and becomes one tool that can be used to achieve liberation.

CHAPTER 8: EARLY BUDDHISM BACKGROUND

Buddhism Rejects Core Beliefs of Hinduism

Buddhism began in India around 500–400 B.C.E., but despite the views of some Hindus, Buddhism is *not* a form of Hinduism. Buddhism rejects the great majority of the core beliefs of the Vedas and *Upanishads*.[1] Buddhism rejects the efficacy of the rituals of the Hindu priests and rejects the spiritual authority of the priests. Buddhism rejects the sacred Vedas and *Upanishads*, rejects the theory of the eternal self-existent immaterial soul (*atman*), and rejects the idea of a sacred absolute, Brahman. Because Buddhism does not accept the sacred authority of the Vedas or *Upanishads*, it is a **heterodox** form of Indian thought.

Nevertheless, Buddhism did arise and develop in the fifth century B.C.E. in northern India, and seems comfortable with many of the ideas accepted by Hinduism. For example, early Buddhism accepts the idea of a cycle of birth-and-death, accepts the idea of karma (good choices produce good consequences, bad choices produce bad consequences), and is comfortable with the variety of techniques we call meditation, accepts the idea of withdrawal away from urban areas to pursue liberation, and utilizes the chanting of words and phrases of power (*mantras*).

There is no single monolithic form of Buddhism; rather there is the Buddhism of the earliest scriptures and commentaries, and there is the practices popular in the communities of followers. It seems clear that the Buddhism of the scriptures corresponds to "Grand Tradition" Buddhism (as described in the introduction), and the popular Buddhism of the householder-followers seems describable as "Little Tradition" Buddhism. In the following chapters, we will focus on the teachings found in the sacred texts, although there will be briefer discussions of the practices in local communities which will involve prayer, rituals, chanting, and adepts who were believed able to perform miracles.

---

[1] Those Hindus who believe Buddhism is a form of Hinduism do so by simply asserting that the Buddhists have misunderstood the Buddha's teachings on *atman*, on *Brahman*, and the other important beliefs and teachings of the Brahmin priests.

CHAPTER 8: EARLY BUDDHISM IN INDIA

8.1 OVERVIEW OF THE CHAPTER

Having explored the wide range of spiritual traditions which Western people refer to as "Hinduism" which ground themselves in the ancient Vedic literature, we now turn our attention to another native tradition of the Indian subcontinent which rejects the great majority of the core beliefs that characterize Hinduism. This is Buddhism, which includes a rejection of the enduring value of priestly ritual, a rejection of the caste system, a rejection of the authority of Brahmin priests, a rejection of the Hindu idea of an eternal unchanging soul (*atman*), a rejection of the idea of an ultimate power behind all the gods (Brahman), and a rejection of the sacred literature of the Vedas, including the *Upanishads* and *Bhagavadgita*, as being of ultimate and transcendental spiritual value. Buddhism is a system which has been successful in many Asian civilizations outside of India, and has achieved substantial popularity in Europe, England, and North and South America.

Buddhism was founded by a forest sage (*muni*) known by the title of Buddha, or "The Awakened One." The Buddha is said to have achieved the goal of nirvana and then taught the pathway to nirvana to his followers. The Buddhist tradition will stress understanding the causal interconnectedness of things in an effort to achieve clarity and understanding of the causes of dissatisfaction, disappointment, frustration, misery, and emotional suffering. Having analyzed the causes of emotional suffering, the Buddha then laid out a pathway by which dissatisfaction and misery can be lessened, and even eliminated.

The goal for the early Buddhist is nirvana, the complete cessation of suffering and emotional misery. The tools to accomplish this are three: insight, morality and focused concentration. Thus early Buddhism can be understood as identifying the numerous causes of misery and suffering, and then devising a strategy to lessen or remove those causes in order to remove misery.

In contemporary times there are two major traditions of Buddhism. The first modern tradition is called **Theravada**[1] and is associated with Sri Lanka, Myanmar (Burma), Thailand, Cambodia, and in the past it dominated in the islands of Java and Sumatra (Indonesia). The majority of the existing Theravada sacred texts are in an Indic language called Pali, which is related to Sanskrit (the dominant religious language of Indian religion).

The other contemporary tradition of Buddhism is called **Mahayana**, and is associated with China, Korea, Japan, Nepal and Tibet. The earliest sacred scriptures of the Mahayana are primarily written in Sanskrit. Neither of these two major traditions correspond precisely to the earliest forms of Buddhism. In this chapter, we will focus on what we know of Buddhism during its formative periods.

---

[1] There is little reason to think that the early conservative Buddhists of Sri Lanka, Cambodia, Thailand, and other places thought of themselves as belonging to a "Theravada" school, or that they used the term "Theravada" (the way of the Elders) to describe their tradition. What we call "Theravada Buddhism" was not a fixed ancient coherent ideology, and was not a homogeneous school of Buddhism, as is implied in the discussion in this chapter. Buddhists of Sri Lanka, Thailand, Cambodia and Burma-Myanmar did not adopt the Theravada label until more recent times. It seems they thought of themselves simply as followers of the teachings of the Buddha (Buddha-dharma). It is mostly as a literary convenience that we will focus upon Theravada when we discuss "conservative Buddhism." A recent substantial volume devoted to this topic is Peter Skilling, Jason A. Carbine, Claudio Cicuzza, Santi Pakdeekham, eds., *How Theravada Is Theravada? Exploring Buddhist Identities* (Chiang Mai: Silkworm Books, 2012). Another book arguing that the school of Theravada is more ancient is Prapod Assavavirulhakarn, *The Ascendancy of Theravada Buddhism in Southeast Asia* (Chiang Mai: Silkworm Books, 2010).

CHAPTER 8: EARLY BUDDHISM

8.2 THE HISTORICAL BACKGROUND

The time period around 600-300 B.C.E. was a crucial time in many world civilizations corresponding with the emergence of large-scale literate and historical cultures, empires, and world religions. The tradition of Buddhism began during this Axial age which we have discussed before. Spiritually, in India this was the time during which some people began abandoning all familial and social responsibilities, and instead they began leaving home and entering the wilderness forest areas for spiritual cultivation and meditation. It is the time of the earliest *Upanishads*, and the earliest practices related to Yoga. New pathways in civilization and religions were appearing everywhere.

In the ancient Indian subcontinent during this time period, the old order of kingdoms based upon tribes and clans and affiliations based on social structures and political structures (republics) was breaking down. The cities were growing larger, and merchants and monarchy were developing. New kingdoms based on geography and territory were beginning to take shape. The result was that people were becoming isolated from the older rural religious traditions which had structured their lives. Society was becoming more complex, and the growth of new technologies increased trade and travel, bringing exposure to other Indian sub-cultures and other ways of worship. These turbulent times encouraged a profusion of new possibilities, and new forms of religion arose, including what we in the West would consider critical thinking and philosophy.

As we saw in a previous chapter, the more ancient religions had been centered on sacred animals (the seals of the Harappans seem to reveal groups which worshiped bulls, snakes, elephants or cows), centered on agricultural imagery (sacred trees), or on personified forces of nature like water, rain, and thunder–but now during the Axial age some new images come to dominate. There is a new stress on the sacred person, and the sacred scripture came to be thought of as having special, pivotal significance for all human experience. The dominant religious symbols became the founder, the liberator, the awakened one, and the collection of sacred teachings. Buddhism belongs to this Axial age. Buddhism begins with a historical person who was aware of many of the current religions, and produced a new pathway and a new goal for followers in India.

8.3 INTRODUCTION TO INDIAN BUDDHISM

Buddhism began about 2,500 years ago in northern India in the Ganges valley, one of several locales where the religious authority of the traditional Brahmin priesthood was not firmly entrenched. As a result, groups of wandering ascetics known as *munis* ("silent sages"), *sramanas* ("ascetics," "recluses") or *yogins* (practitioners of yoga) claimed religious authority based in personal experience, propounded different philosophical and religious ideas, and advocated different religious practices. Buddhism was the most successful of these new systems and religions.

Since the formative period of Buddhism begins with the teachings of an actual person we call the Buddha, we should begin by studying the actual words or writings of "original" or "early" or "primitive" Buddhism. As far as anyone knows, the Buddha himself never wrote anything. He freely answered all questions, but never wrote any books or texts. At best, what we have are the memories of his students.

The words of the Buddha as memorized and recorded by his followers are called sutras.[2] These earliest sutras are an important source for understanding early Buddhism. Another source for early Buddhism is reading what the earliest critics of Buddhism said about the teachings.

---

[2] In Hinduism, the term *sutra* meant a "thread," an extended discourse on a specific topic. In Buddhism, the term *sutra* is reserved for a text which purports to provide the words of the Buddha as remembered by immediate followers. In this sense *sutras* are like Christian Gospels, which are believed to be the memories of the students of Jesus.

CHAPTER 8: EARLY BUDDHISM

Was The Buddha a *Deva*?

Based on the earliest texts, during the lifetime of the Buddha the immediate students did not treat the Buddha as a divinity, as a *deva*. According to the authors of the earliest scriptures, the Buddha does not rule the world, does not punish or reward, and is not a world-creator. The Buddha is not a transcendent divinity, not a *deva*. When asked if he was a god, the Buddha denied he was a *deva*. In an early sutra the Buddha answered a question and replied that he was not a *deva*, not any sort of supernatural being, and not an ordinary person.[3]

It is recorded that a Brahmin priest followed the Buddha into the forest, and then asked him if he was a god or a *deva*. The Buddha answered "No." He then asked if the Buddha were a supernatural spirit, or a ghost, or an ordinary human being. The Buddha explained:

That delusion, Brahmin, that would make me a god, just that delusion is extinguished in me, is torn from the root as a palm-tree is uprooted, is destroyed and will not enter existence again. ...

Just as, Brahmin, the blue, red and white lotus, though born in the water, grown up in the water, when it reaches the surface stands unsullied by the water, just so, Brahmin, though born in the world, grown up in the world, I have overcome the world and now abide unsullied by the world. Wherefore you, Brahmin, may take me as the Enlightened One.[4]

In his teachings, the Buddha seemed to have no interest in religious indoctrination, and instead encouraged individual students to come to a state of deepened understanding of their situation and the causes of their situation. Early Buddhism was principally about ethical action, not fixed belief, not firm faith.

Simple faith cannot produce such understanding. Blind faith in implausible things blocks understanding, preventing the open experience of reality itself, and rational faith becomes obsolete once understanding takes over. ... As the celebrated verse of Matercheta, a well-known author of the third century C.E. says, "Buddhas do not wash away sins with water. They do not heal suffering by laying on of hands, and They do not transmit their understanding into other's minds; They introduce beings to freedom by educating them about reality."[5]

Unquestioning Faith is Not a Virtue in Early Buddhism

Most important was the message of the cessation of misery and suffering (what the Buddhists call *duhkha*), and this was more important than the messenger. The Buddha himself advised students *not* to take what he said without questioning it or testing it to make sure it was correct. Uncritical faith was not a virtue for the Buddha. Religious indoctrination was not a virtue for the Buddha. How you act, what you do, is what is important. The Buddha explained this to a group called the Kalamas:

It is proper for you, Kalamas, to doubt, to be uncertain; uncertainty has arisen in you about what is doubtful. Come, Kalamas. Do not be misled by proficiency in the Collections (of Scriptures), nor by mere logic and inference, nor after considering reasons, nor after reflection on some view and approval of it, not because it fits becoming, not because the recluse (who holds it) is your teacher. But when you know for yourselves: 'These things are not good, these things are faulty, these things are

---

[3] *Anguttara-nikaya* 2.38, paraphrased in David Kalupahana, *Buddhist Philosophy: A Historical Analysis* (Honolulu: University of Hawaii Press, 1976), p. 112.

[4] Translation from Helmuth von Glasenapp, *Buddhism: A Non-Theistic Religion* (London: George Allen & Unwin, 1970), p. 138.

[5] Robert Thurman, *Essential Tibetan Buddhism* (New York: Castle Books, 1997), pp. 11–12.

censured by the intelligent, these things, when performed and undertaken, conduce to loss and sorrow—then do you reject them.[6]

For the Buddha, excessive faith can lead to blind uncritical acceptance of a teacher and the teachings, and this is not a virtue. It is a flaw. Be critical. Test the teacher's claims and see if they do lessen suffering and misery.

In Western religions, faith is invariably associated with accepting a claim without any evidence to support it, accepting a divinity or the claims of those who are priests of the divinity.[7] The Buddhist Sanskrit term *sraddha*, translated as "faith" has no connection to divinity at all.[8] The Buddhists do value *sraddha*, but the meaning of the Sanskrit is closer to the English term "confidence." In Buddhism, doubt is healthy and *sraddha* does not overcome doubt (as Christians understand this virtue, faith overcomes doubt). The Buddha encouraged doubt.

Rather, *sraddha* is essentially sufficient confidence in the teachings to try them out, to put them into practice, which are then tested by practice as described above. One also needs confidence in one's own ability to follow the path and lessen pain and suffering. If you do not have confidence that the Middle Way of Buddhism is effective, then you will not start upon it.[9] Thus, *sraddha* (a positive disposition towards the Buddhist teachings) is necessary to begin.

With practice one recognizes that one's confidence was justified because suffering diminishes. The Buddhist claims at least have been partially verified through practice and the student's own deepening insights. *Sraddha* engenders self-confidence which gives one energy and zeal to follow the teachings. Thus the beginning student does need to give tacit acceptance to the insights of the Buddha which followed from the Buddha's practice and his awakening experience, which in turn led to liberation from pain and suffering. It is felt that over time, one's tacit acceptance will turn into confidence, not blind faith. As pointed out above, Buddhist *sraddha* does not involve a divinity or acceptance of untestable claims; early Buddhism dispensed with the idea of divinity. Buddhist beliefs were explicitly not god-centered. Early Buddhism was non-theistic. The early Buddhists seem to propose a rational and tentative faith which later becomes obsolete once insight has deepened.

Early Buddhism can be understood on a medical model. Human beings are miserable and sick: this is the diagnosis of the disease. The causes are negatives like anger, envy, hatred, ego-centered possessiveness, greed, ignorance, and confusion. The prognosis is that one can eliminate the negatives with morality, mental discipline, and wisdom.

---

[6] *Anguttara Nikaya* 3.65 verse 4. Christmas Humphreys, ed., *The Wisdom of Buddhism* (New York: Random House, 1961), p. 71.

[7] In Christianity, "faith" was connected tightly to the acceptance of a divinity. The Christian theologian St. Augustine (354–430) asserted that one needed complete faith in the divinity of God and faith in the claims of Christianity, but with that faith combined with study of the Greek philosophy of Plato and the Neo-Platonists, the faith would engender understanding of those Christian claims which were not beyond human comprehension. Augustine's motto was "I believe in order to understand," meaning that faith will lead to understanding. In the Old Testament, "confidence" that God will fulfill his obligations seems to be part of the meaning. In the New Testament, "faith" is glossed as "to trust, to show confidence, and to accept as true," including the belief that God exists. Quite often "faith" is glossed as "an acceptance of Jesus Himself as being what He claims to be" including belief that Jesus is the messiah. To become a Christian is to believe in or have faith in the teachings of the Apostles concerning Jesus. These remarks are from the very valuable reference book, John L. McKenzie, S.J., *Dictionary of the Bible* (Milwaukee: Bruce Publishing, 1965), pp. 267–271.

[8] See the entry on *sraddha* in Robert Buswell and Donald Lopez, *The Princeton Dictionary of Buddhism* (New York: Princeton University Press, 2014), pp. 847–848. There is a pathway to liberation by faith, but never by faith alone. The Buddhists had beliefs, but they were non-theistic beliefs. See Wilfred Cantwell Smith, *Faith and Belief* (Princeton, N.J.: Princeton University Press, 1979), ch. 1.

[9] Suppose you wanted to become proficient in martial arts for the purpose of self-defense. If you do not believe the martial art will be useful, you will not begin. You need to have confidence that the skill will be effective, and you need confidence that you will make progress. You see others who are further along that pathway, and they do seem to have achieved something that you value. Your initial confidence is tested as you get better and better, and your own self-confidence increases. Your healthy doubt lessens.

No one can give you wisdom; you must discover it for yourself. The result is nirvana.[10]

Early Buddhism offered a pathway leading to the cessation of dissatisfaction and suffering, a pathway of wisdom and focused meditation, and this appealed especially to the well-educated, and the wealthy, rich and powerful merchants, members of a new rapidly rising class. Many Buddhist monks were from the class of protectors and warriors, *ksatriya/kshatriyas* (the Buddha's family, the Shakya clan, were *kshatriyas*), but many Brahmin priests also were attracted despite the fact that Buddhism minimized the caste society,[11] and the Buddha argued that a worthy Brahmin priest is worthy because of his behavior, not by the *varna* (caste position) of his birth parents. The stress in early Buddhism is on individual responsibility, individual effort and self-reliance, and this must have had great appeal to many within the governing and warrior groups in India.

The Three Jewels

In later centuries, when a student decided to join the Buddhist order, part of the ceremony involved "taking refuge" in what were called the **Three Jewels** or **Three Gems**. These are: the Buddha; the *dharma*; the *sangha*. One takes refuge in the teacher, the **Buddha**; one takes refuge in the content of Buddhist teachings, called the **dharma**, which can lessen or eliminate misery and dissatisfaction. One takes refuge among those who are especially skilled in the teachings, the Buddhist institutional community known as the *sangha*. This chapter on Buddhism is structured around these three. We will begin our discussion with the Buddha, the first of the Three Jewels.

8.4 THE LIFE OF THE BUDDHA: THE FIRST OF THE THREE JEWELS

The students of the Buddha[12] neglected to provide any specific information as to what year the Buddha was born, or what year he died.[13] In fact, we do not even know what language he spoke, although the majority of scholars think the language of his homeland area was very closely related to Pali.[14] This reflects the fact that in early Buddhism, what is most significant about the Buddha is not historical facts about **who** he was, but rather what he understood and could teach others.

One of the earliest Buddhist texts states that the Buddha lived to age 80, so one needs to establish either the

---

[10] This description, although accurate, makes early Buddhism appear opposed to supernatural claims. We will see that supernatural spirits and ghosts, protector deities, magical *mantras* and evil spirits are found throughout all forms of popular Buddhism.

[11] For example, see Vincent Eltschinger, *Caste and Buddhist Philosophy: Continuity of Some Buddhist Arguments against the Realist Interpretation of Social Denominations* (Delhi: Motilal Banarsidass, 2012).

[12] In this book we will follow a standard practice of writing the title of the founder of Buddhism as the "Buddha," and those whom the later traditions considered to be equal to the founder, Siddhartha, as a "buddha."

[13] Christian scriptures fail to provide a date for the birth or death of Jesus. Scholars feel Jesus was born between 6 and 4 B.C.E. and died somewhere around the year 30 of the Common Era, but this date is very uncertain.

[14] Professor Lance Cousins relates in an email from 5-11-2013: We do not know what precise dialect the Buddha spoke.... [or] whether the Buddha spoke only one dialect. ...In effect, then, Pali is the closest we can get to the language spoken by the Buddha. And it cannot have been very different — we are talking about dialect differences here, not radically distinct languages. My thanks to Professor Cousins for allowing me to paraphrase his remarks.

birth year, or death year, and then the other one is established.[15] Possible dates range between 600 B.C.E. to 350 B.C.E. For our purposes we will say the Buddha lived sometime during the fifth to fourth centuries B.C.E.[16]

The person known by the title "Buddha" was born miraculously on the full-moon day of the month which usually falls in late April or May of the Western calendar. He was born in north-eastern India on the border of what is now Nepal and India, in the foothills of the Himalayas.[17] This event is celebrated as Buddha Purnima, the full-moon night of the Buddha, also known as Buddha Jayanti. Although devout Buddhists describe the Buddha's father as a king, scholars describe his father as a leader and nobleman of the Shakya tribe who belonged to the social group of *ksatriyas* (the caste entrusted with guarding, protecting, and governing). Although no biography of the Buddha existed until almost 300 years after his death,[18] later Buddhism supplies the omissions and provides many additional miraculous stories of the previous lives of the Buddha.[19] In the following pages we will summarize the traditional story told by devout Buddhists.

Siddhartha Gautama

The person who was to grow up and be called "The Buddha" was born to the leader of a group known as the Shakyas. The baby's father named him Siddhartha[20] (pronounced Sidd-ART-ah, which means something like "he who has accomplished his aim"). His last name was Gautama. He was a member of the Shakya clan,[21] and often called Shakya-muni,[22] which means the wise teacher, or sage of the Shakyas. In the early Buddhist sutras he refers to himself as the "Tathagata," the "Thus-Come One" or perhaps "One Who Is Just So."

According to the earliest biography, the *Buddhacarita*, "Seven days after the divine child's birth, his mother,

---

[15] Digha Nikaya 16, which is in the Mahaparinibbana sutta, D.II. 100

[16] In Sri Lanka and Southeast Asian traditions, the Buddha's dates are 624–544 B.C.E. It has been common for many Western scholars to date him as 566–486 B.C.E. Other Western scholars prefer 563–483 B.C.E. as the most reasonable dates. Japanese scholars, relying on Chinese and Tibetan texts, provide the birth and death dates for the Buddha as 448–368 B.C.E. In 1998 a symposium of international scholars was held on "The Dating of the Historical Buddha." Although there was not complete agreement, a reasonable conclusion was that the Buddha lived perhaps 500–420 B.C.E. although some argued for dates as late as 430–350 B.C.E. There is an informed and useful summary of the dating issues in Willard Oxtoby, *World Religions: Eastern Traditions* (Oxford University Press, 2002), p. 221.

[17] Although neither of these two nations existed during the lifetime of the historical Buddha, both India and Nepal claim to be the birthplace of the Buddha. The reasons seem to be mostly related to tourism and pilgrim dollars. In India, the city which claims to be the birthplace of the Buddha is Piprahwa, and in Nepal, it is Lumbini. The areas are geographically close to each other.

[18] There are many books with the life of the Buddha. An excellent modern re-telling is David and Indrani Kalupahana, *The Way of Siddhartha: A Life of the Buddha* (University Press of America, 1987). There is also John Strong's *The Buddha: A Beginner's Guide* (Oneworld Publications, 2009) and *The Buddha: A Short Biography* (2001). A recent portrait of the Buddha is found in Stephen Batchelor, *Confession of a Buddhist Atheist* (New York: Spiegel & Grau, 2010), pp. 103-124. Batchelor writes "One of the greatest obstacles to understanding the Buddha's life is the story that Buddhism traditionally tells of it." (p. 103). Batchelor puts great emphasis on the earliest records which portray the Buddha as a social critic and reformer within a dangerous geo-political environment in which the Buddha lived and acted.

[19] Some stories are recounted in Willard Oxtoby, *World Religions: Eastern Traditions*, p. 221–223

[20] In the oldest Buddhist texts, the Pali sutras, the Buddha is referred to as Gautama or Gotama (the family or clan name) or Bhagavat, an honorific meaning "Lord" and sometimes translated "Blessed One."

[21] A clan is a dispersed cluster of people belonging to kinship groups presided over by a hierarchy of male rulers. Clan members were not necessarily biologically related, but they claimed a link to an ancient, often mythical, ancestor.

[22] A later Mahayana text, the *Lotus Sutra*, refer to the Buddha as Shakya-muni, the sage of the Shakyas. Many Mahayana followers use this title, for example: China (Shijia-muni), Korea (Sokka muni), Mongolia (Sigemuni) and Japan (Shakamuni).

the holy vessel of the Savior, was raised bodily, whole and pure, into heaven."[23] Siddhartha was raised by an aunt.

After the child's birth, a fortune-teller examined the infant child and reacted with amazement. Upon seeing significant bodily signs,[24] the fortune teller predicted that he would be either a universal monarch or a supremely awakened sage and great religious leader. If it were your son, which would you prefer?

Preferring that his son be an emperor rather than a forest-dwelling *sramana* (ascetic and beggar), Siddhartha's father attempted to shield his son from negative experiences which might lead the child to embrace a religious life. It was thought that if life poses no problems, there will be little reason for young Siddhartha to become serious about spiritual matters. Siddhartha grew up surrounded by luxuries and pleasures, isolated from human problems like old age, suffering, sickness, and death. In the palace of his father, he was taught proper skills appropriate for the son of a ruler, in an rather hedonistic environment. The intent was to deflect Siddhartha away from spiritual pursuits. He received a superior education, and was trained in skills appropriate to a member of the *ksatriya* (military and political leaders) social caste. At age 16, a marriage was arranged for him with a beautiful princess. Several years later, he became the father of a son.

One day Siddhartha asked his chariot driver to take him to the nearby village, and there he encountered an old man, a sick man and a dead man, symbolizing old age, suffering, sickness, and death, the common lot of all humanity. Siddhartha was face to face with *duhkha* (dissatisfaction, frustration, misery, disappointment, unhappiness, anguish and suffering), and because he had been protected from these all his life, he was stunned when he recognized the true depths of pain and suffering in the world.

Then, for the first time in his life, he also saw a *sunyassin*, a religious ascetic, a wandering hermit wearing only a ragged yellow robe, a mendicant who begged for every meal. The monk's calmness and detachment suggested to Siddhartha that there was a path for overcoming misery and discontent, a path for dealing with a life filled with suffering, sickness, death, in a world where everything is changing and nothing is permanent. Learning that the ascetic sought liberation from suffering, Siddhartha also decided to renounce the world. The desire to resolve the problem of *duhkha* propelled Siddhartha to leave his luxurious home.

The Great Renunciation or Great Departure

Inspired by the beggar he had seen earlier, Siddhartha decided to wander the wilderness far from civilized centers to live the life of a religious recluse and ascetic. On his way out of the palace, Siddhartha passed through the pavilion of beautiful dancing girls provided for his amusement and pleasure, but was not attracted by the sight. Renouncing the life of hedonistic pleasure, he bid goodbye to his sleeping wife and infant son. He climbed the wall surrounding the palace, cut his hair and beard, and put on the saffron yellow robe of a mendicant.[25] Like the other ascetics who wandered the forests and dusty roads of the Ganges valley along the area which later became the Nepal-India border, his robes would have been hand-dyed yellow ochre or brown, made of rags stitched together. His possessions would have included a bowl, needle and thread, a razor and a water strainer to ensure that he did not accidentally swallow any living thing. Siddhartha was 29 years old.

---

[23] From the *Buddhacarita* (Acts of the Buddha) by Ashvaghosa (written around 100 C.E. but a retelling of a story from perhaps 200 B.C.E.). Translated by Arthur Herman and quoted in his *An Introduction to Buddhist Thought*, (University Press of America, 1983), pp. 1–2.

[24] Symbols such as unusually long ear lobes (which means spiritual wisdom); golden complexion; wheel patterns on the soles of his feet; webbed fingers and toes; a mole between his eyebrows; a long tongue. There are 32 of these unusual marks in total.

[25] Siddhartha left his wife and son in the palace of his father, filled with servants, and as the mother of the new prince, she would have had a very good life. The fact that Siddhartha left may have had very little social effect on her. She is now the mother of the child who is next in line for the throne. The story is that both his wife and his son later joined the community of Buddha's followers.

CHAPTER 8: EARLY BUDDHISM

The Period of Study

Siddhartha roamed wilderness areas of northeastern India for the next six years, studying with various teachers. He found *gurus* (spiritual teachers) who meditated and knew how to attain exalted and peaceful states of consciousness. Apparently the first teachers taught Siddhartha what appears to be an early form of Yoga and Siddhartha mastered all the teacher could teach. However, recognizing that the *guru* himself had not achieved liberation from *duhkha*, from the misery of life, Siddhartha sought another teacher, and mastered new doctrines and even deeper levels of concentration. After a year of strenuous effort, once again Siddhartha felt that the teacher had not solved dissatisfaction, frustration, suffering, old age, and death, and so he moved on to seek out a new teacher. As the years passed, he went through several other teachers, and may have been a member of one or more communities of forest dwelling seekers.[26] During this stage he mastered the techniques of each of the teachers but still did not find a satisfactory solution to the problem of *duhkha*.

Finally, he and five other companions decided to go off alone, and push themselves to the limit, denying bodily needs and living a painfully ascetic lifestyle, in an attempt to attain freedom from misery. The six friends wandered in the forest near the city of Banaras. They agreed that if either of them attained the goal, that one would teach what he achieved to the others. Siddhartha pushed asceticism to the limit, starving himself. He practiced breath control and unmoving seated meditation. He stood in the cold rain and hot sun; he practiced severe fasting, living on tiny amounts of water and food per day. He became thinner and weaker because of malnutrition.

After long brutal self-punishment and starvation, Siddhartha realized that the end of suffering cannot be attained by the painful path of self-mortification. Siddhartha accepted nourishment from a passing woman, and his companions left him in disgust, believing that he has given up the noble quest.

At this point, Siddhartha was entirely alone. He had never met anyone who achieved an end to misery and suffering, who had achieved nirvana. There was no path set out for him to follow, and he knew of no one who had successfully traveled the path to awakening. Early Yogic communities and Yogic practices had not worked for him, and neither did extreme and painful asceticism. He had never seen or met anyone who achieved the goal of elimination of *duhkha*. He had no teaching to hold on to, and no doctrine and no path to follow. He had no one to guide him, and he could not even be certain that the goal was achievable.

THE AWAKENING and ACHIEVEMENT OF NIRVANA

Regaining his strength after accepting some food, Siddhartha sat down beneath a fig tree[27] (called the *Bodhi* tree or the Bo tree) and vowed not to get up until he resolved the problem of misery and suffering. Siddhartha focused and stabilized his mind, allowing it to calm down, until it became clear, and manageable. In that state of focused concentration, Siddhartha became aware of many previous lives, and recognized the cause-effect patterns that were active in his own past lives and present life. The insight deepened and he recognized the pattern of death and re-birth in other living beings. He recognized the working of the patterns of karma[28] and understood karmic choices and the

---

[26] Although the standard rendering of the Pali term *aranna* is "forest," the English term is not an exact equivalent. The Pali term signifies wilderness or jungle areas far from centers of urban commerce or political power. It would be sparsely populated rural or "back-country" sorts of places. A forest is an example of such a place, but more literally it is wilderness places far from urban centers. In those days, forests doubtless surrounded many urban areas. Beggars needed to be near human communities which were necessary for monks to collect food.

[27] The *Bodhi* tree, *ficus religiosa*, or pipal tree, is a variety of large fig tree; perhaps because the fig tree was the most impressive of all the trees it was associated with awakening of the Buddha. Images of the pipal tree are also found on ancient Harappan seals

[28] The Buddhist understanding of karma is more complex than the earlier Hindu explanations. The Buddhists assert that the consequences of one's actions are not determined by the action alone, but by other factors such as the nature of the person committing the act, and the circumstances under which the act was performed. See David J. Kalupahana, *Karma and Rebirth* (Sri Lanka: Buddhist Cultural Centre, 2006). Other works by Kalupahana have chapters on the workings of karma from a Buddhist perspective. See also Traleg Kyabgon, *Karma: What It Is, What It Isn't, Why It Matters* (Shambala, 2015).

consequences, and then penetrating more deeply he recognized the causes of *duhkha*. When he understood the causes of suffering and misery, he was able to eliminate those causes. With the causes of *duhkha* removed, so too was the *duhkha* eliminated. One Buddhist text describes the event as follows:

> ... the deities and the Brahma-angels ... came with perfumes, garlands, and other offerings in their hands to the Great Being [Siddhartha] on the throne of wisdom. ...
>
> And the remaining deities, also throughout the ten-thousand worlds, made offerings of garlands, perfumes, and ointments, and in many a hymn extolled him.
>
> ... And then, while the Bo-tree in homage rained red, coral-like sprigs upon his priestly robes, he acquired in the first watch of the night the knowledge of previous existences; in the middle watch of the night, the divine eye; and in the last watch of the night, his intellect fathomed Dependent Origination.
>
> Now while he was musing on the twelve terms of Dependent Origination, forwards and backwards, round and back again, the ten thousand worlds quaked twelve times, as far as to their ocean boundaries. And when the Great Being, at the dawning of the day, had thus made the ten thousand worlds thunder with his attainment of omniscience, all these worlds became most gloriously adorned.
>
> ... the eighty-four-thousand-league-deep ocean became sweet to the taste; the rivers checked their flowing; the blind from birth received their sight; the deaf from birth their hearing; the cripples from birth the use of their limbs; and the bonds and fetters of captives broke and fell off.[29]

To summarize: first Siddhartha remembered previous lives and recognized patterns occurring over and over which have caused misery. Later in the evening, with focused concentration he recognized and eliminated ego-centered grasping and possessive attachment, one of the major causes of *duhkha*. He recognized the cause-effect nature of the world, which Buddhists call **dependent origination**, also called **dependent co-arising**. He recognized and put an end to the causes of suffering (which include ill-will, ego-centered desire, desire for continued existence, mistaken beliefs, and ignorance).

With these causes of suffering removed, Siddhartha Gautama achieved a profound understanding of the causal interconnectedness of all existence, completely comprehending the causes of *duhkha*. In Sanskrit, this profound understanding is called *bodhi*,[30] which is translated "Enlightenment" or "Awakening." Buddhists say that *bodhi* is "the cessation of inverted views," it is seeing things clearly, as they really are.[31]

Siddhartha put an end to the fundamental emotional unsatisfactoriness so typical of our lives. In doing so, with insight into the nature of reality, Siddhartha woke up (*bodhi*). By putting an end to the causes of *duhkha*, Siddhartha has put an end to *duhkha* and just this is the attainment of nirvana. Nirvana is the state characterized by the absence of greed, absence of hatred and anger, and the absence of ignorance or confusion.

Siddhartha achieved awakening through his own reflective and meditative efforts. Siddhartha got rid of all the eliminable causes of human unhappiness, and there are many and they are complex. In early Buddhism, he is a human being who perfected his own spiritual potential, which Buddhists claim is the spiritual potential shared by all human

---

[29] This is from the Jataka tales, the stories of the Buddha and his accomplishments. This is translated in Henry Clarke Warren, *Buddhism In Translations* (New York: Antheneum, 1968), pp. 81–83. Some Buddhists celebrate this event in January.

[30] The term *bodhi* has often been translated as "Enlightenment." The etymology of the Sanskrit term makes no reference to light of any sort. The root of *bodhi* is literally "to wake up." The choice of "Enlightenment" for *bodhi* may reflect European concerns. This text will use "awakening" as the primary translation.

[31] The Four Inverted Views are (1) the mistaken belief about things that are not the self that they are the self; (2) the mistaken belief about things that they are permanent and unchanging or that they are changing and because they are changing, they are not truly real; (3) the mistaken belief about things that they are **intrinsically** beautiful or ugly; (4) the mistaken belief that things which are sources of discomfort are actually sources of comfort. When you do not see things through these inverted views, you now are seeing things as they really are and this is called *bodhi* or Awakening.

beings. Whenever his students asked if he was a divinity, a *deva*, Siddhartha replied in the negative. He is a human being who woke up, and followers can also wake up by following the same pathway.[32]

IMMEDIATELY AFTER AWAKENING

After awakening, Siddhartha sat in meditation for several days. He remembered the promise that he and his companions had made to one another that whoever found the path would share it with the others. He searched for and found his friends. At first they tried to ignore him, but find him profoundly changed. They ask, "Are you Siddhartha?" He replied, "I used to be Siddhartha, but I have awakened." It is from this point on that he is called "The Buddha" or the Awakened One.[33] His explanation of what he had come to understand is the beginning of Buddhism. Siddhartha was 35 years old when he finally awakened to the causes of *duhkha* and eliminated those causes from his personality.

THE FIRST DISCOURSE OF THE BUDDHA AT BANARAS

The Buddha found his five friends in Sarnath, a deer park, and explained what he comprehended: a pathway which runs midway between two extremes. (1) The first is the extreme of **excessive asceticism** (which the Buddha practiced in the wilderness or forest). (2) The other extreme is a life of luxurious pleasures, or **hedonism** (which was his life in the palace of his father). The Buddha's new pathway is a **Middle Way** between the two extremes of self-indulgence (hedonism) and ascetic self-mortification, both of which are painful, useless, and unprofitable. Siddhartha had lived the luxuriously pleasurable hedonistic life of a pampered prince, but that did not lessen emotional dissatisfaction, misery, or suffering. Then in the forest Siddhartha lived the life of a self-torturing ascetic, but that did not lessen *duhkha* or bring him to awakening.

At the deer park, the Buddha taught his friends how suffering is caused, and how it can be eliminated. He pointed out the misery and emotional dissatisfaction (*duhkha*) we experience in life arises because of combinations of (1) a self-centered possessive greediness, (2) anger and hatred, and (3) misunderstanding of or ignorance about the nature of reality. With his friends, the Buddha shared the three basic tools to eliminate dissatisfaction and suffering: mental discipline; morality; wisdom. Mental discipline minimizes anger and hatred, morality minimizes ego-centered greed, and wisdom grows as ignorance declines. Following these methods each of the five friends realized complete awakening, or *bodhi*, and are now known as *arhats* (*arhats* are those worthies who followed the path laid down by the Buddha and ultimately achieved nirvana). They become members and early leaders of the group of those who studied the Buddhist pathway and by following it, eliminated *duhkha*.

The First Turning of the "Wheel of the Teaching" or "Wheel of the *Dharma*"

Buddhists refer to the encounter between the Buddha and his five friends at the deer park as the time when the Buddha first "turned the wheel of the teaching." This allusion to "the turning of the wheel of doctrine" appears

---

[32] The story or myth of the life of Siddhartha Gotama traditionally served as a template or pattern to guide the student's own life.

[33] As indicated before, Siddhartha is also known as *Shakya-muni*, the wise sage (*-muni*) of the Shakya clan, and *Tathagata*, the "one who has come [or gone] thus."

frequently in later Buddhism. After several centuries, later Buddhists recognized a second turning of the wheel, and even a third turning of the wheel of the teaching. After their awakening and achievement of the end of *duhkha*, the five friends left the Buddha and went in different directions, teaching others what they learned.

THE PERIOD OF TEACHING

According to the Buddhist scriptures, the Buddha traveled the Ganges valley in northeastern India as a forest beggar from about age 35 until he was 80 years old. In forty-five years traveling, he taught forest *sramanas* or beggars, and he taught householders. He gave advice to rulers. Large numbers of followers gathered around the Buddha during the later years of his life.[34] It is said that he had over a thousand followers who awakened, and thousands more who counted him as a teacher, or were students of his students.

This community, including both male monks and female monks, is called the *sangha*. Allowing women to join the monastic groups was shocking to traditional Hinduism which rejected any role for women in the religious life, and certainly never allowed women to organize in monastic groups. The Buddha rejected the Hindu claim that some people were better than others due to their birth status, and did not permit followers to organize themselves along caste lines. He stated that a person is noble (a Brahmin) because of behavior, not because of birth parents.

The Buddha rejected the efficacy of Hindu gods and sacrifices, considering them to be of no use for lessening misery and suffering (*duhkha*) and achieving nirvana, the goal of Buddhism. The Buddhists seem to take it for granted that the gods, the *devas*, do exist but even the great Hindu *deva* Indra is merely a human who, because of his good *karma*, now resides temporarily as a *deva* in the heavenly realm.[35] However, even the *devas* are imperfect, subject to laws of nature, and are impermanent.[36] The gods live longer than humans, are more powerful than humans, but are not better than humans. Gods are still trapped in the cycle of death and rebirth, and cannot escape. Humans can escape. In early Buddhism, the stress is on self-reliance, individual responsibility, individual effort and having the right intention.

During the lengthy rainy season in India, in order to avoid slogging through the muddy forests, groups of monks would remain in one place where there might be some protection from the constant rain. They sought a roof and food, and over time, those locations slowly evolved into the sites of fixed communities, where monks practiced and studied year-round. Ultimately these became Buddhist monasteries.[37] As a result, Buddhism slowly shifted from unorganized wandering forest ascetics to numerous settled communities of monks and nuns seeking to end *duhkha*.

---

[34] Several of his early followers became important. They include Shariputra, famous for his wisdom, and Mandgalyayana, famous for possessing and using *siddhis*, or magical powers. Upali was an expert in monastic discipline. Devadatta was a cousin of the Buddha, and was portrayed as jealous of his cousin. It is said that Devadatta led a group of followers in an attempt on Siddhartha's life. Ananda, another cousin of the Buddha, figures prominently in many Buddhist sutras. He was famous for the depth of his philosophical understanding of the Buddhist teachings. Buddhist sutras begin "Thus have I heard," and Buddhists assume that this is Ananda repeating the words of the Buddha at the first council following the death of the Buddha. There was also Mahakasyapa whom the Buddha would call upon to preach to the assembly. It is believed that Mahakasyapa was in charge of the Buddhist community after the Buddha died.

[35] Several recent books assert that Buddhism is quite compatible with the natural world of modern science. For example, see Owen J. Flanagan, *Bodhisattva's Brain: Buddhism Naturalized* (Cambridge, MA: MIT Press, 2011), who describes naturalized Buddhism as providing "a tool for achieving happiness and human flourishing—a way of conceiving of the human predicament, of thinking about meaning for finite material beings living in a material world." See also Stephen Batchelor, *Confession of a Buddhist Atheist*.

[36] Early Buddhist texts acknowledge the existence of the Vedic *devas*, but like the Greek gods, these beings were not morally perfect. S. Bhattacharji, *The Indian Theogony*, p. 11.

[37] The monastic institution in India seems to have originated with Buddhism.

CHAPTER 8: EARLY BUDDHISM

THE DEATH OF THE BUDDHA

The Buddhist literature is filled with stories, miracles, myths and legends. Here is one example about the Buddha's death, which in Buddhist literature is called the "supreme nirvana," or *parinirvana*. Approaching age 80, the Buddha became gravely ill. Recognizing that his own death was near, he announced this fact to his followers.[38] Hearing of the impending death of the Buddha, thousands of prior students and householders came to offer their respect and devotion to this holy teacher. A householder brought eight pints of rice, and four cups of rice as an offering. Using his magical powers, the Buddha multiplied it to create enough food to feed all the thousands of assembled followers.[39]

As death came closer, the Awakened One told the followers that this would be their last chance to ask questions. When his cousin Ananda asked who should be put in charge of the organization of monks, the Buddha refused to establish a successor, instead saying:[40]

> "Behold now, Bhikkhus,[41] I exhort you: Transient are all conditioned things;
> Work out your own liberation with diligence.
> This was the last word of the Tathagata [the Buddha].
> ... And when the Buddha had passed away, simultaneously with his *parinirvana*, there came a tremendous earthquake, dreadful and astounding, and the thunders rolled across the heavens. ... Then, when the Buddha had passed away, some *bhikshus*, not yet freed from passion, lifted up their arms and wept; and some, flinging themselves on the ground, rolled from side to side and wept, lamenting: "Too soon has the Buddha come to his *parinirvana*!" ... But the *bhikshus* who were freed from passion, mindful and clearly comprehending, reflected in this wise: "Impermanent are all conditioned things. How could this be otherwise?"[42]

The Buddha lay down on his right side with his head facing north, and then died, or, as the Buddhists say, entered his final and supreme nirvana, his *parinirvana*. He was now liberated from the cycle of birth and death, escaped the cycle of *samsara*. This was near the village of Kushinagara. His remains were turned over to the villagers of Kushinagara who treated the body with the greatest respect. It seems that devoted followers did not want to believe that an extraordinary person like the Buddha could actually die, and the view that he was eternal and divine was believed by many followers. A magnificent funeral pyre was constructed, the body was cremated, and the ashes and relics taken to the council hall, and were paid respect to with dance and song and music, and with garlands and perfumes.

Non-monastic Buddhist groups of householders requested and received portions of the relics. The ashes were divided into equal parts and distributed. This makes it obvious that the beginnings of a cult of religious zeal for the Buddha, and deep devotion to his relics or ashes, was found among the householders, merchants, and some forest followers. It is believed that one of his followers, Mahakasyapa, was the senior student who then took over the

---

[38] The Pali canon has a text which relates the death of the Buddha, called the *Mahaparinirvana sutra* (Digha II.72–167). There is a later Mahayana text entitled the *Nirvana sutra*, but its contents are unrelated to the earlier Theravada text.

[39] The story is found in the N. *Mahaparinirvana sutra*, roll 10: "At the time of Buddha's nirvana, the last offering was eight dronas and four adhakas of hard rice from a potter named Cunda from Magadha. The Buddha, with his psychic power, multiplied it enough to feed the great assembly."

[40] Paraphrased from the *Mahaparinibbanasutta* VI.7, in *The Last Days of the Buddha: The Mahaparinibbanasutta of the Buddha* (Kandy, Ceylon: Buddhist Publication Society, n.d.), p. 75. This is a Wheel Publication No. 67–69.

[41] Bhikshus are Buddhist monks, literally "beggars."

[42] *Ibid.*, pp. 76-78. This is a paraphrase, replacing the term Bhagava ("Lord") with Buddha and using Sanskrit spellings rather than the Pali spellings in the original translation.

leadership of the Buddhist movement, and guided the creation of the first Buddhist texts.[43]

Pilgrimage Locations

Four sites associated with crucial events in the Buddha's life became important pilgrimage centers: Lumbini Grove (near Kapilavastu) associated with the Buddha's birth; Bodh Gaya, associated with the Bodhi-tree[44] where the Buddha awakened; Deer Park, at Banaras, associated with the first explanation of his teachings to his friends; the sacred grove at Kushinagara, associated with his death. Later, Buddhists would go on pilgrimages to these places in hope of acquiring much good merit that could improve their lives, or grant their wishes. These four places are still sites for pilgrimages among contemporary Buddhists from many different countries, but the birth-place of the Buddha is by far the most popular.[45]

Memorial Monuments

Following his death, the sites which were of great importance during the life of the Buddha had burial mounds built over them, called *stupas*. A *stupa* is a memorial monument built over sacred relics or upon a site that is sacred for some other reason. Over the centuries *stupas* became beautifully carved structures which symbolized the Buddha, represented the Buddha's teachings, and provided a focal point for householder devotion to the Buddha.[46] This created a problem. Among the rules for Buddhist forest and monastic monks was that they could not accept or touch money. Yet *stupas* were the focal points for householders, who participated in Buddhism by offering money to the monastics, and offering gifts to the Buddha. Also, in the vicinity of *stupas* householders engaged in celebrations of the life of the Buddha, including dancing and singing. Buddhist monks had general rules forbidding them to remain present where singing and dancing occurred (because activities which could draw a large crowd were often accompanied by gambling and prostitution).

If knowledgeable monks who practiced meditation and studied the important doctrines could not be present at these important sites, then the result was that non-monastic householders had to take over the business of managing

---

[43] Mahakasyapa is celebrated as one of the ten great awakened students (*arhats*) featured in the earliest Buddhist sutras, and the Buddha would often call upon him to preach to the assembly. Mahakasyapa is supposed to have convened the first Buddhist Council wherein the students recited their memories of the teaching, laying down the foundations of the Buddhist sutras. The later Chinese Ch'an tradition puts Mahakasyapa as the single official successor to the Buddha, and then the *arhat* Ananda as the successor to Mahakasyapa.

[44] The original *bodhi* tree no longer exists; the current *bodhi* tree is the sixth regeneration of the original tree, planted around 1890 after the previous one burned down. A branch of an earlier tree was taken to Sri Lanka, and a sapling from that tree was brought back to Bodh Gaya, where it is growing and is the center of a major pilgrimage site today. Bodh Gaya is a major tourist attraction, with numerous hotels and shops right at the edge of the temple complex. The site is under the control of Hindu Brahmins and Hindu priests have turned parts of the Buddhist holy site into shrines to Hindu *devas*, justifying this by asserting that the Buddha is an *avatar* or incarnation of the Hindu god Vishnu, so the Buddha must have taught Hinduism and Buddhists have misunderstood his real teachings.

[45] The perceptive student will note that our description of the life of the Buddha, and the teachings of the Buddha, have minimized the devotion, beliefs and practices that many in the West would consider superstition. A previous footnote mentioned books which assert the compatibility of science and Buddhism. An interesting book suggests that over the past two centuries Western scholars have turned the historical Buddha into someone more compatible with Western science than the facts support. See Donald S. Lopez, Jr., *The Scientific Buddha: His Short and Happy Life* (New York: Yale University Press, 2012).

[46] The early Buddhist representations were aniconic, that is, they did not use human icons to show the Buddha. Instead they included footprints ("the Buddha stood here") or an empty throne, or a horse with an empty saddle, and so forth. Images of the Buddha as a human being seem to have begun after the Hellenistic influences of the armies of Alexander the Great who conquered north-western India. Greek influence on Buddhist art has been noted in many sources, including Etienne Lamotte, *Histoire du Bouddhisme Indien* (Louvain, Institut Orientaliste: 1958), pp. 469–487, esp. 484–486. Later on, statues of the Buddha had many functions. Certainly they could signify the presence of the Buddha. Also they were intended to be a focus for visual devotion, a locus for story-telling of the life of the Buddha to teach lessons about morality and causality, and an impetus to donate money to the community of Buddhist monks.

these locations.[47] The householders did not study the basic Buddhist philosophy, but instead encouraged devotion to the Buddha and stressed all the benefits that could be obtained by offering money and presents to the Buddhist order. The forest monks and monastic monks do not seem to have been encouraged to be particularly devotional, but lay people were, and householders were encouraged to make offerings to the *sangha* (the organization of Buddhist monks and nuns).

Householder Popular Buddhism

What we have presented here is the traditional account of early Buddhism as portrayed in the sacred scriptures, however it should be noted that in addition to the rather rational attitudes expressed by the Buddha in the earliest texts, anthropological and archaeological evidence reveals that many among the early followers engaged in a wide variety of local religious practices which were not sanctioned in Buddhist scriptures, including the worship of the Buddha as a divinity, and veneration of his relics (bone fragments and ashes). Followers performed rituals at the memorial monuments. Belief in the magical efficacy of sacred sounds and rituals seem to have been important as well. Certainly later Buddhism clearly demonstrates shamanistic elements, and followers worshiped other aboriginal deities and local holy men as well as a divine Buddha. Often Buddhist monks would be fortune-tellers and perform rituals to appease angry spirits and vengeful ghosts, or would exorcize demons and engage in other practices which we do not associate with the Buddha himself. Of course, we do not have access to the "pure" or "original" Buddhism. We do not have any documents written by the Buddha himself, only the memorized stories of some students. We do not have any universally agreed-upon texts from early Buddhism which would allow us to declare some practices "authentic" and others "later accretions."

The Formula of Conversion

Around the year 250 B.C.E., perhaps one or two hundred years after the death of the founder, Buddhism came to be adopted by members of royalty, and began to exert influence in the political realm. Under Buddhist rulers, non-violence (*ahimsa*) was encouraged, capital punishment was banned, and so too were animal sacrifices. As a result of these and other changes, India slowly entered a golden age and the king sent out missionaries to offer Buddhist insights to others, using the formula (later referred to as the Three Jewels):

I take my refuge in the Buddha (Siddhartha Gautama);
I take my refuge in the Dharma (the teachings of the Awakened One);
I take my refuge in the Sangha (the community of advanced Buddhists).

8.5 THE BUDDHA-*DHARMA*: THE SECOND OF THE THREE JEWELS

We have seen the term *dharma* in Hinduism where it denoted caste duty, as well as moral, religious and social duties and obligations. The Buddhists have a different meaning for *dharma*. Although often translated as "truth," one of the most important meanings for the *dharma*, or Buddha-*dharma*, is "teachings of Buddhism which lead to the cessation of *duhkha* and attainment of nirvana."

A Buddhist can take refuge in the *dharma*, can rely on the teachings (*dharma*) as offering successful methods to lessen and ultimately eliminate emotional misery and discontent. The Buddha was not merely the teacher of the *dharma*. In one sense, the physical body of the peaceful smiling Buddha was the embodiment of the teaching, the

---

[47] A scholarly treatment of an important group of these monumental statues is Catherine Becker, *Shifting Stones, Shaping the Past: Sculpture from the Buddhist Stupas of Andhra Pradesh* (New York Oxford University Press, 2014)

dharma. The Buddha himself was the truth (*dharma*) walking on two legs.[48] *Dharma* is considered one of the Three Jewels of Buddhism, in addition to the other two jewels, namely Buddha and the community of advanced Buddhist followers, the *sangha*.

Pratityasamutpada: The Nature of Reality

In our discussion of the awakening of the Buddha under the Bodhi tree, we quoted the Buddhist scriptures which reveal that Siddhartha achieved the cessation of misery and suffering (*duhkha*) when he comprehended **dependent origination**, the dependent causal interconnectedness of all things. The Sanskrit Buddhist technical term for causality is *pratityasamutpada*.[49] This is not merely a philosophical insight into the nature of reality, an insight into metaphysics or ontology. **Understanding causality provides the solution to the problem of suffering**.

Recognizing that all events arise from multiple causes, the Buddha then focused on the **causes** of *duhkha*, misery and emotional suffering, and how to minimize or eliminate those causes. This concept of *pratityasamutpada* is one of the keys to the philosophical teachings of early Buddhism.[50] It is commonly translated as "dependent co-arising," "dependent origination," or "dependent arising." It implies the interrelatedness and contingency of all things. It seems as though it is like "every event has a cause,"[51] however it is more than this.

Buddhists understand events as **arising** out of and **dependent upon** numerous causes and conditions. Take a billiard ball on a pool table. We strike the cue ball with our cue, and the cue ball rolls until it bumps into the 8-ball. The resulting event is that the 8-ball rolls into the corner pocket. However, the motion of the 8-ball does not depend merely on the cue ball. If we strike the cue ball harder or softer, the effect will change. If the table is flat, or tipped at an angle, the effect will change. If we put spin on the cue ball, the effect will change. Clearly, the motion of the 8-ball is <u>dependent</u> upon numerous causes and conditions (not just one), and that particular motion of the ball occurs or <u>arises</u> when all of the causes and conditions are present <u>together</u>.

The EVENT depends upon causes and conditions; "dependent co-arising," or "dependent origination" or "interdependent arising"

I clap my hands together, and a sharp sound follows. The sound depends on how hard I clap my hands, depends upon the angles at which the hands interact, and even depends upon the density of the environment (how much air? what if I do that under water? what if we are in a vacuum chamber?) Thus, the translation of "dependent co-arising" for *pratityasamutpada*. The effect **depends** on the causes, and when all the causes are present together ("present together" is the meaning of "co-"), the effect occurs, or **arises**. We perceive that things around us are changing and are dependently arising (although we do not perceive *dependence* itself).

Buddha does not teach that there are linear causal relationships, where a single cause can bring about a single effect. Buddha teaches that there are many causes and many conditions and always refers to causes and conditions in the plural, never just as cause and effect. We are presented with a very

---

[48] The Buddhist term for this is *dharma-kaya*, "embodiment of truth," "body of truth" or "body of Law." This term will come to have great significance in latter Buddhism.

[49] This is pronounced something like pra - teet - ya sahm-ut paada.

[50] Although most of the Buddhist terminology is also found in non-Buddhist Indian thought, the term *pratityasamutpada* is unique to Buddhism, and seems to have been coined by the Buddha himself. A clear explanation of the etymology of the term is found in David Kalupahana, *A Sourcebook of Early Buddhist Philosophy*, (Sri Lanka: Buddhist Cultural Centre, 2007), p. 3.

[51] Note this is NOT "every **effect** has a cause." That is trivially true because of the definition of "effect" which requires "cause." *Pratityasamutpada* is making an empirical claim about the nature of the world, namely, that **events** arise out of and depend upon numerous causes and conditions. That *everything is caused* is central to understanding events above the quantum level in modern science.

complex picture of how things work. Just because a certain thing seems to have caused something to happen does not mean the particular cause we identified was solely responsible. The effect may not have come into existence at all had it not been for the facilitating conditions supporting its fruition.[52]

For Buddhists, *pratityasamutpada* is key to understanding the nature of reality and central to Buddhist metaphysics, or ontology. There are three fundamental insights (referred to as the "Three Marks" or "Three Characteristics") which follow from this understanding of reality as made up of interdependent causal processes.

The Three Marks / Three Characteristics[53]

The First Insight: Impermanence. The first mark, which follows from the *pratityasamutpada* insight into causality, is impermanence. If each and every thing is dependent upon numerous causes and conditions, then these things will change as causes change, and finally cease when the causes cease. If all events arise dependently, then nothing is independent, nothing is permanent and unchanging, nothing is self-existent, nothing stands alone unaffected by its environment, nothing has an unchanging inner substance or immutable inner essence. To say that something is impermanent means that at some point it arises, and later it ceases.

To the traditional Hindu world-view, this Buddhist claim is terrifying. If the Buddhists are correct, it means that everything everywhere is changing and that nothing survives forever. We all desire stability in our lives, and we want permanence. Permanence is a key belief for traditional Hinduism. For these Hindu thinkers, it is only permanent unchanging things which are truly real. This is not unique just to Hinduism. We humans establish institutions to try to deny or slow impermanence. We pretend we will live forever, and in contemporary times we hide dying by restricting it to hospitals. We focus on the ideals of the past as though they would not change, ever. We look to the past for eternal truths. If everything is changing, then what do we have to hold onto, to what can we cling to maintain stability in our world and in our lives?

The early Buddhists did not flinch from the terrifying consequences of change, of impermanence. It follows that everything is impermanent, including individuals, possessions, institutions, mountains, continents, planets, and galaxies. However, this impermanence is not chaos. Things do not change randomly or chaotically. Things change according to regular causal patterns which we can study, and much change is slow and predictable.

To understand that causes give rise to events is to understand the way the world is, the way things truly are. All things everywhere are impermanent. Even the divinities, the *devas*, are impermanent. For the early Hindus and Buddhists, the *deva* Brahma is not omniscient or omnipotent, but merely a being who, through good *karma*, has achieved the place of the highest of the gods. For the Buddhists, one who achieves the goal of Buddhism, one who has achieved nirvana, has gone beyond the gods.[54]

Pratityasamutpada as a Rejection of Hinduism

Hindu Eternalism: a thing is real only if the thing possesses an eternal unchanging essence.
Hindu Nihilism: if nothing has an eternal unchanging essence, then nothing is real; all is illusory.

As you can see, Buddhist *pratityasamutpada* and its implication of *impermanence* can be understood as a refutation of the non-Buddhist claim that all things that are real exist eternally ("eternalism"). The Hindu thinkers say

---

[52] Traleg Kyabgon, *Karma* (Boston: Shambhala, 2015), p. 2.

[53] In Sanskrit this is the *trilaksana*, literally "three marks" or "three characteristics." Scholars consider these essential to early Buddhism.

[54] "The Buddha acknowledged the existence of Vedic deities. They were regarded as powerful agents somewhat above men who were subject to the laws of nature and had to be redeemed by the Buddha, for they were far from being perfect." Sukumari Bhattacharji, *The Indian Theogony* (Cambridge: Cambridge University Press, 1970), p. 11.

that real things exist eternally because they possess a self-existent immutable inner essence. The Buddhists disagree with eternalism, and point out that at one time something is present, and later it is absent. Things cease, and with cessation, we realize that there is no permanent existence.

We are also aware of the arising of phenomenon, so this is a refutation of nihilism, a refutation of the position which asserts that everything is an illusion, which asserts that nothing exists because nothing has a self-existent immutable essence. The mutual interdependence implied by *pratityasamutpada* is meant to allow us to move freely between the two extremes of eternalism and nihilism. Things are real, but they do not possess an immutable inner essence. Early Buddhism sees the Buddha's teachings as a Middle Way between hedonism and asceticism; later Mahayana Buddhism affirms another Middle Way, this time between eternalism and nihilism.

The Second Insight: Anatman. The Buddhist teaching of *anatman* means "no-*atman*" and is a rejection of the Hindu belief in *atman*.

What is human nature? As discussed in previous chapters, many Hindus believe that we have an immutable inner observer, inner controller, or "soul,"[55] that which hears, feels, and directs and controls the body, an inner controller directing and animating the machine that is the body.[56] The Hindu Brahmins claimed that this *atman*, this inner controller, this agent behind actions, this thinker behind the thoughts, is separate from the physical body and separate from the changing mind, separate from shifting awareness, separate from the flow of consciousness.[57] Our physical body is the container for this eternal inner controller, the way that you are the driver of the physical container called an "automobile."

For traditional Hinduism, the *atman* is a spiritual substance which never was created, never was born. It is the unchanging self-existent essence which transmigrates from one life to the next and makes you not just the "same person," but the *identical* person as the *atman* goes from one year to the next, and then from one life to the next. This immutable *atman* is what carries your good or bad karma from one lifetime to the next. This *atman* is intelligent, aware, and leaves the body at death. For the Hindus, this unchanging essence is responsible for every action we might choose, and in this sense we are responsible for everything we do and have done, and we are responsible for all of the bad things that happen to us, because we create our own bad karma by our bad choices.

Although the Buddhists accept versions of karma, the Buddhists reject the Hindu idea of a self-existent eternal soul, or *atman*. Buddhist thinkers critically explored the Hindu idea of *atman*, and after careful analysis, find it self-contradictory, and therefore impossible. The *atman* is not needed to explain any facet of human experience or existence, because if the *atman* is unchanging, as Hindus insist, then it cannot be the locus of memories or personalities (which do change). The conclusion of the Buddhist analysis is that there is no such thing as an eternal and unchanging spiritual substance called *atman*. The Buddhists use the term *anatman*, where the "*an-*" is a negative. *Anatman* literally means no-*atman*.

---

[55] The Christian term "soul" is misleading. Unlike the Christian idea of soul, the Hindu soul/atman was never created, it is unborn. It is *not* created by a deity or in the image of a deity. The *atman* is not responsible for self-consciousness, and does not have anything resembling the Christian concept of free will.

[56] This is sometimes referred to as the "ghost in the machine."

[57] Buddhist philosophers distinguish flowing consciousness (*vijnana*) from thought processes or mind (*citta*), and from the "mind-faculty" (*manas*). For the distinctions the student can consult *The Princeton Dictionary of Buddhism*, Robert Buswell and Donald Lopez, editors.

CHAPTER 8: EARLY BUDDHISM

Anatman is not "no-self"

Some have rendered *anatman* as "no-self," but this translation is misleading.[58] If "self" means a collection of inner mental states in continuous flux, then the Buddhists would never deny the existence of a flowing stream of fleeting mental images, feelings, memories, emotions, thoughts, and other states. If "self" refers to a gradually changing physical body, the Buddhists would never deny this either. Thus, ordinary everyday notions of "self" are not a problem. It is the idea that the term "self" names an eternal unchanging substance separate from both mind and body that is denied.

A better translation for the Buddhist *anatman* would be something like "no-soul" or "no-**unchanging** inner spiritual substance." Thus, the Buddhist *anatman* is a denial of the existence of the transcendent immutable soul the Hindus call *atman*.[59] If the early Buddhist analysis of causality (dependent co-arising, or *pratityasamutpada*) is correct, it clearly implies that there is nothing existing forever unchanging. It is a denial of the Hindu claim that there is an underlying substratum, an unchanging self-existent nature which gives persons their enduring self-identity over time (in Hinduism, it is the *atman* which transmigrates from one life to the next).

Instead, the early Buddhist thinkers argue that what we think of as our "self" or "personality" arises from a complex network of interdependent processes, and changes over time.[60] Thus, *anatman*. There is continuity connecting you last week with you today, but nothing remains numerically identical and unchanging, physically or mentally, over extended periods of time. The Buddhists are denying that humans have some element or substance within them which never changes.

The Buddhists argue that the Brahmin concept of *atman* is unnecessary and explains nothing. An eternal unchanging soul is not needed to explain emotions, memories, a sense of continuity, a capacity to be self-aware, or the ability to use language. We do not have an eternal unchanging substance called *atman* within us. Most Hindus see our human bodies as containers of an inner unchanging controlling *atman*. Buddhists say we do not have such a thing inside of us; we are **empty of atman**. "Empty of *atman*" does not translate to "no-self."

The Five Bundles of Human Personality

If we do not have an inner unchanging *atman*, then what is human nature? Buddhists analyze the human personality, and conclude that an individual is an embodied person and that person is a psycho-physical unity which arises out of and depends upon five interdependent processes which are referred to as **five bundles** or **five aggregates** (*skandhas*). What we think of as our "self" is a gradually changing stream which arises dependently from these five processes. When all five of the following are present and interdependently interacting, what we call "the self" or "the person" arises. The five are (1) physical bodily processes, (2) feelings and sensations, (3) ideas, (4) impulses, likes and dislikes, and (5) being conscious. None of these five remain unchanging in the process from birth to death that we call human life.

Although the Buddhists did not know what we know about modern human physiology and biology, today we do recognize that we really are dependently arisen from a number of interconnected and interdependent physical

---

[58] In Western thought, a "self" is something unique about a person which allows us to identify the person standing before us as the *same* person we spoke to yesterday. Some argue that it is just the physical body which allows us to identify the person as "the same." Some argue that memories of experiences are primary to the "self" that we recognize and identify. The Hindu *atman* is neither of these: it is separate from body and memories. The *atman* is neither the body, nor the collection of memories or experiences. We may have the same body and the same memories, but the Hindu *atman* is something self-existent, unchanging, and independent of the physical body and the contents of mind. It has existed always. Thus the Buddhist concept of *anatman* or "no-*atman*" is distorted if translated into English as "no-self."

[59] See Steven Collins, *Selfless Persons: Imagery and Thought in Theravada Buddhism* (Cambridge: Cambridge University Press, 1982).

[60] We do not "have a self"; in the Buddhist model it would be more accurate to say we "are a self."

processes. What we call our physical or material self arises out of and is dependent upon the cardiovascular system, respiratory system, nervous system, digestive system, endocrine system, urinary system and the reproductive system. In addition there is our musculo-skeletal system and our immune system. None of these is fixed and unchanging. None of these systems are entirely independent of the others.

The above interdependent processes or systems comprise the physical, or material form. But these changing physical processes are just one of five bundles or aggregates which make up a person; we are not only the physical. We are also feelings, ideas or perceptions, impulses and emotions, and we are conscious, we are aware. Each of these is constantly changing. Sit quietly for a moment and pay attention to the mind; everything in the mental realm is fleeting and changing.[61] There is continuity between the past and the present, but not identity. The person gradually alters over time, but as long as the changes are small and gradual, allowing for continuity, we are comfortable referring to her as the "same person." There is no need for the Hindu *atman* to explain human nature. The concept of *atman* is simply unnecessary.

For the Buddhist, *anatman* is not only a correct description of the human personality; it is also an antidote to the disease of ego-centric greed or possessiveness. Deeply understanding *anatman* can make us less self-centered, it frees us from the belief that we are independent solid beings with an unchanging substance, because these mistaken beliefs can lead to the illusion of a separate self, which can lead to conceit, arrogance, unearned self-confidence, and pride, which are causes of suffering. In a more extreme form, it is narcissism.[62] These attitudes separate us from the world around us and people around us.

Recognizing that we do not have an enduring substance-self is to lessen or lose the illusion of a separate and enduring ego. This will make it easier for us to feel empathy with all other living things, to feel more concern for others and for our environment. Ego-centered people tend not to think about how their choices affect other persons; for people whose desires are less ego-centered, being altruistic is easier because they focus on how their decisions affect others. They can imagine themselves in the situation of another, which makes it easier to be less judgmental and more generous.[63] People who are less self-centered are more generous, more altruistic, more compassionate.

The Buddhists conclude that we are not a container for a substance called *atman*. We do not possess an unchanging immutable *atman* inside ourselves; in fact, if you search inside you will see that the container that is <u>us</u> is **empty of atman**. The term "*atman*" names nothing at all; it accounts for nothing, it is not needed to explain any feature of human existence. For the Buddhists, *atman* is not only misleading, but is an unnecessary concept. Thus, <u>anatman</u>.[64]

Third Insight: Duhkha.

Finally, if we live in the world assuming that we can achieve happiness by accumulating and holding onto enough things which we think will not ever change, or if we assume that our families and siblings will not ever change, or if we believe that we will not change, and then we make choices based on the world using this faulty road map, and

---

[61] The philosopher David Hume wrestled with similar concepts in his *Treatise on Human Nature*, Book I, Part IV.

[62] Narcissism is extreme self-absorption, or grandiose self-regard. Someone who is narcissistic views herself or himself as superior in all situations, feels entitled to special treatment and expects to be admired and praised by those around her or him.

[63] Early Buddhist followers were primarily beggars and monks in monasteries. There was little concern with the social aspect of personality. Socioeconomic status is irrelevant to a monk, but very important to householders. Social support and health needs are provided by fellow monastics, not society. Thus early Buddhism does not comment on the social factors relevant to suffering.

[64] For more on this topic, the reader can consult *anatman* in Robert E. Buswell, Jr. ed., *Encyclopedia of Buddhism* (Macmillan Thomson Gale, 2004), Volume I, pp. 18–19.

the result will be frustration, disappointment, discontent, emotional suffering, dissatisfaction and unhappiness (*duhkha*). Everything is impermanent, everything is flowing change, and this lack of stability in ourselves and the world can be terrifying.

The Three Insights are the Three Marks of Existence

As described previously, Buddhists call these three insights the **Three Marks** or **Three Characteristics** of existence: **impermanence**, *anatman*, and *duhkha*. As we have seen, everything is impermanent because every thing is causally dependent upon previous causes and conditions (*pratityasamutpada*). Careful analysis reveals that there is no permanent unchanging soul (*anatman*).[65] Each one of us is impermanent. If we do not realize the truth that everything changes, including ourselves, our lives will be characterized by frustration and suffering, which is *duhkha*.

Using Buddhist Meditation to Understand the Three Marks

An important element in the Buddhist practice of **insight meditation** (*vipaśyanā* in Sanskrit; in Pali it is *vipassana* meditation)[66] is clearly seeing the three characteristic marks of all phenomena, namely, that all things are impermanent, that no one has an eternal unchanging inner essence (*anatman)* and the reality of dissatisfaction and suffering in our lives (*duhkha*). If you do a meditative exercise of bare attention, awareness of sensations and feelings without judging or reacting to them, which leads to understanding how things arise, then this is called *vipaśyanā* or *vipassana* (insight meditation).

However, this is not the only function of meditation. One can also meditate to calm the mind, in order to reach a peaceful state of equanimity. If you practice awareness of respiration, if you follow the in-breath and the out-breath for the sake of calming the mind, then it is **serenity meditation**.[67] These two forms of meditation work together. A distraught mind cannot achieve insight.

The seated posture and focus of the meditative exercise is the same in each case, but the purpose for doing it differs. Meditating in order to experience calm or serenity brings temporary relief from *duhkha*, while *vipaśyanā/vipassana* works at developing the insight which can eliminate the misconceptions which are the root causes of *duhkha*. Something similar to the Buddhist practice of mindful concentration has been advocated by many in the fields of mental health.[68] To be mindful is to pay attention to the causal connections of our experience; it is non-judgmental awareness focused on the present moment.

---

[65] It also follows that there is no sacred ultimate Brahman either. In fact, the Buddhists argued against the conclusion that all the world came from one source, so Buddhists denied that all the world issued from a sacred ultimate (Brahman), and Buddhist thinkers criticized the Hindu Samkhya/Yoga claims of *prakriti*, *purusha* and *Ishvara* (God) as causes of reality. The Nyaya school of Hinduism also argued for the god *Ishvara*, and the Buddhists produced many texts finding flaws in Nyaya arguments for the existence of a god. See Parimal G. Patil, *Against a Hindu God: Buddhist Philosophy of Religion in India* (New York: Columbia University Press, 2009).

[66] Although in this section of the book we have tried to use only the Sanskrit spellings of technical terms, the stress on mindful meditation in the West has been inspired primarily by South-East Asian forms of Buddhism, and these forms use the Pali spelling, *vipassana*. Consequently we have adopted the awkward mechanism of using both the Sanskrit *vipaśyanā* followed by the Pali.

[67] Monks focused on serenity meditation are encouraged to meditate on the Four Immeasurables, also called the *brahmaviharas*: loving-kindness (*maitri*), compassion (*karuna*), empathetic, appreciative or sympathetic joy (*mudita*), and equanimity (*upeksa*).

[68] A useful book on Buddhist mindfulness is Bhante Henepola Gunaratana, *Mindfullness in Plain English: Revised and Expanded Edition* (New York: Wisdom Publications, 1996). See also Jerry Braza, *Moment By Moment: The Art and Practice of Mindfulness* (Rutland, VT: Charles Tuttle, 1997); Marshall Glickman, *Beyond the Breath: Extraordinary Mindfulness Through Whole-Body Vipassana Meditation* (Rutland, VT: Tuttle, 2002), and Thich Nhat Hanh, *Breathe! You are Alive: The Sutra on the Full Awareness of Breathing* (Berkeley, CA: Parallax Press, 1995).

8.6 THE TWELVE-LINKED CHAIN OF CAUSATION

The Buddhist analysis of causality, *pratityasamutpada*, applies to the entire range of empirical experience. However, there is another formation of dependent co-arising, *pratityasamutpada*, which relates it specifically to the cycle of human existence, how one choice followed by action leads to another, each one conditioning the next, conditioning the person, and ultimately managing to trap us in a continuing cycle of rebirth. This chain with twelve links is an alternative explanation of how causality is related to the pain and misery which we find in our lives.

The elements of existence were contained in a twelve-part, interdependent chain of causation comprising (1) ignorance, (2) impulses and emotions, (3) consciousness, (4) psychological elements, (5) six senses (traditional five senses plus consciousness), (6) contact, (7) feelings, (8) desire, (9) grasping, (10) becoming, (11) old age, and (12) death. These twelve factors produce another analysis of human life using *pratityasamuptada*, this time applied to the cycle of birth-and-death, the cycle of *samsara*.[69] Obviously, old age and death depend on becoming, or birth, but upon what does birth depend?

These twelve links describe the psychological conditions by which humans ensnare themselves in a world of frustration and dissatisfaction, each step conditioning the next step. If a series of twelve steps conditions us to the cycle of birth-and-death, *samsara*, then we can work backwards. If we break the conditioned connection one after another, reverse one link after another, we come finally to the root of it all: ignorance. With ignorance eliminated, we can bring about the cessation of suffering.[70] The awakening experience of Siddhartha under the Bodhi tree can be described as the Buddha working backwards through these twelve until he finally eliminates all the causes of suffering. This same sequence can also serve as a roadmap for the Buddhist follower who seeks to put an end to misery and emotional suffering.

What are the Characteristics of Things that are Real?

The analysis into twelve links of the chain of causation can help us overcome our deep-seated ignorance about the nature of reality. Non-Buddhist Hindu thinkers wondered about the difference between things that are real, and things that are unreal. Hindu thinkers concluded that real things possess a self-existent substance or inner essence, called the *svabhava*. This *svabhava* essence depends on nothing; has always existed, it was never created, and it cannot ever be destroyed. Hindu philosophers reasoned that if something lacks an eternal self-existing and unchanging *svabhava*, then the thing is unreal. According to Hindu thinkers, the reason that Sherlock Holmes or Spider Man or Tarzan or Iron Man are unreal is that they lack *svabhava*, they lack an eternal unchanging inner essence.

After a careful examination of the claims and the evidence, the Buddhists rejected this Hindu theory of eternal self-existent essence. The Buddhist twelve links provide a **Middle Way**[71] or a **Middle Path** between the extremes of the claim that (a) "**everything exists** that has an unchanging self-existent essence (*svabhava*)," and the other extreme, (b) "**nothing exists** because no thing has an unchanging essence."

For the Buddhists, things are real and do exist but it is a mistake to think that what makes something real is that it possesses an unchanging self-existent essence. Humans are real and exist, but humans are flowing processes, each aspect of the processes interconnected and interdependent. There is no inherently self-existing substance anywhere

---

[69] This is explained in detail in many Buddhist texts, such as Etienne Lamotte, *History of Indian Buddhism* (Louvain: Institut Orientaliste Louvain-La-Neuve, 1988), pp. 36–40.

[70] A psychological interpretation of these twelve steps of dependent co-arising is the book by Rune Johansson, *The Dynamic Psychology of Early Buddhism* (London: Curzon, 1975).

[71] Another formulation explains the Middle Path as running in the middle between asceticism and hedonism.

contained inside these processes, and no need for any self-existing essence to explain anything about us. In the *Samyutta-nikaya* 3.90, the Buddha explains this to Kaccana using the idea of a chain of twelve links:

> Kaccana, "Everything exists" is one extreme; Kaccana, "nothing exists" is the other extreme. Not approaching either extreme, Kaccana, the Tathagata [Buddha] teaches you a doctrine in terms of a **middle path**: ignorance depends on action; action depends on consciousness; consciousness depends on name and form; name and form depend on the six sense spheres; the six sense spheres depend on contact; contact depends on feeling; feeling depends on attachment; attachment depends on grasping; grasping depends on existence; existence depends on birth; birth depends on aging and death. Suffering, despair, misery, grief, and sorrow depend on aging and death. In this way, the whole mass of suffering arises. But due to the complete eradication and cessation of ignorance comes a cessation of karmas and so forth. This is the cessation of this whole mass of suffering.[72]

8.7 THE FOUR NOBLE TRUTHS

According to the Buddhist text which tells of the Buddha's initial teaching to his friends after his awakening, the Buddha taught the Three Marks or the Three Characteristics of Existence and the Four Noble Truths.[73] The bedrock of early Buddhism, as his immediate students understood it, is (1) Three Marks, (2) the Four Noble Truths, and (3) the dependent co-arising analysis of causality (*pratityasamutpada*).[74] As we saw above, the Three Characteristics are (a) impermanence, (b) *anatman*, and (c) *duhkha*.

The Four Noble Truths of Buddhism[75] comprise four statements: (1) the existence of *duhkha*; (2) the arising of *duhkha*, (3) the cessation of *duhkha*; (4) the eightfold *marga* or pathway which will lessen or eliminate *duhkha*.

(1) THE FIRST NOBLE TRUTH: the fact of *duhkha*.

Life is *duhkha*. Life is disappointing. We make choices and we experience dissatisfaction. Life is frustrating, dissatisfying, impermanent, imperfect, insubstantial, and all of us experience emotional discontent and suffering. No matter how much you have or how much you have accomplished, life is never perfect and is less than fully satisfactory. Certainly we can feel happiness, and we can feel wonderful. Things go well for a while, but no matter how much happiness we experience, it does not last, it is never permanent. All of existence is trapped in change, and ongoing change produces pain and suffering for those who do not understand the fact of impermanence. Life feeds on death, and time will destroy everything each of us has ever loved. How can we learn to deal with the inevitability of loss?

As we saw in previous discussions, *duhkha* means emotional dissatisfaction, the state of mind that arises from having expectations that are not fulfilled. We feel that things should be better than they are; life is not as good as it could or should be. We are disappointed. We feel dissatisfied—there must be more to life than we have attained so far. Even when things are going well, and we enjoy pleasures, we know these do not last. It feels as though everything we

---

[72] Quoted in James Fieser, John Powers, *Scriptures of the East* 2nd edition (New York: McGraw-Hill, 2003), p. 87. Emphasis added.

[73] Literally, these are the "Four *Satya*." Some linguists explain *satya* as a proposition worthy of being considered, which is not quite equivalent to "truth."

[74] It is interesting that although devotion is so important in later popular Buddhism, in the early Buddhist scriptures devotion is not particularly valuable and not encouraged.

[75] These four are cornerstones of early Buddhism for monks, but are not the cornerstone of popular Buddhism. "Few Buddhists over the course of Asian history would have been able to recite the four noble truths and the eightfold path ..." Donald S. Lopez, Jr., "Belief," in Mark Taylor, ed., *Critical Terms for Religious Studies* (1998).

do is less than perfect, only temporary, and not solid or substantial enough to sustain us in our search for meaning, happiness, contentment, and peace. According to the very first discourse of the Buddha,

> Birth is suffering; old age is suffering; sickness is suffering; death is suffering. Sorrow, lamentation, and dejection are suffering. Contact with what is unpleasant and separation from the pleasant are suffering. Not getting what one wishes is suffering. In brief, clinging to the five aggregates of the personality – body, feeling, perception, disposition, and consciousness – as possessions of 'my self' is suffering.[76]

As we can see, *duhkha* is not limited to just physical or psychological misery or pain. We also experience *duhkha* because we want things to persist unchanging, and we are frustrated when we find that all things are impermanent. Nothing persists unchanging. Finally, there can be *duhkha* because of causal conditions which are independent of ourselves and our choices. It is entirely possible that the airplane upon which we are riding will run into a mountain, or be struck by lightning, and none of that is due to us or our karma. It is just the case that life can be *duhkha*.

This is not intended to provide a pessimistic view of life. Rather, it is meant to be a sober, realistic statement of what life is really like. *Duhkha* is actual, it exists. We all experience it, some more than others. Impermanence is a cause of *duhkha*. All phenomena conditioned by our pulling some things towards us, and pushing other things away from us, lead to *duhkha*.

---

(2) THE SECOND NOBLE TRUTH: the arising of *duhkha*.

Duhkha, these feelings of dissatisfaction, frustration, emotional suffering and misery, arise out of and are dependent upon a complex set of causes and conditions. The Buddha's insight under the Bodhi tree, the insight of *pratityasamutpada*, or dependent co-arising, is focused on the causes of *duhkha*. This second noble truth is also explaining something about human nature. What is going on in our mind, what we think, can and does affect our health. For reasons that the Buddhists do not explain, we human beings tend to be self-centered, and this is one important cause of our misery. Among the many causes of emotional misery are self-centered desire, ego-centered thirst, craving, greed, hatred, and delusion. Although there are several lists of the causes of *duhkha*, most often they can be contained within the **Three Unwholesome Roots**, or the **Three Poisons**.[77] These are the roots of *duhkha*, and we cannot lessen or eliminate *duhkha* as long as these Three Unwholesome Roots dominate our personality.

The First Unwholesome Root/Poison: greed (*raga*), self-centered craving, ego-centered greediness and desires, egocentric attachment, and egocentric possessiveness, including craving or lust. To be egocentric is the tendency to view everything else in relationship to oneself, one's desires, one's values, one's beliefs – thus your own wants, desires, and values are most important and everyone else is less important. This can lead to envy and resentment when our ego-centered desires are obstructed.

In more contemporary terminology, this first poison is something like "I *want* that . . .," whatever it is. We want things we do not have, and we are continually dissatisfied, discouraged, envious. Yes, you do want this, but do you need it? Is it necessary for ease or health? It feels like you *need* something, but actually most of the time it is just *want*. I want a new car, a new home, clothing, and I want the latest gadget or phone, I want what my friends have, my neighbors have. Contentment seems impossible unless one is a billionaire. Our culture spends a great deal of time and effort getting you to *want* things. It is said that we are exposed to 3,500 advertisements every day, on television, on radio, on placards, on signage, on magazines, on busses, on our phones, on the internet and almost every website. That

---

[76] From the *Dhammacakkappavattana-sutta*, translated by and quoted in David Kalupahana, *A History of Buddhist Philosophy: Continuities and Discontinuities* (Honolulu: University of Hawaii Press, 1992), p. 86.

[77] "O Monks, there are three causes from which actions originate: greed, hatred and delusion." *Anguttara Nikaya*, I, p. 263; from Etienne Lamotte, *History of Indian Buddhism* (Louvain: Institut Orientaliste Louvain-La-Neuve, 1988), p. 35.

feeling of "I want . . ." which seems never to be completely satisfied is the first poison.

I want things; I think that if I possess some thing that I want, it will bring me happiness—I make choices and I strive to attain it. Quite often we are successful, we do get what we wanted. However, one cannot help but note that after I get what I want, the object does not satisfy permanently. We have obtained something we wanted, but now we latch onto something else which attracts us. So, then we strive to attain some new thing. This on-going cycle of ego-centered craving can be modified, but it is not easy.

The first poison also includes a desire for and attachment to physical pleasures, a craving, a self-centered attachment[78] and desire for power, for wealth, for correct perspectives or views, holding to opinions, and even a desire to know something we call "the truth."

Being egocentric, it feels that we are the center of creation, it appears to each of us that the cosmos revolves around the point in time and space which we occupy. Wherever we move in time and space, this illusion of being the center goes with us. We move, and the center of everything moves as well. This egocentric illusion continues in another realm as well. We want our selves to continue unchanging through time, from childhood to old-age, and then for that same self to continue on into another realm after death—but reason and experience both tell us that there is nothing permanent and unchanging anywhere in the universe, and certainly nothing permanent and unchanging about us as individuals.

Being self-centered, we interpret our experiences incorrectly. We tend to misunderstand the way things are, and we tend to take things personally that are not personal. We can be offended; our pride can be injured. We become resentful. The less ego-centered we are, the less we are offended. The common phrase "don't take it personally" carries with it some of the sense of not being ego-centered and not being possessive.

Second Unwholesome Root/Poison: hatred (*dosa*), malice, aversion, ill-will, anger, irritation, annoyance, animosity, hostility. Our negative feelings of malice, aversion, ill-will, hatred, and anger, will harm us mentally and physically (in modern times we know that these can damage the immune system and bring on depression and disease). Making choices and decisions grounded upon on these negative feelings are one of the major causes of *duhkha*. Being angry with someone, or especially feeling hatred toward another, will cause *duhkha* in our own lives. Hatred and anger damage us. They are a poison which can cause great pain and suffering.

In the *Sangiiti Sutta* (D. 33 iii 262) we find that malice is stirred by the thought "he has done me an injury," or "he will do me an injury," "he has done a favor to someone who is hateful and unpleasant to me." Malice is overcome by the thought "what good would it do to harbor malice?" Finding myself offended, I can use my awareness of that feeling to observe the illusory ego rearing its ugly head, or I can let it drop, thinking, "What good does it do to feel this way?"

Third Unwholesome Root/Poison: ignorance, confusion, or delusion (*moha*). Being ignorant of the true nature of life (i.e., that everything in life arises from causes and conditions and is impermanent, including our selves), makes us ill-prepared to eliminate this sense of unsatisfactoriness in our life. Being ignorant, we continue to make choices and act upon our self-centered desires to acquire things mistakenly believing that things can provide more than temporary pleasures. Choices based on ego-centric desire leads to activity which generates a never-ending cycle of desire leading to, activity, grasping, greed, craving, which lead to activity, self-centered thirst, leading to activity, and so forth.[79] Not seeing things clearly, we are biased, we are prejudiced, and we are misled by many of the common beliefs of our family, misled by our culture, by our society.[80]

---

[78] The antidote to ego-centered attachment will be to lessen possessiveness, to work on detachment, or non-attachment.

[79] The Twelve-Linked Chain of Causation discussed previously can be understood as an explication of ignorance and its consequences.

[80] Every time I visit some commercial internet site, or turn on a television or read a magazine or newspaper, I am told that the secret to happiness is to purchase things like cars, colas, undergarments, perfumes, shoes, and so forth. We are also bombarded with advertising meant to make us feel inadequate, feel inferior unless we buy and own this product, or that product. We are encouraged to believe that buying things is happiness; if I have enough money to buy enough stuff, I'll be happy. For some reason people with the wealth to buy all

Ignorance most certainly includes mistakenly believing that one does know the truth, and ignorance includes acting on false perspectives, including unexamined belief, dogma, prejudice and wishful thinking, all of which obscure our ability to see things more clearly. We find ourselves in a situation where a choice needs to be made. We assess our options, draw upon dogma, prejudice, and wishful thinking, and then make a choice. No wonder we experience *duhkha*.

Another source of *duhkha* is the assumption that, because we can remember events that happened to us in the past, we imagine that we have an inner unchanging *atman* essence that never changes, a separate independent unchanging self, an isolated personal substance which is fundamentally separate from everything else. For Buddhists, this is a profound confusion.

We might like to think that we have unchanging inner essences, but as discussed previously, the Buddhist analysis of the human personality ("self") reveals that we are not a container for an *atman*, that we do not have eternal souls. We are empty of *atman*. We do change, but we change slowly and gradually (there is **continuity** between past and present), and we mistakenly assume that there must be something about us that remains identical from year to year. We have confused slow gradual *continuity* with unchanging *permanence*. We change gradually, and that continuity over time leads us to assume that something about us has remained identical over time. A permanent or immutable entity called "soul," "self," or *atman*, contradicts the impermanence we see all around, and Buddhists generally argue that the belief in a permanent eternal *atman* supports selfishness and egoism, root causes of ego-centered attachment, greed, possessiveness, and craving. We need to realize that we do not have some sort of self-existing inner controller. We are empty of *atman*. We also need to empty ourselves of these three poisons, and realize a mind totally free from emotional suffering. Then we have achieved the goal of Buddhism.

Thus, we can see that in Indian Buddhism, these three unwholesome roots of anger, greed, and confusion, are the major obstacles to awakening. In the human personality, these three reflect (1) failures of morality, (2) lack of mental self-discipline and (3) conceptual mistakes or lack of wisdom and understanding.

There are other, more detailed lists of various factors (called *klesha*, hindrances or defilements) which lead to *duhkha*, such as believing in an unchanging self, and the mistaken belief that ritual performance invoking supernatural deities can lead to liberation.[81] Most of these can be subsumed under the Three Poisons. There are several other lists including one classic list of ten fetters which keep us in a cycle of *duhkha*.[82]

---

(3) **THE THIRD NOBLE TRUTH**: the cessation of *duhkha*.

It is possible to eliminate the gnawing feeling of dissatisfaction completely and the way to do it is by eliminating its causes (again, the Buddha's insight under the Bodhi tree of *pratityasamutpada* or "dependent co-arising," is insight into the causes of human suffering). Each and every person can actually end emotional frustration, misery, and dissatisfaction, and the end of *duhkha* is what Buddhists call nirvana.

In Sanskrit, the root of the term "nirvana" is "to blow out" or "extinguish," and some mistakenly assume that Buddhists wanted to extinguish the self, a form of suicide. In fact, according to Buddhists, what is extinguished are

---

of these things do not seem to be much happier than the rest of us.

[81] The perceptive student will note that these are foundation beliefs in Brahmanism.

[82] The list includes belief in a permanent self, doubt, belief that morality alone and ritual alone can lead to nirvana, sensual passions, malice, desire to be reborn in other realms, pride, distraction, and ignorance. This and other lists can be found in Edward J. Thomas, *The History of Buddhist Thought* (London: Routledge & Kegan Paul, 1967), pp. 120ff. See also Akira Hirakawa, tr. by Paul Groner, *A History of Indian Buddhism* (Honolulu: University of Hawaii Press, 1990), pp. 153–156.

those things which constrain or obstruct us,[83] the flames of anger, greed, egocentricity, and confusion or ignorance. We extinguish the flames of the Three Unwholesome Roots or Poisons (craving, anger, ignorance) and transform these into positives using Buddhist techniques.

The Third Noble Truth follows from *pratityasamutpada*, the causal analysis of experience. We experience *duhkha*, and *duhkha* has causes. If you can **lessen** the causal factors, lessen your egocentric greed, craving, or thirst, fueled by ignorance, diminish the craving to get something out of life which experience cannot provide, then *duhkha* will lessen. It follows that if you eliminate its causes, you eliminate emotional unsatisfactoriness from your life. If one can **stop** the egocentric desires, self-centered craving, or thirst, fueled by ignorance, the craving to get something out of life which experience cannot provide, then the emotional suffering that is *duhkha* will be extinguished. If we can deal with the world in ways which are not self-centered, not seeking to satisfy egoistic cravings and desires, and can see things without ignorance, see things the way they really are (not the way we have been conditioned to see them as unchanging substances), then our life is nirvana. Liberation from *duhkha* is possible.

The Cessation of *duhkha* is Nirvana: Is Nirvana Unconditioned?

The Third Noble Truth explains that nirvana is the complete elimination of the Three Unwholesome Roots from the personality.[84] Nirvana is the absence of hindrances such as anger, hatred, self-centered possessiveness and ignorance. In the sense that it is just an absence, nirvana is unconditioned. There are several ways to interpret the phrase, "Nirvana is unconditioned." The most famous reference to nirvana as "unconditioned" is found in the *Udana* ("Significant Utterances") 80–81, where we find the following:

> Monks, there is a not-born, not-become, not-made, not-compounded. Monks, if that not-born, not-become, not-made, not-compounded were not, no escape from the born, become, made, compounded would be known here. But monks, since there is a not-born, not-become, not-made, not-compounded, therefore an escape from the born, become, made, compounded is known.[85]

Nirvana is an **absence** of self-centered desires and hindrances. An absence is not a thing in itself. The absence of peanut butter has no conditions; neither does the absence of Santa Claus; the absence of peanut butter is unconditioned. This is one explanation of why nirvana is unconditioned. Nirvana is not some thing in itself; it is a term we use to describe human personality in the absence of the three poisons. However, the mind in which the Three Poisons are absent is still a conditioned mind. The mind of awakening is just not conditioned by the things that cause *duhkha*.[86]

What remains once you have cast off the illusion of *atman*, the illusion of an eternal permanent self, ego? According to Buddhists, the whole universe remains, no longer seen through the distorting filters of ego, ignorance,

---

[83] A good description of these various constraints (physical, psychological, economic, political, social, and ideological views and theories) can be found in David Kalupahana, *A Sourcebook of Early Buddhist Philosophy, op. cit.*, pp. 8–11.

[84] Another explanation of nirvana is the elimination of the two-fold desire concerning becoming: the desire to continue unchanging over time or to be born and reborn (eternalism); the desire to escape the cycle by stopping living entirely (nihilism). As noted before, the root of nirvana is "to eliminate," "to blow out" or "extinguish," and what is extinguished is the flames of the Three Poisons, the flames of hatred, anger, greed, egocentricity, and confusion or ignorance.

[85] Translated in David Kalupahana, *Buddhist Philosophy: A Historical Analysis*, p. 75. Kalupahana's book devotes an entire chapter to this topic. Nirvana as an unconditioned absolute or ultimate is again discussed in chapter 10 of this *Asian Thought* book, in the Madhyamaka tradition of Mahayana Buddhism.

[86] The analysis of nirvana as an absence is associated with the Sautrantika school of conservative Buddhism. The Vaibhasika group of conservative Buddhists held that nirvana (and empty space) were definitely real yet simultaneously unconditioned. Later Mahayana Madhyamaka will hold that the concept of nirvana is a useful fiction, but not an ultimate truth. They argue for the conclusion that no ultimately true claims concerning nirvana are possible.

prejudice, ill-will and self-centered desires. Believing that we were a separate ego or a self-existent *atman*, we believed that we were isolated from others, we were alone. According to Buddhists, it is a mistake to think that you are alone. Rather, you are intimately interwoven into a seamless interconnected interdependent causal web of processes including all living beings. The extinction of egocentric craving allows you to see things as they really are, and you see things without illusions or ignorance, and this is wisdom.

One way of understanding the Buddhist pathway is as a process of practices which will gradually transform these Three Unwholesome Roots into three positives. The motivating force of internal egoistic greed can be transformed into external generosity, the negative feelings of hatred and ill-will can be transformed into compassionate loving-kindness, and finally ignorance or delusion can be transformed into wisdom.[87] The result of the process is nirvana. Thus the result is a person who is generous, loving, non-judgmental, compassionate, and wise. Generosity, loving kindness, and compassion, are the foundation for Buddhist morality. To be compassionate is not to feel pity for someone; rather, it is to share what they are experiencing, to be in oneness with that person. With the lessening of ego-centeredness, altruism becomes a natural response to fellow humans and the creatures with whom we share our world. Buddhist compassion is not limited to our immediate friends and family; it is to be extended to those with whom we do not agree, extended to those of a different ethnicity, those who are mentally or physically challenged, and those who are different.

What is nirvana? As is clear, in early Buddhism, nirvana is not a heavenly state achieved after death, it is not a reward by a supernatural power. Rather, nirvana is a state of joy and happiness in this life, achieved by training the mind and body carefully.[88]

---

(4) THE FOURTH NOBLE TRUTH: the Noble Eightfold Path.

The Fourth Noble Truth explains that there are eight things we can do that will lead to the cessation of *duhkha*, which is nirvana. The fourth of the Four Noble Truths is eight interrelated techniques to achieve insight into the way things really are, and to develop the mental ability to practice techniques which will reduce and ultimately eliminate self-centered desires, grasping, craving, anger and hatred. The goal is realistic insight into the nature of things, and the ending of ignorance, frustration and dissatisfaction, and achievement of loving-kindness and compassion for all living things.

It is important to note that the Noble Eightfold Path is traditionally broken into three areas: wisdom, morality and meditation. The traditional listing of eight begins with wisdom, however in this chapter we will explain wisdom as the summarizing last principle, as the eighth instead of the first.

The Noble Eightfold Path: THREE TECHNIQUES OF MORALITY (*sila*)

If you want to lessen emotional frustration and dissatisfaction, *duhkha*, then you must realize that your own states of mind, actions, and choices are causes of much of your *duhkha*. For a person to live morally is for her or him to live without increasing the *duhkha* in the world. You cannot lessen your own *duhkha* unless you modify your behavior, to bring it into accord with the way things really are (arising from causes, interdependently interconnected, and impermanent). Moral failures comprise a major obstacle to awakening.

---

[87] Many economic systems around the world are dependent upon encouraging greed, for that produces consumers who continually purchase items. Many politicians have encouraged ill-will for political reasons, for without ill-will a nation will not go to war. When our sources of news distort the news to favor visually exciting events rather than important events which can change our lives, to favor celebrity misdeeds instead of important events in the world, then our news sources encourage confusion and ignorance.

[88] For example, see Steven Collins, *Nirvana and Other Buddhist Felicities* (London: Cambridge University Press, 1998).

(1) Right Speech (traditionally #3 on the Buddhist list of eight).

One must use language in the most accurate and compassionate way possible. Language is essential to being human, but language is often used to deceive and this causes suffering. Our words must be motivated by loving-kindness, and this means that we do not cause suffering to others. The Buddhists say that we must pay attention so that our use of language does not mislead another, does not falsify or cover up our actual experience. Only the truth should be spoken. Buddhists do not think that just because something is true, we must speak it no matter what the consequences. We might not want to state it if it is disagreeable, if it increases *duhkha*.

Of course, we must abstain from telling lies, but also abstain from exaggerating, from slander or speech that might bring about disharmony, abstain from hate speech and from idle or useless gossip. There is a positive component to Right Speech as well; use friendly and benevolent words, language which is meaningful, kind and useful.

There is much more to one's best possible speech than just stating the truth. Paraphrasing the Buddha, a guide to Right Speech would be along the lines of:

If it is not true, not beneficial, and disagreeable, don't say it.
If it is true, not beneficial, and disagreeable, don't say it.
If it is true, beneficial, and disagreeable, know when to say it.
If it is not true, not beneficial, and agreeable, don't say it.
If it is true, not beneficial, and agreeable, don't say it.
If it is true, beneficial, and not agreeable, know when to say it.[89]

As you can see, Right Speech does not mean always speaking the truth, no matter what; also it does not mean never saying anything disagreeable. If one's words are true, beneficial and disagreeable, we still need the insight and skill to know whether to speak the words or refrain. Speech motivated by indignation, anger, ignorance, or self-centeredness is to be avoided.

This means we can engage in political speech, we can speak truth to power, and certainly we can speak out against injustice. We just need to do so carefully and skillfully. We create the least amount of *duhkha* when insight, wisdom, and compassion guide our speech.

(2) Right Conduct (traditionally #4 on the Buddhist list of eight)

One must behave in the very best possible way. The Three Unwholesome Roots are causes of *duhkha*, so it follows that acts that result from craving, anger and ignorance must be minimized, because they perpetuate the sources of suffering. All acts of aggression and self-indulgence must be avoided. To be more specific, practice non-violence (*ahimsa*), do not destroy life, do not steal, do not behave dishonestly, avoid immoral sexual behavior, and help others to lead a peaceful and honorable life. These lead to compassionate loving-kindness, the foundation of Buddhist morality and one foundation of the Buddhist pathway to nirvana.

(3) Right Livelihood (traditionally #5 on the Buddhist list of eight).

One's livelihood is one's career or vocation. The Buddhists say that you cannot lessen your own *duhkha* while earning your living by causing *duhkha* to others. If you want to lessen your own *duhkha*, your occupation must be guided by the moral path.

Do not earn your living in ways that increase *duhkha* for living things. The way a person earns his or her living must not be based on aggression, taking advantage of, or misleading others. If you are a Buddhist, you cannot earn your living in a way that harms others, such as selling weapons, selling drugs or alcohol, or selling poisons. As a

---

[89] "Discourse to Prince Abhaya," Discourse 58, translated by I.B. Horner, *The Collection of the Middle Length Sayings* (Majjhima-Nikaya), Vol. II (London: Luzac & Co., 1970), pp. 62-63. The paraphrase was inspired by the skillful words of Franz Metcalf (email communication 2012-08-03).

Buddhist, you cannot earn your living as a gambler, thief, hunter, butcher, drug dealer, pimp, or soldier.[90] As a Buddhist, you should understand that you cannot lessen your own *duhkha* and at the same time cause suffering to other living things. Recommended occupations include that of a monk, a teacher, or a helper and guide. Your livelihood should be one that can help to lessen or eliminate self-centered desire, ill-will and ignorance. The result will be an altruistic personality grounded in loving-compassion for all sentient beings.

The Eightfold Path: THREE TECHNIQUES OF MENTAL DISCIPLINE, or MEDITATION (*samadhi*)

If you want to lessen or eliminate *duhkha*, morality is necessary, but not sufficient. Morality alone is not enough to achieve awakening. In addition you need mental discipline, you need *dhyana*, that is, you need to learn to focus and concentrate your attention, and use that focused attention to work on the causes of *duhkha*.

The term *dhyana* is usually translated "meditation," however in ordinary English, "mediation" can mean sitting quietly thinking about important stuff, or even a mental state that is day-dreaming. In Buddhism, the meaning of *dhyana*, or meditation, is much more specific. Meditation in Buddhism has two aspects:
(a) *shamatha*, calm abiding meditation intended to produce mental tranquility, mental peacefulness;
(b) *vipaśyanā/vipassana*, penetrative insight, experiential awareness or clear vision into the nature of interdependent interconnected phenomena.

(4) Right Effort (traditionally #6 on the list of eight).

If you want to lessen *duhkha*, you need to apply yourself, you need to expend your very best possible effort. You need to act with dedication. You need to clear and calm your mind. You do that if you minimize harmful thinking and encourage good thoughts. You need to understand your mental habits, especially those which are causes of dissatisfaction and frustration. With practice, you can gain some control over your thoughts, your moods, your desires. You can choose to focus on negative thoughts, what you do not have, or you can focus on what you have, those things for which you are genuinely grateful.

Try to maintain states of mind such as being at peace, accepting, and being non-judgmental. Try to avoid hindrances, avoid unwholesome states of mind, such as ill-will, cruelty, lust, self-centered wants and desires, fear, anxiety, and pride. When you cultivate Right Effort diligently, you will notice when negative states of mind are beginning to arise. Use your focus to stop them before they become too strong to deal with. Get rid of such states if they have already arisen, and cause good and wholesome states of mind to arise, and bring to perfection those good and wholesome states of mind which have already arisen. Kindness, compassion, and altruism are to be cultivated. Be grateful for what you have, and to those who have helped make it possible. Right Effort is founded upon morality and concentration. This practice leads to serenity and wisdom.

(5) Right Mindfulness, or Right Attentiveness (traditionally #7).

To be mindful or attentive is developing focused awareness of body, mind, sensations, feelings, actions, and phenomena. Being mindful is the ability to focus on a chosen object without being distracted. Being mindful is a form of self-discipline such that every activity becomes focused in the present, bringing spiritual awareness of the present. Mindfulness involves managing moods and modifying undesirable behaviors by putting attention on one's mind, that is, self-awareness. However, insight and wisdom also play a role. Letting go of our preconceptions and assumptions so we see things clearly is important. Mindfulness[91] has been stressed as a fundamental practice by the early Buddhists,

---

[90] We all know that Buddhists in many countries are soldiers. That people do not always follow their religion's ideals is obvious. For example, one would think that the model of the early Christian martyrs who refused to kill and the dictum "Thou shalt not kill" would require Christians to refuse to be soldiers. Some are conscientious objectors, some warriors.

[91] The Sanskrit term for this is *smrti*.

and is becoming important in the West as a tool to improve mental health.[92]

The Buddhist student begins by being attentive to bodily states, sensations, and emotions. With insight (*vipaśyanā*/*vipassana*) meditation, the student will begin by trying to focus unwavering attention on the inflow and outflow of breathing. When one's focus is starting to settle, one will now focus on the sensation of one's breath as it encounters the upper lip. Concentration becomes even more focused than before. Then the student focuses her attention on the top of the head, and slowly attention flows along the body to the tips of one's toes. One cannot help but note that each sensation, each feeling, each mental activity, each idea, is transitory, that everything is flowing change, that we are constantly changing and impermanent, in an impermanent world. Mindfulness brings wholesome clarity to our perceptual processes. All of this is to be observed impersonally, noticing thoughts, sensations, feelings, gestures. The meditating Buddhist observes these emotional states, but does not try to repress them and does not try to push them away. *The Buddhist does not try to make her mind blank.*

Without being attached to these states of mind, observe them as they arise, and observe them as they fade away. Sensations that we do not like make us unhappy. Sensations we like are ones that we want to repeat or hold onto. However, pleasant or unpleasant, they do fade away. Recognizing this helps us to let go. With practice, mindfulness can be extended to everything we do, when walking, driving, eating, or sitting.

Does concentrating on our experience and sensations reveal that we have some controlling inner self or mind? Focused concentration reveals that the answer is "no." Being attentive to mental states leads to the recognition that what we call "I" or "self" is a group of processes which are changing and interdependent. Mind is not unchanging, and there is no unchanging soul, no unchanging inner substance (the Hindu *atman*). What I think of as my unchanging "self" actually is a continuous series of changing evolving awarenesses, focused upon whatever draws my attention at that moment. There is no permanent unchanging individual self behind the thoughts, no "thinker" who possesses thoughts. In other words, being attentive to the mind helps us realize that there is no permanent self, immutable soul, or *atman*. The Buddhists would say that we are "empty of *atman*." Thus Right Mindfulness helps us to realize *anatman*.

In the *Digha Nikaya sutra* (22) we find this description of mindfulness:

The disciple is clearly conscious in coming and going; clearly conscious in looking forward and backward; clearly conscious in bending and stretching; clearly conscious in eating, drinking, chewing, tasting; clearly conscious in accomplishing all the natural functions of the body; clearly conscious in walking, standing, sitting, falling asleep, and waking; clearly conscious in speaking and in keeping silent.[93]

Focusing attention on all these ordinary activities like eating, drinking, chewing, sitting, or standing, brings our attention to the present and our present experience. Focused attention is a tool that one can use to analyze whether an experience is characterized by transitoriness, imperfection, and lack of substantiality. Can you distinguish whether the sensations are pleasant, unpleasant, or neither?

The Buddhist is mindful of the body, attentive to sensations, states of mind, and finally, she or he pays attention to the world of phenomena. This process leads to a realization that we do not live in a world where we are neutral and things outside of ourselves are intrinsically pleasurable or painful. Our actual experiences are much more complex than this. We begin to realize that it is not just external circumstances which cause our dissatisfaction, but

---

[92] In America, some have attempted to turn mindfulness into a for-profit business and its Buddhist roots become blurred. A book tracing this and its implications is Jeff Wilson, *Mindful America: The Mutual Transformation of Buddhist Meditation and American Culture* (Oxford: Oxford University Press, 2014).

[93] Quoted in G. Constant Lounsbery, *Buddhist Meditation* (New York: Alfred A. Knopf, 1935), pp. 25-26. From Digha Nikaya I.47. There are several useful books on Buddhist mindfulness meditation. For example, Bhante Henepola Gunaratana, *Mindfullness in Plain English: Revised and Expanded Edition* (New York: Wisdom Publications, 1996), and Marshall Glickman, *Beyond the Breath: Extraordinary Mindfulness through Whole-Body Vipassana Meditation* (Tuttle Publishing, 2002), an explanation of a particular form of meditation taught by the Burmese teacher S. N. Goenka. See also Jerry Braza, *Moment By Moment: The Art and Practice of Mindfulness* (Rutland, VT: Charles Tuttle, 1997); and Thich Nhat Hanh, *Breathe! You are Alive: The Sutra on the Full Awareness of Breathing* (Berkeley, CA: Parallax Press, 1995).

our ways of seeing and reacting to our circumstances. We cannot control our external world, and we cannot control others. We need to break the bad habits which we've developed, and we need careful attention and mindful insight to recognize these habits of ours. The only thing that we can control is our own mind, and realizing this is an important key to ending *duhkha*.

Our states of mind, our expectations and mental attitudes can change neutral experiences into pleasurable or miserable or painful experiences.[94] We experience much emotional suffering because of the way we view the world, the way we view our selves. Our mental states, our habits and expectations, and our prejudices affect whether our experiences are pleasant or unpleasant. Our experience of external circumstances is affected by what our culture teaches us about our feelings and our behavior. Our experiences are affected by our conditioning, by ego, affected by our habits, prejudices, and associations, and affected by our misconceptions. However, Buddhists do not declare that we are the only creator of all of our problems, or that we are the only one who can resolve those problems. Those who are farther along the pathway (the *sangha*) are our community of helpers.

Mindfulness is not a miraculous practice that makes all the painful things in life disappear. Instead, with mindfulness we learn to accept grief and loss, and live with the fact that all things are impermanent and must pass away. Mindfulness brings us fully into the present moment, where we all live every moment of the day.

(6) Right Concentration (traditionally the last of the eight).

Samadhi, the most focused concentration, is cultivated in this step. The Buddhists use the term *samadhi* to mean a wholesome focused alertness. It is maintaining one-pointedness of mind on a specific object of concentration. Buddhist *samadhi* is *not* a mind empty of content, not a "trance," but rather it is cultivation of a heightened alertness, a focused concentration which can cut through the distractions which make it difficult for us to deal objectively and dispassionately with life's problems. It is learning to focus and concentrate the mind so that things can be seen clearly, without the confusion, ignorance, and ego-centered craving which cloud our ordinary consciousness. At this stage one works on focusing one's perception and tries to concentrate without being distracted. Ordinarily one practices focused concentration using a seated posture, with the legs crossed in what is often called a lotus posture. By practicing seated meditation, the mind becomes more stable and there will be a state of equanimity.

However, a state of *samadhi*, a stable and peaceful mind is *not* the ultimate goal of a Buddhist. Nirvana is the ultimate goal, and nirvana is *not* the same as the mental state of *samadhi*. The Buddhist goal of *samadhi* is not to stop the mind; rather the goal is insight into the way things really are. Insight into reality produces less self-centeredness, less anger, and less ignorance or confusion. Lessening these three lessens *duhkha*.

The state of *samadhi*[95] is attained through the practice of focused concentration, but *samadhi* is not nirvana. At the worldly level, Right Concentration is a tool for the recognition of the causes of *duhkha* and ultimately eliminating *duhkha*. The elimination of *duhkha* is the attainment of nirvana.

The Noble Eightfold Path: TWO TECHNIQUES OF WISDOM (*prajna*).

The Noble Eightfold Path includes morality and meditation (discussed above), but although both are necessary, they are not sufficient to eliminate *duhkha*. One also needs insight into the way things really are. One needs the wisdom to understand and deal with the real world, and the Buddhist term for such discerning awareness, such wisdom, is

---

[94] A stranger brushes our hand, and we barely notice. The love of our life brushes our hand, and we experience thrills and a feeling of bliss.

[95] The Buddhist use of *samadhi* (to mean wholesome concentration of the mind on a single object) is not identical with the term in Yoga discussed in chapter 4 of this book. On several occasions the Buddha seemed to achieve a cessation of consciousness (the goal of Yoga) in order to deal with pain, but did not treat this as a desirable goal or as nirvana. The Buddhist treats even the highest levels of *samadhi* as merely interesting states of consciousness and not as Yoga understands it, not as union with ultimate reality, not as union with God. For Buddhists, the highest attainment of *samadhi* leads to meditative absorption (*dhyana*). Discussions of *samadhi* can be found various Buddhist dictionaries and Buddhist encyclopedias, and also in Bhikshu Sangharakshita, *A Survey of Buddhism* (Boulder, CO: Shambhala, 1980), pp. 137ff.

prajna.[96] Lack of *prajna*-wisdom is another of the major obstacles to the elimination of *duhkha*.

(7) Right Thought (traditionally this is #2 of eight).

Here the Buddhists work on achieving a state of consciousness that reflects the very best within ourselves. Much of Right Thought involves cultivating a natural spontaneous morality. We must cultivate a selfless compassion, a love for others which is not self-centered. We practice dealing with others and the world without hatred, ill-will, or aversion. We must deal with others without putting our own self first, without considering "what's in it for me?"

We work on developing an effortless benevolent loving kindness, compassion for all who experience *duhkha*, and experience joyful sympathy with the happiness of other living beings. We develop altruistic behavior, a deep empathy for all people we encounter. Thoughts of selfless detachment, ego-less love and non-violence are to be cultivated, which result in deep serenity. True wisdom possesses these moral qualities, and it is a lack of wisdom which produces self-centered craving, ill-will, hatred and violence.

(8) Right Understanding (traditionally the first of the Noble Eightfold Path)

To understand the changing nature of all that is around us is essential if one hopes to bring about the cessation of *duhkha*, which is nirvana. Otherwise, we misunderstand the world and misunderstand the causes of *duhkha*. This understanding is a discernment, a discerning awareness. To understand is to see things as they really are, not as you wish they were, hope they will be, or demand that they must be.

We have been conditioned by family, by the groups we belong to, and by our culture. We see things through our own prejudices, our assumptions and preconceived ideas. We may believe fervently that the important things in our lives will never change, but this is unrealistic. The Buddhists want to see things without confusion, prejudice and bias. The Buddhist wants to see what's there, without adding anything extraneous to her or his perception. When one sees things without ignorance, confusion, anger, or self-centered egocentric perceptions, the Buddhists call it seeing "things as they really are." One lives fully and completely in the present moment. This is the highest wisdom.

According to Buddhists, we see things as they really are, we are actually seeing things as they have become to be (as process). What does one see? The ultimate nature of reality, when seen clearly, reveals a world of flowing change, a world of dependent co-arising (*pratityasamutpada*), a world where events arise from many causes and conditions, a world where nothing is permanent or self-existent, not even an *atman*. When this is perceived with loving-kindness and compassion, without anger, ego, or ignorance, one has achieved the goal, nirvana.

The Four Noble Truths as a Medical Diagnosis

We can see that in early Buddhism the Buddha is neither divinity nor savior; rather the Buddha seems to have seen himself as a healer. We can use the metaphor of a medical diagnosis to understand the Four Noble Truths. The first noble truth is the diagnosis of the problem of the human condition: *duhkha*. The second truth isolates the causes of the condition (the three unwholesome roots, the hindrances, the *kleshas*). The third is the prognosis which is positive; you can cure yourself of *duhkha* (and no one can cure you except yourself). The fourth is the prescription, the remedy, the medicine, the Noble Eightfold Path.

For the Buddhist, these Four Noble Truths are a pathway whereby the fundamental quality of one's life can be changed. The student progresses from suffering and ignorance to compassion, morality, loving-kindness, peace and wisdom. At its core, according to the sutras, early Buddhism as taught by the Buddha was not something to believe in or something to accept with unquestioning faith. The early students of the Buddha understood Buddhism as a pathway of life to be followed with confidence and practiced and perfected: it is self-discipline in body, word and mind. Buddhism is a tool, a method, to lessen suffering, not something to believe in or accept blindly.

---

[96] We have seen the term *jnana* or "wisdom" in Hinduism; the Buddhists use *prajna* for the wisdom that leads to the cessation of *duhkha* and achieves the liberating freedom of nirvana. For Buddhists, perceptual awareness as consciousness is *vijnana*.

8.8 THE GOAL OF THE EARLY BUDDHIST: AN *ARHAT*

According to the early Buddhist sutras, during the lifetime of the Buddha, perhaps over a thousand followers achieved *bodhi* (awakening) and put an end to *duhkha*, thereby achieving nirvana. The Buddhist community referred to a person of such high attainment as an *arhat*, a "worthy one," an "accomplished one," sometimes translated in English as "saint."

An *arhat* is someone who eliminated *duhkha* and achieved nirvana. An *arhat* is free from ego, free from attachment and greed, free from hatred and delusion. Ego-centered desire is gone, replaced by an altruistic loving-kindness and compassion for all living beings. Anger and hatred are gone, replaced by an inner peace. For the early Buddhists, an *arhat* has achieved what the Buddha achieved.[97] However, there is one difference. The Buddha had no teacher and no one to show him the pathway.[98] According to an early Buddhist sutra[99] the Buddha was like a trail-blazer or a path-maker, and the *arhat* is the one who follows the pathway laid down by the Buddha and thereby arrives at the same place at which the Buddha arrived.

We might note here that as the centuries passed, the status of the Buddha grew ever more lofty and exalted and the achievement of the Buddha came to be seen as much more extraordinary than anything achieved by an *arhat*. The later schools of Buddhism, the Mahasanghika and Mahayana traditions, will agree that the *arhat* has achieved nirvana, but they will assert that the nirvana of an *arhat* is still nowhere close to the highest achievement of the transcendent Buddha. This will be one of the several issues that will separate the early conservative traditions of Buddhism from the later Mahayana (discussed in the next chapter).

CAN ONE WITH INSIGHT FALL BACK INTO MISERY AND SUFFERING?

An interesting question arises among Buddhist followers. It was clear that even wise and kind students with a solid grounding in Buddhism can fall back into ego-centeredness, fall back into lust, anger, and increased confusion. Buddhists were certain that the Buddha himself could never fall back into lower states. Where does the *arhat* fit? Can an *arhat* fall back into negative states?

At what stage along the Buddhist path does one become immune from the temptations of egoism, of hedonism, lust and anger? The Buddha never addressed this question, so in the fifth century, a Sri Lankan Buddhist scholar (generally labeled as belonging to the Theravada tradition) wrote a lengthy text entitled the *Path of Purification*, in which he distinguishes five stages of the Buddhist pathway: a beginner's stage, followed by four additional stages in this process.

Beginner: A Preliminary to Stage One

All Buddhists start out as beginners on the pathway to nirvana, but a beginner is not yet considered to be a serious Buddhist because she or he lacks the understanding and insight which arises naturally from following the Buddhist pathway. A true beginner starts the Buddhist path with many assumptions of Indian culture. Indian culture

---

[97] In early Buddhism, "Buddhahood and Arhatship are so closely allied that it is difficult to draw any significant distinction between the two." S. N. Dube, "Arhat Ideal in Early Buddhism" in *Buddhism and Peace: Theory and Practice*, ed. Chanju Mun (Honolulu: Blue Pine, 2006), p. 51.

[98] Buddhists say that the Buddha was not the first human to achieve awakening; other humans in the past achieved awakening but their teachings did not survive to influence Siddhartha Gautama. In addition there have been people in non-Buddhist civilizations who have put and end to suffering and achieved nirvana. They are called "solitary Buddhas."

[99] The early Buddhist sutra is the *Samyutta-nikaya* and is paraphrased from David Kalupahana, *Buddhist Philosophy: A Historical Introduction* (Honolulu: University of Hawaii Press, 1976), p. 114.

encourages us to have blind faith in the superiority of the Brahmin priests, teaches us that some people are so contaminated that even their shadow can cause us to become impure. Indian culture encourages us to seek purity and avoid contamination. We have been taught to rely on the religious value and power of rituals and prayers, and we may believe that we have a self-existing unchanging eternal *atman* or soul moving from life to life. Anyone with this background certainly should have doubts about the Buddha's teachings and their efficacy, considering that the Buddha denied each and every one of these common assumptions.

If one is serious about lessening suffering and attaining nirvana, the beginner will struggle to gain insight into the nature of the world and the nature of the self. A serious student would study *pratityasamutpada*, "dependent co-arising," and as a result he or she begins to comprehend the interconnected interdependent nature of the world. Based on this, the student can begin to understand what sorts of actions cause an increase of *duhkha*, and which choices lead to the lessening of *duhkha*. With the study of dependent co-arising, the Three Marks of (1) impermanence, (2) no *atman*, and (3) *duhkha* begin to be more deeply understood. Although the thought that there is nothing permanent in one's self, and nothing permanent and unchanging in the world, may be disconcerting or even terrifying, as ego-centeredness declines and insight increases, the terror subsides. It is replaced by calmness, energy, and determination to realize the cessation of misery, to attain nirvana.

Stage One: The Stream-Entrant

The first stage of the four stages according to the *Path of Purification* is called the **Stream-winner** or **Stream-entrant**. This person has eliminated doubt about the Buddha's teachings and their efficacy, eliminated blind faith in the religious value and power of rituals and prayers, eliminated the common Indian beliefs in purity and contamination, and eliminated the mistaken belief that we have a self-existing unchanging eternal *atman* moving from life to life. Such people have made substantial progress, but they are not close to the final goal of awakening yet. The Stream-entrant is still subject to self-centered desire for sensual pleasures and can still be angry and behave poorly towards others. Their lives have improved, but they are far from perfect. According to the author of the *Path of Purification*, they can fall back into sensuality, greed, selfishness and ill-will.

Stage Two: The Once-Returner

The second stage is the **Once-returner**. Building on the accomplishment of the previous stage, the Once-returner works on eliminating remaining traces of sensual desires, greed, ego-centered craving, and ill-will from the personality. The flaws of such a person are fewer, and the fall backwards is not so far. This person's insight is continually deepening and nirvana is nearer. When finally they have eliminated self-centered desire and ill-will, they move to the next stage.

Stage Three: The Never-Returner

The third stage is the **Never-returner**. This person has no ego-centered craving for continued existence. The Never-returner has minimized the negative factors of pride, restlessness, and ignorance which tend to dominate the personalities of so many humans. Although minimized, these factors are not non-existent yet. They can return. Some confusion remains. She still has a little more work ahead in order to achieve nirvana.

Stage Four: The *arhat*

The fourth stage is an ***arhat***, the "worthy person," the one who has eliminated completely all traces of self-centered greed or craving, all traces of anger, hatred, and ill-will, and eliminated all ignorance completely. Such people behave with egoless compassion and loving kindness for all living things. This is the achievement of the Buddha, and the achievement of nirvana.[100] Like the Buddha, upon death the *arhat* will not be reborn in the cycle of birth-and-death, the cycle of *samsara*.[101] The *arhat* has achieved liberation from the cycle of *samsara*.

The later Mahayana Buddhist tradition will disagree with this Theravada analysis, and place the achievement of an *arhat* at a level lower than that of the Buddha.

8.9 THE QUESTIONS WHICH TEND NOT TO EDIFICATION

To his students, the Buddha explained the three unwholesome roots as the origins of suffering, of frustration, of *duhkha*, and he explained the noble eightfold path as eight interrelated techniques to lessen or eliminate *duhkha*. But his students had many metaphysical questions[102] about ultimate reality which the Buddha did not answer. The later Buddhists certainly began to treat the Buddha as an omniscient being who knows everything. However, the earliest sutras record that when asked questions about the ultimate nature of reality, or what happened to the *arhat* after death, the Buddha simply refused to answer. In the Buddhist literature these are referred to as the "ten undetermined points," "ten unanswered questions" or perhaps "ten unexplained questions" or even the "ten unanswerable questions."[103] They can be grouped as follows:

The Buddha refused to answer questions about the duration of the universe
    1. The universe is eternal.
    2. The universe is not eternal.
The Buddha refused to answer questions about the extent of the universe
    3. The universe is finite.
    4. The universe is infinite.
The Buddha refused to answer questions about how *atman* is related to the physical body
    5. The *atman* is identical with the physical body.
    6. The *atman* is different from the physical body.
The Buddha refused to answer questions about the existence of the *arhat* after death
    7. The *arhat* exists after death.
    8. The *arhat* does not exist after death.
    9. The *arhat* does and does not exist after death.
    10. The *arhat* neither exists nor does not exist after death.

Why did the Buddha refuse to answer these ten questions? Did he find the wording of the questions to be misleading? Perhaps he found the questions to be irrelevant to the task of eliminating *duhkha*? It seems as though the first four questions cannot be answered because they go beyond all of our present sources of knowledge. Remember

---

[100] See the *Visuddimagga* of Buddhaghosa, *Path of Purification*, (Colombo: A. Semage, 1964), tr. by Vhikkhu Nyanamoli, 2nd ed., Ch. XVII–XXII, pp. 592–885, for a more detailed explication.

[101] The view that an arhat could never fall back was not universally agreed upon in early Buddhism. See S. N. Dube, "Arhat Ideal in Early Buddhism," in *Buddhism and Peace: Theory and Practice*, p. 53.

[102] These metaphysical questions about the ultimate nature of reality cannot be answered by or tested by any possible observation, evidence, or sense experience. Once such a claim about ultimate reality becomes testable, then when tested it becomes either a fact or a mistaken belief. Either way, it is no longer metaphysical. For example, the statement "The world is made of atoms" was untestable until the 1800s; then it went from metaphysical claim about ultimate reality to science fact.

[103] These are discussed in David Kalupahana, *Causality: The Central Philosophy of Buddhism,* pp. 177ff.

that in the Indian world-view (and the early Hindu *Rg Veda* text), the origin of all things is so far in the distant past that not even the gods (*devas*) know the answers to these questions.

Questions about the *atman* are misleading because human beings do not have anything like an *atman*, an eternal unchanging inner essence which is self-existent. Consider "Bob Zeuschner weighs ten pounds" and "Bob Zeuschner does not weigh ten pounds." The first is false, the second is true. Now consider "A unicorn weighs ten ponds," and "a unicorn does not weigh ten pounds." There is something quite different about each; neither is true. Next consider the statement: "the present King of France resides in Paris." This is not true, and it is not false either—there is no such thing as the "present King of France." Any question asking about where the present King of France is located, is misleading or perhaps badly worded. Any question asking how the *atman* is related to the empirical personality is similarly misleading or badly worded.[104]

Questions about the person who has realized nirvana (the *arhat*) become more complicated. Is nirvana a place? Is it some sort of transcendental state realized after death? The Buddha is quoted as stating that "The person who has attained the goal is without measure."[105] This suggests that there is no way of knowing the answer to this question. However, in sutra 63 of the *Majjhima-nikaya*, we find another response to these ten unanswered questions: the parable of the poisoned arrow.

The Parable of the Poisoned Arrow

The student Malunkyaputta asks these ten questions of the Buddha, ten questions about the universe, about life after death, and the soul (*atman*), and Buddha replies:

Malunkyaputta, any one who should say "I will not lead the religious life under the Blessed One until The Blessed One shall elucidate to me either that the world is eternal, or that the world is not eternal, that the world is finite, that the world is infinite, that the *atman* and body are identical, that the *atman* is one thing and the body another, that the *arhat* exists after death, that the *arhat* does not exist after death . . . or that the *arhat* neither exists nor does not exist after death"—that person would die, Malunkyaputta, before the Tathagata[106] had ever elucidated this to him.

It is as if, Malunkyaputta, a man had been wounded by an arrow thickly smeared with poison, and his friends and companions, his relatives and kinfolk, were to procure for him a physician or surgeon; and the sick man were to say "I will not have this arrow taken out until I have learned whether the man who wounded me belonged to the warrior caste, or to the Brahmin caste, or to the agricultural caste, or to the menial caste."

Or again he were to say "I will not have this arrow taken out until I have learnt whether the man who wounded me was tall, or short, or of middle height." . . .

Or again he were to say, "I will not have this arrow taken out until I have learnt whether the man who wounded me was from this or that village, or town, or city." . . .

Or again he were to say, "I will not have this arrow taken out until I have learnt whether the arrow which wounded me was an ordinary arrow, or a claw-headed arrow, or a *vekanda*, or an iron arrow, or a calf-tooth arrow, or a *karavirapatta*." That man would die, Malunkyaputta, without ever having learnt this. . . .

Accordingly, Malunkyaputta, always bear in mind what it is that I have not elucidated, and what it is that I have elucidated. . . .

---

[104] Early Buddhists who were forest ascetics did not perform funerary rituals.

[105] *Ibid.*, p. 179.

[106] As described before, this term "Tathagata" is used of the Buddha and means "One who comes thus."

And what, Malunkyaputta, have I elucidated? *Duhkha*, Malunkyaputta, have I elucidated; the origin of *duhkha*, have I elucidated; the cessation of *duhkha* have I elucidated. And why, Malunkyaputta, have I elucidated this? Because, Malunkyaputta, this does profit, has to do with the fundamentals of religion, and tends to aversion, absence of passion, cessation, quiescence, knowledge, supreme wisdom, and Nirvana. Accordingly, Malunkyaputta, bear always in mind what it is that I have not elucidated and what it is that I have elucidated.[107]

To paraphrase, the Buddha is telling Malunkyaputta that if he wants to know how to lessen or eliminate *duhkha*, then he has come to the right teacher. If Malunkyaputta wants answers to questions about the ultimate nature of reality or human existence, then he should go elsewhere, because the focus of the Buddha is upon lessening *duhkha* and attaining nirvana.[108] Even if the student gets detailed and complex answers to ultimate metaphysical questions, they merely provoke more discussion and these answers will not lessen *duhkha*, so the Buddha does not answer these sorts of questions.[109] In another response to the question about the *atman*, the Buddha points to a fire and asks the questioner, when the fire has gone out, has gone away, in which direction did it go? Did the fire go east, west, north, south, up, or down? To answer in any of these options would not be accurate.[110] The same applies to questions about the existence of the arhat after death. The student acknowledges the insight.

Metaphysical answers to these unanswerable questions (no evidence or observation is relevant to answering them) become a source of dogmatic attachment, and dogma and attachment are not conducive to making progress lessening *duhkha*. Rather, they increase frustration and misery.

For the Buddhas, liberating knowledge is not to be sought in the solution to the great philosophical problems which, for all time, have preoccupied the human mind: Is the world of beings eternal or transitory? limited or unlimited? Does the holy one emancipated from desire exist or not after death? Is the life principle the same as or different from the body? The Buddhas have placed these difficult questions among the "undetermined points" on which they refused to commit themselves. These lofty speculations surpass the capacity of human reason, distract the mind and provoke endless discussions. They are of purely theoretical interest and do not culminate in any practical result . . . The only really efficacious knowledge consists in the liberating vision of the four Noble Truths: the universality of suffering, its origin, its extinction and the path which leads to this extinction.[111]

---

[107] Lucien Stryk, *World of the Buddha* (Garden City, New York: Doubleday Anchor Books, 1969), pp. 144–149. The original dialogue is considerably longer and I have omitted many of the similar related questions. In this quote I have also substituted *duhkha* for the English term "misery," and put back the original term *arhat* which the translator rendered "saint."

[108] Early Buddhists were sure that the Buddha knew the answers to these questions, but simply considered the questions uninteresting and unprofitable to explain.

[109] It is interesting to note that the existence or non-existence of a single all-powerful creator divinity is not on the list of unanswerable questions. The Buddha certainly knew that some Hindus made claims about Brahma as such a divinity. See the *Digha Nikaya* 24, in Maurice Walshe, tr., *The Long Discources of the Buddha—A Translation of the Digha Nikaya* (Boston: Wisdom Publications, 1995), p. 381. It is likely that questions about a "first cause" was of little interest to Buddhists, as the question "are we born awakened or do we have to cultivate awakening?" is of little interest to Christians in the West.

[110] Henry Clarke Warren, *ibid.*, pp. 123–125.

[111] Etienne Lamotte, page vii of his Foreword to *The Teaching of Vimalakirti* (London: Routledge & Kegan Paul, Ltd., 1976), translated by Sara Boin.

8.10 EARLY BUDDHIST TEXTS: *Tripitaka*

A scripture is a body of oral or written traditions accepted by and used in a religious community as especially sacred and authoritative. As the centuries passed after the death of the Buddha, in addition to the memories of the students, there was a growing body of legends about Siddhartha's life, and stories of the lives of the previous buddhas before him. Eventually, the teachings, sermons, predictions, verses of inspiration, and incidents in the Buddha's previous lives, were all grouped into the *Tripitaka*, the **three traditions** or the **three baskets**.[112] These three are (1) sutras, (2) *vinaya*, and (3) *Abhidharma*.

Sutras are a memorized collection of what the Buddha taught (his discourses), and over the centuries these were collected together and studied. The more scholarly students wrote commentaries on and explanations of these sutras.

As Buddhism grew, monasteries developed and a second tradition, or basket, of documents filled with collections of monastic regulations for monks and nuns, was compiled. This was called the *vinaya*. These were rules prohibiting monks and nuns from such things as touching money, from sleeping on expensive beds, or attending carnival events where singing, dancing, prostitution, and gambling would occur. The *vinaya* monastic texts applied only to monks and nuns, and were not to be studied by householders or by any person who was not a monk or nun. Monastic members of the *sangha* were required to meet every two weeks to recite the *vinaya* rules. Both the sutras and the *vinayas* were collected shortly after the Buddha's death.

The third basket comprises doctrinal summaries and systems of analysis with a philosophical and psychological stress, called the *Abhidharma* (the "higher *dharma*" or "higher teachings"). The *Abhidharma* texts base themselves upon physical and psychological elements (which are called *dharmas*) mentioned in the discourses of the Buddha, and breaks these elements down and analyzes them for psychological significance in human experience. Scholastic Buddhist monastics spent their lives putting every teaching of the Buddha into a series of general categories and then subdividing each category, and finally drawing a large number of correlations between one category and another.

Together the sutras, *vinaya* and *Abhidharma*, are the **Three Baskets**, or *Tripitaka*. The *Tripitaka* is the sacred scriptures of early Buddhism, also called the *Pali canon* because so many of these surviving texts were written in the language of Pali (and not written in the closely related language of Sanskrit). The *Tripitaka* is recognized as scriptural, and in early Buddhism it tends to be fixed or closed (no new books can be added).

8.11 EARLY BUDDHIST MONASTIC COMMUNITY: THE *Sangha*
THE THIRD OF THE THREE JEWELS

We have discussed the first two of the Three Jewels or Gems, (1) the Buddha and (2) his teachings, his *dharma*. The third of the Three Gems is the *sangha* (pronounced san-gh), the community of those advanced followers of the pathway set out by the historical Buddha, including both wandering mendicants in the forest and monks and nuns in monasteries. These groups are the third element in defining a Buddhist.

Taking Refuge in the Three Jewels

When a person becomes a Buddhist, there is a ritual wherein one takes refuge in the Three Jewels. To go to refuge to the Buddha means striving to achieve what the Buddha did achieve, including the numerous virtues of a Buddha. Going for refuge to the *dharma* means striving to master the teachings left behind by the Buddha in order to

---

[112] In the Theravada Buddhist language of Pali, the "baskets" are *Nikayas*; in Sanskrit, they are *Agamas*. It is likely that the earliest Buddhist writings were on palm leaves, and many scholars believe that the "three baskets" are just three separate groups of palm leaves which could be grouped and carried around in baskets.

achieve the goal of early Buddhism, that is, to achieve nirvana, which is the elimination of *duhkha*.

Going for refuge to the *sangha* means seeing oneself as a member of a community of folk striving to achieve these goals. Moreover, many in that community have made greater progress than we have, so we must be willing to learn from those who have lessened or eliminated belief in an unchanging *atman*, reduced anger and lust, lessened self-centered possessiveness and those whose ignorance is lessening.[113]

The fact that Buddha died refusing to leave anyone in complete authority affected the *sangha*. When later followers disagreed with one another over meanings or disagreed over what was allowed, there was no single leader to whom all followers granted authority and who could stop disagreements with a ruling. As a result, various interpretations of the teacher's words did develop.

In the earliest times, the Buddhist community was composed primarily of many different groups of wandering mendicants. It seems as though the Buddha's idea was that monks would be wanderers, beggars, or *bhikshu*, seeking their own liberation and also sharing their understanding of the Buddha-dharma, the Buddha-teachings. This lifestyle was solitary, or in small groups. However, the *bhikshu* would gather together for the fortnightly rites of recitation of rules,[114] and for the rainy season retreat.

During the monsoon rainy season, the custom was to suspend wandering, forcing those who had chosen a life as a beggar, a *bhikshu*, to live together for up to three months during the heavy rains. Rules were established to govern the communal residences of the monks during the rainy season. Eventually, for some monks the wandering stopped altogether and full-time monastic environments developed. These monastic groups, which were scattered widely in India, built permanent structures to take care of their needs. Of course, there were other Buddhists who cultivated the life of the ascetic beggar who did not belong to a monastery, but instead lived on the outskirts of the cities, these people practiced solitary meditation, and in doing so, they were echoing the life of Siddhartha himself.

Over the centuries, different *sangha* groups became more individualized and geographically removed from each other, and as a result the possibility of divergent tendencies became stronger. Those who dissented from the understanding of the others simply went to monasteries which shared their ideas. The different schools or traditions of Buddhism starts here. Over the next three hundred years, gradual divisions began to appear at least in part because of the regional pluralism.

The Conservative Schools of Early Buddhism

There really is no standard term to refer to these early scholastic *sangha* traditions which developed in the first three-hundred years of organized Buddhism. Those students who actually heard the teachings of the Buddha were called *sravakas*, or "hearers." A *sravaka* is one who has heard the teachings of the Buddha and seeks the goal of liberation by following the *arhat* pathway of the Four Noble Truths and Noble Eightfold Path. Over centuries, the *sravaka* pathway diverged, and, according to the tradition, perhaps as many as eighteen slightly different systems developed. A later branch of Buddhism, the Mahayana, referred to these early schools as "Hinayana" Buddhism.[115] However, as used in India, "Hinayana" is derogatory, and means something like "the Inferior School" of Buddhism.

Since there is no commonly accepted term for the earliest Buddhist streams of thought and practice, and those that survive into the present, perhaps we can call them the **Conservative Schools** of Buddhism, in the sense that they

---

[113] The *sangha* to which a Buddhist goes in refuge is not the community of beginners. It is those who have attained at least the first of the four stages described previously. That is, those who have achieved Stream-winner or Stream-entrant, Once Returner, Never Returner, or the *arhat* (arhant in Pali).

[114] There was a formula for recitation of rules and confession of transgressions, which monks performed in public every two weeks, known as *prātimokṣa*.

[115] The first appearance of this insulting term is in chapter 4 of the Mahayana *Lotus sutra*, a text from the first century C.E.

believed that they were conserving their understanding of the earliest teachings of the Buddha.[116]

Some scholars refer to these systems as Pali Buddhism, the early forms of Buddhism which used the Pali language in the scriptures. They could also be called "Traditional," in the sense that they believed that they were conserving the tradition handed down by the elders, the students of the Buddha himself. These earliest schools cannot simply be assumed to be identical with the earliest teachings of the Buddha, because these early schools disagreed with one another on many important issues. Also, there is no way to determine how accurate the written records of these followers are to the words of the Buddha. There are many traditions claiming to represent the original teachings of someone called a Buddha and there are differences among them.

8.12 BUDDHIST LIFE STYLES

As we have seen, in early Buddhism the *sangha* followers comprised three groups, forest monks, monastic monks, and householders.

The **forest monks** begged for every meal, and thus were called *bhikshus*,[117] usually translated as "monks" but literally "beggars." This was the original lifestyle of the Buddha and his earliest followers, mendicants, or wandering monks.

The forest monks tended to be more ascetic than the monastic monks (similar to the Hindu tradition of the ascetic *sunnyasin*). The forest monks stressed forms of meditation and physical yoga and apparently valued personal meditative experience more than textual authority. Often they would wander from one sacred pilgrimage site to another, especially these four locations: (1) the Lumbini Grove associated with the Buddha's birth; (2) Bodh Gaya, associated with his awakening; (3) Deer Park, at Banaras, associated with the first discourse to his five friends; (4) the sacred grove at Kushinagara, associated with his death. These forest ascetic mendicants would wander, begging for each meal, except during the rainy season.

Over the centuries many householders regarded these meditating forest monks (and Hindu forest monks) as cultivating *tapas* (heat-energy) and achieving magical powers, such as the power to read another's mind, the power to levitate and even fly through the air, the power to remember previous lives, and the power to hear conversations many miles away.[118]

The second Buddhist life style was the monks who lived in monasteries, the **monastics**. As we have seen, the *sangha* gradually changed from full-time forest dwelling ascetics to include a community of followers, monks and nuns, living more or less permanently in local monasteries. Their material needs were taken care of by senior monks and by donations from householders, so they could devote their efforts to Buddhist practice. However, it was not uncommon for monastic monks to go into the forest for extended periods. The third basket of the *Tripitaka* was the rules of *vinaya* modified to accommodate these monastics, rules which the monks recited in a group meeting every two weeks during

---

[116] Some have suggested calling them the *Śrāvaka-yāna*, the vehicle of those elders who heard the Buddha's teachings.

[117] This is the Sanskrit spelling; in Pali it is *bhikkhu*. The Buddha did accept women into the Buddhist order; they were *bhikshunis* or women beggars.

[118] These are called the six supernatural powers. One list is (1) walking on water or flying, (2) hearing sounds from miles away, (3) seeing things from miles away, (4) memory of previous lives, (5) knowing of the thoughts of others, and (6) knowing one had eliminated all obstacles. The list in Vasubandhu's *Abhidharmakosa sastra*, is almost identical: (1) shape-shifting and the ability to teleport one's body anywhere; (2) ability to see anything anywhere including future births of people; (3) ability to hear sounds far away and understand all languages; (4) mind-reading; (5) knowledge of previous existences of others and oneself; (6) knowing that the passions were eliminated.

the rainy season when everyone was together.[119] The *vinaya* had rules prohibiting behavior like killing, stealing, lying, sexual misconduct, and intoxication. They forbade monks and nuns from touching money, and prohibited attendance at singing and dancing celebrations where prostitution, gambling and general debauchery might occur. The *vinaya* requires celibacy and renunciation of material goods (except for food, clothing, shelter and medicine).

Householders also had an important role to play in Buddhism. The responsibility of the married householder was to support the forest beggars and provide for the needs of the monastics, and as a result of their donations the householders would generate and accumulate good karma, called "merit." In general, householders were expected to follow the Five Precepts, five basic Buddhist moral rules, but were not expected to meditate or study the Buddhist sutras. Householders believed that by giving food or clothing to the monks and nuns (*bhikshus*), good karma would result which would produce rewards in this lifetime, and a better life in the next lifetime. The Five Precepts are the basic set of moral guides practiced by all followers of Buddhism. The Five Precepts might fall under "Right Conduct" in the Noble Eightfold Path (discussed previously).

8.13 THE FIVE PRECEPTS AS A GUIDE TO MORALITY

For the Buddhists, moral goodness is whatever genuinely lessens *duhkha*. Whatever increases *duhkha* is not good. The Five Precepts are five guidelines to help the householder determine what sorts of behavior in general is likely to lead to *duhkha*. These five precepts are not vows, they are not commandments, and they are not rules in any legalistic sense. These are the Five Precepts:

(1)   Refrain from killing or hurting (*ahimsa*) living creatures (do not increase the *duhkha* for any living thing).
(2)   Refrain from taking anything not given, respect what others have.
(3)   Refrain from misuse of sensual pleasures. Do not engage in intimate relationships which are likely to increase misery and suffering. Do not engage in sexual exploitation. Respect your own committed relationship, and the relationships of others. Refrain from sexual relations with another's spouse, with someone promised in marriage to another, or with someone who has chosen a celibate lifestyle.
(4)   Refrain from speaking untruths; do not intentionally say something untrue. Speak clearly. Speak honestly. Do not claim to know something that you do not know. Speak with non-judgmental loving-kindness.
(5)   Refrain from self-intoxication (including non-medicinal drugs and alcohol) which lessen our awareness of causes of suffering, which distorts our ability to see things as they really are and makes us more likely to engage in behavior which is harmful to ourselves or to others. Of course, self-intoxication can lead to substance abuse, which is a profound source of much misery and suffering.

These five apply to householders. In previous paragraphs, we pointed out that members of the Buddhist clergy follow these five, plus many additional precepts.[120]

Buddhist Morality Applied to Real Life

The Buddhist practitioner who follows these five and lessens ego-centeredness will also develop loving kindness, compassion, honesty, forgiveness, tolerance, contentment, patience, and some self-discipline. Following these

---

[119] These days were called *uposatha*, 'days of observation,' which were held on the days of the new moon, and full-moon days, when the monastic rules were recited by the *bhikshus*.

[120] As mentioned briefly in the material on the monastic monks, there are five additional precepts for Buddhist clergy: (1) Abstain from eating after noon (because the Buddha did not eat after noon). (2) Abstain from watching dancing, singing, and shows (because prostitution and gambling occurred at places where singing and dancing occurred). (3) Abstain from adorning oneself with garlands, perfumes and ointments (because attempting to make oneself more attractive was symptomatic of ego-centered states of mind). (4) Abstain from using a high bed (typical of wealthy and nobility). (5) Abstain from receiving gold and silver.

five leads to nonviolence and harmlessness even to animals Those who practice seated meditation seriously (which leads to insight and calmness) and explore the implications of dependent co-arising (*pratītyasamutpāda*) should be peaceful exemplars of loving-kindness and compassion for all living things. With ego lessened, self-centered pride lessened, with anger and ill-will lessened, such a person will be tolerant and forgiving. With ignorance and confusion lessened, one can recognize how little one truly needs to be secure and content, and such a person develops equanimity and wisdom. Of course, to regularly engage in seated meditation is to develop self-discipline. Thus it is that Buddhists claim that morality flows naturally from cultivating the Buddhist pathway.

8.14 BUDDHISM IN THE MAURYAN EMPIRE: KING ASHOKA

The Buddha died somewhere in the hundred-year period between 486 and 380 B.C.E., and over the succeeding centuries a new political and social order developed. Alexander the Great (356–323 B.C.E.) of Macedonia (north of Greece) was conquering much of the ancient world, and in 326 B.C.E. his troops broke through into the Indus valley in the part of India that today is Pakistan. The military regime which he set up lasted just three years, after which the Greeks were driven from northern India. Nevertheless, Greek (Hellenistic) cultural influences began to spread through northern India.

In 322 B.C.E., a year after Alexander died, an Indian soldier named Chandragupta Maurya drove out the Macedonian Greek armies and then used his army and military skills to found the Maurya dynasty, which controlled most of northern India for more than a century. The grandson of this Indian soldier and warrior was King Ashoka, who was one of the most famous rulers of ancient India. He ruled c. 270 B.C.E.-230 B.C.E.

King Ashoka

Ashoka (Asoka, pronounced Ah-sho-ka) continued expanding the empire of his father and grandfather. In the eighth year of his reign, his armies invaded a kingdom to the south. Written records indicate that some 200,000 people were killed or taken prisoner. Coming face to face with the pain and suffering that he had caused, Ashoka was shocked to his very core. He then rejected military expansionism.

Ashoka adopted a particular form of early Buddhism, Theravada Buddhism, and strongly supported Buddhist ethical virtues of nonviolence, honesty, compassion, and harmlessness even to animals. He prohibited animal sacrifices which were a part of standard Hindu ritual, and substituted Buddhist pilgrimages to holy sites in place of hunting expeditions. He became an enthusiastic supporter of Buddhist monks and Buddhist monasteries, endowing many monasteries with money, land, and food.[121]

As a result of disagreements between various Buddhist groups, he called a Buddhist council at which his own school of conservative Buddhism, Theravada Buddhism, was declared the official orthodox form of Buddhism. Although Ashoka practiced Theravada, he still supported all forms of Buddhism which based themselves on the Three Jewels (the Buddha, the Buddha-*dharma*, and the *sangha*). His reign also supported non-Buddhist Hindu groups as well.

Buddhism Is Carried Beyond India

It is during the reign of King Ashoka that Buddhism grew from a small non-Brahmin sect located in the Ganges valley to spread throughout India, and then beyond into South East Asia. Ashoka sent missionaries all over India, and to Afghanistan and Southeast Asia. According to some texts, a mission was sent to Sri Lanka (Ceylon) under the direction of a family member. Other missions may have traveled to Burma or central Thailand.

He instigated a policy of tolerance for all religions, not just Buddhism. Ashoka placed Buddhist inscriptions all over India, and built many shrines in honor of the Buddha. He even had a fence put up to protect the Bodhi tree from over-zealous followers of the Buddha. Under Ashoka, India entered a golden age of Indian art, and a time of

---

[121] Nayanjot Lahiri, *Ashoka in Ancient India* (Cambridge, MA: Harvard University Press, 2015).

tolerant and humane religious and governmental policy.

During much of the period from about 250 B.C.E. to about 200 C.E. Buddhism was supported by wealthy and powerful merchants and royalty.

THE BUDDHIST COUNCILS

The earliest collection of the memories of the students of the Buddha, called sutras, began in several meetings, or councils, held by followers of the Buddha. According to tradition, the first council was held three months after the death of the Buddha, when, five hundred senior students (*arhats*) came together to clarify the teachings of the Buddha.[122] The senior monks spent the three months going over and reciting their memories of the actual words and teachings of the Buddha. Two of the three baskets of the *Tripitaka* (sutras and *vinaya*) begin as an oral tradition during this time. Different monks were supposed to be proficient in different areas, and they were called upon to explain words and their interpretations.

Approximately one hundred years after the death of the Buddha, a second council was held,[123] but by this time there were no monks alive who had heard the Buddha speak. Different groups of monks provided incompatible interpretations of key issues. There were disagreements about monastic rules, disagreements about the status of and accomplishment of *arhats*, disagreements about the true nature of the Buddha, and disagreements about doctrines. These tensions were not satisfactorily resolved in this second council. There was no one with central authority to determine which interpretations were correct, and which were not, so the council ended without settling these important issues.

8.15 BUDDHISM SLOWLY DIVIDES: MAHASANGHIKAS AND STHAVIRAVADINS

According to tradition, thirty-seven years after the Second Council, another council was held to continue the discussion of issues which remained unresolved.[124] There were issues concerning the rules of discipline for followers.[125] The *arhat* issue was raised again. At the council, the monks argued whether one could achieve awakening abruptly or suddenly, or must it be gradually. One monk asserted that *arhats* were still subject to temptation (but the Buddha was not). *Arhats* may have some things of which they were ignorant (but the Buddha was not ignorant of anything). *Arhats* may have doubts (but not the Buddha). *Arhats* gain their understanding through the help of others (but the Buddha was not helped by anyone). Was the achievement of an *arhat* equal to that of the Buddha? Some said "yes," and others said "no." Was the Buddha a *deva*, a divinity, or merely an extraordinary human being who had achieved the ultimate goal of complete unexcelled awakening? Some asserted the former, and others the latter. The Buddha had died refusing to put anyone in charge, so there was no one with the authority to decide such issues. These and other points of contention were finally settled by a simple majority vote.

---

[122] This book is very highly recommended: Charles Prebish, *Buddhism in a Modern Perspective* (University Park, PA: University of Pennsylvania, 1975), pp. 21ff; see also K. N. Upadhyaya, *Early Buddhism and the Bhagavadgita* (Delhi: Motilal Banarsidass, 1971), pp. 42ff.

[123] There is much discussion about the status of these "councils," and whether (a) they were minor local meetings of a few Buddhist groups, or (b) a major meeting of all Buddhist teachers of the time (as portrayed by legend), or even (c) pious legends with little historical evidence to support their existence.

[124] K. N. Upadhyaya, *ibid.*, p. 42.

[125] For example, could a monk accept an offering of money? The Elders said "no."

The majority group was the **Mahasanghikas,** literally "the majority (*maha*) of the *sangha*," and they declared that the Buddha was more than human, that he was a divinity, a *deva.* The smaller losing group was not willing to accept the vote of the majority, asserting that several of the new interpretations contradicted explicit statements by the Buddha in the sutras as remembered by the earlier generation of Elders (*Sthaviras*). The minority asserted that the understanding of the Elders (*Sthaviras*) was correct, and the majority was wrong. This group referred to itself by the Sanskrit term **Sthaviravadins** (Followers of the Elders).

Although the more liberal Mahasanghikas and more conservative Sthaviravadins agreed on most of the teachings, they did not agree on everything.[126] The Buddha had encouraged his students to think for themselves, and accept doctrines only after they had been tested and found to be true. This led to a genuine tolerance for differing interpretations of Buddhist doctrines, so the two major interpretations of Buddhist traditions existed side by side.

New issues continued to be debated and as a result, both Mahasanghikas and Sthaviravadins subdivided again, until there would be as many as eighteen viewpoints or schools of conservative Buddhism including Vibhajyavadins (Ones who make Distinctions), Sarvastivadins (those who assert "all exists"), Sautrantikas (those who base themselves on sutras) and the group which called itself Theravadins (those who follow the Elders). The only group which survives into the present uses the Pali term **Theravadins** to describe themselves.[127]

After the collapse of the Mauryan empire the new Brahmin rulers supported Hinduism. In the name of Hinduism they looted Buddhist monasteries, and during the upheaval and chaos, new forms of Buddhism slowly emerged which treated the Buddha as a deity. These in turn developed numerous variations, some of which analyzed the nature of the elements of existence into mere processes, and believed that all humans are born fundamentally good with the nature of a Buddha. Several centuries later these diverse tendencies become known as Mahayana Buddhism.

8.16 BUDDHISM SPREADS OUT OF INDIA

During the period between c. 50 B.C.E. and 220 C.E., newer forms of Mahayana Buddhism were encouraged, especially the branches which worshiped a Buddhist goddess of wisdom named *Prajnaparamita* (Perfect Wisdom). It was also during this general period that Buddhism went to Afghanistan and Afghani rulers promoted Buddhism through central Asia, although the form of Buddhism they promoted tended towards the more devotional Mahayana forms.

The many forms of Hinduism were strongly challenged by Buddhist ideas and practices, and Hindu thinkers responded with new ideas and new forms. Hindu rituals that had been suppressed by the Buddhists (the horse-sacrifice, a Vedic ritual) became popular again. The Buddhists had minimized the caste system, but the resurgence of Hinduism resulted in the caste system being reinforced, and there were new developments in astronomy and mathematics, including the discovery of and use of zero and decimals.

This is also the period during which Hindu worship of gods and goddesses became quite strong, and during this same period the ancient Vedic gods (*devas*) acquire most of the images and symbols that become associated with

---

[126] Do not think of this as involving violence as it did in the Western model of Catholics versus Protestants. For nearly a thousand years the two Buddhists groups lived side by side in the same monasteries and ultimately wound up separated by geography. Buddhism has been tolerant of differences in doctrine, and this attitude did allow for a wide variety of interpretations. Of course, Buddhism was not exempt from politicians and others who used religion to instigate violence and establish their own political supremacy. Although Buddhist teachings stress non-violence, many individual Buddhist politicians and others have used religion to justify violence. Indeed, in some countries Buddhism has been confused with nationalism. See Michael Jerryson and Mark Juergensmeyer, *Buddhist Warfare* (New York: Oxford University Press, 2010). Of course, if you judge any religion by the worst behavior of some of its followers, no religion looks good. If you judge a religion by the highest and most noble followers, every religion looks good.

[127] An excellent clear summary can be found in David Kalupahana, *Buddhist Philosophy: A Historical Analysis,* pp. 97–111. For more details see Nalinaksha Dutt, *Buddhist Sects in India* (Calcutta: Mukhopadhyay, 1970).

them in later times. After 400 C.E., traditional Vedic religion was assimilated into popular *bhakti* devotionalism, and goddess worship became important. This is the time period when the secret and magical Tantric forms of Hinduism were beginning to develop and continued to gain in strength during the following centuries. All of these tendencies in Hinduism affected Indian Buddhism as well, and Tantric forms of Buddhism are found by the eighth century.

Buddhism as State Religion

During this same period of 100 B.C.E. to 400 C.E. Buddhism spread along the trade routes of Central Asia to the Far East, past the borders of northern China and into Korea. In many of these countries, Buddhism became an official religion of the state, with many new political implications (especially for India, Sri Lanka, Burma, and Thailand). When a religion becomes the state religion, it adapts to the needs of the empire. State religion will function to legitimize rulers, and will become a vehicle for disseminating popular culture as well as religious culture.

The official religion of the state needs clearly defined texts and doctrines so that it is clear which aspects the state supports and which it rejects. The religious hierarchy tends to move into the empire's bureaucratic structure, so that church and state reinforce each other. State officials become church officials, and church officials become bureaucrats and even rulers. Religious rituals become state rituals.[128] Seasonal agricultural festivals become religious rituals and are state-supported. Pilgrimage sites receive state funds and political figures are appointed to run them and become wealthy. There are ceremonies of sacred kingship wherein the ruler is recognized as a religious figure as well, perhaps a saint or even a buddha. Popular forms of religion prosper, with wayside shrines, charms and amulets. Through these elements, the people are brought into the group, and simultaneously are brought into the imperial order and submit to religious and political authority. The obligation of the government becomes to preserve the eternal truths of the official state religion. The obligation of the religion becomes to preserve the power and authority of the state.[129]

8.17 DIFFERENCES BETWEEN EARLY BUDDHISM AND HINDUISM

Early Buddhism grows out of the combination of a society with Vedic Hinduism and with pre-Aryan meditative and ascetic religious trends. There was a wide variety of practices, and there were other non-Aryan religious practices occurring in the rural areas as well.

Buddhist doctrines contradict several key features of Hinduism. Buddhists assert the impermanence of the personality, and argue against the existence of an eternal unchanging *atman* and they deny the existence of the sacred ultimate, Brahman. The Buddhists rejected the privileged status the Brahmin caste claimed for itself, and rejected Brahmin claims to hold the ultimate truth when it comes to ritual, spiritual practices and insights. In fact, Buddhism denied that rituals and sacrifices were of any advantage in lessening suffering. The Buddha specifically rejected the caste system among his followers, and socially, Buddhist rules minimized caste differences, resulting in more social egalitarianism. In Buddhism, women are allowed into the order as female monks, although in Hinduism women were not allowed to be present for many rituals. In Buddhist literature many women are recorded as attaining nirvana, and

---

[128] We must not think of south-east Asian Buddhism as a rigid sect which held to one set of beliefs and rejected others. Indian religion in general had entered these countries along with Buddhism, and quite often Buddhism specialized in morality, meditation, and metaphysics, and Hindu rituals became central for rulers. Hindu and Buddhist rituals and beliefs developed side-by-side in south-east Asia and influenced one another. Much about modern Buddhism in south-east Asia is easily identifiable as originally Hindu, including numerous gods and goddesses.

[129] The perceptive student might note that these remarks apply to Western religion and political systems as well as eastern.

there exists a collection of the poetry of these awakened women of the earliest era.[130]

Although numerous deities, or *devas*, are mentioned by name in the early Buddhist sutras, these are not morally superior transcendental beings above and beyond this world. Buddhists and many Hindus thought the *devas* exist, as much as fleas, elephants and pine trees exist, but that what set the *devas* apart was their greater powers and their longer life. However, for Buddhist monks, *devas* are without significant transcendental or moral value, so that gods are not essential to the teaching of the Buddha.[131]

8.18 FEATURES BUDDHISM SHARES WITH THE INDIAN MILIEU

Despite the important differences between Buddhism and Hinduism, they both arise out of a common culture, and share many attitudes and world-views. For example, they recognize and share the cluster of ideas relating to karma[132] and the continuing cycle of birth and death, *samsara*. For both Hinduism and Buddhism, each of us is reborn into successive lives.[133]

Early Buddhism and the monastics are clearly continuous with the previous Indian traditions of asceticism (the *sunyassin* or *sramana*), where the ascetic withdraws from family life and enters the forest. Phrases filled with sacred powers (*mantras*) are chanted in Buddhist monasteries, similar to Hindu practices. Despite the fact that in early Buddhism the Hindu *devas* are placed lower than Buddhas and *arhats* (and thereby minimized), there are numerous references to *devas* such as Indra and also goddesses and demons from the narratives of the Little Tradition, or the folk traditions of popular Buddhism.

8.19 SUMMARY OF THE CHAPTER

In early and conservative Buddhism, a forest monk named Siddhartha left his hedonistic existence at home in order to find out how to lessen misery and suffering. He experienced a liberating insight (*bodhi*) into the causally

---

[130] These books are the *Therigatha*, or "verses of the women monks." This is a collection of 73 poems composed by women who had achieved insight. Women are the equal of men when it comes to Buddhist attainment. See Caroline Rhys Davids, *Poems of Early Buddhist Nuns: Therigatha* (London: Pali Text Society, 1989).

[131] Some scholars use the label "Non-Theistic" to describe the Buddhist attitude.

[132] Neither Buddhists nor Hindus provide arguments to demonstrate or support the existence of the cycle of birth-and-death (*samsara*) or karma; both groups seem to merely assume it is true because wise sages assert that it exists. Buddhist thinkers consider their formulation of karma to be much more sophisticated and nuanced than the popular Hindu understanding. If you recall, traditionally there are five karmic destinations into which we are continually reborn: heavens, human realm, animal realm, realm of anguished spirits who are manifest as hungry ghosts, and then the hells. Later in Tibet the heavenly realm is distinguished into two: gods and jealous gods. A clear description can be found in David J. Kalupahana, *Ethics in Early Buddhism* (Honolulu: University of Hawai'i Press, 2007), chapter 11.

[133] Of course, the Hindus assert that the unchanging *atman* is reincarnated. The Buddhists deny this, and claim that the slowly changing interdependent cluster of processes (like a river) continues from one life to another, and is reborn, but nothing permanent remains identical from one life to the next. You and I are related to the self in a previous life the way we are related to the person who used to be us when we were five years old. We share a lot in common with that individual, but there are many changes as well. Ultimately nothing remains unchanged. See David J. Kalupahana, *Karma and Rebirth* (Sri Lanka: Buddhist Cultural Centre, 2006). Other works by Kalupahana have chapters on rebirth from a Buddhist perspective. A later Mahayana Buddhist school called Yogacara asserts that there is an underlying container for the mind, which they call the "seed storehouse consciousness" which accounts for rebirth and for karmic influences. Yogacara is discussed in chapter ten of this book.

interdependent nature of existence (*pratityasamutpada*, dependent co-arising). Using his deepened understanding of causality, he analyzed the causes of misery. He then cultivated morality, meditation, and insight, and with these he eliminated the causes of emotional suffering, thereby achieving nirvana, the cessation of suffering. Siddhartha then taught his realization to those who were interested in his teachings.

In early Buddhism, nirvana is the goal and it is defined as the elimination of the Three Poisons, or Three Unwholesome Roots, which are (a) ego-centered craving, thirst and greediness, (b) hatred, anger, and ill-will, and (c) ignorance or delusion. Causality is the heart of early Buddhism. The Three Marks, or Three Characteristics, are the result of an insight into the implications of causality. The Three Poisons are the *causes* of suffering. The Four Noble Truths are a causal analysis of suffering, and steps to take to eliminate the *causes* of suffering. Nirvana is defined as putting an end to the *causes* of suffering, the cessation of suffering. Thus a Buddha is someone for whom a causal insight into the nature of suffering and elimination of those causes has resulted in a human who is wise, generous, and filled with non-judgmental loving compassion.

Early Buddhism explained awakening or enlightenment (*bodhi*) as seeing all things as they really are (impermanent and arising from prior causes) and as the cessation of inverted views. The four inverted views are (1) the mistaken belief that something is your true self when it is not the self; (2) the mistaken belief that things are permanent and unchanging, or the mistaken view that they are impermanent and therefore not real (eternalism versus nihilism); (3) the mistaken belief that things are *intrinsically* beautiful and ugly; (4) the mistaken belief that things are sources of comfort, when actually possessing those things becomes ultimately a source of discomfort.

When you no longer see things through these inverted views, you see things as they really are and this is called awakening, *bodhi*. The resultant elimination of the *causes* of misery and suffering (*duhkha*) from the personality and the inner peaceful state which results, is the goal of early Buddhism, a life of freedom. Nirvana is the goal, and *bodhi* is seeing things clearly, and this is essential for attaining nirvana.

About a hundred and fifty years after the death of Siddhartha, Buddhism began to separate slowly into many different traditions. Two major traditions of Buddhism survive into the modern world: Theravada Buddhism and Mahayana Buddhism. The roots of each of these are quite ancient. These early forms of Theravada and Mahayana will be discussed in the next chapter.

Many people in the West have been attracted to the philosophical ideas of early Buddhism, have used the Buddhist precepts as an effective guide for moral judgments, and have practiced focused concentration. These are part of the Buddhist monk's life, but in Buddhist communities, popular Buddhism is much more than these features. Buddhism is a religion embedded in the cultures of the Theravadin and Mahayana civilizations. For ordinary Buddhists living a family life, Buddhist philosophy and Buddhist meditation are rarely studied or practiced. For the majority of Buddhists, Buddhism is more a stress on ritual and prayer, devotion, repetition of magical chants, and other aspects of popular religion.

8.21 TECHNICAL TERMS

anatman   Literally, "no-atman," i.e., no unchanging and eternal essence or soul to any thing. Humans are processes which arise dependently.

Ashoka   King Ashoka/Asoka (Ah-sho-ka) adopted Buddhism and sent missionaries throughout India and Southeast Asia. He ruled c. 270 B.C.E.-230 B.C.E.

atman   the unchanging self-existent substance, the inner controller, the eternal soul, according to Hinduism. Buddhism rejects the existence of the *atman*.

bhikshu   literally, a "beggar." These are Buddhists who chose to live in the wilderness areas and beg for their meals, while they attempted to eliminate *duhkha*. The term is also used for monastic monks.

bhikshuni	a female bhikshu.
bodhi	literally, "awakening." To awaken is to see things as they truly are, things arising in dependence upon numerous causes and conditions, everything impermanent and without eternal essence. It is the cessation of inverted views. It is often translated "Enlightenment" in English texts.
Buddha	Literally, The One Who Woke Up, or The Awakened One, and is a title, not a name. There are many Buddhas in Buddhism. When one refers to "The Buddha," usually this is Siddhartha Gautama.
dharma	In Buddhism, one meaning of dharma is the teachings of the Buddha, teachings which are philosophical, psychological, and spiritual.
duhkha	Dissatisfaction, frustration, misery, unhappiness, and emotional suffering. Note that duhkha is NOT the cause of suffering; "duhkha" *means* "suffering." The elimination of *duhkha* from life is the goal of early Buddhism (the Pali spelling is *dukkha*).
hedonism	The philosophical position that the highest good in life is pleasure.
Hinayana	The Mahayana used this derogatory term to designate conservative Buddhism, including (but not restricted to) the Theravada tradition. The Mahayana authors of the *Lotus Sutra* used this as a term of insult, literally meaning "inferior vehicle," or "little vehicle." Theravada Buddhists would never describe their pathway as "inferior" or "junk" and it is a mistake to use the term to refer to Theravada. Some Mahayana Buddhists use the term simply to refer to the early practices and teachings of the Buddha, and are not sensitive to the fact that it is disrespectful.
klesha	hindrance, or defilement. The things which need to be removed to achieve the end of *duhkha*: greed, hatred, ignorance. Nirvana is the absence of the hindrances.
Mahasanghikas	One of the two earliest Buddhist traditions, literally the "majority of the *sangha*." This group held the Buddha to be a transcendent being, a *deva*, not merely a human, and asserted that *arhats* were decidedly inferior to the Buddha.
Mahayana	Literally, the "Big Vehicle." This names a group of Buddhist traditions which begin to arise about a hundred years following the initial division of Buddhism into Sthaviravada and Mahasanghika, perhaps 200 B.C.E.
Nirvana	Literally, to *blow out* the flames of hatred and anger, to *blow out* the flames of ego-centric craving and greed, and to eliminate delusion and ignorance from the personality. The elimination of these causes of *duhkha* is nirvana.
Pali	Pali is the language that is used for the Theravada Buddhist sacred texts. The Tripitaka is written in Pali. Pali is related to Sanskrit but not identical with Sanskrit (Sanskrit is the language of Hinduism and Mahayana Buddhist texts).
parinirvana	The final nirvana, the ultimate nirvana. Used to signify the death of the Buddha.
prajna	liberating wisdom, the insight into reality, understanding the way things really are, i.e., impermanent

and without any inner essence. Prajna is the wisdom that eliminates suffering.

pratityasamutpada	"dependent co-arising," the empirical claim that all events arise out of numerous causes and conditions, and depend upon numerous causes and conditions. It would follow that events are impermanent, that there is no permanent unchanging *atman*, and we experience *duhkha* if we do not recognize these insights.
sangha	The community of those advanced followers of the teachings of Buddhism.
Sarvastivadins	One of the early eighteen schools of conservative Buddhism, derived from the earlier Sthaviravada tradition.
Sautrantikas	One of the early eighteen schools of conservative Buddhism, derived from the earlier Sthaviravada tradition.
sramanas	Wandering ascetic monks in ancient India, including Brahminism, Jainism and Buddhism. A sramana renounces the world and leads an ascetic life in order to achieve liberation. Personal exertion involving meditation combined with ascetic self-control are the tools of sramanas. Sramanic traditions generally dispense with the rites and rituals of popular religion as factors in the attainment of liberation.
sravaka	A *sravaka* is a "hearer," that is, one who was alive when the Buddha was alive, and who heard the teachings of the Buddha and seeks the goal of liberation.
Theravada	The only surviving one of the early eighteen schools of Buddhism, derived from the earlier Sthaviravada tradition. Later developments of the Theravada tradition continue today in Sri Lanka, Burma, Thailand, and other places in S. E. Asia.
Three Jewels	The Three Jewels, or Three Gems, constitute (1) the Buddha, (2) the teachings, or Buddha-*dharma*, and (3) the *sangha*.
Three Marks	These are the three characteristics of reality which follow from *pratityasmutpada*: (1) all things are impermanent; (2) nothing has an *atman* or eternal and unchanging soul; (3) we experience *duhkha* if we do not realize things are impermanent and that we are impermanent (the first two marks).
Three Poisons	These Three Unwholesome Roots are the causes of *duhkha*: (1) ego-centered craving, greed, possessiveness; (2) anger, hatred, ill-will; (3) ignorance, confusion, delusion.
vipaśyanā/vipassana	Insight meditation; focused concentration whose goal is to achieve insight into the nature of reality, that things are impermanent, without an *atman*, and are the cause of *duhkha* if we do not understand the nature of reality clearly.

8.22 QUESTIONS FOR FURTHER DISCUSSION

1) Many Hindus considered Buddhism to be a form of Hinduism, but the Buddhists deny this. What features of Hinduism do the Buddhists disagree with, and which features do the Buddhists share?

2) Briefly explain the Four Noble Truths of Buddhism and consider: is it really true that our lives are pervaded by *duhkha*?

3) The Noble Eightfold Path can be explained in terms of three general categories: morality; mental discipline; wisdom. Explain each these general categories.

4) Right Livelihood (one of the Noble Eightfold Path) limits the sorts of occupations available to traditional Buddhists. What sorts of careers would be available or unavailable to Buddhists in modern times? Could a Buddhist sell used cars? Could a Buddhist work for an advertising agency? Could a Buddhist be a sheriff or *ninja*?

5) What are the Three Characteristics (Three Marks) which follow from *pratityasamutpada*?

6) What are the Three Poisons which cause *duhkha*? Can you think of any other causes of misery or suffering which are not included in the Three Poisons?

7) Many Buddhists would say that *pratityasamutpada* is an empirical claim, that is, it is supported by our observations of the world. Are there any things in our empirical world which are not dependently co-arisen? Are there any things which are self-existing, eternal, self-arising, and not dependent or conditioned by other processes?

8) Some Western descriptions of Buddhism suggest that the goal of a Buddha is to become free from all desire, to be emotionless, to be without any affect. Is this what early Buddhism asserts? Discuss.

A SELECTED BIBLIOGRAPHY

Buswell, Robert E., Jr., ed., *Encyclopedia of Buddhism* (New York: Thomson Gale, 2004). Excellent source of information on all aspects of Buddhism.
Buswell, Robert E., Jr., and Donald S. Lopez, Jr., *The Princeton Dictionary of Buddhism* (New York: Princeton University Press, 2014). Very highly recommended.
Irons, Edward A., ed., *Encyclopedia of Buddhism* (New York: Facts On File, 2008)

Early Buddhism: Original Source Texts

Beyer, Steven, tr. and ed., *The Buddhist Experience: Sources and Interpretations* (Belmont, Ca.: Dickenson Publishing, 1974)
Conze, E., et. al., *Buddhist Texts Through the Ages*, (London, Oneworld and New Delhi, Munshiram Manoharlal, 1995)
de Bary, Theodore and W. T. Chan, *The Buddhist Tradition in India, China and Japan* (New York, Vintage, 1972)
Kalupahana, David J., *A Sourcebook of Early Buddhist Philosophy* (Sri Lanka: Buddhist Cultural Center, 2007) [www.buddhistcc.com] A fine collection of original texts.
Koller, John and Patricia, *Sourcebook in Asian Philosophy* (New York: Macmillan, 1991)
Lopez, Donald S. Jr., *Buddhist Scriptures* (New York: Penguin Classics, 19)
Miles, Jack, and Donald S. Lopez, Jr., *Buddhism* (N.Y.: Norton, 2015) This Norton Anthology of World Religions has a good collection of original sources.
Walshe, Maurice, tr., *The Long Discources of the Buddha–A Translation of the Digha Nikaya* (Boston: Wisdom Publications, 1995)
Warren, Henry Clarke, *Buddhism In Translations* (New York: Antheneum, 1968)

CHAPTER 8: EARLY BUDDHISM

Buddhism: General

Batchelor, Stephen, *Buddhism Without Beliefs: A Contemporary Guide to Awakening* (New York: Riverhead, 1996)

Bechert, H. and Gombrich R., eds. *The World of Buddhism: Buddhist Monks and Nuns in Society and Culture* (London, Thames and Hudson, 1991).

Becker, Catherine, *Shifting Stones, Shaping the Past: Sculpture from the Buddhist Stupas of Andhra Pradesh* (New York Oxford University Press, 2014)

Beyer, Steven, tr. and ed., *The Buddhist Experience: Sources and Interpretations* (Belmont, Ca.: Dickenson Publishing, 1974)

Bronkhorst, Johannes, *Buddhist Teaching in India* (Boston: Wisdom Publications, 2009)

Burton, David, *Buddhism, Knowledge and Liberation* (Burlington, Vt.: Ashgate Publishing, 2005)

Buswell, Jr., Robert, Editor-in-Chief, *The Encyclopedia of Buddhism*, Two Volumes. (New York: Macmillan Reference USA, 2003).This is a highly recommended set with articles by scholar specialists in various areas of Buddhism.

Caplow, Zenshin Florence, Susan Moon, eds., *The Hidden Lamp: Stories from Twenty-Five Centuries of Awakened Women* (Boston: Wisdom Publications, 2013)

Carrithers, Michael, *Buddha: A Very Short Introduction* (London: Oxford, 2001)

Conze, E., et. al., *Buddhist Texts Through the Ages*, (London, Oneworld and New Delhi, Munshiram Manoharlal, 1995)

Cooper, David E., and Simon P. James, *Buddhism, Virtue and Environment* (Burlington, Vt.: Ashgate Publishing, 2005).

de Bary, Theodore and W. T. Chan, *The Buddhist Tradition in India, China and Japan* (New York, Vintage, 1972)

Dube, S. N., *Cross Currents in Early Buddhism* (New Delhi: Manohar, 1980) - a careful analysis of the "points of controversy" in early Buddhism as found in the *Kathavatthu* book of the Abhidharma.

Encyclopedia of Buddhism (Farmington Hills, MI: Thomson Gale, 2004), two volumes.

Gethin, Rupert, *The Foundations of Buddhism*, (Oxford and New York, Oxford University Press, 1998)

Gowans, Christopher, *Philosophy of the Buddha: An Introduction* (New York: Routledge, 2003)

Gross, Rita M., *Buddhism After Patriarchy: A Feminist History, Analysis, and Reconstruction of Buddhism* (New York: SUNY Press, 1992).

Gudmunsen, Chris, *Wittgenstein & Buddhism* (New York: Barnes and Noble Books, 1977).

Harvey, Peter, *An Introduction to Buddhism: Teachings, History and Practices* (New York: Cambridge University Press, 1990)

Hanh, Thich Nhat, *The Heart of the Buddha's Teaching* (Berkeley, CA: Parallax Press, 1999)

Herman, A. L., *An Introduction to Buddhist Thought: A Philosophic History of Indian Buddhism* (New York: University Press of America, 1983).

Irons, Edward A., ed., *Encyclopedia of Buddhism* (New York: Facts on File, 2008)

Jackson, Roger, and John Makransky, *Buddhist Theology. Critical Reflections by Contemporary Buddhist Scholars* (London: Routledge, 1999)

Jerryson, Michael and Mark Juergensmeyer, eds., *Buddhist Warfare* (New York: Oxford University Press, 2010).

Keown, Damien, *Buddhism: A Very Short Introduction* (London: Oxford, 2000)

Keown, Damien, *The Nature of Buddhist Ethics* (New York: Palgrave-Macmillan,)

Keown, Damien and Charles S. Prebish, eds., *Encyclopedia of Buddhism* (Routledge, 2004)

Koller, John and Patricia, *Sourcebook in Asian Philosophy* (New York: Macmillan, 1991)

Lopez, Donald S. Jr., *Buddhist Scriptures* (New York: Penguin Classics, 19)

Mitchell, Donald W., *Buddhism: Introducing the Buddhist Experience* (New York: Oxford, 2002)

Mizuno, Kogen, *Buddhist Sutras: Origin, Development, Transmission* (Tokyo: Kosei Publishing, 1982)

Murcott, Susan, *First Buddhist Women: Poems and Stories of Awakening* (Parallax, 2006).

Olson, Carl, *The Different Paths of Buddhism: A Narrative-Historical Introduction* (New Brunswick, NJ: Rutgers University Press, 2005)

Oxtoby, Willard, *World Religions: Eastern Traditions* (London: Oxford University Press, 1999)

Powers, J., *A Concise Encyclopedia of Buddhism* (Oxford, One World, 2000).

CHAPTER 8: EARLY BUDDHISM

Rahula, Walpola, *What The Buddha Taught* (New York: Grove Press, 1962)

Robinson, Richard, Willard Johnson and Thanissaro Bhikkhu, *Buddhist Religions: A Historical Introduction* 5th edition (Belmont, CA: Thomson Wadsworth, 2005)

Skilton, Andrew, ed., *A Concise History of Buddhism* (Windhorse Publications, 2013)

Strong, J. S., *The Experience of Buddhism: Sources and Interpretation* (Belmont, Ca., Wadsworth: 2002 second edition)

Trainor, Kevin, *Buddhism: The Illustrated Guide* (London: Oxford, 2004)

Williams, Paul, *Buddhist Thought: A Complete Introduction to the Indian Tradition* (London and New York., Routledge and Kegan Paul, 2000)

Early Buddhism in India: History and Analysis

Akira, Hirakawa, *A History of Indian Buddhism: From Sakyamuni to Early Mahayana* (1989).

Assavavirulhakarn, Prapod, *The Ascendancy of Theravada Buddhism in Southeast Asia* (Chiang Mai: Silkworm Books, 2010)

Bechert, Heinz, ed., *When Did The Buddha Live? The Controversy on the Dating of the Historical Buddha* (Academy of Sciences in Gottingen, 1995)

Braza, Jerry, *Moment By Moment: The Art and Practice of Mindfulness* (Rutland, VT: Charles Tuttle, 1997)

Buddhaghosa, *Path of Purification*, (Colombo: A. Semage, 1964), tr. by Vhikkhu Nyanamoli, 2nd ed.

Burton, David, *Buddhism, Knowledge and Liberation* (Burlington, Vt.: Ashgate Publishing, 2005)

Choong, Mun-keat, *The Notion of Emptiness in Early Buddhism* (Delhi: Motilal Banarsidass, 1999)

Collins, Steven, *Nirvana and Other Buddhist Felicities* (London: Cambridge University Press, 1998)

_____, *Selfless Persons: Imagery and Thought in Theravada Buddhism* (Cambridge: Cambridge University Press, 1982)

Conze, Edward, *Buddhist Thought in India* (Ann Arbor, Mi: Univ. of Michigan Press, 1967)

Davidson, Ronald M., "An Introduction to the Standards of Scriptural Authenticity in Indian Buddhism," in Robert E. Buswell, *Chinese Buddhist Apocrypha* (Honolulu: University of Hawaii Press, 1989)

Dube, S. N., "Arhat Ideal in Early Buddhism" in *Buddhism and Peace: Theory and Practice*, ed. Chanju Mun (Honolulu: Blue Pine, 2006)

Dutt, N., *Early Monastic Buddhism* (Calcutta: Firma K. L. Mukhopadhyay, 1971)

Eltschinger, Vincent, *Caste and Buddhist Philosophy: Continuity of Some Buddhist Arguments against the Realist Interpretation of Social Denominations* (Delhi: Motilal Banarsidass, 2012)

von Glasenapp, Helmuth von, *Buddhism: A Non-Theistic Religion* (London: George Allen & Unwin, 1970)

Glickman, Marshall, *Beyond the Breath: Extraordinary Mindfulness Through Whole-Body Vipassana Meditation* (Rutland, VT: Tuttle, 2002)

Gombrich, Richard, *Theravada Buddhism: A Social History from Ancient Benares to Modern Colombo*, Routledge and Kegan Paul, London and New York, 1988)

Gombrich, Richard, *How Buddhism Began: The Conditioned Genesis of the Early Teachings* (Curzon, School of Oriental and African Studies, 1996)

_____, *What the Buddha Thought* (London: Equinox, 2009)

Griffiths, Paul J., *On Being Buddha: The Classical Doctrine of Buddhahood* (Albany: State University of New York Press, 1994)

Gunaratana, Bhante Henepola, *Mindfullness in Plain English: Revised and Expanded Edition* (New York: Wisdom Publications, 1996).

Hamilton, Sue, *Identity and Experience: The Consitution of the Human Being According to Early Buddhism* (London: Luzac Oriental, 1996)

Haldar, J. R., *Early Buddhist Mythology* (New Delhi, India: Manohar, 1977)

Hoffman, Frank J., *Rationality and Mind in Early Buddhism* (New Delhi: Motilal Banarsidass, 1987)

Horner, I. B., *The Collection of the Middle Length Sayings* (Majjhima-Nikaya), Vol. II (London: Luzac & Co., 1970)

Humphreys, Christmas, ed., *The Wisdom of Buddhism* (New York: Random House, 1961)

Jayatilleke, K. N., *Early Buddhist Theory of Knowledge* (London: Allen & Unwin, 1963)

CHAPTER 9: THERAVADA vs MAHAYANA BUDDHISM

Johansson, Rune, *The Dynamic Psychology of Early Buddhism* (London: Curzon, 1975)

Kalupahana, David J., *Buddhist Philosophy: A Historical Analysis* (Honolulu: University Press of Hawaii, 1976)

_____, *Causality: The Central Philosophy of Buddhism* (Honolulu: University Press of Hawaii, 1975)

_____, *Ethics in Early Buddhism* (Honolulu: University of Hawaii Press, 1995)

_____, *A History of Buddhist Philosophy* (Honolulu: University of Hawaii Press, 1992).

_____, *Karma and Rebirth* (Sri Lanka: Buddhist Cultural Centre, 2006)

_____, *A Sourcebook of Early Buddhist Philosophy* (Sri Lanka: Buddhist Cultural Center, 2007)

Kalupahana, David and Indrani Kalupahana, *The Way of Siddhartha: A Life of the Buddha* (University Press of America, 1987)

Kyabgon, Traleg, *Karma: What It Is, What It Isn't, Why It Matters* (Shambala, 2015)

Lamotte, Etienne, *History of Indian Buddhism*, tr. from French by Sara Webb-Boin (Paris: Peeters Press, 1988).

Lopez, Donald S., Jr., ed., *Buddhism in Practice* (Princeton, NJ: Princeton University Press, 1995)

_____, *The Scientific Buddha: His Short and Happy Life* (New York: Yale University Press, 2012)

Prebish, C. S., *Buddhism in a Modern Perspective* (Univ. of Pennsylvania, 1975) (an excellent collection of many articles on all aspects of Buddhism from India to China to Korea to Japan to Tibet)

Pande, G. C., *Studies in the Origins of Buddhism* (1974).

Rahula, Walpola, *What the Buddha Taught*, 2nd ed. (New York: Grove Press, 1978)

Rhys Davids, Caroline, *Poems of Early Buddhist Nuns: Therigatha* (London: Pali Text Society, 1989)

Sangharakshita, Bhikshu, *A Survey of Buddhism* (Boulder, Co.: Shambhala, 1980)

Skilling, Peter, Jason A. Carbine, Claudio Cicuzza, Santi Pakdeekham, eds., *How Theravada Is Theravada? Exploring Buddhist Identities* (Chiang Mai: Silkworm Books, 2012)

Stryk, Lucien, *World of the Buddha* (Garden City, New York: Doubleday Anchor Books, 1969)

Thomas, E. J., *The History of Buddhist Thought* (London: Routledge, Kegan, Paul, 1933)

Thich Nhat Hanh, *Breathe! You are Alive: The Sutra on the Full Awareness of Breathing* (Berkeley, CA: Parallax Press, 1995)

Upadhyaya, K. N., *Early Buddhism and the Bhagavadgita* (Delhi: Motilal Banarsidass, 1971)

Vetter, Tilmann, *The Ideas and Meditative Practices of Early Buddhism* (1988).

Walshe, Maurice, tr., *The Long Discources of the Buddha–A Translation of the Digha Nikaya* (Boston: Wisdom Publications, 1995)

Warder, A. K., *Indian Buddhism* (Delhi: Motilal Banarsidass, 1970)

Warren, Henry Clarke, *Buddhism In Translations* (New York: Antheneum, 1968)

CHAPTER 9: THERAVADA and MAHAYANA BUDDHISM

9.1 OVERVIEW OF THE CHAPTER

Two slightly different yet overlapping interpretations of Buddhism slowly separated out over the centuries following the death of the Buddha. Although contemporary scholars have distinguished as many as eighteen early conservative *Sthaviravada* (Pathway of the Elders) interacting systems, after a thousand years there remained just one lasting system belonging to the *Sthavirvada* group, which called itself **Theravada**. Meanwhile, there was a cluster of new developments which slowly evolved to became known as the **Mahayana** (the Great Vehicle). Historical details are extremely difficult to ascertain, but the earliest forms of Mahayana seem to date to about 200–100 B.C.E., perhaps two- or three-hundred years after the death of the Buddha. Although these two groups shared the great majority of their doctrines and insights, there are interesting differences. In this chapter we will focus on the differences between Theravada and the developing Mahayana traditions.[1]

In comparing the Conservative Theravada and the Mahayana forms, we will note three interrelated approaches to Buddhist practice in this chapter. They are Buddhism which tends to be (a) *dharma*-centric, centered on the concepts, doctrines and texts of Buddhism, or (b) *sangha*-centric, centered on the community of advanced followers, or (c) Buddha-centric, centered on the person, relics, and divine nature of Buddhas.

Although these three were not separate and distinct, there is a tendency in early Buddhism towards being both *dharma*-centric and *sangha*-centric. In this case, the *dharma* in Conservative Theravada is the doctrines contained in the early discourses of the Buddha (and as such serve as the actual speech of the Buddha), and this also includes the third basket of the *Tripitaka* collection, the Abhidharma ("higher dharma") texts. Thus the *dharma*-centered forms place emphasis on sacred texts and philosophy.

The *sangha*-centric aspect concerns itself with the Buddhist community, which ordinarily is the center of one's practice. If one is living in a monastery, the *sangha* is the senior monastic community. In addition to monastics, fellow advanced Buddhists in the social community constitute the *sangha*. The *sangha* community supports the monk and nun in his or her quest to achieve the ultimate goal, that is, to become an *arhat*, one who has followed the pathway laid out by the Buddha, who has eliminated all *duhkha* and achieved nirvana.

In contrast with Theravada, the developing sets of traditions which came to be called Mahayana Buddhism slowly elaborated a new goal. Instead of trying to become an *arhat*, these newer schools will pursue what they consider a superior pathway, the **bodhisattva** pathway, the pathway of universal compassion and universal liberation. The Mahayana will also have a stronger tendency to treat the Buddha as far superior to human beings, superior to the *arhat*, and more like a Hindu divinity, or *deva*. The Mahayana will be a little more open to the possibility of householders and women achieving the goal of nirvana, not limiting it to monastics. Many new and different Buddhas will be added

---

[1] In the interests of clarity, the author has had to simplify the historical complexities of these issues, and the author stressed differences to make clear the ways in which the two major approaches differed. As is true in all intellectual endeavors, however, the actual lines are not as clear or as precise as we have presented them in this chapter, and the traditions overlapped much more broadly than suggested here. Many of these issues are still under historical examination, and leading scholars often disagree with one another on the finer details.

to the Buddhist pantheon by the various Mahayana schools. The worship of Buddha-relics[2] will become a centerpiece of much of devotional Mahayana Buddhism.

New and quite different sutras will appear in the various Mahayana groups, and smaller groups of Buddhists will tend to pick out just a few of these new sutras and focus their intellectual and devotional energies upon those few. The sutra itself can become an object of reverence, separate from its contents.

Finally, the Conservative Buddhist view of the nature of reality was established within the philosophical and psychological speculation found in the Abhidharma texts. Some of the Mahayana will ignore, minimize or reinterpret Abhidharma claims, thereby offering a different view of the nature of ultimate reality.

In 2002, it was estimated that there were about 350 million Buddhists, making it the fourth largest world religion (that would be about 7% of the world). Approximately 62% belong to Mahayana groups, and 38% are Theravadins. It is estimated that there are approximately 700,000 Buddhists monks and nuns, most in monasteries.[3]

9.2 THE THERAVADA (CONSERVATIVE) TRADITION

We have used the term "Conservative Buddhism" to refer to the variety of schools in early Buddhism, not just the surviving group called Theravada. "Conservative" also refers to the Sthaviravadins and the early Mahasanghikas, and several schools which divided from the two earlier traditions.[4] The author's use of the term signifies that these traditions attempted to **conserve** their understanding of the early teachings and early practices of Buddhism.[5]

The earlier Sthaviravadin pathway, and the later Theravada path, was the path of the Elders, the senior monks, the traditionalists. These groups tended to understand the Buddha to be an extraordinary human, and tended to emphasize the spiritual superiority of monks over householders and the conservative Buddhist groups tended to treat *arhats* as having attained the same nirvana in the same way the Buddha did.

Modern Theravada Buddhism (centered in Sri Lanka, Burma, Thailand, and south-east Asia in general) is one of several sub-groups of the Sthaviravadin branch. One distinguishing feature of the Theravada group is that they preserved their sacred *Tripitaka* texts in the Pali written language.[6] Theravada monastics were often associated with

---

[2] Concern with the relics of the Buddha and various *arhats* is common in Asia, and in Western communities as well. Consider that in February 2015 the Lu Mountain Temple in Rosemead California opened its huge collection of Buddhist relics to the public, noting that these bones, teeth, and crystals, were the only known bodily pieces in the U.S. and 'are sacred religious artifacts highly revered throughout the world.' Of course this is not unique to Buddhism. In the West, holy relics of founders and saints is common. Consider the Western concerns with the search for relics from Noah's ark, the search for fragments of the "true cross," adoration for the Shroud of Turin, and with bone fragments of famous Christian saints which serve as centerpieces of many churches.

[3] John Esposito, Darrell Fasching, Todd Lewis, *World Religions Today* (Oxford: Oxford University Press, 2002), pp. 353–356.

[4] These conservative schools argued among themselves over many topics, which were called "points of controversy." These points included the status of the *arhat* (or *arahant* in Pali), the status of the Buddha himself, spiritual stages of development, the meaning and role of the groups of senior monastics, whether or not we possess an inner "person" that was not an undying eternal *atman* yet offered some sort of enduring personal identity, whether nirvana was some sort of supernatural unconditioned ultimate reality, or rather simply an **absence** which by definition has no conditions. One of the Abhidharma books written during the time of King Ashoka focuses on these issues. It is called the *Kathavatthu* and for more information on this one can consult S. N. Dube, *Cross Currents in Early Buddhism* (New Delhi: Manohar, 1980).

[5] The student should note that no single chapter like this can incorporate all the many Buddhist groups and their ways of seeing and experiencing Buddhist teachings.

[6] Pali is a standardized and slightly Sanskritized version of the spoken dialect parts of the "Greater Magadha" region (where the Buddha lived and wandered). There were many Conservative Buddhist groups whose writings were not in Pali.

orange or yellow robes, and put some emphasis on rationality, individual effort, and ascetic self-discipline for monks and nuns.[7]

The more liberal branch of Conservative Buddhism was the Mahasanghikas (whose name means something like "the majority of the *sangha*"), who tended to devalue the attainment and perfection of the *arhats*. The Buddha was understood to be perfect, but clearly *arhats* were not perfect. The Mahasanghikas asserted that the Buddha had numerous superhuman powers and transcended all human limitations. Although both Theravada and Mahasanghika followers had a tendency to revere and even pray to the Buddha, the Mahasanghikas may have been more comfortable with religious devotion (*bhakti*) focused on the Buddha and other saints, thereby making room for Buddhists who wanted to worship the Buddha as a *deva*, instead of treating him merely as an exceptional and extraordinary human being. These more devotional schools were strong in northern India and what is today known as Pakistan. Although the Theravada was not the most popular form of Conservative Buddhism in India, it is the only branch of Conservative Buddhism active in the world today.

When Western scholars of the past first encountered Buddhism in a serious manner, they had a tendency to understand these early Buddhist groups on the model of Christian sects who firmly separated themselves from other Christian sects because of specific doctrinal positions and warred with one another, each insisting that it was the sole possessor of ultimate truth, and each was the only group who truly understood God's message. This was not true for Buddhism. Recent scholarship has revealed that the Buddhist schools, although often geographically separated, continuously interacted and influenced one another. This means that separate and unique doctrines were not as clearly delineated as previously believed, and none insisted they were the sole possessor of ultimate truth.

One area that both Conservative Buddhism and Mahayana Buddhism shared was its relationship with the community of householders, or non-monastic laypersons. The householders donated food, clothing, land, and other important items to the monasteries. In return, Buddhist priests, whether Theravada or Mahayana, performed protective rituals for the benefit of donors and the community of followers. They promised relief from sickness, drought, flood, and other natural disasters. The rituals involved chanting *mantras*, reciting words and phrases of power. The monks and priests participated in and encouraged cults of devotion to images in the hope of receiving benefits from the buddhas or divinities portrayed. All the Buddhists shared a large group of ideas and rituals in common, although different systems had different emphases.

9.3 THE MAHAYANA TRADITION: HISTORICAL ORIGINS

A very loose conglomeration of new and various approaches to Buddhism (later calling themselves "Mahayana") began to appear about 200–100 B.C.E, and continued to develop over the thousand years following the

---

[7] Modern Theravada temples are much more devotional, and more eclectic, than the early forms of Theravada described in this chapter. Popular Buddhism in Thailand focused on the worldly concerns of practitioners is described in Pattana Kitiarsa, *Mediums, Monks, and Amulets: Thai Popular Buddhism Today* (Chiang Mai: Silkworm Books, 2012). On page 2, the author writes "popular Buddhism in Thailand is a large-scale, cross-social spectrum of beliefs and practices–incorporating the supernatural power of spirit, deity, and magic—that have emerged out of the interplay between animism, supernaturalism, folk Brahmanism, the worship of Chinese deities, and state-sponsored Theravada Buddhism." A "Little Tradition" Thai temple was described in 2013 as having statues of Kwan Yin, Avalokiteshvara, Tara, Confucius and Ganesha, and a large white statue of some great physician. The attendee was assured that if he made offerings and prayed all ailments would be gone. There was another cabinet filled with crystals of semi-precious stones and weird rock formations—and people were placing their hands in front of these to get energy. Another shrine was surrounded by children's toys — including a huge stuffed Winnie the Pooh. On the sides were glass cabinets with lifelike waxwork figures of monks, a "bodhi tree" where you could write your name and a prayer on golden bodhi leaves, and numerous other shrines—all heaped with offerings and flowers. Right at the center was a large black image of Rudra the Howler surmounted by a golden Garuda (a bird-like creature) and figure of the Hindu divinity Vishnu or Rama—in front of this, people were offering black candles. Upstairs was another large temple with regular Thai Buddhas and a very large image of the Thai King—next to this was another large hall with many monks and lay people listening to a Dharma talk.

death of the Buddha. There are no written accounts of earliest years of this development. The origins of the earliest strains of Mahayana are not clear and contemporary scholars have several different yet complementary hypotheses. Older theories are slowly being shown to have been based on incorrect assumptions, and new theories continue to arise.

We do know that around the first century B.C.E. there appeared in northern India several groups which offered a broad range of rather liberal interpretations of the teachings of the Buddha. These groups shared some tendencies of the more conservative Mahasamghikas, but they were also influenced by both Abhidharma analysis and popular devotional religion among householders.

In one case a Mahayana sub-group pursued extraordinary elevated philosophic analysis (the Madhyamaka school), and in the other extreme there were Mahayana sub-groups of monks in monasteries who meditated upon and visualized an ideal Buddhist heavenly realm referred to as the "Pure Land" or the "Western Paradise," and that powerful image inspired *bhakti*-devotion among later followers in the Far East (in China and Japan this became the Pure Land traditions of Buddhists).

Although the Buddha had been dead for three hundred years, new sutras slowly begin to appear in these more liberal Buddhist communities. Some of these texts described new and different buddhas[8] in addition to Siddhartha Gautama. One theory about the origin of Mahayana stresses the role of these new Mahayana sutras. Many of these sutras encourage Buddhists to pray to and make worship offerings to these new buddhas. Some tell of the good "merit" which will accrue to the follower who worships the sutra itself. Other Mahayana sutras are quite technical and scholastic, and spend many pages on the minutia of later Buddhist philosophy. Contemporary scholars using linguistic techniques tend to date the earliest of these sutras as several hundred years after the death of the Buddha, and some of these texts are much more than a thousand years following the death of the Buddha.[9]

These new sutras express a wide variety of interpretations of Buddhism. Often the newer texts contradicted other sutras and were incompatible with earlier teachings. It seems as though there was a tendency for groups of monks to create, focus on and venerate particular sutras or groups of sutras. As a result, an especially popular new sutra could possibly have served as the seeds for a later Mahayana school. The Mahayana texts vary considerably, and this may help account for the fact that in the earliest centuries, there was not just one Mahayana school; rather it refers to loose clusters of followers at least some of which focused on different techniques of practice as outlined in different sets of these new sutras.[10]

Until very recently, Theravada Buddhist countries simply ignored the Mahayana sutras. The Conservative Buddhists did not have these Mahayana scriptures in their Theravada *Tripitaka* collections, and believed that the Mahayana groups were creating new sutras to fit their own purposes.

The Mahayana followers needed to defend themselves against this charge, justifying their reliance on texts which were unknown to the earlier Buddhist communities. They claimed that their own Mahayana texts were genuine, and were special teachings which Buddha had given to his most advanced students, and that they were not in the conservative *Triptaka* collections because the majority of his early conservative followers could not understand this difficult and higher teaching. The Mahayana claimed that the Elder monks were persons of low ability and these monks set aside the Mahayana sutras, to be preserved until a time arrived when followers would have the intellectual and spiritual abilities to understand them. The Theravada followers said "nonsense," but the idea took root in the wide

---

[8] In this book we will follow a standard practice of writing the title of the founder of Buddhism as the "Buddha," and those who are not the founder as a "buddha."

[9] Those Buddhists who focus on the various sutras are certain that they contain the authentic words of the Buddha, even if they appear to be several centuries later. There is not just one buddha, and so a later sutra might be attributed to a buddha other than Siddhartha.

[10] This wide variety of genuinely contradictory holy sutras generated a serious problem in later Chinese and Japanese Buddhism. In the early period the Chinese and Japanese did not know that there were so many schools of Buddhism which disagreed with one another. Chinese and Japanese Buddhists assumed that every single Buddhist sutra was the actual words of the Buddha himself. As a result, Chinese Buddhists had to come up with some kind of explanation for the contradictory claims and assertions apparently made by the same holy person. The Chinese T'ien-t'ai school decided that the texts were spoken by the Buddha but tailored to different audiences of vastly different capabilities and insight. This is discussed in greater detail in *Asian Thought*, Vol. II, chapter 20 on Chinese Buddhism.

variety of Mahayana communities.[11]

In addition to groups focusing on subsets of sutras, another possible source for some Mahayana groups may be devotional communities focused around religious monuments, especially those sites which were focal points for pilgrimages such as the birthplace of the Buddha, the Bodhi tree, and the place where he passed away. Householders or lay supporters who gathered at *stupas* (monuments dedicated to important Buddhist sites) took care of the monetary donations, the gifts and offerings to the Buddha, and they engaged in celebratory behavior such as dancing, and singing. These sorts of activities were believed to produce good merit, or good karma leading to a better rebirth in the next life.

However, ordained Theravada monks were strictly forbidden to be present where there was singing and dancing, and forbidden to touch money.[12] Thus knowledgeable monks were not present at these religious sites, and it was householders who answered questions of the fellow householders and visitors. In general, for their sustenance the monks relied upon householders who were encouraged to make offerings to the monastic *sangha* (organization of Buddhist monks and nuns) in exchange for good merit, rituals to heal and protect, and a better life in the next life.[13]

The distinction between the two traditions of Conservative Theravada and Mahayana was slow to develop; monks we now think of as non-Mahayana Conservative Buddhists and monks we call Mahayana lived side-by-side in the same monasteries for centuries. They studied with teachers in common. They chanted common phrases of power and performed rituals. The differences were mostly differences in emphasis and practices rather than differences in doctrines. The distinction for "Conservative" versus "Mahayna" for both teachers and students seems to have been which sutras they devoted the most attention to.

After about five hundred years, this newer tradition began to think of itself as the Maha-yana, the Greater Vehicle, and in at least one important Mahayana sutra, the derogatory term "Hina-yana" (the Inferior Vehicle, the Lesser Vehicle, or the Smaller Vehicle) was used to denigrate the remaining conservative traditions including the Theravada.

Mahayana Doctrines Originate in Theravada

The Mahayana doctrines are not a rejection of or a complete break with the earlier traditions. Most of what we identify as Mahayana has its origin in prior Conservative Buddhist practices and doctrines. Much of Mahayana simply adopts Theravada texts, traditions, rituals, chants, mythologies, biographies of the Buddha, and several variations upon the rules for monastic life. It has been noted that there was a tendency in both Conservative Buddhism and Mahayana Buddhism to deify the Buddha. At the simplest level, to deify someone is to exalt him or her (and this can include entertainers and athletes as well as religious leaders) whether in public or privately. Stories are told about the one deified, and legends can arise. Such a person is now thought of as more than human.

The Mahayana followers tended to stress the positive benefits of *bhakti* devotion or having faith in the Buddha. Some scholars have suggested that perhaps some Mahayana followers felt that the Theravadin tradition had become too strongly focused on monastics, and lost sight of the householders. Indeed, many Theravada monks believed that householders could not become *arhats* and could not achieve the goal of nirvana. The majority of Mahayana schools stressed the possibility of nirvana for everyone.

---

[11] Later, the same strategy will be employed by Tantric Buddhism against Mahayana Buddhism.

[12] A traveling circus with singing and dancing tended to be the locus for gambling and prostitution as well. Buddhists did not think singing or dancing was inherently evil; rather it was inappropriate for monastics to be in the area where unsavory activities tended to occur.

[13] This view is proposed by Akira Hirakawa, *A History of Indian Buddhism: From Sakyamuni to Early Mahayana* (Honolulu: University of Hawaii Press, 1990), although not all scholars find this compelling. For an excellent summary of a variety of positions, see Gregory Schopen, "Mahayana" in Robert E. Buswell, Jr., ed., *Encyclopedia of Buddhism* (New York: Macmillan and Thompson-Gale, 2004), Vol. 2, pp. 492–499.

CHAPTER 9: THERAVADA vs MAHAYANA BUDDHISM

Although Theravada accepted that the Buddha had achieved the ultimate nirvana and thus was gone, Mahayana disagreed. Perhaps in response to the devotional needs of householders, Mahayana asserted that the Buddha, and other buddhas, could be prayed to, meditated upon, and experienced in visions. Mahayana created a rich Buddha-centered mythology.

Mahayana Groups Organize Around Scriptures

Several very general tendencies (not yet schools or traditions) of Mahayana Buddhism developed slowly, focusing on new sutras and the accompanying commentary literature. These traditions included a broad range of practices. As mentioned previously, there were some monks in monasteries who stressed a group of texts called the Pure Land sutras, which was a rather *bhakti*-devotional Buddha-centered form of Buddhism emphasizing visualizing various Buddhist paradises, praying to and worshiping the historical Buddha, and other buddhas and various supernatural beings called bodhisattvas (beings who aspired to the full awakening of the Buddha). This was not a particularly popular form of Buddhism in India.

In addition, some more philosophical Mahayana followers calling themselves "Middlers," or Madhyamikas,[14] stressed a collection of sutras called the *Prajna-paramita* (the perfect wisdom which carries one over to the other shore). The writings of the Madhyamika thinkers offered a very analytic and philosophical form of Buddhism, based upon insights explained by a great Buddhist philosopher named Nagarjuna (c. 150–250 C.E.), which he derived from the *Prajna-paramita* collection of sutras.

A few hundred years after the growth of Madhyamaka, another group diverged which accepted the Madhyamaka insights, but believed that the Madhyamaka had mistakenly overlooked the importance of meditation and ignored the centrality of the mind. This tradition became known as *Yogachara* or *Yogacara* ("one who practices yoga" pronounced yog-AH-CH-ara), or *Vijnapti-matrata* ("mind-only" or "consciousness-only"). This form is also known as Buddhist idealism, that ideas shape our experience of the world. Yogacara argues that for human beings, knowledge of all that exists is completely dependent upon consciousness. It is based on the idea that there must be some part of human consciousness which is not tainted by ignorance and error, and this is what makes awakening possible.

Meanwhile, some new and different Buddhist Mahayana sutras appeared which made reference to something they called *Tathagata-garbha*, popularly referred to as "Buddha-nature." The assertion was that all living beings have *Tathagata-garbha* or buddha-nature, and have the inborn capacity of a buddha, and therefore can achieve buddhahood by realizing this inborn buddha-nature. This was a new Buddhist tradition just beginning to develop.

The last Mahayana group to appear in India focused around an entirely new class of Buddhist texts, called Tantras. This group, the *Vajrayana* (Diamond or Thunderbolt Vehicle), began to develop shortly before Buddhism diminished in importance in India. In many respects it seems similar to Tantric Hinduism which developed at the very same time in India.[15]

The first four general strains of Mahayana Buddhism gradually flowed into China, Korea, Japan, and other places in S. E. Asia. The devotional strain, Pure Land Buddhism became especially important in Korea and Japan. The analytic philosophical Nagarjuna strain had a great influence upon many of the Chinese schools, and especially the Ch'an/Zen schools and the Tibetan traditions. The Tantric Vajrayana form of Mahayana will come to dominate in Tibet and Nepal.

---

[14] The Buddhist school is called Madhyamaka; those who belong to the school are called Madhyamikas. This is analogous to Buddhism, and those who follow, Buddhists.

[15] It is important to note that the followers of the Vajrayana are quite certain that the Buddha himself taught the Tantric Buddhism to his most capable students, and would reject the idea that non-Buddhist Tantric ideas associated with the worship of Shiva had any influence over their fundamental insights. However, for scholars the evidence of influence of Shaivite Hinduism seems reasonably convincing.

CHAPTER 9: THERAVADA vs MAHAYANA

These various Mahayana traditions will be examined in detail in the next chapter. In this chapter, we will focus on outlining the most significant differences between the two traditions of Theravada and early Mahayana. We will begin with a comparison of (a) the goal of the Theravadin versus the goals for a Mahayana follower, (b) the attitude towards awakening in both traditions, (c) the attitude towards the status of the Buddha, (d) the sacred books of the two traditions, (e) and the attitudes towards the nature of reality.

9.4 THE GOAL OF THE THERAVADA: THE *ARHAT*

As we discussed in the previous chapter, the early Buddhist community used the term *arhat* to refer to one who followed the pathway laid down by the Buddha and ultimately achieved *bodhi* (awakening, enlightenment) and put an end to *duhkha*, thereby achieving nirvana.

> It seems that originally Arhat was a popular appellation given to ascetics. In Buddhism, however, it assumed a technical significance as denoting only the fully and finally emancipated saints. The Buddha is generally called an Arhat. In the earliest Buddhist usage, Buddhahood and Arhatship are so closely allied that it is difficult to draw any significant distinction between the two.[16]

For the early Buddhists, an *arhat* has achieved what the Buddha achieved. However, whereas the Buddha struggled and then found the path by himself, without a teacher, an *arhat* is the one who follows the pathway laid down by the Buddha yet nevertheless arrives at the same nirvana that the Buddha achieved.[17]

9.5 THE GOAL OF THE MAHAYANA: THE BODHISATTVA

The Mahayana groups acknowledged that an *arhat* had achieved nirvana and achieved liberation from the cycle of *samsara*. However, the Mahayana groups were certain the Buddha was a supernatural being, far superior to a fully-human *arhat*. They asserted that being an enlightened buddha was far more than the mere cessation of *duhkha*. Mahayana agreed that the *arhat* had put an end to suffering, but claimed that the *arhat* did not achieve the highest most complete full awakening of the omniscient Buddha. The Mahayana tradition offered what it considered a higher and more noble goal, and thus treated an *arhat* as considerably less than a buddha.

The Theravada's ideal was an *arhat*, but the Mahayana ideal was a **bodhisattva**.[18] A bodhisattva is a being (-*sattva*) who aspires to the full awakening of the Buddha (*bodhi*). A bodhisattva does ***not*** aspire to be an *arhat*, but aspires to surpass the *arhat* and become a fully awakened buddha. The bodhisattva path included both devotional and intellectual elements.

What puts one on the path to being a bodhisattva is a compassionate vow to help liberate all living beings from *duhkha* (a vow of altruism), a vow to eliminate all obstacles (the practice of morality), and a vow to exceed the achievement of an *arhat* and actually become an omniscient buddha (a vow of wisdom). The motive which the bodhisattva is trying to cultivate is altruistic loving compassion for all living things. The bodhisattva is supposed to

---

[16] S. N. Dube, "Arhat Ideal in Early Buddhism," pp. 50–51, in *Buddhism and Peace: Theory and Practice* (Honolulu: Blue Pine, 2006). ed. Chanju Mun.

[17] Paraphrased from David Kalupahana, *Buddhist Philosophy: A Historical Introduction* (Honolulu: University of Hawaii Press, 1976), p. 114.

[18] The term "bodhisattva" appears in conservative Buddhism and Theravada, but there it referred to the previous merit-filled lives of Siddhartha Gautama before he attained final awakening. In previous lives, Siddhartha was a being (-*sattva*) who aspired to awakening (*bodhi*).

seek awakening for the sake of others and not for selfish reasons.[19] The bodhisattva becomes the ideal role model and goal for Mahayana Buddhism.

Some Mahayana followers made the rather surprising claim that the goal of becoming an *arhat* is fundamentally selfish. Why selfish? Mahayana agrees that the *arhat* has eliminated his or her own *duhkha* and achieved nirvana. Nirvana is liberation from *samsara*, the cycle of birth-and-death. That means that the *arhat* will never be reborn. After death, the *arhat* will not return to this world of suffering in his or her future lives. The Mahayana claimed that the more compassionate goal, the more altruistic goal, would be to continue to return to the cycle of birth-and-death to help liberate **all living beings**—lifetime after lifetime. Mahayana asserted that because an *arhat* does not return to *samsara* for another life where he could help others who suffer, the *arhat* must be selfish. The Mahayana understood their goal to be a bodhisattva, someone who will return to the cycle of birth-and-death out of loving compassion. Therefore the Mahayana concluded that the *arhat* is not on the same level of altruistic compassion as a Buddha.

Beginning the Bodhisattva Pathway

One begins the Mahayana bodhisattva path when one takes the bodhisattva vow to liberate all living beings.[20] That is all it takes to become a bodhisattva. If you take that vow, then you are a bodhisattva, but you are a bodhisattva only on level one. Of course, there are numerous stages along the way, and the bodhisattva path only terminates when one goes from being a beginning-stage bodhisattva to becoming a fully awakened buddha. An awakened buddha understands the true nature of reality, that both (a) selves are empty of inner unchanging *atman*, and (b) that all things are empty of inner unchanging essences.

Thus, according to the Mahayana traditions, a bodhisattva is a human being who, from one life to the next, continues to work on achieving the full and complete awakening of the Buddha. In the course of this practice, the bodhisattva is reborn over and over, and although, at the higher levels of achievement, he or she could achieve the inferior nirvana of the *arhat*, instead, motivated by compassionate love for all living things, the bodhisattva remains in *samsara* (the cycle of birth and death) to achieve the much more difficult goal of complete Buddhahood.

Because of this, the bodhisattva is able to help living beings for all of those additional lifetimes. This makes the bodhisattva a hero of extraordinary compassion. Lifetime after lifetime, the insight of the bodhisattva continually deepens, while he or she continues doing deeds which help others to lessen *duhkha*. In helping others, the bodhisattva generates oceans of good karma or merit. In fact, after many lifetimes advanced bodhisattvas are supposed to have acquired miraculous powers and abilities, and have also developed immense compassion.[21]

The Image of the Raft

An image used in Mahayana is that of the raft which carries passengers from this shore (*duhkha*) to the other shore (nirvana). Out of compassion, the bodhisattva chooses to be the pilot of the raft or driver of the vehicle, not merely a passenger on the raft. After piloting, guiding and carrying one load of passengers from *dukkha* to the other

---

[19] The Mahayana interpreted the goal of the *arhat* as striving to achieve an end to *duhkha*, but Mahayana asserted that the *arhat* was not concerned with lessening the *duhkha* of others.

[20] We might note that contemporary Western Buddhists often interpret this vow as liberating individuals from social *duhkha* as well as individual pain and suffering. This then encourages social activism, with the bodhisattva attempting to change social conditions so that misery is minimized. This would involve becoming an altruistic society. To achieve an altruistic society involves changing from a society that idolizes individual wealth and acquisitions, and encourages purely personal satisfactions, which Buddhism would think a self-centered pursuit of goods and fame. This in turn encourages greed and envy, which Buddhism considers sources of *duhkha*.

[21] There are stories of bodhisattvas engaging in violence in order to prevent others from causing great harm. This will lessen the suffering of others, and this raises interesting questions about the morality of the bodhisattva.

shore of nirvana, the bodhisattva-pilot chooses to return the raft back to the original shore, and pick up a new batch of passengers. The bodhisattva chooses be reborn and return to the world of *dukkha*. Even though the advanced bodhisattva knows how to escape *samsara*, the realm of human suffering, he or she is seeking the perfection of buddhahood and in all the additional lifetimes this requires, the compassionate bodhisattva is continually reborn and continually helps living beings lessen or escape *duhkha*. Some Mahayana texts portray the bodhisattva as postponing entrance into final buddhahood because of his or her compassion for all beings, because of her desire to help all living beings.

According to the Mahayana, the bodhisattva pathway is a path of spiritual growth for the follower. The bodhisattva pathway encourages each person to discover the perfect quality of buddha-nature within. The foundation for this bodhisattva path is ethical discipline, a commitment to a life of non-violence and compassionate selfless service to others. The bodhisattva pursues the goal of full awakening and works incessantly for the welfare and salvation of all beings, while offering praise and flowers to the Buddha, and cultivating sympathetic delight in the merit of the buddhas and bodhisattvas. It is clear that for many Mahayana followers, the bodhisattva path is a *bhakti* devotional path, and the bodhisattva an ideal role model.

The most advanced bodhisattvas do not merely live on earth; they occupy heavenly realms and have extraordinary powers. In Mahayana, they become objects of worship, like Hindu gods or *devas*. Bodhisattvas will help those who call on them for help, or who pray to them, or offer sacrifices to them.[22] In fact, for the majority of Mahayana groups, different bodhisattva images have a tendency to replace Shakyamuni, the "sage of the Shakya clan" (Siddhartha), as the central image of Mahayana Buddhism. There are countless numbers of buddhas and bodhisattvas, each of whom will assist you if you ask with loving devotion.

The Two Functions of the Bodhisattva in Mahayana Buddhism

We can see that bodhisattvas fulfill at least two very different functions in Mahayana Buddhism. The first is to serve as a practical **role model** of compassion for those who aspire to follow the Mahayana path and take a vow to become a bodhisattva. The second function is to serve as a **supernatural helper** and locus for **devotion and worship**, thus serving a function similar to a Hindu *deva*, or an angel or a saint in Western religions.

9.6 METHODS TO ACHIEVE THE GOALS

THERAVADA METHODS

The primary Theravada methods for achieving the status of an *arhat* are the three clusters of techniques of the Noble Eightfold Path: (1) morality; (2) mental discipline; (3) insight or wisdom. These lead to nirvana, the cessation of dissatisfaction, frustration, and suffering (*duhkha*). Like the other Indian religions who believed in the supernatural powers generated from repeated sounds, the early Buddhists also utilized the technique of chanting words and phrases of power, that is, *mantras* or mantra-like devices. For example, the conservative Mahasanghikas utilized phrases that were chanted and were thought to provide protection.[23] The Theravada Buddhists chanted constantly repeated formulas to prevent or cure diseases, to preserve peace, and for other benefits. Certainly the primary methods involved meditation to bring about a peaceful mind, and meditation which cultivates insight into the nature of reality.

---

[22] In this respect, bodhisattvas come to resemble Hindu *devas* and also have some similarity with the role of a "guardian angel" in Western religion.

[23] Agehananda Bharati, *The Tantric Tradition* (New York: Anchor Books, 1970), p. 104.

MAHAYANA METHODS

The Mahayana did not put much emphasis upon the texts of the Elders (the *Tripitaka*), and so the stress upon the Noble Eightfold Path became weaker. The Mahayana goal was not to become an *arhat*, but rather to become a bodhisattva. Both early Theravada and Mahayana shared the "four immeasurables,"[24] which include loving kindness, compassion, empathetic joy, and equanimity. However, Mahayana needed additional techniques to enable the student to surpass the *arhat* goal, and such techniques were devised. The characteristic compassion of a bodhisattva can be achieved in the cultivation of the "four immeasurables," but the primary methods for the Mahayana still included devotion combined with focused concentration or meditation,[25] done for the two-fold purpose of calming the mind and achieving insight into the nature of reality. Like the Theravada, the Mahayana utilized chanted *mantras* for protection and as an aid to meditation.

The major difference between Theravada and Mahayana would be the greater willingness of the Mahayana to practice devotional techniques like prayers and rituals as instruments leading to nirvana. The Mahayana developed numerous buddhas in addition to Siddhartha Gautama, and these buddhas and various bodhisattvas became objects of intense devotion for some Mahayana followers.

9.7 ATTITUDES TOWARDS AWAKENING

In the conservative Theravada tradition, *bodhi* awakening is difficult to achieve, but it is possible to achieve it in this very lifetime. After all, the *Tripitaka* sutras are filled with stories of nuns and monks who heard the Buddha teach, applied the teachings and then achieved awakening and put an end to *duhkha*. However, most often these stories refer to monks and mendicants, not householders or lay persons. Also, as the centuries progressed, the number of monks regarded as *arhats* became fewer and fewer. The stress in Theravada continues to be primarily on the monk or nun in a monastery for whom the goal is nirvana.

On the other hand, several Mahayana sutras make it clear that everyone can achieve *bodhi* awakening but it will not be achieved easily. For the Mahayana, human beings are born with the buddha-nature, the innate quality of a buddha, but that innate buddha potential is covered over and obscured by anger, hatred, self-centered desires, and ignorance. Humans need to practice morality in order to remove the defilements of anger, ego, and confusion to achieve *bodhi*. However, the Mahayana understood their goal of becoming a perfect buddha as one both exceptionally difficult and exceptionally rare. It seemed obvious to the Mahayana schools that becoming an advanced bodhisattva and then a buddha is much more difficult than being an *arhat*. It can take hundreds of thousands of lifetimes to achieve the goal of buddhahood.

---

[24] These four are common to both Theravada and later Mahayana. Nyanaponika Thera describes these: "These four attitudes are said to be excellent or sublime because they . . . provide, in fact, the answer to all situations arising from social contact. They are the great removers of tension, the great peace-makers in social conflict, and the great healers of wounds suffered in the struggle of existence. They level social barriers, build harmonious communities, awaken slumbering magnanimity long forgotten, revive joy and hope long abandoned, and promote human brotherhood against the forces of egotism." From the 1994 book by Nyanaponika Thera, *The Four Sublime States*, which can be found online at http://www.accesstoinsight.org/lib/authors/nyanaponika/wheel006.html.

[25] See B. Alan Wallace, *The Attention Revolution: Unlocking the Power of the Focused Mind* (Wisdom Publications, 2006), and Wallace's *Stilling the Mind* (Wisdom, 2011), which focuses on Tibetan Buddhist meditation.

9.8 ATTITUDE TOWARDS HOUSEHOLDERS

THERAVADA ATTITUDES TOWARDS HOUSEHOLDERS

In the Theravada, monks are the focus of spiritual practice. It is monks and mendicants who are most important when it comes to achieving *bodhi* and nirvana. The early sutras emphasized the spiritual superiority of monks and nuns who transform themselves with insight and meditation to achieve the exalted perfection of *arhats*. To do so, monks and nuns develop morality, mental discipline, and *prajna*-wisdom.[26] Ordained monks seek to eliminate suffering as the Buddha did, but it is not easy.

Buddhist monks are also ritual specialists, so they preside over numerous Buddhist ceremonies, including funerals. Monks can chant magical words which can protect individuals and the community from malevolent spirits. Monks can provide amulets and talismans to deal with the dangers encountered in the process of life. Monks are the ones who preserve the Buddha's teaching, and communicate it to the householders. The monks provide talks on the teaching on holy days and at sacred ceremonies. Monks may even serve as ministers in the government. Buddhist monks belong to the *sangha*, which provides the opportunity for householders to earn good karma, or merit, by doing things for the *sangha* (groups of monastics). The role of the householder was to support the monks and nuns on their noble quest.

In Theravada, householders in the Buddhist communities were not expected to strive for awakening or practice meditation. Householders were encouraged to donate to the monasteries (thereby acquiring merit) and could hope to achieve a better life when reborn, or even hope to become a monk in this life or a next life if they generate enough good karma. Householders may pray to buddhas, and offer food and clothing and medicines to the monasteries, thereby earning merit. They also tended to believe in the magical protective properties of the chants and talismans obtained from the monks.

In the Theravada, householders were not expected to study the Four Noble Truths, and were not expected to meditate, or study the sutras and *Abhidharma* texts. They were expected to observe the Five Precepts which guide the moral conduct of the Buddhist layperson[27] as follows:
(1) Refrain from killing or hurting living creatures.
(2) Refrain from taking anything not given.
(3) Refrain from misuse of sensual pleasures.
(4) Refrain from speaking untruths.
(5) Refrain from self-intoxication with drinks or drugs.[28]

These Five Precepts are fundamental for an individual to live a good life, but also they can be understood as encouraging a healthy community. Ideally, in a Buddhist lay society, there is stress on respect for the lives of all living things, as well as respecting property and the environment. In addition, the Buddhist householder lifestyle rejects harmful pleasures, such as alcoholism and drug addiction. If the householder follows the Five Precepts, the society composed of such people will itself minimize much *duhkha*. The Buddhists feel that if householders try to guide their

---

[26] Morality, mental discipline, and wisdom are the three components of the Noble Eightfold Path, the fourth of the Four Noble Truths.

[27] The earliest form of Buddhism was primarily concerned with those who had retired from the worldly life and were living the celibate life of a mendicant and the Noble Eightfold Path was originally intended for such people. The Five Precepts is probably a later adaptation for the use of householders.

[28] If a person wants to lessen *dukkha*, then the person needs to understand clearly the causes of *dukkha*. Alcohol and drugs lessen our ability to see things clearly, and in fact under the influence of these we notice a tendency to say and do things which cause misery and suffering to one's self and to others.

lives by these five, they can expect a better life in this life, or in the next life. However, merely following these five is not sufficient to achieve nirvana. Going beyond the householder, the monastic also perfects mental discipline and wisdom, and these are also important to attain nirvana.

MAHAYANA ATTITUDES TOWARDS HOUSEHOLDERS

In several Mahayana sutras,[29] the attitudes towards householders can be a bit different. Although the ordained monk's path seems preferred, householders can achieve awakening, can achieve advanced states of bodhisattva-hood and ultimately buddhahood. Within the Mahayana literary tradition, one of the greatest and wisest of all the Buddhists was a householder, or a layman, named Vimalakirti, described in the Mahayana sutra entitled the *Vimalakirti-nirdesa-sutra*.[30] This entertaining sutra is filled with Mahayana philosophy exemplified with a great sense of humor.

In the Mahayana, householders are expected to fulfill pretty much the same support functions as Theravada, but there may be greater stress on *bhakti* devotion. A householder can call on bodhisattvas for help, and a bodhisattva will fly down from heavenly realms to help those who call on them, or who pray to them, or offer sacrifices to them. In fact, it is not just older male householders, but even women and pre-teens are capable of the bodhisattva path.

9.9 ATTITUDES TOWARD THE BUDDHA

Background for both Theravada and Mahayana

The early conservative Buddhist text, the *Nirvana-sutra*, provides a vivid description of the death of the Buddha. It is clear that for the majority of students in the first generations, the Buddha was an extraordinary human being who discovered the path to nirvana and then established the most effective way for others to attain the same liberation (i.e., the Middle Path of Buddhism). For these Buddhists, the Buddha was a perfect exemplar of the moral virtues: compassionate to the extent that, if you remembered him, said his name, visited some place where he had lived, this could inspire you to make greater and faster progress along the path to nirvana and liberation from the cycle of birth-and-death, *samsara*.

There is another element to the status of the Buddha. There are those who knew the Buddha personally, who studied with him, and some of whom even achieved nirvana. Then, there are those householders who had heard about this extraordinary individual whose achievements went well beyond those of ordinary human beings. Even in the earliest Buddhist tradition, inspirational tales[31] were composed which purported to tell about many of the previous lives before Siddhartha achieved Buddhahood, tales about this teacher whose abilities exceeded those of mortal men. In these tales, even though Siddhartha was not yet a fully awakened buddha, already he was exceptionally moral and

---

[29] Although it is commonly accepted that Mahayana was friendlier towards householders, this is not true for all the Mahayana sutras. Jan Nattier's book, *A Few Good Men: The Bodhisattva Path According to the Inquiry of Ugra* (Honolulu: University of Hawaii Press, 2003) points out that the impression of Mahayana inclusiveness is true of many sutras, but not all. She also indicates that Japanese scholars, who influenced much of Western understanding of Mahayana Buddhism, may have placed undue emphasis on this aspect of Mahayana because East Asian forms of Buddhism tended to prefer the inclusive aspects.

[30] There are several translations of this text, the best and most scholarly being the French translation by Etienne Lamotte, *L'Enseignement de Vimalakirti* (Louvain, Belgium: Universite de Louvain Institut Orientaliste, 1962). This exceptional translation and study has been rendered into English by Sara Boin in Etienne Lamotte, *The Teaching of Vimalakirti: From the French Translation with Introduction and Notes* (London: Routledge & Kegan Paul, Ltd., 1976). See also Robert Thurman, *The Holy Teaching of Vimalakirti* (Pennsylvania State, 2009).

[31] These are the Jataka tales, many of which date to prior to the second century B.C.E.

selfless. Many of these portray Siddhartha as possessing miraculous powers, but he always uses these powers in egoless striving to help humans and animals. These seem mostly folkloric stories, although some appear inspired by discourses of the Buddha where an important moral point was stressed.

During the period of the development of early Mahayana, and for Indian religions in general, devotional activities were becoming more important. Buddhists did not make icons of the Buddha in the first four-hundred years after the death of the Buddha, so the earliest Buddhist images portrayed symbols like footprints (i.e, "the Buddha stood here"), or a wheel with eight spokes (the eightfold path). Devotional images of the Buddha begin to appear by the beginning of the Christian era, between 100 B.C.E. and 100 C.E., approximately the same time devotional images of the Hindu deity Shiva were appearing.

These devotional icons provide a focus for the great majority (who were illiterate) to come and venerate the Buddha, because of his divine nature, his loving compassion and spiritual powers.[32] In the popular forms of Buddhism, Siddhartha is thought of as a great being who has much in common with the Hindu gods like Vishnu and Brahma. Even in the Conservative Buddhism of the Traditionalists, one can see a tendency to elevate the Buddha into the status of someone more than human. Scholars tend to believe that originally this was a tendency for the householders rather than the earliest monks, but some of the Mahasanghika monastics (an early branch of conservative Buddhism) made devotion a central tenet in their pathway.

Buddhist developments competed with Hindu theistic forms of devotion and meditative visualization. Scholars note that in the process Buddhism was slowly becoming more like Hinduism, and in turn, Hinduism was being influenced by Buddhism. This tendency is clearly seen in contemporary Buddhist temples in Thailand, Burma, and South-east Asia. Many Theravada Buddhist temples in north America are quite eclectic.

The Buddha Becomes Divine: Theravada

The conservative Theravada followers did not think that Siddhartha Gautama was the only human to achieve ultimate awakening and nirvana, or the first to achieve this goal. Belief in other buddhas who lived before Siddhartha Gautama was not uncommon for the early Buddhists—but these prior buddhas were not gods and were not *devas*. Rather, they were just awakened beings from previous eras. In fact, Buddhist awakening was not limited to Buddhists only. One did not need to be a Buddhist to achieve awakening and nirvana. One needed to eliminate *duhkha* and see the causal interconnectedness of existence (*pratityasamutpada*). The result was a human who had freed herself of *duhkha*.

According to later Theravada, there have been many buddhas in the past, but only one appears in each world period, and the Buddha Siddhartha Gautama (Gotama in Pali) was the buddha for our time period. The Buddha taught the true *dharma*, and after it was comprehended, the Buddha disappeared into ultimate nirvana (*parinirvana*). For the early generations of Elder monks, after he died the Buddha was no longer in the world and could not be communicated with, could not respond to prayers or ritual sacrifices.

Even if the Buddha himself may be gone, one can acquire good karma and merit by taking a devotional attitude toward the Buddha. In Theravada, a monk can imagine that the Buddha is here and teaching, and this can serve as an aid to meditation or seeking awakening, but the closest thing to the Buddha is actually the community of advanced followers, the *sangha*, and the *dharma* or teachings.

The Two Bodies of the Buddha in Theravada

Speaking loosely, we have the physical body of the teacher himself, and then we have a collection of the teachings of that teacher. The collection of teachings can be described as a "body of teachings." Conservative Buddhists began to talk about the *physical body* of the Buddha, and then they talked metaphorically about the *body of teachings* that

---

[32] A good book on this topic is Robert Decaroli, *Haunting the Buddha: Indian Popular Religions and the Formation of Buddhism* (Oxford University Press, 2004). Decaroli's study collected materials on spirit cults popularly ongoing during the early Buddhist eras.

the Buddha had left behind, the body of teachings (*dharma*) that were memorized by his students. Over time these became referred to as the **two bodies of the Buddha**.

There was the completely human physical body of Siddhartha (called the *nirmana-kaya*, "Transformation-Body"), the physical body that all of his followers encountered and learned from. Then there was another body, the cluster of *dharma*-teachings, the *dharma* body, the "body of truth" or *dharma-kaya*. In the earliest layers of the sutras, the *dharma* body is a reference to the body of doctrines or a body of teachings taught by the Buddha. However, the more devotional (*bhakti*-oriented) sects seized upon this term as referring to a supernatural divinely ultimate body which transcended our world, while the human physical body in our world was reduced in importance.

Maitreya—The Future Buddha

Siddhartha Buddha is the Buddha for our time period, but there is a bodhisattva who will become a buddha and who will appear in the future when the time is right. The future buddha is named **Maitreya**, ("benevolence"), but presently he resides patiently in a heavenly realm where he waits the appropriate time to be reborn into the world. At the right time, he will appear and will teach, and many of his new students will eliminate *duhkha* and achieve nirvana. With a perfectly realized buddha to teach us, we will find it easy to awaken and then teach others.

Maitreya became the center of focus in some Buddhist strongholds in northwestern India and central Asia including China. Knowing that Maitreya will appear in the future, some followers tried to cultivate good deeds so that they could be alive at the same time that Maitreya descended into the human world. With a living buddha to teach one, liberation would be easy. With a living buddha in our world, all the people around him would be affected for the better, world societies would practice virtues and lessen *duhkha* and the key to liberation would be available to all.

Thus, the historical Buddha, Siddhartha Gautama, or Shakyamuni,[33] is the central figure in Theravada Buddhism, the teacher and the inspiration, and he can be recalled in meditation and can be encountered by reading the sutras which give the Buddha's dharma (teachings).

Mahayana Attitudes Towards the Buddha

The Theravada *Nirvana-sutra* portrays the death of the Buddha, as described by his immediate followers, as entering his final nirvana, or *parinirvana*. The Mahayana traditions had a tendency to treat the Buddha as a divinity, a *deva*, which meant that it was not appropriate to think of him as dying of old age. The Mahayana needed to explain why the early texts portrayed the Buddha's death. The Mahayana offered a reinterpretation of the apparent death of the Buddha. He did not really die.

The Apparent Death of the Buddha was merely a Skillful Teaching Device

Only the Buddha's physical-appearance-body (*nirmana-kaya*) had passed away. His apparent death was merely a skillful pedagogical teaching device which leads one to liberation (*upaya* is the name for this skillful teaching device)[34] utilized by the divine Buddha in order to reinforce the truth of impermanence for the Elder monks. However, the Mahayana asserted that the historical Buddha and an infinite number of other buddhas have always existed, and always will exist, and have always been awakened. There are as many buddhas as there are specks of dust, as many as there are grains of sand in the Ganges river. The buddhas transcend this world. The buddhas are omniscient and are perfect in

---

[33] The "wise sage" (*-muni*) of the Shakya clan.

[34] *Upaya* is stressed in Mahayana Buddhism, and a great teacher (or bodhisattva) has the ability to teach in ways which are tailored to the abilities of the audience, teach in ways that can bring the listeners to adopt Buddhist ways, or perhaps even bring the listener to insight and awakening.

every way.[35]

In the pantheon of divinities there are also the bodhisattvas, human beings who have been on the Buddhist path for so long that they have acquired miraculous powers and abilities, and have cultivated immense compassion and oceans of good karma or merit. They tend to become quasi-divine focal points for householders and monks to worship.

Skillful Teaching Devices (*upaya*)

With this new interpretation of the divine status of the Buddha, much of the entire teaching in the *Tripitaka* (the sacred books of the conservative Buddhists) would have to be reinterpreted. Did Siddhartha Gautama actually achieve awakening under the Bodhi tree and only then become a Buddha? Not according to Mahayana. The Mahayana assert that the Buddha's birth and apparent struggle to awakening was just an expedient means, or a "teaching trick" (*upaya*) to inspire unawakened beings to make greater efforts to achieve awakening. By pretending to be a human and pretending to achieve awakening, the Buddha could inspire ordinary humans to believe that it is possible for them to achieve awakening too. Believing the Buddha to be a human being who achieved nirvana, ordinary folk could believe that they too could achieve the goal. And, according to Mahayana, ordinary folk could believe that they too can becomes buddhas.

Use of skillful teaching devices, or *upaya*, is one of the skills of a buddha and advanced bodhisattvas. Using *upaya*, buddhas and bodhisattvas can lead people from this shore of *duhkha* to the other shore of nirvana. The apparent death of the Buddha was an *upaya*, a device to stress the impermanence of all things in the minds of his followers, but the infinite and eternal Buddha himself could never die.

Mahayanists argued that over many millions of lifetimes the Buddha had built up a giant field of good karma which he no longer needed, and which could be made available to Buddhist followers who needed it. The self-transforming "do it yourself with great effort" aspect of conservative traditional Buddhism was gradually being replaced by "ask and receive help from divine buddhas and bodhisattvas" as the pathway of Buddhism. Like buddhas, advanced bodhisattvas preach, teach, and lead us to liberation. The numberless buddhas and bodhisattvas can be contacted and they can perform miracles for our benefit. Buddhas and bodhisattvas can help us through meditative visualization, and we can pray to them and get our prayers answered. Like the gods of the Hindus, Buddhist bodhisattvas reward those who worship them and pray to them.

Some Buddhist texts describe ten stages for the bodhisattva pathway.[36] As noted previously, the first stage is simply taking the vow to help all living beings achieve Buddhahood. At the tenth stage, a bodhisattva is an immensely powerful being, capable of doing miraculous feats. At the tenth level, the bodhisattva is said to enter a *vajra* or "diamond" state with an awakened mind with the power of the diamond. The diamond is the hardest substance, able to cut through the obstacles to the spiritual path. The term *vajra* also carries the meaning of a lightning-bolt, or thunderbolt. The awakened mind is filled with awesome and overwhelming power. The only step after the tenth-level bodhisattva is that of full buddhahood.

The Three Bodies of the Buddha in Mahayana

A later development originally stressed in the Yogachara school of Mahayana is the idea that the divine

---

[35] There is an extensive discussion of the original Pali, Sanskrit and Chinese sources which consider the conflict over whether the Buddha was omniscient in Etienne Lamotte, *La Traite de la Grande Vertu de Sagesse de Nagarjuna (Mahaprajnaparamitasastra)*, Vol. I (Louvain: Institut Orientaliste, 1949) p. 13, fn. 4.

[36] Har Dayal, *The Bodhisattva Doctrine in Buddhist Sanskrit Literature* (London: Kegan, Paul, Trubner, Trench & Co., 1932). See also "Mahayana Holy Beings" in Peter Harvey, *An Introduction to Buddhism* (London: Cambridge University Press, 1990), p. 135.

Buddha has three different ways to appear to various beings.[37] These are:
  (1) *Dharma-kaya*, the Dharma-body;
  (2) *Nirmana-kaya*, the transformation-body;
  (3) *Sambhoga-kaya*, the bliss-body.

Since the Buddha is now understood to be an infinite divinity, then he must possess an infinite body, which Mahayana called the *dharma-kaya* ("dharma body"). For the earlier Theravada followers, *dharma-kaya* would mean the "Body of Dharma-Truths," or the collection of wisdom teachings, but for the Mahayana the sense is better captured by something like "Eternal-Truth Body." D. T. Suzuki describes this body as ". . . the highest being which is the ultimate cause of the universe and in which all existences find their essential origin and significance."[38] Of course, no human being could perceive this infinite manifestation of the eternal Buddha. This means that the Buddha is now a divinity as worthy of veneration and worship as the Hindu gods.

The body which humans could perceive and which taught followers for eighty years, is the *nirmana-kaya*, the "Transformation-Body." Finally, various bodhisattvas and buddhas inhabit countless blissful heavenly realms, and the body that the Buddha uses to enjoy the bliss of nirvana and to interact with these heavenly beings and heavenly realms is called the *sambhoga-kaya*, the "Body of Bliss."

9.10 IMPORTANT MAHAYANA BUDDHAS & BODHISATTVAS

Although in the Mahayana there are an infinite number of bodhisattvas and buddhas, some are featured in Mahayana sutras and gain special importance.[39] Buddhists talk about five transcendent buddhas who correspond to the four points of the compass and the center. These five (plus the historical Buddha, Siddhartha) can also symbolize the various aspects of awakened consciousness.

Six Different Buddhas

Vairochana Buddha ("He Who Is Like the Sun" or "The Illuminated One") presides over a pure realm in the cosmic center, and in artistic representations, he makes the hand gesture of supreme wisdom.[40] About the 10th century Vairochana became identified with the personification of the *dharma*-body of the primordial Buddha. Vairochana thus becomes the Eternal Truth Body of the Buddha.[41]

Akshobhya Buddha ("Immovable" or "Imperturbable") inhabits a pure realm in the eastern quarter and reigns over this eastern paradise and has taken a vow never to feel disgust or anger towards any being—thus Akshyobhya symbolizes overcoming passions. He can be recognized because his hands typically point to the earth, or touch the

---

[37] These three originated with the Sarvastivadin school of conservative Buddhism, but the Yogacara tradition elaborated on that idea in the way it appears in Mahayana. The three bodies also appear very early in the Mahayana *Lotus* sutra.

[38] D. T. Suzuki, *Outlines of Mahayana Buddhism* (New York: Schocken Books, 1963), pp. 73-74.

[39] Taigen Dan Leighton, *Bodhisattva Archetypes: Classic Buddhist Guides to Awakening and their Modern Expression* (New York: Penguin Arkana, 1998).

[40] These "hand gestures" are called *mudra*, and are described in Meher McArthur, *Reading Buddhist Art: An Illustrated Guide to Buddhist Signs and Symbols* (London: Thames & Hudson, 2002). Vairocana's *mudra* are described on page 35 of the McArthur book.

[41] Vairochana is of special importance in esoteric forms of Buddhism. In Japan, Vairochana is called *Dainichi* ("Great Sun") and is the Supreme Buddha, the Cosmic Buddha. Tibetan Buddhists consider Vairochana the primordial omniscient Buddha who created the universe and everything in it, including all the other Buddhas. In some Tibetan Buddhist representations, he is portrayed in embrace with his female consort.

237

earth, an image also associated with the awakening of Siddhartha under the Bodhi tree.[42] Many Buddhists consider him as Shakyamuni or Gautama Buddha.

Ratnasambhava Buddha ("Jewel-Born One" or "Source of Precious Things") is in the southern quarter of the universe, and is associated with the earthly Buddha, and makes the gesture of wish-granting,[43] and is riding on a lion or a horse.

Amoghasiddhi Buddha ("Unfailingly Successful" or "He Who Unerringly Achieves His Goal") reigns over the northern quarter, and is usually depicted making the hand gesture symbolizing fearlessness, and his emblem is a double *vajra*-thunderbolt, symbolizing the awakened mind with its awesome and overwhelming power. In Tibetan art he is sometimes depicted in embrace with his female consort, Tara.

Amitabha ("Infinite Light," the Buddha of the Western Paradise) is featured in several Mahayana sutras, where, as an advanced bodhisattva, he makes forty-eight vows. After lifetimes of supreme effort, he becomes a Buddha presiding over a Western Pure Land, and his followers can be assured of being reborn in this paradise if they call upon him with faith. Amitabha is the personification of Buddhist compassion. A standard image portrays Amitabha as seated on a lotus blossom. The lotus is a flower which grows out of muddy ponds but upon opening, is pure and untainted by the mud. Similarly a bodhisattva or buddha grows up in our muddy defiled world, but remains pure and untainted while still in the world.[44]

In addition to these five transcendent Buddhas, there is also the historical Buddha, a heavenly Buddha whose historical manifestation was Siddhartha Gautama Buddha. He is called **Shakyamuni** Buddha in the Mahayana *Lotus sutra*.

Various Bodhisattvas

In addition to these six buddhas, there are countless bodhisattvas at the highest tenth level. **Avalokiteshvara** Bodhisattva ("The Lord Who Looks Down on the World" or according to the Chinese, "He Who Hears the Sounds of the World") is the bodhisattva embodiment of unlimited compassion and is one of the most important of all bodhisattvas. He looks in all directions in an effort to save living beings from suffering. He is the subject of the twenty-fourth chapter of the Mahayana text, the *Lotus Sutra*. Some myths assert that Avalokiteshvara was born from a ray of light emanating from the right eye of Amitabha, the Buddha of infinite compassion.

The icons[45] associated with Avalokiteshvara[46] symbolize his limitless compassion and protection. One powerful image of power and compassion are the thousand arms and a thousand eyes. The arms symbolize his powers and protection, but also they are reaching out to help anyone who asks. The hands are symbolic of helpful compassion and

---

[42] McArthur, *op.cit.,* p. 37.

[43] *Ibid.*, p. 41.

[44] Amitabha was not particularly important in India, but later becomes of supreme importance in the Pure Land traditions of Buddhism in China, Korea, and Japan, and even Tibet. After death, the Pure Land devotee will be greeted by Amitabha and other heavenly beings, and taken to the wonderful Pure Land Paradise of the West. As Chinese forms of Buddhism came to influence south-east Asian Buddhism, Amitabha statues are found in many Theravada temples in Thailand.

[45] It is interesting to note that icons of the various buddhas tend to wear robes associated with beggars and monastics. Unlike the buddhas, the bodhisattvas tend to be depicted wearing earrings, bangles, garlands, necklaces, and other forms of decoration, and wear the garments of the aristocracy. See *In the Footsteps of the Buddha* (Hong Kong: University of Hong Kong, 1998), p. 24.

[46] David Snellgrove points out that one title of Avalokiteshvara is the same as Shiva's title, "Lord of the World." David Snellgrove, *Indo-Tibetan Buddhism* (Boston: Shambhala, 2002), p. 61.

represent his ability to lead all to liberation. Sometimes the hands have eyes in them, symbolizing omniscience and his constant efforts to see and to know when human beings need his assistance. His hands often hold a blue lotus blossom and a rosary.[47] After the third century C.E. Avalokiteshvara will become the most popular of all the great bodhisattvas, with sutras devoted to him[48] and cults devoted to him.[49]

Maitreya Bodhisattva (Bodhisattva of Benevolence, or All-Encompassing Love) has already been discussed because in Theravada he is to become the buddha of the future. He is important in Mahayana as well, where he is venerated as the next earthly buddha. He is currently a bodhisattva but will become a buddha and the successor to Siddhartha Gautama. In China he has absorbed many popular myths about lucky folk divinities, and is often associated with the chubby "Laughing Buddha." In Tibet, he is expected in about 30,000 years.[50]

Manjusri

Manjusri Bodhisattva ("He Who Is Noble And Gentle" or "Beautiful and Virtuous") is the bodhisattva who resides in the east, and who is the personification of liberating wisdom (*prajna*). Seated on a lotus, he carries two items. One is a sword (which cuts through the bonds which tie us to ignorance and confusion) and the other a scripture (the *Prajnaparamita* collection of Mahayana sutras). He is sometimes portrayed as riding a white lion whose roar is a symbol of the Buddha's wisdom. He is the symbol for awakening as manifested in intellectual endeavor, that is, *prajna*, perfect wisdom. In the same way that wisdom is paired with compassion, Manjusri is often paired with the next bodhisattva, Samantabhadra.[51]

Samantabhadra is the Bodhisattva of Universal Knowledge who rides a white six-tusked elephant (the elephant symbolizes the power of wisdom to overcome all obstructions). Very generally he is considered the bodhisattva of awakened activity, or activated wisdom, applied in the world. His other icons include a wish-fulfilling jewel, and the lotus (Japanese Buddhists tend to associate Samantabhadra, who they call Fugen, as the patron of the *Lotus sutra* and a prolonger of life).[52]

There is also **Vajrapani** ("Thunderbolt-in-Hand") who in early Mahayana texts is a protector of higher stage bodhisattvas. He represents the fearsome power of the buddhas, and he removes obstacles and conquerors demons. In later Tantric forms of

---

[47] It has been pointed out that the Christian rosary, which becomes popular in Christianity in the fourteenth century, may have had its origins in the much earlier use of a rosary in Indian religions.

[48] The *Prajnaparamita sutra* entitled the *Heart sutra* is taught by Avalokiteshvara.

[49] In China, Avalokitesvara is venerated as Kuan-yin (Guanyin in Pinyin, Kannon in Japanese, Kwanum in Korean) and is generally considered female. In Tibetan forms of Buddhism, Avalokitesvara is known as Chenresi and in Tibet several kings and the Dalai Lama are believed to be human incarnations of Avalokiteshvara. In Tibet he is closely associated with his female counterpart, Tara.

[50] *Shambhala Dictonary of Buddhism and Zen*, p. 137

[51] Manjusri is known as Wenshu in Chinese and Monju in Japanese.

[52] The Samantabhadra discussed in Tibetan Buddhism is apparently a different figure from the Samantabhadra Bodhisattva of India. In some forms of Tibetan Buddhism, his body can be green, yellow or deep blue (symbolizes that all things are empty of inner essences) and he can be depicted in sexual union with his consort.

Mahayana, the blue-skinned Vajrapani becomes one of the most important of all the bodhisattvas.[53]

9.11 SACRED SCRIPTURES OF BUDDHISM

THERAVADA SACRED WRITINGS: The *Tripitaka*

The earlier conservative schools and the later Mahayana schools had different collections of scriptures, accepted by and used in the various religious communities as sacred and authoritative. Among the Elders, the Sthaviravadins and the several groups that separated from the Sthaviravadin conservative traditions, eventually the teachings, verses of inspiration, and incidents in the Buddha's life, were all grouped into the sutra basket of the *Tripitaka* or "Three Baskets." The first basket is the sutras, and the second basket was the monastic regulations, or *vinaya*.

Later, after the death of the Buddha, more scholarly monks assembled dense and detailed doctrinal summaries and systems to explain the world and the mind. These became the third basket, the *Abhidharma* ("higher dharma"). These were the earliest explanations and commentaries. In the *Abhidharma* texts, concepts such as *karma*, self, mind, merit, and rebirth, were analyzed. The *Abhidharma* texts analyzed and classified all those processes and events in our world which were relevant to the goal of attaining nirvana.[54] One set of *Abhidharma* texts provided the basis for the Sarvastivada school (which no longer exists) and a different set was the foundation for the Theravada school in Sri Lanka (which still exists). The analysis of experience into aggregates, elements, and faculties (elements of existence) was a primary concern.

The Two Truths: Conventional and Ultimate

The *Abhidharma* texts distinguished between a conventional truth and an ultimate truth. If we assume that our everyday sort of speech and descriptions were absolutely real ("I am going to school," or "It is noon on Tuesday"), then we had confused the conventional truth with an ultimate truth. Conventional truth uses terms like "I" and place names like "school," but in fact the Buddhists agreed there was no eternal atman, that there was no ultimate "I" but only a continuous collection of processes that we conventionally referred to as "I." And "school" has no essence, but is constantly changing. Consider "I am going to a baseball game." There isn't a real unchanging "I" and what we call a "baseball game" is merely a conventional shorthand phrase indicating a constantly changing process where nothing real is named, only changing players, changing activities, and even changing playing fields and changing owners.

Abhidharma authors asserted that the only things in the universe which were truly real are tiny factors or constituents of reality which they called *dharmas*. These dharmas are the tiniest ultimate building blocks of all that is real, including psychological factors as well as the physical In the Sarvastivada Abhidharma collection, these dharmas were claimed to possess an unchanging essence, an eternal substance, an intrinsic self-existent nature (*svabhava*) which is what makes them real and the ultimate building blocks of all reality, even including mind and consciousness.

MAHAYANA SACRED WRITINGS: New Sutras

There is no single collection of Mahayana sutras equivalent to the *Tripitaka*. As described earlier, by 200–100

---

[53] The various Bodhisattvas, including Vajrapani, are discussed in David Snellgrove, *Indo-Tibetan Buddhism* (Boston: Shambhala, 2002), pp. 58-61. Snellgrove also points out that there are interesting parallels with Vajrapani and Vedic *devas*, Indra and Brahma.

[54] There are two different collections of Abhidharma texts; the conservative school of Theravada had their own Abhidharma texts, and the conservative school of Sarvastivada had another set of Abhidharma texts. The Sarvastivadins asserted that reality is made of dharmas, and dharmas have a self-existing essence, a *svabhava*.

B.C.E. new sutras begin to appear which offered a different emphasis than those of the Elders, and Mahayana monks tended to pick out some of these new texts and base their practice and understanding of Buddhism on just a few of these. Although the conservative Buddhists rejected these sutras as inauthentic, the Mahayana claimed that these were teachings which the Buddha had given to his most advanced disciples while he was still alive, but because majority of the conservative Buddhist followers could not understand this teaching, the Mahayana sutras were omitted from the conservative Buddhist *Tripitaka*. The implication is clear: Mahayana implied that conservative Buddhism was inferior and for monks of limited abilities; Mahayana claimed to be a superior pathway which reflects a higher truth.[55]

The *Prajnaparamita* Group of Sutras

Among the very earliest of the new Mahayana sutras is a collection of many different scriptures stressing *prajna*-wisdom, called *Prajna-paramita*, or "The Prajna-wisdom which carries one over to the other shore," but could also be rendered as the "Perfection of Wisdom" or even "Perfect Wisdom."[56] The earliest sutras of this group, such as the *Prajnaparamita in 8,000 lines*, date to circa 200 B.C.E. and 100 C.E. Another sutra which belongs to the *Prajna* family of texts, although it has a very different structure, is the *Vimalakirti-nirdesa-sutra*, which features a householder named Vimalakirti as the wisest of all the followers of the Buddha, who in clever and profound dialogue proves that he is fully the equal of Manjusri, the bodhisattva who embodies highest wisdom (*prajna*). Two of the most famous *Prajna-paramita* texts are the Diamond Sutra (*Vajracchedika*)[57] and the Heart Sutra (*Hrdaya*).

The *Saddharmapundarika Sutra* (The *Lotus sutra*)

In East Asia, one of the most popular Mahayana texts is the *Lotus of the Marvelous Dharma*, or *Lotus of the Marvelous Law*. In Sanskrit it is the *Saddharma-pundarika sutra*, in Chinese it is the *Miao fa lien hua ching*, and in Japanese it is the *Myo-ho-renge-kyo* (or *Hokekyo*). This text teaches that there is only one supreme vehicle of Buddhism, not two (the text refers to the two as "Hinayana and Mahayana"). The Buddha is elevated to an omniscient eternal deity whose bodhisattvas work to achieve salvation and liberation for all sentient beings. The text uses images and parables to teach that all who believe can achieve buddhahood. It also uses the term Shakyamuni[58] for the historical Buddha, Siddhartha Gautama, and many Asian Buddhists know the historical Buddha as Shakyamuni. The bodhisattva of compassion, Avalokiteshvara ("The Lord Who Looks Down on the World" or "He Who Hears the Sounds of the World"), is featured in the twenty-fourth chapter (or twenty-fifth in some translations) of the *Lotus Sutra*. Among all the Mahayana texts, this one very strongly and in no uncertain terms insults and abuses the non-Mahayana schools

---

[55] This is especially stressed in the *Lotus sutra*, the *Saddharma-pundarika sutra*.

[56] The scholar Edward Conze devoted his life to the study and analysis of this literature, and there are at least a dozen books written by Conze which explain these seminal texts. For example, there is Conze, *Buddhist Wisdom Books: The Diamond Sutra; The Heart Sutra* (London: Allen & Unwin, 1958), and Conze, *The Perfection of Wisdom in Eight Thousand Lines* (Bolinas: Four Seasons Foundation, 1973); Conze, *The Large Sutra on Perfect Wisdom* (Berkeley: University of California Press, 1975). The largest text of this group is the *Mahaprajnaparamita-shastra* or *Prajnaparamita sutra in 100,000 lines* which has been partially translated into French in five encyclopedic volumes by Etienne Lamotte, *La Traite de la Grande Vertu de Sagesse de Nagarjuna* (Louvain: Institute Orientaliste, 1949-1980). The earliest of these is explored in Gil Fronsdal, *Dawn of the Bodhisattva Path: The Early Perfection of Wisdom* (Honolulu: University Press of Hawai'i, 2014).

[57] The Diamond sutra is thought to have been composed perhaps fifty years before the lifetime of Nagarjuna, the most famous and influential of all Mahayana thinkers. This seminal text has been translated many times into English. A quality study and translation is Mu Soeng, *The Diamond Sutra: Transforming the Way We Perceive the World* (Boston: Wisdom Publications, 2000). A very thorough translation and study of the text is by Red Pine (Bill Porter), *The Diamond Sutra: The Perfection of Wisdom* (Washington, D.C.: Counterpoint, 2001). Another valuable translation based entirely on the Sanskrit is Edward Conze, *Buddhist Wisdom Books: The Diamond Sutra; The Heart Sutra* (London: Allen & Unwin, 1958).

[58] The sage or wise teacher of the Shakya tribe.

referring to the traditions of the Elder monks as *Hinayana*, or followers of "Inferior Vehicle"[59] of Buddhism.[60]

9.12 BUDDHIST ATTITUDES TOWARDS REALITY

THE CONCEPT OF DHARMAS IN CONSERVATIVE BUDDHISM

As we discussed earlier, the scriptures of early Buddhism included the *Abhidharma* texts, which were the basis for the conservative Sarvastivada school and the Theravada school in Sri Lanka. These texts go beyond the words of the Buddha, and begin to speculate on metaphysical issues relating to the ultimate nature of reality.

The *Abhidharma* texts give an additional meaning to the term *dharma*. The standard meaning was "Buddhist teachings." However, in the Abhidharma texts *dharma* is used to denote something similar to fundamental constituents of reality. The mind perceives *dharmas*, discrete elements, point-sources of energy, or dependently-arisen phenomena. *Dharmas* are factors of experience which compose all existence[61] including the factors which can cause misery, or *duhkha*. *Dharmas* are the tiniest building blocks of reality (in this sense they are like atoms). *Dharmas* even include thoughts.[62]

The early *Abhidharma* texts analyzed reality (and the self) into *dharmas* to demonstrate that what Hindus think of as an unchanging *atman* ("soul" or "self") which has no parts, is actually made up of smaller changing processes. What we call the *atman* is not singular, eternal, or unchanging. Instead, what we think of as "self" is actually made up of uncountably many smaller *dharmas*. The self is dependently arising. There is no permanent and unchanging self (the Buddhist insight of *anatman*). All the things you and I see are changing and impermanent. This provides a tool for Buddhist thinkers to demonstrate that Hindu Upanishadic concepts of an absolute Brahman or eternal *atman* are mistaken. The analysis of reality into *dharmas* also could show how conditioned *dharmas* (the causes of existence and *dukkha*) could be uprooted so that the unconditioned nirvana could be achieved.

It seemed clear to these Conservative Buddhists that some qualities which we tend to attribute to the world are actually mind-dependent. Is the world precisely as we experience it? Clearly it isn't. For example, heat is how we humans react to vibrating molecules. In the world itself there are only molecules which vibrate, some slowly (which humans experience as cold), some fast (which humans experience as heat). Without human taste buds, nothing is sweet or sour. What we experience as a fragrant odor is simply specific molecules in the air to which our nostrils are sensitive, and which we enjoy. There are vibrations in the air, some of which our ears can perceive, and others that we cannot perceive.

But the Conservative Buddhists were sure that if minds were to disappear, the world would not disappear. There must be something that does not depend on human sense organs, something that exists independent of our sense organs. The world is made of independent substances, substances like earth, air, empty space, fire and water. The substance of earth does not depend on fire, or air, or water. It is independent. These substances are the constituents of reality and do not depend on human consciousness.

---

[59] No Buddhist school ever referred to itself as the Hinayana/Inferior Vehicle or thought of itself as inferior. It is rare for Buddhist sutras to use such an insulting and derogatory term to refer to fellow Buddhists the way the *Lotus sutra* does.

[60] Some Japanese Buddhists chant the title of this sutra as a powerful *mantra*, chanting **nam-myo-ho-renge-kyo**, literally "homage to the Lotus of the Wonderful Dharma."

[61] The term *dharma* has at least four related uses in early discourses, but in this context it denotes dependently-arisen phenomena or elements of experience. For additional meanings, see David Kalupahana, *Nagarjuna: The Philosophy of the Middle Way* (New York: SUNY), p. 15.

[62] An extensive explanation of the dharma theory can be found in Buswell, *Encyclopedia of Buddhism*, Volume One, pp. 220ff.

CHAPTER 9: THERAVADA vs MAHAYANA BUDDHISM

These ultimate substances are *dharmas* and the substance of a *dharma* is independent of consciousness. However, this *Abhidharma* analysis of the constituents of reality in Conservative Buddhism (especially the Sarvastivada group of Conservative Buddhists) led to a problem. If every aspect of reality changes every instant, then how is the present connected to the past? The past changed, and then the present seems to arise but how could it arise without any causal connection between past and present? The same problem arises with the future. How is the next instant connected to the previous instant? One solution to the problem is to consider *dharmas*, these small tiny discrete elements of reality, as having an inner aspect which is constant which moves unchanging from past to present to future, and this constant aspect could explain continuity from past to present to the future moment.

This unchanging aspect contained within a *dharma* is called *svabhava*, (literally "self-existing," or existing independently of cause-and-effect). For many early Buddhists, all real things are made of *dharmas* which contain an enduring self-existent essence which moves from past to present to future.[63] These *dharmas* are in constant motion, so when one considers the world from the perspective of tables, chairs, and mountains, all things are constantly changing. Although the tables and chairs of our empirical world are impermanent, the underlying *dharmas* (out of which they are made) exist permanently, contain inner immutable self-existence, persist unchanging and are real. In this case *dharmas* function a bit like atoms did in science a hundred and fifty years ago, as the ultimate building blocks of reality (however in contemporary science, atoms are neither permanent nor unchanging).

Svabhava is the "intrinsic and essential quality of ultimately real objects."[64] *Svabhava* is what distinguishes a real lake from a mirage, *svabhava* is what distinguishes dreams and illusions from reality.

The *Abhidharma* authors asserted that the only things in the universe which were truly real, are these tiny factors or constituents of reality. These dharmas include the psychological factors as well as the physical. Dharmas are simple and unchanging but the phenomenal realm of human experience is in constant change. All the impermanence in the world is due to changes in the manner in which the dharmas shift and regroup.[65] Change is due to recombinations of dharmas, differing arrangements of dharmas, which in turn differ in size and shape. Dharmas themselves do not change. These dharmas each possess an unchanging essence, an eternal substance, an intrinsic self-existent nature (*svabhava*) which is what makes them real and the ultimate building blocks of all reality, even including mind and consciousness. These details are the philosophical and psychological speculations of later Buddhists.

THE UNDERSTANDING OF DHARMAS IN MAHAYANA BUDDHISM

The Mahayana philosophers found claims that *dharmas* contain something which exists permanently, or persist unchanging, to be logically and conceptually impossible. The Mahayana analysis is not something done in a laboratory; rather, when one draws out the implications and consequences of the idea of enduring *dharmas*, she will find the concept simply self-contradictory. Mahayana thinkers denied the Hindu claim that some sort of enduring permanent existence is the essence of what makes things real. Mahayana thinkers produced careful arguments which attempted to demonstrate that these Abhidharma claims made about *dharmas* were self-contradictory, therefore *dharmas* could not have the properties attributed to them.

Mahayana thinkers argued for the conclusion that if there are small building blocks which constitute reality and which we call *dharmas*, then they must be merely impermanent flowing processes which are not substantial and which do not contain self-existence (*svabhava*).

---

[63] As noted previously, this is especially associated with the Sarvastivada ("all-exists") group of Conservative Buddhists.

[64] Jan Westerhoff, *Nagarjuna's Madhyamaka* (New York and London: Oxford University Press, 2009), p. 30.

[65] This suggests similarities with the traditional Greek atomists who asserted that there were four basic elements: earth, air, fire, water.

CHAPTER 9: THERAVADA vs MAHAYANA

There is **nothing anywhere** which is permanent and unchanging.

Mahayana philosophers argued that there is no such thing as *svabhava*, which Abhidharma thinkers claimed to be the essence of these fundamental elements of reality. *Dharmas* do not contain some inner substance or essence which allows them to persist unchanging.[66]

Svabhava-sunyata

For the Mahayana, *dharmas* are not containers of some self-existing substance. *Dharmas* are **empty of inner permanent essence.** In Sanskrit, they say that *dharmas* are empty (*sunya*) of an inner unchanging self-nature (*svabhava*). Thus, *dharmas* are *svabhava-sunyata*, literally "empty of self-existent inner essence." For Mahayana, *dharmas* are ever-changing interdependent processes, not unchanging ultimate constituents of reality.

If the world is *pratityasamutpada*, or interdependent interconnected processes, that means that everything depends on prior causes and conditions. If something were self-existent, it would depend upon nothing but itself. Mahayana texts were produced demonstrating that all things depend on prior causes, all things are part of the causal interconnected network of processes, so nothing is immutable or self-existent, that nothing contains or possesses inner *svabhava*. If these arguments are strong, the conclusion is that there are no inner unchanging self-existent essences anywhere. Then all things are "empty of essence" (*svabhava-sunyata*), including *dharmas* themselves.

For the Mahayana traditions concerned with the analysis of reality, the world is ever-changing flux, composed of inter-dependent processes. There is nothing like an independent self-nature, no *svabhava*, nothing unchanging, no *atman*, no Brahman, no ultimately real unchanging substances making real things real, no substances which allow us to separate out reality from illusion the way we assumed. Reality is just changing processes. Reality is **empty** of self-existent essences. It is human mental processes which create the illusion that there are enduring substances which make up reality.

9.13 SUMMARY OF THE CHAPTER

We have analyzed the significant differences between the Conservative (especially the Theravada) schools of Buddhism, and the Mahayana traditions. Claims about differences between early Conservative Buddhism and early Mahayana Buddhism are contested by scholars, and thus our discussion had to be tentative. Although both traditions revered the Buddha, the early Theravada monks tended to understand Siddhartha as an incredible and extraordinary person who worked his way to awakening, attained nirvana, and when he died, he escaped the cycle of *samsara*, leaving behind him a clearly explained pathway, the Middle Way, made up of the Four Noble Truths and grounded in the insight into the nature of reality, that is, dependent co-arising (*pratityasamutpada*).

The Mahayana tended to think of Siddhartha as a super-being, a god, a *deva* who has always been awakened and was neither born nor died. Instead, the eternal Buddha (the *Dharma-kaya*) transformed himself into the Siddhartha we know. Out of love and compassion, that being pretended to be born and pretended to be human (the transformation-body, the *Nirmana-kaya*) so that he could teach humans how to lessen or eliminate misery, frustration, suffering, i.e., *duhkha*. He also pretended to die in order to stress the truth that all things are impermanent. However, the Mahayana followers assert that in truth the divine Buddha neither achieved awakening nor died. Instead, these are merely skillful teaching devices, or *upaya*, used by the compassionate Buddha to teach followers to achieve the cessation of *dukkha* and nirvana.

---

[66] This seems similar to the discovery that atoms are not eternal and unchanging, but instead arise from sub-atomic processes which in turn arise from more fundamental sub-atomic processes. There is nothing solid and unchanging about the atomic processes.

244

CHAPTER 9: THERAVADA vs MAHAYANA BUDDHISM

The Theravada was inclined to put much of its attention on those who have renounced the householder's life and pursued the path to awakening in the forest as beggars and meditators, or in the monastery. However Theravada monks did perform devotional rituals for householders. Mahayana was primarily a monastic religion, but the Mahayana were more open to the householder as someone who could achieve awakening and nirvana. It is possible that one of the sources of the various groups that constitute Mahayana was the beliefs and practices of householders who took care of the numerous Buddhist monuments scattered throughout Buddhist India, and who encouraged devotion to Buddhas.

The sacred scriptures for the Theravada were all contained in the three baskets which compose the *Tripitaka*, but new Mahayana sacred sutras continued to appear for a thousand years after the death of the Buddha. Mahayana schools tended to focus their intellectual and devotional energies upon particular groups of sutras, and this is likely another possible source for the origins of Mahayana followers.

Finally, basing itself on the *Abhidharma* basket of the *Tripitaka*, the Theravadins analyzed reality into a changing interdependent world whose ultimate constituents were point-instants of energy, which they called *dharmas* and they thought of as having *svabhava*, an unchanging inner self-existing self-nature. Possessing *svabhava* made something real; lacking *svabhava* made something unreal like a mirage, a dream, a hallucination.

The Mahayana thinkers argued philosophically against this, and instead asserted that it is impossible for things to contain an immutable self-existent *svabhava*. Rather, all things are empty of *svabhava*, empty of self-existence or empty of unchanging permanent substance. Thus, all dharmas are *svabhava-sunyata*, empty of immutable self-nature. Mahayana texts often assert that all things are **empty**, or that reality is **emptiness** (*sunyata*). Some translators render *sunyata* as "void" or "voidness." "Empty" does not mean non-existent, unreal, or illusory; rather it means that like a coin purse that is empty of coins, the object (the coin purse) is without an internal self-existent essence or substance (empty of coins).

9.14 TECHNICAL TERMS

Abhidharma	The "higher dharma" or "higher teachings," which are technical treatises by philosophers who analyze all the sayings of the Buddha, and then produce technical treatises on the nature of the mind and reality.
arhat	A noble one. In early and Conservative Buddhism, an arhat puts and end to duhkha, achieves nirvana, and does so by following the pathway laid out by the Buddha in the sutras of the *Tripitaka*.
bodhi	Awakening, to wake up. Some scholars translate this as "enlightenment" but "bodhi" shares the same root as the Sanskrit term for waking up in the morning, and does not have any reference to light.
bodhidsattva	A being (-*sattva*) who aspires to the complete awakening (bodhi) of a buddha.
bhikkshu	Literally a "beggar." These are the followers of the Buddha who abandoned the life of a householder and lived by begging.
dharma	The teachings of the Buddha, contained in the sutras. Some translators render this as the "Laws" of the Buddha.
dharmas	The smallest perceivable constituents which make up the processes we call reality. Some conservative Buddhists thought of dharmas as having an enduring unchanging inner essence, making them independent of the causal nexus. The Mahayana followers denied that dharmas have a self-existing

essence (*svabhava*).

Dharmakaya	The eternal "Truth-Body" of the Buddha, when he is thought of as an eternal god-like being.
guru	A spiritual guide or a spiritual teacher, one worthy of the highest respect because he or she had achieved great insight and great powers, or *siddhi*.
Hinayana	This is the "Inferior Vehicle" or the "Small Vehicle" and is an insulting and disrespectful term used by some Mahayana (especially in the *Lotus sutra*) followers to describe Theravada, Sarvastivada, or other groups of conservative Buddhism.
Mahayana	The "Greater Vehicle," a self-congratulatory term used to describe a broad variety of later developments in Buddhism, ranging in some groups to complete devotion to a buddha, to other Mahayana groups which provided incredibly detailed and careful analyses of the nature of reality.
Nirmanakaya	The "Transformation-body" of the eternal Buddha, the body which was a projection of the infinite Dharmakaya, but this body is visible to human beings and is the body that the Buddha used to teach students, and the body with which his followers interacted, according to the Mahayana.
Sambhogakaya	The "Bliss-body" in which the eternal Buddha experiences the bliss of nirvana, and the body used to appear to various other buddhas and bodhisattvas in their heavenly realms.
Sangha	The followers of the Buddha, or the Buddhist community made up of those senior and advanced members who look up to the Buddha as their teacher.
Sarvastivada	This was one of the most important of the eighteen schools of Conservative Buddhism. The Sarvastivada held that all *dharmas* truly existed because they have an unchanging self-nature or essence.
siddhi	Supernormal powers achieved by meditating and other yogic spiritual practices. They include hearing people speaking from many miles away, or flying through the sky, or reading another person's mind. These were not restricted only to Buddhist monks; it was thought that anyone who practiced hard enough could learn *siddhis*.
shunya/sunya	Pronounced "shun-ya," literally, "empty," an abbreviation for "empty of inner self-nature" or "empty of essence."
shunyata/sunyata	Pronounced "shun-ya-TA," literally, "emptiness," an abbreviation for "emptiness of self-nature." Often written *sunyata*.
Sthaviravada	Early Buddhism divided into two traditions: a pathway as taught by the *arhats* or Elders (Sthaviravada) and another group, the majority of the *sangha* (Mahasanghika) which tended to see *arhats* as inferior to the Buddha, and tended to see the Buddha as a *deva*.
stupa	A monument constructed over the ashes of the Buddha or later Buddhist follower, or erected to commemorate some important place where a significant event occurred.
sutra	The discourses of the Buddha as remembered by his students.
svabhava	Literally, "self-existing" or "self-becoming." It is an eternal unchanging inner essence which depends on nothing. Mahayana thinkers produced arguments showing that it is impossible for anything in our

changing world to possess *svabhava*.

svabhava-sunyata	Svabhava means "self-existent." "Sunyata" means "emptiness." So, the term means that all things are without any internal permanent substance or essence, that elements of existence are without an inner self-existing unchanging substance. This can be expressed by saying that things are "empty" of substance. So, "emptiness of essence" or "emptiness of inner unchanging self-nature." This is a key concept of much of later Mahayana Buddhism.
Theravada	One of the eighteen early schools that make up Conservative Buddhism, one that developed from the earlier Sthaviravada tradition. In Sanskrit, "Sthaviravadin" literally means "one who follows the pathway of the Elders," and Theravada is the Pali language equivalent of "one who follows the pathway of the Elders." However, the Theravada is a later development of Sthaviravada and not identical with the earlier Sthaviravada.
Tripitaka	The "three baskets" which make up the sacred scriptures of Theravada Buddhism. They include sutras, vinaya (rules for monks and nuns), and Abhidharma texts.
vajra	Literally, "diamond." A bodhisattva of the highest achievement is said to have a *vajra* or "diamond" mind, able to cut through the obstacles to the spiritual path. The term *vajra* also carries the meaning of a lightning-bolt, or thunderbolt. The awakened mind is filled with awesome and overwhelming power.
vinaya	The rules for monks and nuns. These were one of the three "baskets" included in the *Tripitaka*, but the Indian Mahayana followers pretty much used the same sets of rules in their monasteries.

9.15 QUESTIONS FOR FURTHER DISCUSSION

(1)   In early Conservative schools of Indian Buddhism, is the Buddha a deity? Did monastic monks have a different understanding of the nature of the Buddha than householders?

(2)   In Mahayana Buddhism, is the Buddha more than human, even a deity? Is there more than one Buddha?

(3)   In Mahayana Buddhism, does the Buddha reward some and send them to heaven? Do Buddhas curse some and send them to torture in hellish realms? If not, why not?

(4)   Are the sacred scriptures of Buddhism divine and infallible?

(5)   Historians often point out that the two major divisions of Indian Buddhism did not engage in violence towards one another. In fact, monks of both traditions lived side by side in the same monasteries. What features of Buddhism might account for this?

(6)   If a Buddhist wanted to eliminate suffering, what techniques are available to accomplish this? Morality? Meditation? Devotion? Ritual? Discuss.

(7)   Mahayana Buddhism claims that the Buddha has three bodies. Distinguish between these three. What is the purpose of each?

(8)   The attitude of Mahayana towards the basic constituents of matter (*dharmas*) differs from that of the conservative Theravadins who accepted *svabhava* (eternal self-existent essence). This disagreement is one of the central issues behind the later division of Buddhism into Theravada and Mahayana. Explain the position of each.

(9)   There are many Theravada groups and temples in the Western world. You might consider visiting such a contemporary group and seeing its understanding of the Buddha and the Buddhist pathway. You might be surprised to discover that different temples and groups may have very different understandings of the Buddha and the Buddhist pathway.

(10)   A search of the internet for Buddhist-based web sites will reveal a huge number of such sites. Some focus upon translations of sacred texts, some encourage the practice of meditation, some are devotional, and some are modern Western sites which can show profound misunderstandings of Buddhism as it is practiced. What tendencies seem to dominate? Why?

A SELECTED BIBLIOGRAPHY

Translations of Original Texts

Beyer, Steven, tr. and ed., *The Buddhist Experience: Sources and Interpretations* (Belmont, Ca.: Dickenson Publishing, 1974)
Conze, E., et. al., *Buddhist Texts Through the Ages*, (London, Oneworld and New Delhi, Munshiram Manoharlal, 1995)
Conze, Edward, *Buddhist Wisdom Books: The Diamond Sutra; The Heart Sutra* (London: Allen & Unwin, 1958)
Conze, Edward, *The Perfection of Wisdom in Eight Thousand Lines* (Bolinas: Four Seasons Foundation, 1973)
Conze, Edward, *The Large Sutra on Perfect Wisdom* (Berkeley: University of California Press, 1975)
de Bary, Theodore and W. T. Chan, *The Buddhist Tradition in India, China and Japan* (New York, Vintage, 1972)
Koller, John and Patricia, Sourcebook in Asian Philosophy (New York: Macmillan, 1991)
Lamotte, Etienne, *La Traite de la Grande Vertu de Sagesse de Nagarjuna* [the *Mahaprajnaparamita-shastra* or *Prajnaparamita sutra in 100,000 lines*] (Louvain: Institute Orientaliste, 1949-1980), 5 volumes.
Lamotte, Etienne, *The Teaching of Vimalakirti: From the French Translation with Introduction and Notes*, tr. by Sara Boin (London: Routledge & Kegan Paul, Ltd., 1976)
Lopez, Donald S. Jr., *Buddhist Scriptures* (New York: Penguin Classics, 19)
Miles, Jack, and Donald S. Lopez, Jr., *Buddhism* (N.Y.: Norton, 2015) This Norton Anthology of World Religions has a good collection of original sources.
Soeng, Mu, *The Diamond Sutra: Transforming the Way We Perceive the World* (Boston: Wisdom Publications, 2000).
Thurman, Robert, *The Holy Teaching of Vimalakirti* (Pennsylvania State, 2009)
Warren, Henry Clarke, *Buddhism In Translations* (New York: Antheneum, 1968)

Developments in Indian Buddhism

Bunce, Fredrick W., *Mudras in Buddhist and Hindu Practices: An Iconographic Consideration* (DK Printworld, 2005)
Buswell, Robert E., Jr., ed., *Encyclopedia of Buddhism* (New York: Macmillan and Thompson-Gale, 2004), 2 volumes.
Conze, Edward, *Buddhist Wisdom Books: The Diamond Sutra; The Heart Sutra* (London: Allen & Unwin, 1958)
_____, *The Large Sutra on Perfect Wisdom* (Berkeley: University of California Press, 1975)
_____, *The Perfection of Wisdom in Eight Thousand Lines* (Bolinas: Four Seasons Foundation, 1973)
Dayal, Har, *The Bodhisattva Doctrine in Buddhist Sanskrit Literature* (London: Kegan, Paul, Trubner, Trench & Co., 1932)

CHAPTER 9: THERAVADA vs MAHAYANA BUDDHISM

Decaroli, Robert, *Haunting the Buddha: Indian Popular Religions and the Formation of Buddhism* (Oxford University Press, 2004)

Dube, S. N., *Cross Currents in Early Buddhism* (New Delhi: Manohar, 1980)

Fronsdal, Gil,, *Dawn of the Bodhisattva Path: The Early Perfection of Wisdom* (Honolulu: University Press of Hawai'i, 2014)

Harvey, Peter, *An Introduction to Buddhism* (London: Cambridge University Press, 1990)

Herman, A. L., *An Introduction to Buddhist Thought: A Philosophic History of Indian Buddhism* (New York: University Press of America, 1983).

Hirakawa, Akira, *A History of Indian Buddhism: From Sakyamuni to Early Mahayana* (Honolulu: University of Hawai'i Press, 1990)

Katz, Nathan, *Buddhist Images of Human Perfection (The Arahant of the Sutta Pitaka Compared with the Bodhisattva and the Mahasiddha* (Benares, India: Motilal Banarsidass, 2010)

Kitiarsa, Pattana, *Mediums, Monks, and Amulets: Thai Popular Buddhism Today* (Chiang Mai: Silkworm Books, 2012)

Lamotte, Etienne, *La Traite de la Grande Vertu de Sagesse de Nagarjuna* [the *Mahaprajnaparamita-shastra* or *Prajnaparamita sutra in 100,000 lines*] (Louvain: Institute Orientaliste, 1949-1980), 5 volumes.

_____, *The Teaching of Vimalakirti: From the French Translation with Introduction and Notes* , tr. by Sara Boin (London: Routledge & Kegan Paul, Ltd., 1976)

Leighton, Taigen Dan, *Bodhisattva Archetypes: Classic Buddhist Guides to Awakening and their Modern Expression* (New York: Penguin Arkana, 1998)

McArthur, Meher, *Reading Buddhist Art: An Illustrated Guide to Buddhist Signs and Symbols* (London: Thames & Hudson, 2002).

Nattier, Jan, *A Few Good Men: The Bodhisattva Path According to the Inquiry of Ugra* (Honolulu: University of Hawaii Press, 2003)

Red Pine (Bill Porter), *The Diamond Sutra: The Perfection of Wisdom* (Washington, D.C.: Counterpoint, 2001)

Pye, Michael, *Skilful Means: A Concept in Mahayana Buddhism* (London: Routledge, 2004)

Schopen, Gregory, "Mahayana" in Robert E. Buswell, Jr., ed., *Encyclopedia of Buddhism* (New York: Macmillan and Thompson-Gale, 2004), Vol. 2.

Soeng, Mu, *The Diamond Sutra: Transforming the Way We Perceive the World* (Boston: Wisdom Publications, 2000).

Snellgrove, David, *Indo-Tibetan Buddhism: Indian Buddhists and their Tibetan Successors* (Boston: Shambhala, 2002)

Thurman, Robert, *The Holy Teaching of Vimalakirti* (Pennsylvania State, 2009)

Wallace, B. Alan, *The Four Immeasurables: Practices to Open the Heart* (Boston: Snow Lion, 2010)

Westerhoff, Jan, *Nagarjuna's Madhyamika: A Philosophical Introduction* (London: Oxford University Press, 2009)

CHAPTER 9: THERAVADA vs MAHAYANA

CHAPTER 10: MAHAYANA BUDDHIST SCHOOLS–PART I
THE PURE LAND
THE MADHYAMAKA
THE YOGACHARA
THE TATHAGATA-GARBHA

10.1 OVERVIEW OF THE CHAPTER

Comparing the conservative Theravada and Mahayana in the previous chapter, we distinguished three approaches to Buddhist practice. They are (a) centered on the doctrines and books of Buddhism, or *dharma*-centric, (b) centered on the community of followers, or *sangha*-centric, (c) centered on the nature and relics of the Buddha, or Buddha-centric.

The first two approaches typify early conservative Buddhism, which tends towards being both *dharma*-centric and *sangha*-centric. In this case, the *dharma* is the doctrines contained in the early discourses of the Buddha, and the *Abhidharma* texts. The *sangha* or Buddhist community is where the center of practice can be found.

Several of the Mahayana traditions also focus on the *dharma*, but this is the *dharma* as explained in Mahayana *sutras*, the Mahayana philosophical implications of the discourses of the Buddha (which are not identical to the Theravada interpretations), in addition to their focus on the divine nature of the Buddha. More than Theravada, Mahayana traditions tended to stress *bhakti*, devotion to or having faith in buddhas. It is rather clear that popular Buddhism in Buddhist nations is mostly devotional, and the worship of numerous gods and goddesses of India and local spirits is very common.[1]

In the Pure Land school of Mahayana, the historical Buddha, and other buddhas and bodhisattvas, could be prayed to, meditated upon, and experienced in visions. Mahayana created a rich Buddha-centered mythology of the three bodies of the Buddha and worship of other buddhas. In addition, Mahayana stressed the possibility of nirvana for everyone, monk, nun, or householder.

Several Mahayana Buddhist schools developed quite sophisticated forms of philosophical analysis. One school, the Madhyamaka, analyzed the ultimate nature of reality as a means to the achievement of nirvana. Another, Yogachara/Yogacara (pronounced Yoog-ACH-ara), analyzed the nature of consciousness and discovered that there is a deep unconscious level in all of us which can be explored using meditation. That deep level can become free from error using focused concentration. Several Mahayana texts assert that all living things possess the potential for awakening, or possess the "Buddha-nature" and no things are excluded.

The last development of Buddhism in India is Tantric Buddhism, which was not the most important form of Buddhism in India, but later came to dominate Tibetan forms of Buddhism. This will be discussed in the next chapter.

---

[1] For example, see Miranda Shaw, *Buddhist Goddesses in India* (Princeton, N.J.: Princeton University Press, 2006). The author describes popular female divinities, which include tree spirits, maternal nurturers, potent healers and protectors, transcendent wisdom figures, cosmic mothers of liberation, and dancing female buddhas.

10.2 THE FORMS OF MAHAYANA BUDDHISM

The various Mahayana schools of Buddhism tended to focus upon and ground their traditions in groups of specific Mahayana texts, texts not found in the Pali canon (the *Tripitaka*) of sacred texts. The Mahayana traditions based themselves on unique groups of sutras, and also put much weight on *shastras*, or commentaries.[2] These Mahayana schools or traditions include:

(1) PURE-LAND:
A rather *bhakti*-devotional Buddha-centered form of Buddhism, which places more emphasis on praying to and worshiping the relics of Buddhas and bodhisattvas; the emphasis is on devotion, miracles, and supernormal events.

(2) MADHYAMAKA:
A very analytic philosophical form of Buddhism established around insights explained by possibly the greatest Mahayana Buddhist philosopher, named Nagarjuna, which were inspired by the collection of various Mahayana sutras called the *Prajna-paramita* (the "perfection of wisdom," or the "wisdom which carries one over to the other shore").

(3) YOGACHARA / YOGACARA:
Drawing on the insights of Nagarjuna, but with a new stress on meditation combined with detailed and careful analysis of the mind and mental events, this tradition became known as *Yogachara* ("one adept at yoga," pronounced Yoog-ACHa-ra), *Cittamatra* ("mind-only," pronounced Chitta-ma-tra) or *Vijnapti-matrata* ("consciousness-only," pronounced Vij-nyahp-ti Ma-tra-tah).

(4) BUDDHA-NATURE or TATHAGATA-GARBHA:
In India another strain of Mahayana was just beginning, centering around Mahayana texts which stress the *Tathagata-garbha* or "Buddha-nature." This Mahayana tradition asserts that all living things, without exception, have "Buddha-nature" which means we have the capacity to awaken and become buddhas. We are all the same when it comes to spiritual potential. No one is better or higher or more spiritual than anyone else; similarly, no one is inferior and incapable of attaining awakening (*bodhi*).

(5) DIAMOND or THUNDERBOLT VEHICLE:
Another Indian Mahayana group, the *Vajrayana*, began to develop around the 7th century C.E., several centuries before Buddhism diminished in importance in India. It shares many commonalities with Tantric Hinduism which developed at the very same time in India.[3] This will be discussed in the next chapter.

These general approaches to Buddhism then flow into China, Korea, Japan, and other countries in S. E. Asia. The devotional strain becomes the "Pure Land" schools. The analytic Nagarjuna strain is associated with many of the Chinese schools, and especially the Ch'an/Zen schools and the Tibetan traditions. The Vajrayana will become dominant in Tibet.

---

[2] An excellent treatment of Mahayana Buddhism is Paul Williams, *Mahayana Buddhism: The Doctrinal Foundations* (London: Routledge, 1989).

[3] It is important to note that the followers of the Vajrayana are quite certain that the Buddha himself taught Tantric Buddhism to his most capable students, and would reject the idea that Tantric Hindu ideas in India had any influence over their fundamental insights, and would reject the idea that Tantric Buddhist texts are significantly later than the earliest conservative Theravada texts.

10.3 HISTORICAL BACKGROUND

POPULAR BUDDHISM

As we discussed in a previous chapter, it was during the medieval period[4] in India (6th - 11th century C.E.) that Vedic Hinduism became thoroughly devotional (a *bhakti* religion), and Hindu cults devoted to many different *deva* (divinities) proliferated. In chapter 5 we studied the worship of Vishnu, Shiva, Kali, Durga, Gopala Krishna, Ganesha and others. We also discussed a strong trend (affecting all Indian religions) to substitute a much more physical and colorful popular ritual for the prior abstract meditations.

Popular Buddhism was responding to the same forces as Hinduism, and the same tendencies are reflected in Buddhism of this period as well.[5] By 500 C.E., Buddhism was thoroughly integrated into Indian civilization. Differing Mahayana communities continued to grow and develop, especially in the north of India. As a result, popular Buddhism had a tendency to become more and more devotional. Popular Buddhism stressed special beings (bodhisattvas) whose powers were virtually indistinguishable from Hindu *devas*. Popular Mahayana continued to develop and expand its pantheon of bodhisattvas. New Mahayana texts continued to appear and new rituals and ceremonies continued to evolve.

For the first 500 years in the common era, several branches of conservative Buddhism remained strong. The majority of the Conservative (Theravada) Buddhist monks and nuns resided in monasteries, but there remained others who choose the difficult ascetic pathway of the forest monks, the *bhikshu*, the beggar. However, in India in general, the attitude toward the forest dweller was changing. The belief became stronger and stronger that these forest dwellers, whether Buddhist or non-Buddhist, were charismatic figures who have acquired magical powers (*siddhis*) due to their ascetic exertions.

Conservative Theravada, with its stress upon monastic monks and solitary mendicants, came to have less and less influence on Indian culture in general. Supported by the wealthier segment of Indian society, the major monasteries acquired power, wealth, and land from wealthy donors, and, as a result, became self-sufficient. This also had the effect of isolating the monasteries from the householder communities although these monks did provide rituals for the benefit of the community and benefactors.

It was the newer Mahayana practices which came to dominate in popular Buddhism in India. Many larger Buddhist monastic centers became cultural centers of learning, like universities. As such, they preserved and passed on not only Theravada and Mahayana Buddhism, but also Brahmanic culture as well, and taught subjects related to arts and sciences.

Some were centers of intellectual activity, with conservative Buddhists intermingling with the various Mahayana monks all under one roof. Several of these Buddhist monastic institutions were famous throughout Asia and students would travel from as far away as China and South-East Asia to attend these centers of learning. The lifestyles varied from one monastery to another. Some areas had wealthy patrons who donated land, buildings, and other sources of wealth to the monasteries, so these groups had large grounds and extensive libraries. The majority of the Buddhist institutions were more modest, neither wealthy nor extensive. One of the most famous was Nalanda, which in the seventh century had nine monasteries, eighteen temples, and was reported to cover an area of forty-eight square miles. It was the largest Buddhist university in all of Asia. It was said that there were more than a thousand professors and tens of thousands of students studying all facets of early and Mahayana Buddhism. The Buddhists lived together without sectarian competition.

For a while Buddhism was favored by kings and rulers and the educated merchants and wealthy middle class tended to follow their lead. Impressive Buddhist rituals and ceremonies were employed by rulers to legitimize their

---

[4] The term "medieval period" originally was used by European historians, but when applied to India, it is quite vague. In fact, there is no agreement among scholars as to precisely when the "medieval period" in India begins, or ends. Some have dated this period as beginning as early as 200 C.E. although 500-600 C.E. is more common for a beginning date. Although some scholars mark the ending as late as 1600 C.E., a more common range of ending dates would be 1100-1400 C.E.

[5] A. K. Warder, *Indian Buddhism* (Delhi: Motilal Banarsidass, 1970), p. 490.

authority (implying that the ruler has the approval of various buddhas to rule). Monks in rural villages carried on Buddhist learning, but also served as spiritual guides and performed rituals for local spirits and non-Buddhist religious traditions. It is no longer just Hinduism, but Buddhism as well became integrated into popular mythology, tales, themes, and folklore.

Buddhism appealed to many of the Brahmin priests and the *ksatrya* caste, the politicians, bureaucrats, and protectors, and the merchants. These were the most educated groups, which were the top three layers of Hindu society.

Mahayana Communities Continue to Develop

For the Grand Tradition, the Mahayana path included both devotional and intellectual elements. The intellectual elements include understanding the causally interdependent interconnected nature of all things, *pratityasamutpada*, and not being frightened by a world where everything is impermanent and changing, where there is nothing to hold onto, nothing solid, nothing substantial, nothing but swirling interdependent processes. Each of these Buddhist claims contradicted popular Brahmin teachings that real things were permanent and unchanging because each real thing possessed an immutable eternal essence (*svabhava*), and that humans possessed an immutable soul (*atman*). In contradicting the popular view, many people in India found that Buddhist world-view of impermanence to be unsettling.

The basic practice of Mahayana was compassion for all living things, exemplified by the bodhisattva who works incessantly for the happiness, welfare and liberation of all beings. It was believed that bodhisattvas had been on the spiritual pathway so long that they had acquired characteristics and powers of divinities as a result of all their good karma. They had also acquired a large amount of good merit or karma which they did not need, and which they could share with those who asked for help.

For the householder, it is very good to cultivate a relationship with these powers, by offering praise to the Buddha and bodhisattvas, by making offerings of flowers, money and food. The Buddhist householder is to observe the five Buddhist precepts,[6] but it doesn't hurt to keep in mind the name of your favorite bodhisattva who will help you when you need help. These beings can share their good merit with us, easing our own lives.

As this process continued for hundreds of years, the village *puja* rituals of praise of Hindus for their *devas* became nearly indistinguishable from the Buddhist rituals of praise for their bodhisattvas. Popular Buddhism and popular Hinduism were becoming more similar to one another, especially for the common folk.[7]

Northwestern India was an area particularly prone to foreign invasions, and Buddhism was especially strong in the northwest. During the sixth century, the White Huns swept northwestern India from central Asia, and destroyed Hindu and Buddhist institutions. In the eighth century, Muslim Arabs arrived at the Indus River, and by the thirteenth century, they had all of northern India under their control. The Muslim Turks vigorously destroyed Buddhist universities, executing entire communities of nuns and monks, and leveling monasteries, scattering their libraries and burning the sacred texts.

10.4 THE PURE LAND TRADITION OF THE MAHAYANA

The Pure Land form of devotional Mahayana Buddhism began as a monastic movement about the end of the

---

[6] Discussed in the previous chapter.

[7] There is disagreement among scholars on the details of early Mahayana, whether it originated due to social issues, whether it was an institutional development, or perhaps arose because of new doctrines or perhaps simply new rituals. It is not even clear whether the primary audience for early Mahayana was monks in monasteries, or householders seeking Buddhist gods to worship.

first century C.E. in northern India. In India, Pure Land Buddhism was neither a separate group nor a popular movement practiced by householders. There were just a few groups of monks who practiced an elite monastic meditation technique involving the visualization of the celestial home of the Buddha Amithabha[8] ("Infinite Light"), the Buddha of the Western Paradise. However, there was no separate devotional sect of Buddhism in India devoted to Amitabha Buddha.

It is likely that the earliest Pure Land images were *mandala* maps which served as a focal point for monkish meditation.[9] Over time these maps of the mind were thought of as maps of an actual paradise not in our universe. Focusing on a visual image of a Buddhist paradise is certainly useful as a mind-calming practice, whether one is an academic scholar or a monk or layperson inclined to have love and devotion to buddhas and bodhisattvas.

Indian Pure Land Buddhism can be seen as arising at the same time as the growing popularity of *bhakti* (devotional) Buddha-worship in India at this time. Pure Land developed greater popularity in northern India and Central Asia from the second century C.E. However, in India, householders were not devoted to Amitabha Buddha.

We have seen that to achieve the Mahayana goal of bodhisattvahood required uncountably many lifetimes, and in the course of those lifetimes ego-less bodhisattvas kept returning to the realm of *samsara* to perfect themselves, but also to help others lessen their *duhkha*, even though the bodhisattva knew how to escape from the cycle of birth and death. In the process of helping living beings, lifetime after lifetime, it was thought that, because of the depth of their compassion, some bodhisattvas had acquired so much good karma or merit that they developed the power to create a "purified" land, and set it aside expressly for the deliverance of sentient beings who express faith in them.

Human beings have different capabilities, but even those of the lowest spiritual capability can achieve rebirth in the Pure Land because it is the result of the compassion of the bodhisattva, not the spiritual development of the individual human. The ancient celestial Buddha Amitabha, the buddha of longevity and infinite light, emerged as the most popular of these bodhisattvas and stories about Amitabha took form as books, or sutras.

The Pure Land Sutras

Indian Pure Land Buddhism based itself on three primary Mahayana Buddhist texts, especially the *Sutra of Infinite Light* (*Sukhavati-vyuha sutra*). It tells the story of the celestial Buddha Amithabha ("Infinite Light," the Buddha of longevity), who lived in the ancient past long before Siddhartha was born, and the forty-eight vows[10] he made while still a bodhisattva named Dharmakara who was working towards buddhahood.

The Bodhisattva Dharmakara took a vow to establish a pure land of bliss wherein all beings could be free of *duhkha* (misery, frustration, suffering). Using his supernatural bodhisattva powers, Dharmakara inspected vast numbers of buddha lands[11] to select distinctive features of each, in order to establish a perfect land of his own, based on the best features of all other buddha lands. Most importantly, all beings who live in Dharmakara's buddha-land shall be certain of achieving awakening quickly and easily.[12]

Then Dharmakara made forty-eight vows in which he promised he would not leave the cycle of birth and death

---

[8] Amitabha is also known by the name Amitayus, "Infinite Life." In China he is Omitofo, Amitofo or Emitofo, in Japan he is Amida Butsu.

[9] In this context see Paul M. Harrison, *"Buddhaanusmrti in the Pratyutpanna-buddha-sammukhaavasthita-samaadhi-suutra"* in the *Journal of Indian Philosophy*, Vol. 6, 1978:35–57.

[10] The story of the sutra is summarized in Alfred Bloom, *Shinran's Gospel of Pure Grace* (Association for Asian Studies, 1965), on pages 1–4. See also Allen Andrews, *Teachings Essential for Rebirth: A Study of Genshin's Ojoyoshu* (Tokyo: Sophia University, Monumenta nipponica monograph, 1973), pp. 8–11.

[11] In Mahayana, there are uncountably many buddhas, and each presides over his own buddha-land.

[12] Andrews, *Teachings Essential for Rebirth, op. cit.*, p. 9.

unless he could be certain that he could create such a perfect buddha land. Dharmakara labored for uncountably many lifetimes until he finally accomplished all forty-eight vows. Then he went beyond the status of a bodhisattva to became a buddha and came to preside over his own buddha land. Now he is called Amitabha Buddha, the Buddha of Infinite Light.

The 18th Vow of Dharmakara

> The 18th Vow is the foundation for Pure Land Buddhism. Dharmakara vowed:
> > If, after my obtaining Buddhahood, all beings in the ten quarters should not desire in sincerity and trustfulness to be born in my country, and if they should not be born by only thinking of me for ten times, except those who have committed the five grave offences and those who are abusive of the true Dharma, may I not attain the Highest Enlightenment.[13]

In Mahayana Buddhism, Amitabha Buddha presents a new way of salvation or liberation for all beings. The sutra stresses the recitation of the name of Amitabha Buddha and the value of praising this sutra. Even if one committed the five grave offences, by reciting the name of Amida Buddha ten times his offences would be erased and he could be reborn in the Pure Land.

Followers of Pure Land who possess sincere faith in Amitabha's powers can be certain that they will be reborn in his Western Pure Land paradise. Amitabha Buddha does not care about your beliefs or your moral condition. Amitabha does not care if you are a Buddhist or a Christian. Amitabha does not judge your moral worth. Amitabha rewards perfect faith and the recitation of his name is a chanted phrase of power (a *mantra*).

None of us are spiritually accomplished enough to achieve nirvana on our own — thus we need the loving help of a loving buddha. The Pure Land school relies on the compassion of Amitabha Buddha, and his "chief lieutenant," Avalokiteshvara (bodhisattva of compassion) who will greet and lead followers to the Pure Land after their death.

Those reborn in his Pure Land[14] will never fall back to lower realms, and in the Western Paradise the meditating monk will find it easier to attain nirvana there than to try to achieve nirvana in this world of pain and *duhkha*. People can be assured of being reborn in this paradise if they call upon Amitabha with total faith and confidence. That powerful feeling of faith generates a sympathetic response from Amitabha, who greets and welcomes the follower to the Pure Land.

The Western Paradise is Not the Ultimate Goal

Amitabha's Western Paradise, the heavenly Pure Land, is exceedingly beautiful but it is important to realize that, according to the Pure Land sutras, the heavenly Pure Land is **not** the follower's ultimate destination; rather it is a realm in which Amithabha Buddha himself will personally teach the follower. Being reborn in the Pure Land allows for additional training provided by an actual buddha which will guarantee that the Buddhist student will succeed in the attempt to achieve final nirvana. There are numerous practices taught to ensure the follower of rebirth in the Pure Land, but probably the most common is simply single-minded chanting or recitation of the name of Amitabha with total concentration and complete confidence.

---

[13] This idea of thinking about a divinity at the moment of death has ancient roots. In the *Bhagavad-Gita*, Lord Krishna tells Arjuna: (4) A man who dies remembering me at the time of death enters my being when he is freed from his body, of this there is no doubt (5) Whatever being he remembers when he abandons the body at death, he enters, Arjuna, always existing in that being. Barbara Stoller Miller, *Bhagavad-Gita* (New York: Columbia University Press, 1986), pp. 77-78.

[14] There is more than one way to interpret being reborn in the Pure Land. For example, the Pure Land might be understood as nowhere other than your own mind. Some Chinese Pure Land masters expected you to realize that the Amitabha Buddha that you visualized was you and the Pure Land was simply your mind. Thus, some Pure Land practice identifies one's own mind with the Buddha, or at least we realize that the two were not ultimately different.

Although a small and relatively unimportant form of Buddhism in India, over the centuries, Pure Land Buddhism became one of the most important forms of Buddhism in China, Korea and especially Japan.

10.5 THE MADHYAMAKA TRADITION OF MAHAYANA

The name "Madhyamaka" literally means the "Middlers," in the sense of "Middle Path" or "Middle Way" school.[15] In early Buddhism, the term "Middle Way" referred to the Four Noble Truths as a middle way between the two extremes of <u>practice</u>, one extreme is asceticism and the other extreme is unbridled hedonism. The Madhyamaka tradition re-conceived Buddha's middle way as a path which is free from two extreme <u>views</u> about reality:

(1) The Middle Way is free from the mistaken view of *eternalism* (eternalism is the view that things that are truly real possess something about them which is permanent, an eternal unchanging substance or essence which are uncaused and self-existing)

(2) The Middle Way is free from the mistaken view of complete *nihilism* (nihilism is the view that nothing is real because nothing has an eternal substance or essence, and thus nothing truly exists, it is all illusory, nothing is important, nothing matters).[16]

According to the Madhyamaka, both of these views are extremes and are mistaken. The Madhyamaka "Middlers" pathway is to steer a middle path between eternalism and nihilism. Things are real and do exist (so nihilism is wrong) but at the same time nothing possesses an unchanging self-existing substance (so eternalism is wrong). For the Madhyamika thinkers, the truth is between the two extremes; nothing possesses an eternal self-existent inner essence, but at the same time these flowing processes we call "things" are real and do exist.

It must be stressed that Madhyamaka is a Buddhist school, and so it too is concerned with eliminating misery, frustration, and suffering, *duhkha*. It will argue that most of us have a fundamental misunderstanding about the nature of reality, and this is one major cause of *duhkha*. The problem is that this misunderstanding is grounded in the language which we speak daily, and so these misconceptions are at a very deep level. So, the primary concern is with the true nature of reality.

The focus on the ultimate nature of reality is called ontology, or metaphysics. Basing itself on the Buddhist explanation of causality as dependent co-arising (*pratityasamutpada*), Madhyamaka will build upon the implications of this fundamental concept to explicate their analysis of ultimate reality. The Madhyamaka will also analyze knowledge and the limitations of language to express that knowledge (called "epistemology" in Western philosophy).

Madhyamaka Rejects Abhidharma Teachings

To understand the Madhyamaka school of Mahayana Buddhism, we need to review briefly the position on ultimate reality contained in the Abhidharma texts (discussed in the previous chapter). The Abhidharma texts of early Buddhism ask, "What are the ultimate building blocks of real things? What is reality made of?" The Abhidharma texts answer: real things are composed of *dharmas*, the tiny discrete point-instants of energy which are constantly in motion, and this is what makes up reality. Everything, even human beings, are made of moving *dharmas*, so therefore everything changes.

---

[15] The name of the school is Madhyamaka; the followers of the school are Madhyamikas. This is analogous to the Western school of Existentialism, whose followers are Existentialists.

[16] The Advaita Vedanta school of Hinduism holds both of these views. Shankara declared that to be real is to have an eternal unchanging substance. Shankara concludes that the realm of appearances is ultimately unreal precisely because things lack any enduring substance. Some Hindus criticized Shankara as a "Buddhist in disguise" because he asserted that the things in this world lack enduring *svabhava*; this is his theory of *maya*, discussed in section 4.8 of this volume of *Asian Thought*.

In some schools of Conservative Buddhism these discrete elements of reality were asserted to be containers of an enduring inner self-existing substance. The things in the world made up of collections of *dharmas* (like tables and chairs) are always changing, but the ultimate smallest parts that underlie things, the *dharmas* themselves, are truly real because they contain a permanent a self-existent essence.

Many Indian thinkers (not just Abhidharma Buddhists) asserted that real things possesses an unconditioned and unchanging inner essence, some self-existing nature, an inherent existence, or some aspect of a thing which is not affected by any causes or conditions. Hindu thinkers argued that a thing is ultimately real if it does not depend on other things for its existence. If a thing changes, then it is not ultimately real. This inherent existence never changes, so it is never created or destroyed.

In Sanskrit this unchanging essence is called **svabhava**,[17] a technical term which translated literally is "own-being" or "self-existent," and in English is often translated substance, essence or inherent existence. For those who accept this claim, a real thing exists because it possesses *svabhava*, an independent permanent essence which never changes and that does not arise from causes. For Indian thinkers, things which possess this unchanging substance are truly real; things which lack inherent existence are ultimately unreal. For the Abhidharma Buddhists, the tiny building blocks of reality, *dharmas*, possess **svabhava**, self-existence, or inherent existence, and so are real. If metaphysics is the study of ultimate reality, then *svabhava* is the basic principle which tells us which things are real, and which are not. The Madhyamaka school will disagree with *svabhava* and will argue that *svabhava* is a word which describes or names nothing at all.

Emptiness: the Key Organizing Concept of Madhyamaka

The Madhyamaka school will analyze this metaphysical concept of *svabhava*, self-existent essence, and then argue that if anything actually possessed *svabhava*, the world that we observe around us would be impossible. Causality and change would be impossible. Growth and development would be impossible. Nirvana would be impossible. The building blocks of reality, *dharmas*, may exist but they could not possibly have an eternal unchanging inner self-existent nature.

In fact, the Madhyamaka will argue that there is **nothing anywhere** which is permanent and unchanging. There are no substantial entities which are independent of causality. It is perfectly fine to refer to *dharmas* as the building blocks of reality, but at the same time we must realize that *dharmas* are not a container for eternal self-existent essences. In fact, *dharmas* are **empty of any self-existing inner essence**. The Sanskrit term for this is *svabhava-sunyata*. As we have seen, *svabhava* means "self-existing" or "independently existing." **Sunyata** (pronounced shun-ya-TA) means "emptiness," the state of being empty of an inner eternal substance.[18]

Empty of What?

"Empty" is a relative term; it expresses a relationship. If something is empty, we do not yet know what is missing. If my wallet is empty, we know that I mean that there is no money in it. A vacuum container is empty of air;

---

[17]   In traditional India, what makes a dog a real dog is that real dogs have a permanent dog essence, an essential "dog-hood" or "dogness." Cats share an immutable essence of "catness," and that's why they are different from dogs. Water has "wetness." Fire has "heat." Tables have "tablehood." Human beings have "human nature," or our "common humanity." Unreal things, like a dream, a mirage or illusion, have no inherent essence, no inner unchanging substance, and that is why they are unreal. Madhyamika Buddhists disagree with each of these beliefs.

[18]   The Sanskrit term *sunya* (empty; pronounced shun-ya) is of great historical and mathematical importance to the West. The possibility of both zero and infinity were rejected by Aristotle and Greek and Roman thinkers. In the seventh century, when the Muslims conquered northern India, what we call "Arabic numerals" were adopted by the Muslims from the Indian mathematicians, and carried back into the Muslim empire. In the end of the thirteenth century the ideas were introduced into European mathematics. The Indian term *sunya* is the origin of the words "zero," and "cypher." See Charles Seife, *Zero: The Biography of a Dangerous Idea* (New York: Penguin Books, 2000); chapter 3 discusses the origins of zero in India and its influence upon Arabic numerals.

a cup is empty of tea. The tank of an automobile is empty of gasoline. To say that "all things are empty" raises the question: empty of what?

Defining "Emptiness"

The Madhyamika thinker says that "all things are empty" simply means that all *dharmas* are empty of *svabhava*, empty of an inner self-existing unchanging essence or substance.[19] Every thing you see or touch or taste or smell is without an eternal inner self-existent essence. Even *dharmas*, the building blocks of the things we experience, are without any inner self-existent essence. *Dharmas* is simply a name for changing processes, none of which possess an unchanging ultimate eternal essence. Things are not non-existent, but no thing possesses an immutable inner substance. Things are real and exist, but they are flowing processes, not containers for an inner permanent substance.[20] If we think about things as containers, then every container is empty of inner unchanging self-existent essence.

The Perfection of Wisdom Sutras

The insights into the nature of *dharmas* is incorporated in the approximately thirty-eight volumes[21] that comprise the Mahayana *Prajnaparamita* (Perfection of Wisdom)[22] group of new sutras. These texts inspired the philosophical analysis and conclusion that *dharmas* are empty of unchanging self-existent essences. Two of these sutras are quite popular: (1) the "Diamond Sutra" (*Vajracchedika*, which is the Perfection of Wisdom in 300 Lines),[23] and (2) the "Heart Sutra" (*Hrdaya*, the Perfection of Wisdom in 25 lines).[24] These sutras explain the insight of the bodhisattva which leads to awakening, which is the insight into emptiness. This is the heart of the *Prajnaparita* group of Mahayana sutras.

No Eternal Essences Could Exist If Things Arise From Multiple Causes

If everything in the world arises dependent upon numerous prior causes and conditions as described by *pratityasamutpada*, dependent co-arising, then everything is impermanent; there are no inner unchanging essences anywhere. If what we call "things" arise from multiple causes, and change as the causes change, then all things are

---

[19] We have already encountered this idea in early Buddhism with the assertion that human beings are **empty** of an *atman* — the human body is not a container for an *atman*, we do not possess an inner unchanging soul or essence. Human personality arises from a collection of interdependent processes, with no single aspect remaining unchanging. One way to say this is to say that "selves are empty" of *atman*.

[20] There are many books attempting to explain this idea of "empty of permanent essence." One is *Emptiness: The Foundation of Buddhist Thought* by Tsering, Geshe Tashi & Gordon McDougall, eds., (Boston: Wisdom Publications, 2009). See also C. W. Huntington, Jr., *The Emptiness of Emptiness: An Introduction to Early Indian Madhyamika* (Honolulu, HI: University of Hawai'i Press, 1989).

[21] Edward Conze, *Buddhist Wisdom Books* (New York: Harper Torchbooks, 1958), p. ii.

[22] More than any other individual, the scholar Edward Conze (1904–1979) translated and studied the *Prajnaparamita* texts in several dozen different books, including translations of the titles listed in this paragraph. See the bibliography.

[23] A clearly-written historical and philosophical explanation of the *Diamond* sutra (emphasizing the connections with Ch'an/Zen Buddhism) is Mu Soeng, *The Diamond Sutra: Transforming the Way We Perceive the World*. The *Diamond* sutra is also famous for being the earliest book published with movable type, printed perhaps six-hundred years before the Guttenberg bible. See Frances Wood, and Mark Barnard, *The Diamond Sutra: The Story of the World's Earliest Dated Printed Book* (Oxford: The British Library, 2010)

[24] The *Diamond* and *Heart* sutras are of supreme importance in the East Asian traditions, those of Chinese Ch'an, the Korean Son, and the Japanese Zen schools of Buddhism, and are translated and discussed in much of the Zen literature. It has been argued that the *Heart* sutra was not composed in India, but rather is a Chinese text which summarizes Indian texts. See Jan Nattier, "The *Heart Sutra*: A Chinese apocryphal text?" *Journal of the International Association of Buddhist Studies*, Vol. 15, no. 2, 1992, pp. 153–223.

"empty of unchanging essence" (*svabhava sunyata*), including *dharmas* themselves, the building blocks of our world. If *dharmas* are to exist, they cannot have self-existing essences, *svabhava*. All things in the world arise from changing clusters of causes and conditions. This raises an interesting question. How can fixed language capture truths related to a world of ever-changing processes? Language can direct our attention to the swirling realms around us, but not describe it accurately. This means that even the fundamental insights of the Buddha when expressed in language are not eternal sacred truths. Buddhism too arises from numerous causes and conditions and is empty of essence. This insight leads to the next, about the relationship of form (the physical things that make up our world) to emptiness.

"Form is Emptiness, Emptiness is Form"

Here is a passage from the *Heart sutra*, which is one of the most famous of the quotations from the *Prajnaparamita* group of sutras:

> Listen, Shariputra,[25] form, just as it is, is emptiness (*sunyata*), emptiness, just as it is, is form; form does not differ from emptiness, emptiness does not differ from form.[26]

Everything that is solid we call "form." "Form is emptiness" means that everything we see, hear, touch, taste, or smell, is empty of *svabhava*. Everything we see, hear, touch, taste, or smell, is without an unchanging self-existent substance, without *svabhava*. The table is before us, and the table is real, but the table is not a container for an unchanging substance; nothing about the table is permanent and unchanging. We perceive the impermanent and mistakenly assume it to be permanent. "Form is emptiness" is a corrective for this mistake.

"Emptiness is form" means that the swirling changing universe which is without permanent unchanging essences is precisely the real world of apparently solid forms. Everything solid we call "form," yet "form" arises from multiple causes which themselves are impermanent and changing, so form is without self-existing substance, form is emptiness. All things are empty, and these empty processes constitute forms. Thus, "emptiness is form."

Interdependent causal arising (the insight of *pratityasamutpada*) leads to the understanding of emptiness, and emptiness (the insight that things in the world lack unchanging self-existing substance) is itself describing the world of form.[27] Madhyamika Buddhists will say that tables, chairs, doorways, and living beings, are all various ways in which emptiness appears to us, and ways that we refer to as "forms." All is change, so there is nothing permanent anywhere. To see all as *pratityasamutpada* (dependent co-arising) is to see things as they really are, and is the insight which leads to awakening.

We have a psychological tendency to think of our world as made of relatively stable and unchanging objects, where the substance (*svabhava*) we call "water" has the property of wetness, and the substance we call "fire" has the property of heat. The insight of emptiness (*sunyata*) tells us that our common understanding is not completely accurate. There are no unchanging substances which possess properties and primary and secondary qualities. There are qualities, but no substance to which the qualities belong. The world is ever-changing flux, it is process, with nothing substantial anywhere, nothing unchanging, no *atman*, no essences underlying things.[28]

---

[25] Shariputra was one of the closest friends of the Buddha, and was famous for the depth of his philosophical understanding and insight.

[26] Translated by Robert Zeuschner from the Chinese with reference to the Sanskrit text of Edward Conze and the Alex Wayman commentary, "Secret of the *Heart Sutra*" in Lewis Lancaster, ed., *Prajnaparamita and Related Systems* (Berkeley, CA: Berkeley Buddhist Studies Series, 1977), p. 141.

[27] It is correct to say that all that we experience is empty of immutable substance. However, "emptiness" is a universal generalization dependent upon instances of things which are empty of *svabhava*. We must be careful not to reify "emptiness," not to treat this abstract generalization as though it were something sacred, something absolute or something ultimately transcendent.

[28] Some scholars have noticed that this emptiness claim appears to be compatible with modern quantum physics, where things are ever-changing processes. The table is composed of atoms, yet atoms are almost entirely empty space, tiny electron-processes circling neutrons and protons, which in turn are processes, not self-existent substances.

Nagarjuna: Founder of Madhyamaka

Scholars of Buddhism regard Nagarjuna as the single most important Buddhist thinker[29] after the Buddha himself. Apart from his writings, we do not know much about Nagarjuna. Early biographies claim he was born in south India and most probably lived between 100-250 C.E. Biographies say he studied conservative Buddhism but it did not resolve his deepest questions. He then met a monk who told him that lake-dwelling serpents had hidden and preserved the *Prajnaparamita sutras* ("Perfection of Wisdom sutras") which revealed the truth of *sunyata* (emptiness). The serpents gave these texts to Nagarjuna. Reading these, all of his doubts were settled. Then with his new insights prompted by these sutras, Nagarjuna began writing, began explaining this liberating insight.[30]

Nagarjuna seems to have written extensively about a number of topics. His single most influential and important text is the *Mulamadhyamakakarikas*, or *Verses on the Fundamental Middle Way*. This text was read and studied in India, and then in China, in Korea, in Japan, and in Tibet. Each country produced a large amount of secondary literature commenting upon Nagarjuna's insights and the ultimate implications of his work. Schools of Buddhism based on Nagarjuna proliferated in each country. The influence of Nagarjuna on Mahayana Buddhism is analogous to the importance of Plato or Aristotle's influence on the Western world view.

Nagarjuna on Language and Concepts

Nagarjuna did not just claim that all things are empty (*sunya*) of inherent existence (*svabhava*). Nagarjuna did not expect anyone to accept anything he wrote on faith. He provided extensive philosophical arguments for the conclusion that all the observables that make up reality, *dharmas*, must be empty of essence or empty of substance, for if objects have some self-existing eternal essence like *svabhava*, cause-and-effect would be impossible. To do this, Nagarjuna explores how our conceptual and linguistic conventions structure our understanding of the world.

Obviously, we use language to communicate with one another. We try to describe reality using words. We tend to assume that the grammar and structure of our words reflects the structure of reality, but do they? Can language accurately describe reality? If things arise from numerous causes, and change when the causes change, then every thing in the world is continually changing processes.[31] Consider a waterfall or a river. Its name stays the same, but the actual physical flowing river changes constantly. We tend to think that our words and names describe enduring fixed objects ("desk" "chair" "whiteboard" "Colorado River") but the physical things that the words denote are not fixed, they are dependent and impermanent. The things those words conceptualize, the things that the noises (words) point to are swirling change.[32]

It is obvious that words and concepts have a practical value ("Please pass the salt") and there is no problem when we understand that language is conventional ("Gasoline is $5 per gallon this week"). The difficulty is that the structure and function of language can cause us to misunderstand the nature of the world in which we live.

Words are relatively fixed so it is very natural to assume that words correspond to and pick out relatively fixed objects in the world. Thus language can reinforce mistaken ideas about the nature of reality. Because we have the word

---

[29] The literature on Nagarjuna and the Madhyamaka tradition is vast, and many are listed in the bibliography at the end of this chapter. Two of the very best philosophical treatments are Mark Siderits and Shoryu Katsura, *Nagarjuna's Middle Way* (Boston: Wisdom Publications, 2013), and Jan Westerhoff, *Nagarjuna's Madhyamaka* (New York and London: Oxford University Press, 2009).

[30] A Tibetan biography of Nagarjuna can be found in Donald S. Lopez, Jr., *A Study of Svatantrika* (Ithica, N.Y.: Snow Lion, 1987), pp. 245–249.

[31] Again, the perceptive student might note that this description is implied by modern physics and the sub-atomic realm of processes, of changing atoms within nothing solid and unchanging, with nothing permanent.

[32] Please note that spoken or written language is not the only means by which we communicate. We communicate with a snap of the fingers or a wink of the eye, we communicate by the way we walk, and even by the tone of our voice.

"I" we assume that because we used the term "I" fifteen years ago, and then we used "I" five years ago, and then again yesterday, the term "I" refers to something unchanging within us, a true self, a soul, an *atman*, but in fact when we look and search within, we find that we are empty of *atman*.

Another problem is that some people have a regrettable tendency to confuse symbols with reality. They mistakenly assume that because we have a name for something (like "time" or "truth"), then there must also be some existing thing that corresponds to that name (i.e., "time itself" or "truth itself"). Language is conventionally useful, but we have a tendency to assume that its structure corresponds to reality and provides an accurate description of reality. As a result, we experience *duhkha*.

Making it more personal, people refer to me as "Bob." The noise "Bob" does not change, but the person picked out by that name (me) is continually changing. I'm learning new things, I'm forgetting old things, I'm gaining weight, I'm losing weight. I find new things to like. I learn a new acoustic blues piece from the 1930s. I forget tunes I used to be able to play on the guitar. Experiences are occurring regularly which change me. If you knew me twenty years ago, and assume that because my name has not changed, that therefore some inner enduring thing about me has never changed (i.e., an *atman*), then you've made a conceptual mistake and have been fooled by language.

Whenever we mistakenly believe our words and concepts of things are accurately referring to unchanging objects which make up reality, we have a mistaken understanding of the nature of reality. We have been confused by a useful form of speech when we take the word or concept to refer to some actual separate entity; we take a concept and turn it into a thing.

Reification: turning words into things

When we mistakenly think that terms naming abstract ideas like "time," "truth," or "being," correspond to real things, then we are **reifying**[33] the words and our error produces great confusion. There is no immutable substance called "mind," but there are flowing mental states. There is no substance called "time" but there are measurable durations which are relative to our systems of descriptions. Words are useful. Words can draw our attention to what is around us, but language is nothing more than a limited system of symbols, which cannot adequately describe reality, especially if we believe that real things have an unchanging essence.

Describe what it feels like to hold the hand of someone you care about deeply. You cannot do it. I cannot describe the taste of mango to someone who has never tasted something like a mango. I cannot describe what it feels like to be in love to someone who has never experienced it. I cannot explain the feeling of surfing on a wave to someone who never had a similar experience. I can try to find experiences in the person's life which are analogous to surfing, but I cannot describe it without saying "it is like . . .."

Who Cares Whether Words Describe Reality?

Ordinary people use language without worrying about whether words and concepts adequately describe reality, but there are several groups of people for whom language is very important. These include people who believe that sacred scriptures contain inerrant descriptions of reality because they were spoken by a god, by a *deva* or a buddha. These are monks, priests, true believers and theologians.[34] Their business is sacred words, sacred texts, and they seek ultimately inerrant correct descriptions of sacred reality.

---

[33] When we reify, we treat an abstract idea as though it was a physical thing in the world, we make a thing out of an idea. Self, Mind, Time, Truth, and Being are Western examples of this process. We understand "What time is it?" perfectly well, but we become confused when we are then asked, "What is Time itself?" We have reified the term "time." We understand "I am going to the market" perfectly well, but we become confused when we ponder, "What is this 'I', what is this 'self'?" The technical Buddhist term for the tendency to "thingify" words is *prapañca*.

[34] We human beings are infamous for killing one another over our words, our descriptions of the sacred. "The words in my sacred book are completely correct, and therefore the words in your sacred book are all mistaken" or "The earth is the center of the universe," or "God created the earth and all living things just 6,000 years ago." The history of Western religion is filled with groups killing other groups over their descriptions of reality.

Those deeply immersed in religion treat scriptures as sacred objects, instead of what they really are: pieces of paper filled with black marks which are only symbols. They regard the names of their deities as sacred sounds of power and are offended when those names are uttered, written down or slandered.

Philosophers are another group who spend much effort analyzing the nature of reality, and the tools philosophers use to describe reality are words, concepts, and language. Philosophers and theologians both are prone to mistakenly believing that words or concepts can capture accurately or describe ultimate reality.

The Madhyamika philosopher asserts that we do not notice that our ideas and concepts are merely conventional symbols pressed on paper, just vibrations of the air which issue from our mouths. These are just symbols. Symbols cannot be described as being real, or being correct, and symbols are not adequate to describe reality just as it is.

"The map is not the territory"

Perhaps you've heard the phrase "the map is not the territory." The map stands for the territory, the map symbolizes the territory. The map is marks on a piece of paper which point to the actual physical territory and help us figure out how to go from one point to another. Thus the map is useful. But the map is not the territory. The word (and concepts symbolized by the word) is not the thing. Similarly, the menu is not the meal. A photographic menu points to the meal, but it is a visual or written description. It cannot satisfy hunger. The menu is not the meal. Words and concepts, even the deepest most profound religious words may be useful, but they are just concepts, are just noises, just puffs of wind, just symbols—but not ultimate truths.[35]

When we focus our attention on the words and concepts, we can miss what the words are symbolizing, what they point to. There is no problem as long as we realize that religious language and philosophy give us a partial view of reality, a perspective on reality, and words are the useful tools we use to describe this perspective or viewpoint of reality. According to the Madhyamaka analysis, all of our philosophical and religious views are, at best, partial views of reality. This is not a problem unless we confuse our symbols with reality. The Madhyamika Buddhists argue that every religious claim, every philosophical claim, is a perspective which cannot help but be incomplete, misleading and **cannot be held as absolute truth**. This confusion about language, then, is a source of *duhkha*, frustration, dissatisfaction, and suffering.

In Madhyamaka thought, the way we understand *what a thing is* depends on the perceiver as well as the world. Our language and our concepts can pre-determine how we will interpret what we see. I look at someone, and I see a brother, you see a student, and the recruiter sees a soldier. Someone who is biased may see someone of a different race, different religion, and may even see an "enemy." Our views are relative to many interdependent factors. What is reality like apart from our linguistic conceptions of things? Is it possible to see things without any preconceptions at all? Perhaps we can see things through their relative interconectedness, but a Madhyamika Buddhist adept would not take any of those relative perspectives as absolutely true.

When you and I have a distorted misunderstanding of the way things really are, and we act on that misunderstanding, we are going to be frustrated, dissatisfied, and miserable. The implication of the idea of *sunyata* is that because all things lack ultimate unchanging reality, being possessive and attached to things as though they could provide enduring happiness, is acting confusedly. There is no enduring substance, no enduring substantiality, and no enduring value. This can be frightening, but it is the way things are. Of course, this is why there is *duhkha*.

---

[35] In the United States, there is a red, white and blue flag which symbolizes the country and symbolizes the values of the country. Those people who want to put someone in jail for burning the flag are confusing the symbol with what is being symbolized. These people want to put others in jail because they have set fire to several pieces of dyed cloth that have been sewn together.

Madhyamaka Criticisms of the *Arhat*

From the Mahayana perspective, the goal of the conservative Buddhist, the *arhat*, has achieved nirvana, has successfully eliminated *duhkha*, and understands that persons are empty of *atman*, but the *arhat* does not yet understand that **all things are empty of inherent existence** (*svabhava-sunyata*). Mahayana followers claim that the Theravada *arhat* has an incomplete understanding, and has not removed all ignorance. An *arhat* may have mastered the tools to escape from the cycle of *samsara*, but she does not have the all-encompassing understanding of a Buddha (according to the Mahayana).

Nagarjuna's Method

If someone says something that I disagree with, I am inclined to assert "you are mistaken." This is simply to disagree with the person. Nagarjuna does *not* simply disagree, and Nagarjuna does not quote Buddhist thinkers to show you are wrong. Rather, Nagarjuna begins and says "Let's assume that everything you have said is completely and totally correct." Nagarjuna then logically derives implications from your view which you yourself recognize are absurd and impossible. In mathematics and philosophical logic, this is called the method of *reductio ad absurdam*, to "reduce to an absurdity." Nagarjuna, the logical philosopher, uses logic to reveal that all attempts to describe a reality believed to be composed of self-existent substances result in absurdity, in self-contradiction.[36]

Most people mowing the lawn, shopping for food, and in general going about their everyday affairs have no interest in describing reality. But the status of language is a crippling problem for those who hold their own view or description of reality to be absolute, to be completely correct. These are philosophers and religious people who study texts in an attempt to know what is ultimately true.

The goal of the Madhyamaka process is to help you realize that the problem is your mistaken conception of the nature of reality. Can you realize that your concepts—the unconscious assumption that reality is made of objects which possess self-existing *svabhava*—are the cause of all the absurd self-contradictory conclusions?

The result of the Madhyamaka process of Nagarjuna: (a) first you analyze then reject the non-Buddhist Hindu views of *atman* and Brahman as self-contradictory and thus impossible; (b) then you analyze and show that conservative *Tripitaka* Buddhist views of truly real *dharmas* which possess *svabhava* are not correct descriptions of reality; (c) although you try holding onto Mahayana descriptions, you find them too demonstrated to be self-contradictory and incorrect; (d) and when you think you've got the final truth, that **all things are empty** of *svabhava*, you find not even that statement is an ultimately correct description of things such as they are. There is no position or perspective at all which can be correct.

Sunyata and *Pratityasamutpada*

Nagarjuna points out that emptiness, *sunyata* (shun-ya-TA), is not some new concept which he has added to Buddhism. He thinks the concept is already implied in the earliest teachings of the Buddha. Consider the early Buddhist key organizing concept of *pratityasamutpada*, or dependent co-arising. Nagarjuna argues that when a person completely understands the implications of causality (dependent co-arising or *pratityasamutpada*), the central concept in early Buddhism, one recognizes that this is simply equivalent to *sunyata*, "emptiness" or "empty of inherent existence" (*svabhava-sunyata*).

---

[36] Mark Siderits and Shoryu Katsura offer a brief analysis of the basic types of arguments used by Nagarjuna in their book, *Nagrjuna's Middle Way* (Somerville, MA: Wisdom Publications, 2013), pp. 7–9.

Emptiness means that nothing in the world is self-created, self-existent, eternal and uncreated, and nothing in the world stands alone, unrelated to other things. Nothing exists in itself, in isolation. Everything exists in relation to other things. There is nothing anywhere with a solid permanent substance; it is all flowing processes. But this is precisely what *pratityasamutpada* implies. If you understand that all things are dependent upon changing causes and conditions and nothing stands independent and alone, then you understand that nothing possesses *svabhava*. Only then do you understand *sunyata*.[37]

Both *pratityasamutpada* and *sunyata* amount to a denial of the Hindu substantialist claim that there is an underlying substratum, an unchanging self-existent nature (*svabhava*) which gives things their enduring self-identity over time (which in humans is named *atman* and supposedly transmigrates from one life to the next). Instead, the Buddhists argue that changing things (or events) arise from a network of many different interdependent causal processes, and what they are (their name, their identity) depends on convention and changes over time. Thus, *anatman*, no-atman, no eternal unchanging essence to a human being.

If a *svabhava* (unchanging essential feature) existed, then one of the causes of an event would have conveyed that essence from prior cause to subsequent event. The result (the event, the "thing") would be some thing with an unchanging essence which defined it. In that case, the other causes and conditions would be irrelevant. The other causes and conditions would have no essential effect on the event, because the essence (*svabhava*) had been transmitted and nothing else is relevant.

Nagarjuna explicitly states that *sunyata* is the same as dependent origination or dependent co-arising, or *pratityasamutpada* properly understood, in chapter 24, verse 18 of his classic text *Verses on the Fundamental Middle Way*. In their translation from the Sanskrit, Mark Siderits and Shoryu Katsura translate:

Dependent origination we declare to be emptiness;
It [emptiness] is a dependent concept; just that is the middle path.[38]

Pratityasamutpada properly understood is *sunyata*, and the verse indicates that these are simply conventional terms, but neither term identifies some self-existent reality denoted by the words *"pratityasamutpada"* or *"sunyata."* Whatever things arise dependently, those things are empty of self-existence or inherent essence. Since everything arises dependently, then everything is empty.[39] "Emptiness" is a useful noise or sound, but it is just a conceptual fiction.

The term "emptiness" draws our attention to the insight that nothing sustains its existence by itself, without causes and conditions. Nothing has inherent existence or self-existence (*svabhava*). Nothing is independent. All the things that exist, exist because they arise out of numerous causes and conditions and have no inner unchanging essence, no "own-being" (*svabhava*) or self-nature. Thus, all things are *svabhava-sunyata*.[40]

Does Buddhism have a True Description of Reality?

Is anything the Buddha is quoted to have said a correct description of reality? The only consistent answer has to be "no" if we assume that the Buddha is making accurate claims about ultimate reality in which we are supposed

---

[37] Some Buddhists disagree with this claim, that emptiness is the simple absence of *svabhava*, self-existing essence. They will argue that emptiness is an experience which transcends both existence and non-existence, something transcendental. In this view, emptiness becomes something closer to god-like.

[38] Siderits and Katsura, *op. cit.*, p. 277.

[39] In the *Heart Sutra*, this is the meaning of "Form itself is emptiness."

[40] In an interesting quirk of history, due to the nature of the translation of the Sanskrit verse into Chinese, the later Chinese T'ien-t'ai school understood this verse to be teaching three truths, (1) emptiness, (2) dependent origination (the conventional), and (3) the highest truth which transcends both, i.e., the Middle Way.

to have faith. However, if we understand the Buddha's language as conventional, as symbols to draw our attention to the processes that surround us, then the problem disappears. The realization that all things are empty of *svabhava* (no self-existing intrinsic nature) stops our human disposition to believe that there are ultimately real objects in the world, instead of recognizing that all our words provide are merely useful concepts.

But, what happens to Nagarjuna's own claim that all *dharmas* are empty? Nagarjuna uses language when he asserts this position. Is emptiness a correct description of reality?

The result of the method of Nagarjuna is that when you think you've got the final truth, that **all things are empty** of self-existence, you find not even that is an ultimately correct description of things such as they are. Nagarjuna asserts that the view that "all things are empty" must not be held onto as though it were some ultimately correct description of reality. It is not.

Emptiness is Empty

Nagarjuna concludes that in the final analysis, **emptiness itself is empty**. "Emptiness" is an expedient device, not a description of reality. The goal of Madhyamaka is *not* to produce a statement about ultimate self-existent elements of reality. Instead, the goal is to have the student let go of trying to conceptualize reality as composed of ultimately real self-existing essences; this is the function of the useful concept of emptiness. If one clings to the concept of emptiness, then emptiness becomes an obstacle instead of a helpful tool designed to lessen clinging.

With the statement "emptiness itself is empty," Nagarjuna asserts that emptiness is *not* an ultimate truth which describes reality accurately. Emptiness is not a truth to believe in, not a truth to assert and hold to, not even a description of reality. Rather, emptiness is a medicine, a tool to use as an antidote against dogma, against mis-conceptualization, against thinking that we have enduring souls and that things have self-existing substances or essences.

Emptiness is a tool to help us realize that ideas and concepts cannot be accurate representations of reality. When you deeply understand emptiness, you no longer assume that things remain unchanging over time. You live fully in the present, fully in things just as they are.

Emptiness is not a truth about the world. The concept of "emptiness" is merely a tool whose function is to get you to let go of concepts[41] and live fully in the present moment. A hammer is a tool, but it is not correct to call a hammer "true," or "accurate." Certainly one would not want to put the hammer on an altar and bow down to it. Thus emptiness, like the hammer, is not true or accurate; but it is useful.

Emptiness is simply a poetic way of referring to two facts. (1) One fact is that everything that exists does so because of a multiplicity of causal factors, so that nothing is independent or self-existing (nothing has an unchanging essence, a self-nature, a *svabhava*). (2) The other is the fact that every concept we use to understand the world (such as the concepts of "cause," "effect," "time," "space," "conditioned," "unconditioned," "bondage," "liberation," "samsara" and "nirvana") makes sense only in the context of contrasting concepts, that no concept is primitive and absolute. "All such dichotomies, in other words, contribute to suffering when we take them to reflect the nature of reality and fail to see them as mere useful tools."[42]

But if one ever forgets that one is speaking poetically, or if one forgets what that poetic image refers to, then one is liable to reify emptiness, to treat it as some absolute truth describing ultimate reality. And, as Nagarjuna warns so eloquently, when one turns emptiness, the cure to all views, into an eternal truth, then one becomes incurable.

Nagarjuna knows we can use language and concepts as long as we realize that language is like a finger pointing

---

[41] Some might note a similarity between this and the later philosophy of Ludwig Wittgenstein. See Chris Gudmunsen, *Wittgenstein & Buddhism* (New York: Barnes and Noble Books, 1977).

[42] Siderits and Katsura, *op. cit.*, p. 198.

at the moon;[43] the finger is a device to get you to focus your attention on the moon. If you focus your attention exclusively on the finger, you miss the moon! The finger (language, concepts) is not true. It is just a way of drawing and focusing your attention, a way of helping you to see the moon. One can use concepts without thinking that concepts are ultimately correct and true. One uses language without being confused by language.

There is no single reality called "emptiness" any more than there is some ultimately real entity called "time." I can assert "all *dharmas* are empty of essence," without believing in a mysterious entity called "emptiness."[44]

Many deeply religious people have a desire to possess the highest truth, the ultimate truth, the absolute truth. There is a natural tendency for the Madhyamika student to hold tightly to *sunyata* or emptiness as that final truth that the student has been seeking. Nagarjuna warns us not to do that. Those who take *svabhava-sunyata* as an ultimately correct description of reality have it wrong. Those who **believe** in emptiness have got it wrong! Do not have faith in emptiness, do not fixate on *sunyata*. To genuinely understand emptiness is to relinquish the belief that any view is absolutely correct. Emptiness does not offer religious certainty, or conviction. Rather, it offers freedom from the traps of concepts and language.

"Emptiness is not an ultimately real entity nor a property of ultimately real entities. Emptiness is no more than a useful way of conceptualizing experience."[45] "Emptiness" is just black marks on white paper, it is a sound we make, a conventional and useful term whose function is to point us to a way to see the world and lessen *duhkha*.

Emptiness is like an aspirin. The aspirin pill is neither true or false, but merely used to accomplish a purpose. The same is true for emptiness. Emptiness is like a ladder which gets us onto the roof, like a boat which carries us to the other side of the river. A ladder is simply a tool like a hammer or a saw.

Emptiness has accomplished its purpose when we no longer hold to any view as absolute, as ultimate and correct. *Sunyata* is not ultimate truth and it is not a description of anything; rather it is like a medicine; take the medicine to bring about health. When we are healthy, we do not need the medicine any longer. We use the ladder to climb to the roof, but we do not pull the ladder up after ourselves and strap it to our back.

Buddhism is Empty

For Madhyamaka, the Four Noble Truths and other teachings of Buddhism are not truths at all; they are a finger pointing to the moon. Buddhism, like emptiness, is like the raft that we use to get to the other shore. When you get to the other shore (the end of *duhkha*), leave the raft behind! Do not hold onto the raft, do not carry it on your back. Do not hold onto Buddhism or *sunyata* as ultimate truth. Every truth, even Buddhist truths, are only conventionally true. According to Nagarjuna, none are ultimately true.

Even the truth that "all truths are only conventionally true" is merely conventionally true. If you treat this as an ultimate truth, you've made a mistake. If you recognize that it is a useful statement intended to affect behavior and minimize mistaken assumptions, then it can help us to understand how to lessen *duhkha*.

For Nagarjuna, the value of Buddhism is not that it correctly describes reality. The Buddha was not trying to describe reality with his discourses, but instead trying to get us to change our behavior, to change the way we conceptualize and deal with the world, in order to lessen *duhkha*. According to Madhyamaka, to ask "Is Buddhism

---

[43] "The one who sees only the literal, does not see reality—like one who wants to see the moon, [but instead is] gazing at the finger [pointing at it]." Candrakīrti, *Pradīpoddyotana*. The later Mahayana *Lankāvatāra Sūtra* also comments on the delusion of mistaking the finger that points as the object, the moon.

[44] A good book which explores this is C. W. Huntington, Jr., *The Emptiness of Emptiness: An Introduction to Early Indian Madhyamika* (Honolulu, HI: University of Hawai'i Press, 1989). This is the interpretation offered by the ancient thinker named Candrakirti including a translation of Candrakirti's commentary, "The Entry into the Middle Way."

[45] Siderits and Katsura, *op. cit.*, p. 278.

true?" is to miss the point. The Buddhists ask us to judge Buddhism by its fruits: does the practice of Buddhist techniques turn one's life into a positive life experience? If so, that is the entire point.

The Four Noble Truths (*duhkha*, arising of *duhkha*, cessation of *duhkha*, Noble Eightfold Path) are not ultimate truths to believe in or accurate descriptions of unchanging reality; they are a prescription for action ("Take two pills every four hours"). The ideas of Buddhism are like signposts pointing the direction to your goal. If going in the direction of the signpost will lessen *duhkha*, then it works. But the signpost itself is just a symbol, is neither true nor false.

The value of Madhyamaka Buddhism is that it can help you to recognize that all theories are a potential trap of attachment which then are potential causes of *duhkha*. Do not cling to Buddhism or Buddhist philosophy. According to the Madhyamaka analysis, no religious or philosophical theory can give us truth; Buddhist thought is a **method** which helps you to let go of your attachment to theories, concepts, representations, views, and even let go of your attachment to religion. The result: you live fully in reality!

THE TWO TRUTHS

It may be true that the world is made up of shifting processes, but most of us do not use language as though we were trying to describe reality. It is a network of social conventions that makes me a college professor. It is interdependent social relationships that determine who counts as "teacher" and who is a "student." In a different context, I may be the student and you be the teacher.

It is conventionally true that my college has 28,000 students, even though "being a student" is relative to the time, place, and culture, and even though no student has an independent unchanging personal essence (*atman*) and every student is slowly changing every day. It is conventionally true that we live in a world filled with *duhkha*, and seek nirvana. If all mental constructs are inadequate, then so too the construct of the duality between *samsara* and nirvana must be incorrect. In the Indian world view, we all live in the cycle of birth and death, in *samsara* and we seek liberation from *samsara*. Nagarjuna asserts that even the distinction between nirvana and *samsara* is not ultimate truth.[46]

In the *Mulamadhyamakakarikas*, chapter 25 is on nirvana and in verses 19-20, Nagarjuna writes:

There is no distinction whatsoever between samsara and nirvana.
There is no distinction whatsoever between nirvana and samsara.
What is the limit of nirvana, that is the limit of samsara.
There is not even the finest gap to be found between the two.[47]

Neither *samsara* nor nirvana have an unchanging essence; the terms point to processes. Neither exist independently from one another. In fact, they depend upon and define one another. Nirvana does not name some alternate realm separate from *samsara*. Nirvana is life when the emotional pain and frustration called *duhkha* no longer arises and our ignorance is gone. Like all things, both nirvana and *samsara* are dependently arisen. Ultimately, the limits of *samsara* are the same limits of nirvana. They both share a common nature—that they are empty of essence. Nirvana is just *samsara* perceived without anger, hatred, ego, and confusion. Then we see things clearly.[48] This would seem to be a higher truth which can free us from the conventional truths that have confused us.

---

[46] Esoteric Buddhism will stress that the distinction between nirvana and samsara is conventional, not ultimate. The same will be true for the common Hindu distinction between "purity" and "polluted."

[47] Siderits and Katsura, *op. cit.*, p. 302.

[48] The Japanese Zen Buddhist teacher Hakuin (1686-1768) offers this comment: "Nirvana and samsara, [are] riding whips carved from rabbit horn." Of course, there is no such thing as "rabbit horn." Norman Waddell, *Zen Words for the Heart* (Boston: Shambhala, 1996), p. 37.

Note, however, that this says nothing about the conventional status of nirvana and samsara. A Madhyamika can still hold it to be conventionally true that nirvana and samsara are very different states, that the former should be sought while the latter should be stopped, and so on.[49]

From this comes the Madhyamaka thesis of **two truths**, or **two goods**, or two goals.

The Conventional Truth

The first is the **provisional, conventional, worldly truth, mundane truth**, or **conventional good**. This includes ordinary conversation, such as "today is Tuesday," that I am a person writing and you are a person reading, that rivers flow, that it is better to be paid $50 per hour than $15 per hour. It is only because there is consensual agreement among the entire community that we agree to call this day "Tuesday" that it is Tuesday. Tuesday is a conceptually created entity, and such things exist by common agreement, by convention. The conventional truth also corresponds to *Tripitaka* teachings such as the Four Noble Truths, *dharmas* and the distinction between the realm of *samsara* and the state of release from *samsara*, nirvana.

The Buddhists are not trying to devalue conventional truth. It is essential to our lives. The conventional truth makes nirvana possible, it is the realm of Buddhist practice. If we agree to talk on the level of conventional reality, all of this is just fine.

The Ultimate Truth

However, there is the *paramartha*, usually rendered into English as the highest truth, supreme truth or **ultimate truth**. The term *-artha* in Sanskrit has the meaning of a worthy good, or a worthy goal.[50] The **highest truth** is that when we let go of all claims to an ultimate reality, we realize there is no content to the highest truth. The highest truth is merely abandoning the grasping of any view as the ultimate one. The ultimate truths do not describe some different realm or reality apart from the conventional.

For Nagarjuna, things are neither ultimately real nor ultimately unreal. "Reality" is just a concept, just an idea. Things are just what they are, things are "Suchness," such as they are. Whatever is said about the ultimate nature of reality can only point toward it, not fully describe it.

One cannot help but wonder if the doctrine of the Two Truths is an ultimate truth itself, or merely a conventional truth. To be consistent, the goal of the Two Truths is to allow us to free ourselves from attachment to truth. The ultimate truth seems to be that there are no ultimate truths; thus the doctrine itself must be conventional, in the same way that the distinction between *samasara* and nirvana is merely conventional.

Is Nirvana Conditioned or Unconditioned?

Some Buddhists believe that a phrase from an early Pali *sutra* (*Khuddaka-nikaya*) asserts that nirvana must be some sort of transcendental Ultimate Absolute. In *Udana* ("Significant Utterances") 80–81, we find the following:

Monks, there is a not-born, not-become, not-made, not-compounded. Monks, if that not-born, not-become, not-made, not-compounded were not, no escape from the born, become, made, compounded

---

[49] Siderits and Katsura, *op. cit.*, p. 303.

[50] In traditional Hinduism, in life there are four goals or aims, four *artha*: virtuous living in accord with duty, wealth, pleasure, liberation. As we have seen, the "ultimate goal" of the Buddhist is nirvana. So a truth is *parama-artha* if it conduces to nirvana. What leads to nirvana is the elimination of the three root causes of *duhkha*.

would be known here. But monks, since there is a not-born, not-become, not-made, not-compounded, therefore an escape from the born, become, made, compounded is known.[51]

Nirvana is the Absence of Duhkha

It is easy to see why many take the above quote as evidence that nirvana is some sort of ultimate truth or eternal realm which transcends conventional reality. However, the Third Noble Truth (that nirvana is the absence of the three unwholesome root causes of *duhkha*) asserts that nirvana is not a thing, it is the absence of the root causes of *duhkha*.

Nirvana is Not the Absence of Duhkha

In Chapter 25 of Nagarjuna's classic *Verses on the Fundamental Middle Way*, the Madhyamaka analysis of nirvana results in a rejection of the claim that nirvana is an absence, or a presence, or both, or neither. To say "nirvana is an absence" is not useful. To say "nirvana is not an absence" is also not useful. For the Madhyamika thinker, statements like "Nirvana exists" or "Nirvana does not exist" are both obstacles or impediments to the lessening of suffering.

If we accept the Two Truths (discussed previously), then the "truth of nirvana" is a conventional truth, a useful fiction, a helpful and skillful device to aid us in the elimination of frustration and misery. To speak of and advocate practices to lessen suffering and conduce to nirvana is a compassionate thing to do. It is conventionally useful for us to strive for nirvana. However, at the end of the process, to claim that nirvana has been attained is only conventionally true. It is no more than a fruitful fiction.[52]

At the level of highest truth, no ultimately true statements can be made (including the statement that "no ultimately true statements can be made"), only statements that are conventionally true. At the level of the highest truth, nothing [with an enduring essence] has been obtained and no one [no enduring *atman* or essence at the heart of the processes which constitute the "self"] exists to achieve nirvana. There are no ultimately real entities, just processes which interact. It follows that no possible view concerning nirvana and the person who attains nirvna, can be ultimately true.[53]

10.6 THE MAHAYANA YOGACHARA: A Stress on Mind and the Unconscious[54]

Sometime prior to 300 C.E. several new Mahayana sutras appeared which placed stress on consciousness.[55] Basing its insights on these and several additional texts and commentaries, the Yogachara Mahayana Buddhist tradition

---

[51] David Kalupahana, *Buddhist Philosophy: A Historical Analysis*, p. 75. Kalupahana's book devotes an entire chapter to this topic.

[52] It is conventionally true that today is May 12th, but that is true only because we all agree to talk about the process called "today" with a useful label, "the 12th," but nothing in nature, nothing in reality supports that label. In fact, for many other world cultures, today would not be labeled "the 12th." It is conventionally true, but not ultimately true.

[53] Paraphrasing Siderits and Katsura, *Nagarjuna's Middle Way*, p. 303–304.

[54] An excellent summary treatment of Yogachara and all aspects of Mahayana in general is Paul Williams, *Mahayana Buddhism: The Doctrinal Foundations*, (London: Routledge, 1989). A more detailed treatment is found in William S. Waldron, *The Buddhist Unconscious: The Alaya-vijñana in the context of Indian Buddhist Thought* (London: Routledge, 2006). See also Dan Lusthaus, *Buddhist Phenomenology: A Philosophical Investigation of Yogacara Buddhism* (London: Routledge, 2002). The Lusthaus volume places special emphasis on Chinese understandings of Yogacara.

[55] These included the *Samdhinirmochana sutra (Resolving the Underlying Meaning)* and the *Lankavatara* ([Buddha's] *Descent into Lanka*).

developed. This new Mahayana tradition which stressed consciousness is known by several names: **Yogachara** (mastery of yogic meditation); *Cittamatra* (mind-only); *Vijnapti-matrata* (consciousness-only).

The Yogacara/Yogachara[56] school will claim that human beings possess a consciousness which can become free from all error, free from those complications and discriminations which cause us suffering. There must be a deep untainted consciousness in the mind or otherwise awakening would be impossible. Yogacara will argue that this consciousness contains "seeds" which are pure, and "seeds" which are impure. To become a buddha is to use focused concentration to eliminate the impure aspects of consciousness.

New Questions

Yogacara accepts the emptiness arguments of Nagarjuna and the *Prajnaparamita* sutras (which teach emptiness), but there is a deep psychological dimension to Yogachara thought that is not typical of the Madhyamaka traditions. The Yogacharins are asking new questions. What is the relationship between consciousness and reality? How are sense perceptions, feelings, memories and ideas related to reality? How is consciousness related to nirvana? If all things are empty of essence, then consciousness is also empty of any self-existent substance, but then what relates one moment of consciousness with the moment that follows? How do we remember the past, and how is the future moment of consciousness related to the past moments? What sort of connection is possible between past, present, and future? How can karma connect past actions to future consequences unless there is a connection?

Yogachara acknowledges the emptiness of *dharmas*, and agrees with Nagarjuna's arguments that ultimately there are no fixed marks to distinguish *samsara* and nirvana, and that all mental or linguistic constructions are conventional and relative. However, these thinkers were not completely happy with Nagarjuna's conclusion that all things are empty and nothing ultimately true can be asserted.

From the Yogachara perspective, Madhyamaka seems too negative. The stress on the emptiness of all things is a stress on the **absence** of *svabhava*, or on the **lack** of unchanging essences. It seemed that the positive message of the Buddha was lost in emptiness. What about the positive fact of ending the psychological state of *duhkha*? What about the positive fact that a follower can become a bodhisattva, or even a buddha? Where is the positive side of Buddhism? Who is it who awakens? Who is ignorant and where is ignorance? Who becomes a bodhisattva or a buddha? How is the consciousness of a buddha different from the consciousness of an ordinary person?

Yogachara thinkers shift the focus from Nagarjuna's metaphysical analysis of the nature of reality and language to a more meditative and detailed psychological analysis of the <u>mind</u> which awakens. How does our <u>mind</u> experience the world where all things are dependently-arising processes, and <u>who</u> is it who experiences processes which are empty of self-nature? What is the difference between an awakened mind, and an unawakened mind? Is there some deeper underlying subliminal consciousness which serves to connect each moment of shifting and transitory experience? Can this deeper unconscious connect one life to the next in the constant round of rebirth, or *samsara*? Can this deeper consciousness account for karma? The Yogachara seeks to analyze the nature of consciousness or mind, and the primary tool to understand mind is focused concentration.

Yogachara Practices

The fundamental Yogachara practice is meditation, or focused concentration, which emphasizes perception, awareness, consciousness and the purification of consciousness. When I see a world of empty flowing processes, I have mental images. When I am deeply focused in concentrated meditation, there are also images. When I am dreaming,

---

[56] Yoga-achara is the term **Yoga** as focused meditation plus **-achara** (an adept practitioner). The standard transliteration of the Sanskrit is Yogacara, but the "c" is pronounced "ch." English speakers will approximate the correct pronunciation with the spelling "Yo-guh-AHch-ara."

there are images (and these are so vivid that usually I do not know that I'm dreaming). What is the difference between the images when awake, when meditating, and when dreaming?

Consciousness creates our world

Normally we think that images and sensations reflect exactly what is out there is the external world. The Yogachara thinkers argue that this is mistaken. All images, no matter what their causes may be, are grounded in mind and mind-produced. Our consciousness creates the world in which we are aware. You and I create the entire world in our own consciousness. This is a rather startling conclusion. Ordinarily we think that we are the subject, and our senses come in contact with externally existing objects, and the coming together of both subject and object produce the conscious experience of things in the world. Yogacara thinkers reverse this.

When the eyes are open, visual information flows from the retina through the optic nerve and into the brain, which assembles this raw information into objects and scenes. Then we interpret our mental images and believe that these are accurate re-creations of some objective external reality. This belief is being challenged by Yogacara thinkers.

For Yogachara, consciousness generates the world which in itself has neither subject (the perceiver) nor object (thing perceived). I experience colors, shapes, textures, odors, flavors and sounds. There is the experience of sensations and perceptions. The problem is each of these is present only in consciousness. All we can ever experience is our own mental images, our own mind. I can never escape from my own consciousness to experience things directly. I cannot tell whether my senses are giving me accurate information about the world which I believe to be independent of my senses. My senses are the only way I can know the world. Our minds generate vivid and realistic images when we dream, when we daydream, when we hallucinate, and when we perceive the tree in the garden.

Consciousness is all we can ever know

What is the world like apart from my sense experiences? I can never know. The only world we know and can know, is the world filtered through our own consciousness. For us, consciousness creates the world. Thus Yogacara/Yogachara is known as the school of "consciousness-only" (*vijnapti-matrata*), or "mind-only" (*cittamatra*). Mind is the pre-condition for all experiences, all ideas, all concepts. Without consciousness, there are no sights, no sounds, no flavors, no textures, no fragrances. As a Western scientist remarks, "From tiny slivers of sensations, scraps of memories and flashes of emotion, the mind makes something much bigger. In the blink of an eye, the brain creates the entire world."[57]

A basic Buddhist claim is that there is no *atman*, there is no mysterious eternally self-existing unchanging agent (*atman*) behind consciousness.[58] The term "consciousness" does not name some thing; rather it directs our attention to the *experience of being conscious*. Consciousness is a transitory flowing series of interdependent processes, including attention and awareness. These are not fixed. Like a waterfall, like a river, there is merely flowing consciousness. There is no ultimate enduring dichotomy between subject (the consciousness doing the seeing, hearing, tasting, smelling and touching) and object (the conscious experience of things seen, heard, tasted, smelled, and touched). All we can ever be aware of is flowing consciousness.

Using language, we mentally construct what we think of as fixed enduring objects from our flow of perceptions and sensations. We have a fundamentally wrong understanding of the world, and we try to live in that misunderstood world, and so this error creates both *duhkha* (emotional misery) and *samsara* (the cycle of birth and death). Yogacara

---

[57] An excellent summary of recent scientific findings on the nature of consciousness can be found in Laura Sanders, "Consciousness Emerges," in *Science News*, Vol. 181, No. 4, February 25, 2012, p. 21. A much more technical article about the brain processes which create images is Najib J. Majaj, et al., "Simple Learned Weighted Sums of Inferior Temporal Neuronal Firing Rates Accurately Predict Human Core Object Recognition Performance," *The Journal of Neuroscience*, 30 September 2015.

[58] An agent is something that engages in an activity aimed at some goal, the goal being something the agent intended to bring about.

thinkers assert that we need to wake up to the true nature of things, the way the Buddha did under the Bodhi tree. We need to awaken to the true nature of things, and when we do this with clarity, we have achieved nirvana.

Consciousness or mind[59] is required for *bodhi*, for awakening. Without the flowing of consciousness, there could be no *samsara* and no nirvana. The same flow of experience when misunderstood creates *duhkha*; the same flow of experience clearly understood is Suchness, is nirvana. As Nagarjuna said, the limits of *samsara* are the limits of nirvana. They are not two ultimately different things. Ignorance of the way things really are, anger and ego-centered grasping of things that cannot be grasped (because they are flowing change) are indeed causes of *duhkha*.

Yet, consciousness must exist in order for consciousness and perceptions to create unreal worlds. Even though there is no subject-object duality in mind, nevertheless mind itself must have some real existence, some inherent self-existence.

Yogachara Disagreement with Madhyamaka

Mind must have some organizing principle which holds it together, the way the bank of the river underlies and holds the river together. The Yogachara assert that there must be some substratum or container of consciousness. That container is to be discovered in focused concentration, or meditation, but the self-existing substratum cannot be conceptualized (because all concepts are mistaken). For Yogacara followers, mind must truly exist. That means that mind must have some self-existing essence.

It is this stress on the real existence of mind that we see the real separation from the Madhyamaka. Nagarjuna's Madhyamaka asserts that **all things are empty of inherent self-existence** (*svabhava*). At least some Yogacara thinkers hold that **mind has inherent self-existence**. For Yogachara, mind is *not* "empty of inherent essence" (*svabhava-sunyata*).[60]

The Eight Levels of Consciousness

Yogachara texts analyze the container of consciousness (*vijnana*) into eight levels. The first through the fifth are seeing, hearing, touching, tasting, and smelling, five separate channels (eyes, ears, nose, skin, tongue) of input of information to the brain. The sixth is consciousness where we unify these incoming disparate senses and combine them to create unitary objects in the world.[61] This sixth level is where the mind unifies the chaotic flux of internal and external messages into a single seamless experience.

The next is the seventh level of consciousness which is where focused attention occurs; this consciousness places its attention on sense experience and mistakenly concludes that there are external objects independent of consciousness which have the objective properties which we know through our sensations and perceptions. This seventh level is dimly aware that there is some further, deeper subliminal level of consciousness which it cannot quite grasp, and so concludes mistakenly that the deeper eighth level is an *atman*, some eternally unchanging self-existent true self.

---

[59] In this brief explanation of Yogachara the author is intentionally ignoring the subtle differences between "mind" or "thought processes" (*citta*) and "consciousness" (*vijnana*) discussed in numerous commentaries in Buddhist philosophy. There is also "mentality" (*manas*). A brief but accurate description can be found in Robert E. Buswell and Donald S. Lopez, Jr., eds., *The Princeton Dictionary of Buddhism*, p. 194 ("*citta*") and p. 968 ("*vijnana*").

[60] Paul Williams, *Mahayana Buddhism: The Doctrinal Foundations*, p. 86.

[61] You touch an orange, you hear the sound of your finger tapping the orange, you see the orange, you taste the orange, and you smell the orange. But these are five different channels of information flowing through five different sense paths into the brain; the sixth level of consciousness unifies these inputs into one thing, an orange. The seventh level conceptualizes it as belonging to an external world.

The Eighth Level: The Seed Storehouse Consciousness

Yogachara refers to this eighth level as the "seed storehouse consciousness" or *alaya-vijnana*, the repository of all perceptions, memories, emotions, and dispositional tendencies accumulated through one's behavior, and the seed storehouse consciousness is also the container of karma. Everything you have ever experienced in this life (and previous lives) is deposited in this eighth-level of consciousness. These memories and dispositions will then affect our perceptions. These dispositions are referred to as seeds stored in the container of the mind, and the image of a seed which germinates is a powerful image for the Yogachara.

A memory deposited in the *alaya-vijnana* is like a seed, and the later arising of the memory into consciousness (i.e., remembering) is analogous to the germination of the seed. Seeds are potentialities for resultant phenomena to arise, such as consciousness, feeling, faculties, and so forth—when appropriate conditions arise. Some conditions cause seeds of anger to arise, or seeds of self-centeredness. Thus there are seeds which are responsible for the Three Poisons (ego-centered greed, anger, ignorance).

Since there are defiled seeds in the mind, this means that the mind is not innately pure (as some Mahayana texts assert), but rather is a combination of pure seeds and defiled seeds. The seeds are only one of the conditioning factors that give rise to what we think of as a consciousness of the world.

This eighth level *seed storehouse consciousness* is like a flowing torrent of processes which underlies all of *samsara*. Consciousness may be flowing change, but there must be a container for those changing processes. It is the eighth-level *alaya-vijnana* which is the enduring "jar" or container for consciousness. It is reborn lifetime after lifetime, and it is the *alaya-vijnana* which connects past, present, and future, and which ensures that we are the same person lifetime after lifetime.[62] The *alaya-vijnana*, the seed storehouse consciousness, makes karmic consequences possible. It is in the *alaya-vijnana* where we possess the seeds of buddhahood that allows us to become a buddha.[63]

Yogacara Meditation Techniques

For Yogacara, the key to liberation is removing the tainted or defiled seeds from the seed storehouse consciousness so that all that remains is pure consciousness. To accomplish this we must focus our meditative energies inwardly on the eighth and deepest level of our consciousness, focus on the actual origins of awareness. One must find the place where thoughts and images arise from. Using focused concentration one can revolve one's attention 180° from an apparently external world to the internal sub-conscious level and become clearly aware of the *alaya-vijnana* (seed storehouse consciousness) and see how it creates worlds out of dispositional seeds and karmic energies generated from our past, and our past lives.[64]

To become a buddha requires a radical transformation of consciousness so that all the seeds of defilement are eventually removed and the mind remains filled exclusively with pure seeds.

This results in a rather unique Yogachara meditation technique. After mental tranquility and focus are achieved, the follower focuses attention upon a complex painted image (*mandala*) and tries to hold that image in the

---

[62] Many Madhyamika Buddhists criticized Yogachara, claiming that they were trying to smuggle an *atman* back into Buddhism. Madhyamika students had a tendency to interpret the *alaya-vijnana* as simply a Hindu *atman* by a different name.

[63] A very controversial aspect of Yogachara is the assertion by some followers that some beings only possess *arhat* seeds, so they cannot become buddhas. Some even lack the seeds required for being an *arhat*, so they can never achieve an end to *duhkha*. The majority of the Mahayana schools disagreed and instead asserted that everyone has the nature of a Buddha.

[64] There are interesting similarities between the fourth century Buddhist concept of the "storehouse consciousness" and the twentieth century **unconscious** as originally explored by Freud and Jung. There are also major differences between these two concepts. A technical analysis of this issue reflecting current interpretations of the unconscious is the chapter "Beneath the Waves: Conceiving the Unconscious" by Richard K. Payne in Sarah F. Haynes, Michelle J. Sorensen, eds. *Wading into the Stream of Wisdom: Essays in Honor of Leslie Kawamura* (Honolulu: University of Hawai'i Press, 2013).

mind even after the eyes are closed. When the meditator gets good at that, she then works on projecting entirely imaginary alternative worlds and tries to hold that mental world in focused consciousness until it gradually fades away. The process is repeated and repeated for years until ultimately the mentally created world becomes so realistic in appearance, durability, and detail, that it seems as real as ordinary experience. This process of mastery of yogic meditation (the meaning of "Yoga-acara/Yogachara") allows us to realize that the mentally created realm and the apparent external world are not two separate realms; both are merely flowing consciousness (*vijnapti-matrata*) or just mind (*cittamatra*). And finally we eliminate the defiled or tainted seeds, and with a pure mind we perceive the world as it really is, flowing process. Some Yogacara Buddhists might nod their heads "yes" when they read, "Of course it is happening inside your head, Harry, but why on earth should that mean that it is not real?"[65]

10.7 INSIGHTS INTO THE BUDDHA-NATURE

Another still-developing form of Mahayana Buddhism in India is the "Buddha-nature" tradition. In Sanskrit, this is the *Tathagata-garbha* (pronounced something like ta-TA-ga-ta gar-bha) which, like Yogachara, developed during a time of flourishing development of Hindu devotionalism and the strong domination of Hindu culture over all aspects of life in India.

Around 200 to 250 C.E. more new Mahayana Buddhist sutras appeared, teaching that each person has the potentiality of buddhahood within, which they refer to as the *tathagata-garbha*.[66] The term *tathagata-garbha* means the "womb" or "embryo" (*garbha*) of the *Tathagata* ("the one who goes thus," another name for the Buddha). The image is that all people have the embryonic potential to become a buddha. In other words, we all have the nature of a buddha, we have the essential feature of a buddha, we have the seeds of buddhahood, innate within us. Each and every one of us are born potential buddhas, but we just do not realize it. Liberation or salvation is available for all.

Buddha-nature (*Tathagata-garbha*) followers describe Buddha-nature as a pure luminous awareness. The listener, you or I, hear the teachings of the Buddha for the first time, and something within us resonates to those teachings, feels comfortable with those ideas, and wishes to follow them and learn more. According to the Buddha-nature tradition, our own *tathagata-garbha* responds to Buddhist teachings by generating the desire or thought to achieve buddhahood for the benefit of all living beings. Unlike some Yogachara Buddhists who felt that some humans were lacking the potential to become *arhats* or buddhas, the Buddha-nature texts assert that the potential to become a buddha, or Buddha-nature, is universal to all.

Buddha-nature shines like the sun in the sky

Mahayana Buddhism uses the analogy of the *Tathagata-garbha*, or Buddha-nature, as being like the bright sun shining overhead. On an overcast dense cloudy rainy day we cannot see the sun, but the sun is shining nevertheless. The sunlight is obscured or hidden by clouds.

In the case of the Buddha-nature, the clouds which obscure our Buddha-nature are a metaphor for the Three Poisons, (1) anger and hatred, (2) aversion, ignorance and confusion, and (3) ego-centered possessiveness. These defilements, these three unwholesome roots, keep us from recognizing the eternally shining Buddha-nature which is our true nature. Your consciousness is innately pure; defilements are external to consciousness, the way the clouds are external to the sun.

No human could become a buddha if she or he had no trace of potential buddhahood. We cannot change wood into metal. We cannot transform a brick into a mirror. If in the end we want something worked of wood, it can

---

[65] I assume the reader will recognize this line from J. K. Rowling, *Harry Potter and the Deathly Hallows* (New York: Scholastic, 2007).

[66] These include the *Tathagata-garbha sutra* ("Womb/Matrix of the Tathagata"), the *Srimaladevi Simhananda sutra* ("The Lion's Roar of Queen Srimala"), and the *Ratnagotra-vibhaga* ("Analysis of the Gems and Lineages"). We should note that these texts are before the Yogachara school developed, so the roots of *Tathagatagarbha* thought are probably before early Yogachara.

only happen if we start with wood from the very beginning. No amount of polishing a brick can transform it into a mirror. You cannot become a buddha unless you already have the nature of a buddha.

According to this set of Buddha-nature scriptures, becoming a buddha is not a goal so very far away; it is closer than you think. The process of becoming a buddha is the process of removing the defilements (clouds), and allow the Buddha-nature to shine through. We discover that we have always been a buddha, and there is no point in looking outwardly to try to gain something called buddhahood. Rather, we must find what we have always had but simply did not recognize.

The person who directly recognizes the Buddha-nature within herself has awakened; she has not only eliminated the defilements, but she can also see the shining Buddha-nature in all living beings. When one can see all *dharmas* as empty of *svabhava* (independent self-existence), one recognizes that there is no Hindu *atman* and that there is no thing which is separate and independent, so there is nothing to grasp onto, and no one to do the grasping. There is no enduring unchanging person to be angry with, and no enduring person to be angry. Thus, the Madhyamaka insight into *sunyata* is still the foundation of the *Tathagata-garbha*, however, the experience of emptiness results in the clear vision of the Buddha-nature in all living things.

The *Tathagata-garbha* Was Never an Independent Buddhist Tradition

In India the *Tathagata-garbha* was not a separate independent school of Buddhism in the same way the Madhyamaka and Yogachara were. It is doubtful that any Buddhist monk of the era thought of himself as belonging to a Buddha-nature school. Perhaps it is more accurate to describe the "Buddha-nature" ideas as a tendency. These ideas do not seem to have exerted much influence over any of the major Indian Buddhist thinkers, but the ideas in these sutras laid the groundwork for much of East Asian and Tibetan Buddhism. Some scholars have suggested that in India the *Tathagata-garbha* tradition was absorbed into Yogachara before *Tathagata-garbha* could develop into a separate school.[67]

10.8 SUMMARY OF THE CHAPTER

The major traditions of Mahayana discussed in this chapter include the Pure Land (devotion to Amitabha Buddha), the Madhyamaka (founded by Nagarjuna basing his "emptiness" ideas on the *Prajnaparamita sutras*), the Yogachara (accepting emptiness but analyzing consciousness and knowledge), and Buddha-nature (*Tathagatagarbha sutras* which teach that all living beings possess the potential for full buddhahood). In addition there is the Tantric Buddhist pathway to be discussed in the next chapter.

These Mahayana ideas are found in the world today, with the Pure Land tradition very popular in East Asia, and with the Tantric pathway as the Buddhism of Tibet and Nepal. The Madhyamaka and Yogachara pathways were of central importance for many schools of Chinese, Korean, and Japanese Buddhism, however the more devotional Pure Land traditions tended to dominate. The basic ideas and insights of the Buddha-nature tradition were simply absorbed into the other schools.

However varied these schools are, they agree about the essentials. Buddhism is about compassion, generosity, morality, and concentration. It is about gaining insight through focused observation. It is realizing that all is interconnected and interdependent. It is about diminishing ego, and as ego fades, ego-less love and compassion arise and are focused upon all the living things in this world.

---

[67] Some Yogachara thinkers were quite comfortable equating the eighth level of consciousness, the storehouse *alaya* consciousness, with the *tathagata-garbha*. See Paul Williams, *op. cit.*, pp. 96–97. Chinese Buddhist thinkers made this claim explicitly, however they understood the *tathagata-garbha* as the essence of substance of mind, and the *alaya-vijnana* as the functioning of the mind.

10.9 TECHNICAL TERMS

Amitabha   The Buddha of the Western Paradise, whose realm is a Pure Land.

cittamatra   "Mind-only," another name for Yogachara Buddhism.

guru   A spiritual teacher or guide, especially important to Tantric Buddhism.

Madhyamika   A follower of the Madhyamaka school inspired by the philosopher Nagarjuna.

Madhyamaka   The school of Indian Mahayana which was inspired by the *Prajnaparamita* literature, and brought to fruition by the philosopher Nagarjuna.

Tathagatagarbha   The Buddha-nature, also a school of Mahayana Buddhism.

Tantra   A special Buddhist manual or book with esoteric instructions, associated with Tantric Buddhism .

Vijnaptimatrata   "Consciousness-only," another name for Yogachara Buddhism.

Yogachara   The Mahayana school (also Yogacara) which asserts that all of our knowledge of the external and internal realms comes via consciousness, but consciousness creates much more of our world than we realize. The name is Yoga-achara, a person who has mastered yogic meditation (pronounced Yo-guh-AHch-ara or Yoog-ACHa-ra).

10.10 QUESTIONS FOR FURTHER DISCUSSION

(1)   We discussed three Buddhist approaches to Buddhism: (1) centered on the founder, the Buddha; (2) centered on the teachings; (3) centered on the religious groups in monasteries or wilderness areas working on nirvana. Are there any equivalent approaches to Western religions? Are there similar approaches in the history of Christianity? Do some Christians focus their religious energies on the founder, Jesus? Do some followers of Western religions focus their religious energies on sacred texts and the ideas found therein? Do some commit themselves to live in monasteries and follow monastic rules? What would be the purpose of such activities? Discuss.

(2)   Mahayana Buddhists accused the Theravada tradition of being selfish, of being concerned only for themselves, of seeking the status of an *arhat* but not helping others. Does this criticism seem justified to you? Discuss.

(3)   The earlier Theravada traditions stressed individual attainment of nirvana. The later Pure Land tradition says that in contemporary times none of us are good enough to achieve that on our own, and we need a savior who will respond with loving compassion as we are dying. Why do you think that some Buddhists would prefer one approach, and others prefer the second approach? Discuss.

(4)   In the West, it used to be believed that atoms were the smallest particles and existed, indestructible. Later we discovered that atoms were mostly empty space, a tiny nucleus encircled by whirring electrons. More recently we discovered that even the what we thought were the smallest solid particles, even neutrons, electrons, and

protons were made up of even tinier constituents, called quarks. Are quarks solid, or are they just flowing processes? Would the Madhyamaka view of all things as "empty of self-existing essence" be in agreement with modern physics? Discuss.

(5)   One of the most famous of all Mahayana Buddhist quotations is the one from the *Heart Sutra*, "form, just as it is, is emptiness (*sunyata*), emptiness, just as it is, is form; form does not differ from emptiness, emptiness does not differ from form." Explain what this means.

(6)   Madhyamaka Buddhism argues that everything is empty of inner self-existent enduring essence (*svabhava-sunyata*), that it is all flowing change. If nothing is fixed, nothing permanent, nothing eternal, then does anything have value? If nothing will last, does it make any difference if we destroy it now, or wait for it to decompose? Discuss.

(7)   The Yogachara school of Mahayana claims that all of our knowledge of the "external world" is based on consciousness, on sense experience. We can see the orange, hear the orange, touch the orange, and taste and smell the orange – what is the orange itself like independent of our various sensory input? Can we escape our consciousness to examine the "orange itself"? Do you agree with the Yogacara that everything is "mind-only"?

A SELECTED BIBLIOGRAPHY

Mahayana Buddhism

Akira, Hirakawa, tr. Paul Groner, *A History of Indian Buddhism: From Sakyamuni to Early Mahayana* (Honolulu: Univ. of Hawaii Press, 1989).

Conze, Edward, *Buddhist Thought In India* (Ann Arbor: The University of Michigan Press, 1967)

Conze, Edward, *Buddhist Wisdom Books: The Diamond Sutra; The Heart Sutra* (London: George Allen & Unwin, Ltd., 1958), reprinted by Harper Torchbooks, TB 1659, 1972.

Conze, Edward, *The Short Prajnaparamita Texts* (London: Luzac & Co., 1974).

Conze, Edward, *Selected Sayings from the Perfection of Wisdom* (London: The Buddhist Society, 1955)

Conze, Edward, *The Perfection of Wisdom in Eight Thousand Lines & Its Verse Summary* (Bolinas, CA.; The Four Seasons Foundation, 1973).

Conze, Edward, *The Large Sutra on Perfect Wisdom* (Berkeley: University of California Press, 1975)

Dayal, Har, *The Bodhisattva Doctrine in Buddhist Sanskrit Literature* (London: Routledge & Kegan Paul, 1931).

de Jong, J.W., Kogen Mizuno, *Essentials of Buddhism: Basic Terminology and Concepts of Buddhist Philosophy* ( )

Dutt, Nalanaksha, *Aspects of Mahayana Buddhism and its Relation to Hinayana* (1930).

Hanh, Thich Nhat, *The Diamond that Cuts Through Illusion: Commentaries on the Prajnaparamita Diamond Sutra* (Berkeley, CA: Parallax Press, 1992)

Hanh, Thich Nhat, ed. by Peter Levitt, *The Heart of Understanding: Commentaries on the Prajnaparamita Heart Sutra* (Berkeley, CA: Parallax Press, 1988)

Herman, A. L., *An Introduction to Buddhist Thought: A Philosophic History of Indian Buddhism* (New York: University Press of America, 1983)

Huntington, Jr., C. W., *The Emptiness of Emptiness: An Introduction to Early Indian Madhyamika* (Honolulu, HI: University of Hawai'i Press, 1989)

Jamieson, R. C., ed., *The Perfection of Wisdom, Illustrated with Ancient Sanskrit Manuscripts* (Viking Press, 2000)

Lancaster, Lewis, ed., *Prajnaparamita and Related Systems* (Berkeley, CA: Berkeley Buddhist Studies Series, 1977) These are some very technical studies of the literature in honor of Edward Conze (1904-1977), the preeminent explorer of these texts.

Lopez, Donald S., Jr., *The Heart Sutra Explained: Indian and Tibetan Commentaries* (Albany: State University of New York Press, 1988).

Pine, Red [Bill Porter] *The Diamond Sutra: Text and Commentaries Translated from Sanskrit and Chinese* (New York: Counterpoint, 2001)

Pye, Michael, *Skilful Means: A Concept in Mahayana Buddhism* (London: Routledge, 2004)

Ruegg, David Seyfort, *The Symbiosis of Buddhism with Brahmanism/Hinduism in South Asia and of Buddhism with 'Local Cults" in Tibet and the Himalayan Region* ( )

Schopen, Gregory, *Figments and Fragments of Mahayana Buddhism in India* (Honolulu: University Press of Hawaii, 2005)

Suzuki, Daisetz, T., *Studies on the Lankavatara Sutra* (1930).

Thomas, E. J., *The History of Buddhist Thought* (London: Routledge, Kegan, Paul, 1933)

Warder, A. K., *Indian Buddhism* (Delhi: Motilal-Banarsidass, 1970)

Williams, Paul, *Mahayana Buddhism: The Doctrinal Foundations* (London and New York, Routledge and Kegan Paul, 1989)

Wood, Frances, and Mark Barnard, *The Diamond Sutra: The Story of the World's Earliest Dated Printed Book* (Oxford: The British Library, 2010)

Nagarjuna and the Madhyamika Origins

Batchelor, Stephen, *Verses From the Center: A Buddhist Vision of the Sublime* (New York: Riverhead Books, 2000).

Conze, Edward, *Buddhist Thought in India*

Daye, Douglas D., "Madhyamika" in C. S. Prebish, ed., *Buddhism in a Modern Perspective* (Univ. of Pennsylvania Press, 1975)

Garfield, Jay, *The Fundamental Wisdom of the Middle Way* (Oxford University Press, 1995)

Glass, Newman R., *Working Emptiness: Toward a Third Reading of Emptiness in Buddhism and Postmodern Thought* ( )

Hopkins, *Meditation on Emptiness* (Boston: Wisdom Press, 1996)

Huntington, Jr., C. W., *The Emptiness of Emptiness: An Introduction to Early Indian Madhyamika* (Honolulu, HI: University of Hawai'i Press, 1989)

Inada, Kenneth, *Nagarjuna: A Translation of his Mula-Madhyamika-karika with an introductory essay* (Tokyo: Hokuseido Press, 1970)

Kalupahana, David, *Nagarjuna: The Philosophy of the Middle Way* (State University of New York Press, 1986).

Lindtner, Christian, *Nagarjuniana: Studies in the Writings and Philosophy of Nagarjuna* (Delhi: Motilal Banarsidass, 1982)

Murti, T. R. V., *The Central Philosophy of Buddhism: A Study of the Madhymaika System* (London, Allen & Unwin, 1960). (NOTE: this is a Hindu absolutistic Vedanta interpretation of Nagarjuna, and absolutism is rejected by most Buddhist scholars)

Ramanan, K. V., *Nagarjuna's Philosophy as Presented in the Maha-Prajñapāramitā-Sastra* (India: Motilal Banarsidass, 1966, reprinted 1975).

Robinson, Richard, "Did Nagarjuna Really Refute All Philosophical Views?" (*Philosophy East and West*, Vol. 22, No. 3, pp. 325-331).

Robinson, Richard, *Early Madhyamika in India and China* (1967).

The Root Stanzas of the Middle Way: The Mulamadhamakakarika (translated from the Tibetan text by the Padmakara Translation Group: Boston: Shambhala, 2016)

Ruegg, David Seyfort, *The Literature of the Madhyamaka School of Philosophy in India* (Weisbaden: Otto Harrassowitz, 1981)

Siderits, Mark, and Shoryu Katsura, *Nagarjuna's Middle Way: Mulamadhyamakakarika* (Boston: Wisdom Publications,

2013)

Sprung, Mervyn, *Lucid Exposition of the Middle Way: The Essential Chapters from the Prasannapada of Chandrakirti Translated from the Sanskrit* (Prajna Press, 1979).

Streng, Frederick, *Emptiness: A Study in Religious Meaning* (1968).

Tuck, Andrew P., *Comparative Philosophy and the Philosophy of Scholarship: On the Western Interpretation of Nagarjuna* (New York: Oxford University Press, 1990)

Tola, F. and Dragonetti, C., "Nagarjuna's Conception of 'Voidness' (*Sunyata*) (*Journal of Indian Philosophy*, Vol. 9, pp. 273-282).

Walser, Joseph, *Nagarjuna in Context: Mahayana Buddhism and Early Indian Culture* (N.Y.: Columbia University Press, 2005)

Westerhoff, Jan, *Nagarjuna's Madhyamiaka: A Philosophical Introduction* (London: Oxford University Press, 2009)

Williams, Paul, *Mahayana Buddhism: The Doctrinal Foundations* (1989).

On the "Mind-Only" School in India: Yogacara Buddhism

Conze, Edward, *Buddhist Thought in India*

Dasgupta, S. *Indian Idealism* (Cambridge University Press, 1969)

Garfield, Jay L. "Three natures and three naturelessnesses: comments on cittamatra conceptual categories." *Journal of Indian Philosophy and Religion*, Calcutta: vol. 1, 1996. vol. 2, 1997.

Harris, Ian Charles, *The Continuity of Madhyamaka and Yogacara in Indian Mahayana Buddhism* (Leiden: Brill Academic Publishers, 1991).

Jiang, Tao, *Contexts and Dialogue: Yogacara Buddhism and Modern Psychology on the Subliminal Mind* ( )

Lusthaus, Dan, *Buddhist Phenomenology: A Philosophical Investigation of Yogacara Buddhism and the Ch'eng Wei-shih Lun* (London: Routledge Curzon, 2002).

----. "The Heart Sutra in Chinese Yogacara: Some Comparative Comments on the Heart Sutra Commentaries of Wonchuk and K'uei-chi," *International Journal of Buddhist Thought and Culture*, Seoul: 2003. pages 59-104.

Mueller, Charles, *Living Yogacara: An Introduction to Consciousness-Only Buddhism* ( )

Powers, John, *The Yogacara School of Buddhism: A Bibliography* ( )

Ueda, Yoshifumi, "Two Main Streams of Thought in Yogacara Philosophy" in *Philosophy East and West*, Vol. 17, 1967, pp. 155-165.

Verdu, Alfonso, *Dialectical Aspects in Buddhist Thought – Studies in Sino-Japanese Mahayana Idealism*, vol. 8 (Lawrence, Kansas: International Studies, East Asian Series Research Publication, 1974)

Wood, Thomas, *Mind Only: A Philosophical and Doctrinal Analysis of the Vijnavada* (1989).

CHAPTER 11: TANTRIC BUDDHISM IN INDIA

THE TANTRIC VAJRAYANA IN INDIA
THE DECLINE OF BUDDHISM IN INDIA
MODERN DEVELOPMENTS OF INDIAN BUDDHISM

11.1 OVERVIEW OF THE CHAPTER

Comparing the Theravada and Mahayana in the previous chapter, we distinguished three approaches to Buddhist practice. In this chapter we will expand on those three and add one more, the focus on the *guru*, or the spiritual guide and teacher who may possesses supernormal powers. The four approaches to Buddhism are those (a) centered on the doctrines explained in the scriptures of Buddhism, or *dharma*-centric, (b) centered on the community of followers, or *sangha*-centric, (c) centered on the nature and relics of the Buddha, or Buddha-centric, and one not discussed in the previous chapter, (d) *guru*-centric Buddhism centered on the nature of the *guru*, a teacher and spiritual guide believed to have very special supernormal powers.

The first two approaches typify early conservative Buddhism. Several of the Mahayana traditions also focus on the Mahayana philosophical implications of the discourses of the Buddha, in addition to their focus on the divine nature of the Buddha. Mahayana traditions tended to place more stress on *bhakti*, devotion to or having faith in buddhas. Buddhas and bodhisattvas could be prayed to, meditated upon, and experienced in visions. Mahayana created a rich Buddha-centered mythology and many sacred rituals.

Several Indian Buddhist schools developed quite sophisticated forms of philosophical analysis. The Madhyamaka which argued that all things are empty of an unchanging inner essence (*svabhava-sunyata*), or emptiness, and the Yogacara, which argued that there is a deep unconscious level in all of us which can be explored using meditation, and awakening can result. Several Mahayana texts assert that all living things possess the potential for awakening, or possess the "Buddha-nature" and no things are excluded.

The last development of Buddhism in India is Tantric Buddhism, whose origins are traced to the seventh century in India. This esoteric teaching and practice was not the most important form of Buddhism in India, but later dominated Tibetan forms of Buddhism. It was exported into China, but did not establish a large following there and began to decline after a hundred years. During this brief period of popularity, Tantric Buddhism was carried from China to Japan where it flourished as the Japanese Shingon sect.

What is Tantric Buddhism? Christian Wedemeyer explains that:

... Tantric Buddhism comprehends those forms of esoteric Buddhism which are nondualist in their conceptualization of ritual purity and pollution and are, accordingly, antinomian[1] or transgressive[2] in their ritual praxis and scriptural discourses. What, then, is esoteric Buddhism? This expression

---

[1] "Antinomian" means that the tradition encourages the student to violate the established rules of the social order, including the violation of caste rules concerning purity and impurity, and, in this case, rules for Buddhist monks and nuns.

[2] In this case, "transgressive" means that these forms of Buddhism transgress against the traditional moral precepts and rules which guide the lives of ordinary Buddhist monks and nuns.

distinguishes those forms of Buddhism that require a special initiation ritual to authorize their central practice (excluding those not so initiated from access to ritual and doctrine) and are thus *esoteric*: 'Designed for, or appropriate to, an inner circle of advanced or privileged disciples; communicated to, or intelligible by, the initiated exclusively.'[3]

A major focus of Tantric Buddhism is freeing the student from the socially imposed discriminations we make, such as the powerful and important dualism between "purity" and "impurity" in Hindu society.[4] However, Tantric Buddhism was not merely nondual. Using rituals and chanted phrases of power, it was believed that worldly goals could be achieved, and protection from danger was possible.

Later, the Tantric Buddhists understand their pathway to awakening as both radical and dangerous, but for those with the requisite superior capability and training, it could produce a shortcut to final liberation. The danger is due to the fact that in Buddhist Tantra, things that would be regarded as impure and polluting in Indian culture (such as meat-eating, drinking alcohol from human skulls, celibate monks engaging in sexual intercourse) are put to ritual use to overcome dualities.

There are difficulties in studying Tantric Buddhism because the experts do not agree on many important points. For our purposes, the most serious difficulty is whether to treat the Tantric doctrines and statements as meaning what is literally written down in the texts, or to interpret these apparently immoral and shocking claims as figurative, as metaphor, as symbols which need to be interpreted by a teacher.

A third possibility is that the language of the Tantras is not primarily literal or figurative, but instead is grounded in Tantric ritual, and designed to be shocking because its intention is to challenge and overturn (in the mind of the practitioner) deeply ingrained cultural assumptions about purity and pollution which were widespread in the ritual and social mores of India.[5] The result will be that the student no longer understands dualities (pure versus impure, sacred versus profane, awakened versus ignorant, *samsara* versus nirvana, etc.) to be of ultimate significance, and now perceives the world with clarity, a world of non-dual flowing processes each of which is empty of self-existing essence (*svabhava-sunyata*). The practitioner is no longer trapped by dichotomies or differentiation. This is liberation.

This chapter ends with a brief account of the disappearance of Buddhism in India after the twelfth century of the common era, and a summary of the practice of Indian forms of Buddhism into the contemporary world.

11.2 THE FORMS OF MAHAYANA BUDDHISM (A REVIEW)

(1) PURE-LAND:
> a rather *bhakti*-devotional Buddha-centered form of Buddhism, which places more emphasis on praying to and worshiping the Buddha of the Western Paradise.[6]

---

[3] Christian K. Wedemeyer, *Making Sense of Tantric Buddhism* (New York: Columbia University Press, 2013), p. 9.

[4] The importance of purity and impurity to Hindu society cannot be emphasized strongly enough. Ritual purity was especially important because the gods are of transcendent purity, so the priests must be extra careful so as not to offend these powers. The entire social system was established on purity. The caste *varna* groups are sharply distinguished based on their degrees of purity and impurity. Different duties are proscribed, different rights, different obligations of behavior and ritual, with different social value or dignity assigned to them, with the Brahmins as the most pure.

[5] *Ibid.*, p. 126. The result will be liberating insight into the ultimate non-dual nature of reality, and the student with a pure mind will perceive reality as a buddha or a divinity perceives it.

[6] The Pure Land (Ching-t'u/Qingtu) became the dominant form of popular Buddhism in China, Korea and Japan.

(2) MADHYAMAKA:

a very analytic *dharma*-centered form of Buddhism established around the "emptiness" insights of Nagarjuna, based on various *sutras* called the *Prajna-paramita* (the "perfection of wisdom," or the "wisdom which carries one over to the other shore").

(3) YOGACARA, CITTAMATRA or VIJNAPTI-MATRATA:

drawing on the insights of Nagarjuna, but with a new stress on meditation combined with detailed and careful analysis of consciousness, the unconscious, and mental events, which argues that all knowledge of what exists is available to us only through consciousness.

(4) BUDDHA-NATURE or TATHAGATA-GARBHA:

This tradition stress the *Tathagata-garbha* or "Buddha-nature" and asserts that all living things, without exception, have "Buddha-nature" which means we have the capacity to awaken and become buddhas.

The focus of this chapter is on the fifth tradition, the *Vajrayana*.

(5) DIAMOND or THUNDERBOLT VEHICLE:

The Indian Mahayana group, the *Vajrayana*, began to develop slowly around the sixth and seventh centuries, about five-hundred years before Buddhism diminished in importance in India. It shares many commonalities with Tantric Hinduism which developed at the very same time in India.[7]

11.3 HISTORICAL DEVELOPMENT OF BUDDHISM IN INDIA

For the first 500 years in the common era conservative Buddhism in India remained strong. Theravada monks and nuns took up residence in monasteries, but there remained others who choose the difficult ascetic pathway of the forest monks, the *bhikshu* or beggar. However, in India in general during the period of the fourth and fifth centuries C.E., people began to believe that these forest dwellers, whether Buddhist or non-Buddhist, were charismatic figures who had developed magical powers (*siddhis*).

Over the following centuries, the more conservative Theravada, with its stress on recluse monks and wandering mendicants, came to have less and less influence on Indian culture in general. Many Theravada monasteries acquired power, wealth, and land from wealthy donors, and, as a result, became self-sufficient. This also had the effect of isolating them from the householder communities.

The newer Mahayana practices came to dominate popular Buddhism in northern India. By 500 C.E., the many differing Mahayana communities continued to grow and develop in the north of India. Many larger Buddhist monastic centers became cultural centers of learning, where they taught subjects related to arts and sciences: logic, literary studies, astronomy, astrology, medicine, as well as Buddhist thought. Conservative Buddhists intermingled with the various Mahayana monks all under one monastery roof.

Buddhism had become favored by wealthy middle class merchants and by kings and rulers. Impressive Buddhist rituals and ceremonies were employed by rulers to protect their kingdom and legitimize their authority, demonstrating that *god*-like buddhas approve of their rule. Kings were identified with buddhas and bodhisattvas, and statues of kings were installed in monasteries and were the focus of rituals designed to ensure the safety of the ruler and the success of his rule.

Monks in villages carried on Buddhist learning, but also served as spiritual guides for local non-Buddhist religious traditions. During this period village religion was no longer just forms of Hinduism, but Buddhism as well became integrated into popular mythology, tales, themes, and folklore.

---

[7] It is important to note that the followers of the Vajrayana assert that the Buddha himself taught the Tantric Buddhism to his most capable students, and would reject the idea that Tantric Hindu ideas in India had any influence over their fundamental insights. This topic is hotly debated by scholars of Tantric Buddhism. Many scholars find that "There is decidedly such a thing as a common Hindu and Buddhist tantric ideology ..." See Agehananda Bharati, *The Tantric Tradition* (New York: Anchor Books, 1970), p. 20.

CHAPTER 11: MAHAYANA SCHOOLS–PART II

Buddhism also appealed to the better educated groups, which were the Brahmin priests and the *ksatryas*, the politicians, bureaucrats, and protectors. In an earlier chapter, we explained a distinction between a religion as a Grand Tradition, and an oral tradition, a Basic Religion, or a Little Tradition; at this stage of history the sort of Buddhism that appealed to the elite cultured classes tended towards the Grand Tradition. Although Hindu rulers dominated India during this era, Buddhism persisted as a religious tradition among the well-educated. Little Tradition householder Buddhism certainly existed, but it existed within a dominant Hindu sensibility. Even Buddhist villagers participated in Vedic rituals and the Vedic *devas* (divinities) were celebrated with sacrifices and rituals. In terms of the rural villages, the most popular forms of religion were still a wide variety of Hindu beliefs and practices. Buddhist temples could have statues of popular Hindu divinities, such as Ganesha.

Popular Mahayana Communities Continue to Develop

For the Grand Tradition, the bodhisattva path included both devotional and intellectual elements. The intellectual element is understanding that both selves and things are empty of inner essence, and not being frightened by a world where there is nothing to hold onto, nothing solid, nothing substantial, nothing but swirling interdependent processes. Although Nagarjuna and Yogacara were studied in highly intellectual universities, these were not the heart of Mahayana for the householder, or for the majority of Mahayana monks.

Popular Mahayana continued to place great stress on compassion for all living things. Popular Mahayana ("Little Tradition") was *not* a practice of realizing that all *dharmas* are empty of self-existence. In the more popular forms of Mahayana, the object of one's attention is devotion focused on the bodhisattva who works incessantly for the happiness, welfare and liberation of all beings. Amitabha Buddha was a popular focus for devotional Buddhism.

Some bodhisattvas, such as Avalokitesvara, had been on the Buddhist pathway of loving compassion for so long that due to all their good karma they acquired characteristics and powers of divinities. For the householder, it is obvious that the best reaction is to offer praise to the Buddha and various bodhisattvas. A prudent Buddhist will make offerings of flowers and money and food. Certainly one must observe the five precepts, but keep in mind the name of your favorite bodhisattva who will help you when you need help. Cultivate an inner attitude of sympathetic delight in the oceans of good karma and merit of the Buddhas and bodhisattvas. These beings can share their good merit with us, easing our own lives.

As this process continued for hundreds of years, the village *puja* rituals (prayers and offerings to images) of Hindus for their gods (*devas*) became nearly indistinguishable from the Buddhist rituals of praise for their bodhisattvas. Popular Buddhism and popular Hinduism were becoming more alike. Philosophical Hinduism and philosophical Buddhism were also influencing one another.

The Mahayana goal was to become a buddha and not just an ordinary human *arhat*. A buddha was an incredible divine figure with properties and powers that were beyond comprehension. The status of a buddha is far, far above us, perhaps impossibly far above us. The space between the human realm and the divine realm of the buddha is filled with the bodhisattva. Bodhisattvas are human, and only slightly more powerful than ordinary people. Bodhisattvas are like us, and can relate to us.

Although becoming a buddha may be beyond reach in this life, one can still get the help of a bodhisattva. How is this attained? Though the practice of *bhakti* or devotion. Pray to the bodhisattvas. Make offerings of love and devotion (*puja*) to bodhisattvas. Ask for help, ask for less *duhkha*, ask for your child to get well, ask the bodhisattva to drive out evil spirits, ask to win the next lottery, ask for a male child, ask to make a profit in your business, and ask for divine assistance to defeat the enemy in battle.

11.4 THE ROOTS OF INDIAN TANTRIC BUDDHISM

As we discussed in chapter 5, it was during the medieval period in India (5th - 12th century C.E.) that Vedic Hinduism became a thoroughly *bhakti* religion, and Hindu cults devoted to many different *deva* gods proliferated. In chapter 5 we studied the worshipers of Vishnu, Krishna Vasudeva, Shiva, Kali, Durga, Gopala Krishna, Ganesha and others. We also discussed a strong trend (affecting all Indian religions) to substitute a much more physical and popular ritual for abstract meditation. Temples and monasteries became richly decorated intentionally making use of all the arts, including painting, music, sculpture, dance, and drama. Instead of meditation, the tendency was for the performance of these theatrical richly ceremonial rituals themselves to become the way to liberation.

This was not limited to Vedic Hinduism. Popular Buddhism was responding to the same forces, and the same tendencies are reflected in early popular Buddhism but become much stronger during this seventh century period.[8]

Visually stimulating images and rituals became the basis for faith, which in turn was needed to achieve progress towards awakening.[9] As a result, popular Buddhism became more and more devotional and stressed bodhisattvas whose powers are virtually indistinguishable from the gods and goddesses (*devas*) of Hindu devotionalism. Popular Mahayana imagery continued to develop and expand its pantheon of bodhisattvas, and in the popular mind they became much like the Hindu *devas*. New texts continued to appear and new ceremonies continue to evolve. The Buddhists had a tendency to adopt the Hindu divinities and explain them as converts to Buddhism, or as compassionate manifestations of bodhisattvas, and so devotional Buddhism became very much like devotional Hinduism.[10]

It was a combination of the Mahayana and popular *bhakti* forces and forest monks which led to the last development of Mahayana in India.[11] The forest dwellers now included non-monastic male and female ascetics on the fringes of the Hindu and Buddhist community. It was believed that by following secret methods, these ascetics had developed supernormal powers, called *siddhis*. Often the behavior of these ascetics was shocking to Indian sensibilities, involving actions prohibited to monks and nuns. In addition to eccentric dress and transgressive behaviors, these ascetics used words and phrases of power, *mantras* (pronounced mahn-tra) which amplified the supernormal powers (*siddhi*) developed by their difficult spiritual practices. It was also thought that these difficult spiritual practices could give the follower the magical ability to control the world through rituals and chants, but even more importantly, they provided a shortcut to liberation, for those who were sufficiently prepared.

Tantric Buddhism is *Guru*-centered

The last development of Mahayana Buddhism in India is Tantric Buddhism is clearly in evidence by the

---

[8] A. K. Warder, *Indian Buddhism* (Delhi: Motilal Banarsidass, 1970), p. 490.

[9] See Andy Rotman, *Thus Have I Seen: Visualizing Faith in Early Indian Buddhism* (London: Oxford, 2008).

[10] David Snellgrove, *Indo-Tibetan Buddhism* (Boston: Shambhala, 2002), p. 150.

[11] Theories about the origins of Buddhist Tantrism are debated and there are several possibilities. Because Tantric Buddhism allows drinking alcohol, eating meat and fish, allows sexualized rituals, and other such behaviors, some have argued that Tantric Buddhism originated with degenerate monks who needed some Buddhist authority for breaking the monastic rules regarding sexuality and alcohol, and so invented fictitious sermons of the Buddha justifying their transgression. This view is not considered likely by the majority of scholars. Others have attempted to trace Tantric Buddhism and Tantric Hinduism back to the pre-Aryan groups, perhaps Indus Valley goddess worship, shamanism and magical impulses. In this view, Tantric Buddhism and Tantric Hinduism, although similar, originated from the same shamanistic roots but originated independently from one another. However, if one adopts this analysis, Tantric Buddhism was never taught by the Buddha and did not originate with the Buddha, as followers assert, but would be pre-Buddhist. Yet another commonly-held theory is that Tantric Buddhism began, not with the Buddha, but rather in esoteric Shaivism, with Buddhists influenced by the Hindu communities which worshiped Shiva and drawing inspiration and ideas from Tantric Hindu Shaivist traditions. Of course, mutual influences are very likely. This is a popular explanation of Tantric practices.

seventh century. It tended to put much more emphasis upon the *guru*,[12] an accomplished spiritual guide and teacher who not only communicates with spirits, but also possesses secret knowledge which provides control over spirits, which gives power. The *guru* is not only to be treated with respect; the *guru* is to be treated with the respect owed a god, a *deva*.

Tantric Buddhism in Tibet has Four Jewels, not just three: Buddha; dharma; *sangha*; *guru*. It is in this sense that Tantric Buddhism is said to be *guru*-centric. Tantric Buddhism held that one cannot make progress towards the goal of liberation unless the student had been ritually initiated by a *guru* into particular practices and certain texts. Initiation empowerment rituals were necessary if one was to make progress towards bodhisattva-hood and nirvana.

For the student undergoing these rituals, the belief is that the deeper the insight and attainment of the *guru*, the more effective the magical initiation ritual, which can help prepare the student for nirvana either in this life, or in a future existence. The *guru* is the teacher, and the student is the servant, serving his *guru* with complete trust.

The earliest Tantric texts begin to appear late in the fourth century, and are often associated with the Buddhist university of Nalanda in northern India. This final phase of Buddhist development in India continued to grow stronger from the sixth to the twelfth centuries.

One interesting feature of Tantric Buddhism is a very strong tendency to emphasize goddess worship and to practice popular rituals which occur in richly decorative settings. The visual element was becoming stronger and stronger. In earlier forms of Mahayana, ritual practices were thought to be preliminary to serious study, but in Tantric India, rituals become the higher, more advanced practices, a short-cut to liberation.

Tantric Buddhists made use of bright colors, active colorful rituals, painting, sweet-smelling incense, music, sculpture, intricate patterns, dance, and drama. Tantric Buddhism utilizes the entire body as an instrument for liberation, including chanting. Tantric Buddhism will develop a very complex system of meditation, which utilizes magic, a rich variety of symbols, and very colorful rituals.

In India those who went into the forest to master Tantric accomplishments were mostly males, although some females were included. These Buddhists lived as beggars wearing rags, or wearing nothing at all. A person who lives this way is often referred to as a *yogi*, that is, someone who places great stress on yogic meditation practice. These yogis attached themselves to specific deities, they cultivated spiritual supernatural powers, and focused upon the importance of the human body. Rituals which were contrary to moral rules were carried out to destroy dualism and destroy relative dichotomies (such as destroying the distinction between divine and secular, nirvana and *samsara*, male and female, good and evil, purity and impurity, and subject and object). Whether these rituals happened as described in the texts, or whether the texts are giving us metaphors and figurative language whose social connotations must be interpreted properly by one's teacher, is debated. Of course, they could be doing both.

11.5 TANTRIC BUDDHISM: THE VAJRAYANA

The Tantric form of Buddhism was the final phase of Buddhism in India, but it never achieved as much importance in India as it did in Tibet and Nepal, and to a lesser extent, in China and Japan. Before the seventh century, it is thought that esoteric Buddhism in India was perceived as simply one form of Mahayana Buddhism.[13] However, as Vajrayana developed, rulers and people in authority began to adopt some Tantric forms because they believed that these esoteric rituals gave the rulers magical power and some control over the dangerous world.

Within a few centuries, Tantric Buddhists began to consider themselves an alternative and improved form of Buddhism, in the same way that Mahayana saw itself as an improvement over Theravada. In the north, earlier forms of Buddhism slowly gave way to the newer form of Buddhism, Mahayana, and the Tantric Buddhists consider the Mahayana giving way to their form, a higher, richer, and ultimate form of Buddhism.

---

[12] In Tibetan Buddhism, the *guru* is also called a *lama*, that is, a "superior one."

[13] Paul Williams, Anthony Tribe, *Buddhist Thought: A Complete Introduction to the Indian Tradition* (London: Routledge, 2000), p. 197.

CHAPTER 11: MAHAYANA SCHOOLS–PART II

Tantric Buddhism is the "Third Vehicle" or "Third Turning of the Wheel"

As we learned in the previous chapters, some of the Mahayana followers referred to the Conservative Buddhists as "Hinayana," or the "Smaller Vehicle" or "Inferior Vehicle." They then referred to themselves as the "Greater Vehicle." Using this same strategy, Tantric Buddhists consider themselves a "third vehicle" or *yana*, the *Vajrayana*, with *vajra* explained as "diamond-like" (the hardest natural substance which cannot be scratched), or "Lightning" or "Thunder Bolt." The *vajra* icon has a long association with the thunderbolt as a weapon of the Hindu *deva*, Indra.[14] It can symbolize what Mahayana Buddhists call "skillful means" (*upaya*), but also the indestructible (diamond-hard) character of the highest teaching. Awakening is sudden like a crash of thunder, so this is the Way of the Thunderbolt.[15] Tantric Buddhism was also referred to as *Mantrayana*, that is, the vehicle which makes extensive use of *mantras*, chanted phrases of power.

Another way to explain Tantric Buddhism draws on a popular image of the "turning of the wheel of *dharma*." Buddhists say that the Buddha first "turned the wheel of the *dharma*" when he explained *pratityasamutpada* and the Four Noble Truths to his five friends in the forest. Mahayana describes itself as a second turning of the wheel of the *dharma*, where the more profound teachings involving emptiness, Buddha-nature, and the storehouse-consciousness were first taught by the Buddha. Tantric Buddhists describe their teachings as a third "turning of the wheel of the dharma" where the Buddha taught only a select few monks this highest teaching of rituals, mantras, mandalas, gods, and magic.

The Roots of Tantric Buddhism

Historians generally feel that the roots of Tantric Buddhism developed during the same period when Hindu Tantric ideas flourished and became solidified.[16] Buddhist Tantric followers are confident that their doctrines go all the way back to buddhas of the past including Siddhartha Buddha, or Shakyamuni[17] and are as original as the doctrines of the conservative Elders. According to the Tantric Buddhists, the Buddha explained *Vajrayana* to the Elder Conservative monks, but the Tantric ideas were so complex, and so profound that the conservative Buddhists were incapable of understanding them. Thus the texts containing the teachings of Tantric Buddhism are not for all, but only for a very select subset who have first mastered the Conservative Buddhist teachings (the Four Noble Truths and the Noble Eight-fold Path) and then mastered the Mahayana Buddhist teachings (empty of self-existing substance, or emptiness, eight-levels of consciousness, and Buddha-nature), and were now ready for the ultimate and the highest teachings grounded in devotion to gods and goddesses, constant practice of ritual and chanted mantras which connect us with those divinities. For those who had the higher ability and are ready, the Vajrayana claims that it offers the fastest path to buddhahood (because one does not have to go through countless thousands of lifetimes as a bodhisattva). However, this pathway is dangerous and not for everyone.

---

[14] "The vajra as an instrument plays an essential part in all Vajrayana ritual, where it is used in conjunction with a bell, of which the handle is a half-vajra. Treated thus as a form of duality, the vajra represents the active principle, the means toward enlightenment and the means of conversion, thus the actual Buddha-manifestation, while the bell represents the Perfection of Wisdom, known as the Void (*sunyata*). In the state of union, however, the vajra comprehends both these coefficients of enlightenment, the means and the wisdom." David Snellgrove, *op. cit.*, pp. 131–132.

[15] The term "*vajrayana*" does not appear until the late seventh century in India, so earlier forms of Tantric Buddhism would not have referred to themselves as *Vajrayana*. Paul Williams, Anthony Tribe, *Buddhist Thought: A Complete Introduction to the Indian Tradition*, p. 196.

[16] Hindu Tantrism regards the Buddhist Tantras as Buddhist adaptations of Hindu Tantric literature. David Kalupahana, *A History of Buddhist Philosophy: Continuities & Discontinuities* (Honolulu: University of Hawaii Press, 1989) p. 217.

[17] Shakyamuni ("the sage of the Shakya clan") Buddha is a common Mahayana name for Siddhartha Gautama.

11.6 THE TEXTS: TANTRAS

We have previously seen how many Mahayana Buddhist traditions grew out of specific clusters of Mahayana sutras. We can see something similar for Tantric Buddhism. The combination of rituals, chants and meditation (which resemble Hindu Tantric practices) are explored in a group of texts called Tantras, from which we get the name "Tantric Buddhism."

The original meaning of the Sanskrit term *tantra* draws on the imagery of weaving, where it can signify a continual sequence of threads, and by extension, a continuity of ideas or words. The Indo-Tibetan exegetical tradition understands the term to mean "continuity," extending this to the continuum that exists between the Buddha level and the human level, especially in terms of body, speech and mind. Thus, according to Tantric Buddhism, a *tantra* is a kind of a scripture, a technical manual which contained the difficult and profound instructions which the Buddha had given to certain spiritually advanced disciples.

These new texts are not like the earlier sutras. Tantras use an intentionally esoteric language, a paradoxical description style relying heavily on symbolism, especially arcane symbols to express the various positive categories in Buddhist doctrine. There is much about Tantras which is obscure, because Tantras were never intended to be a philosophical commentary which would be clear to outsiders. Here is a brief excerpt from a Tantra:

> SRI-HERUKA! And I myself become the Blessed Cakrasamvara, Father & Mother, and from my mouth there issues forth:
> A AA I II U UU R RR L LL A AI O AU AM AH KA KHA GA GHA NA CA CHA JA JHA NA TA THA DA DHA NA TA THA DA DHA NA PA PHA BA BHA MA YA RA LA VA SA SHA SA HA KSHA HUM HUM PHAT PHAT!
> And from these syllables there radiates an immeasurable brilliance of white & red light: and it serves the aims of all beings, and it is gathered back & fills all the places of my body. ...
> The syllable A appears in my heart & transforms into a moon: and above the moon is the syllable HUM.
> And light radiates forth from that syllable HUM: and the light is the light of the five knowledges, which invites the lineage of my masters to sit above my head, in the upper part of the mandala of the Blessed Cakrasamvara. And I pay homage to them: NAMAH TE HUM! MANAH ME HUM! NAMO NAMAH HUM!
> And from my own heart there emanate goddesses of offerings for them: OM AH diamond lady of the lute HUM HUM PHAT! OM AH diamond lady of the flute HUM HUM PHAT! OM AH diamond lady of the tambourine HUM HUM PHAT! OM AH diamond lady of the drum HUM HUM PHAT![18]

The *guru* would explain the hidden meanings within Tantras to special students who had been carefully taught secret insights and were now deemed ready, and the *guru* would provide an oral explanation for the vowels, the terms, the symbols, the rituals, and all the details. The foundation of study for Vajrayana Buddhism is the Tantric texts.

Although not unique to Tantric Buddhism, complex ritual is one of the core practices of Tantric Buddhism. Tantras were recited aloud in rituals and ceremonial occasions and so Tantras utilize effects which are appropriate to ritual, such as chanted repetition. Tantras conclude with *dharani*, a magical formula of special and secret knowledge comprised of syllables with symbolic content. A *dharani* is an incantation which is thought to convey the essence of

---

[18] Steven Beyer, *The Buddhist Experience: Sources and Interpretations* (Belmont, CA.: Dickenson Publishing, 1974), pp. 141–142. These are just a brief excerpt of the longer Preliminary Meditations from the Tibetan text "The process of generalization of the wishing gem of the ear-whispered teachings." The original translation uses diacritical marks which have been omitted, however these were suggested for the long vowels by typing AA where the translated text has Ā, and so forth.

a teaching, or a particular state of mind. That state of mind is created by the constant repetition of a *dharani*.

Tantric texts were intentionally esoteric,[19] intentionally difficult to interpret and understand. These texts were secret, were meant to be understood *only* by insiders who had undergone initiation rituals. As we saw before, a tantric text may break into what appear to be alliterative non-sense syllables. Tantras utilize esoteric symbolism of correspondences to such an extent that they are almost unintelligible to anyone lacking a *guru* to explain the correspondences and match them to Buddhist tradition and history. The oral explanation provided by a properly trained *guru* was essential to comprehend the symbols utilized.

For example, it has been revealed that in these chanted tantric texts, philosophical concepts of Mahayana are correlated with the chanting of names of demons we fear (personifications of tremendous power and sometimes, evil), chanting names of *devas* we respect (embodiments of pleasurable existences or experiences), and chanting names of buddhas and bodhisattvas we venerate (teachings of ultimate goal of Buddhist life). These various devices made the text more interesting during chanted *mantra*-recitation ceremonies.

In the previous chapter, we discussed a number of key Buddhas in Mahayana. These names of Buddhas become correlated with philosophical symbols in Tantras. When we discussed the self in early Buddhism, we saw that Buddhists analyzed the self into five groups or five bundles of processes, including physical form and the body, feelings, perceptions, dispositions, and consciousness. In the Tantra, the human personality consists in Vairocana, Ratnasambhava, Amitabha, Amoghasiddi, and Aksobhya. When the name Vairocana appears, it symbolizes the body and ethics; when the name Ratnasambhava is chanted, it symbolizes feelings and concentration. Amitaabha corresponds to perception and appreciation; Amoghasiddhi is dispositions and freedom; and Aksobhya is consciousness.[20]

11.7 VAJRAYANA DOCTRINES

The Triple Body of the Buddha

All of the central Mahayana insights and doctrines are found and accepted in early Tantric Buddhism and its later development, Vajrayana Buddhism. For example, in the Yogachara form of Mahayana there developed the theory of the triple body of the Buddha, which include the body of the Buddha that his students saw (*nirmanakaya* or transformation body), the enjoyment body (*sambhogakaya*, the body clothed in light and beauty which visits bodhisattva heavens) which is the perfected body which appears to us as a Buddha such as Amitabha who enjoys the Pure Land of the West, and then there is the Cosmic body (*dharmakaya*), the ultimate and non-dual reality.[21] Thus the single Buddha can appear in many different forms and many different places, all united in one cosmic absolute Buddha which can be understood by those who achieve awakening. This three-body doctrine is accepted by the Tantric Buddhists, although they do offer additional interpretations of the ideas. The devotional aspect of this doctrine is obvious.

When a student achieves a profoundly transformative awakening experience, and is filled with bliss, this is now described as the *sambhogakaya*, a bliss-filled beatific body with which the student can converse with fellow enlightened beings. Yet another deeper experience can follow where the student loses all sense of self and becomes indistinguishable from and identified with ultimate reality. This is now the *dharmakaya*, the Cosmic body. Finally, recognizing the pain

---

[19] Esoteric is designed for, or understood by the specially initiated alone; requiring knowledge that is restricted to a small group; limited to a small circle. The element of secrecy is quite important in Tantric Buddhism.

[20] David Kalupahana, *A History of Buddhist Philosophy* (Honolulu: University of Hawaii Press, 1992), pp. 223ff.

[21] The Tantric acceptance of the three body doctrine is an important feature of devotional Mahayana Buddhism which separates Tantric Buddhism from the corresponding Hindu forms of Tantric religion. There is no teachings of three bodies in Hindu Tantrism.

and suffering of all those who remain behind, the adept returns to the world and teaches students how to eliminate suffering. The body with which the person uses to teach others is the *nirmakaya*, the physical body.

Emptiness

Like the earlier Mahayana schools, Tantric Buddhism was primarily concerned with the attainment of buddhahood and relied heavily upon Nagarjuna's Madhyamaka tradition and the *Prajnaparamita sutras* which emphasize emptiness, i.e., all things are *svabhava-sunyata* or empty of inner unchanging substance (discussed in the previous chapter). Everything can be described as *sunyata*, it is all dependently co-arising (*pratityasamutpada*), interdependent and interconnected. Nothing has any intrinsic qualities; all of reality is flowing process, and everything is relative to the changing causes.

If we see the world as composed of things which are intrinsically good, and things which are intrinsically bad, then we see the world dualistically, and we think of reality as composed of separate independent self-existing contraries. For the Madhyamaka tradition of the Mahayana, this is a mistake. Reality is not composed of opposites which are ultimately separate and independent of each other. Reality is just flowing interdependent processes which cannot be conceptualized accurately because every concept is merely a snapshot of a constantly changing series of processes. No term accurately describes Reality, so the Buddhists say "Reality is Suchness," and despite the Hindu insistence to the contrary, everything is real while at the same time everything is empty of essence.

Tantric Buddhism perceives the mistaken tendency to see reality in terms of opposites, or dualities, as one of the biggest problems for the unawakened.[22] There is a strong tendency in people to believe that purity and impurity, good and evil, liberation and bondage, were objective qualities residing in things, person and actions. Some things are believed to be pure, and other things impure. Some things are regarded as good, and others as evil. The insight of emptiness reveals these are dualisms which exist only in the mind, not in the world.

Ritual

Tantric Buddhism used rituals for the express purpose of destroying the trap of dualism. It used rituals to destroy these relative dichotomies (such as the distinction between sacred and secular, between pure and impure, the distinction between nirvana and *samsara*, the duality of male and female, the good and evil duality, and the division between god and human, the division between awakened and unawakened). If one wants to use a ritual to destroy the human perception of some things as pure and others as impure, it must include behaviors which ordinary people perceive as impure, as polluted. Thus the Tantric rituals are often contrary to popular Buddhist and Hindu moral strictures, and shocking to ordinary people. For example, death was regarded as polluting in India, and if the Tantric follower who stood as a beggar before your door, dressed in the clothing of a dead body at a funeral, it was frightening and shocking.

Devotionalism in Tantric Buddhism

Bhakti ("devotion") is also extremely important in Tantric Buddhism. The practitioners of yogic meditation were attached to deities, especially goddesses, and cultivated spiritual powers (magic). Special *mantras* are recited to put us into contact with divinities. Followers practice visualization of a special guardian deity as the focus of one's meditation.

---

[22] Tantric and Madhyamaka Buddhists think ordinary people tend to divide the world up into ultimate opposites. Ordinary people think in terms of dualistic categories and do not recognize that reality is flowing change. Ordinary people see things as Good versus Evil, Sacred versus Profane, you are with me or you are against me, humans are good or they are evil, and so forth. Buddhists, Taoists, Confucianism, and Shintoism all reject the belief that the world is composed of ultimate dualistic opposites.

CHAPTER 11: MAHAYANA SCHOOLS–PART II

Buddha-Nature

The idea that each of us has the buddha-nature is also essential for Vajrayana Buddhism. The Buddha's awakening is not something that we lack. Ultimately it is to be found within our own mind, which means we are already a buddha. It is only our ignorance which keeps us from actualizing our Buddha-nature. Purity and impurity are merely concepts, nothing more. The illusion that opposites and duality are some sort of ultimate properties in the world, external to ourselves, is the key form of ignorance.

The goal of Tantric Buddhism is the transformation of our body, speech, and mind into those of a buddha by the means of special esoteric practices. Part of the problem is that we are trapped in duality: we think our self is different from a buddha. We do not realize that we have always had the buddha-nature, and we live as though we are not buddhas, and as though we are lacking something and so we are trying to seek something outside ourselves to attain awakening. This attitude is part of the problem; it traps us in a duality of unawakened versus awakened.

Each of the doctrines discussed above should be familiar to the reader. They all derive from earlier forms of Mahayana Buddhism in India. It is not unique doctrines that distinguish Tantrism from the other Buddhist schools. Rather, it is methods and techniques which set Tantrism apart. Tantric Buddhism puts stress on apparently bizarre rituals and psychological methods of experimentation which are minimized or not used in other Mahayana traditions.

11.8 TANTRIC BUDDHIST PRACTICES IN INDIA

The Tantric practices are esoteric, and not for everyone. Tantric Buddhists believe that their practices are dangerous, and only for those who have surpassed the Theravada and Mahayana pathways, and are ready for something even higher. These practices are done in the context of a *guru*, the teacher with powers (in fact, the goal for Theravada is the *arhat*, the goal for the Mahayana is the bodhisattva, the goal for the Vajrayana is the *guru* with paranormal powers). Originally it is likely that the emphasis was probably upon rites and rituals, but increasingly it became identified with shocking rituals, with chanted *mantras*, meditation used to visualize gods and bodhisattvas, symbols, and powers.[23] Distinguishing Mahayana Buddhism from Vajrayana, David Snellgrove writes:

> The main difference derives from the Vajrayana use of incantation and ritual as means toward the ultimate goal, whereas in the earlier phases of Buddhism their use was largely peripheral. By their means one gains power over beings in other spheres of existence, either dominating them, so that they may do one's will, or identifying onself with them, so that one may enjoy their higher states of existence.[24]

The Sanskrit term for these powers is *siddhis*. Tantric Buddhism recognizes *siddhas*, special spiritual teachers who possess *siddhis*, powers achievable with advanced meditation and magical phrases. Tantric Buddhists assert that there are numerous miraculous powers, including the ability to make onself invisible, to walk through solid walls, to walk on water, to fly through the air, to levitate and control physical objects without touching them, to be able to hear conversations miles away. One can also read the minds of others and even be in more than one place at the same time. In addition, one can dominate and control spirits in parallel realms. A special term for a *guru* who possesses *siddhis* is a *mahasiddha*. Thus one could say that the goal of the conservative schools of Buddhism is the *arhat*, the goal of the Mahayana schools is the bodhisattva, and the goal of the Tantric schools is a *mahasiddha*. Of course a buddha is higher than all of these.

---

[23] A. K. Warder, *Indian Buddhism, op. cit.*, p. 485.

[24] David Snellgrove, *Indo-Tibetan Buddhism* (Boston: Shambala, 2002), p. 130. The reader should recognize what was described as "Shamanism" in the introductory chapter.

Tantric Buddhism came to place great stress on the visualization of diagrams (*mandalas*), and the diagram can be small or can also be as large as a farmer's field, an open site, a large area where fire rituals are carried out, symbolizing the burning up of passions and delusions in the fire of understanding.[25]

The Goal of the Vajrayana

The ultimate goal of Tantric Buddhism is the supreme full awakening of a buddha in this very life, and the goal does not require thousands of lifetimes (as is suggested for traditional Mahayana followers). Vajrayana claims that the *guru* who cultivates supernatural powers (*mahasiddha*) and who utilizes the decidedly unconventional techniques can achieve buddhahood in this very life. The Tantric pathway is an abrupt and difficult path to traverse, but its followers assert that its power comes from its unconventional practices. Vibrant colors are used in artistic creations and rituals. Tantric Buddhism uses music, sweet-smelling incense, bright colors, intricate patterns, and monks chanting. The student travels through the senses to a higher realm of reality (a *mandala* is a road map for this sort of journey). Tantric Buddhism also utilizes sexual imagery, goddess worship, and rituals which involve behavior such as sexuality, alcohol consumption, consumption of meats, song and dance, all of which are intentionally contrary to Buddhist moral precepts.

A key insight of Tantric Buddhism is that the Buddha's awakening is ultimately to be found within your own mind. You are already a buddha: do not live as though you are un-awakened, and are trying to attain enlightenment – that traps you in duality. There is nothing ultimate in the nirvana-*samsara* duality.

11.9 PRACTICES WHICH DISTINGUISH VAJRAYANA FROM OTHER FORMS OF BUDDHISM

The new practices of Vajrayana were esoteric techniques, intentionally secret techniques. The abstract concepts of "the wisdom which carries one over to the other shore" is transformed into actual bodily experiences of emptiness (*sunyata*). Rituals are essential. Empowerment transmissions are essential. Sounds of power were chanted, secret diagrams were constructed, secret hand positions were mastered (*mudra*), and fire rituals were performed. One central practice involves visualization of oneself as a divinity.

Visualization of Buddhas and Bodhisattvas

Tantric Buddhism is devotional and places great emphasis upon the visualization of deities, and establishing relationships with deities. The deities do not live merely in the heavenly realms; they live within us, and can be visualized. In the process of visualizing, we come into contact with deep pools of unconscious energy which can be terrifying. This energy and subliminal anger can be directed to eradicate those features of one's personality which were hindering the free flow of sympathetic compassion; channeling and using the apparently negative energy for good.

> In learning to produce mentally such higher forms of emanation and eventually identifying himself with them, the practitioner gradually transforms his evanescent personality into that higher state of being. Thus belief in them [divinities] is essential ...[26]

---

[25] A detailed discussion of the various stages of meditation, or visualization, including all various aspects mentioned above, is found in A. K. Warder, *Indian Buddhism*, op. cit., pp. 492–499.

[26] Snellgrove, *Indo-Tibetan Buddhism*, op. cit., p. 131.

With the mastery of guided visualization, the student is believed to be able to re-create herself from ordinary to divine. These are called self-creation yogas or methods of magical and religious practices allowing the practitioner to be reborn, to acquire a new identity. The Tantric adept could acquire magical powers of the *devas* by visualizing and conjuring them up from depths of human consciousness. The external and internal worlds could be seen as relative and not absolute. The Buddhist deities dissolve into emptiness. The practitioner of yoga experiences emptiness, the diamond essence, or reality.

The central aim of this self-creation yoga is for the practitioner to do away with the perception of herself as ordinary — as well as the pride that is believed to be associated with that perception — and to replace it with a perception of herself as a divine, enlightened being, with the sense of proud empowerment and universal efficacy that characterizes such a being. Such a profound transformation is not considered to be an undertaking that can be accomplished just so; rather, it is a highly ramified process that involves meditatively dying from the previous, unenlightened embodiment and ritually taking rebirth with a new, perfected identity.[27]

Use of *Mandala*

Like the Hindu Tantric practitioners, as an aid to meditation the Buddhist Tantric adepts utilized the *mandala*, the circular image, drawing, or pattern, inside a square. A *mandala* is interpreted as a map of sacred space. In some sense, Tantric Buddhism asserts that buddhas and bodhisattvas reside within the mind of every human being and *mandalas* are special sacred maps which correlate external realms with internal states of consciousness. The totality of reality, the macrocosm, is replicated in the human body, and with practice and the guidance of the *guru*, it can be visualized.

The correspondences extend to the various elements of reality, and associated properties and symbols which the student can use to clarify many levels of doctrine. Various colors used in the *mandalas* are also part of the system of symbols. Buddhist concepts and doctrines are symbolically represented in special patterns that described the interrelationship between the different teachings and various forces in the teaching.

Thus a colorful *mandala* presents Buddhist doctrines in a physical form, as a multi-colored picture where each color has a special meaning, and where the various shapes also have hidden meanings. In this way esoteric Buddhist teachings could be encoded in diagrams conveyed in simplified forms which the *guru* could reveal to the student who is ready, through the medium of the *mandala*.

When you are ready, your *guru* will provide the appropriate *mandala* for your level of spiritual accomplishment. Using the *mandala* assigned by one's teacher, the student visualizes the body as the dwelling or palace of a pure being, a buddha or bodhisattva. This image is not merely an intellectual symbol. Tantric *gurus* teach that the *mandala* are maps of our own personal spiritual journey in which the student can discover and comprehend secret doctrines which can awaken spiritual potentials buried deep in the subconscious. The presence of an accomplished *guru* to guide the student is essential to this Tantric pathway; no one can simply stare at a *mandala* on her own. An advanced female student who has recreated herself using secret yoga methods will find herself in the *mandala* palace of a god or a buddha.

She then imaginatively creates a divine environment for this recreated personality to inhabit: the *mandala*, with its glorious palace suitable as the residence of a full-enlightened divinity. The yogini then "enters the mandala of ultimate reality" (i.e., dies, leaving her ordinary personality), and arises in a thoroughly-accomplished, perfected form whose mind is suffused with the great compassion and

---

[27] Christian K. Wedemeyer, *Making Sense of Tantric Buddhism, op. cit.*, p. 117.

wisdom of voidness cultivated previously. A variety of yogas involving the arraying and recitation of mantras and/or manipulation of vital airs are then prescribed to reinforce and consecreate this identity ...[28]

The Use of *Mantras*

We discussed *mantras* in the chapter explaining the Vedas, and then again in chapter 5 about Tantric Hinduism. *Mantras* are found in early Buddhism and Mahayana schools, but the Vajrayana puts much more stress on *mantras* than the previous forms of Buddhism.

Some scholars suggest that Buddhist Tantricism may have borrowed the emphasis upon sacred sounds which give power from Vedic Hinduism. *Mantras* are thought to be highly compressed, power-packed terms or phrases, drawn from Sanskrit, and charged with deep meaning and magical potency. Although a popular Tibetan explanation of *mantra* is that it is something which protects the mind, the actual Sanskrit etymology does not support this. According to Sanskrit scholars, the original Vedic meaning of *mantra* is that by which one thinks, or an instrument of thought. In Vedic times, *mantra* referred to the sacred sounds of the Vedic verses, so that a Brahmin priest who chants or sings the verses from the early Vedas is uttering *mantras*; but in a Buddhist context, it acquires a slightly different meaning.

For a Buddhist, the truth was in the words spoken by the Buddha. Because the sacred Awakened One spoke those words, words spoken by the Buddha become sacred sounds and syllables which, when properly chanted, contain magical powers. However, there are numerous Mahayana sutras, and there are many different buddhas presiding over many different realms. It was believed that each buddha had a special sound which reflected the pure mind of that buddha.

For example, the special *mantra* of the bodhisattva of compassion, Avalokiteshvara, is *OM MANI PADME HUM*. If this is the sound which encapsulates the compassionate consciousness of Avalokitesvara, then constant repetition of this sound must affect the pupil's mind for the better. It will nourish the egoless compassion of the bodhisattva that resides in the mind of the student. The student comes to understand some of the symbolism of this *mantra* when the *guru* explains the meaning of each syllable. For example, in the context of describing the syllable HUM carved into the *vajra* instrument, a Tibetan explains as follows: "The syllable HUM ... indicates the unsurpassable essential truth: H representing freedom from causality, U representing freedom from argumentation and M the groundlessness of all *dharmas*."[29]

Mantras can be recited verbally, but their power extends beyond the sound itself. *Mantra* can be visualized, and repeatedly written down as spiritual practice. They can be carved in stone, or written on paper. One can internally recite a *mantra* as a device to help develop and nurture one-pointed focused concentration. An example of this is the following:

OM SUNYATA JNANA VAJRA SVABHAVA MAKO 'HAM

which might be translated as "Om! I am the essential nature of the diamond insight of emptiness." Chanting this helps to bring about this exalted state of mind.

These *mantra* are believed to be like a key to the mind and the powers that reside deep in the unconscious. Through knowledge and manipulation of appropriate sounds, the psychic forces could be brought under control, and

---

[28] *Ibid.*, p. 118.

[29] David Snellgrove, *Indo-Tibetan Buddhism*, p. 133. The phrase "groundlessness of all dharmas" is a reference to *sunyata*, "empty of unchanging essence." In the quote I have omitted some Sanskrit technical terms and diacritical marks.

various levels of attainment are possible.[30] In the Tantric traditions, one needs the guidance of a *guru* to gain anything from the chanting of *mantra*s.

There are various ways to understand the powers of *mantra*. Is it the specific sound of the Sanskrit word that is powerful, or is it the state of mind of the person who chants the sound that creates the power? If it is the **sound** itself which is powerful, then proper pronunciation is essential and mis-pronunciation is a serious problem. Without knowledge of the ancient sounds of the Sanskrit language no one could get any benefit from *mantra* unless they have a teacher who has learned the correct pronunciation from his teacher.[31] A second understanding is that it is the **state of mind** of the person chanting the sound that gives the power to the *mantra*, so proper Sanskrit pronunciation is not essential.

A third understanding is that the potency of the sound is initially generated and then amplified because the sound has been repeated over and over by a long line of teachers, all of whom chanted the same sound. In this third case, no one can simply recite a *mantra* and expect results.[32] Rather, the Tantric empowerment ritual in which the *guru* transmits the secret *mantra* to the student is precisely when the *mantra* becomes effective. The empowerment transmission rituals are the key to the effective power of a *mantra*.

In any case, Tantric Buddhism asserts that recitation of a *mantra* is a daily practice which purifies speech, helps to focus concentration, maintains a constant spiritual connection, and it helps to disperse mental chatter.[33] It might be understood as a tool of inward cultivation and exploration, or as an instrument to activate the energies of external bodhisattvas and other spiritual beings.

Shakti (female partners and goddesses)

Sexual symbolism plays an important role in Tantric Buddhism as it does in Tantric Hinduism.[34] The term *shakti* refers to a goddess and a sexual partner, and refers to a symbol of the divine feminine energy to create and transform. The *shakti* in Hinduism is the female consort, or wife, of a Hindu deity. For the Hindu followers of the god Shiva, the term **shaktism** draws our attention to the *shakti*, the feminine creative energy of Shiva, the power to transform. *Shakti* simply means force or transformative energy. The follower of Shiva can cultivate a relationship with and worship the feminine *shakti* dimension of Shiva as well as the masculine aspect. The feminine *shakti* is the *devi*, the Great Goddess, symbolic of the feminine side of the divine male-female polarity, symbolic of the **active creative** natural processes in the universe.[35]

In Hinduism the gods are certainly sexually active, however in early Buddhist iconography the great bodhisattvas remain celibate, and the goddesses serve as handmaidens, not sexual partners.[36] Thus "female partner" has

---

[30] Several books in English contain Tantric texts with *mantras*. For example, see Steven Beyer, tr. and ed., *The Buddhist Experience: Sources and Interpretations* (Belmont, CA: Dickenson Publishing, 1974), pp. 125–153.

[31] This would reflect the ancient Vedic Hindu insistence upon proper pronunciation as essential.

[32] Thus, buying a book of mantras and chanting them on one's own is a waste of time if one expects to achieve Tantric goals thereby.

[33] John Snelling, *The Buddhist Handbook* (Rochester, VT: Inner Traditions, 1991), p. 96.

[34] Previously we discussed Hindu Shaktism in chapter five, section 5.5.

[35] See David R. Kinsley, *Hindu Goddesses: Visions of the Divine Feminine in the Hindu Religious Tradition* (Berkeley: University of California, 1998).

[36] David Snellgrove, *op. cit.*, p. 150. There do seem to be some exceptions, however, especially in Tibetan forms of Buddhism.

been suggested to render *shakti* in the context of Tantric Buddhism in India.

The Female Partner or Handmaiden

In Tantric Buddhism, female partners of bodhisattvas are not merely lowly helpers or unimportant handmaidens, but become important symbols of wisdom and liberation. They are goddesses, or *devi*. Much of the artistic expression of the *shakti*-energy in Buddhism is explicitly sexual. The sexual union of male and female is symbolic of the self-division of primal unity into a bi-polar dualism. It is the subsequent interaction of the two poles which produces all the things in the world. By reversing that process of creation, the male energy and female energy are united and we bring about a conscious return to unity. It is also symbolic of the union of calm wisdom and active compassion, the two becoming one. In meditation, one can imagine the dynamic male energy uniting with the passive wisdom which is the female energy, in a sexual symbol of oneness.[37] Pure Wisdom without compassion is cold and hard, empathy with other living things is difficult or impossible. Pure Compassion without wisdom is misdirected and can lead to harm. One of the most powerful images of two becoming one, or non-duality, is sexual imagery and sexual symbols.[38]

Tantric Practices Forbidden to those Lacking Sufficient Spiritual Accomplishment

According to Tantric Buddhist teachers, the philosophical grounding in Madhyamaka (things are empty of self-existing essence), Yogachara (eight levels of consciousness), and Buddha-nature (Tathagata-garbha) forms of Buddhism, combined with the Tantric techniques, provide the foundation of ethical and spiritual purity needed before one can attempt the more dangerous and more powerful Vajrayana practices. The student-practitioner does have the buddha-nature, which means that the potential for buddhahood is innate within. Each of us is already a potential buddha but we are ignorant of this fact and so we do not live that way. With adequate meditative and moral training, we are ready for the next level.

Buddhist philosophers argue that what we think of as Reality is flowing processes, not separate and independent entities. In Madhyamaka Buddhism, there are two truths, the ultimate highest truth (the absolute truth), and the conventional truth (the relative truth). Although grounded in Madhyamaka insights, Tantric Buddhists insist upon the complete identity of all opposites, including the conventional and ultimate truths — not just in theory, but also in practice.

The universe is flowing processes and nothing has an unchanging inner essence; thus no duality is ultimate. This includes the duality of purity versus impurity, sacred versus worldly, or subject versus object. Dualities belong to the level of convention, to the conventional truth, not ultimate truth. We must not be trapped into dividing the world up using the categories created by these false dichotomies. There is no real separation between sacred and secular. Do not think that there is an absolute transcendent realm of awakening, and a completely different separate realm of suffering in the relative world. The realm of nirvana is not different from the realm of birth-and-death, *samsara*.

Do not live as though you are unawakened, as though you are trying to attain some new quality called "enlightenment" that you do not now possess — this mistaken belief traps you in a conceptual duality of awakened

---

[37] The Hindu Tantric pathway considers the male as passive and knowledge, and the female pole is the active and the dynamic aspect of reality. Shiva is passive and the *shakti* female energy is active. The Buddhist Tantric pathway tends to be just the opposite; the male is compassionate, active and dynamic, and the female is the passive and the wisdom pole. Agehananda Bharati, *The Tantric Tradition* (New York: Anchor Books, 1970), p. 19, p. 31, pp. 201–203.

[38] It is interesting to note that religious Taoism in China places great emphasis upon sexual intercourse, but there the belief was that when a female achieves orgasm, the male sex organ could absorb her emitted *yang* energy, and thereby prolong the life of the male (sex with 1200 girls could give immortality) or cure illness. See *Asian Thought*, Volume II, section 18.7, "Techniques of Inner Alchemy." After Tantric Buddhism was introduced into China in the eighth century, the religious Taoists incorporated much of Indian analysis into their schema.

versus not-awakened and is a cause of your *duhkha*. For Tantra, there is no ultimate awakened-unawakened duality, no subject-object duality, no deity-human duality, no purity-impurity duality — so live that way.

Some Tantric Rituals Transgress Against Morality

Many esoteric Tantric rituals are purposely designed to shatter socially acceptable ways of conceptualizing the world. These esoteric practices designed to push the student beyond these ordinary ways of perceiving the world include sexual rituals, eating meat and fish, living unclothed or wearing clothes associated with a dead body, singing and dancing, drinking alcohol and even consuming excrement and other bodily fluids.

These Tantric practices transgress against traditional Buddhist morality. Some Tantric rituals involve bodily experiences, including sexual intercourse between the practitioner and his or her partner. The male visualizes himself as a divinity, the masculine energy. The female visualizes herself as a divinity, the feminine energy. During the ritual, the masculine and feminine forces, corresponding to active compassion and passive wisdom, are activated and reunited. However, in the Tantric tradition these forbidden rituals are suitable only for advanced practitioners who have the spiritual insight and moral training to undertake these practices. Some scholars believe that it is likely that most of the Tantric sexual practices are visualization exercises rather than physical encounters, but there is no unanimous agreement on this. Of course, these could be both visualization exercises and actual physical encounters.[39]

These forbidden practices are the result of teachers trying to push their students to see the world non-dualistically, as genuinely empty of self-existent essences (*sunyata*). If there are no unchanging substances or essences, then nothing has an unchanging essence (*svabhava*). If nothing has an essence, then nothing is inherently, in its essence, good. Nothing is, in its essence, evil. Things as changing processes certainly are conventionally good or evil, but not ultimately or absolutely good or evil.

To help the advanced student understand this, activities normally forbidden in earlier forms of Buddhism (and thought of as evil) serve as teaching instruments: meditation in areas associated with decomposing corpses, imbibing alcoholic beverages, eating fish, meat eating, and sexual intercourse. Thus, passions themselves are not evil, not intrinsically bad, or impure — passions and emotions do not possess an evil or impure inner nature (because all things are empty of an inner essence). It must be our mind that makes certain desires and passions impure.

Advanced Buddhist Tantric adepts seem to have thought that deliberate transgression of conventional norms could generate the liberating insight that propels one to liberation, to the achievement of buddhahood. Tantric Buddhism celebrates rites which make real the student's attainment with actual physical bodily experiences of buddhahood.[40]

Tantric Deities As Spiritual Practice

Tantric Buddhism employs a wide variety of gods and demons, both male and female, some benign offering help and compassion, some fearsome, snarling, wreathed in flames, drinking out of skulls. These deities are forces that can help us. If you want to get rid of ignorance, you can fight it with a "Destroyer of Ignorance," a deity who has a threatening or fear-generating personality. There is also a secret *mantra* for each divinity, which can connect us to each of them, revealed to the student by the *guru*. The *guru* knows the words of power for this wide pantheon of deities, and can share that knowledge, but not until the student is ready. In the following quotation, the author uses "Void" to translate *sunyata*, or what we have consistently translated as "emptiness."

---

[39] Historical records reveal that there were Tantric Buddhist monastics who were married and had children, and so their partner would have been their spouse. Wedemeyer, *op. cit.*, p. 183.

[40] As was noted in the section on Tantric Hinduism, contemporary Western techniques which are called "Tantric sexuality" have almost no connection at all with what was done among Tantric followers in India or Tibet.

The student of tantric Buddhism must accustom himself to a bewildering variety of Buddha-names, many of which relate to distinctive iconographic forms, but which in their true essence know of no diversity. Scarcely any other religion can display so many different divinities, some appearing singly, some appearing in sets, all treated by the simple Tibetan believer as the many gods of his religion, yet recognized by the true adept as mere expressions of absolute buddhahood adapted to his own special circumstances. Thus all these divine forms are dissolved by him into the luminous state of the Void, and it is out of the Void that they are duly summoned by means of his meditative practice.[41]

For the Tantric adept, these supernatural divinities can be understood as archetypal images symbolic of primordial energies all of which are found within ourselves. You have the wisdom of awakening within you, but there are the negatives as well. You have hatred and fear simmering inside of you. You have lust, you have anger, you have ignorance. These Tantric deities are the passions transformed and personified.

The Symbolism of the Five Buddhas

One special group of deities is the fundamental five Buddhas described in a previous chapter, Vairochana (the Supreme Buddha), Akshobhya, Ratnasambhava, Amitabha, and Amoghasiddhi. As described in a previous paragraph, these symbolize five primary energies which provide a structure by which all of reality can be understood and interpreted. The bodhisattva of compassion, Avalokitesvara, is singularly important as well.

As was pointed out earlier, in Tantric Buddhism there are the *shakti* goddesses as well as male divinities. In Tantric Buddhism, the sacred *Prajnaparamita* ("Perfection of Wisdom") is not just a scripture, or a Buddhist concept; *Prajnaparamita* becomes a goddess. A Buddhist text describes her as follows:

> She bears a head-dress of twisted hair; she has four arms and one face. With two of her hands she makes the gesture of expounding the dharma and she is adorned with various jeweled ornaments. She blazes like the colour of gold and in her (second) left hand she holds a blue lotus with the Prajnaparamita-book upon it. She wears various garments both below and above and with her (second) right hand she makes the gesture of fearlessness. She is seated cross-legged on the lunar disk and on a red lotus.[42]

One of the most important of all the Tantric goddesses is Tara, "One who Saves."[43] In the form of the White Tara, the White Goddess,

> ... she manifests herself as a Great Goddess, indeed as the greatest of all Buddhist Goddesses, in her own right. ... She becomes a feminine version of Avalokitesvara rather than his partner in that both of them remain major celibate divinities. Tara also tends to replace Prajnaparamita in that she comes to be regarded as the Mother of all Buddhas. Her remarkable success appears to be an exclusively Buddhist development for which no convincing Hindu parallel can be found.[44]

Each of these Buddhas in turn arise out of, and return to the emptiness of the one supreme Tantric Buddha, Vairocana.

---

[41] David Snellgrove, *Indo-Tibetan Buddhism*, op. cit., p. 207.

[42] Translated by D. L. Snellgrove in E. Conze, ed., *Buddhist Texts Through the Ages* (New York: Harper Torchbooks, 1964), p. 253.

[43] See Steven Beyer, *The Cult of Tara* (Berkeley: University of California Press, 1978).

[44] David Snellgrove, *Indo-Tibetan Buddhism*, op. cit., p. 151.

11.10 THE VAJRAYANA COMMUNITY IN INDIA

The heart of the Vajrayana Tantric Buddhist community was mostly monastics, composed primarily of *gurus*, teachers and their students. It seems likely that these teachers developed Buddhist Tantric liturgies which were specially designed for the use of kings. The kingdom could be protected by the *siddhis* and powerful *mantras* and by Buddhist divinities. Demons and evil forces could be driven out of the nation. There were monks who could invoke gods and force them to protect the ruler and the nation. The status of the ruler could be enhanced by magical rituals which emphasized the king or ruler as a bodhisattva or even a buddha. It made the rule and ruler legitimate.[45]

Sometimes the local ruler was blessed and consecrated as a bodhisattva or living buddha. The Buddhists and the kings believed that the powers of the buddha or advanced bodhisattvas could protect the ruler and the kingdom against disruptions, or even evil forces.[46] However, these very similar liturgies were already in place in Hindu India functioning in the same way; Tantric practices were very popular, but they were also making Buddhism look more and more like Hinduism.[47]

11.11 THE DECLINE OF BUDDHISM IN INDIA

From the growth of the *bhakti* (devotional) and Tantric approach to Hinduism until the invasion of India by the Arab and Turkish Muslims, the several forms of Buddhism were only one of many religious traditions in India, and although popular among the more affluent merchants and the administrators who belonged to the protector-warrior (*ksatriya*) groups, Buddhism did not dominate at the level of popular religion. Although institutional Buddhism did disappear from India, we must remember that it did not disappear all at once, or in all places simultaneously. For some areas accommodations occurred, in others it was destruction, in some there was tolerance, and in some there was the equivalent of ethnic cleansing. These events occurred over the centuries. Although the decline of Buddhism is a complex topic, for our purposes we will pay special attention to five factors which played an important role in the slow decline and the ultimate disappearance of institutional Buddhism in India.

ECONOMIC CONSIDERATIONS

The strongest support for Buddhism was in the upper levels of Hindu society, including priests, rulers and administrators, and wealthy traders and merchants. This allowed institutional Buddhism to centralize their monks in the equivalent of universities, with massive libraries, and these impressive institutions encouraged additional support from the ruling classes. When the ruling classes were overturned or when rulers were replaced with new rulers unsympathetic to Buddhism, Buddhism's centralization became a lethal weakness. To feed a lot of monks requires lots of food and requires patronage. Buddhist monastic institutions required support, and much of its support was from the rulers.

In exchange for food and money, Buddhist institutions legitimized the ruler and gave religious support for the ruling classes and provided them with the right to rule. Things began to change from the seventh century on. Political instability became the order of the day. Much of India was embroiled in clan warfare and other forms of

---

[45] Throughout its history, Buddhist monks have repaid the donations of the community with community-protecting rituals. The shamanistic roots of these activities should be obvious to the reader.

[46] Fenton, *et. al., Religions of Asia*, 3rd. ed. , p. 129. Indeed, some Americans seem to believe that posting bumper stickers on their automobiles that say "God Bless America" can bring a divine blessing down and protect the country from outside evildoers.

[47] Ronald M. Davidson, *Indian Esoteric Buddhism: A Social History of the Tantric Movement* (New York: Columbia University Press, 2002).

incessant conflict for several centuries. New local dynasties would appear, would start wars for political hegemony and then disappear. One consequence was that there was no more imperial support for large Buddhist monastic institutions, and weakened support for important pilgrimage centers.

In the eighth century, invading armies of Muslims took control and exerted power over many kingdoms in the north and further fed the resentments. The wealthy classes became impoverished and weakened as a result of political and military clashes. The Buddhist monastic institutions, wedded to their patrons, were severely weakened in turn with the destruction of the financial order on which they depended. When rulers changed religion, those who depend upon the rulers for their livelihood also change their religions. As for those who did not, they were no longer wealthy or successful. Political and economic change thus affected these higher class followers of Buddhism more than it did popular Hinduism.

SOCIOLOGICAL CONSIDERATIONS

As noted above, the strongest support for Buddhism was in the upper levels of Hindu society, including priests, rulers, and wealthy traders and merchants. The sociology of the day was such that a ruler's populace largely followed the lead of the rulers. If the ruler supported a religion, so did many of his citizens, at least nominally. If he or his successor subsequently changed religion, so did the populace directly influenced by the rulers, or those hoping to interact with the rulers.[48]

Buddhism tended to be a well-educated, high-culture sort of religion, and did not have as strong roots in the popular religious sensibility of the majority of the population, who tended to be poor yet ordinary Hindus in the rural villages. The Buddhists had become associated with the wealthy, upper layers of society, whom the peasants generally resented. Thus, a religion associated with the wealthy and powerful was not very popular with the farmers, with the poor and lower castes.

ISOLATION OF THE MONASTERIES: MONKS versus LAITY

The conservative Theravada Buddhism was primarily a pathway for monks who would break away from the social order and either beg or belong to a monastery. The primary role for householders and laypersons was to support the spiritual aspirations of the monks. Later, due to political connections and tax benefits, many of the monasteries acquired power, wealth, and land and, ultimately became self-sufficient. Monks in these monasteries became more isolated from the general population. The Buddhist monks continued to perform social rituals to benefit patrons and the community, but donations from householders were no longer essential to survival. As a result, the connection between rural householders and Buddhist monks was weakened. The popular support from earlier times was slowly withering.

At the same time, devotional *bhakti* tendencies within Buddhism were satisfied equally well by popular Hindu *devas* and popular Buddhism became less important as the self-sufficient monasteries became more and more remote from everyday Indian society. Among the majority, Tantric practices of Buddhists became indistinguishable from Hindu Tantricism.

THE VITALITY OF THE BRAHMANIC HINDU TRADITION.

What we have called Hinduism was the social foundation for India; it justified the caste system which structured the lives of all ordinary people. The ceremonial rituals of the Brahmin priests were believed essential to the universe, and devotion to *devas* was becoming more popular. Whether the people lived in large cities or rural villages,

---

[48] There is a popular Chinese proverb: "When the wind blows the grass bends," or those who are below will respond to or imitate those who are above. Often those below have no choice.

CHAPTER 11: MAHAYANA SCHOOLS–PART II

Hinduism determined their occupation, the four stages of their lives, and even their social responsibilities. Every Hindu wanted to achieve a better life in the next life, and every Hindu knew how to do that. The key to a good life in the next life was to follow one's social duty as ordained by one's caste. For popular religion, there were four stages (four ashrama)[49] to a person's life, and everyone was somewhere on that ladder leading to a better life.

Over time, Hinduism incorporated some of the insights of Buddhism. Hinduism generated a monastic system similar to that of Buddhism, but it was more closely tied to the everyday lay devotional society. Hinduism responded more strongly to the popular needs of devotional religion, but in the earlier centuries the Buddhist monasteries did not stress devotionalism as much as popular Hinduism.

Popular Buddhism, in turn, may have denied the existence of a supreme creator god, but popular Buddhism is otherwise opulently shamanistic, with spirits, protector deities, ghosts, and evil spirits. As such, it was becoming similar to popular Hinduism. Mahayana bodhisattvas were prayed to and offered sacrifices and as such were treated as *devas* by Buddhists. In this popular Buddhism was becoming almost indistinguishable from Hinduism; so why not be a Hindu instead of a Buddhist? For the householders, there did not seem to be any significant differences between the two.

FOREIGN INVASIONS

Northwestern India was an area particularly prone to foreign invasions,[50] and Buddhism was strongest in the northwest. In the sixth century, a group referred to as the "White Huns" swept Iran and into northwestern India and destroyed Buddhist monasteries.[51] In the eighth century, armies of Muslim Arabs arrived at the Indus River, and by the thirteenth century, they had all of northern India under their control. Muslim kingdoms were created, and they battled among themselves for power and wealth. The Muslim Turks arrived later in the eleventh century, and in addition to their military conquests they vigorously persecuted and destroyed the Buddhist universities and monasteries, and slaughtered unresisting communities of nuns and monks.[52] Muslim sources describe killing "clean shaven Brahmins,"[53] all of whom were "put to the sword."

The Turkish troops came upon a Buddhist university [Bihar] where they found a great library. They killed all the people in the area and scattered all the books. Later, when they wondered what those books were about, they could find no one left alive who could read the contents.[54] The monks and nuns who managed to escape the massacre fled north into Nepal and Tibet, and into the south of India. Monks who fled to Tibet left some quite graphic descriptions of the massacres at the Nalanda Buddhist university.[55] Records indicate that Hindu temples were destroyed as well. The

---

[49] Student, householder with a family and business, hermit, and forest ascetic.

[50] A thorough discussion of the Islamic religion entering India is Marshall Hodgson's monumental three-volume work, *The Venture of Islam* (Chicago: University of Chicago Press, 1977), especially volume 2: *The Expansion of Islam in the Middle Periods*. A book with a different perspective is Derryl N. MacLean, *Religion and Society in Arab Sind* (Leiden: Brill Academic Publishers, 1997).

[51] It is unclear whether this group who invaded India had any relationship to the nomadic military group who invaded southeastern Europe in 370 C.E. and conquered much of Germanic Europe, and received tributes from the Roman empire. Atilla the Hun (d. 453) is the most famous of the European Huns. The group that dominated India are technically called Hephthalites.

[52] Ira M. Lapidus, *A History of Islamic Societies* 2nd edition (Cambridge: Cambridge University Press, 2002).

[53] Monastic Buddhists shaved their heads; Brahmins did not shave their heads.

[54] Vincent Smith, *The Oxford History of India*, 1928, p. 221. The violent role Islam played is debated. For more recent research, see Giovanni Verardi's *Hardships and Downfall of Buddhism in India* (Manohar, New Delhi: Institute of SouthEast Asian Studies, 2011).

[55] George N. Roerich, *Biography of Dharmasvamin, Chag lo-tsa-ba Chos-rje-dpal, A Tibetan Monk Pilgrim*, with an historical and critical introduction by Dr. A. S. Altekar (Patna: K.P. Jayaswal Research Institute, 1959). Reprinted in George N. Roerich, *Izbrannie Trudi* (Moscow: Nauka, 1967), 453-571. My thanks to Dr. Dan Lusthaus for pointing me to this important resource.

Jain followers in northern areas of India suffered a similar fate. The Jains and various Hindu groups recovered, but the Buddhists did not.

As a result, Buddhist monks and Buddhist monasteries disappeared in all areas of India under the control of Islam.[56] Eastern India and the Bengal regions were the least affected. Popular Buddhism did not utilize the traditional Hindu idea of four stages of life, which could have fed the top layers of Buddhist endeavor. With the monasteries destroyed and knowledgeable teachers and monks gone, popular Buddhism did not have a foundation or momentum to sustain its existence.

With a combination of all the factors described above, by early thirteenth century, Buddhism was almost extinguished in northeastern India, but continued in the south until approximately the fifteenth century where ultimately it was absorbed by popular Hinduism. However, it continued an independent existence in Sri Lanka, southeast Asia, China, Korea, Japan, Nepal, Tibet, and neighboring regions.

11.12 MODERN DEVELOPMENTS IN BUDDHISM

Within a hundred years after the death of the Buddha, there was no single leader for the Buddhist community, and to this day there is no official doctrinal interpretation. There is no single core of behaviors which can be called the "practice of Buddhism." There is no common Buddhist text, no common Buddhist belief, and no common Buddhist rituals. There is no creed to which a Buddhist must profess, and there are no dogmas. Although in these chapters we have stressed the practice of Buddhism as an attempt to achieve awakening and the end to *dukkha*, that is not the only possible pathway. As we have noted, Buddhist pathways can include faith, devotion, creation of art, meditation, rituals, visualization, and more.

Contemporary Buddhism is practiced by people ranging from Sri Lanka, from South Asia into the tallest mountains in the world, the Himalayas, and into Myanmar (Burma), Thailand, Cambodia and Vietnam throughout southeast Asia, into China and Korea and Japan, but there are Asian Buddhists and Western converts to Buddhism in Alabama and Texas, in Paris, in Mexico City and Rio de Janeiro, in Moscow, Berlin, and in London.[57] There has been a major resurgence of Buddhism in India itself, especially among the lower castes, due to Dr. Bhimrao Ambedkar (1891–1956), an extraordinary Indian politician, economist, lawyer, jurist, philosopher, anthropologist, and historian, whose conversion and activities inspired the modern Buddhist movement in India.[58]

Practicing Buddhism

For a Tibetan monk, the practice of Buddhism may involve many thousands of full prostrations on the ground, chanting and undergoing empowerment rituals followed by years spent in solitary meditation in a cave high in the snow. A Buddhist in Tokyo might wear a Western suit and vest, and spend a week or two in the year practicing meditation at a monastery so that it can improve his business. In Singapore "practicing Buddhism" might mean venerating bones or sacred relics that might once have been those of a Buddhist saint. For someone in Taiwan or

---

[56] "With the defeat of the Hindus under Prithviraj at the hands of Muslim invaders in A.D. 1192, Buddhism disappeared as an organized force in India ..." Sukumari Bhattacharji, *The Indian Theogony,* p. 19.

[57] It is estimated that there are about 350 million Buddhists today, making it the fourth largest world religion. Approximately 62% belong to Mahayana groups, and 38% are Theravadins. It is estimated that there are approximately 700,000 Buddhists monks and nuns, most in monasteries. John Esposito, Darrell Fasching, Todd Lewis, *World Religions Today,* pp. 353–356.

[58] Dr. Ambedkar's importance has been ranked alongside Gandhi, and he is discussed in chapter 7 of this volume. A book analyzing his importance is Aishwary Kumar, *Radial Equality: Ambedkar, Gandhi, and the Risk of Democracy* (Stanford: Stanford University Press, 2015).

CHAPTER 11: MAHAYANA SCHOOLS–PART II

Kyoto, the name of the Buddha is chanted in the hope of achieving rebirth in the Western Paradise.

Modern Theravada countries do not practice Buddhism exactly like the earliest practitioners in the first centuries.[59] In Theravada Buddhism as practiced in Asia, there is the praying to the Buddha as a god, there is worship of the Buddha's relics, there are many rituals with priests encouraging devotional behavior which will result in good karma. There are blessing rituals which are colorful and devotional. Buddhist temples have statues of many popular Hindu deities, and devotion to these various buddhas, bodhisattvas, and Hindu *devas* are expected.

For many, both in the conservative Theravada and later Mahayana, the name of the Buddha is chanted merely in the hope of achieving a better rebirth in the next life. Some Buddhists practice complex rituals in the hope of inspiring bodhisattvas to shower good merit upon the entire community. In cities throughout the United States, such as Los Angeles, Portland, Boulder, and New York, American college students may practice cross-legged meditation in the hope of achieving *satori* (a breakthrough insight experience in Zen Buddhism). All of these are some form of "practicing Buddhism."

In the West, many Buddhist ideas have become quite popular, and some non-Buddhist religious groups have incorporated concepts such as quiet mindfulness-meditation and non-violence. These groups may read and study Buddhist texts, and even hold regular meditation retreats based on insight meditation (*vipassana*) or Zen *zazen* (seated focused concentration) and the cultivation of loving-kindness (*metta-bhavana*) towards all living things. Buddhist ideas are also utilized in Christian groups.[60] Some Buddhist beliefs are major obstacles for many Western Buddhists, because these are perceived as superstitions which can be ignored, such as the many gods and goddesses, and the numerous supernatural claims, especially reliance on rituals and the acceptance of the doctrine of rebirth.

Western Modifications to Buddhism

Some people disparage those westerners who follow specific Buddhist practices without seriously adopting the totality of traditional Buddhism. Many Western students do not accept Indian Buddhist beliefs in things like rebirth, nirvana as the complete cessation of all dissatisfaction, perfect enlightenment or awakening, *arhats*, and spiritual powers, and the efficacy of Buddhist rituals. For many Western Buddhists, things like rebirth are simply ancient cultural assumptions and superstitions which a well-educated student can ignore.

Those who believe that all aspects of historical Buddhism must be accepted in order to call oneself a "Buddhist" refer to Western Buddhism disparagingly as "Buddhism Lite." On the other hand, many contemporary Buddhists find Buddhism of value even when shorn of its apparently superstitious, supernatural and devotional components. In the West, Christians used to believe that god forbade eating shellfish and pork for all time, but later decided that these were dietary rules that made sense in the past, but are no longer relevant. Something similar can be true for Buddhism. For example, that celibacy was important to those who begged for every meal is a historical fact about ancient India. However celibacy seems less important to the lifestyles of contemporary Western students. The Buddhist scholar Stephen Batchelor writes:

> But in a modern society, where one has access to greater leisure, education, financial provision, and
> — crucially for women — the means of controlling one's fertility, does such a rule of sexual abstinence
> still make sense? Is someone in a stable and loving sexual relationship, who is capable of supporting
> him- or herself by leading a life of simplicity, intrinsically less able to realize the fruits of a Buddhist
> way of life than a celibate monk or nun?[61]

When Martine [Mrs. Batchelor] and I started teaching Buddhism in England, it became clear that such a division between monks and laity no longer seemed relevant. The people who read my books and attended our retreats were well-educated men and women, often with families and careers, who

---

[59] The same can be said for all religions including Christianity. Christian practices of the first two hundred years were not much like anything done in contemporary Christianity.

[60] This is especially true for groups such as some of the Unitarian-Universalist churches.

[61] Stephen Batchelor, *Confession of a Buddhist Atheist*, p. 91.

had sufficient leisure time to pursue their religious and philosophical interests, but no wish at all to be ordained as a celibate monk or nun. For many of them, the traditional practices of lay Buddhism appeared uncritically devout, simplistic, and superstitious. They were looking for a coherent and rigorous philosophy of life, coupled with a meditative practice that made an actual difference in their lives here and now, not a set of consoling beliefs and aspirations that promised rewards in a hypothetical future existence.[62]

It is becoming rather clear that for many Western Buddhists, worshiping a buddha or a bodhisattva holds little appeal, and accepting Indian cultural ideas like rebirth literally (as opposed to metaphorically) is not compatible with the modern age. Several scholars have noted that Buddhism is in the process of being changed into something fully compatible with secular society. The people doing the reforming are deeply respected Buddhist practitioners and scholars, people who know the original languages, people who have mastered the philosophy, and who have devoted their lives to various forms of Buddhism.

Is it possible for the ancient texts of Buddhism to address the needs of contemporary married people living active, engaged lives in the world of the twenty-first century? Many have argued that the answer is "yes." Can one be an atheist and be a Buddhist? Clearly, the answer is "yes." Can one seek the deepening of wisdom, the encouragement of altruism and compassion, and not belong to a devoutly religious group of fellow Buddhists? Again, the answer is "yes." Is humanism compatible with Buddhism? Yes. Several recently published books have dealt with these issues; the student interested in a secular form of Buddhism might want to read some of these.[63]

In addition, there are numerous books by Buddhist practitioners and scholars which advocate an engaged form of Buddhism, Buddhist paths which encourage us to take seriously the ecological interconnectedness and to advocate and act on behalf of the planet.[64] Can a Western Buddhist be involved in contemporary politics? Again, the answer is "yes." Buddhist teacher Wendy Egyoku Nakao advises her students to accept the fact that we do not know what is going to happen in our crazy political universe, encourages us to pay attention to our own experience of what is happening, and take action in a way that does not encourage ill-will or anger, self-centered craving or greed, and see clearly the interconnected interdependence that is our world.[65]

11.13 SUMMARY OF THE CHAPTER

The major traditions of Mahayana include (1) the Pure Land (devotion to Amitabha Buddha), (2) the Madhyamaka (associated with the "emptiness" ideas of Nagarjuna based on the *Prajnaparamita sutras*), (3) the Yogachara/Yogacara or "Consciousness-Only" (accepting emptiness but analyzing consciousness and knowledge), (4) the Buddha-nature (*Tathagatagarbha sutras* which teach that all living beings possess the potential for full buddhahood), and (5) the Tantric Buddhist pathway (basing itself on esoteric Tantras, and combining devotion, philosophy, meditation, chanting, magic, sexual imagery, and very colorful rites and ceremonies).

The Vajrayana doctrines are grounded in Nagarjuna's analysis of things being empty of unchanging inner essence, but the idea of levels of consciousness are also important. Chanting magical phrases of power and devotional

---

[62] *Ibid.*, p. 92.

[63] For example, see Stephen Batchelor, *After Buddhism: Rethinking the Dharma for a Secular Age* (Yale University Press, 2015), or Batchelor's *The Faith to Doubt* (Counterpoint Press, 2015) or *Buddhism Without Beliefs* (Riverhead Books, 1998).

[64] There are many such books, such as *Time to Stand Up: An Engaged Buddhist Manifesto for Our Earth – the Buddha's Life and Message through Feminine Eyes*, by the nun Thanissara (North Atlantic Books, 2015). See also David R. Loy, *A New Buddhist Path: Enlightenment, Evolution, and Ethics in the Modern World* (Wisdom Publications, 2015). These books contain useful bibliographies.

[65] David Loy, *The Great Awakening: A Buddhist Social Theory* (Boston: Wisdom Publications, 2003).

rituals are also important. Visualization of buddhas, bodhisattvas, and other deities play a significant role. The elite or advanced Vajrayana followers included practices like alcohol and meat-eating which the larger Mahayana community rejected.

By the thirteenth century, several factors combined to bring about the extinction of Buddhism in north India, and then its eventual disappearance even in the south. It had to do with economic and political forces, as well as the invasion of north India (Pakistan) by groups who were not tolerant of religious other than their own.

The Mahayana forms of Buddhism did not disappear everywhere. They are found in the world today, with the Pure Land tradition dominating in China, Korea, and Japan, and with the Tantric pathway as the Buddhism of Tibet and Nepal. The Madhyamaka and Yogachara pathways were of central importance for many schools of Tibetan, Chinese, Korean, and Japanese Buddhism, but never matched the Pure Land traditions in the number of followers. The basic ideas and insights of the Buddha-nature tradition was simply absorbed into the other schools.

There are non-Asian American-born teachers of Buddhism found in major Western centers. Like their Asian counterparts, Western Buddhists tend to stress ego-less compassion, kindness, focused concentration, and insight into the ever-changing nature of reality. Many Western Buddhist groups devote themselves to social activities which activate their compassion and love, such as assisting prisoners in prison, baking bread and feeding the hungry, clothing the homeless, and generally trying to exemplify ego-less love founded upon insight into the self and into the nature of an ever-changing interdependent reality. Through personal experience helping others, the students are to learn that everything is in flux, everything changes, and accept that fact. To accomplish this the student must pay attention. This too is an aspect of Western Buddhism.

11.14 TECHNICAL TERMS

Amitabha   The Buddha of the Western Paradise, whose realm is a Pure Land.

cittamatra   "Mind-only," another name for Yogachara/Yogacara Buddhism.

dharani   a chanted magical formula of special and secret knowledge comprised of syllables with symbolic content

dorjes   small double-ended scepters, usually made of bronze, which represent lightning bolts.

guru   a spiritual teacher or guide, especially important to Tantric Buddhism.

mandala   a complex image which provides a map of the journey into consciousness, used in focused concentration.

mahasiddha   a *guru* who has mastered *siddhis*, or spiritual magical powers.

mantras   chanted phrases of power.

Mantrayana   the Buddhist vehicle (*-yana*) which makes extensive use of *mantras*, chanted phrases of power, i.e., Vajrayana Buddhism.

Tantra   a special book with esoteric instructions.

Vajrayana   the *vajra* vehicle. *Vajra* is often explained as either "Lightning" or "Thunder Bolt" (The *vajra* symbol is traditionally associated with the thunderbolt of the Hindu *deva*, Indra).

Vijnaptimatrata "Consciousness-only," another name for Yogachara Buddhism.

yana   literally, "vehicle," as in the Maha-yana, or the Great Vehicle.

Yogachara   the Mahayana school which asserts that all of our knowledge of the external and internal realms comes via consciousness, but consciousness creates much more of our world than we realize. The name is Yo-g-ACHara, a person who has mastered yogic meditation.

11.15 QUESTIONS FOR FURTHER DISCUSSION

(1)   Tantric Buddhists make use of the abstract diagrams called *mandala* and these are used as a spiritual map to guide the seeker to deeper religious experience. Some Christians go through the "Stations of the Cross" which seems as though it might serve a similar function. Discuss.

(2)   We have seen that feminine energies (*shakti*) play a role in Tantric Buddhism. Scholars say that there were early forms of Christianity which worshiped wisdom as a goddess. Are there any feminine aspects to Western religions. Does the mother of Jesus have any features which suggest a goddess? Discuss.

(3)   Little Tradition or Popular Tantric Buddhism treats the gods and buddhas as external beings of great power. How does the Grand Tradition of Tantric Buddhist philosophers understand Buddhist deities? Discuss.

(4)   What are the key doctrines of Tantric Buddhism? Are any of these doctrines also found in earlier forms of Indian Buddhism? Discuss.

(5)   Scholars say that it is Tantric practices which set Vajrayana apart from other forms of Mahayana. What are these unusual Tantric practices?

(6)   Tantric Buddhists claim that the world is flowing change (so too modern physics seems to suggest everything is mostly empty space filled with electrons circling a nucleus). But then Tantric Buddhists go on to assert that it follows that all the ultimate dichotomies are false, that good versus evil, liberated versus trapped, and even heaven versus hell, are a mistaken perception. Even male/female is a dichotomy to be transcended. Why is it that the modern Western view (all is mostly empty space and whirling electrons) did not come to a similar conclusion? Why do so many in the west see so many stark contrasting dualities as ultimately real? Discuss.

(7)   According to Tantric Buddhism, if we see evil everywhere we look, we are not seeing clearly. If we see good at war with evil, we are not seeing clearly. Even if we see good and evil, we are not seeing clearly. So, what does an accomplished Tantric Buddhist see when he or she is "seeing clearly"? Discuss.

A SELECTED BIBLIOGRAPHY

Tantric Buddhism in India

Beyer, Steven, tr. and ed., *The Buddhist Experience: Sources and Interpretations* (Belmont, Ca.: Dickenson Publishing, 1974)
Bharati, Agehananda, *The Tantric Tradition* (London: Rider & Co., 1965)
Conze, Edward, *Buddhist Thought In India* (Ann Arbor: The University of Michigan Press, 1967)
Dasgupta, S., *An Introduction to Tantric Buddhism* (Berkeley: Shambhala, 1974)
Davidson, Ronald M., *Indian Esoteric Buddhism: A Social History of the Tantric Movement* (New York: Columbia University Press, 2002).
Hopkins, Jeffrey, *Emptiness Yoga* (Prasanghika Madhyamika) (New York: Snow Lion, 1987)
Kalupahana, David J., *A History of Buddhist Philosophy: Continuities & Discontinuities* (Honolulu: University of Hawaii Press, 1989)
Lessing, F. D., and Alex Wayman, *An Introduction to the Buddhist Tantric Systems* (Delhi, MB, 1978)
Lopez, Jr., Donald S., *A Study of Svatantrika* (Ithica, N.Y.: Snow Lion, 1987)
Snelling, John, *The Buddhist Handbook* (Rochester, Vt.: Inner Traditions, 1991)
Snellgrove, D. L., *Indo-Tibetan Buddhism: Indian Buddhists and their Tibetan Successors* (Boston: Shambhala, 2002)
Warder, A. K., *Indian Buddhism* (Delhi: Motilal Banarsidass, 1970)
Wayman, Alex and Hideko. *The Lion's Roar of Queen Srimala* (New York: Columbia University Press, 1974)
Williams, Paul, *Mahayana Buddhism: The Doctrinal Foundations* (London: Routledge, 1989).
Wedemeyer, Christian K., *Making Sense of Tantric Buddhism: History, Semiology, and Transgression in the Indian Traditions* (New York: Columbia University Press, 2012)

Buddhism and the West: History and Psychology

Aronson, Harvey, *Buddhist Practice on Western Ground: Reconciling Eastern Ideals and Western Psychology* (Boston: Shambhala, 2004)
Batchelor, Stephen, *Awakening of the West: The Encounter of Buddhism and Western Culture* (Berkeley: Parallax, 1994).
Batchelor, Stephen, *Living With the Devil: A Meditation on Good and Evil* (New York: Riverhead Books, 2004).
Brazier, Caroline, *Buddhism on the Couch: From Analysis to Awakening Using Buddhist Psychology* (Ulysses Press, 2003)
Cadge, Wendy, *Heartwood: The First Generation of Theravada Buddhism in America* (Chicago: University of Chicago Press, 2004)
Magid, Barry, and Charlotte Joko Beck, *Ordinary Mind: Exploring the Common Ground of Zen and Psychotherapy* (Boston: Wisdom Publications, 2002)
Trungpa, Chogyam, *Cutting Through Spiritual Materialism* (Berkeley: Shambhala, 1973)
Young-Eisendrath, Polly, and Shoji Muramoto, eds., *Awakening and Insight: Zen Buddhism and Psychotherapy* (London: Brunner-Routledge, 2002)

Buddhism in the Modern Age

Batchelor, Stephen, *After Buddhism: Rethinking the Dharma for a Secular Age* (Yale University Press, 2015)
_____, *The Faith to Doubt* (Counterpoint Press, 2015)
_____, *Buddhism Without Beliefs* (Riverhead Books, 1998)
Coleman, James W., *The New Buddhism: The Western Transformation of an Ancient Tradition* (New York: Oxford, 1992)
Cooper, David E., and Simon P. James, *Buddhism, Virtue and Environment* (Burlington, Vt.: Ashgate Publishing, 2005).

Dumoulin, Heinrich, *Buddhism in the Modern World* (New York: Collier, 1976)

Fields, Rick, *How the Swans Came to the Lake* (Boston: Shambhala, 1992)

Flanagan, Owen J., *Bodhisattva's Brain: Buddhism Naturalized* (Cambridge, Ma: MIT Press, 2011)

Keown, Damien, ed. et. al, *Buddhism and Human Rights* (1997)

Loy, David R., *A New Buddhist Path: Enlightenment, Evolution, and Ethics in the Modern World* (Wisdom Publications, 2015).

Prebish, Charles, *American Buddhism* (Duxbury Press, 1979)

_____, *Luminous Passage: The Practice and Study of Buddhism in America* (Berkeley: University of California Press, 1999)

_____, *Westward Dharma: Buddhism Beyond Asia* (2002)

Prebish, Charles, and Kenneth Tanaka, eds., *The Faces of Buddhism in America* (1998)

Prebish, Charles and Steven Heine, eds, *Buddhism in the Modern World: Adaptations of an Ancient Tradition* (2003)

Prebish, Charles, ed., *Buddhist Studies from India to America* (2005)

Queen, Christopher, ed., *Action Dharma: New Studies in Engaged Buddhism* (2003)

Rapaport, Al, and Brian Hotchkiss, *Buddhism in America* (Rutland, Vt.: Tuttle, 1998)

Seager, Richard, *Buddhism in America* (New York: Columbia University, 2000)

CHAPTER 12: THE TANTRIC BUDDHISM OF TIBET

12.1 OVERVIEW OF THE CHAPTER

The topic of Buddhism in contemporary Tibet is complicated by the political problems which arise due to the Chinese claim that Tibet is a proper part of China. It is also complicated by the fact that the official Communist party in China has the power to approve who gets to be a monk, which monasteries receive support, and which monks get recognized as official incarnations of previous generations of Tibetan teaching lineages. The political arm of the Communist party nominates and controls high-ranking Tibetan Buddhist teachers and monks. Because this situation is very controversial and is continually changing, this aspect is about politics and as such will not be stressed in this chapter. Instead, we will focus on the historical background for Tibetan religion.

In previous chapters we have studied both Traditional (or Conservative) Buddhism, and the later Mahayana forms of Buddhism in India. Tibetan Buddhism is generally categorized as belonging to the Mahayana branch of Buddhism. Some Mahayana traditions focus on the Mahayana philosophical implications of the discourses of the Buddha (things like emptiness, Buddha-nature, and the eight levels of consciousness), in addition to their focus on the divine nature of the Buddha and the worship of his relics. Mahayana traditions also tended to stress devotion to or having faith in buddhas and bodhisattvas, who could be prayed to, meditated upon, and experienced in visions. The rituals and spectacle stressed in Mahayana becomes amplified and this evolved into the final development of Mahayana Buddhism in India, the *Vajrayana* (the indestructible diamond thunderbolt vehicle), or Tantric Buddhism. Although Tantric forms were not the most important forms of Buddhism in India, the Vajrayana forms dominated Tibetan forms of Buddhism from the eighth century on.

Tantric Buddhism is also known as esoteric Buddhism, which means that the teachings are to be taught only to specially initiated students, and require knowledge restricted to a small group of specially chosen people. The element of secrecy is essential to Tantric Buddhism. Tantric Buddhists describe their tradition as a speeded-up yet dangerous pathway of secret powerful magical techniques that propels the student to awakening in this very life instead of thousands of lifetimes from now.

A contemporary student who devoted many years to the practice of Tibetan Tantric Buddhism with the Dali Lama's group in northern India summarizes the Tibetan practices as follows:

In order to become a Buddha as quickly and effectively as possible, the Tibetans practice a unique body of teachings inherited from India called the "Diamond Vehicle" (Vajrayana, i.e., Tantric Buddhism). Unlike the Buddha's sutras, which were discourses given to the general public, the tantras were taught only to select disciples. These were secret teachings, which to receive and practice one had to be "empowered" by a qualified tantric master, who in turn had been empowered by an unbroken lineage of teachers going back to the Buddha himself. The highest class of tantra entailed imagining onself as "a god" at the heart of a resplendent mandala, thereby replacing one's "ordinary perception" of being a mundane ego with the "divine pride" of being a fully enlightened Buddha. Once this perceptual transformation was achieved, one could then proceed with the actual transformation of oneself into a Buddha by means of yogic practices involving subtle energies, nerve channels and chakras. Having taken the bodhisattva vow and come to an adequate understanding of the sutra teachings, we were strongly encouraged to receive a tantric empowerment in order to enter the "swift path" to complete enlightenment.[1]

Tantric Buddhism relies heavily on esoteric symbolism to express various categories in Buddhist doctrine. One central practice of Tantric Buddhism is visualization and communion with a divinity, identifying oneself with the speech, body, and mind of the deity. These practices are embedded within a wide variety of rituals involving things like blindfolds, postures, tying bands of cloth around the head, visualization of colors, throwing flowers while blindfolded, ringing of bells, rubbing of eyes as symbolic of removing ignorance, mirror images, and sexual rituals with a consort.[2]

Another name for Tantric Buddhism is **Mantrayana**, that is, the vehicle which makes extensive use of *mantras*, chanted phrases of power.[3] A wide variety of deities are worshiped and invoked with these chanted phrases. Tantric texts often utilize these *mantra* sounds as magical formula which could be recited and would produce physical effects in the world.

Vajrayana monks carried Tantric Buddhism from India to Southeast Asia, Central Asia, and to Japan. However, the Tantric schools were only a minor influence in Southeast Asia and China. The Tantric path was most important in Tibet and the Himalayan areas of Nepal, Bhutan and Kashmir. Japanese forms are also significant.

Although Tantric Buddhism considers itself separate from and superior to Mahayana Buddhism, many scholars tend to see this form of Buddhism as a form of religious practice which puts great emphasis on rituals and deities using esoteric symbolism, and on unusual special techniques and approaches within a Mahayana philosophical and doctrinal framework. In terms of philosophical insights on the nature of reality, Tantric Buddhism is in complete agreement with Mahayana.[4]

12.2 TIBET BEFORE BUDDHISM

Tibet is "the land of snows," a country in broad upland plateaux surrounded by the tallest mountains on the planet. The average height of the Tibetan plateau is 15,000 feet. Tibet is high, rocky, dry and desolate, and is the ancient home of various tribes of nomadic herding peoples, in a land with few natural resources. Although we tend to think of Tibet as a Buddhist country, the actual popular religion of the people is a mixture of numerous shamanistic religious practices combined with Tantric Buddhism originating in the seventh to twelfth centuries in India.

Buddhism first came to Tibet in the seventh century, but the religious traditions of Tibet prior to Buddhism are shrouded in confusion. Undoubtedly there were indigenous religions in the Tibetan region long before Indian Tantric Buddhism came to Tibet. The problem is that our knowledge of these religions is fragmentary. Prior to

---

[1] Stephen Batchelor, *Confession of a Buddhist Atheist* (New York: Spiegel & Grau, 2010), p. 22.

[2] Many scholars have noted that Buddhist Tantras share a remarkable similarity to non-Buddhist Shaivite Hindu Tantras from the same period in India. Bharati writes "Among scholars, two views have been held – that Buddhism was influenced by non-Buddhist Indian tantric or similar ideas in the process of creating the Vajrayana school which was then transplanted into Tibet; the other, more recent and nowadays more usually accepted view is that tantric notions, especially the ones using sexual polarity symbolism, are originally Buddhist and that the left-handed Hindu tantric schools derived their inspiration from them. Both views have much to commend them and the final word has yet to be said." Bharati himself holds that some Buddhist Vajrayana goddesses were borrowed from Hindu Indian female energies (*shakti*), while other goddesses originated within Vajrayana involving Prajnaparamita goddesses. A. Bharati, *The Tantric Tradition* (New York: Anchor Books, 1970), pp. 201-202.

[3] The Tibetans refer to their Buddhism as Vajrayana but also "Mantrayana," "Secret Mantra-Vajrayana," "Secret Mantra of the Mahayana," or "Inner Secret Mantra" and so on.

[4] This view is standard in scholarly Buddhist studies written by non-Tantric practitioners. For example, Rupert Gethin, *The Foundations of Buddhism* (London: Oxford University Press, 1999), p. 268.

Buddhism there was no written language in Tibet and there are no documents about religion from pre-Buddhist times. The general term for the religion of Tibet prior to Tantric Buddhism is Bon (pronounced "pern"),[5] and the best scholarship suggests that it was a form of ancient animism, or shamanism, a religious attitude which was widespread in Siberia, Turkestan, Mongolia, Manchuria and northern China. The Bon religion of ancient Tibet is not identical with the more modern Bon religion which was changed profoundly by the arrival of Buddhism into Tibet. It is the post-Buddhism Bon religion that we will describe below.

Followers of Bon, called Bon-po, feel that the visible and invisible realms were filled with natural and powerful non-human influences. Tibetans feel they are living in a world filled with a wide variety of spirits who affect human life, and who could be contacted by numerous methods, including ecstatic dances, drumming, magical chants and secret chanted formulas. The spirits are understood to be forces of nature, good and evil spirits which swirl around our everyday world, and can include animals, rivers and mountains. These spirits can be flattered, can be offended, and can help or hurt humans.[6]

Shamans with special esoteric knowledge can manipulate these forces for the benefit of people. Life in Tibet has always been very difficult, and the Bon religion promised to offer some degree of control over powerful and unpredictable natural forces. The Bon priests developed a highly complicated system of magical and occult rituals to interact with the realm of spirits, which is also the realm of the powers of nature. Wearing elaborate headdresses and robes of blue, the shaman priest believed he could enter a trance which would allow spirits to take possession of the shaman priest, who in a state of trance could speak for the spirits and even manipulate them. The proper formulas, the proper incantations, and even dances can be used to control forces of nature.

The Bon priests utilized small drums that were considered essential to the efficacy of rituals. There are stories of Bon priests who would fly through the air. It was commonly believed that some of these spirits must have special knowledge, perhaps even knowledge of the future. Therefore the shaman utilizes his or her abilities in the process of divination (predicting the future).

The spirits include *nagas*, powerful entities who live in watery realms, who can adopt the shape of water snakes whenever they wish it. They are also described as dragons. They live on the bottom of lakes and rivers, and they guard hoards of secret treasures. There are other spirits who are masters of the earth, who roam on mountains and valleys, and live in trees and rocks, in woods and ditches. These are easily annoyed by human beings, and they send sickness, plague, and death to those who bother them. Some spirits resemble winged insects. There are also spirits who resemble vampires and their realm is the air. The Bon priests try to protect the people by many elaborate rituals which stress purification. Some spirits reside inside each human being and function as a guardian angel to ward off demonic influences.[7]

Bon also sacrificed to the gods of heaven and earth utilizing animal sacrifices, sacrificing sheep, dogs, monkeys, horses, oxen, donkeys and even human beings.[8] In more recent times the Tibetans use effigies, representations of yak, sheep, and wooden carved deer heads.

Scholars generally believe that Bon religion before Buddhism was especially focused upon death and the proper

---

[5] Rendering Tibetan words into English is a problem. The word "Bon" uses the scholarly system devised by Turrell Wylie published in 1959, but unless one is a scholar, words romanized in this system will not be pronounced correctly by English speakers. Many Tibetan proper names and words are often well-known in the Wylie spelling, but this is misleading for non-Tibetan scholars. Jeffrey Hopkins has devised a system which allows us to reproduce the dialect of Lhasa, and in Hopkins' system Bon is transliterated to reflect the way the word is actually pronounced, that is "pern." See Jeffrey Hopkins, *Meditation on Emptiness* (London: Wisdom Publications, 1983), Technical Notes, pages 19–22. See also Donald S. Lopez, Jr., *A Study of Svatantrika* (Ithaca, NY: Snow Lion Press, 1987), pp. 11–12.

[6] A recent book on Bon is Latri Khenpo and Nyima Dakpa, *Opening the Door to Bon* (New York: Snow Lion Publications, 2005).

[7] These beliefs are found in contemporary Tibetan *lamas* as well as in the folk religion.

[8] Helmut Hoffmann, *The Religions of Tibet* (New York: The Macmillan Company, 1961), p. 22.

rites to deal with death. It was important that rituals be performed to allow the soul safe passage to an existence in a land beyond this one. Another factor is that Bon priests wanted to prevent the dead from returning and harming the living. Many of these Bon ideas about handling the dead body, rituals to be performed immediately after death, and the eventual fate of the soul, can be found incorporated into the "Tibetan Book of the Dead" or *Bardol Thodol*.

Although there was ongoing tension between Bon and Indian Buddhism, these Bon beliefs and practices slowly affected and reshaped the Tantric Buddhist ideas from India to produce the modern religion of Tibet. Sometimes the religions of Tibet are called "Lamaism," the religion of the *lamas* (or "superior ones"), but to some the term seems to be disrespectful because it implies that Tibetan Buddhism is not genuine Buddhism, but rather a degenerate form of Buddhism, merely "Buddhism of the *lamas*." As used among Tibetan Buddhist monastics, the term *lama* can refer to one's religious instructor, but it is commonly used to describe a reincarnated *guru*, a person of excellent moral quality and high spiritual attainment.[9]

The religion of the ordinary Tibetan in the twenty-first century is still heavily influenced by Bon shamanistic practices and beliefs. However, popular Bon religion has also absorbed so much of Buddhist ideas that Bon ". . . has become a form of Buddhism that may fairly be regarded as heretical, in that those who follow it have persisted in claiming that their religion was taught not by Shakyamuni Buddha, but by gShen-rab [Shenrap]. . ."[10]

The society of Tibet was dominated by the religions of Bonpo and Tibetan Vajrayana, and was a land of aristocrats, monks, peasants, serfs or indentured farmers, nomads, warriors, merchants, and others. Originally it was ruled by kings and aristocrats, and later the rulers were heads of great monastic orders and powerful aristocratic families. Thus, Tibet was a theocracy until modern times. Clearly the topic of Tibetan society is too complex for us to discuss in any detail in this chapter.[11]

12.3 A REVIEW OF TANTRIC BUDDHISM IN INDIA

As we saw in previous chapters, for the first several centuries in the common era devotional Hinduism and the beginnings of Tantric Hinduism dominated, but there were also several forms of Theravada and Mahayana Buddhism in India. There were conservative Theravada monks and nuns who saw themselves as preserving the authentic teachings and traditions of the Buddha. Some of these monks and nuns resided in monasteries, and others chose the ascetic pathway of the forest monks. As the centuries progressed Indians believed that these forest dwelling ascetics, whether Buddhist or non-Buddhist, were charismatic figures who cultivated *tapas* (the heat or energy cultivated by ascetic practices) and have *siddhis* (magical powers).

Strongest in northern India, there were also Mahayana practices involving devotion to buddhas who had become supernatural divine figures with properties and powers that were beyond comprehension, such as omniscience.

---

[9] Although "lama" (in Tibetan, *bla ma*) is most often used to designate a superior monk who possesses both inner and outer excellent qualities, the term can also be used in a non-religious way to describe a socially superior and important person in authority (such as a landlord, restaurant owner, or head farmer) and is not exclusively a religious or spiritual title. A lama does not have to be a Buddhist. Considering this usage, the term "Lamaism" is not all that useful to describe the Buddhism of Tibet. Consult the entry "Lama" in Robert Buswell, ed., *Encyclopedia of Buddhism* (New York: Thompson Gale, 2004), Vol. 1, pp. 450–451.

[10] David Snellgrove, *Indo-Tibetan Buddhism* (Boston: Shambhala, 1987), p. 390. Because Bon priests say that the origins of Bon lie outside of Tibet and not in Tibet, it is probably a mistake to describe Bon as an "indigenous" religion of Tibet.

[11] Over the past hundred years there have been many very fanciful claims made about Tibet as an ancient land of spiritual perfection. As always, the truth is much more complex. A recent book traces the origins and manifestations of the Tibetan myth leading to the World War II era, in which China claimed Tibet. The modern geopolitical intrigues are spelled out with clarity. The book is by Lezilee Brown Halper and Stefan Halper, *Tibet: An Unfinished Story* (New York: Oxford University Press, April 2014).

CHAPTER 11: MAHAYANA SCHOOLS–PART II

The compassionate pathway of Mahayana is personified by bodhisattvas, who have taken a vow to do whatever is necessary to lessen the suffering of all living beings, and who seek awakening in order to help all living things. As such, advanced bodhisattvas are human beings who have been on the pathway toward Buddhahood so long that by egoless compassion they have acquired extraordinary powers. They have the power to eliminate bad karma or even give those who ask a share of the oceans of good karma which each bodhisattva had accumulated.

Like popular Hinduism during the same period, in popular Buddhism one can get the help of a bodhisattva though the practice of *bhakti* or devotion. During the medieval period in India (fourth through the eleventh century C.E.) Indian religions saw the proliferation of devotional cults focused upon many different *deva*. During this same period we also discussed a strong trend to practice physical and popular ritual instead of abstract philosophy or focused meditations. Temples and monasteries became richly decorated intentionally making use of all the arts, including painting, music, sculpture, dance, and drama. In India Tantric Buddhists made use of bright colors, colorful rituals, painting, sweet-smelling incense, music, sculpture, intricate patterns, dance, and drama. Tantric Buddhism uses the entire body as an instrument for liberation, including powerful emotions such as anger, lust, and fear. Tantric forms of Indian Buddhism placed special emphasis upon richly decorative settings, which appeal to our aesthetic apprehension, not our intellect. In Tantric India, rituals with secret meanings become the higher, more advanced practices. The tendency was for these richly ceremonial rituals themselves to become the way to buddhahood. Tantric Buddhism developed a very complex system of meditation, which utilizes visualization, identification with deities, magic, a rich variety of symbols, and very colorful rituals.

Tantric Buddhism draws on a popular image called the "turning of the wheel of *dharma*." Because the *dharma* is the teachings, Buddhists say that the Buddha first "turned the wheel of the *dharma*" after his awakening when he explained *pratityasamutpada* (dependent co-arising) and the Four Noble Truths to his five friends in the forest. Mahayana describes itself as a second turning of the wheel of the *dharma*, where the more profound teachings involving emptiness (*sunyata*), Buddha-nature, and the storehouse-consciousness were first taught by the Buddha. Tantric Buddhists describe their teachings as a third "turning of the wheel of the dharma." Thus Tantric Buddhists do not consider themselves to be a later development of Mahayana Buddhism, but a higher, richer, and ultimate culmination of Buddhism. They consider their practices and doctrines to be more advanced and beyond the abilities of the Theravada and Mahayana followers. Tantric Buddhism is the *Vajrayana*, with *vajra* often explained as either "Diamond," "Lightning" or "Thunder Bolt."[12] As mentioned above, another name for Tantric Buddhism is *Mantrayana*, that is, the vehicle which makes extensive use of *mantras*, chanted phrases of power.

Forest Dwellers With Powers

Tantric practices in India draw heavily upon the practices of forest ascetics who lived on the fringes of society. Those who went into the nearby forest to master Tantric accomplishments included both females and males, who might wear rags, or nothing at all. These ascetics or yogis had a personal attachment to particular deities, often goddesses, and cultivated spiritual powers, and focused upon the importance of the human body. Rituals were carried out to destroy dualism and relative dichotomies (such as the distinction between *nirvana* and *samsara*, male and female, good and evil, and so forth). Ultimate oneness is achieved if the ascetic could unify all these opposites. It was also believed that these ascetics had developed supernormal powers, or *siddhis*.

One's *guru* is to be treated with the respect owed a *deva*. Thus Tantric Buddhism tends to be *guru*-centric. In fact, in Tibetan Tantric Buddhism the *guru* has been added to the previous Three Jewels producing Four Jewels: Buddha,

---

[12] As mentioned previously, the *vajra* is derived from the thunderbolt sceptre of the Hindu *deva*, Indra (Indra was the deity of thunderstorms and the hourglass-shaped *vajra*-thunderbolt sceptre carried by Indra symbolized his power). In the *Vajrayana* the *vajra* can symbolize skillful means, but also the indestructible character of the highest teaching. Awakening is sudden, so this is the Way of the Thunderbolt. The *vajra* is also a symbol of the fact that all things are empty of unchanging essence (*svabhava-sunyata*).

dharma, *sangha*, *guru*.[13] Tibetan Tantric Buddhism held that one cannot make progress towards the ultimate goal of Buddhism unless the student had undergone initiation rituals by a *guru* into particular secret practices and certain esoteric texts. The initial rituals were necessary if one was to make progress towards Buddhahood and nirvana.

SIDDHIS: Supernatural Powers

In the chapter on early Buddhism, we discussed the fact that forest-dwelling hermits in both the Hindu and Buddhist traditions were believed to possess extraordinary powers which resulted from their meditations, and from engaging in physical practices which produce pain. This was especially true for Tantric Hindus and Tantric Buddhists who accept what we would call magic.[14] Tantric Buddhism accepts *siddhis*, powers achievable with advanced meditation and magical phrases. The Tantric Buddhist believes that chants, words, and gestures can affect physical reality.

There are numerous powers, including the ability to turn base metals into gold, to discover hidden treasures, the ability to change one's physical appearance, the ability to make onself invisible, to walk through solid walls, to fly through the air, to be able to hear conversations miles away. They also include levitation, going for long periods without sleep, and warming the body using the energy of internal heat (*tapas*). The guru with *siddhis* is believed to be able to read the minds of others and even be in more than one place at the same time. There are higher powers, but there are also lower powers, and these lower powers involve things like curses to cause bad luck, pain and suffering.

TANTRAS

The advanced esoteric scriptures of Tantric Buddhism are *Tantras*. Tantric Buddhists believe that these texts are accurate records of the Buddha's secret teachings to a few special monks, but following the death of the Buddha the texts were preserved and hidden by demons until a thousand years later. Modern scholarship indicates that these texts were first composed a thousand years after the death of the Buddha, and are texts which evolved as part of a general Tantric approach to religion in northern India.[15]

A *Tantra* is a kind of technical manual written in a style relying heavily on metaphor and symbolism, especially arcane symbols to express vivid personal experiences as well as the various positive categories in Buddhist doctrine. The language of Tantras is also intended to evoke profound experiences. There is much about Tantras which is intentionally obscure, because Tantras were never intended to be mere descriptions clear to outsiders. The symbolism of the Tantra conceals as it reveals.

Tantras were also intended to be recited in complex rituals and ceremonial occasions and so focus on effects which are appropriate to ritual, such as constant repetition.[16] A Tantric text may break into what appear to be alliterative non-sense syllables. Tantric texts were intentionally esoteric, intentionally difficult to interpret and understand. Tantras utilize obscure symbolism of correspondences to such an extent that they are almost unintelligible to anyone lacking a *guru* to explain the correspondences and match them to Buddhist tradition and history. Elaborate

---

[13] Robert E. Buswell, Jr., ed., *Encyclopedia of Buddhism*, Vol. 1 under "Lama."

[14] Magic (not stage magic of professional magicians) is the belief that the world is controlled by forces that can be manipulated by means of processes such as prayers, spells, incantations, and dance, and the result might be rain, abundant crops, successful hunts, things which benefit friends and harm enemies. If the right words or bodily motions are engaged in, the world will grant the wishes of the magician. Belief in magic is rather common for most world religions. It is obvious in our culture in the wide variety of superstitions held by some athletes.

[15] Rupert Gethin, *The Foundations of Buddhism* (London: Oxford University Press, 1998), p. 268.

[16] A valuable overview of the different ways to interpret a Tantra is found in David Kalupahana, *A History of Buddhist Philosophy* (Honolulu: University of Hawaii Press, 1992), pp. 217–223.

symbolism connects visualizations, liturgy, and ritual to fully engage body, speech and mind.[17]

The *guru* would explain specific tantras to special students who had been carefully taught secret insights and were now deemed ready, and the *guru* would provide an oral explanation for the symbols and details. The secret explanation provided by a properly trained *guru* was essential to comprehend the symbols utilized. Even the alphabetic letters that make up a word can have symbolic importance. Tantras conclude with magical formulas of special and secret knowledge comprised of syllables with symbolic content. The Buddhist scholar, Edward Conze, who had translated hundreds of Mahayana sutras from the Sanskrit, was so baffled by the Tantras that, in 1967, he wrote:

> . . . the original documents in which any study of Tantric thought must be based, are written in a code which no one has yet been able to break. Their language is not only cryptic and designed to conceal rather than reveal their meaning; they are deliberately so constructed that they remain a dead letter in the absence of the holy *guru* whose oral teachings are held to be absolutely indispensable for the explanation of these texts.[18]

This situation has changed in recent decades because following the "peaceful liberation" of Tibet by the Chinese army in 1950, Tibetan teachers have been forced to flee Tibet and as they came into Western countries they carried their knowledge and traditions with them. As a result, Western students have had the opportunity to study with Tibetan lamas who have accepted them as students, and have provided much of the framework needed to understand Tantras. Many of these students have now become professors in major universities and very scholarly studies of Tibetan thought have resulted.

There are "lower" Tantras and "higher" Tantras, whose goals differ. The practice of the "lower" Tantras emphasize external rituals and devotions focused on gods and goddesses. The "higher" Tantras stress meditative strategies to focus energy centers, intended to transmute the body of the student into the body of a transcendent Buddha.

Every Buddha and Bodhisattva Was Born of a Woman

The highest Tantras, the Supreme Yoga Tantras, focus on the ritualized performance of sexual union. These texts traditionally begin: "Thus have I heard: at one time the Lord reposed in the vaginas of the Vajra-maidens—the heart of Body, Speech and Mind of all Buddhas."[19] These references to the feminine are not intended to be erotic. In fact, the Buddhists recognize that every buddha who ever lived was born from the vagina of a woman. In popular Buddhism, the embodiment of the highest wisdom is a goddess named *Prajñāpāramitā*. Edward Conze translates this about the goddess, from the *Prajnaparamita in 8,000 Lines*:

> For she is their mother and begetter, she showed them this all-knowledge, she instructed them in the in the ways of the world. From her have the Tathagatas come forth. For she has begotten and shows that cognition of the all-knowing, she has shown them the world for what it really is. The all-knowledge of the Tathagatas has come forth from her.[20]

She is the Perfect Wisdom who gives birthless birth to all buddhas.

---

[17] Gethin, *ibid.*, p. 269.

[18] Edward Conze, *Buddhist Thought In India* (Ann Arbor, Mi.: University of Michigan Press, 1979), p. 271.

[19] Translation from the Hevajra Tantra by D. Snellgrove, *Indo-Tibetan Buddhism*, p. 312.

[20] Edward Conze, *The Perfection of Wisdom in Eight Thousand Lines and Its Verse Summary* (Bolinas, CA: The Four Seasons Foundation, 1973), p. 172.

And through the sublimely Awakened Ones,
it is Mother Prajnaparamita alone
who turns the wheel of true teaching.[21]

12.4 VAJRAYANA DOCTRINES

It is not doctrines that distinguish Tantrism from the other Buddhist schools. Rather, Tantric Buddhism puts stress on methods which are minimized, or rejected in other Mahayana traditions. The unique and special Tantric practices are esoteric, and not for everyone. These practices are done in the context of a *guru*, the teacher with powers (in fact, the goal for Theravada is the *arhat*, the goal for the Mahayana is the bodhisattva, the goal for the Vajrayana is the *guru* with powers). Originally the emphasis was probably upon rites and rituals, but increasingly it became identified with meditation,[22] visualization, symbols, and powers.[23]

Nagarjuna's Madhyamaka Insights

Like the earlier Mahayana schools, Tantrism relied heavily upon the *Prajnaparamita sutras* and Nagarjuna's Madhyamaka thought which emphasize "emptiness," *svabhava-sunyata*, or "empty of unchanging inner essence." The insight is not complicated. We come to recognize that there are no unchanging essences anywhere. Nothing has an unchanging substance which underlies reality. Everything is flowing process, is empty of unchanging inner essence, it is *sunyata*, it is all interdependently arising (*pratityasamutpada*), dependently co-arising. There is nothing solid and unchanging to which one could cling, and no unchanging person to do the clinging. No words, no descriptions, and no philosophical explanations are able to describe reality completely. There is no philosophical position to which one can hold as ultimately true. No thing has any intrinsic qualities; it is all process, everything is relative to all that is going on all around.

If things do not have any intrinsic (*svabhava*) qualities, that means that nothing can be intrinsically evil, intrinsically bad or intrinsically impure (it is all process and change; nothing is intrinsically anything). Reality is just "such-as-it-is," it is Suchness, it is flowing processes which are empty of essence. Nirvana is what happens when we perceive *samsara* (the realm of birth and death) without anger, hatred, envy, or ignorance. A brief verse summarizes the Madhyamaka insights of Nagarjuna as understood within the Tantric tradition:

If you cling to this life, then you are not a dharma practitioner.
If you cling to existence, then you do not have renunciation.
If you are attached to your own interests, then you do not have the mind of awakening.
If you hold to [a position], then you do not have the correct view.[24]

Buddha-Nature Doctrines

The Mahayana *Tathagata-garbha* (the "matrix of the Thus-come One") idea that each of us has the Buddha-nature (the potential to become a buddha) is also essential to Tantric Buddhism. The Buddha's awakening is ultimately

---

[21] Quoted by Judith Simmer-Brown in "Look, Look," *Shambhala Sun*, Volume 22, No. 2, November 2013, p. 18.

[22] Tibetan meditative practices within a Western scientific perspective are discussed in B. Alan Wallace, *Buddhism With An Attitude: The Tibetan Seven-Point Mind Training* (Boston: Snow Lion, 2003).

[23] A. K. Warder, *Indian Buddhism*, p. 485.

[24] Verses within the Sakya tradition spoken to a twelfth century monk by Manjushri; quoted in James Fieser, John Powers, *Scriptures of the East* 2nd edition (New York: McGraw-Hill, 2003), p. 114.

to be found within our own mind, which means we are already potential buddhas. The goal of Tantric Buddhism is the transformation of our body, speech, and mind into those of a buddha by the means of special esoteric practices such as visualizing buddhas, or identifying with buddhas.[25]

Part of the problem is that we do not realize that we have always had the buddha-nature, and we live as though we are not buddhas. We believe we are lacking something and are trying to seek something outside ourselves to attain awakening. This attitude is part of the problem; it traps us in a false duality of unawakened versus awakened. This claim that we are all potential buddhas is not merely symbolic. One central feature of Tibetan Tantric Buddhism is the clear conviction that buddhas are alive and share our world, that many lamas are genuinely living buddhas, and that it is actually possible to utilize esoteric Tantric techniques to turn an individual student or monk into a living buddha, in this very life.

Devotion to Gods and Buddhas

The strong devotional tendencies typical of the Mahayana are also extremely important in Tantric Buddhism. The forest dwelling men and women cultivated relationships to specific deities, and cultivated spiritual powers. Followers practice visualization of a special "guardian deity" as the focus of their meditation. The Buddha of the Pure Land Western Paradise of Amitabha, also plays a role in Tibetan devotional practices.[26]

12.5 TANTRIC BUDDHISM COMES TO TIBET

Buddhism moved from north-east India into the region of the Himalayan mountains including Nepal, Bhutan, and Kashmir, and then to Mongolia and Tibet. Buddhism first came to Tibet during the seventh century, during the time period when the Tantric form dominated in northern India. Consequently another name for this form of Buddhism is "Northern Buddhism" because it is north of the birthplace of the historical Buddha. By this reckoning, Theravada Buddhism is Southern Buddhism, and most forms of Mahayana would be Eastern Buddhism (China, Korea, Japan).

Buddhism had been strongest in the north-east of India, but following the growth of devotional Hinduism, and economic and political changes including the movement of Islam into northern India, by 1150 C. E. Mahayana Buddhism was nearly destroyed in India, and Indian monks were dispersed northwards into the Himalayas, and to coastal urban centers. However, Tantric Buddhism first entered Tibet several centuries before the period of destruction.[27]

Around 600 C. E. the central area of the wild realm of Tibet had been unified under a lineage of kings who ruled together with numerous noble families, and at the same time Tibet had become a significant military force. It was influenced by Sui dynasty China (590-618 C.E.) for models of civilized social behavior and politics, as well as

---

[25] Tantric Buddhists accept the Mahayana doctrine that the Buddha has three bodies: a "transformation body," an "enjoyment body," and an "ultimate body." Some Tantric texts interpret the three bodies of the Buddha as metaphors for the achievement of awakening on the part of the Tantric adept. Upon awakening and achieving buddhahood, the Tantric adept teaches others (this is the "transformation body," the *nirmanakaya*). The adept experiences the bliss of enlightenment (this is the "enjoyment body," or *sambhogakaya*). The adept loses ego and subject-object are no longer distinguished; as a result he identifies with all of existence (this is the *dharmakaya* or "ultimate body.").

[26] For more on this aspect of Tibetan thought see Georgios T. Halkias, *Luminous Bliss: A Religious History of Pure Land Literature in Tibet* (Honolulu, HI: Pure Land Buddhist Studies Series. University of Hawaii Press, 2012).

[27] Tibetan Buddhism is discussed in detail in John Powers, *Introduction to Tibetan Buddhism* (Ithica, NY: Snow Lion Publication, 1995).

CHAPTER 12: TIBETAN THOUGHT

India, Kashmir and East Turkestan which influenced Tibetan understanding of spiritual and religious matters. Since China, northern India and Kashmir were Buddhist, Buddhist influences on Tibet were significant.[28] At this time Tibet did not have a written language. The Tibetans adopted the written language of Kashmir, based on written Sanskrit, to develop a written form of Tibetan. The capital was established at Lhasa.

Founders of Tibetan Buddhism

In the middle 600s, the king of Tibet had numerous wives, but for political reasons, married a Chinese princess from the east, and a Nepalese princess from the south, both of whom were devout Buddhists. Both princesses brought religious statues and texts with them to their new homes, contributing to the Buddhist influence upon Tibet. Under the influence of his new wives, the king wanted to establish some Buddhist temples in honor of various buddhas, but local Bon deities and demons interfered. The king summoned a Buddhist missionary and sorcerer from neighboring Kashmir named Padmasambhava, who was reputed to have magical powers obtained by secret rituals, austerities, and concentrated meditation. Using his supernatural powers, Padmasambhava was said to have overcome and defeated the malevolent Bon spirits of Tibet. In fact, many of the Bon gods and goddesses were adopted into the Buddhist pantheon as guardian deities, and other aspects of Bon were incorporated into Tibetan Buddhism. Padmasambhava[29] is credited with founding the first Buddhist temple in Tibet, in Lhasa. He was given the name Guru Rimpoche ("Precious Guru") and is reputed to have established a community of "superior ones," or lamas.

In 710 a later king repeated the process of marrying a Chinese Buddhist wife, and used Buddhism in an effort to strengthen his control over the other ruling families, but the aristocracy allied themselves with the old native religion of Bon to limit the power of the ruler. To compete with Buddhism, the Bon religion became more sophisticated philosophically, and clearly it was influenced by Buddhism. There was a constant political conflict between the forces of the king, supporting Buddhism, and the politically important aristocratic families supporting Bon.

Between 792 and 797, there was a debate between a representative of Indian Tantric Buddhism, and a Chinese representative of the Ch'an school, and the Tibetans seem to have decided that they preferred the Tantric form. Tibetan monks were sent to India to retrieve Tantric texts, which were then the beginnings of Tibetan thought. Things did not stay healthy for Buddhism. In succeeding eras, many rulers attempted to eliminate Buddhism from Tibet via assassination and violence.

Then around the year 1000, a second importation of Buddhism into Tibet occurred. A Buddhist teacher named Atisha (c. 982-1054) came to Tibet with new doctrines to reform Tibetan lamas. The story is that Tibetan Buddhists of the time were freely indulging in sexuality and liberally imbibing alcohol as part of their practices, and Atisha corrected their misunderstanding of Buddhist techniques. One generation later Tibetan monks Naropa (1016-1100) and Marpa (c. 1012-1096) traveled to India and brought back the latest Tantric texts.

12.6 SCHOOLS OF TIBETAN BUDDHISM

INTRODUCTION

During most of its history, Tibet was a feudalistic country with hereditary aristocratic families, serfs, farmers, merchants, herders, slaves, and monastics. As Buddhist schools arose in Tibet, there was violent conflict between

---

[28] A good anthology of articles on the historical background of Tibet is Gray Tuttle, Kurtis R. Schaeffer, eds., *The Tibetan History Reader* (New York: Columbia University Press, 2013).

[29] In popular Tibetan religion, Padmasambhava, Atisha, and Tsongkhapa (pronounced Dzong-ka-ba) are regarded as living buddhas, not merely as missionaries. Cf. Robert Thurman, *Essential Tibetan Buddhism* (New York: Castle Books, 1997), p. 1.

aristocratic families, Bon religious powers, and Buddhist orders over secular and political power, within a feudalistic framework.

In most of Mahayana Buddhism, the schools of Buddhism focus upon particular texts. Tibetan Buddhism generated schools based upon teaching lineages. The stress upon secret techniques has generated Buddhist traditions that separate themselves from one another by the esoteric teachings passed on from *guru* to disciple. There are numerous sub-schools within any particular teaching lineage. In this chapter we will discuss only the four major Tibetan schools and not the sub-schools.

SCHOOLS OF TIBETAN BUDDHISM: NYIMGMAPA

The school of Nyingma (the "Old Ones") traces its history back to the first diffusion of Indian Tantric Buddhism into Tibet. It counts Padmasambhava as its founder, and Nyingmapa (the school of Nyingma) is a mixture of the ancient Bon shamanistic attitudes combined with Buddhist teachings. Nyingmapa claims that Padmasambhava concealed many "hidden treasures" of technique which were then discovered over the following centuries by a series of later *gurus* and taught to their students.

Nyingmapa monks are allowed to marry and have families. This group was never strong on central authority. It tended to be a loose confederation of quite individualistic monks who were closely associated with their own local communities. In addition to meditation, the Nyingma school stresses divination, agricultural rituals, and exorcism. A variety of Tantric rituals are stressed very strongly in the Nyingmapa lineages.

Another important Nyingmapa tradition is the unified system of focused practice called *dzogchen*, literally "great perfection" which according to legend was passed to Padmasambhava by *dakinis*, naked female demons who consort with deities and who have access to the highest levels of reality. The stress in *dzogchen* is meditation upon the innate purity of the mind, and the goal is for the student to realize the innate purity of her or his own mind by immediate and direct personal experience. These "Great Perfection" practices have elicited much interest among scholars and students.[30]

SCHOOLS OF TIBETAN BUDDHISM: SAKYA SCHOOL

The Sakyapa (Sakya school) was named after the "Grey Earth" (Sakya) monastery, founded in 1073 in southern Tibet. The teaching system of Sakya studies Tantric texts, Mahayana Buddhist texts, Buddhist logic, and stresses a Tantric text called the *Hevajra Tantra*. The leadership of the Sakya school belongs to the same family and is hereditary, passing from father to son, and then later from uncle to nephew in the same extended family.

Mongols had conquered and ruled northern China from 1222–1368, but did not attempt to rule Tibet at this time. They appointed a member of the Sakya order to rule as viceroy for the region, and from this time the kings of Tibet faded away and the rulers of Tibet have been associated with Buddhist monastic orders. In effect, Tibet became a theocracy, a governmental form run by religion. The Buddhist ruler was not absolute; he ruled with a council and the aid of the ruling aristocratic families.

SCHOOLS OF TIBETAN BUDDHISM: THE KAGYU SCHOOL.

The Kagyu ("Whispered Transmission") school claims to have been founded by the married lama Marpa (c. 1012–1096) and his famous student, Milarepa (1052–1135). Marpa and Milarepa were famous as monks and as miracle workers who could control and even defeat the strongest demons. Milarepa was also a great poet and singer. The center

---

[30] See B. Allen Wallace, *Heart of the Great Perfection* (Boston: Wisdom Publications, 2016). See also B. Allen Wallace, *Meditations of a Buddhist Skeptic: A Manifesto for the Mind Sciences and Contemplative Practice* (New York: Columbia University, 2013).

of power for the Kagyu school is eastern Tibet, and the head of the Kagyu lineage wielded considerable political power in eastern Tibet.

The Kagyu school is credited with originating the institution of "official reincarnations," the idea that each generation's spiritual leader is the previous leader reborn once again. Such a person is referred to as a *tulku*, a "transformation body" of the previous *lama*. The head *lama* in the Kagyu line is called the Black Hat Lama (named for his official headgear), and the Kagyu claimed that when one Black Hat Lama passed on, because of his great spiritual power he had the ability to choose to be reborn in an area where he was needed.

Following the death of the Black Hat Lama, Kagyu *lamas* would search for a child of the appropriate age who seemed to have unusual spiritual powers and similar qualities and characteristics of the deceased *lama*. If the child seemed to have a psychological connection with the deceased Black Hat Lama, the child would become a monk and would be educated in Buddhist thought and practice and would be formally recognized as the previous Black Hat Lama reincarnated.[31]

A compassionate bodhisattva is supposed to choose continual rebirth for the benefit of living beings, so many of these Tibetan *gurus* were also understood to be advanced bodhisattvas. In accepting official reincarnations, Tibetan civilization also accepted the idea that buddhas and bodhisattvas are not merely abstract ideals, but in fact are also living human beings who exist physically in the world of Tibet. "Real Buddhas—living, breathing, teaching, helping, blessing—could be found among them right there in Tibet."[32]

One aspect of Kagyu is the supreme practice of *Mahamudra* ("great seal"), where the student dispenses with deity visualization, Tantric rituals, and instead focuses upon the natural state of the mind. The goal is the clarity and luminosity that comes with the realization of *sunyata* (all things are empty of unchanging essence, pronounced "shun-ya-TA"), and the consequent ending of the rebirth cycle.

The natural state of the mind is one's Buddha-nature, so it is clear, luminous and yet constantly in flux (no aspect of mind is unchanging; mind is empty of any inner essence). Achieving pure conceptually unstructured awareness of one's Buddha-nature, the student focuses upon the ever spontaneous clear light of consciousness, and as a result the student moves more quickly towards awakening.[33] An example of this *Mahamudra* practice is found in the following poem by a contemporary Kagyu teacher:

FREE AND EASY: A Vajra Song
by Ven. Lama Gendun Rinpoche[34]

Happiness cannot be found
through great effort and willpower
but is already present, in relaxation and letting go.

Don't strain yourself;
there is nothing to do.
Whatever arises in the mind

---

[31] Western scholarship indicates that the modern Chinese communist party has attempted to take over this Tibetan model of reincarnation, and Chinese communist party officials are determining who gets chosen as the appropriate rebirth of an eminent *lama*. For more on this from a Western scholarly perspective, see John Powers, *The Buddha Party: How the People's Republic of China Works to Define and Control Tibetan Buddhism* (New York and London: Oxford University Press, 2016), especially chapters 3 and 4.

[32] Robert Thurman, *Essential Tibetan Buddhism* (New York: Castle Books, 1997), p. 31.

[33] Many scholars find similarities between Tibetan *Mahamudra* and Chinese Ch'an Buddhism, and will refer to *Mahamudra* as Tibetan Zen. The similarities between the following poem and Chinese Taoist insights should also be obvious.

[34] Lama Gendun was the retreat master for the Kagyu three-year retreat center in France. There is a web site with more information: http://www.dhagpo-kundreul.org/anglais/gendun/bost_gendun4_en.html

has no real importance at all,
because it has no reality whatsoever.
Don't become attached to it;
don't identify with it and pass judgment upon it.

Let the entire game happen on its own,
springing up and falling back like waves --
without changing or manipulating anything --
and everything vanishes and reappears, magically, without end.

Only our searching for happiness
prevents us from seeing it.
It's like a rainbow which you pursue
without ever catching.

Although it does not exist,
It has always been there
and accompanies you every instant.

Don't believe in the reality
of good and bad experiences.
They are like rainbows in the sky.

Wanting to grasp the ungraspable
you exhaust yourself in vain.
As soon as you open and relax this grasping,
space is there — open, inviting, and comfortable.

Don't search any further.
Don't go into the tangled jungle
looking for the great elephant
who's already quietly at home.

Nothing to do,
Nothing to force.
Nothing to want — and everything happens by itself.[35]

Following the initial movement of Chinese armies into Tibet in October 1950, and the later repression following a popular revolt in 1959, it was the Kagyu lineage monks who were the first to travel outside of Tibet and India to Europe and to north America, carrying authentic Kagyu esoteric teachings to outsiders.

---

[35] From the French Dhagpo Kundreul Ling web site which includes numerous references to Lama Gendun's teachings. The poem is found here: http://www.dhagpo-kundreul.org/anglais/gendun/bost_gendun10_en.html

CHAPTER 12: TIBETAN THOUGHT

SCHOOLS OF TIBETAN BUDDHISM: THE GELUKPA

The school of Tibetan Buddhism best known in the West is the politically dominant order to which the Dalai Lama belongs, the Gelukpa (the "Virtuous school" perhaps more commonly romanized as Gelug or Gelugpa). The Gelugpa, or the Yellow Hat school, whose members wear distinctive yellow hats, began as a reform movement by Tsongkhapa (1357-1419), minimizing magical practices, minimizing sexual yoga, minimizing alcohol usage, and encouraging the scholarly study and proper interpretation of texts (especially Nagarjuna's Madhyamaka philosophy of emptiness), and enforcing greater monastic discipline. The Gelugpa eventually became the dominant Buddhist tradition in Tibet.

In the sixteenth century the Mongolians ruled northern China and Tibet and the third spiritual leader of the Gelugpa (the scholar-monk Sonam Gyatso 1543-1588), converted the Mongol ruler to Buddhism. The Mongolian ruler gave the third spiritual head of the Gelugpa order the title (Third) Dalai Lama ("dalai" is Mongolian for "ocean," and this is usually explained as the *lama* who is an "Ocean of Wisdom"), and each succeeding leader was understood to have the qualities and characteristics of the previous leader reborn. Thus, in the sixteenth century, Tibet became a theocracy and continued as such until recently.

The Dalai Lama is an Incarnation of the Bodhisattva Avalokiteshvara

Each Dalai Lama was not merely a *tulku*, that is, the incarnation of the previous Dalai Lama; in addition, he was perceived to be a rebirth of the Bodhisattva Avalokitesvara, famous as the bodhisattva of compassion. In addition to the Dalai Lama, there is also a Panchen Lama, the "superior one who is also a great scholar," who was declared to be an incarnation of the Buddha of the Western Paradise, Amitabha Buddha. The Panchen Lama had no political responsibilities except for acting as a spiritual representative of the Dalai Lama upon his death.[36] The Dalai Lama is not the formal head of the Gelug order; that position is held by the Ganden Tripa, the abbot of Ganden monastery, a rank awarded to the most accomplished masters of the Gelug lineage. Although the Dalai Lama is held in high esteem, the Gelug order is not automatically obedient to the Dalai Lama.

The Buddhist orders often battled each other for political power and wealth. The fifth Dalai Lama directed Mongol armies to annihilate all traces of the Karmapa lineage, who were their political rivals,[37] and he was appointed ruler of all Tibet in 1642 by the Mongolians (who also ruled north China). He is responsible for the construction of the magnificent Potala palace in Lhasa.

The position of Dalai Lama continued as a succession of heads of state which only ended when the twenty-three-year-old Tenzin Gyatso, the fourteenth Dalai Lama, fled from Tibet into northern India in 1959.[38] Although in many ways he is quite modern, the shamanistic background of Tibet is clear in his thinking because the Dalai Lama is known to consult oracles and uses divination in day-to-day decision making on matters of religion and state.

---

[36] The Chinese Communist party has claimed the right to determine who is to be the true Panchen Lama.

[37] Michael Parenti, "Friendly Feudalism: The Tibet Myth," on line at http://www.michaelparenti.org/Tibet.html . See also Donald Lopez Jr., *Prisoners of Shangri-La: Tibetan Buddhism and the West* (Chicago and London: Chicago University Press, 1998).

[38] Several filmmakers have made Hollywood movies about Tibet during this era. For example, Martin Scorcese filmed a version the story of the fourteenth Dalai Lama in 1997, entitled *Kundun* and *Seven Years in Tibet* starring Brad Pitt deals with the Dalai Lama.

12.7 TIBETAN VAJRAYANA DOCTRINES

TIBETAN BUDDHISM DOES NOT STRESS THE NOBLE EIGHTFOLD PATH

Scholars view Tantric Buddhism in Tibet as a creative combination of (a) the animism and shamanism of the Bon religion, (b) the Mahayana teachings of emptiness (*svabhava-sunyata*), Buddha-nature, and levels of consciousness, (c) popular *bhakti* devotion to and faith in male and female divinities, (d) the magically powerful forest monks, including meditating non-monastic male and female ascetics on the fringes of the society, and (e) earlier non-Buddhist texts and practices.[39]

The earlier central importance of the Four Noble Truths and Noble Eightfold Path have been demoted in Tantric Buddhism to a preliminary practice appropriate for beginners and intermediate students. The Tibetans refer to these as "Hinayana," that is "Inferior Vehicle"[40] or "Little Vehicle" practices. In Theravada and Mahayana schools, the teachings of Buddhism are based on the Noble Eightfold Path, stressing wisdom, morality and mental discipline (mediation). For traditional monks and nuns of the Theravada traditions, the central practice is (a) focused meditation intended to quiet the roaming mind and develop tranquility (*samatha*) and (b) deepening insight into the nature of reality (*vipaśyanā/vipassana*). Students pay attention to their own emotional states, observing them, but not being attached to them. In a non-judgmental state, even the strongest emotions are allowed to rise and then fade.

In Tibetan Buddhism the early Buddhist techniques of *samatha* calmness and *vipaśyanā/vipassana* insight are considered preliminary practices appropriate for beginners and those of limited spiritual abilities, but not a higher practice for advanced monks. For an advanced student, tantric practice is dynamic rituals centered upon deities who embody manifestations of the energy of the universe. Tibetan Tantric Buddhism uses the physical body, erotic energy, and other passions as sources of energy which can be redirected to achieve powerful goals. Instead of observing emotions and allowing them to subside naturally, in Tibetan Tantric practices the emotional energy is harnessed as a source of energy which can be used to speed the processes leading to buddhahood. The world is bound by lust, and can be released by the energy of lust when properly directed.

> Those things by which evil men are bound, others turn into means and gain thereby release from the bonds of existence. By passion the world is bound, by passion too it is released, but by heretical Buddhists this practice of reversals is not known.[41]

Although in the West, Tibetan teachers have taught standard Buddhist meditation techniques of *samatha* (calming) and *vipaśyanā/vipassana* (insight) to their American followers, in actual practice, for more advanced students the main meditative practice in Tibetan Buddhism is recitations and deity visualizations.

---

[39] Although Tibetan Tantric Buddhist followers reject the idea, there is substantial scholarship which argues that Tantric Buddhism is heavily influenced by very similar non-Buddhist Shaiva Tantras. Some scholars appeal to some unknown older tradition common to both Shaiva Tantra and Buddhist Tantra. For example, see Oxford professor Alexis Sanderson, "Vajrayana: Origin and Function," Chapter 5 of *Buddhism into the Year 2000* (Los Angeles and Bangkok: Dhammakaya Foundation, 1994), pp. 87–102. On page 92 he writes "The present author's view is that almost everything concrete in the [Buddhist Tantric] system is non-Buddhist in its origin even though the whole is entirely Buddhist in its function." See also Alexis Sanderson, "Saivism and the Tantric Traditions," in Friedhelm Hardy, ed., *The World's Religions: The Religions of Asia* (London: Routledge, 1990), pp. 128–172.

[40] As was explained in chapter 9, no Buddhist school ever referred to itself as the Hinayana/Inferior Vehicle or thought of itself as inferior. Tibetan Buddhism puts great stress on the Mahayana *Lotus sutra* which uses this insulting and derogatory term to refer to the pre-Mahayana Buddhists.

[41] From the *Hevajra-tantra*, I.ix.2-3, tr. David Snellgrove, *Indo-Tibetan Buddhism* (Boston: Shambhala, 1987), vol. I, pp. 125–126.

CHAPTER 12: TIBETAN THOUGHT

Ritual Transmissions (*abhisheka*) Empower the Pupil

The Tibetan lamas assert that to make acceptable progress in Tantric Buddhism, one must receive ritual "transmissions of power," and the transmission is given only after one has completed preliminary practices, and earned the confidence of the teacher. Before being accepted on the tantric pathway, the potential student must demonstrate tenacity and dedication. Preliminary practices can include full prostration (laying flat on your stomach full length on the floor and then returning back to a standing position) which should be performed one hundred thousand times as preliminary practice. As a part of one's preliminary practice, one must make offerings for the good of all living things, and there is the recitation of the practitioner's own personal sequence of sacred syllables (*mantra*), given to him by his *guru*. It is believed that these preliminary techniques provide the foundation of ethical and spiritual purity needed before one can attempt the more dangerous and difficult Vajrayana practices. Next the student studies the Mahayana scriptures and commentaries, and undertakes the bodhisattva pathway of egoless compassion. These practices can take many years, perhaps as many as 15 or 20 years, before moving on to the higher secret teachings.

With the preparation completed, the ritual transmissions or consecrations (*abhisheka*) can be given. The Tantric followers believe that there is some subtle awareness or insight or knowledge that is not entirely available to the student unless it is accompanied by non-verbal, ritualized and secret transmission. The ritual empowers the student to carry out more advanced Tantric practices.

The *guru* who is advanced in training and possessing *siddhis* officiates at the initiation of the student.[42] The Tibetans believe that the deeper the insight and attainment of the *guru*, the more effective the initiation ritual, which can help prepare the student for nirvana either in this life, or in a future existence.

The *guru* is the teacher, and the student is the servant, serving her or his *guru* with complete trust. One's *guru* is a superior one (*lama*), a divinity, and as one makes spiritual progress, one's *guru* also becomes a friend. Friendship with a god (or gods) will deepen the student's realization of the similarity of the student and the divinity. Friendship deepens trust, and with trust, fear of the gods diminishes.[43] Ultimately, the student is identified with the divine.

These ritual transmissions not only authorize the student to move on to more advanced topics, but they are believed to actually empower the student as well. Following the empowerment ritual, when the student recites the appropriate *mantra*, it is believed to have more power. With the empowerment ritual, deeper levels of the secrets of the *mandala* can be revealed.

The goal of *Vajrayana* is supreme awakening (Buddhahood) in this very life, and monks believe that this is achieved by many very unconventional practices. Tantric Buddhism believes that it is superior because it has a higher secret teaching for the select few, not available to ordinary folk. A central insight of that esoteric teaching is that the Buddha's awakening is ultimately to be found within your own mind. You are already a buddha: do not live as though you are un-awakened, and are trying to attain enlightenment — this is to be trapped in a conceptual duality. If everything is flowing process and change, concepts do not adequately describe reality, especially dualistic concepts that see absolute differences and separations. There is no awakened-unawakened duality, no subject-object duality — no nirvana-*samsara* duality — so we must live that way.

Like its Indian antecedents, Tibetan Buddhism believes in using the entire body as an instrument for liberation; sweet-smelling incense, vibrant colors, intricate patterns, monks chanting -- one travels through the senses to a higher realm of reality (a *mandala* is a road map for this sort of journey).

---

[42] Ritual transmissions are often given to a large crowd, and members of the audience seem to feel they have received a blessing, rather than special powers allowing them to comprehend abstract doctrines.

[43] Herbert V. Guenther, *Buddhist Philosophy In Theory and Practice* (Baltimore, MD: Penguin Books, 1972), p. 179.

CHAPTER 11: MAHAYANA SCHOOLS–PART II

The Use of *mandala*

Buddhas and bodhisattvas reside within every human being and there are special sacred maps which we can use to correlate the external realms with states of consciousness. These maps are the *mandala*. Like the Hindu Tantric practices, as an aid to meditation the Buddhist Tantric adepts utilized the circular image, drawing, or pattern, inside a square. A *mandala* is a symbolic diagram which represents the interconnections between cosmic forces. A *mandala* is a map of sacred space, which depicts equivalence between the macrocosm and the microcosm. Under the guidance of a *guru*, the same *mandala* might be a symbol of the entire universe, and then it might be a symbol of the palace of a heavenly being or a terrifying demon, and it most certainly can symbolize states of mind of the person who meditates.

Each of the important Tantric deities belongs to a family of deities, and each grouping has an appropriate *mandala*. The deity dwells in the center of the *mandala*, guarded by the deities who surround it, and the surrounding spirits belong to that family. The macrocosm is replicated in the human body, and with practice and the guidance of the *guru*, it can be visualized.

For each human being, we have a center of consciousness, guarded by dreaded guards, where an ultimate sacred being resides, an ultimate buddha. Properly visualized, it is in three-dimensions, and it has correspondences with all directions in the universe, above, below, north, east, south, west. It is a model of both the cosmos and of the total human being. When you are ready, you can be guided to that place. Your *guru* gives you the appropriate *mandala* for your level of spiritual accomplishment. You are to visualize the *mandala* as the dwelling or palace of a pure being, a buddha or bodhisattva. This image is not merely an intellectual symbol. It is a road-map. *Mandala* are maps of a spiritual journey in which the pupil's *guru* guides the student to awaken spiritual potentials buried deep in the subconscious. Ultimately the student identifies himself with the divine buddha in the center of the *mandala*. As a result, the student recognizes his own divinity. In your deepest nature, you are a buddha.

The Use of *Mantras*

As mentioned earlier, another name for Tantric Vajrayana Buddhism is the *Mantrayana*, the vehicle (*yana*) which makes extensive use of *mantras*. We discussed *mantras* in the chapter explaining the Vedas, and then again with Tantric Hinduism. There is limited use of *mantras* in early Buddhism,[44] but scholars suggest that the great stress placed on chanting *mantras* in Buddhist Tantrism may have been borrowed from some forms of earlier Hinduism. Some who reject direct Hindu influence on Tantric Buddhism have suggested that perhaps both Tantric Hindu and Tantric Buddhist traditions drew from a common source which is still unknown.

Mantras are highly compressed, power-packed phrases, drawn from Sanskrit, and charged with deep meaning and magical potency. In addition to their ordinary meaning, in Tantric religions *mantras* are believed to have special secret meanings which can only be passed on to the student by a *guru* who has been initiated into these hidden powers.

In Mahayana, there are many different buddhas presiding over many different realms. It was believed that each buddha had a special sound which invoked that deity, but also reflected the pure mind of that buddha. For example, one of the most important buddhas in Tibet is Avalokiteshvara,[45] and Avalokiteshvara's special *mantra* is *Om Mani Padme Hum.* Literally this is "*Om*[46] jewel lotus – ah." Originally, chanting this sound was simply invoking

---

[44] Early Buddhist texts refer to the Buddha himself instructing students to use chanted phrases called *dharani* which would banish evil and offer protection from harm. Cf. David Kalupahana, *A History of Buddhist Philosophy*, p. 227.

[45] In Tibet, Avalokiteshvara is known as Chenrezi (and known as Kuan-yin/Guanyin in China and Kannon Bosatsu in Japan).

[46] *Om*, the most sacred sound which contains all other sacred sounds, was discussed in chapter 4 on the Hindu wisdom traditions.

Avalokiteshvara,[47] however later Tibetan commentators provided numerous explanations of the mystic significance of the *mantra*. For example, the jewel can symbolize male and the lotus can symbolize the female, or the jewel can symbolize the Buddha-nature and the lotus can symbolize the world of birth-and-death. The symbolism is sexual if we translate this as "the jewel IN the lotus," and it is philosophical if we render the *mantra* as "the jewel IS the lotus." Contemporary scholars reject both of these popular readings as merely later Western projections on Tibet.[48] There are many possible ways to interpret this key *mantra*.

If this is the sound which encapsulates the compassionate consciousness of Avalokiteshvara, then constant repetition of this sound must affect the pupil's mind for the better. Tibetans believe that chanting *Om Mani Padme Hum* will nourish the egoless compassion of the bodhisattva that resides in the mind of the student.

Mantras can be recited verbally, but their power extends beyond the sound itself. *Mantra* can be visualized, and repeatedly written down as spiritual practice. Tantric Buddhists believe that a *mantra* can awaken powers that reside in the unconscious. Through knowledge and manipulation of appropriate sounds, the psychic forces could be brought under control, and various levels of attainment are possible.[49]

Following empowerment rituals between teacher and student, the *guru* is to provide the student with a specific deity, and the *mantra* of that deity.

In addition to **Om Mani Padme Hum**, some other well-known *mantras* used in Tibetan Vajrayana are **Om Ah Hum**, and **Om Vajradake Hum**. The Tibetan *mantra* for the deity Vajrasarasvati (originally a Hindu *deva*) is **Om Picu Picu Prajnavardhani**. The *mantra* for the goddess Ekajata is **Om Hum Vajra Ange Mama Raksha Phat Svaha**.[50]

These combination of sounds, each *mantra*, is believed to have great power. The student is to meditate on the phrase, at all times and all places, and by reciting the *mantra* one is in constant spiritual communication with the deity. With the *mantra* and the appropriate *mandala*, the student can identify with his or her god and ultimately identify with the clear light of awakening.

For many in India, the powers of *mantra* result from the properly pronounced sound of the Sanskrit words. If it is the actual **sound** which is divine and that divine sound produces the powerful effect, then proper pronunciation is essential and mis-pronunciation is a serious problem. Tibetans pronounce *mantras* according to the phonetic rules of Tibetan and do not pronounce Sanskrit words in the ancient and accurate manner. Hence, from the Indian perspective, *mantras* chanted using Tibetan pronunciation (or English pronunciations) should be worthless.

The Tibetans have a solution to this problem. In Tibet it is believed that it is the **state of mind** of the person chanting the sound that gives the power to the *mantra*, so what is important is ritual empowerment, not proper Sanskrit pronunciation.[51] Tibetans also feel that the potency of the sound is intensified due to the sound having been repeated over and over by a long line of *gurus* or lamas, all of whom chanted the same sound. In any case, Tibetan

---

[47] Donald Lopez, Jr., *Prisoners of Shangri-La: Tibetan Buddhism and the West* (Chicago and London: Chicago University Press, 1998)

[48] The most thorough study of this mantra, both grammatically and historically, is Alexander Studholme, *The Origins of Om Manipadme Hum: A Study of the Karandavyuha Sutra* (New York: SUNY Press, 2002).

[49] Several books in English contain Tantric texts with *mantras*. For example, see Steven Beyer, tr. and ed., *The Buddhist Experience: Sources and Interpretations* (Belmont, Ca.: Dickenson Publishing, 1974), pp. 125–153.

[50] These mantras are quoted without Sanskrit diacritical marks, and taken from Agehananda Bharati, *The Tantric Tradition* (New York: Anchor Books, 1970), pp. 133–134.

[51] It follows that any person who recites *mantras* but is ignorant of their hidden inner meaning will get limited or no effect from the recitation.

Buddhists believe that recitation of a *mantra* is a daily practice which purifies speech and protects the mind by maintaining a constant spiritual connection, and it helps to disperse mental chatter.[52]

12.8 TANTRIC DEITIES

Tantric Buddhism is clearly polytheistic, employing a wide pantheon of deities, both male and female. Some of these divinities offer kindness, compassion, and help. Others are fearsome, snarling, wreathed in flames, wielding skulls. Among the spirits are the gods of the Hindus, Bon deities and buddhas and bodhisattvas. For the advanced Tantric adept, these are not so much external deities as archetypal images symbolic of primordial energies, such as anger, fear, aversion, hatred, rage, compassion, pain, and love. These are the passions and emotions given visual images, transformed and personified. To focus on these is to be aware of them, and the roles they play in our lives.

Although these can be thought of as manifestations of one's own consciousness, it seems clear that for the majority of practitioners they are external deities who will obey the will of a trained adept. One can invoke spirits to attack one's enemies, as well as for positive results. This is ritual magic, it is based on a cause-effect model whereby magical sounds (*mantras*) and rituals become causes and can bring about the desired effects in the physical universe.

Deities are not just external spirits, and not just internal mental states. They are also abstract concepts given physical form. For example, philosophical concepts of Mahayana are symbolized by names of demons we fear (which become personifications of tremendous power and sometimes, evil), *devas* we respect (who become embodiments of pleasurable existences or experiences), and buddhas and bodhisattvas we venerate (each buddha or bodhisattva embodies teachings of ultimate goal of Buddhist life). These various devices made the text more interesting during *mantra*-recitation ceremonies.

Vajrayana classifies various buddhas and bodhisattvas into groups, or families, and these groupings become the basis for practice and for visualization. The most important of these is the fundamental five buddhas described in a previous chapter, Vairochana (Mahavairochana), Akshobhya, Ratnasambhava, Amitabha, and Amoghasiddhi. These symbolize five primary energies which provide a structure by which all of reality can be understood and interpreted.

In Chapter 8 on early Buddhism, we saw that Buddhists analyzed the self into five groups or five bundles of processes, including physical form and the body, feelings, perceptions, dispositions, and consciousness. In the Tantra, the human personality is symbolized by buddhas. When the name Vairocana appears, it can symbolize both the body and ethics; when the name Ratnasambhava is chanted, it symbolizes feelings and concentration. Amitabha corresponds to perception and appreciation; Amoghasiddhi is dispositions and freedom; and Aksobhya is consciousness.[53] Each of these buddhas in turn arise within one supreme Tantric Buddha.

Do not think of these frightening Tibetan deities as demons or devils from hellish realms. Rather, these fearsome beings can come to our aid, they can frighten away the evil forces that we want to eliminate. The deities wreathed in flames, snarling, carrying skulls and severed heads, are very powerful forces that can help us. If you want to get rid of ignorance, you can fight it with a "Destroyer of Ignorance," a deity who has a threatening or fear-generating personality.

The *mandala* diagrams are an actualization of these families of divinities. A *mandala* will place a buddha at its center, and will have others buddhas and bodhisattvas belonging to the same family circling the central image. Secret relationships are diagramed within the *mandala*, and the student needs the *guru* to reveal the many levels of symbolism.

---

[52] John Snelling, *The Buddhist Handbook* (Rochester, VT: Inner Traditions, 1991), p. 96.

[53] David Kalupahana, *A History of Buddhist Philosophy* (Honolulu: University of Hawaii Press, 1992), pp. 223ff.

12.9 VAJRAYANA PRACTICE: VISUALIZATION as *SADHANA*

A basic rite called a *sadhana* is literally an "accomplishing" or "effecting." There are many such rites, including fire ceremonies, offerings of ritual cakes, rites of prosperity or curing, dedicating statues, and other such rituals. A meditative communion with a divinity is also a *sadhana*. The abstract concept of "the wisdom which carries one over to the other shore" is personified into a goddess to be prayed to and worshiped,[54] and also transformed into actual bodily experiences of emptiness (*sunyata*). Instead of stressing *samatha* (tranquility) and *vipaśyanā/vipassana* (insight), Tantric Buddhism utilizes visualization of gods as a central meditative practice. This is *sadhana*, a method, or technique in Tantric Buddhism involving meditative communion with a deity, a buddha or a bodhisattva.[55]

Tibetan meditation stresses visualization of deities, buddhas and bodhisattvas more than previous Mahayana schools. We all possess the Buddha-nature, and so we are all potential buddhas already. Visualization of ourselves as a specific buddha could be an aid to our realization. We need to identify with a buddha, the body of that buddha, the mind of that buddha, and the speech of that buddha.

If we believe that the *siddhas* (*gurus* with *siddhi* magical powers) in the past did achieve what the tradition asserts, that these *gurus* became buddhas, and that these *gurus* recorded their actual practices in *sadhana* texts, then when the sacred texts tell us that a *guru* experienced a deity as the embodiment of awakening, we too can utilize that technique with confidence. During earlier stages of Tantric practice, the student is to focus upon her or his *guru* as a divinity, as a living Buddha.[56] This is done in the context of focused concentration or meditation.

After undergoing the proper preparation, the student focuses upon an image of a buddha or bodhisattva as chosen by the *guru*. The student has received ritual transmission which empowers her to use the buddha or bodhisattva as the means to lead to buddhahood. The *guru* has chosen the appropriate buddha or bodhisattva for the student's stage and understanding. That buddha or bodhisattva is already awakened, so visualizing that being is important. A *mandala* can be used at this stage.

The student may visualize the buddha or divinity, focusing upon the image until it remains unshaken in the mind. The deity holds his or her hands in a certain way, and each hand position and hand gesture (*mudra*) has esoteric significance, and is to be imitated by the student. The deity may be seated upon a lotus or riding an elephant or a lion. One can then modify the mental image by visualizing rays of light emanating from these heavenly beings. One may visualize the deity surrounded by geometric shapes (*mandala*) and surrounded by members of that family of buddha images. One is taught the sacred sounds (*mantra*) that correspond to the buddha or bodhisattva, and may chant or recite them in the process of visualization. In the process the student is supposed to feel that she is establishing a communion, a connection with the supernatural being.

---

[54] Edward Conze, "The Iconography of the Prajnaparamita" in *Thirty Years of Buddhist Studies* (Oxford: Bruno Cassirer Publishers, 1967), pp. 243ff.

[55] A Tantric ritual designed to receive powers (*siddhi*) from a deity. In one type the deity is requested to appear before the meditator, and then worshiped in the expectation of receiving blessings. In the other type of tantric *sadhana*, the meditator imagines himself or herself to be the deity at this very moment. Often this can involve the creation of a body *mandala*, in which deities take residence in the meditator's body. Robert Buswell Jr., Donald S. Lopez Jr., eds, *The Princeton Dictionary of Buddhism* (Oxford: Princeton University Press, 2014), p. 731b.

[56] As has been pointed out before, all systems which emphasize the superiority of the *guru* and blind obedience from the student, have the potential to be misused. A student who attributes supernatural insight to the teacher, and unquestioning faith in whatever the teacher asks, is at risk. There are many documented case studies of authoritarian teachers claiming to be liberated, demanding and receiving financial and sexual favors from students. When devotion to a teacher overrides one's conscience, there is great potential for harm.

CHAPTER 11: MAHAYANA SCHOOLS–PART II

Deity Practice

Having built up a visualization of the deity in the first stage amplified by reciting the deity's specific *mantra*, the meditator then moves to "deity practice," a stage in which she may identify with the visualized supernatural being, the goal being to lose the sense of separation between the person and the deity. The visualized deity is not different from the student, and so the energy centers of the deity are now available to the student. In the mind of the meditator, he or she becomes a deity, for, in essence, the student and the god are identical.

With complete identification with the awakened being, the student has now realized his or her own buddha-nature. The student is no longer a student; she or he is not different from the Buddha himself. But that is not enough. There is another step.

The Clear Light of Emptiness

In the next step of this practice, the visualized deity is dissolved into formlessness. This is described in the *Guhyasamaja-tantra* as follows:

> Everything from the crown of the head to the feet dissolves into the heart; you engage in the perfect yoga (meditation on emptiness). ... All sentient beings and all other phenomena dissolve into clear light and then dissolve into you; then you yourself, as the deity, dissolve into your heart. . . . Just as mist on a mirror fades toward the center and disappears, so does everything — the net of illusory manifestation — dissolve into the clear light of emptiness. Just as fish are easily seen in clear water, so does everything — the net of illusory manifestation — emerge from the clear light of emptiness.[57]

The process is more complicated than outlined above. For example, the *guru* may instruct the student to visualize the bodhisattva of loving compassion, Avalokitesvara, as a calm, peaceful, smiling radiant deity. That is not too difficult. But supernatural beings have aspects which are frightening, and these too must be visualized and then identified with. Roaring beasts, fearsome fanged figures stamping their feet and growling at the student are also part of the visualization. This apparently negative and fearsome energy and embodied anger are within each of us.

For the more advanced student, the gods are not outside; each deity and each demon is an aspect of our own consciousness. These are graphic symbols of hatred, envy, greed, anger, and neurotic behavior. With this deepened understanding, it is hoped that one's *guru* can direct and guide one to minimize those features of one's personality which were hindering the free flow of sympathetic compassion which is defining of buddhahood; channeling and using the apparently negative energy for good is another goal.

With the mastery of guided visualization, new magical and religious practices follow. The Tantric adept could acquire magical powers of the gods by visualizing and conjuring them up from depths of human consciousness. The external and internal worlds could be seen as relative and not absolute. The Buddhist deities dissolve into emptiness. The practitioner experiences the clear light of emptiness, the diamond essence of reality.[58]

---

[57] Quoted in James Fieser, John Powers, *Scriptures of the East*, 2nd edition (New York: McGraw-Hill, 2003), p. 109.

[58] A Western student who devoted years to learning Tibetan and practicing Gelug Tantric Buddhism ultimately found it ineffective. Stephen Batchelor writes, "I was drawn to [non-Tantric] Buddhist practices that did not require the visualization of complex deities and mandalas and the endless recitation of mantras. I was finding the daily obligation of chanting devotional *pujas* and reciting the tantric *sadhanas* of Yamantaka and Vajrayogini increasingly meaningless. I continued to do them out of loyalty rather than conviction. They had no discernable effect on the quality of my lived experience." Stephen Batchelor, *Confession of a Buddhist Atheist* (New York: Spiegel & Grau, 2010), p. 55.

12.10 FORBIDDEN TANTRIC PRACTICES

Some Tantric practices are forbidden for those who were felt to be insufficiently developed in morality. Each of the students must spend years mastering the Mahayana sutras and commentaries, and cultivating the foundations of Buddhist morality before being allowed to proceed to the forbidden practices. The moral foundation provided by the precepts of traditional conservative Buddhism, plus the philosophical grounding in the emptiness tradition of the Madhyamaka, the Mind-Only insights of Yogacara, and Buddha-nature forms of Indian Mahayana Buddhism, combined with the basic Tantric techniques, provide the essential foundation of ethical and spiritual purity needed before one can attempt the more dangerous and difficult Vajrayana practices which separate Tantric Buddhism from other forms of Mahayana. In theory, the supremely moral *guru* decides when the student has sufficient moral foundation, and then guides the student to more advanced Tantric practices. The student-practitioner does have the buddha-nature, which means that the potential for buddhahood is innate within. Each of us is already a buddha but ignorance clouds this fact and so we do not live that way. With adequate meditative and moral training, we are ready for the next level.

According to Nagarjuna's insight into emptiness (*svabhava-sunyata*), reality is *not* made up out of separate and independent entities, but rather is interconnected flowing processes. Everything is flowing process; nothing has an unchanging defining inner essence. If there are no unchanging essences, then nothing is innately or intrinsically evil or good. Good and evil are relative to the context. To help the advanced student understand this, behavior normally forbidden in earlier forms of Buddhism can serve as teaching instruments in Tibetan Buddhism: meditation in areas associated with corpses, imbibing alcoholic beverages, meat eating, and participating in a variety of sexual activities including intercourse. Meat in itself is not evil. Although alcohol is forbidden to other Buddhists, Tantra insists that alcohol in itself is not evil.[59]

Tantric Buddhism celebrates rites which make real the student's attainment with actual physical bodily experiences of buddhahood. These sorts of rituals transgress against conventional morality and the Buddhist Five Precepts,[60] but if the student mistakenly believes that some things are innately good and other things are innately evil, then the student cannot progress to the state where all things are seen as flowing processes. To use formal rituals to push the student to act in ways which are contrary to ordinary moral rules can help the student realize that the duality between good and evil is not ultimate. The Tantric Buddhists assert that we need to collapse this duality; we need to unify the duality so that the two are now non-dual. Two become one.

These regulated and formal transgressive rituals can include sexual intercourse between the practitioner and his or her partner (often a spouse). Sexual union is the ultimate image of two becoming one. The masculine and feminine forces, corresponding to compassion and wisdom, are activated and reunited. The unifying bliss of orgasm is transformed into the bliss of awakening. However, these forbidden rituals are suitable only for advanced students who have the spiritual insight and moral training to undertake these practices. These practices are not supposed to be an excuse to enjoy a sexual interlude; rather they are choreographed rituals which have been sexualized.

---

[59] A bottle of alcohol is simply a bottle of chemicals. Alcohol itself is not evil. Intoxication does not reside in alcohol. Alcohol in the bottle is not intoxicated. It is the effect of the chemicals *upon us* that is known as intoxication. The good or evil is in our reaction, not in the world. The author would be remiss if he did not point out that at least a few famous teachers from Tibet seemed to exhibit the symptoms of alcoholism.

[60] (1) Refrain from killing or hurting (*ahimsa*) living creatures (do not increase the *duhkha* for any living thing). (2) Refrain from taking anything not given, respect what others have. (3) Refrain from misuse of sensual pleasures. (4) Refrain from speaking untruths. (5) Refrain from self-intoxication (including non-medicinal drugs and alcohol) which lessen our awareness of causes of suffering.

CHAPTER 11: MAHAYANA SCHOOLS–PART II

Shakti: Sacred Energy as Male and Female Sexuality

We discussed Hindu *shaktism* in chapter 5 of this volume. In Tantric Hinduism and Tantric Buddhism, female divinities become important *devas* and the consorts of buddhas and bodhisattvas. The primordial energy (or the primordial deity) is not just masculine; it is both masculine and feminine. The role of the female is connected to the pathway of liberation and wisdom.[61] The feminine principle is essential to the nature of reality. Sacred reality can be conceptualized as masculine and feminine energies. One of the most powerful images of non-duality, of two becoming one, is sexual imagery and symbols. The spiritual union of those forces recreates the original unity, and for the devotee the manipulation of that erotic force can be used to fuel the goal of awakening.

Female *devas* were associated with various specific bodhisattvas, in the same way Radha is the consort of Krishna, the same way Durga or Parvati[62] is attached to Shiva. It is symbolic of the self-division of primal unity into a bi-polar dualism. It is the subsequent interaction of the two poles which produces all the things in the world. By reversing that process of creation, we bring about a conscious return to unity. The sacred erotic love of a divine pair can be reenacted by the union of the male with his female consort, his *yogini*. The sexual union is a ritual recreation of unity. For monks who have taken a vow of chastity, or "right handed Tantra," this sexuality is not physical but rather is symbolic and the becomes the focus of visualization and meditation.

For advanced students of "left-handed Tantra," sexual intercourse is a choreographed ritual, with one's partner visualized as a deity, and the sexual act is a ritual recreation of unity. Sometimes the *guru* participates in the sexual activities. Male and female identify with and assume the roles of male buddhas and their female consorts, both enlightened beings. The sexual union of the male and female student can be utilized to unify the two energies, the female wisdom or *prajna* energy, and the male *upaya* energy, the union of wisdom (*prajna*) and skillful teaching means (*upaya*).

Sexualized ritual can also be symbolic of the union of wisdom and compassion, the two becoming one. In meditation, one can imagine the feminine wisdom uniting with the masculine compassion in a sexual symbol of oneness. Pure Wisdom without compassion is cold and hard, empathy with other living things is difficult or impossible. Pure Compassion without wisdom is misdirected and can lead to harm. The aesthetic union of inspiration and appreciation is another symbolic interpretation. The Tantric follower can interpret the dual energies of male and female in an almost limitless number of ways. Although we have been describing possible symbolic interpretations of the sexual act, we must also acknowledge that the sexual climax is important. The bliss of sexual orgasm is to be transformed into the bliss of the awakened mind.[63]

Some divide the tantras into four groups. The first is "Action Tantra," where the partners gaze into each others eyes as god and goddess. Then there is "Performance Tantra" where the partners hold hands. The "Yoga Tantra" involves embracing. What is called the "Highest Yoga Tantra" is sexual union. For some monastics who had taken a vow of celibacy, this is imagined or visualized. For others, it could be actual sexual intercourse, most often with one's spouse. In both cases, sexual desire is aroused and then transformed to become a tool for liberation.[64]

---

[61] As was noted in previous chapters, there is a tendency in Western religions to perceive sexuality as the enemy of spirituality, as dirty, impure, and something of which we should be ashamed. This attitude is not shared by all world religions, as we see in Tantric Hinduism and Tantric Buddhism. Of course, in the hands of a *guru* (or priest) who is not as moral as we assume the *guru* to be, the teacher can easily take sexual advantage of students who are taught never to question or doubt. Resistance to the sexual advances of the teacher on the part of the student can be explained as a failure of the student, an ego-problem of the student.

[62] These are goddesses discussed in the prior chapter 5 on devotional Hinduism.

[63] For more details on the role of the female, see Miranda Shaw, *Passionate Enlightenment: Women in Tantric Buddhism* (Princeton, 1995).

[64] Seminar with Guy Newland, 1989.

A typical ritual involves the *guru* offering a feast where the student and a female partner enjoy a meal. Then the *guru* leads the student in a ritual which begins with the teacher having intercourse with the female, and then the student is to swallow a drop of semen of the *guru*, and then the female gives the student a taste of her own sexual fluids. The student and the female then enjoy the "four blisses" of sexual intercourse. Then the couple is joined by a garland of flowers and the *guru* explains that the female must be visualized as a goddess, and the man as a buddha.[65] In Tibet many of the monks are married, and so their consort is in fact their spouse. Lust is confronted, and the energy of sexuality is channeled for spiritual goals.

Consuming Alcohol, Eating Meat

This same approach can be applied to alcohol, meat-eating, and other sorts of behavior which are traditionally interpreted as forbidden to Buddhist monks. Consider the negative emotions generated by sights and smells that a human would experience sitting alongside a decomposing human body day after day. A feeling of revulsion, disgust, and worse, will arise. It is our *reaction* to the corpse that is the problem.

All of us have our own inner fears, our own anger, or rage which can be triggered by images or by behavior. Tantric Buddhism feels that negative acts and negative passions need not be avoided, rejected, or allowed to fade away. Instead, Tantric teachers assert that a skilled *guru* can guide the student into techniques whereby these negatives are generated, focused and harnessed and brought into use to overcome their negativity. One can use lust to overcome lust; one can use disgust to overcome disgust, one can use anger to overcome anger, one can use meat-eating to overcome the negatives of eating meat, and other such techniques. A verse from a Tantric master summarizes this:

> Water in the ear is removed by more water,
> A thorn [in the skin] is removed by another thorn.
> So wise men rid themselves of passion
> By yet more passion.[66]

12.11 MODERN TIBET

Although some authors tend to portray Tibet before the Chinese invasion as a land of peace, happiness, and great spirituality, others tend to find a society that was ". . . little more than a despotic retrograde theocracy of serfdom and poverty, so damaging to the human spirit, where vast wealth was accumulated by a favored few who lived high and mighty off the blood, sweat, and tears of the many."[67] Those with sympathy for the Chinese takeover of Tibet tend to stress the non-spiritual behavior of many of the famous lamas,[68] stress the violence and inequity, and those who are sympathetic followers of Tibetan lamas have a tendency to see Tibet of the past as a land of peace and deep religious

---

[65] More details can be found in Alexis Sanderson, "Vajrayana: Origin and Function," in *Buddhism Into the Year 2000* (Bangkok and Los Angeles: Dharmmakaya Foundation, 1994), pp. 89–91. The possibility of misuse is obvious.

[66] From the *Cittavishuddhiprakarana*, in Embree, *Sources of Indian Tradition*, pp. 195–196.

[67] Michael Parenti, "Friendly Feudalism: The Tibet Myth," which can be accessed at http://www.michaelparenti.org/Tibet.html

[68] "To elevate his authority beyond worldly challenge, the first (a.k.a. third) Dalai Lama seized monasteries that did not belong to his sect, and is believed to have destroyed Buddhist writings that conflicted with his claim to divinity. The Dalai Lama who succeeded him pursued a sybaritic life, enjoying many mistresses, partying with friends, and acting in other ways deemed unfitting for an incarnate deity. For this he was done in by his priests. Within 170 years, despite their recognized status as gods, five Dalai Lamas were murdered by their high priests or other courtiers." Michael Parenti, "Friendly Feudalism: The Tibet Myth," *loc. cit.*

commitment.[69] As one might expect, it is probable that an accurate portrayal lies somewhere between the two extremes.

Books on the history of Tibet describe a long history of tension and violence between the various orders of Tibetan Buddhism. As was pointed out in the introduction to this book, in virtually every human civilization, religion and politics were not separated. In Tibet, political power was usually at the center of conflicts between Buddhist orders, and wars and assassinations were utilized. Over the centuries the number of Tibetan monasteries increased, and some of the Buddhist orders also accumulated a great deal of real estate, farmed by feudalistic serfs. At least some of the lamas accumulated great wealth. Monasteries were not independent of the business world. Much of the wealth of some monasteries was accumulated "through active participation in trade, commerce, and money lending."[70] The wealth of the monasteries rested in the hands of small numbers of high-ranking lamas. Of course, the majority of ordinary monks lived modestly and had no direct access to great wealth. One source reports that the current Dalai Lama admits to having owned slaves during his years reigning in Tibet.[71]

Chairman Mao sent Chinese Communist troops into Tibet in 1950 and using military force the army began the systematic destruction of Tibetan Buddhist religion and culture. The People's Liberation Army, followed by the barbaric destructiveness of the Red Guard between 1966–1976, brought about the death of over a million Tibetans and the destruction of over 6,000 monasteries.[72] According to the Tibetan Buddhist scholar Robert Thurman, of 6,267 significant monasteries in Tibet, only thirteen remain undamaged.[73] The drive to transform Tibet into a Chinese land continues to this day as huge numbers of Chinese families have been forcibly relocated into Tibet. According to Western scholarship, the People's Republic of China (PRC) communist party is attempting to rewrite the history of Tibet and its relationship with China in favor of Chinese communist claims. The attempt is also to redefine how Tibetans practice Buddhism. Scholarly research in China has been criticized, and it is noted that in the year 2000 the Chinese Tibetological academic community was instructed to counter scholarly claims of Western scholars working in the field of Tibet studies. The PRC blames the current Dalai Lama for protests among the Tibetan community, and even claims that the Dalai Lama trains Tibetan terrorists to travel to China and foment trouble. They claimed that the Dalai Lama wished to turn Tibetan Buddhism "into a religion of suicide and self-immolation in the services of his own political purposes."[74]

---

[69] On the **Students for a Free Tibet** website, in "A Lie Repeated," Joshua Michael Schrei writes "But perhaps there is no more telling testament to the Tibetan people's sentiment towards their own culture than the fact that in the early 1980's— when the Chinese government finally relaxed some of its draconian policies towards Tibet— the first thing Tibetans set about doing is rebuilding and repopulating monasteries — the very symbols of 'old Tibet.' The next thing they did was take to the streets and protest for freedom and for the Dalai Lama's return. This is not the behavior of a people who are trying to cast off their old ways. It sounds more like a people who are trying to get their culture back." See the **Students For a Free Tibet** website, www.studentsforafreetibet.org/

[70] Dalai Lama quoted in Donald Lopez Jr., *Prisoners of Shangri-La: Tibetan Buddhism and the West* (Chicago and London: Chicago University Press, 1998), p. 205. A reviewer comments: In this fine scholarly work, Lopez (Asian Languages and Cultures/Univ. of Michigan) warns his readers away from romanticized visions of Tibet, which ultimately harm that beleaguered nation's prospects for independence. Buddhism, the religion of enlightenment, takes as its task the dispersal of human misconceptions of reality. It is only fitting that, in the wake of heightened popular interest in Tibet, Lopez should write a corrective to both positive and negative misconceptions of Tibetan Buddhism (review Copyright ©1998, Kirkus Associates).

[71] Michael Parenti, *op. cit.*, quoting from the pro-Chinese-occupation authors Stuart Gelder and Roma Gelder, *The Timely Rain: Travels in New Tibet* (New York: Monthly Review Press, 1964), p. 119, p. 123.

[72] Estimates placing the number of Tibetans killed between one million and 1.2 million are very common. John Powers, *Introduction to Tibetan Buddhism* (New York: Snow Lion Press, 1995), pp. 169–187; Donald S. Lopez and Cyrus Stearns, "A Report on Religious Activity in Central Tibet," *Journal of the International Association of Buddhist Studies* 9 (1986), pp. 101–107.

[73] Robert Thurman, *Essential Tibetan Buddhism*, p. 7.

[74] John Powers, *The Buddha Party: How the People's Republic of China Works to Define and Control Tibetan Buddhism* (New York: Oxford University Press, 2016), p. 83.

CHAPTER 12: TIBETAN THOUGHT

12.12 TANTRIC BUDDHISM COMES WEST

In the Western world, the best-known Tibetan Buddhist lamas come from the Kagyu order, the Nyingma and the Geluk orders. Following the initial Chinese invasion of Tibet in October 1950, and the later repression following a popular revolt in 1959, it was the Kagyu lineage monks who were the first to take the initiative and leave their temporary homes in northern India and travel to Europe and to north America. A consequence of this was carrying authentic Kagyu esoteric teachings to outsiders, thereby expanding the influence of the Kagyu order. The Kagyu tradition of Tibetan Buddhism was very active in Europe and north America, with its most famous exponent the "crazy wisdom" lama Chogyam Trungpa (1939-1987). Trungpa lived a very unconventional and controversial life and was described by students and friends as a heavy drinker. He established centers in Scotland and then came to the USA where he founded a Buddhist community and training group in 1973 called Vajradhatu and the next year he established an accredited university, Naropa University, in Boulder, Colorado. He was the author of a number of quite popular books as well. Many students continue his teaching line.

The Nyingmapa tradition, which utilizes the unified system of practice called *dzogchen*, literally "great perfection" (which stresses the innate purity of the mind), also expanded into Europe and the US. In north America, the Tibetan Nyingma lama Tarthang Tulku (author of a popular book on *dzochen* entitled *Time, Space, and Knowledge* [Berkeley, CA: Dharma Publishing, 1977]) established an ongoing publishing house and a teaching center in Berkeley, California.

As mentioned before the Dalai Lama belongs to the Gelukpa tradition. Tenzin Gyatso (b. July 6, 1935), the fourteenth Dalai Lama in the lineage, was the religious head of state in Tibet until 1959. Due to renewed hostility and a popular uprising against Chinese forces that was crushed, the twenty-three-year-old Dalai Lama was forced to flee Tibet to a hill town named Dharmasala in northern India. Tenzin Gyatso has been continually involved in the attempt to free Tibet from Chinese control, and to free Tibetan Buddhism from Chinese attempts to destroy it. He has gained much support for his position (including receiving a medal from President George W. Bush in 2007 and the Nobel Peace Prize in 1989) because of his insistence upon non-violent ways to pursue freedom and independence for Tibet. Preaching peace and compassion, the Dalai Lama has been an international religious figure respected in international politics.[75]

12.13 SUMMARY OF THE CHAPTER

We have discussed the history and doctrines of Tibetan religion, beginning with the Tantric Buddhist ideas and practices found in India before Tantric Buddhism made its way to Tibet. We discussed briefly the more ancient shamanistic religion of Tibet, called Bon, and saw how it both influenced later Buddhism but also pointed out that Bon experienced continuous deadly conflicts with Tantric Buddhism.

We discussed the introduction of Indian esoteric Buddhism into Tibet in the seventh century, and outlined the arising of the four major groups of Tibetan Vajrayana Buddhism: the Sakya, the Nyingma, the Kagyu, and the Gelug orders. We discussed the stress upon rituals, music, ceremony, *mantras*, *mandalas*, Tantras, deity visualization, and the practices which were contrary to previous generations of Buddhists, such as sexual intercourse, alcohol

---

[75] A source for this material which traces the history of Tibetan religion from the earliest days to the contemporary fourteenth Dalai Lama is Alexander Norman, *Secret Lives of the Dalai Lama: The Untold Story of the Holy Men Who Shaped Tibet from Pre-History to the Present Day* (New York: Doubleday, 2010).

334

consumption, and meat-eating.

We finished the chapter with a very brief discussion of modern Tibet following the Chinese claim that Tibet belonged to China, and the military conquest of Tibet and the systematic deconstruction of Tibetan Buddhist culture.

The philosophical ideas of Mahayana Buddhism, combined with the supernatural and magical aspects of Tibetan Tantric Buddhism appealed to and fascinated many people in the West. The chanted formulas of power combined with the visualization methods of Tibetan meditation are not the same as the focused concentration of Theravada Buddhism, but the Tibetans believe their methods to be more effective. It is important to recognize that these are part of the Buddhist monk's life, but popular Tibetan forms of Buddhism are much different for the person who does not live in a monastery. Tantric forms of Buddhism are embedded in the cultures of Tibet and the assumptions of Tibetan civilization. Even for monks in monasteries, Tibetan Buddhism places great stress on ritual and prayer, aspects of popular religion which have held little interest for many Western students.

12.14 TECHNICAL TERMS

abhisheka	a ritual initiation transmission given by the guru which authorizes and empowers the student to carry out more advanced esoteric practices. Tantric followers believe that the deeper the attainment of the *guru*, the more effective the initiation ritual.
Amitabha	The Buddha of the Western Paradise, whose realm is a Pure Land. The Panchen Lama of Tibet is supposed to be a reincarnation of Amitabha.
Avalokiteshvara	The bodhisattva of compassion and assistant to Amitabha. The Dalai Lama is supposed to be Avalokiteshvara reborn.
Bon	The popular religion of Tibet (pronounced "pern") which exists alongside Tantric Buddhism. Bon is a form of ancient animism, or shamanism, a religious attitude which was widespread in Siberia, Turkestan, Mongolia, Manchuria and northern China.
Dalai Lama	in the ancient past, this was the scholar-monk belonging to the Gelugpa tradition who was named the secular ruler of Tibet by the Mongolians. The term Dalai Lama literally means "ocean *lama*," or the "superior one (*lama*) [whose wisdom is as deep as the] ocean," and each succeeding leader was understood to be the previous Dalai Lama reborn; in addition, he was perceived to be a rebirth of Avalokiteshvara, famous as the bodhisattva of compassion.
dorjes	small double-ended scepters, usually made of bronze, which represent lightning bolts.
guru	A spiritual teacher or guide with knowledge of secret rituals and techniques, especially spiritual powers. In Tibetan, guru is *lama*.
lama	A lama is a "superior one". When used correctly, the term *lama* is not a synonym for monk; rather a *lama* is an advanced *guru*, a person of superior spiritual attainment higher than a mere monk.
Mahamudra	Kagyu practice for the realization of emptiness and escape from the cycle of birth-and-death, where the student focuses upon the natural state of the mind, which is one's Buddha-nature.

CHAPTER 12: TIBETAN THOUGHT

Mandala	a complex image of colorful circles and squares which provides a map of the journey into consciousness, used in focused concentration.
mantras	chanted phrases of power.
Mantrayana	the vehicle which makes extensive use of *mantras*, chanted phrases of power. This is another name for Vajrayana.
nagas	In India, nagas are serpents; in Tibet they are Bon spirits who live in watery realms, who can adopt the shape of water snakes or dragons. They live on the bottom of lakes and rivers, and they guard secret treasures, including guarding Buddhist texts.
Nagarjuna	The Indian Buddhist teacher who lived during the second century C.E. and developed the implications of *sunyata*, or emptiness, as taught in the Perfection of Wisdom sutras. The Madhyamaka school bases itself on Nagarjuna's writings.
Tibetan orders	The Gelugpa, the Nyingmapa, the Sakyapa, and the Karmapa.
Padmasambhava	A Tantric miracle worker contemporary with a ruler of Tibet who lived between 755-797. He is considered a founder of the Nyingmapa. He drove away Bon demons using ritual and magical powers. He is venerated under the name Guru Rinpoche ("Precious Teacher").
sadhana	a ritual practice, or a text which describes a ritual practice which leads to perfection. In Tantric Buddhism one's *sadhana* is meditative communion with a deity, a buddha or a bodhisattva, as well as activities like a fire ritual, and other such activities.
siddhis	extraordinary powers achievable with ascetic practices, advanced meditation and magical phrases. Powers might include the ability to change one's physical appearance, the ability to make onself invisible, to walk through solid walls, to fly through the air, to be able to hear conversations miles away. They also include reading the minds of others and even be in more than one place at the same time. There are higher powers, but there are also lower powers, curses to cause bad luck, pain and suffering.
Tantra	A special book with esoteric instructions to guide students to the achievement of buddhahood.
tulku	A tulku is the official reincarnation of a bodhisattva or a buddha. The Dalai Lama is a tulku, namely the Bodhisattva Avalokiteshvara reborn.
Vajrayana	the *vajra* vehicle. *Vajra* is often explained as either "Lightning" or "Thunderbolt" (the *vajra* symbol is traditionally associated with the thunderbolt of the Hindu *deva*, Indra).
yana	literally, "vehicle," as in the Maha-yana, or the Great Vehicle.
Yogachara	The Mahayana school which asserts that all of our knowledge of the external and internal realms comes via consciousness, but consciousness creates much more of our world than we realize. Pronounced "Yog-ACH-cha-ra." The term Yoga-achara names a person who is a master of yogic-style meditation.

12.15 QUESTIONS FOR FURTHER DISCUSSION

1) Tibetan forms of Buddhism have become popular in the West in the past thirty years. What features of Tibetan Buddhism do you think appeal most strongly to college-age students? Do you think it is relevant that popular entertainment figures are associated with Tibetan forms?

2) Are there any Tibetan Buddhist centers in your area? If so, you might consider calling and setting up a visit where your questions can be answered.

A SELECTED BIBLIOGRAPHY

Robert Buswell, ed., *Encyclopedia of Buddhism* (New York: Thompson Gale, 2004), Vol. 1 & 2.

Tibetan Buddhism

Bachelor, S., ed., *The Jewel in the Lotus: A Guide to the Buddhist Traditions of Tibet* (Boston: Wisdom, 1987)

Beyer, Steven, tr. and ed., *The Buddhist Experience: Sources and Interpretations* (Belmont, Ca.: Dickenson Publishing, 1974)

Dasgupta, S., *An Introduction to Tantric Buddhism* (Berkeley: Shambhala, 1974)

Davidson, Ronald, *Tibetan Renaissance: Tantric Buddhism in the Rebirth of Tibetan Culture* ( )

Hopkins, Jeffrey, *The Tantric Distinction: An Introduction to Tibetan Buddhism* (Boston: Wisdom, 1984)

Halkias, Georgios T., *Luminous Bliss: A Religious History of Pure Land Literature in Tibet*, Pure Land Buddhist Studies Series (Honolulu, HI: University of Hawaii Press, 2012).

Hopkins, Jeffrey, *Emptiness Yoga* (Prasanghika Madhyamika) (New York: Snow Lion, 1987)

Hopkins, Jeffrey, *Emptiness in the Mind-Only School of Buddhism* ( )

Kalupahana, David J., *A History of Buddhist Philosophy: Continuities & Discontinuities* (Honolulu: University of Hawaii Press, 1989)

Kapstein, Mathew T., *The Nyingma School of Tibetan Buddhism: Its Fundamentals and History* ( )

Lessing, F. D., and Alex Wayman, *An Introduction to the Buddhist Tantric Systems* (Delhi, MB, 1978)

Lopez, Jr., Donald S., *A Study of Svatantrika* (Ithica, N.Y.: Snow Lion, 1987)

Lopez, Donald S., Jr., *Prisoners of Shangri-La: Tibetan Buddhism and the West* (Chicago and London: Chicago University Press, 1998)

Novick, Rebecca McClen, *Fundamentals of Tibetan Buddhism* ( )

Norman, Alexander, *Secret Lives of the Dalai Lama: The Untold Story of the Holy Men Who Shaped Tibet from Pre-History to the Present Day* (New York: Doubleday, 2010)

Powers, John, *Introduction to Tibetan Buddhism* (New York: Snow Lion Press, 1995)

The Root Stanzas of the Middle Way: The Mulamadhamakakarika (translated from the Tibetan text by the Padmakara Translation Group: Boston: Shambhala, 2016)

Snelling, John, *The Buddhist Handbook* (Rochester, Vt.: Inner Traditions, 1991)

Snellgrove, D. L., *Indo-Tibetan Buddhism: Indian Buddhists and their Tibetan Successors* (Boston: Shambhala, 2002)

Tarthang Tulku, *Time, Space, and Knowledge* (Berkeley, CA: Dharma Publishing, 1977)

Thurman, Robert, *Essential Tibetan Buddhism* (New York: Castle Books,)

Wallace, B. Allen, *The Attention Revolution: Unlocking the Power of the Focused Mind* (Boston: Wisdom Publications, 2006)

Wallace, B. Allen, *Buddhism With An Attitude: The Tibetan Seven-Point Mind Training* (Boston: Snow Lion, 2003)

Wallace, B. Alan, *The Four Immeasurables: Practices to Open the Heart* (Boston: Snow Lion, 2010)

Wallace, B. Allen, *Heart of the Great Perfection* (Boston: Wisdom Publications, 2016).

Wallace, B. Allen, *Meditations of a Buddhist Skeptic: A Manifesto for the Mind Sciences and Contemplative Practice* (New York: Columbia University, 2013)

Wallace, B. Allen, *Stilling the Mind* (Boston: Wisdom Publications, 2011)

Wayman, Alex and Hideko Wayman, *The Lion's Roar of Queen Srimala* (New York: Columbia University Press, 1974)

Williams, Paul, *Mahayana Buddhism: The Doctrinal Foundations* (London: Routledge, 1989).

Wedemeyer, Christian K., *Making Sense of Tantric Buddhism: History, Semiology, and Transgression in the Indian Traditions* (New York: Columbia University Press, 2012)

Bon

Karmay, Samten G., *Treasure of Good Sayings: A Tibetan History of Bon* (Delhi: Motilal Banarsidass, 2001)

Karmay, Samten G., and Yasuhiko Nagano, eds., *New Horizons in Bon Studies* (New Delhi: M. Saujanya, 2004)

Kvaerne, Per, *The Bon Religion of Tibet: The Iconography of a Living Tradition* (Boston: Shambhala, 2001)

Snellgrove, David L., *The Nine Ways of Bon* (Boulder, CO: Prajna Press, 1980)

Credits

Introduction

Excerpt from Stephen Batchelor, *Confession of a Buddhist Atheist* (New York: Spiegel & Grau, 2010), p. 58.

Excerpt from Konrad Talmont-Kaminski, "The New Atheism and the New Anti-Atheism," *Skeptic*, Vol. 15, No. 1, 2009, p. 68.

Chapter 1

Excerpt from John L. Esposito, Darrell J. Fasching, Todd Lewis, *World Religions Today* (London: Oxford University Press, 2002), p. 7.

Chapter 2

Excerpt from Rig-Veda 1.3; James Fieser and John Powers, *Scriptures of the East*, Second edition (New York: McGraw-Hill, 2004), p. 10, p. 11.

Excerpt from Atharva-Veda 6.20 and 6.9, in Robert E. Van Voorst, *Anthology of Asian Scriptures* (Wadsworth, 2001), p. 51.

Excerpt From Rig-veda 10.72, from Wendy Doniger O'Flaherty, *The Rig Veda, An Anthology* (London: Penguin, 1981).

Chapter 3

Excerpt from Rig-Veda, 10.90; Robert E. Van Voorst, *Anthology of Asian Scriptures* (Wadsworth, 2001), p. 37, pp. 43-44, p. 45.

Bhimrao Ambedkar, *What Congress and Ghandi Have Done to the Untouchables* (Bombay, India: Thacker and Company, 1934), pp. 307-308.

Chapter 4

Excerpt from Lama Govinda, *Foundations of Tibetan Mysticism* (London: Rider & Co., 1960), p. 22, p. 23, p. 47.

Excerpt from Chandogya Upanishad 6:9-11; in Robert E. Van Voorst, *Anthology of Asian Scriptures* (Wadsworth, 2001), pp. 34-35.

Excerpt from Shankara's "Crest-Jewel of Discrimination," in James Fieser and John Powers, *Scriptures of the East*, Second edition (New York: McGraw-Hill, 2004), p. 25.

Excerpt from Eliot Deutsch, *Advaita Vedanta: A Philosophical Reconstruction* (Honolulu: University of Hawaii Press, 1969), p. 28.

Excerpt from David Snellgrove, *Indo-Tibetan Buddhism* (Boston: Shambhala, 2002), pp. 124-125.

Excerpt from Radhakrishnan, *Indian Philosophies*, vol. 2 (New York: Macmillan and Company, 1958), p. 337.

Excerpt from Thomas J. Hopkins, *The Hindu Religious Tradition* (Belmont, Ca: Wadsworth, 1971), p. 68.

Chapter 5

"The Shiva Lingam" photo by Dr. Philip Ricards; used by permission.

"Dancing Shiva" photo by Danae Michelle Zeuschner, used by permission.

Excerpt from Ananda K. Coomaraswamy, *The Dance of Shiva* (N.Y.: Noonday, 1957), p. 78.

Excerpt from Max Muller, trans., *The Upanishads, Sacred Books of the East*, vols. 1 and 15 (Oxford University Press, 1878, 1884).

Excerpt from Christian Wedemeyer, *Making Sense of Tantric Buddhism: History, Semiology, and Transgression in the Indian Traditions* (New York: Columbia University Press, 2012) p. 158.

Excerpt from Agehananda Bharati, *The Tantric Tradition* (New York: Anchor Books, 1970), p. 130.

Excerpt from Nanditha Krishna, *The Book of Vishnu* (New York: Penguin Group, 2003), cover.
Excerpt from Sri Purohit Swami, *Bhagavad Gita*, pp. 99-101, pp. 40-42.
John Y. Fenton, *et. al.*, *Religions of Asia*, 3rd edition (New York: St. Martin's Press, 1993), p. 73
Randal Helms, *Gospel Fictions* (Prometheus Books, 1988) p. 24.

Chapter 6
Excerpt from Robert E. Van Voorst, *Anthology of World Scriptures* (Belmont, Ca.: Thomson Wadsworth, 2008), p. 114.

Chapter 7
Excerpt from John Esposito, Darrell Fasching, Todd Lewis, *World Religions Today* (New York: Oxford University Press, 2002), p. 313.

Chapter 8
Excerpt from Helmuth von Glasenapp, *Buddhism: A Non-Theistic Religion* (London: George Allen & Unwin, 1970), p. 138.
Excerpt from Robert Thurman, *Essential Tibetan Buddhism* (New York: Castle Books, 1997), pp. 11-12.
Excerpt from Christmas Humphreys, ed., *The Wisdom of Buddhism* (New York: Random House, 1961), p. 71.
Excerpt from Henry Clarke Warren, *Buddhism In Translations* (New York: Antheneum, 1968), pp. 81-83.
The Parable of the Poisoned Arrow from Lucien Stryk, *World of the Buddha* (Garden City, New York: Doubleday Anchor Books, 1969), pp. 144-149.
Excerpt from Etienne Lamotte, page vii of his Foreword to *The Teaching of Vimalakirti* (London: Routledge & Kegan Paul, Ltd., 1976), translated by Sara Boin.
Excerpt from *The Last Days of the Buddha: The Mahaparinibbanasutta of the Buddha* (Kandy, Ceylon: Buddhist Publication Society, n.d.), p. 75. This is Wheel Publication No. 67-69.
Excerpt from Robert E. Buswell, *Chinese Buddhist Apocrypha* (Honolulu: University of Hawaii Press, 1989), p. 294.
Brief excerpt from Traleg Kyabgon, *Karma* (Boston: Shambhala, 2015), p. 2.
Excerpt from James Fieser, John Powers, *Scriptures of the East* 2nd edition (New York: McGraw-Hill, 2003), p. 87.
Excerpt from David Kalupahana, *A History of Buddhist Philosophy: Continuities and Discontinuities* (Honolulu: University of Hawaii Press, 1992), p. 86.
Excerpt from David Kalupahana, *Buddhist Philosophy: A Historical Analysis*, p. 75.

Chapter 9
Excerpt from S. N. Dube, "Arhat Ideal in Early Buddhism," pp. 50-51, in *Buddhism and Peace: Theory and Practice* (Honolulu: Blue Pine, 2006). ed. Chanju Mun.
"Manjusri" photo by Danae Michelle Zeuschner, used by permission.

Chapter 10

Excerpts from Mark Siderits and Shoryu Katsura, *Nagarjuna's Middle Way: Mulamadhyamakakarika* (Boston: Wisdom Publications, 2013), p. 277, 302, 303.
Excerpt from David Kalupahana, *Buddhist Philosophy: A Historical Analysis*, p. 75.

Chapter 11

Excerpts from Christian K. Wedemeyer, *Making Sense of Tantric Buddhism* (New York: Columbia University Press, 2013), p. 9, p. 117, p. 118.
Excerpt from Steven Beyer, *The Buddhist Experience: Sources and Interpretations* (Belmont, CA.: Dickenson Publishing,

1974), pp. 141-142.

Excerpts from David Snellgrove, *Indo-Tibetan Buddhism* (Boston: Shambala, 2002), p. 130, p. 131, p. 133, p. 151, p. 207.

Excerpt from Edward Conze, ed., *Buddhist Texts Through the Ages* (New York: Harper Torchbooks, 1964), p. 253.

Excerpt from Stephen Batchelor, *Confession of a Buddhist Atheist* (New York: Spiegel & Grau, 2010), p. 92.

Chapter 12

Excerpts from Stephen Batchelor, *Confession of a Buddhist Atheist* (New York: Spiegel & Grau, 2010), p. 22.

Excerpt from Edward Conze, *Buddhist Thought In India* (Ann Arbor, Mi.: University of Michigan Press, 1979), p. 271.

Excerpt from Edward Conze, *Selected Sayings from the Perfection of Wisdom* (London: The Buddhist Society, 1955), p. 107.

Excerpt from Edward Conze, *The Perfection of Wisdom in Eight Thousand Lines and Its Verse Summary* (Bolinas, CA: The Four Seasons Foundation, 1973), p. 172.

Excerpt from Judith Simmer-Brown in "Look, Look," *Shambhala Sun*, Volume 22, No. 2, November 2013, p. 18.

Excerpt from James Fieser, John Powers, *Scriptures of the East* 2nd edition (New York: McGraw-Hill, 2003), p. 109, p. 114.

Excerpt from the French Dhagpo Kundreul Ling web site: http://www.dhagpo-kundreul.org/

Excerpt from David Snellgrove, *Indo-Tibetan Buddhism* (Boston: Shambhala, 1987), vol. I, pp. 125-126.

Excerpt from Agehananda Bharati, *The Tantric Tradition* (New York: Anchor Books, 1970), pp. 133-134.

Excerpt from Embree, *Sources of Indian Tradition*, pp. 195-196.

Index

CPSIA information can be obtained
at www.ICGtesting.com
Printed in the USA
LVOW04s0036070318

568948LV00004B/91/P

9 781635 6170